THE GOOD BIRDWATCHERS GUIDE

PETER JENNINGS

FICEDULA BOOKS

cover: Abernethy Forest & The Cairngorms
Pied Flycatcher by Alan Harris

© Ficedula Books

ISBN 0-9513070-1-0

Published in 1991 by Ficedula Books, PO Box 10, Llandrindod Wells, Powys, UK, LD1 5ZZ.

Typeset by BP Integraphics, Upper Bristol Road, Bath
Printed and bound by The Bath Press, Lower Bristol Road, Bath

CONTENTS

PREFACE

Some birdwatchers stay indoors and birdwatch through the window; others go outside and stand there – watching. This book is for the latter although the indoor type could throw it at the cat which ate 'the little bird with the blue tail and red bits'!
A few facts:-

- The number of birdwatchers is increasing daily whilst the number of birds to watch is decreasing.
- More than 30,000 copies of 'Birdwatching'magazine are sold every month.
- There are some 9,000 members of the British Trust for Ornithology.
- More than 1,000 birdwatchers would turn up tomorrow if a Gray's Grasshopper Warbler was seen at Gib. Point.
- There were 7,500 members of the RSPB in 1958 and 750,000 in 1990.
- At the present rate of increase everyone in the world will be a member of the RSPB by the year 2050 – but there will be no birds to watch by then – or not enough for one each anyway! (Fortunately most RSPB members stay indoors – but generally do not throw things at cats!)

The popular view of the birdwatcher is the rather unkempt, woolly-hatted fellow occasionally appearing in the tabloid press, or on the News at Ten, arriving in hoards at some distant corner of the country to see a little yellow bird from half way around the planet; or the retired army type with World War I binoculars who's always saying that he remembers this or that species from Abyssinia/Burma/off Jutland etc. These archetypes are now largely passé along with dibs and bubble-cars. Birdwatchers are in fact from all walks of life; doctors, actors, housewives, W.I. stalwarts, Kalahari bushmen, skivers, layabouts and citizens on the run from the Poll Tax.

One thing you can say about all birdwatchers is that they are all 'twitchers'. Oh yes! every last one of them! No one would buy 'Housesparrowwatching' magazine or 'Housesparrowing World 'would they? No, it would be pretty dull stuff if we only had one species of bird to look at. So, if you've ever 'noticed'more than one species of bird you qualify as a 'twitcher'. Admittedly there are subspecies of the birdwatcher/twitcher (**Ornithoptikos**):-

domesticus: stays at home – birdwatches through the window; throws things at cats with blue and red feathers stuck to their whiskers.

vulgaris: the everyday, bog-standard twitcher who just follows everyone else about with a tripod extended over his shoulder.

garrulus: talks too much, usually a lot of hot air, about birds he thinks he saw yesteryear or yesterday but are now gone (ah! you've met him too!).

solitarius: either very good or very bad birdwatchers. Usually seen alone (!); in the corner of a hide, sat huddled on some storm-swept promontory doing a six hour seawatch or, when it's dark, propping up the bar with a long shot of 'Wild Turkey'in deep thought on hybrid calidrids, Empidonax flycatchers, pipits' greater-coverts or (if one of the bad'uns)- whether they were Gannets or Snow Geese passing the point all day at 200 per hour.

peregrinus: the wanderer: you see him everywhere, St.Ives, Sumburgh, Sandwich and Kakamega. Determined, relentless, often boring, he's drawn inexorably, like Odysseus to the Sirens, to the next new species. Needs a good whacking about the greater-coverts with a tripod now and then to bring him back to the real world!

So every birdwatcher is a twitcher of some sort. Seeking variety in the birds they watch to a greater or lesser degree. Seeking variety in this way is to be encouraged, in the young especially. It has positive survival value and is a characteristic innate in primitive man. Do you know how many species of food plant are utilised by a Kalahari bushman? Well, it's more than the number of bird species ever seen in Radnorshire, I know that! Nobody likes eating pot-noodles all the time, everyday (?) or doing the same routine. Variety (and hence birdwatching) is the spice of life – ask any Kalahari bushman.

So now you've got this book you can set off and do a bit of peregrinating! And if you discover any possibly useful contributions report back. For instance this edition has pubs where Tawny Pipit, Ivory Gull (and 'Wild Turkey') have been seen from the bar and a guesthouse boasting Osprey from the breakfast table. Helpful sites such as this are rare but if you discover one let us know. You could be in the running for a free copy of the 2nd edition of the Good Birdwatchers Guide!! Or you could simply work out when the number of RSPB members will exactly equal the number of birds in the world!

Several years work and many thousands of miles have gone into putting this guide together. On reflection it would never have been started had the true extent of the work required been envisaged. I would like to thank everyone who has helped make it as complete and accurate as possible and Ruth A. Lowther, my wife, for her innumerable hours on the word processor.

Although every effort has been made to ensure the accuracy of the information in this guide errors are bound to have crept in or gone uncorrected and no responsibility can be accepted for those with blind faith in it! Nor for good birdwatching sites disappearing under the plough/bull-dozer/nuclear power-station/oil terminal/ 'thrown-up'housing development/shopping mall etc etc! Also **take care**! Birdwatchers are usually well aware of the dangers in the countryside generally but often have the basic faults of looking up, and not down at their feet, and wanting to 'get a bit closer'rather a lot! These are greater dangers at coastal sites with cliffs of course; take a friend along (if you can), or at the very least tell someone exactly where you are going. Although there can be few safer pursuits than birdwatching sadly a few birdwatchers manage to get themselves into 'scrapes'(!) or worse each year.

Ed. Edw Valley 1.1.91

HOW TO USE THIS BOOK

**Site Name   Ordnance Survey Landranger map no. (1-204)
approx. location**
Directions with road numbers and/or Ordnance Survey grid references.
The types of bird you are likely to see at the site, or for which it is best known.

> ***secondary site*** *worth a look but generally less good for bird-watching than the main sites.*

Maps:-   Ordnance Survey Landranger Series (1.25″ to the mile)
1–204 £3.70. Complete set £680.
Ordnance Survey Pathfinder Series (2.5″ to the mile)
1–1373 £3.25 each. Complete set ca. £4,150.
A list of Ordnance Survey agents/stockists, Price List, and catalogue of all Ordnance Survey publications can be obtained from:-
Information & Enquires, Ordnance Survey, Romsey Road, Southampton, SO9 4DH tel: 0703 792763

Road Maps:-
The vast majority of the sites can be found using a good motoring atlas. Some of the best for the birdwatcher are:-
AA G.B. Road Atlas 1991 (£16.95)
AA Maxi-Scale Atlas of Britain (£8.95)

These two have nearly every lane shown and many more place-names than most. They also use the O.S. grid system – essential to the travelling birder.

Almost as good are:-
Ordnance Survey Motoring Atlas of G.B. (£5.99)
Ordnance Survey Superscale Atlas of G.B. (£8.95)
Ordnance Survey National Atlas of G.B. (£20.00)

Useful books for those not familiar with using large scale Ordnance Survey maps are:-
'Ordnance Survey Map Skills Book' (£4.95)
'Simply Map Reading' (£2.95)

Both are published by the Ordnance Survey. The latter is also available from 'Telegraph Books' tel: 071 537 2207.

A free and very useful booklet guide to your rights of access and your responsibilities in the countryside can be obtained from The Countryside Commission, John Dower House, Crescent Place, Cheltenham, GL50 3RA tel: 0242 521381. It is titled 'Out in the Country – where you can go and what you can do'.

The Law is different in Scotland but a brief guide titled 'Access to the Scottish Countryside: Rights and Responsibilities'can be obtained free from The Information Section, Countryside Commission for Scotland, Battleby, Redgorton, Perth, PH1 3EW tel: 0738 27921.

TIC   'Tourist Information Centres run by the Tourist Boards of England, Scotland and Wales. Those marked with an asterisk * are only open in the summer, usually Easter to the end of September/October. The staff at these centres are usually brilliant and able to put you in contact with exactly the type of accommodation in the area you want – if it exists! We have often just turned up at a TIC mid-afternoon after birding all day, been found perfect accommodation, and are out birdwatching again within the hour. Usually the centres also have lots of information on local nature reserves, nature walks etc.

YH   The nearest Youth Hostel(s) to the group of sites. Administered by: Youth Hostels Association (England & Wales), Trevelyan House, 8 St.Stephens Hill, St.Albans, Herts, AL1 2DY. tel: 0727 55215. or – Scottish Youth Hostels Association, 7 Glebe Crescent, Stirling, FK8 2JA. tel: 0786 51181.

Membership of the Associations costs from ca. £1.70 to £7.60 a year at present, depending on age and the Association. There is no upper age limit by the way – you can still stay at a youth hostel aged 100+, but accompanying children must be aged 5 or over. Accommodation is in unisex dormitories usually although some hostels have family rooms or annexes. Some hostels provide breakfasts, evening meals and packed lunches very cheaply or you can self-cater. Overnight charges are about £2–£6 per person and generally in the price bracket of £2–£4, costs varying with age of the hosteler and category of the hostel. Membership of either of the above Associations permits use of the others' hostels and to youth hostels in more than 50 countries abroad – very useful for the birdwatcher on a budget. Much more information from the addresses above.

H/B   Other hostels or bunkhouses in the area but run independently. Vary greatly but many are along youth hostel lines and with similar charges or cheaper. Increasing in number in rural Britain by way of converted barns etc.

RF   An inn or pub offering refreshment (R) or refreshment and meals (RF). Selected as convenient to the grouped sites or the most important of them. Usually traditionally brewed beers are available (rare in Scotland) and 90% serve coffee and 70% tea. Reasonably priced good food is available in most both at lunchtime and in the evening.

BBE   A hotel, guesthouse, farmhouse or inn offering bed and breakfast (BB) with an evening meal if required (BBE). Again selected for convenience to the sites, offering good value and a rural setting where possible. There are a very few places included which are more than £25 per person B & B and the vast majority are well below this. Generally speaking a comfortable, warm, double-room with colour television and en suite is rarely worth more than £20 per person, including breakfast, and there are a great number available much cheaper than this. There are many superb places for birdwatchers the length and breadth of Britain in this book for less than £15 B & B per person and there are doubtless hundreds more to be discovered!

SC   Self-catering cottage or other property in the area. Usually in a rural and/or good birdwatching setting. Costs vary considerably but not necessarily with quality. Most National Trust/Landmark Trust properties are on the expensive side, it has to be said, and are much in demand but usually superb! There are many other very good self-catering cottages for the birdwatcher and this style often suits keeping strange hours and flexible eating arrangements. Many are available for weekend bookings but usually properties are bookable by the week, Saturday to Saturday.

Your reports/comments on all types of accommodation, pubs and inns mentioned are always welcome: Good Birdwatchers Guide, PO Box 10, Llandrindod Wells, Powys LD1 5ZZ.

When you are birdwatching always remember the 'Good Birdwatchers'code of conduct:-

- The welfare of the bird comes first.
- Do not damage the environment in any way.
- Keep to public rights of way or access and if you have any near where you live *use them*!
- Park sensibly especially in rural areas.
- Have consideration for other countryside users.

- Take all your litter home, where you can ensure it's safe collection/disposal.
- If you find a rare migrant bird think before you tell anyone. Will hundreds of other birdwatchers cause problems for the bird, the environment, or other land users? *But* do not be selfish with the birds you find.
- If you find a nationally rare breeding bird which is not under any apparent threat from human influence say nothing to anyone until after fledging, then firstly contact the Nature Conservancy Council or the new equivalents in Wales and Scotland. If it is in immediate or obvious danger ring Species Protection Dept, RSPB (0767 680551).
- Send in your bird records to the appropriate County Bird Recorder (see list of CR's at the back of this book).
- Do not keep cats as pets. Ten million birds are killed by feral and domestic cats annually in Britain.
- If you have a garden improve it's attractiveness to birds at all seasons.
- Join at least two of the following: British Trust for Ornithology, Woodland Trust, your local county nature trust, Scottish Ornithologists Club, Campaign for the Protection of Rural Wales, Council for the Protection of Rural England, Scottish Wildlife Trust, Wildfowl and Wetlands Trust.
- Never bring birdwatching into disrepute.
- Enjoy your birdwatching whilst there are still birds to watch!

Bedfordshire

Odell & Harrold Country Park   153   6m S of Rushden
Car-park and information centre by minor road on east side of
Harrold village at SP956567. Then tracks around pits and beside
river.
Winter wildfowl; summer warblers and Hobby; passage waders;
migrants.

Felmersham Gravel Pits   153   6m SE of Rushden
Park by minor road just N of Felmersham over the bridge at
SP991580. Then footpath to pits and beside river.
Summer warblers; wildfowl; migrants.

Odell Great Wood   153   5m S of Rushden
Park by church ¼m NE of Odell village at SP967580. Then footpaths
north to the woods.
Woodland birds including Nightingale and Hawfinch.

Radwell Gravel Pits   153   1m NE of Felmersham
Park by minor road ½m N of Radwell at TL007583. Then footpaths
north and east between the pits.
Passage waders and terns; wildfowl; migrants; summer Hobby.

TIC	10 St. Pauls Square, Bedford (0234 215226)
YH	Manor Farm, Vicarage Road, Bradwell, Milton Keynes (0908 310944)
RF	Bell, Odell
	Mad Dog, Odell
	Swan, Radwell
BB	Newton Park Farm, Turvey, nr Bedford (023064 250)
SC	New Gains Farm, Bedford Road, Turvey (023064 281)

The Lodge   153   1½m SE of Sandy
Car-park and reception centre, ½m S of B1042, at TL187478. Then
nature trails and hide.
Woodland birds including Crossbill.

Priory Country Park   153   1½ m SE of Bedford centre
Car-park ¼m N of A603 just E of its junction with A5134 at
TL079488. Then tracks around pit and beside the river.
Passage waders and terns; winter wildfowl; passerine migrants.

Blunham Gravel Pits   153   6m E of Bedford
Park by minor road ½m N of Blunham at TL155519 and take foot-
path south by River Ivel and the pits.
Wildfowl; passage terns.

> ***Home Wood***   *153   TL140463   6m SE of Bedford*
> *Woodland birds.*

> ***Rowney Warren Wood***   *153   TL124405   8m SE of*
> *Bedford*
> *Woodland birds.*

> ***Willington Wood***   *153   TL097503   3m E of Bedford*
> *Woodland birds.*

> ***Henlow Pits***   *153   TL184387   3m S of Biggleswade*
> *Summer warblers; wildfowl; passage waders and terns.*

TIC   As previous entry.
YH   97 Tenison Road, Cambridge (0223 354601)
RF   Hare and Hounds, Old Warden, nr Biggleswade
          Crown, Willington
BB   Orchard Cottage, 1 High Street, Wrestlingworth, nr
          Sandy (076 723 355)
          Church Farm, 41 High Street, Roxton, nr Bedford (0234
          870234)
BBE   Highfield Farm, Sandy (0767 82332)

Stewartby Lake Country Park   153   6m SW of Bedford
Car-park by A5140 1½m NW of Stewartby at TL006429. Then track
around the lake.
Winter wildfowl and gull roost; passage waders; summer
warblers.

Marston Thrift   153   3m E of Stewartby
Car-park at end of minor road 1½m E of A5140 at SP974413. Then
footpath through woods.
Woodland birds including Nightingale; summer warblers.

Chimney Corner   153   4m SW of Bedford
View from minor road between A418 and A5140 at Kempston
Hardwick, TL034443, and from beside A5140 1m N at TL036445.
Passage waders and winter wildfowl.

Brogborough Pit   153   SP975395   *8m SW of Bedford*
Winter wildfowl and gulls; passage terns.

Maulden Wood   153   TL074395   *3m NE of Ampthill*
Woodland birds including Hawfinch and Lady Amherst's
Pheasant.

Kings Wood   153   TL045403   *2m NE of Ampthill*
Woodland birds.

Flitwick Moor   153   TL046355   *1m E of Flitwick*
Woodland birds; summer warblers; Water Rail; river birds.

Ampthill Park & The Firs   153   TL026382   *1m NW of*
Ampthill
Woodland birds including Hawfinch; summer warblers.

TIC   12 Dunstable Street, Ampthill (0525 402051)
YH   Manor Farm, Vicarage Road, Bradwell, Milton Keynes
(0908 310944)
RF   Green Man, Lidlington
BBE   Pond Farm, 7 High Street, Pulloxhill (0525 712316)
SC   Priestly Farm, Church Road, Flitwick (0525 712978)

Stockgrove Country Park & Kings Wood   165   **3m N of
Leighton Buzzard**
Car-park by minor road 1½m SE of Great Brickhill at SP919294.
Then many paths north and south.
Woodland birds including Hawfinch and Redstart, summer
warblers.

Wavendon Heath & Charle Wood   165   **6m N of Leighton
Buzzard**
Car-park by minor road 1m W of A5 at SP926336. Then footpath
north and south.
Woodland birds including Redstart, Nightjar and Lady Amherst's
Pheasant.

Aspley Wood   153   SP937350   *6½m N of Leighton*
Buzzard Woodland birds and summer warblers.

TIC   *Heritage Centre, 12 Bedford Street, Woburn
The Library, Vernon Place, Dunstable (0582 471012)
YH   As previous entry.
RF   Old Red Lion, Great Brickhill
Magpie, Woburn

Sundon Hill & Sharpenhoe   166   **5m N of Luton**
Car-park by minor road 1m N of Streatley at TL065296. Then foot-
paths east and west.
Woodland and downland birds; migrants.

Deacon Hill   *166*   *TL126298*   *4m W of Hitchin*
Summer warblers; downland birds; migrants.

Barton Hills   *166*   *TL095300*   *5m N of Luton*
Downland birds; migrants.

Warden & Gulley Hills   *166*   *TL092265*   *3m N of Luton centre*
Downland birds; migrants.

TIC	Grosvenor House, 45–47a Alma Street, Luton (0582 401579)
YH	As previous entry.
	The Old Brewery House, Ivinghoe, Leighton Buzzard (0296 668251)
RF	Live and Let Live, Pegsdon, nr Barton-le-Clay

Berkshire

Horton, Wraysbury & Hythe End Pits   176   **3–4m SE of Windsor**
Park at the end of lane ¼ m S of Horton, ½ m E of B376, at TQ013756, then path between the pits, under the railway line, and across the road to Wraysbury Pits. Also, from Wraysbury railway station, ¾ m E of Wraysbury at TQ014742, take the path SE beside the line and then S under it to Hythe End Pits.
Passage and winter wildfowl; summer warblers; migrants.

Queen Mother Reservoir   176   **2–3m E of Windsor**
Car-park by minor road along east shore ¾m N of Horton at TQ014769 and view from the adjoining bank.
Winter wildfowl and gull roost; passage terns.

Windsor Great Park   176   **4m S of Windsor**
Car-parks at the SW end of Virginia Water by the A329 e.g. at Blacknest, SU961686, then paths north and west.
Wildfowl and woodland birds.

> *Sunnymeads Gravel Pit*   176   *TQ001760*   *¾m W of Horton*
> *Passage and winter wildfowl; passage terns.*

TIC	Central Station, Thames Street, Windsor (0753 852010)
YH	Edgeworth House, Mill Lane, Windsor (0753 861710)
RF	Union, Old Windsor
BB	41 Frances Road, Windsor (0753 861207)

Summerleaze Pit   175   **1¼ m NE of Maidenhead centre**
Park by minor road ¾m W of A4094 at SU893825, then path north beside the west side of the lake.
Passage and winter wildfowl; passage waders and terns; Little Ringed Plover.

Maidenhead Thicket   175   2m W of Maidenhead centre
Car-park ¼m N of A423, 1m N of A4 at SU855816, then path SW
across the main road and through the woods.
Woodland birds.

Cock Marsh & Winter Hill   175   3m N of Maidenhead
Car-park at Cookham by B4447, ¼m W of its junction with A4094 at
SU894854, then paths north beside the River Thames and under
the railway line toward Winter Hill. Also car-park at Winter Hill at
SU870860 and paths west or east through the woods.
Woodland, river and meadow species.

> *Ashley Hill   175   SU825812   4m W of Maidenhead*
> *Woodland birds.*
>
> *Bowsey Hill   175   SU806797   5m W of Maidenhead*
> *Woodland birds and summer warblers.*

TIC   The Library, St. Ives Road, Maidenhead (0628 781110)
YH   As previous entry.
RF   Shire Horse, Littlewick Green
          Jolly Farmer, Cookham Dean, nr Marlow
BBE   Laurel Cottage, Bath Road, Knowl Hill, nr Maidenhead
          (062882 5046)
SC   New Cottage, National Trust, Cliveden, Taplow, nr
          Maidenhead (0628 605069)

Twyford Pits   175   0.5–1m SW of Twyford
Car-park by minor road ½m SE of A3032, just S of the railway line
at SU779751. Then paths east around the pits.
Winter wildfowl and gulls; passage waders.

Dinton Pastures Country Park   175   3m S of Twyford
Car-park by B3030 1m N of its junction with A329 at SU784718.
Then many paths around and between the lakes and to the hides.
Winter wildfowl; summer warblers; Little Ringed Plover and
Common Tern.

TIC   Town Hall, Blagrave Street, Reading (0734 566226)
YH   As previous entry.
RF   Black Swan, by Dinton Pastures
          Green Man, Hurst, nr Wokingham
BBE   Inverloddon, Wargrave, nr Twyford (073522 2230)

Englemere Pond   175   2½m E of Bracknell centre
Car-park by B3017 0.3m S of its junction with A329 at SU903684.
Then paths east through the woods and to the pond.
Woodland birds; wildfowl; Reed Warbler and other reedbed
species.

Crowthorne Wood   175   2–3m S of Bracknell centre
Car-park by B3430 ½m E of its junction with A3095 at SU862661, then many tracks south.
Woodland birds.

Edgebarrow Woods & Broadmoor Bottom   175   4m SW of Bracknell
Car-park by A3095 1m S of its junction with B3348 at SU838631. Then tracks east through the woods and Owlsmoor Bog and on east to Broadmoor Bottom.
Woodland and heathland birds including Woodlark and Hobby.

> *Finchampstead Ridges   175   SU813636   2m SW of Crowthorne*
> *Woodland birds and summer warblers.*

TIC   Central Library, Town Square, Bracknell (0344 423149)
YH   As previous entry.
RF   Crooked Billet, Honey Hill, nr Wokingham
BB   Beechwood House, Vicarage Road, Yateley Green, nr Camberley (0252 872395)

Burghfield & Theale Gravel Pits   175   3–4m SW of Reading centre
View from minor roads 1.5–2m NE of Burghfield e.g. SU685700, and SU670703 1m W. Also 1m SE of Theale from A4 at SU649697. Winter wildfowl and gull roost; passage terns and waders; summer Little Ringed Plover and Common Tern.

Padworth Common   175   2m SW of Burghfield Common
Park by minor road ½m S of Ufton Nervet at SU635666, then tracks west and south.
Woodland birds and summer warblers.

> *Moor Copse   175   SU635742   2m N of Theale*
> *Woodland and river birds.*

TIC   Town Hall, Blagrave Street, Reading (0734 566226)
YH   Hill House, Reading Road, Streatley, Reading (0491 872278)
RF   Queens Head, Bradfield, nr Theale
        Old Boot, Stanford Dingley, nr Theale
        Bull, Stanford Dingley, nr Theale
BB   Boot Farm, Southend Road, Bradfield, nr Reading (0734 744298)

Thatcham Reedbeds & Gravel Pits   174   2m E of Newbury
Car-park at the end of track ½m S of A4, ¼m SE of the sewage works, at SU505667. Then paths west, east and south under the railway line.
Passage and winter wildfowl; passage waders; reedbed species; summer warblers; migrants.

Buckleberry Common   174   2m NE of Thatcham
Car-park by minor road 1m NE of Upper Buckleberry, 1½m N of A4, at SU556692, then many tracks and paths.
Woodland birds and summer warblers.

Snelsmore Common Country Park   174   3m N of Newbury
Car-park by B4494 2m N of its junction with A4 at SU 463710, then paths and tracks westwards.
Woodland and heathland birds.

> *Bowdown Woods*   174   *SU502655   2m SE of Newbury*
> *Woodland birds.*

> *Brimpton Gravel Pit*   174   *SU571654   3½m SE of Thatcham*
> *Passage terns and waders; winter wildfowl; reedbed species.*

TIC	The Wharf, Newbury (0635 32196)
YH	As previous entry.
RF	Pineapple, Brimpton, nr Thatcham
	Blade Bone, Buckleberry, nr Thatcham
BB	Manor Farm, Brimpton (0734 713166)
BBSC	Red Shute Hill, Hermitage, nr Newbury (0635 201100)
BBE	Woodlands Park Farm, Ashford Hill, nr Heath End (063523 258)
SC	Zinzan, Upper Buckleberry, nr Reading (0635 64751)

Inkpen & Walbury Hills   174   7m SW of Newbury
Car-park by minor road 1½m S of Inkpen, 1m S of Upper Green at SU370620. Then track east up Walbury Hill to West Woodhay Down, or west along the ridge to Inkpen Hill then south down the Test Way to Sheepless Hill and Combe Wood.
Downland and woodland birds including Hobby; migrants.

TIC	As previous entry.
YH	Red Lion Lane, Overton, Basingstoke (0256 770516)
RF	Swan, Inkpen
	White Hart, Hamstead Marshall, nr Newbury
RFBBE	Jack Russell, Faccombe, nr Newbury (026487 315)

Buckinghamshire

Black Park Country Park   176   2–3m S of Gerrard's Cross
Large car-park by minor road ½m N of A412 1m W of its junction
with A4007 at TQ005833, then paths and tracks eastward.
Woodland birds; summer warblers.

Langley Park   176   3½m S of Gerrard's Cross
Car-park ¼m down minor road (Billet Lane) south of A412, ¼m west
of its junction with A4007, at TQ015823. Then paths west.
Woodland birds.

Church Wood   176   1½m W of Gerrard's Cross
Park beside track running east from the village of Hedgerley, 1m E
of A355 at SU970873, then track and path east to the woods.
Woodland birds.

Burnham Beeches   175 or 176   3m SW of Gerrard's Cross
Car-parks ¼m W of A355 3m S of junction 2 of M40 at SU956850,
then many tracks and paths west and north.
Woodland birds and summer warblers.

> ***Little Britain Country Park***   *176*   *TQ045806*   *2m SE of*
> *Iver Heath*
> *Woodland birds; summer warblers; wildfowl; winter gulls;*
> *passage terns.*

> ***Farnham Common***   *176*   *SU970848*   *2m SW of Gerrard's*
> *Cross*
> *Woodland birds.*

> ***Stoke Common***   *176*   *SU985855*   *1½m S of Gerrard's*
> *Cross*
> *Woodland birds.*

TIC   The Library, St. Ives Road, Maidenhead, Berks (0628
781110)
YH   Welders Lane, Jordans, Beaconsfield (02407 3135)

RF   One Pin, Hedgerley, nr Gerrard's Cross
           Black Horse, Fulmer, nr Gerrard's Cross
           Royal Oak, Farnham Common
           Fox and Pheasant, Stoke Poges
           Blackwood Arms, Littleworth Common, nr Farnham
           Common
BBE   Bridgettine Convent, Fulmer Common Road, Iver Heath
           (0753 662073/662645)

Little Marlow Pits   175   2m E of Marlow
Park down lane at S end of Little Marlow village, ½m S of A4155 at
SU875877 and take track and path south beside the pit. Also car-
park on east side at SU884876.
Winter wildfowl and gull roost; passage waders and terns;
migrants.

> **Hambleden Great Wood**   175   SU770875   5m W of
> Marlow
> Woodland birds.

> **Heath Wood**   175   SU805870   3m W of Marlow
> Woodland birds.

TIC   *Court Garden Leisure Complex, Pound Lane, Marlow
           (06284 3597)
YH   As previous entry.
RF   Yew Tree, Frieth, nr Marlow
           King's Head, Little Marlow
           Old Sun, Lane End, nr Marlow
           Peacock, Lane End, nr Marlow
RFBBE Stag and Huntsman, Hambleden, nr Henley (0491
           571227)
BBE   The Old Bakery, Skirmett, nr Marlow (049 163 247)
SC   Myosotis, Widmoor, Wooburn Green, Bourne End
           (06285 21594)

Penn Wood   165   4m SW of Amersham
Park in Penn Street ½m S of A404 at SU922958 and take track and
path north through the woods.
Woodland birds; summer warblers.

Hearnton Wood   165   3m NW of High Wycombe centre
Car-park ¼m N of A40 from West Wycombe at SU827952 then track
and paths north.
Woodland birds; summer warblers.

Philipshill Wood & Newland Park   176   4m SE of Amersham
Park by minor road 1m SE of B4442, 1m N of Chalfont Common, at TQ007936 and paths north through the park and woods.
Woodland birds and summer warblers including Hawfinch and Firecrest.

Shardeloes Lake   165   SU940982   2m W of Amersham
Wildfowl; migrants.

Naphill Common   165   SU840970   1m W of Naphill
Woodland birds; summer warblers.

Hodgmoor Woods   175 or 176   SU965935   3m NE of Beaconsfield
Woodland birds.

Chesham Bois Woods   165   SP962003   1m N of Amersham centre
Woodland birds.

TIC   As previous entry.
YH   The Village Hall, Bradenham, High Wycombe (024 024 2929)
RF   Hit or Miss, Penn Street
Red Lion, Little Missenden
Pink and Lily, Lacey Green, nr Princes Risborough
Queens Head, Winchmore Hill, nr Amersham
BBE   The Elms, Radnage, nr High Wycombe (024 026 2175)

Weston Turville Reservoir   165   1m N of Wendover
Park by minor road ½m N of A413 from Worlds End, 1m S of Weston Turville at SP858097, then paths around the reservoir to the east.
Winter gulls; passage and winter wildfowl; woodland birds and summer warblers.

Wendover Woods   165   1–2m NE of Wendover
Several car-parks and picnic sites about 1m SE of A4011. Access from minor road near Aston Hill ¼m S of A4011 at SP887105. Then many tracks, paths and forest walks.
Woodland birds; summer warblers.

Pulpit Hill   165   2m NE of Princes Risborough
Park by A4010 just south of Great Kimble church at SP826057 and take track and path SE to wooded hill.
Woodland and downland birds; summer warblers.

Coombe Hill   *165*   *SP849067*   *1½m SW of Wendover*
Woodland and downland birds; summer warblers.

Grand Union Canal   *165*   *SP873140*   *4m N of Wendover*
Summer warblers; water birds including Kingfisher.

TIC   The Clock Tower, Wendover (0296 623056)
YH   As previous entry.
RF   Rising Sun, Little Hampden, nr Princes Risborough
RFBBE   Chandos Arms, Weston Turville
BB   The Haven, 7 Lower Icknield Way, Aston Clinton, nr Tring (0296 630751)

Ivinghoe Hills & Common   **165**   **4½m SW of Dunstable centre**
Park beside minor road S of B489 to Ringshall 1m NE of Ivinghoe e.g. SP961164 or SP964158 or SP975146. Then paths and tracks east or west.
Woodland birds including Hawfinch, Redstart and Wood Warbler; summer warblers; downland birds; migrants.

College Lake   **165**   **1½m NE of Tring**
Car-park and visitor centre by B488 just NE of Bulbourne at SP935139 then nature trails and hide.
Passage terns and waders; winter wildfowl; summer Little Ringed Plover and Common Tern.

TIC   The Library, Vernon Place, Dunstable (0582 471012)
YH   The Old Brewery House, Ivinghoe, Leighton Buzzard, Beds. (0296 668251)
RF   Greyhound, Aldbury, nr Tring
   Valiant Trooper, Aldbury, nr Tring
   Kings Head, Ivinghoe
BBE   Bellows Mill Cottage, Bellows Mill, Eaton Bray, nr Dunstable (0525 220548/220205)

Calvert Jubilee   **165**   **6m S of Buckingham**
Park by minor road between the two lakes 1½m N of Edgcott at SP681252 and path east to the lake and hide.
Winter wildfowl and gulls; summer warblers.

Shabbington Woods   **165 or 164**   **3½m N of Wheatley**
Car-park by minor road 2m W of B4011 from Oakley at SP612117, then tracks and paths east and south.
Woodland birds; summer warblers.

Rushbeds Wood   **165**   **1½m NE of Brill**
Park by the railway line 2½m E of B4011, 1½m S of Ludgershall at SP674154. Then paths through the woods to the west of the line.
Woodland birds.

TIC   County Hall, Walton Street, Aylesbury (0296 382308)
YH   As previous entry.
RF   Greyhound, Marsh Gibbon, nr Bicester
        Pheasant, Brill, nr Aylesbury
        Clifden Arms, Worminghall, nr Wheatley
BB   Poletrees Farm, Brill (0844 238276)
        Manor Farm, Shabbington (0844 201103)
BBSC   Wallace Farm, Dinton, Stone, nr Aylesbury (0286 748660)
BBE   Manor Farm, Waterperry, nr Wheatley (08447 263)

Brickhill Woods   152   S & E of Bow Brickhill
Park by Bow Brickhill church at the top of the hill ¼m E of the village at SP912344, then paths through the woods north or south.
Woodland birds including Nightjar, Hobby, Golden and Lady Amherst's Pheasants.

Caldecote Lakes   152   1m NW of Bow Brickhill
View from minor road 1m N of A45, ¼m N of Bow Brickhill railway station at SP900350.
Passage and winter wildfowl; passage waders and terns; winter gull roost.

Willen Lake   152   2m S of Newport Pagnell
Car-park by minor road (V10, Brickhill Street) ½m N of A509 1½m W of junction 14 of M1 at SP876402. Then path around the northern half of the lake.
Winter wildfowl and large gull roost; passage and winter waders; passage terns and passerines; summer Little Ringed Plover.

Stony Stratford Wildlife Conservation Area   152   ½m E of Old Stratford
Park by minor road 1m SE of junction of A422, A5 and A508 at SP785409, or in the car-park at east end of lakes, and footpath around.
Passage and winter wildfowl; passage waders; summer warblers.

Great Linford Pits Wildfowl Centre   152   2m SW of Newport Pagnell
Signposted car-park from minor road 1m SW of M1, just N of Great Linford at SP847426 and view from lane beside western end of the lake. Entrance to reserve and hides by permit available on site Sept-Feb.
Winter wildfowl; passage waders and terns; summer warblers.

>*Emberton Park Country Park   152   SP885504   1m S of Olney*
>*Winter wildfowl; passage terns and waders.*

>*Stokepark Wood   152   SP825492   4½m NW of Newport Pagnell*
>*Woodland birds.*

TIC	Saxon Court, 502 Avebury Boulevard, Milton Keynes (0908 691995)
YH	Manor Farm, Vicarage Road, Bradwell, Milton Keynes (0908 310944)
RF	Black Horse, Great Linford
	Old Red Lion, Great Brickhill
	Weathercock, Woburn Sands
	Magpie, Woburn
BB	Milford Leys Farm, Castlethorpe, nr Wolverton (0908 510153)
	Haversham Grange, Haversham, nr Wolverton (0908 312389)
BBE	Chantry Farm, Pindon End, Hanslope, Stony Stratford (0908 510269)
	Mill Farm, Gayhurst, nr Newport Pagnell (0908 611489)

Foxcote Reservoir   152   1½m NE of Buckingham

View from minor road by S end of reservoir 1m NE of A413 from Maids Moreton at SP716364.

Wildfowl; passage waders and terns.

Hyde Lane Pits   152   2m NE of Buckingham

Car-park ¼m down track S off A422 at the S end of the lakes at SP724349, then path along east side.

Winter wildfowl including Whooper Swan; woodland birds; summer warblers.

TIC	As previous entry.
YH	As previous entry.
RF	Bull and Butcher, Akeley, nr Buckingham

Cambridgeshire

Grafham Water   153   5m SW of Huntingdon
Car-park at West Perry by B661 along the south shore at TL143672, then track west to hide. Also car-parks 1½m further east along B661, and along the north shore at TL166681.
Winter wildfowl; passage waders and terns.

Little Paxton Gravel Pits   153   2m N of St. Neots
Park at east side of Little Paxton, 1m E of A1, at TL195629. Then footpaths north and south around the pits.
Wildfowl; passage waders and terns; summer warblers.

Fen Drayton Pits   154   3m SE of St. Ives
Park in Fen Drayton, TL339686, then footpaths north around the pits.
Wildfowl; passage waders and terns.

Gransden & Wavesley Woods   153   6m SE of St. Neots
Park by minor road 1m SW of Great Gransden at TL257552. Then track east and footpaths through the woods.
Woodland birds.

Hayley Wood   153   TL290530   *8m SE of St. Neots*
Woodland birds.

Hemingford Grey & Fenstanton Pits   153   TL302697 & TL303685   *2–3m S of St. Ives*
Wildfowl; passage waders and terns; summer warblers; woodland birds.

Little Paxton Wood   153   TL167635   *3m NW of St. Neots*
Woodland birds.

St. Ives Pits   153   TL325715   *1m SE of St. Ives centre*
Wildfowl; passage waders and terns.

TIC	The Library, Princes Street, Huntingdon (0480 425831)
YH	97 Tenison Road, Cambridge (0223 354601)
RF	New Tavern, Great Staughton
	Three Tuns, Fen Drayton
	Crown and Cushion, Great Gransden
BBE	Molesworth Lodge Farm, Molesworth (08014 309)
	Cross Keys Inn, Molesworth (08014 283)
	Arden House, 4 Pettitts Close, Dry Drayton, nr Cambridge (0954 80975)

Fowlmere   154   4m NE of Royston

Car-park by minor road 1½m west of Fowlmere ¾m east of A10 at TL407461. Then tracks to hides.

Reedbed species; summer warblers; winter woodland birds and roost.

> ***Wandlebury Country Park*** *154* *TL495535* *4m SE of Cambridge centre*
> *Woodland birds; summer warblers.*

> ***Shepreth Moor*** *154* *TL385475* *4m NE of Royston*
> *Woodland birds; summer warblers.*

TIC	Wheeler Street, Cambridge (0223 322640)
YH	As previous entry.
RF	Royal Oak, Barrington
	Swan House Inn, Fowlmere
	Plough, Shepreth
BBE	Worsted Barrows Guest House, Babraham, nr Sawston (0223 833298)

Wicken Fen   154   6m NW of Newmarket

Car-park ¼m south of A1123 in Wicken at TL565706. Then paths around the reserve and to the hides.

Summer warblers including Cetti's, Savi's and Grasshopper; occasional Spotted Crake and Marsh Harrier in summer; Bearded Tit; winter Hen Harrier roost; winter wildfowl.

Chippenham Fen   154   4m N of Newmarket

Park by minor road 1m SW of B1085 from Chippenham at TL656686. Then track NW and footpath across the fen and woodland.

Woodland birds; summer warblers; Long-eared Owl.

TIC	Oliver Cromwell's House, 29 St. Mary's Street, Ely (0353 662062)
YH	Ely 6th Form Centre, St. Audrey's, Downham Road, Ely (0353 667423)

RF   Bell, Kennett
              Lazy Otter, Stretham
BB   The Old Rectory, Green End, Landbeach, nr Cambridge
              (0223 861507/861348)

Ouse Washes   143   4m E of Chatteris
Car-park and visitor centre at end of minor road 3m south of
Manea at Welches Dam, TL471862.
Summer and winter wildfowl; winter gulls; passage and winter
waders; summer Black-tailed Godwit; winter Hen Harrier roost;
migrants.

Roswell Pits & Ely Nature Trail   143   1–2m E of Ely
Park by minor road 2m NE of A142 on the east side of River Great
Ouse at TL563804. Then footpaths west and north around the pits.
Summer warblers; reedbed species; woodland birds; passage
waders and terns; winter wildfowl.

TIC   As previous entry.
YH   As previous entry.
RF   Ship Inn, Purls Bridge
              Fenlands Lodge, Stuntney, nr Ely
BB   The Black Hostelry, The College, Firmary Lane, Ely (0353
              2612)
              The Old Bow House, 52 West End, March (0354 53793)
SC   Greenways Lodge, Queen Adelaide, nr Ely (0353 666706)
              56 St. Marys Street, Ely (0353 664780)

Holme Fen   142   6m SE of Peterborough
View from minor roads which cross the reserve NE of Holme off
B660 e.g. at TL203894 and TL215885.
Woodland birds; summer warblers; Nightingale.

Aversley Wood   142   10m SW of Peterborough
Woodland Trust. Park by minor road ¾m SW of A1, 1½m south of
Sawtry, at TL173814. Then track NW to the wood.
Woodland birds.

Monks Wood   142   6m N of Huntingdon
Permit in advance from NCC, Northminster House, Peter-
borough.
Entrance by minor road 1m SW of B1090 1½m SW of Woodwalton at
TL202797.
Woodland birds including Nightingale.

TIC   45 Bridge Street, Peterborough (0733 317537)
YH   As previous entry.

RF	Bell, Stilton
	Admiral Wells, Holme
BBE	25 Bury Road, Ramsey, Huntingdon (0487 813221)

Ferry Meadows Country Park   142   2m W of Peterborough centre

Car-park ½m N of A605, 1½m W of its junction with A1260, at TL148974.

Wildfowl; passage waders and terns; summer warblers, Little Ringed Plover and Common Tern.

Castor Hanglands   142   4m NW of Peterborough

Park by minor road off A47 2½m north of Ailsworth at TF124024. Then track west and footpath south through the woods.

Woodland and scrub species including summer warblers and Nightingale.

Peakirk Wildfowl Refuge   142   5m N of Peterborough centre

Entrance by minor road just north of Peakirk village ¼m N of B1443, at TF168069.

Wildfowl; passage waders.

Nene Washes   142   6m E of Peterborough

Park by minor road just east of B1040 1½m N of Whittlesey on the south side of River Nene at TF276992.

Summer waders and Marsh Harrier; passage waders and winter wildfowl.

> ***Barnack Hills***   *142   TF076044   7m NW of Peterborough*
> *Woodland birds; summer warblers.*

TIC	45 Bridge Street, Peterborough (0733 317336)
YH	Capstone, 16 High Street, Thurlby, Bourne, Lincs (0778 425588)
RF	Golden Pheasant, Etton
	Royal Oak, Castor
	Dog in a Doublet, nr Whittlesey
BBE	Castle Farm, Fotheringhay, nr Peterborough (08326 200)

Cheshire, Merseyside & Greater Manchester

Burton Marsh   117   2½m S of Neston
View from car-park by minor road 1½m W of Burton, ¼m W of railway line, at SJ303746. Also paths by marshes north and south. Passage and winter waders and wildfowl; winter raptors, Short-eared Owl and Twite; migrants.

Little Neston   117   1m S of Neston centre
Car-park at end of minor road at west end of Little Neston, ¾m W of railway line at SJ288762, and footpaths north and south.
Birds as at Burton Marsh and reedbed species.

Gayton Sands & Neston Marshes   117 & 108   1½m-2½m NW of Neston centre
Car-park ¼m N of B5135 at NW extremity of Neston (Parkgate), SJ274791. Then footpath northwest.
Passage and winter waders, wildfowl and raptors; marsh and reedbed species.

West Kirby Marine Lake, Red Rocks & Hilbre   108   1–2m SW of Hoylake
Park ¼m W of A540 at west end of West Kirby, at the north end of the lake, SJ210867, and take footpath north to Red Rocks Point or across the sands to Hilbre at low tide.
Passage terns; passage and winter waders; winter seaduck, divers and northern gulls; migrants.

New Brighton   108   N extremity of Wirral peninsula
Park by A554, on the north side of New Brighton by the marine lake, and view from Perch Rock, SJ310945.
Seawatching; winter seaduck, divers and northern gulls; passage and winter waders.

Eastham Woods Country Park   108   1m NE of Eastham
Car-park at end of minor road N of Eastham near Eastham Ferry, SJ363820. Then footpaths through the woods and along the foreshore.
Woodland birds; passage and winter waders and wildfowl; migrants.

> **Thurstaston Common**   108   SJ245855   2m SE of Hoylake
> *Woodland birds; summer warblers; migrants.*

> **Wirral Country Park**   108   SJ237835   2m W of Heswall
> *Passage and winter wildfowl; migrants.*

> **Leasowe Common & Mockbeggar Wharf**   108   SJ253914
> *2m W of Wallasey*
> *Seawatching; passage and winter waders; migrants.*

> **Caldy & The Wirral Way**   108   SJ222850   4m NW of
> *Heswall*
> *Passage and winter waders and seaduck; scrub species; migrants.*

> **Dibbinsdale**   108   SJ345827   2m NW of Eastham
> *Woodland and river birds; summer warblers; reedbed species.*

> **Burton Wood**   117   SJ314745   2m SE of Neston
> *Woodland birds and summer warblers.*

> **Caldy Wood**   108   SJ230858   ½m N of Caldy
> *Woodland birds including Redstart and Lesser Spotted Woodpecker.*

> **Storeton Woods**   108   SJ314850   ½m NE of Storeton
> *Woodland birds and summer warblers.*

TIC	Marine Parade, New Brighton, Merseyside (051 638 7144)
YH	Hough Green House, 40 Hough Green, Chester (0244 680056)
RF	Magazine, New Brighton
	Harp, Neston
	Seven Stars, Thornton Hough
	Yacht, Puddington, nr Burton

RFBBE Pollard Inn, Hadlow Road, Willaston, nr Neston (051 327 4615/6695)

BBE Park Hotel, Westbourne Road, West Kirby (051 625 9319)
Sea Level Hotel, 126 Victoria Road, New Brighton (051 639 3408)

Delamere Forest   117   7m NE of Chester
Car-parks by minor road, 1m W of B5152, 1½m NE of Kelsall, e.g. at SJ543716. Then many tracks north or south.
Woodland birds including Crossbill, Long-eared Owl, Pied Flycatcher, Goshawk and Redstart.

Little Budworth Common Country Park   117   5m W of Winsford
Car-park ¼m W of Little Budworth, 1½m E of A49, at SJ592655. Then footpaths NW across the common.
Woodland and heathland birds.

Frodsham Marsh & Weaver Bend   117   1–2m NW of Frodsham
Park 1m NW of A56 along track over M56 from Marsh Green at SJ507787. Then tracks east to Weaver Bend and ICI tank, west around the sludge bed and to the pools by Manchester Ship Canal.
Passage waders and terns; winter widlfowl; summer Little Ringed Plover; migrants.

Marston Flashes   118   1m NE of Northwich
View from B5075 along the east side, e.g. ½m N of A559 at SJ670747, and from minor road along the western banks.
Passage terns and waders; winter wildfowl and gull roost; summer Little Ringed Plover.

Marbury Country Park   118   N of Northwich
Car-park by minor road, 1½m N of A553 1m S of Comberbach, at SJ652763. Then footpaths north to the woods and Budworth Mere hide.
Woodland birds; summer warblers; wildfowl; passage waders.

> *Foxhill Woods*   117   SJ510760   *2m SW of Frodsham*
> *Woodland birds; migrants.*

> *Nunsmere*   117   SJ590690   *5m SW of Northwich*
> *Wildfowl; woodland birds; summer grebes.*

> *Eaton Estate*   117   SJ418615   *3m S of Chester*
> *Woodland birds; summer warblers; river birds including Mandarin Duck.*

TIC   Chester Visitor Centre, Vicars Lane, Chester (0244 351609)

YH   As previous entry.

RF   Spinner and Bergamot, Comberbach
Ring o'Bells, Overton, nr Frodsham
Fishpool, Delamere

BBE   Beechwood House, 206 Wallercote Road, Weaverham, nr Northwich (0606 852123)
Wincham Hall, Wincham, nr Northwich (0606 43453)
Springfield Guest House, Chester Road, Oakmere, nr Northwich (0606 882538)

Peckforton Hills   117   8m NW of Nantwich
Park just east of Higher Burwardsley, 1½m N of A534, at SJ526566. Then footpaths and tracks north and south through the woods. Woodland birds including Pied Flycatcher and Redstart; migrants.

Marbury Mere   117   3m NE of Whitchurch
Park in Marbury village, SJ562457, and take footpath along south side of the lake.
Wildfowl.

Oss Mere   117   SJ566440   2m NE of Whitchurch
Wildfowl; summer warblers.

Bickerton Hill   117   SJ500530   9m W of Nantwich
Woodland birds and summer warblers; scrub species.

Raw Head   117   SJ506547   9m W of Nantwich
Woodland birds.

Baddiley Mere Reservoirs   117   SJ595503   4m SW of Nantwich
Wildfowl including Ruddy Duck.

TIC   Civic Centre, High Street, Whitchurch, Shrops (0948 4577)
Beam Street, Nantwich, Cheshire (0270 623914)

YH   As previous entry.

RF   Pheasant Inn, Higher Burwardsley
Cholmondeley Arms, Bickley Moss
Swan, Marbury
Dusty Miller, Wrenbury

BBE   Millhey Farm, Barton, nr Malpas (082 925 431)
Tilston Lodge, Tilston, nr Malpas (082 98 223)
Sproston Hill Farm, Wrenbury, nr Whitchurch (0270 780241)

SC   Woodworth Lodge, Birds Lane, Bunbury, nr Nantwich (0829 260581)

Sandbach Flashes   118   **2m W & SW of Sandbach**

> *Watch Lane Flash*   *1m SW of Elworth*
> View from minor road (Watch Lane) 1m SW of Sandbach railway station along the northern side e.g. at SJ727606.
>
> *Fodens Flash*   *½m SW of Sandbach Railway station*
> View from minor road ½m N of Watch Lane Flash at SJ730614.
>
> *Elton Hall Flash*   *2m SW of Sandbach Railway station*
> View from minor road (Clay Lane) running between the flashes ¼m W of the railway line at SJ725595.
>
> *Railway Flash*   *1m SW of Elton Hall Flash*
> View from footpath leading southwest from above site for about ½m to SJ720589.
>
> *Crabmill Flash*   *1m W of Watch Lane Flash*
> View from minor road 1½m SE of Warmingham at SJ718607. Also from footpath from the minor road between the flash and River Wheelock.
> Passage waders and terns; wildfowl; summer warblers and Little Ringed Plover; migrants.
>
> *Brereton Heath*   *118*   *SJ797648*   *4m NE of Sandbach*
> Woodland birds; wildfowl; summer warblers.

TIC   Sandbach Motorway Service Area, M6 Northbound, Sandbach, Cheshire (0270 760460/761879)
YH   As previous entry.
RF   Bears Paw, Warmingham, nr Sandbach
BB   Forge Mill Farm, Warmingham, nr Sandbach (027 077 204)
        Curtis Hulme Farm, Bradwall Road, Middlewich (0606 843230)

Alderley Edge   118   **5m NW of Macclesfield**
Park by minor road ½m E of Alderley Edge, ½m E of A34, at SJ850784. Then footpaths southeast through the woods along the ridge.
Woodland birds; migrants; summer warblers.

Tegg's Nose Country Park   118   **2½m SE of Macclesfield**
Car-park by minor road ½m SW of A537, ½m SW of Walker Barn, at SJ949732. Then take footpaths south.
Woodland and moorland birds; wildfowl.

Trentabank Reservoir & Macclesfield Forest   118   4m SE of Macclesfield
Car-park by minor road along south shore of the reservoir 1½m SE of Langley at SJ964712. Also footpath south through the forest.
Winter wildfowl; woodland birds including Crossbill, Redstart, Pied Flycatcher, Wood Warbler and Goshawk.

Bosley Reservoir   118   5m S of Macclesfield
View from A54 at north end, SJ920666 and from minor road along the south side, SJ927657.
Winter wildfowl; passage waders and terns.

*Redes Mere   118   SJ847867   5m SW of Macclesfield
Wildfowl.*

*Lamaload Reservoir   118   SJ974750   3½m E of
Macclesfield
Winter wildfowl.*

*Sutton Reservoir   118   SJ920702   2½m S of Macclesfield
Winter wildfowl.*

*Withington Hall Lake   118   SJ810730   7m W of
Macclesfield
Wildfowl; woodland birds.*

*Shell Brook   118   SJ946650   6m SE of Macclesfield
Woodland and river birds; summer warblers.*

TIC	Town Hall, Market Place, Macclesfield, Cheshire (0625 21955 ext 114/5)
YH	Sherbrook Lodge, Harpur Hill Road, Buxton, Derbyshire (0298 2287)
	Gradbach, Quarnford, Buxton, Derbyshire (02607 625)
RF	Hanging Gate, Higher Sutton, nr Langley
	Queens Arms, Bosley
BB	Goose Green Farm, Oak Road, Mottram St. Andrew, nr Macclesfield (0625 828814)
	Sandpit Farm, Messuage Lane, Marton, nr Macclesfield (0260 224254)
BBE	Hardingland Farm, Macclesfield Forest (0625 25759)
SC	Mill House Farm Cottage, Bosley, nr Macclesfield (02606 265)

Rostherne Mere   109   3m SW of Altrincham
View from Rostherne church 1m SE of A556, south of the mere at SJ743837.
Winter wildfowl and gull roost; passage terns.

Woolston Eyes   109   3m E of Warrington centre
Park ½m S of A57, south of Martinscroft at SJ654887. Then footpaths south and east.
Wildfowl; winter raptors; summer warblers; passage waders and terns; migrants.

Risley Moss   109   4m NE of Warrington centre
Car-park and visitor centre by minor road ½m E of A574, 1m S of M62, at SJ664921. Then footpaths and nature trail and observation tower.
Woodland birds; summer warblers; wildfowl; passage waders.

> *Chorlton Water Park   109   SJ820918   2m E of Sale*
> *Winter wildfowl and gulls; passage terns and waders; migrants.*

> *Sale Water Park   109   SJ800930   1½m NE of Sale*
> *Birds as Chorlton.*

> *Carrington Moss   109   SJ745915   1m S of Carrington*
> *Winter wildfowl.*

> *Tatton Mere & Park   109 & 118   SJ755800   5m W of Wilmslow*
> *Woodland birds.*

> *Styal Country Park   109   SJ833833   2m N of Wilmslow*
> *Woodland birds.*

> *Appleton Reservoir   109   SJ603843   2½m S of Warrington centre*
> *Passage and winter wildfowl; passage terns and gulls; marshland birds.*

TIC   Rylands Street, Warrington, Cheshire (0925 36501)
YH   Peak National Park Hostel, Crowden, Hadfield Hyde, Cheshire (04574 2135)
RF   Bears Paw, High Legh, nr Lymm
Farmers Arms, Heatley, nr Lymm

Etherow Country Park   109   2m E of Romiley
Car-park and visitor centre just E of B6104 in Compstall, SJ965908. Then footpaths east up the valley.
Woodland and river birds including Dipper; wildfowl and passage waders.

Audenshaw & Gorton Reservoirs   109   1½m NW of Denton
View from B6390 along the north side of Audenshaw Reservoirs, e.g. SJ914973, and from track SW across the golf course and by Gorton Reservoirs.
Passage terns and waders; winter wildfowl and gulls; migrants.

Lyme Park Country Park 109 SJ976835 *3m E of Poynton*
Wildfowl and woodland birds.

Walkerwood Reservoir 109 SJ990990 *1½m NE of Stalybridge*
Winter wildfowl.

Daisy Nook Country Park & Medlock Valley 109
SD920010 *2½m S of Oldham centre*
Woodland birds; wildfowl; migrants.

TIC	84 Union Street, Oldham, Lancs (061 678 4654)
YH	As previous entry.
RF	Boundary, Audenshaw
	Andrew Arms, Compstall, nr Romily
BBE	Shire Cottage, Benches Lane, Chisworth, nr Marple (0457 866536)
	Needhams Farm, Werneth Low, Gee Cross, nr Hyde (061 368 4610)

Saddleworth Moor & Reservoirs 110 **6m E of Oldham**
Car-park ½m S of A635 at west end of Dovestone Reservoir, at
SE014034. Then tracks east and north.
Upland birds including Ring Ousel, Golden Plover and Red
Grouse; winter wildfowl.

Hollingworth Lake 109 **1m S of Littleborough**
View from roads around the north and east sides e.g. SD937153.
Also track around the southern shore. Visitor centre and hide.
Winter wildfowl and gulls; passage waders; migrants.

Healey Dell 109 **2m NW of Rochdale centre**
Car-park and visitor centre just west of the junction of B6377 and
A671 at SD880159. Then footpaths and nature trail.
Woodland and river birds including Dipper, Kingfisher and Pied
Flycatcher.

Tandle Hill Country Park 109 SD907087 *4m S of Rochdale centre*
Woodland birds.

Watergrove Reservoir 109 SD910180 *2m NW of Littleborough*
Winter wildfowl.

Blackstone Edge Reservoir 109 SD970180 *2½m NE of Littleborough*
Winter wildfowl.

TIC	as previous entry.
	The Clock Tower, Town Hall, Rochdale (0706 356592)
YH	As previous entry.
H/B	Globe Farm, Huddersfield Road, Delph, nr Oldham (0457 873040)
RF	Farrars Arms, Grasscroft, nr Mossley
	Cross Keys, Uppermill, nr Oldham
BB	Leaches Farm, Ashworth Valley, nr Rochdale (0706 41116/228520)
BBE	Globe Farm, Huddersfield Road, Delph, nr Oldham (0457 873040)
SC	Lower Hill Top Cottage, Grains Road, Delph (0457 872357)

Pennington Flash   109   2m NE of Golborne
Signed car-parks and visitor centre on south and east sides by A572, 2½m NE of junction with A580 at SJ644985. Then footpaths around the flash west and north.
Passage and winter wildfowl and gulls; passage terns and waders.

Ince Flashes   108   1½m-2½m S of Wigan centre
Park by B5238 1m NE of its junction with A49, by Poolstock church at SD578045. Then towpath beside canal and between the pits to the south.
Wildfowl; winter gulls; passage terns; Kingfisher; summer warblers.

> **Car Mill Dam**   108   SD525980   1m N of St. Helens
> Passage and winter wildfowl and gulls.

> **Haig Hall Country Park**   108 & 109   SD595085   2m NE of Wigan
> Woodland birds.

> **Sankey Valley Park**   108   SJ547956   between St. Helens & Newton le Willows
> Woodland and river birds; summer warblers.

TIC	Trencherfield Mill, Wigan Pier, Wigan, Lancs (0942 825677)
RF	Red Lion, Lowton, nr Leigh

Seaforth Nature Reserve   108   by Mersey 5m N of Liverpool centre
Park by Freeport entrance just W of A565 at its junction with A5036, at SJ324973. Then foot access only along road to the west and hides etc.
Spring Little Gull; winter northern gulls; passage waders and terns; migrants; seawatching.

Hale Head   108   1m S of Hale
Park by minor road south of Hale, SJ473814. Then track south to the point and coastal path (The Mersey Way).
Passage and winter waders and wildfowl; migrants.

Garston Channel   108   by Mersey 4m SE of Liverpool centre
Car-parks by the front ½m S of A561 2m NW of Garston, e.g. SJ375861.
Passage and winter waders and gulls.

> ***Garston Rocks***   *108   SJ396835   W side of Garston*
> *Waders and wildfowl.*

> ***Calderstones Park***   *108   SJ405875   2m N of Garston*
> *Woodland birds.*

> ***Croxteth Country Park***   *108   SJ406943   5m NE of Liverpool centre*
> *Woodland birds.*

> ***Pickerings Pasture Country Park***   *108   SJ486836   1½m NE of Hale*
> *Passage and winter waders; migrants.*

> ***Mill Wood***   *108   SJ457837   1m NW of Hale*
> *Woodland birds.*

> ***Sefton Park***   *108   SJ376877   1m N of Garston Channel*
> *Woodland birds; passage wildfowl.*

TIC   Atlantic Pavilion, Albert Dock, Liverpool (051 708 8854)

Formby Point & Hills   108   1½m NW of Formby centre
Car-park at end of minor road 1½m W of railway line at SD274084. Then tracks south to the point and north to the dunes and woods.
Migrants; winter seaduck; seawatching.

Ainsdale & Birkdale Hills & Sands   108   4m N of Formby
Park in Ainsdale-on-Sea, SD302127. Then footpaths and marked trails north and south.
Migrants; woodland birds; waders and wildfowl; seawatching.

Crossens Marsh & Pool   102   4m NE of Southport centre
View from minor road 1–3m NW of A565 e.g. SD370210.
Passage and winter waders, wildfowl, raptors and Short-eared Owl.

> ***Marshside Golf Course & Southport Sands***   *108*
> *SD350195   N side of Southport*
> *Winter wildfowl; migrants.*

Southport Marine Lake   *108*   *SD334182*   *W side of*
Southport
Winter wildfowl and gulls.

TIC	112 Lord Street, Southport, Merseyside (0704 33133/500175)
RF	Hesketh Arms, Churchtown, nr Southport
	Punchbowl, Churchtown, nr Southport
BB	Sandy Brook Farm, Scarisbrick, nr Southport (0704 880337)
BBE	Garden Hotel, 19 Lathom Road, Southport (0704 30244)
	Lockerbie House Hotel, 11 Trafalgar Road, Birkdale (0704 65298)
SC	Strawberry Cottage, 89 King Street, Southport (0704 36282)

Cornwall

River Lynher   201   2–4m W of Torpoint
Car-park overlooking the estuary by A374 2½m W of Torpoint, ½m
W of Antony at SX390552. Also view from Wilcove, 1m N of
Torpoint, ¼m N of A374 at SX430564, and from St. Germans Quay,
¼m SE of St. Germans railway station, at SX364572.
Passage and winter waders, wildfowl and grebes.

St. John's Lake   201   1m S of Torpoint
View from minor road ¼m-½m SW of the Torpoint ferry terminal
at SX436546 and from the western end at St. John, 1m S of A374,
at SX411539.
Passage and winter waders, wildfowl and grebes; passage terns
and gulls.

Millbrook Lake & Pool   201   2m S of Torpoint
View the 'lake' from minor road along the southern shore ½m-1m E
of Millbrook, east of B3247. Also from coastal path further to the
east e.g. SX445528. The Pool lies between the 'lake'and the centre
of Millbrook at SX426523.
Birds as St. John's Lake.

Rame Head   201   4½m S of Torpoint
Car-park at the end of minor road 2½m S of B3247 from Millbrook at
SX420487. Then path south to the point and Cornwall Coast Path
eastward to Penlee Point and the east side of the hill.
Migrants; seawatching; winter seaduck, divers and grebes.

> *Mount Edgcumbe Country Park*   201   SX457517   *3m SE
> of Torpoint*
> *Woodland birds; migrants.*

TIC   Civic Centre, Royal Parade, Plymouth (0752 264849)
Granada Motorway Services, Carkeel Roundabout, nr
Saltash (0752 849526)
YH   Belmont House, Devonport Road, Stoke, Plymouth (0752
562189)

R   Edgcumbe Arms, Cremyll
RFBBE Copley Arms, Hessenford, nr Liskeard (05034 209)
BBE   Liscawn Hotel, Crafthole, Torpoint, Cornwall (0503 30231)
         The Old Mill, Polbathic, nr Liskeard (0503 30596)

Cargreen & Kingsmill Lake   **201**   **1½m-2½m N of Saltash**
Park and view from the waterfront at Cargreen 2½m E of A388 from Halt at SX436626. For Kingsmill Lake, 1m south, park by the church at Landulph, SX433615, and take track and path south to the shore.
Passage and winter waders including Avocet.

TIC   As previous entry.
YH   As previous entry.
R   Rising Sun, Botusfleming, nr Saltash
RFBBE The Spaniard Inn, Cargreen, Saltash (0752 842830)
SC   Lantallack Farm, Landrake, Saltash (075538 281)
         Crylla Valley Ltd, Notter Bridge, Saltash (0752 842187)
         (Cotehele Cottages) National Trust, Lanhydrock Park, Bodmin (0208 73880)

Siblyback Lake   **201**   **5m NW of Liskeard**
Car-park at the east shore 2m N of St. Cleer at SX237706.
Passage and winter wildfowl; passage waders and terns.

Colliford Lake   **201**   **7m NW of Liskeard**
Several car-parks by the minor road which encircles the reservoir 2–3m S of A30 e.g. at SX165733 and SX186727 on the east side. Also Dozmary Pool by the northeast corner at SX193746.
Passage and winter wildfowl; passage terns and gulls.

TIC   Shire House, Mount Folly Square, Bodmin (0208 76616)
YH   Penquite House, Golant, Fowey (072 683 3507)
RF   Crow's Nest, Crows Nest, nr Tremar
         Colliford Tavern & Restaurant, Colliford Lake
         London, St. Neot
         Caradon Inn, Upton Cross
BB   Upton Farmhouse, Upton Cross (0579 62689)
SC   Rivermead Farm, Twowatersfoot, nr Liskeard (020 882 464)
         Greatlands, Pensilva, Liskeard (0579 62491)

Tamar Lakes   **190**   **6m NE of Bude**
Car-parks 2½m E of A39 from Kilkhampton at SS287117 (upper lake); and SS294107 (lower lake). Then paths and hide.
Passage waders; passage and winter wildfowl; migrants.

Coombe Valley   190   4m N of Bude
Car-park by minor road 2m W of A39 from Kilkhampton at
SS222116. Then footpaths and nature trail west and east through
woods and beside the river.
Woodland and river birds including Dipper and Kingfisher;
migrants.

> ***Bude Haven***   *190   SS203067   ¾m NW of Bude centre*
> *Passage waders; gulls.*

> ***Bude Marshes***   *190   SS207062   ¼m W of Bude centre*
> *Reedbed species; summer warblers; passage waders.*

TIC	The Crescent Car-park, Bude (0288 4240)
	Market House Arcade, Market Street, Launceston (0566 2321)
YH	Elmscott, Hartland, Bideford, Devon (02374 367)
RF	Tree Inn, Stratton
RFBBE	Bullers Arms, Marhamchurch (028 885 277)
BBE	Cornakey Farm, nr Morwenstow (028 883 260)
	Fosfelle, Hartland, Devon (0237 441273)

Crowdy Reservoir   200   2½m E of Camelford
Car-park at west end 2½m E of A39 from Camelford at SX138834
and path around the reservoir.
Passage waders and winter wildfowl.

Davidstow Airfield   200 & 201   3m NE of Camelford
View from the minor road which crosses the disused airfield 1–2m
E of A39 e.g. SX148853.
Passage waders; winter and passage raptors.

> ***Lye Rock***   *200   SX064898   1m N of Tintagel*
> *Summer seabirds.*

> ***Trevelga Cliffs***   *190   SX075906   1½m W of Boscastle*
> *Summer seabirds.*

TIC	*North Cornwall Museum, The Clease, Camelford (0840 212954)
	Market Place Arcade, Market Street, Launceston (0566 2321)
YH	Palace Stables, Boscastle (08405 287)
	Dunderhole Point, Tintagel (0840 770334)
RFBBE	Mill House Inn, Trebarwith (0840 770200)
	Masons Arms, Camelford (0840 213309)
RFSC	Port William, Trebarwith, Strand (0840 770230)
BBE	Trevervan Hotel, Trewarmett, Tintagel (0840 770486)

Camel Estuary   200   1–4m NW of Wadebridge
Park at Tregunna 1m N of A39, 2m NW of Wadebridge at
SW966736. Then track N to shore and The Camel Trail beside the
estuary west and east.
Passage and winter waders, wildfowl and gulls.

Padstow   200   NW end of Camel Estuary
Park in Padstow SW917753. Then coast path north or south from
the harbour.
Passage and winter waders; winter divers, grebes and gulls.

> ***Rumps Point***   *200   SW935808   1½m N of Polzeath*
> *Seawatching; migrants.*
>
> ***Stepper Point***   *200   SW915785   2m N of Padstow*
> *Passage and winter waders; winter divers and seaduck;*
> *seawatching; migrants.*
>
> ***Trevose Head***   *200   SW851766   4m W of Padstow*
> *Seawatching; migrants.*
>
> ***River Amble Marshes***   *200   SW988744   1½m N of*
> *Wadebridge*
> *Passage waders; winter wildfowl.*

TIC	*Wadebridge Town Hall, Wadebridge (020 881 3725)
	Shire House, Mount Folly Square, Bodmin (0208 76616)
YH	Tregonnan, Treyarnon, Padstow (0841 520322)
RF	Maltsters Arms, Chapel Amble
RFBBE	London Inn, Padstow (0841 532554)
BBE	Coimbatore Hotel, West View, Trevone Bay, Padstow
	(0841 520390)

Gannel Estuary   200   1m SW of Newquay centre
Car-park on the southern side ½m N of Crantock, 2m NW of A3075
at SW789609. Then path by the estuary to the east. On the northern side, view from minor road at west end, SW806607, and car-
park at Pentire, SW787615 and track west.
Passage and winter waders and gulls.

Towan Head   200   1½m NW of Newquay centre
Park ½m NW of the railway station at SW806624 and take Cornwall
Coast Path northwest to the point.
Seawatching; winter divers and seaduck.

TIC	Cliff Road, Newquay (0637 871345)
YH	Alexandra Court, Narrow Cliff, Newquay (0637 876381)
	Droskyn Point, Perranporth (0872 573812)
RF	Treguth Inn, Holywell Bay
BBE	Crantock Cottage Hotel, West Pentire Road, Crantock,
	Newquay (0637 830232)

Crantock Plains Farmhouse, Crantock, Newquay (0637 830253)

Fowey Estuary   200   2–4m SW of Lostwithiel
On the east side park at St. Winnow church, SX116570, and coast path south. Also view from Cliff, 1½m SW of Lerryn, at SX128555. Passage and winter waders.

> ***Deviock Wood*** 200 *SX105680 5m N of Lostwithiel*
> *Woodland and river birds.*

> ***Fowey Mouth*** 200 *SX126516 SE side of Fowey*
> *Winter gulls, grebes and divers.*

> ***Par Sands*** 200 *SX085530 2m W of Fowey*
> *Gulls; passage waders and terns.*

> ***Gribbin Head*** 200 *SX097497 2½m SW of Fowey*
> *Migrants; seawatching.*

> ***Goss Moor*** 200 *SW950600 3m SE of St. Columb Major*
> *Raptors; heathland birds; summer warblers.*

> ***Innis Downs & Criggan Moors*** 200 *SX015625 4m NW of Lostwithiel*
> *Heathland birds.*

TIC The Post Office, 4 Custom House Hill, Fowey (072 683 3616)
YH Penquite House, Golant, Fowey (072 683 3507)
RF Fishermans Arms, Golant
  Old Ferry Inn, Bodinnick
SC (Triggabrowne cottages) National Trust, Lanhydrock Park, Bodmin (0208 73880)

St. Anthony Head   204   1½m S of St. Mawes
Car-parks at the end of minor road at the point, 1m SW of St. Anthony at SW847314. Then coastal path north to the mouth of the Percuil River and northeast to Porthmellin Head.
Migrants; seawatching; passage waders; winter divers and seaduck.

Nare Head & Gerrans Bay   204   7m SE of Truro
Car-park at Carne Beach 1m SE of A3078 at SW906383. View from here and coast path southeast to Nare Head.
Winter divers and seaduck; migrants; seawatching.

> ***Dodman Point*** 204 *SX003394 3½m S of Mevagissy*
> *Migrants; seawatching.*

St. Just Pool   204   SW845356   2½m N of St. Mawes
Passage waders.

Percuil River   204   SW856341   1½m NE of St. Mawes
Passage and winter waders.

TIC   Municipal Buildings, Boscawen Street, Truro (0872 74555)
YH   Boswinger, Gorran, St. Austell (0726 843234)
RF   New Inn, Veryan (0872 501362)
         Rising Sun, St. Mawes (0326 270233)
SC   (Porth & Bohortha cottages) National Trust, Lanhydrock Park, Bodmin (0208 73880)
         (Penare & Veryan cottages) As above.

Tresilian River   **204**   **2m SE of Truro**
Park at St. Clement 2m SE of A39 at SW853439. Then track beside the estuary toward the northeast.
Passage and winter waders.

Restronguet Point & Creek   **204**   **5m S of Truro**
View from the point 1m S of Feock at SW817373 and from minor road on the northern side of the estuary between Devoran and Penpol e.g. SW804387.
Passage and winter waders.

Swanpool & Pennance Point   **204**   **1–1½m S of Falmouth centre**
Park by Swanpool 1m SW of the town centre at SW803314 and take track south to the sewage outfall at Pennance Point, SW804305.
Gulls.

Truro Estuary   204   SW838430   1½m S of Truro
Passage and winter waders.

Falmouth Harbour   204   SW814325   E end of Falmouth
Winter gulls.

TIC   As previous entry.
YH   Pendennis Castle, Falmouth (0326 311435)
RF   Heron, Malpas (0872 72773)
          Pandora Inn, Restronguet Passage (0326 72678)
BBE   Driffold Lodge Hotel, Devoran (0872 863314)
SC   (Trelissick Estate) National Trust, Lanhydrock Park, Bodmin (0208 73880)
          (Mawnan Smith cottages) As above.

Goonhilly Downs   **204**   **4m E of Mullion**
View from minor road ½m–1½m SW of B3293 from Traboe Cross e.g. SW732196.
Winter and passage raptors; migrants.

Church Cove, Lizard   203   1m E of Lizard
Park by church ¾m E of Lizard at SW712127. Then track east and
coast path south to Bass Point.
Migrants; seawatching.

Kynance Cove   203   1½m NW of Lizard
Car-park 1m W of A3083 above the cove at SW687133. Then coast
path west.
Migrants.

Predannack Airfield   203   2m S of Mullion
Car-park 1m S of Mullion Cove at Predannock Wollas, SW668162.
Then tracks southeast.
Passage waders; winter raptors.

Church Cove, Gunwalloe   203   3m S of Helston
Car-park 3m SW of A3083, 1m S of Gunwalloe at SW659209. Then
tracks south and east along the coast and beside the marsh and golf
course.
Reedbed species including Cetti's Warbler; migrants including
regular autumn Aquatic Warbler.

The Loe   203   2m SW of Helston
Car-park 1m SW of A3083 at Degibna, SW654252. Then track west
and path beside The Loe and Carminowe Creek.
Passage and winter wildfowl; passage terns.

TIC	Laity, Carnbone, nr Helston (0326 40899)
	28 Killigrew Street, Falmouth (0326 312300)
YH	Parc Behan, School Hill, Coverack, Helston (0326 280687)
RF	New Inn, Manaccan
	Blue Anchor, Helston
	Halzephron, Gunwalloe
	Old Inn, Church Town, Mullion
BBE	Gallen Treath, Porthallow, St. Keverne (0326 280400)
BBESC	Old Inn, Church Town, Mullion (0326 240240)
	Penmenner House, Penmenner Road, Lizard (0326 290370)
SC	(Frenchmans Creek, Helford) Landmark Trust, Shottesbrooke, Maidenhead, Berks (0628 825925)
	(Ruan Minor & Loe Pool cottages) National Trust, Lanhydrock Park, Bodmin (0208 73880)

Hayle Estuary   203   1m SW of Hayle
View from car-park and hide next to the 'Old Quay House Inn',
200yds NE of the junction of B3301 and A30, 1m SW of Hayle at
SW545364. Also walk NE by B330 and the footpath west around
Carnsew Pool, SW553374.
Passage and winter waders and wildfowl; winter grebes, divers
and gulls; summer and passage terns.

St. Ives Island   203   ½m N of St. Ives centre
Car-park by the headland at the north end of St. Ives, SW519409.
Then path up to the lookout across St. Ives Bay and sewage outfall.
The best seawatching in Britain in a NW gale; gulls at sewage
outfall; winter divers and seaduck.

Godrevy & Navax Point   203   4m NE of Hayle
Park by B3301 ¾m N of Gwithian at SW587421. Then Cornish Coast
Path northwest around the peninsula.
Seawatching; summer seabirds; migrants.

Stithians Reservoir   203   4m S of Redruth
View from minor road and hides at southern end 1m E of Pen-
marth, 2½m E of B3297 at SW715352. Also view from northern end
1½m N of Penmarth, SW708373, and path along the west shore.
Also car-park at east end by the dam, SW719364.
Passage waders, terns and gulls; passage and winter wildfowl.

> ***Copperhouse Creek***   203   SW564379   *between Hayle &*
> *Copperhouse*
> *Passage waders; gulls including regular Ring-billed Gull.*

> ***Porth Kidney Sands***   203   SW545385   *2m SE of St. Ives*
> *Passage and summer terns.*

> ***Cargenwen Reservoirs***   203   SW654353   *3m S of Cam-*
> *borne*
> *Passage waders and wildfowl.*

TIC	The Guildhall, Street-an-Pol, St. Ives (0736 796297/797600)
YH	Castle Horneck, Alverton, Penzance (0736 62666)
RF	Old Key House Inn, Hayle
	Angarrack Inn, Angarrack
	Bird in Hand, nr Hayle
BBE	Old Springfields, Lelant Downs, Hayle (0736 756590)
	Sandsifter Hotel, Godrevy Towans, nr Hayle (0736 753314)
SC	Polmanter Farm, Hasletown, St. Ives (0736 795640)
	Orchard House, Wall, Gwinear, Hayle (0736 850201)

Marazion Marsh   203   2½m E of Penzance
View from car-parks along the front ½m-1m E of Longrock, ½m
S of A394 – A30 junction, at SW506313 and SW514312.
Reedbed and scrub species including Cetti's Warbler; passage
waders; migrants including regular autumn Aquatic Warbler and
Spotted Crake; winter diver and grebes offshore.

Drift Reservoir   203   2½m W of Penzance
Park at the southern end ¼m NW of A30 from Lower Drift at
SW436287. Then path around the reservoir.
Passage waders, gulls and terns.

> *Longrock Beach   203   SW490310   1m NE of Penzance
> centre*
> *Gulls and passage waders.*

> *Newlyn Harbour & Sewage outfall   203   SW465286
> 1½m SW of Penzance centre*
> *Gulls.*

> *Lamorna Valley   203   SW447244   4m SW of Penzance*
> *Migrants; woodland birds.*

TIC	Station Road, Penzance (0736 62207)
YH	As previous entry.
RF	Mexico Inn, Longrock
	Dolphin, The Quay, Penzance
RFBBE	Cutty Sark, The Square, Marazion (0736 710334)
BBE	Chymorvah-Tolgarrick Hotel, Marazion (0736 710497)
SC	Lynfield Farm, Perranuthnoe, Penzance (0736 710547)
	Trenow Farm, Perranuthnoe, Penzance (0736 710421)
	Sarah's Cottage, Lamorna, Penzance (0736 731227)

Porthgwarra   203   2½m SE of Land's End
Car-park 1½m S of Poligigga from B3315, at SW370218. Then
tracks and paths NW as far as Zawn Reeth, east to St. Levan
church and SW to Gwennap Head.
Migrants; seawatching.

St. Just Airfield & Nanquidno   203   3m NE of Land's End
View the airfield from minor road near its junction with B3306 e.g.
SW374294. For the wooded valley park beside the road 1m further
west e.g. SW364292.
Passage waders and pipits; migrants.

Cot Valley   203   1m SW of St. Just
Follow signposts west from the church in St. Just and park by the
road at the head of the valley at SW364306. Then walk the road,
tracks and paths westward.
Migrants.

Pendeen Watch   203   3m N of St. Just
Park near the lighthouse at SW380358, signposted from the B3306
north of Pendeen.
Seawatching.

> *Porthcurno   203   SW386224   3–4m SE of Land's End*
> *Migrants.*

Land's End   203   *SW345250*   *W end of A30*
Migrants; seawatching.

Kenidjack Valley   203   *SW368319*   *½m N of St. Just*
Migrants.

Cape Cornwall   203   *SW353319*   *1½m W of St. Just*
Seawatching.

Penberth to Logan Rock   203   *SW400225*   *½m SE of*
Treen
Migrants.

TIC	As previous entry.
YH	Letcha Vean, St. Just, Penzance (0736 788437)
RF	Logan Rock Inn, Treen
RFBBE	Wellington Hotel, St. Just, Penzance (0736 787319)
BB	The Old Count House, Boscaswell Downs, Pendeen (0736 788058)
BBE	Bosavern House, St. Just, Penzance (0736 788301)
	Kenython, St. Just, Penzance (0736 788607)
	Boswednack Manor, Zennor, St. Ives (0736 794183)
SC	(Lower Porthmear, Zennor) Landmark Trust, Shottes-brooke, Maidenhead, Berks (062 882 5925)
	Carrallack Cottage, Cot Valley, St. Just (0736 788858)
	(Kenylack cottage) Kookaburra, St. Levan, Penzance (0736 810465)
	Tregeseal Cottages, 4 Fore Street, St. Just (0736 788317)
	(Nanquidno cottage) 4 Tyler Street, Stratford-on-Avon (0789 299338)

Scilly Isles   **203**   **28m SW of Land's End**
Reached by boat, helicopter or plane to St. Mary's. Many inter-island boats.
Boat; 'Isles of Scilly Steamship Co. Penzance tel: 0736 62009
H'copter; 'British International Helicopters, The Heliport, Penzance tel: 0736 63871
Plane; 'Isles of Scilly Skybus Ltd, St. Just Aerodrome tel: 0736 787017
'Brymon Airways, Roborough Airport, Plymouth tel: 0752 707023
The best site in the U.K. for spring and especially autumn migrants; summer seabirds.

TIC	Porthcressa Bank, St. Mary's, Isles of Scilly (0720 22536)
RF	Mermaid, Hugh Town, St. Mary's
	Bishop and Wolf, Hugh Town
	Turks Head, St. Agnes
	Seven Stones, St. Martins
	Porthcressa Restaurant, Hugh Town
BBE	The Wheelhouse, Porthcressa, St. Marys (0720 22719)
	Carnwethers Country House, Pelistry, St. Marys (0720 22415)

Santa Maria, Sally Port, St. Marys (0720 22687)
Coastguards, St. Agnes (0720 22373)
Covean Cottage, St. Agnes (0720 22620)
Bank Cottage, Bryher (0720 22612)
Chafford, Bryher (0720 22241)
Glenmoor Cottage, Higher Town, St. Martins (0720 22816)
Polreath, Higher Town, St. Martins (0720 22046)
SC Holy Vale Farm, St. Marys (0720 22429)
Lunnon Cottage, St. Marys (0720 22422)
Trenoweth Farm, St. Marys (0720 22474)
Porthloo Farm, St. Marys (0720 22636)
South Hill, Bryher (0720 22411)
Veronica Farm, Bryher (0720 22862)
Carron Farm, St. Martins (0720 22893)
2 Coastguards Cottages, St. Martins (0720 22814)
Tresco Estate, Tresco (0720 22849)

Campsites
St. Marys (0720 22670)
Bryher (0720 22886)
St. Martins (0720 22888)
St. Agnes (0720 22360)

Cumbria

Foulshaw   97   **6m SW of Kendal**
Park by minor road. 1½m SE of A590, 1m NE of Meathop, at
SD449812. Then footpath SE by river and NE along the sea wall.
Passage and winter waders; gull roost.

Humphrey Head & Out Marsh   97   **3m SW of Grange-over-Sands**
Car-park at end of minor road 2m S of B5277, 2½m SW of Flookburgh, at SD389742. Then footpaths west to the marsh and east to
the wood and point.
Passage and winter waders; migrants; winter wildfowl.

Sandgate & Low Marsh   97   **4m SW of Grange-over-Sands**
Park at Sand Gate ¾m W of Flookburgh at SD354757. Then footpath south around the marshes.
Passage and winter waders and wildfowl; migrants; winter
raptors.

Park Head   97   **4½m W of Grange-over-Sands**
Car-park by the estuary at end of minor road 1½m W of B5278 at
SD336786.
Winter gull roost; passage and winter waders and wildfowl.

> *Meathop Marsh*   97   *SD427797*   *2m NE of Grange-over-Sands*
> *Waders and wildfowl.*

> *Killington Reservoir*   97   *SD590910*   *4m E of Kendal*
> *Winter wildfowl.*

> *Whitbarrow Scar*   97   *SD450845*   *5m SW of Kendal*
> *Woodland and upland birds including Pied Flycatcher, Pere-grine and Ring Ousel.*

> *Roudsea Wood*   97   *SD327826*   *6m NW of Grange-over-Sands*
> *Woodland birds.*

Colton Woods   97   *SD324863*   *2m NW of Haverthwaite*
Woodland birds including Pied Fycatcher and Redstart.

TIC	Town Hall, Highgate, Kendal (0539 725758)
	Victoria Hall, Main Street, Grange-over-Sands (05395 34026)
YH	Highgate, Kendal (0539 24066)
	Oakfield Lodge, Redhills Road, Arnside, Carnforth (0524 761781)
RF	Cavendish Arms Hotel, Cartmel, nr Grange-over-Sands
	Hare and Hounds, Levens, nr Kendal
BBE	Priory Hotel, The Square, Cartmel (05395 36267)
	Grammar Hotel, Cartmel (05395 36367)
	Greenacres County Guest House, Lindale, nr Grange-over-Sands (05395 34578)
SC	Longlands Farm, Cartmel (05395 36406)
	Longlands, Cartmel (05395 36475)

Grizedale   **97 or 96**   **5m SW of Windermere**
Car-park by minor road in Grizedale, 1½m N of Satterthwaite, SD336944. Then paths and nature trails west and east.
Woodland birds including Pied Flycatcher, Redstart, Crossbill, Black Grouse and Goshawk.

Dodgson Wood   **97 or 96**   **7m SW of Windermere**
Car-parks beside Coniston Water along the eastern shore e.g. SD299927. Then footpaths through the woods.
Woodland birds including Pied Flycatcher, Wood Warbler and Redstart.

Claife Heights   97 or 96   *SD375975*   *2½m SW of*
Windermere
Woodland and moorland birds; winter wildfowl.

Brantwood   97 or 96   *SD314957*   *1½m SE of Coniston*
Woodland birds.

TIC	*Glebe Road, Bowness (09662 2895)
	Victoria Road, Windermere (09662 6499)
YH	Esthwaite Lodge, Hawkshead, Ambleside (09666 293)
	High Cross, Bridge Lane, Troutbeck, Windermere (09662 3543)
	Coppermines House, Coniston (05394 41261)
	Holly How, Far End, Coniston (05394 41323)
RF	Drunken Duck, Barngates, nr Hawkshead
	Towerbank Arms, Near Sawrey, nr Windermere
RFBBE	Kings Arms, Hawkshead (09666 372)
	The Sawrey Hotel, Far Sawrey (09662 3425)
BBE	Summer Hill Cottage, Hawkshead Hill (09666 311)
	Sawrey House Country Hotel, Near Sawrey (09666 387)

BBE   Force Mill Farm, Satterthwaite, Grizedale (022 984 205)
SC   Townhead Cottage, Satterthwaite (022 984 203)
       1 Church Cottage, Satterthwaite (0229 860336)
       (Rose Cottage, Satterthwaite) Forestry Commission, 231
       Corstorphine Road, Edinburgh (031 334 0303)

Plumpton Hall & Ashes Point   97 or 96   2m NE of Ulverston
Park at end of minor road 1½m SE of 590 ¼m SE over railway line, at SD314786. Then track and footpaths north and south.
Passage and winter waders and wildfowl.

Ulverston Sands   97 or 96   2m SE of Ulverston
Car-park by A5087 at Bardsea, SD304744, and track NE.
Passage and winter waders; winter seaduck and divers.

Rampside & Foulney Island   96   3m SE of Barrow-in-Furness
View from minor road to Roa Island, SD234657, and walk SE to Foulney Island.
Passage and winter waders and wildfowl; summer terns; winter seaduck and divers.

South Walney   96   4m S of Barrow-in-Furness
Car-park and entrance to reserve 1m SE of South End at SD215621. Then nature trails to the hides.
Migrants; passage and winter waders and wildfowl; winter raptors and Short-eared Owl; summer Eider and terns; seawatching.

North Walney   96   3m NW of Barrow-in-Furness
Car-park at end of minor road at North Walney, 1½m NW of A590, SD171698. Then track and coastal paths north.
Migrants; winter seaduck and divers; passage and winter waders and wildfowl; winter raptors.

Duddon Estuary   96   3m NE of Millom
Park in Foxfield, 1½m SW of A595, SD211853. Then walk south over the railway line and beside the estuary and marshes.
Passage and winter waders and wildfowl; winter raptors.

> ***Cavendish Dock*** *96   SD214686   S side of Barrow-in-Furness*
> *Winter wildfowl, grebes, divers and gulls.*

> ***Urswick Tarn*** *96   SD270745   2m SW of Ulverston*
> *Winter wildfowl.*

> ***Sandscale Haws*** *96   SD190750   3m N of Barrow-in-Furness*
> *Migrants; passage and winter waders and wildfowl.*

White Moss 96 *SD220856* *4m NE of Millom*
Heathland birds; summer warblers; Nightjar; winter raptors.

TIC	Town Hall, Duke Street, Barrow-in-Furness (0229 870156)
	Coronation Hall, County Square, Ulverston (0229 57120)
YH	As previous entry.
RF	Queens Arms, Biggar, Walney Island
	Bradylls Arms, Bardsea, nr Ulverston
	Greyhound, Grizebeck, nr Broughton-in-Furness
RFBBE	Red Lion Inn, Market Street, Dalton-in-Furness (0229 62180)
BB	Hill Farm, Heathwaite, Grizebeck, Kirkby-in-Furness (022989 706)
SC	Walney Bird Observatory, Coastguard Cottage, Walney Island (0229 41066)
	Mill House, Lowick Bridge, nr Ulverston (022985 685)
	The Falls, Mansriggs, nr Ulverston (0229 53781)

Millom Marsh 96 **2m NE of Millom**
Park at end of minor road ½m E of A5093, ½m E of The Hill at
SD186828. Then under the railway line and footpaths east and
south.
Passage and winter waders and wildfowl; winter raptors.

Hodbarrow 96 **1m S of Millom**
Car-park at end of minor road S from Millom, 1m NE of Haverigg,
at SD174792. Then track and footpaths east and south.
Migrants; seaduck; winter wildfowl, grebes, divers and raptors;
passage and winter waders; passage terns; seawatching.

Eskmeals Dunes 96 **5m SE of Seascale**
Park by minor road ½m W of Newbiggin, just west of the railway
line at SD089943. Then path west across the dunes north of the
fence to the estuary.
Migrants; summer terns; passage and winter waders and
wildfowl.

Ravenglass & Mite Estuary 96 **4½m SE of Seascale**
Park in Ravenglass, west of the railway, SD085964. Then footpaths
south beside the Esk estuary and north beside the Mite.
Passage and winter waders.

Devoke Water & Water Crag 96 **4m E of Ravenglass**
Park by minor road across Birker Fell, 3m SE of Eskdale Green, at
SD171977. Then track and path southwest around the lake and
onto the moor.
Wildfowl and raptors; Red Grouse and other upland birds.

Irt Estuary & Drigg Dunes   96   2–3m S of Seascale
Park near the end of minor road 1m SW of Drigg, at SD053986.
Then track south by the dunes and to the estuary shoreline.
Passage and winter waders; winter wildfowl and raptors; summer
terns; seawatching.

> *Newbiggin & Waberthwaite Marshes   96   SD095944*
> *1½m SE of Ravenglass*
> *Passage and winter waders and wildfowl.*

> *Eskholme Marsh   96   SD112965   1½m E of Ravenglass*
> *Winter wildfowl.*

TIC	12 Main Street, Egremont (0946 820693)
	*Ravenglass & Eskdale Railway Co., Ravenglass (06577 278)
	*Millom Folk Museum, St. Georges Road, Millom (0229 772555)
YH	Boot, Holmrook, Eskdale (09403 219)
RF	Mineers Arms, Silecroft, nr Millom
	Bower House, Eskdale Green, nr Ravenglass
	Ratty Arms, Ravenglass
BBE	Foldgate Farm, Corney, Bootle, nr Millom (06578 660)
	Croft Cottage, Kirksanton, nr Millom (0657 2582)
	Whicham Old Rectory, Silecroft, nr Millom (0657 2954)
SC	Fisherground Farm, Eskdale (09403 319)

St. Bees Head   89   3m SW of Whitehaven
Car-park by shore ¾m W of St. Bees, ¾m W of B5345, at NX961118.
Then coastal path north to North Head and beyond. Or park in
Sandwith 2m N of St. Bees and take tracks and footpaths west.
Summer seabird colonies including Black Guillemot; seawatching;
migrants.

> *Siddick Ponds   89   NY002303   1m N of Workington*
> *Wildfowl; passage waders and terns; reedbed species.*

> *Longlands Lake   89   NY014127   2m N of Egremont*
> *Winter wildfowl.*

TIC	Civic Centre, Lowther Street, Whitehaven (0946 695678)
	12 Main Street, Egremont (0946 820693)
YH	Cat Crag, Ennerdale, Cleator (0946 861237)
	Double Mills, Cockermouth (0900 822561)
H/B	Rowrah Hall, West Cumbria Field Centre, Frizington (0946 816029)
RF	Queens Hotel, St. Bees
RFBBE	Shepherds Arms Hotel, Ennerdale Bridge (0946 861249)
BBE	Glenlea House, Glenlea, Lowca, nr Whitehaven (0946 3873)

SC   Routen Farm, Ennerdale (0946 861270)
Mireside Farm, Ennerdale (0946 861276)

Wythop Woods & Bassenthwaite Lake   89 or 90   4m E of Cockermouth
Park at Beck Wythop by A66 on west side of the lake at NY215285.
Then footpath north and south beside the lake and tracks west through the woods.
Woodland birds; winter wildfowl.

Braithwaite Moss   89 or 90   2m NW of Keswick
Park by A66 ¼m N of Braithwaite at NY234242. Then track and footpaths east across the moss.
Summer warblers; winter raptors.

Lodore Wood   89 or 90   3m S of Keswick
Car-park by minor road ¼m E of B5289 at NY268188. Then paths through the woods and by the beck.
Woodland and river birds including Pied Flycatcher, Wood Warbler and Dipper.

Bowness Bay   89 or 90   NY223294   3m NW of Keswick
Winter wildfowl.

Mungrisdale Common   90   NY310295   5m NE of Keswick
Upland birds.

Castlerigg Fell   90   NY285185   3m SE of Keswick
Upland birds.

TIC   Moot Hall, Market Square, Keswick (07687 72645)
YH   As previous entry.
Station Road, Keswick (07687 72484)
Barrow House, Borrowdale, Keswick (059684 246)
The Old School, Stanah Cross, Keswick (07687 73224)
H/B   The Trekkers Lodge, 32 Lake Road, Keswick (07687 72267)
RF   Pheasant, nr Dubwath
Salutation, Threlkeld, nr Keswick
RFBBE   Coledale Inn, Braithwaite, nr Keswick (059 682 272)
BBE   Link House Hotel, Bassenthwaite Lake, Cockermouth (059 681 291)
Ivy House Hotel, Braithwaite (059 682 338)
Beckstones Farm, Thornthwaite, nr Keswick (059 682 510)
SC   Lakeland Cottage Holidays, Keswick (059 682 626)
Grey Abbey Properties, Coach Road, Whitehaven (0946 693346/693364)
Old Farmhouse, Braithwaite (059 682 431)
Beckside, Thornthwaite (059 682 395)

Seldom Seen Cottages, Braehead, Papcastle, Cockermouth (0900 823138)

Rydal Water   90   2m NW of Ambleside
Car-parks by A591 at W end of the lake at NY347065. Then footpath through the woods beside the southern side of the Water. Wildfowl and woodland birds.

Dovedale & Brothers Water   90   4½m N of Ambleside
Park by A592 at the northern end of the lake by Goldrill Beck, 1m S of Bridgend, NY404134. Then track south by the woods and lake and up Dovedale to Hart Crag.
Winter wildfowl; woodland birds; Ring Ousel and Peregrine.

Brockhole   90   2½m SE of Ambleside
Car-park at visitor centre between A591 and Lake Windermere at NY390010. Then footpaths beside the lake and neighbouring woodland.
Woodland birds including Pied Flycatcher.

Ullswater   90   8m N of Ambleside
Park in Patterdale by A592 at NY395162. Then track and path east and north beside the lake and through woodlands.
Woodland and upland birds; gull roost.

TIC	As previous entry.
	*Old Courthouse, Church Street, Ambleside (05394 32582)
YH	Waterhead, Ambleside (05394 32304)
	High Close, Loughrigg, Ambleside (09667 313)
H/B	Ambleside Bunkroom, Low Gate, Ambleside (05394 33311)
	Sykeside Farm, Brotherswater, Patterdale (08532 239)
RF	Wordsworth Hotel, Grasmere
	Glen Rothay Hotel, Rydal
	Kirkstone Pass, nr Brothers Water
	Travellers Rest, Glenridding (by Ullswater)
RFBBE	Britannia Inn, Elterwater, nr Ambleside (09667 210/382)
BBE	Fellside, Elterwater (09667 678)
	Crow How Hotel, Rydal Road, Ambleside (05394 32193)
	Woodland Crag, Howhead Lane, Grasmere (09665 351)
SC	Wheelwrights, Elterwater (09667 635)
	Loughrigg Cottage, White Crags, Clappersgate, Ambleside (05394 32120)
	Lane Ends Cottage, Elterwater (09667 678)

Haweswater   90   7m NE of Ambleside
Car-park at south end of the reservoir at NY470107. Then tracks south and west and observation post if eagles are nesting.
Upland birds including Golden Eagle, Peregrine and Ring Ousel.

Longsleddale   90   7m E of Ambleside
Park at Sadgill, NY484056. Then track north along the valley.
Upland and river birds including Ring Ousel, Peregrine and
Dipper.

> *Shap Fells   90   NY530085   4m SE of Haweswater*
> *Upland birds.*

TIC	Victoria Street, Windermere (09662 6499)
YH	As previous entry.
	The Old School, Tebay, Penrith (05874 286)
RF	Crown and Mitre, Bampton (nr Haweswater)
RFBBE	Eagle & Child, Staveley, nr Windermere
BBE	Murthwaite Farm, Longsleddale, nr Kendal (053 983 634)
	Beckfoot Country House, Helton, nr Penrith (09313 241)
	Haweswater Hotel, nr Bampton, Penrith (09313 235)
SC	Capplebarrow House, Longsleddale (053 983 686)
	Brunt Knott Farm, Staveley (0539 821030)

Geltsdale   86   12m E of Carlisle
Park by minor road 1½m E of Castle Carrock, 1½m E of B6413, at
NY557556. Then tracks east over River Gelt.
Upland birds including Red Grouse, Golden Plover and Ring
Ousel

River Gelt Valley   86   4m NE of Warwick Bridge
Park in Low Geltbridge on the north side of the river, NY521593.
Then path south beside the river and through the woods.
Woodland and river birds including Pied Flycatcher, Wood
Warbler, Redstart, Dipper and Goshawk.

> *Talkin Tarn   86   NY546590   5m NE of Warwick Bridge*
> *Wildfowl and woodland birds.*

TIC	*The Moot Hall, Brampton (06977 3433)
	M6 Service Area, Southwaite (06974 73445/6)
YH	Etterby House, Etterby, Carlisle (0228 23934)
RF	Hare and Hounds, Talkin
	Stone Inn, Hayton, nr Warwick Bridge
BBE	Hullerbank, Talkin (06976 668)
	Oakwood House, Longtown Road, Brampton (06977 2436)
SC	Long Byres, Talkin Head, Brampton (06976 262)
	Netherton Farm, Talkin (022 870 276)

Milburn Forest   91   7m NE of Appleby-in-Westmorland
Park in Knock, 4m N of Apleby at NY680270. Then tracks, paths
and Pennine Way northeast for 4 miles.
Upland birds including Red Grouse, Golden Plover and other
summer waders.

TIC	Moot Hall, Boroughgate, Appleby (07683 51177)
YH	Redstones, Dufton, Appleby (07683 51236)
H/B	George & Dragon, Garrigill, by Alston (0498 81293)
RFBBE	New Inn, Brampton, nr Appleby (0930 51231)
BBE	Slakes Farm, Milburn, nr Appleby (07683 61385)
SC	Milburn Grange, Knock (07683 61867)

Grune Point   85   3m NE of Silloth
Park in Skinburness, 2m NE of Silloth at NY127557. Then track
northeast to the Point.
Passage and winter waders and wildfowl.

Anthorn   85   3m NW of Kirkbride
View the estuary from minor road on the north side of Moricambe
Bay e.g. NY200584 at Anthorn, and 2m east at NY174576.
Passage and winter waders and wildfowl.

Campfield Marsh   85   2½m N of Anthorn
View from minor road SW of Bowness-on-Solway e.g. NY197616.
Winter waders and wildfowl.

Burgh Marsh & Eden Estuary   85   6m NW of Carlisle
Park by minor road 1m N of Burgh by Sands at NY328604. Then
track and footpath N across the marsh to the estuary.
Passage and winter waders and wildfowl.

> *Drunburgh Moss   85   NY248586   9m NW of Carlisle*
> *Moorland birds including Red Grouse, Curlew and Snipe.*

> *Rockcliffe Marsh   85   NY330630   3m SE of Gretna*
> *Winter waders, wildfowl and raptors.*

TIC	Old Town Hall, Green Market, Carlisle (0228 512444)
	*The Green, Silloth (06973 31944)
YH	Etterby House, Etterby, Carlisle (0228 23934)
R	Greyhound, Burgh-by-Sands
	Bird in Hand, Oulton, nr Wigton
RF	Drovers Rest, Monkhill, nr Burgh-by-Sands
	Rose and Crown, Kirkbampton, nr Carlisle
RFBBE	Royal Oak Hotel, Wigton (0965 42393)
BBE	Nith View, Pine Terrace, Silloth (06973 31542)
	How End Farm, Thursby, nr Carlisle (06973 42487)
SC	32 Skinburness Drive, Silloth (09666 432)

Derbyshire

Hope Forest   110   5m SE of Glossop
Car-park by A57 4½m SE of Glossop at SK109914. Then paths east up through woods and onto the moors.
Woodland and moorland birds including Red Grouse, Golden Plover, Twite, Goshawk and Crossbill.

Ladybower & Derwent Reservoirs   110   9m SE of Glossop
Car-parks by minor road along the western shores north of A57 e.g. SK173894. Then many tracks and footpaths west and north through woodland and by the reservoirs.
Woodland birds including Crossbill, Goshawk and Black Grouse.

Edale Moor   110   4m E of Hayfield
Car-park and information centre at Edale, 2m N of A625, at SK125856. Then Pennine Way and other tracks north and east up onto Edale Moor and Kinder Scout.
Upland birds including Peregrine, Dunlin, Golden Plover, Ring Ousel and Twite.

Bleaklow   110   4m NE of Glossop
Car-park by B6105 on the southern side of Torside Reservoir, SK068984. Then tracks and Pennine Way south and east up onto the moor.
Upland birds.

> *Longdendale Reservoirs   110   SK025970–SK100995*
> *2–4m N & NE of Glossop*
> *Winter and passage wildfowl.*

TIC Station Forecourt, Norfolk Street, Glossop (04574 5920)
YH Rowland Cote, Nether Booth, Edale, Sheffield (0433 70302)
H/B Snake Pass Inn Bunkhouse, Ashopton, Bamford (0344 51480)
R Yorkshire Bridge, Bamford (nr Ladybower Reservoir)

RF	Derwent Hotel, Bamford, nr Hathersage
	Poachers Arms, Hope
	Ladybower, by Ladybower Reservoir, nr Bamford
RFBBE	Cheshire Cheese Inn, Hope
BBE	The Old Vicarage, Church Bank, Hathersage (0433 51099)
	Birds Nest Cottage, 40 Primrose Lane, Glossop (04574 3478)
SC	Shatton Hall Farm, Bamford (0433 20635)
	9 The Croft, Bamford (0433 51543)

Goyt Valley   119   4m NW of Buxton
Car-parks by minor road on west side of Errwood Reservoir, 2m W of A5002, e.g. SK014757 & SK013748. Then many tracks and nature trail beside reservoirs and through the woods.
River and woodland birds including Dipper, Common Sandpiper, Redstart, Wood Warbler and Crossbill.

> *Combs Reservoir   119   SK040795   4½m N of Buxton*
> *Passage and winter wildfowl.*

TIC	The Crescent, Buxton (0298 25106/77889)
YH	Sherbrook Lodge, Harpur Hill Road, Buxton (02982 2287)
RF	Beehive, Combs
BB	Hawthorn Farm Guest House, Fairfield Road, Buxton (0298 23230)
BBE	Fernilee Hall, Fernilee, nr Whaley Bridge (06633 2258)
SC	Sittinglow Farm, Dove Holes, nr Buxton (0298 812271)

Monsal & Taddington Dales   119   3½m NW of Bakewell
Car-park by A6, 2m W of Ashford, at SK170706. Then paths north and west through woods and beside the River Wye.
Woodland and river birds including Wood Warbler, Redstart, Dipper and Kingfisher.

Cressbrook & Millers Dale   119   4½m NW of Bakewell
Park in Cressbrook SK170731 and take tracks and paths north or west. Also by B6049 1m S of Tideswell, at SK154743, and track and path south beside river.
Woodland and river birds.

Chatsworth Park   119   3m E of Bakewell
Car-park by A623 (formerly B6012) 1m N of Beeley, at SK257686. Then path north on west side of River Derwent.
River and woodland birds including Kingfisher and Hawfinch.

Longshaw Country Park, Barbrook Reservoir & Big Moor   119
6m N of Bakewell
Car-park at junction of B6054 and B6055, SK268790. Then tracks
and footpaths west through woodland and east to moorland and
reservoir.
Woodland and moorland birds including Pied Flycatcher, Hawfinch, Wood Warbler, Red Grouse; Merlin and Hen Harrier in
winter; passage waders and winter wildfowl.

Linacre Wood & Reservoirs   119   3m NW of Chesterfield
Car-park ½m S of B6050 at east end of reservoirs, SK337726. Then
tracks and footpaths through woods and beside reservoirs.
Woodland birds; summer warblers and winter wildfowl.

Lathkill Dale   119   2–3m SW of Bakewell
Car-park in Over Haddon, 1m S of B5055, at SK203664. Then path
west beside the river toward Monyash. Or park in Monyash at
SK150665 and walk the valley from west to east.
Woodland and river birds including Redstart, Hawfinch and
Dipper.

> ### Beeley & East Moors   119   SK295677   5m E of Bakewell
> *Moorland birds including Golden Plover; winter Merlin and
> Hen Harrier.*

> ### Monk's Dale   119   SK135745   4m E of Buxton
> *Woodland birds.*

TIC	Old Market Hall, Bridge Street, Bakewell (0629 813227)
YH	Fly Hill, Bakewell (062981 2313)
RF	Monsal Head Hotel, Monsal Head
	Three Stags Heads, Wardlow
RFBBE	Chequers, Froggatt Edge (0433 30231)
BB	Bubnell Cliff Farm, Bubnell, nr Bakewell (024 688 2454)
	Highfield Farm, Ashford-in-the-Water (062 981 2482)
SC	The Rest, Foolow, Eyam, nr Bakewell (0433 30186)

Dovedale   119   4m NW of Ashbourne
Car-park by minor road 1m NW of Thorpe by River Dove,
SK146508. Then short walk back down road to footpath north up
the dale along the east bank.
Woodland and river birds including Redstart, Pied Flycatcher,
Dipper and Grey Wagtail.

Osmaston Park   119   3m SE of Ashbourne
Park in Osmaston, 1m S of A52, SK201436. Then tracks and foot-
paths SW and SE across the park.
Woodland birds and wildfowl.

TIC	13 The Market Place, Ashbourne (0335 43666)
YH	Ilam Hall, Ashbourne (033529 212)

RF Coach and Horses, Fenny Bentley, nr Ashbourne
BBE Hillcrest House, Thorpe (033529 436)
BBESC Little Park Farm, Mappleton, nr Ashbourne (033529 341)
SC Gateham Grange Farm, Alstonefield, nr Ashbourne (033527 349)

Ogston Reservoir 119 5m E of Matlock
Car-parks on W shore, ½m S of B6014, at SK374605, and by B6014 at north end, SK376609.
Winter gull roost including northern gulls; winter wildfowl; passage waders and terns; migrants.

Shiningcliff Wood 119 4m N of Belper
Park just west of A6, ¾m NW of Ambergate at SK342523. Then tracks and footpaths north and west.
Woodland birds including Redstart, Wood Warbler, Hawfinch and large winter finch roost.

Cromford Canal 119 1½m S to 4½m SE of Matlock
Car-parks at Cromford Wharf, ¼m N of A6 at SK300570. Then footpath south beside canal, and at Whatstandwell by junction of A6 and B5035, SK333543, and paths north and south.
Woodland and river birds including Hawfinch, Pied Flycatcher, Dipper and Kingfisher.

> ***Birdholme Wildfowl Reserve*** *119* *SK386690* *1½m S of Chesterfield centre*
> *Summer warblers; wildfowl; migrants. (Open Sat pm & Sun only).*

> ***Wyver Lane*** *119* *SK344495* *1½m NW of Belper centre*
> *Wildfowl; summer warblers and Hobby; migrants.*

> ***Butterley Reservoir*** *119 & 120* *SK400520* *1m N of Ripley*
> *Winter wildfowl.*

> ***Carsington Reservoir*** *119* *SK245520* *5m NE of Ashbourne*
> *Winter wildfowl; passage waders, terns and gulls.*

TIC The Pavilion, Matlock Bath (0629 55082)
  Peacock Info & Heritage Centre, Low Pavement, Chesterfield (0246 207777)
YH 40 Bank Road, Matlock (0629 582983)
RF White Horse Inn, Woolley Moor (nr Ogston Reservoir)
  White Lion, Starkholmes, nr Lea, Matlock
BBE Henmore Grange, Hopton Carsington, nr Wirksworth (062985 420)
  Fairhaven, Stonerows Lane, Ashover, nr Matlock (0246 590405)

BBESC Lydgate Farm, Aldwark (062 985 250)
SC Ivy Dene Cottage, Sandy Lane, Crich, nr Matlock (077 385 2416)
Barncroft, Well Street, Elton, nr Matlock (062 988 645)

Mapperley Reservoir   129   2m S of Heanor
Car-park by minor road ½m N of Mapperley, 1½m N of A609, at SK435436. Then paths around reservoir to hide at western end.
Passage waders; winter wildfowl; summer warblers.

Church Wilne Pits & Reservoir   129   1½m SE of Draycott
Park by Church Wilne church, 1m S of Draycott, SK447318. Then footpaths and tracks around pits and by western end of reservoir.
Passage and winter wildfowl, waders and gulls; summer warblers, Common Tern and Little Ringed Plover; reedbed species; passage terns and raptors.

> *Elvaston Castle Country Park*   129   SK410330   1½m SW of Borrowash
> *Woodland and river birds; summer warblers.*

> *Shipley Lake*   129   SK445442   2m SE of Heanor
> *Winter wildfowl.*

TIC Central Library, The Wardwick, Derby (0332 290664)
YH Shining Cliff, c/o 24 Bank View Road, Nether Heage (077385 3068)
RF Canal Tavern, Shardlow, nr Draycott
Harrington Arms, Elvaston, nr Derby
BBE Ockbrook House, Flood Street, Ockbrook (0332 662208)

Cresswell Crags   120   5m SW of Worksop
Car-park and visitor centre ¾m E of A616 at SK537744. Then footpaths around the gorge.
Woodland birds and summer warblers.

Whitwell Wood   120   4m W of Worksop
Park by minor road ½m N of A619 at SK517777. Then tracks east through the woods.
Woodland birds.

Hardwick Hall Country Park   120   2½m SE of Holmewood
Car-park and visitor centre 1m E of Astwith, 1½m E of B6039 at SK454640. Then many paths.
Woodland birds; summer warblers; winter wildfowl.

Williamthorpe Reservoirs   120   4½m SW of Bolsover
Park by minor road on north side of Holmewood, ½m E of B6039 at
SK433664. Then track north by the reservoirs.
Summer warblers; reedbed species; autumn and winter roosts;
occasional Bearded Tit; passage waders and terns.

> *Scarclie Park*   120   SK516706   *2m E of Bolsover*
> *Woodland birds.*

> *Pleasley Vale*   120   SK520650   *3m NW of Marsfield
> centre*
> *Woodland and river birds including Kingfisher and Hawfinch.*

TIC	Public Library, Memorial Avenue, Worksop (0909 501148)
YH	The Edge, Eyam, Sheffield (0433 30335)
R	Jug and Glass, Whitwell
RF	Hardwick Inn, Hardwick Park
BB	Norton Grange Farm, Norton, nr Warsop (0623 842666) Old Orchard Cottage, Holbeck, nr Cresswell (0909 720659)
BBSC	Blue Barn Farm, Cuckney, nr Warsop (0623 742248)

**Staunton Harold Reservoir & Calke Park   128   1½m SW of
Melbourne**
Car-parks at southern end of reservoir ½m N of Calke, SK375227,
and ½m E at SK378219, and at the northern end by the dam, ¼m
S of B587 at SK377245. For Calke Park signed car-parks 1m S of
Ticknall then many paths.
Wildfowl; passage waders and terns; winter gull roost; migrants;
woodland birds.

Foremark Reservoir   128   3m NE of Swadlincote
Car-parks at northern end, down track south of minor road 2m
NW of Ticknall, SK336241, and at the southern end ¼m west of
A514, SK334226. Then take paths around reservoir.
Winter wildfowl and gulls; passage terns; woodland birds and
summer warblers.

**Drakelow Wildlife Reserve   128   2m SW of Burton-upon-
Trent**
Permit from CEGB, Drakelow Power Station, Burton-upon-Trent.
Entrance to car-park, centre and hides from minor road 1½m NE of
Walton-on-Trent at SK228191.
Passage waders and terns; winter wildfowl and gulls; summer
warblers, Common Tern and Little Ringed Plover; reedbed
species.

Swarkestone Gravel Pits   128   2½m NW of Melbourne
View from minor road 1m SW of Swarkestone ½m SW of A514 at
SK363279.
Winter wildfowl; passage terns and waders.

Egginton Gravel Pits   128   *SK257286 & SK275276*
1m NW & 1m SE of Egginton
Wildfowl; passage waders and terns.

Willington Gravel Pits   128   *SK292283   W end of*
Willington
Winter wildfowl.

Hilton Gravel Pits   128   *SK250315   ¾m NE of Hilton*
Winter wildfowl; grebes; summer warblers; woodland birds;
passage terns.

Melbourne Pool   128   *SK390248   SE edge of Melbourne*
Winter wildfowl.

TIC   Town Hall, King Edward Place, Burton-upon-Trent, Staffs (0283 45454)
YH   Little Ranger, Oakamoor, Stoke-on-Trent, Staffs (0538 702304)
RF   John Thomson, Ingleby, nr Swarkestone
Chequers, Ticknall
White Swan, Egginton
Horseshoe, Tutenhill, nr Burton-upon-Trent
BB   High Barn Farm, Isley Walton, nr Castle Donington (0332 810360)

Devon

Plym Estuary   201   W side of Plymouth
Park and view from A374 on the west side of the estuary at
SX515563 and from path along the east side off A38.
Passage and winter waders and gulls.

Wembury & Yealm Estuary   201   4m SE of Plymouth centre
Car-park at end of minor road above the shore at SX519484. Then
coast path east to the estuary or west.
Passage and winter waders; migrants; Cirl Bunting.

Lopwell Dam & River Tavy   201   5m N of Plymouth centre
Park by the dam at end of minor road 2½m W of A386 at SX475650.
Then path through woods on the west side if crossing is possible,
and south beside the estuary.
Passage waders; woodland birds.

Burrator Reservoir   202   8m NE of Plymouth
View from minor road around reservoir or park at north end 1½m
E of B3212 at SX567694 and take tracks through woods.
Passage and winter wildfowl and gulls; woodland and hill birds
including Crossbill.

> *Millbay Docks*   201   *SX470540   1m SW of Plymouth
> centre*
> *Winter gulls.*

> *Warren Point*   201   *SX444606   3m NW of Plymouth
> centre*
> *Passage and winter waders and wildfowl.*

TIC   Civic Centre, Royal Parade, Plymouth (0752 264849)
         *Town Hall Buildings, Bedford Square, Tavistock (0822
         612938)
YH   Belmont House, Devonport Road, Stoke, Plymouth (0752
         562189)

RF	Who'd Have Thought It, Milton Combe, nr Yelverton
	Royal Oak, Meavy, nr Yelverton
	Odd Wheel, Wembury
BBE	Uppaton House, Buckland Monachorum, nr Yelverton (0822 853226)
	Broadmoor Farm, nr Yealmpton, Plymouth (0752 880407)
SC	(The Mill Cottage, Wembury Beach) National Trust, Killerton House, Broadclyst, nr Exeter (0392 881691)

Thurlestone & South Milton Ley   202   4m NW of Salcombe
Car-park at end of minor road 2m SW of South Milton at SX677416, then footpaths north to sewage outfall and south to Bolt Tail. Reedbed species including Bearded Tit and Cetti's Warbler; winter wildfowl and gulls; migrants; Cirl Bunting.

Avon Estuary   202   5m NW of Salcombe
Car-park at end of minor road 3m SW of A379, 1m NW of Thurlestone, ½m W of Bantham at SX664436. Then coastal path.
Passage and winter waders and wildfowl.

> ***Bolt Head***   *202   SX725364   2m SW of Salcombe*
> *Migrants; sea watching; winter seaduck and divers.*

> ***Kingsbridge Estuary (west)***   *202   SX742392   NE corner of Salcombe*
> *Passage and winter waders.*

TIC	The Quay, Kingsbridge (0548 3195)
	*66 Fore Street, Salcombe (054 884 3927)
YH	Overbecks, Sharpitor, Salcombe (054 884 2856)
RF	Old Inn, Malborough, nr Salcombe
	Church House, Churchstow, nr Kingsbridge
RFBBE	Sloop Inn, Bantham, nr Kingsbridge (0548 560489)
BBESC	Fern Lodge, Hope Cove, nr Salcombe (0548 561326)
SC	Brook Cottage, Inner Hope, Hope Cove (039 287 4120)

Slapton Ley   202   5½m E of Kingsbridge
Car-parks by A379 between the Ley and the sea e.g. at SX824424 and at northern end SX828442. Footpaths and nature trail west from the northern end behind the Ley and through woods.
Reedbed species; winter wildfowl, grebes and divers; large winter gull roost; Cetti's Warbler; migrants; summer warblers and woodland birds.

Start Point   202   6½m SE of Kingsbridge
Car-park at end of minor road 1½m SE of Kellaton, ¾m from the point at SX821376. Then track east to the point and coast path north and south.
Summer seabird colonies; seawatching; migrants; Cirl Bunting and Raven.

Prawle Point   202   3½m SW of Start Point
Car-park at the end of minor road south from East Prawle at
SX775355. Then coast path east around fields and west to the point
and the wooded Pigs Nose Valley.
Migrants; seawatching; Cirl Bunting.

Kingsbridge Estuary (east)   202   4m S of Kingsbridge
View from minor road east and west of East Portlemouth on east
side of estuary e.g. at SX755390 and SX743382.
Passage and winter waders; winter wildfowl, grebes and divers.

TIC	As previous entry.
YH	Parish Hall, Strete, Dartmouth (0803 770013)
RF	Pigs Nose, East Prawle
	Millbrook, South Pool
	Start Bay Inn, Torcross
RFBBE	The Tower, Slapton (0548 580216)
BBE	Old Walls, Slapton (0548 580516)
	Oddicombe House Hotel, Chillington, nr Kingsbridge (054 853 234)
	Wyngates, East Prawle (054 851 443)
BBESC	Maelcombe House Farm, East Prawle (054 851 300)
	Sloutts Farmhouse, Slapton (0548 580872)

River Dart Estuary   202   3m W of Brixham
View from ferry terminal on the east side 1½m W of A379 at
SX870548 and from Stoke Gabriel 2m upstream at SX848573.
Passage and winter waders and wildfowl.

Berry Head   202   1½m NE of Brixham centre
Car-park at top of road 1½m NE of B3205 at SX941563. Then foot-
paths and nature trail NE to the point.
Seabird colonies; seawatching; migrants.

**Brixham Harbour & Fishcombe Point   202   NW side of
Brixham**
Park near the harbour at SX926565 and take the Devon South
Coast Path NW to Churston Cove and Fishcombe Point.
Winter seaduck and divers; migrants.

Hope's Nose   202   2m SE of Torquay centre
Park at top of minor road nearest to the point at SX945635 and
footpath east to the point and sewage outfall.
Seawatching; gulls; Kittiwake colony; migrants.

> *Goodrington Sands & Saltern Cove* 202   *SX895590*
> *1m S of Paignton*
> *Winter seaduck and divers.*

> *Higher Brownstone & Newfoundland Cove* 202
> *SX903497 1½m SE of Kingswear*
> *Migrants; winter seaduck and divers.*

TIC	The Old Market Place, The Quay, Brixham (08045 2861)
YH	Maypool, Galmpton, Brixham (0803 842444)
RF	Church House, Stoke Gabriel
	Ship, Kingswear
BBE	Greenbrier Hotel, Victoria Road, Brixham (0803 882113)
SC	(New cottages, Nethway Cross, Kingswear) National Trust, Killerton House, Broadclyst, nr Exeter (0392 881691)
	(Colt Cottage, Higher Brownstone Farm, Kingswear) As above.

Yarner Wood   191   2m W of Bovey Tracey

Car-park by minor road at east end of reserve 1m N of B3387 at SX786788. Then paths and nature trails west through the woods. Woodland birds including Pied Flycatcher and Redstart.

Fernworthy Reservoir & Forest   191   3m SW of Chagford

Car-park along the southern side of the reservoir 1½m NW of B3212 at SX669838. Then tracks beside the reservoir and through woods.
Woodland birds including Crossbill and Nightjar; winter and passage wildfowl.

Challacombe Down & Headland Warren   191   4½m S of Chagford

Car-park by B3212 2½m NE of Postbridge at SX676811. Then track and footpaths west.
Upland birds including Ring Ousel and Raven; winter Hen Harrier roost.

Teign Valley   191   3m NE of Chagford

Car-park at end of minor road on south side of the river 1m SE of Drewsteignton at SX744898. Then tracks and paths east and west beside the river and through woods.
Woodland and river birds including Dipper, Pied Flycatcher, Wood Warbler and Redstart.

TIC	*Lower Car-park, Station Road, Bovey Tracey (0626 832047)
	8 Sherbourne Raod, Newton Abbot (0626 67494)
YH	Bellever, Postbridge, Yelverton (0822 88227)
	Steps Bridge, Dunsford, Exeter (0647 52435)
RFBBE	Rock, Haytor Vale, nr Bovey Tracey (03646 305)
	Sandy Park Inn, Sandy Park, nr Moretonhampstead (06473 3538)
	Ring of Bells, North Bovey, nr Moretonhampstead (0647 40375)
BBE	Bly House, Chagford (06473 2404)

SC	Clifford Bridge Park, Clifford, Drewsteignton (0647 24226)
	(The Mill Cottage, Chagford) National Trust, Killerton House, Broadclyst, nr Exeter (0392 881691)
	(Glebe cottages, Drewsteignton) National Trust, as above.

Cranmere Pool Letterbox 191 6m S of Okehampton

Minor road south from centre of Okehampton passes over bypass. Continue beyond the gate at the army camp *if red flags are not flying* (dates and times from Okehampton Post Office or Police Station). Continue south for 4 miles and park at the top of Okement Hill at SX604877. Then walk south to plateau area around SX605855. It is also possible to walk northwest from Fernworthy Forest.

Upland birds including Red Grouse, Dunlin and Golden Plover.

Roadford Reservoir 190 2m W of Bratton Clovelly

View from lay-by at the north end of the reservoir by Southweek Viaduct, 1m S of Germansweek at SX434930. Also large car-park at the south end by the east end of the dam, 1m NW of Broadwoodwidger at SX423899.

Wildfowl; passage terns and waders; passage and winter gulls; raptors; migrants.

> **Lydford Gorge** *191 SX504840 SW of Lydford*
> *Woodland and river birds.*

TIC	*3 West Street, Okehampton (0837 53020)
YH	As previous entry.
RF	Clovelly, Bratton Clovelly
	Oxenham Arms, South Zeal
	Arundel Arms, Lifton, nr Launceston
RFBBE	The Tors Inn, Belstone, nr Okehampton (0837 840689)
	Castle Inn, Lydford
BBE	Upcott House, Upcott Hill, nr Okehampton (0837 53743)
	Lifton Cottage Hotel, Lifton (0566 84439)
SC	East Hook Cottages, West Hook Farm, Okehampton (0837 2305)

Haldon Forest 192 6m SW of Exeter centre

Car-parks and viewing points by minor roads north and south of A38 2m SW of Kennford e.g. just south of the main road at SX904838; Bird of Prey Viewing Point on the north side at Bullers Hill, SX882847; and Tower Hill, SX877855. There are also many tracks and forest walks from the car-parks.

Woodland birds including Crossbill, Nightjar, Turtle Dove, Honey Buzzard and Hobby; migrants.

Exminster Marshes   192   1m E of Exminster
Car-park 200yds east of roundabout on A379 by 'Swan's Nest' inn,
¾m SE of Exminster at SX954873. Then track east to estuary and
path south to Turf Inn.
Passage and winter waders and wildfowl including Avocet; winter
raptors and Short-eared Owl; migrants; Cirl Bunting.

Powderham   192   3m SE of Exminster
Park by the church 2m SE of A379 at SX973844. Then track and
path north beside the estuary.
Passage and winter wildfowl and waders including in winter up to
500 Black-tailed Godwit; passage Osprey and Hobby.

Dawlish Warren   192   3m NE of Dawlish
Car-park just east of Dawlish Warren railway station at SX981787,
then paths to point and hide.
Passage and winter waders and wildfowl; winter raptors and
Short-eared Owl; winter divers, grebes, seaduck and gulls; Cirl
Bunting; migrants.

TIC	The Lawn, Dawlish (0626 863589)
YH	47 Countess Wear Road, Exeter (039 287 3329)
RF	Anchor, Cockwood, nr Dawlish
RFBBE	Nobody Inn, Doddiscombsleigh (0647 52394)
	Turf Inn, nr Exminster (0392 833128)
SC	Shell Cove House, Old Teignmouth Road, Dawlish (0626 862523)

Exmouth   192   extreme W of Exmouth
Car-park overlooks the estuary just west of railway station ¼m W
of A376 at SX997810.
Passage and winter waders and wildfowl; winter seaduck, divers
and grebes; passage terns and gulls.

**Otter Estuary & Budleigh Salterton   192   4–5m E of
Exmouth**
Car-park at east end of Budleigh seafront at SY073820. Then tracks
north beside the estuary and southeast to the point.
Passage and winter waders and wildfowl; marshland species;
migrants; a few Serin usually singing in conifers in the town in the
spring.

Aylesbeare Common   192   6½m NE of Exmouth
Car-park by A3052 1m SE of its junction with B3180 at SY057897.
Then tracks and path north.
Heathland birds including Dartford Warbler, Nightjar and Wood-
lark; winter raptors; woodland birds including Hawfinch.

Bicton & Woodbury Commons   192   2m E of Woodbury
Car-parks by B3180 at SY032872 and ½m further south at junction
with B3179. Then tracks and paths south and north.
Heathland and woodland birds.

East Budleigh & Lympstone Commons   192   2½m SE of Woodbury
Paths south from above sites and car-park by minor road 1m NE of B3179, 2m W of East Budleigh at SY042848 and paths westwards. Heathland and woodland birds.

> *Ashclyst Forest   192   SY001995   2m NE of Broadclyst*
> *Woodland birds.*

TIC	*Alexandra Terrace, Exmouth (0395 263744)
	Exeter Services, M5 Sandygate Junction 30, nr Exeter (0392 437581)
YH	As previous and following entries.
RF	Sir Walter Raleigh, East Budleigh
BBE	Crossways, Oakhayes Road, Woodbury, nr Exmouth (0395 32673)
	Tidwell House Country Hotel, Budleigh Salterton (03954 2444)
SC	(Ashclyst Forest cottages) National Trust, Killerton House, Broadclyst, nr Exeter (0392 881691)

Axe Estuary   192 or 193   1m E of Seaton
View from B3172 south of Axmouth on the east side of the estuary e.g. SY256910. Also track and footpath beside the river mouth to the southeast of the bridge at SY255898.
Passage and winter waders and wildfowl.

Culverhole Point & Dowlands Undercliff   193   2–4m E of Seaton
Take South Devon Coast Path east from the mouth of River Axe (see previous site). Wooded and scrubby undercliff continues almost to Lyme Regis.
Woodland birds and summer warblers including Nightingale; migrants; passage waders; winter seaduck.

TIC	The Esplanade, Seaton (0297 21660)
YH	Bovey Combe, Townsend, Beer, Seaton (0297 20296)
RF	Kingfisher, Colyton, nr Seaton
	Ship, Axmouth
BB	The Old Rectory, Colyton (040 487 300)
BBE	Garlands, Stovar Long Lane, Beer, nr Seaton (0297 20958)
	Swallows Eaves Hotel, Swan Hill Road, Colyton (0297 53184)
SC	(Forge Cottage, Branscombe, nr Seaton) National Trust, as previous SC entry.

Heddon Valley & Highveer Point   180   **4m W of Lynton**
Car-park by Hunter's Inn, 2½m NW of A39 from Martinhoe Cross, at SS655482. Then paths and nature trail south and north through woods, beside river and to the Point.
Woodland and river birds including Redstart, Pied Flycatcher and Dipper; migrants; summer seabirds; seawatching.

Countisbury Common & Foreland Point   180   **2m NE of Lynton**
Car-park by A39 ½m E of Countisbury at SS754496. Then many paths north across the common and to the point.
Migrants; summer seabirds; seawatching.

> **Wistlandpound Reservoir** 180 SS644415 7m SW of Lynton
> Passage and winter wildfowl.

> **Woody Bay** 180 SS673494 3m W of Lynton
> Woodland birds; migrants; summer seabirds.

TIC   Town Hall, Lee Road, Lynton (0598 52225)
YH   Lynbridge, Lynton (0598 53237)
RF   Exmoor Sandpiper, Countisbury
BBE   Seawood Hotel, North Walk, Lynton (0598 52272)
        Bridge Cottage, Brendon, nr Lynton (0598 7247)
        Red House Hotel, Woody Bay (05983 255)
SC   Martinhoe Manor, Woody Bay (05983 424)
        (Countisbury Hill Cottage, Countisbury, nr Lynton)
        National Trust, Killerton House, Broadclyst, nr Exeter (0392 881691)

Borough Valley   180   **2½m SW of Ilfracombe**
Park at Lee 1½m NW of B3231 at SS483464 and take footpath south through woods and beside river.
Woodland and river birds; migrants.

Morte Point   180   **1½m NW of Woolacombe**
Park by the church in the centre of Mortehoe at SS456453 and take track and path west to the point.
Migrants; seawatching.

Baggy Point & Morte Bay   180   **3m SW of Woolacombe**
Car-park at the south end of Woolacombe Sand, 1½m NW of B3231 fron Georgeham at SS447407. Then coast path west to the point.
Migrants; seawatching; winter seaduck and divers.

Taw Mouth & Braunton Marsh   180   **2–3m SW of Braunton**
View marsh from minor road SW of A361. Car-park at end of the road at SS466327, then paths south to Crow Point, across the dunes to the shore and NE beside the estuary to the River Caen.
Passage and winter waders and wildfowl.

Bassett's Ridge & Heanton Court   180   SS514347   2m
SE of Braunton
Passage and winter waders and wildfowl.

Capstone Point   180   SS519481   N end of Ilfracombe
Seawatching.

TIC	The Promenade, Ilfracombe (0271 63001)
	The Car-park, Braunton (0271 816400)
YH	Ashmoor House, 1 Hillsborough Terrace, Ilfracombe (0271 65337)
RF	Ship Aground, Mortehoe, nr Ilfracombe
	Rock, Georgeham, nr Braunton
BB	Croyde Manor, Croyde
BBE	Pebbles Hotel, Chapel Hill, Mortehoe (0271 870426)
	Gull Rock, Mortehoe (0271 870534)
SC	Bloomfield, Hills View, Braunton (0271 812398)
	(Croyde Hoe Farmhouse, Croyde) National Trust, Killerton House, Broadclyst, nr Exeter (0392 881691)

Muddlebridge & Penhill Point   180   **3m W of Barnstaple**
Park by A39 1m W of Bickington at SS523325 and take track NW on the east side of the estuary and on to Penhill Point and the Taw Estuary.
Passage and winter waders and wildfowl.

Instow Sands   180   **½m-1m n of Instow**
Car-park on north side of Instow at SS474310, 200yds west of A39. Then coast path north.
Passage and winter waders.

Northam Burrows Country Park   180   **3m N of Bideford**
Signed car-park 1m N of B3236 from Westward Ho! along the coast road, at SS437306. Also road to the point and beside estuary NW from A386 ¼m south of Appledore.
Passage and winter waders; migrants.

TIC	North Devon Library, Tuly Street, Barnstaple (0271 47177)
	*The Quay, Bideford (0237 477676)
YH	Worlington House, Instow, Bideford (0271 860394)
RF	Quay, Instow
BBE	4 Marine Parade, Appledore, nr Bideford (02372 78649)

Buck Mills – Clovelly   190   **7m W of Bideford**
Car-park in Buck Mills ½m N of A39 at SS358233. Then lane NW and North Devon Coast Path westwards through woodland and scrub.
Migrants; woodland birds.

Hartland Point   190   3m NW of Hartland
Car-park near the point 5m NW of A39 at SS236275. Then walk
along the road which continues to the lighthouse and coastguard
lookout and to the coastal path.
Summer seabirds; seawatching; migrants; winter divers and
raptors.

> *Marsland Valley   190   SS217174   6m SW of Hartland*
> *Migrants and woodland birds.*

TIC   The Crescent Car-park, Bude, Cornwall (0288 4240)
       *The Quay, Bideford (0237 477676)
YH   Elmscott, Hartland, Bideford (02374 367)
RF   Hartland Quay, Hartland Quay
       Farmer's Arms, Woolwardisworthy
BBE   Fosfelle, Hartland (0237 441273)
       West Titchberry Farm, Hartland (02374 287)
SC   (The Tatches, Peppercombe, nr Clovelly) National Trust,
       Killerton House, Broadclyst, nr Exeter (–392 881691)
       (5 Forest Gardens, Buck's Mills) Court Barn Cottage,
       West Bradley, Glastonbury, Somerset (0458 50349)

Lundy Island   180   20m NW of Bideford
Boat from Bideford or Ilfracombe; 'MS Oldenburg' run by the
Landmark Trust tel: 0237 470422 for details.
Also the Trust's 32ft launch 'Islander' can be hired from Clovelly
when 'MS Oldenburg' is not sailing (except Sundays), minimum
charge £125.
Self catering cottages, hostel accommodation and camping avail-
able, all details from: The Landmark Trust, Shottesbrooke,
Maidenhead, Berkshire, SL6 3SW. Tel: 062 882 5925
Migrants including many rarities; summer seabirds.

Dorset

Charmouth & The Spittles   193   0–1m W of Charmouth
Car-park by the front at Charmouth just west of the river at
SY365931. Then coastal paths west to Black Ven and The Spittles
and east to Cains Folly.
Migrants; summer warblers; passage waders; river birds.

Lamberts Hill Woods   193   3½m N of Charmouth
Car-park by B3165 3½m NE of its junction with A35 at SY366987.
Then tracks and footpaths around the hill.
Woodland birds and summer warblers including Redstart and
Wood Warbler.

> *Marshwood Vale*   193   *SY400964*   *3m NE of Charmouth*
> *River and woodland birds.*

TIC   The Guildhall, Bridge Street, Lyme Regis (02974 2138)
YH   Bovey Combe, Townsend, Beer, Seaton (0297 20296)
            West Rivers House, West Allington, Bridport (0308
            22655)
RF   Pilot Boat, Lyme Regis
            Bottle, Marshwood
BBE   Newlands House, Stonebarrow Lane, Charmouth (0297
            60212)
            Penn Farm, Axminster Road, Charmouth (0297 60428)
            Church Ground Farm, Salway Ash, nr Bridport (030 888
            282)
SC   Willowhayne Farm, Chideock, nr Bridport (0297 89042)
            (St. Gabriels cottages, Golden Cap, nr Chideock)
            National Trust, Filcombe Farmhouse, Morecombelake,
            Bridport (0297 89628)

Powerstock Common   194   3m W of Maiden Newton
Car-park by minor road 1¼m SW of Toller Porcorum, 2m SW of
A356 at SY547974. Then tracks westwards through woodland.
Woodland birds and summer warblers.

West Bexington   194   3m NW of Abbotsbury
Car-park by the front 1m SW of B3157 at SY532864. Then coast
path NW to reedbeds and meres.
Reedbed species; passage waders and wildfowl; migrants; gull
roost; seawatching.

Abbotsbury   194   1½ m SW of Abbotsbury centre
Car-park by the beach 1m SW of B3157 at SY560845. Then coast
path SE to reedbeds and the northwest end of the Fleet.
Reedbed species; passage waders, wildfowl, gulls and terns;
migrants.

**Herbury Gore & Rodden Hive   194   4m NW of Weymouth
centre**
Park by minor road just before the entrance to the Moonfleet
Hotel, 1½m SW of B3157 at SY619807. Then Dorset Coast Path NW
to Herbury Gore and Rodden Hive and SE to East Fleet.
Passage and winter waders and wildfowl; passage terns and gulls;
migrants.

> ***Black Down*** *194   SY610875   3m NE of Abbotsbury*
> *Heathland birds; migrants.*
>
> ***Lower Kingcombe*** *194   SY554991   3m NW of Maiden
> Newton*
> *River birds including Dipper and Kingfisher.*

TIC   32 South Street, Bridport (0308 24901)
YH   Litton Cheney, Dorchester (03083 340)
RF   Spyway Inn, Askerswell, nr Bridport
            Manor Hotel, Burton Bradstock
            Ilchester Arms, Abbotsbury
BBE   Swan Lodge, Abbotsbury (0305 871249)
            Millmead Country Hotel, Portesham (0305 871432)
SC   Tamarisk Farm, West Bexington (0308 897784)

Deadmoor Common   194   3m SW of Sturminster Newton
Park by minor road 2½m SW of A357, ½m W of Fifehead Neville at
ST759107. Then track NW to the woods.
Woodland birds; summer warblers including Nightingale.

Piddles Wood   194   1m SE of Sturminster Newton
Car-park by A357 1m E of its junction with B3091 at ST801134.
Then track SW through the woods and by the River Stour on the
north bank.
Woodland and river birds; summer warblers.

Ringmoor   194   4m SE of Sturminster Newton
Car-park by minor road at top of the hill 1½m SE of Okeford
Fitzpaine. Then track and paths southwest.
Woodland and downland birds; summer warblers; migrants.

Whatcombe Wood   194   *ST824030*   *2m NW of Winter-borne Whitechurch*
Woodland birds.

TIC	Marsh & Ham Car-park, West Street, Blandford Forum (0258 451989/454770)
YH	2 Crane Street, Cranborne, Wimborne (07254 285)
R	Antelope, Hazelbury Bryan
RF	Green Man, King Stag
	Brace of Pheasants, Plush
RFBBE	Fox, Higher Ansty (0258 880328)
BB	The Old Bakery, Milton Abbas (0258 880327)
	Manor House Farm, Ibberton, nr Blandford (0258 817349)
BBE	Holebrook Farm, Lydlynch, nr Sturminster Newton (0258 817348)
SC	The Drove, Higher Ansty (0258 880441)
	Bere Marsh Farm, Shillingstone, nr Sturminster Newton (0258 860339)

Radipole Lake   **194**   **by Weymouth centre**
Large car-park just west of Weymouth railway and bus stations at SY677796. Then tracks north to hides.
Reedbed species including Cetti's Warbler and Bearded Tit; wildfowl; passage waders and terns; gulls; migrants.

Lodmoor   **194**   **1m NE of Weymouth centre**
Car-park by A353 at SY687807. Then track around the reserve and to hides.
Birds as Radipole.

Portland Harbour & The Nothe   **194**   **1½ m S of Weymouth centre**
Park down Old Castle Road (a no through road) ½m S of A354 at SY675774. Walk across the park and view harbour from the ruins of Sandsfoot Castle. Coast path NE along the Western Ledges past the breakwater and to the Nothe Fort at SY687787.
Winter divers, grebes and wildfowl; migrants.

Ferrybridge   **194**   **2½ m SW of Weymouth centre**
View from car-park by A354 as it crosses the causeway to Portland at SY668755.
Passage and winter waders and gulls; passage and summer terns; winter wildfowl, grebes and divers.

Ringstead Bay & White Nothe   **194**   **6m NE of Weymouth**
Car-park at the end of minor road 1½m SE of A353, 2m E of Osmington, at SY759825. Then tracks and paths south and south-east.
Migrants; summer warblers.

TIC	Pavilion Theatre Complex, The Esplanade, Weymouth (0305 772444)

YH	Little Cheney, Dorchester (03083 340)
RF	Cove House, Chesil
	Old Ship, Upwey
BBE	Maiden Castle Farm, nr Dorchester (0305 262356)
SC	The Creek, Ringstead, Dorchester (0305 852251)

Portland Bill   194   6½m S of Weymouth
Large car-park at the southernmost end of Portland, SY677685.
Then paths and tracks north and east and south to the obelisk.
Migrants; seawatching.

Church Ope Cove   194   2m NE of Portland Bill
Park by minor road between Southwell and Easton at SY696712
and take paths down by the Museum and below the Pensylvannia
Castle Hotel.
Migrants.

> *Verne Common & Cemetary*   194   SY692741   *NW corner*
> *of Portland*
> *Migrants.*

> *East Weares*   194   SY703730   *½m NE of Grove*
> *Migrants.*

> *Reep Lane & Southwell Quarries*   194   SY685707
> *N end of Southwell*
> *Migrants.*

TIC	As previous entry.
YH	As previous entry.
RF	Eight Kings, Southwell
	George, Reforne
BBE	Pennsylvannia Castle Hotel, Wakeham, Portland (0305 820561)
SC	Portland Bird Observatory, Old Lower Light, Portland (0305 820553)

Puddletown Forest   194   2½m NE of Dorchester
Car-park at Higher Brockhampton ½m south of A35 at SY725922.
Then paths and tracks east through the woods.
Woodland birds.

Bryants Puddle Heath   194   2m N of Bovington Camp
Car-park by minor road 1m E of B3390, ½m S of Briants Puddle at
SY815925. Then tracks south and west.
Woodland birds including Nightjar, Turtle Dove, Crossbill and
Redstart.

TIC	7 Acland Road, Dorchester (0305 67882)
YH	As previous entry.
RF	Frampton Arms, Moreton, nr Dorchester
	Kings Arms, Puddletown

BB	The Old Vicarage, Affpuddle, nr Dorchester (0305 848315)
BBE	Vartrees House, Moreton, nr Dorchester (0305 852704)
SC	The Rambles, Bradford Peverell, nr Dorchester (0305 64523)
	Higher Waterston Farm, Piddlehinton, nr Dorchester (0305 848208)

Durlston Head & Country Park   195   1m S of Swanage
Car-park at end of minor road south of Swanage at SZ033774. Then many paths along the coast and inland.
Migrants; seawatching; summer seabird colonies; winter seaduck and divers.

Studland Heath & Little Sea   195   4m N of Swanage
Car-parks at northern end of peninsula near South Haven Point at SZ035863 and at the southern end overlooking Studland Bay, ½m N of Studland at SZ034835. Then coastal path and tracks to the hides.
Heathland birds including Dartford Warbler and Nightjar; wildfowl; passage and winter waders and wildfowl; passage terns; winter divers and grebes; migrants.

St. Aldhelm's Head, Chapmans Pool & The Winspit Valley 195   4–5m SW of Swanage
For the Winspit Valley park near the church in Worth Matravers at SY974775 and take track south. Otherwise car-park near Renscombe Farm ¾m W of Worth Matravers at SY964775. Then track south to the point or west to the valley above Chapmans Pool.
Migrants; seawatching; summer seabird colonies.

Arne   195   3m E of Wareham
Car-park 3m NE of A351 just south of Arne Village at SY972877. Then track and nature trail east to the hides and Shipstal Point.
Dartford Warbler, Nightjar and Hobby; passage and winter waders, wildfowl and raptors.

> ***Frome Estuary***   *195*   *SY941879*   *1m E of Wareham*
> *Passage and winter waders and wildfowl.*

> ***Godlingston Heath***   *195*   *SZ016825*   *3m NW of Swanage*
> *Heathland birds; raptors.*

> ***Handfast Point***   *195*   *SZ052823*   *3m NE of Swanage*
> *Migrants; seawatching; winter divers and grebes.*

> ***Townsend Quarries***   *195*   *SZ025783*   *½m SW of Swanage centre*
> *Migrants.*

TIC	The White House, Shore Road, Swanage (0929 422885)
	*Town Hall, East Street, Wareham (0929 552740)

YH	Cluny, Cluny Crescent, Swanage (0929 422113)
	School Lane, West Lulworth, Wareham (092941 564)
R	Square & Compass, Worth Matravers
RFBBE	Bankes Arms Hotel, Studland (092944 225)
BB	Redcliffe Farm, nr Wareham (09295 2225)
BBE	Bradle Farm, Church Knowle, nr Corfe Castle (0929 480712)
	Knitson Farm, nr Swanage (0929 422836)
BBSC	Creech Barrow Farm, East Creek, nr Wareham (0929 480548)
SC	(1 London Row, Worth Matravers) 54 Hillway, Highgate, London (081 348 9815)
	(Isle of Purbeck cottages) National Trust, Marine Terrace, Studland, nr Swanage (0929 44259)

Wareham Forest   194 & 195   1–3½ m N & NW of Wareham
Car-parks at Stroud Bridge by minor road 3m NW of Wareham at
SY888915, and at Sherford Bridge by B3075, 3m N of Wareham at
SY918927. Then tracks and footpaths east and west.
Woodland and heathland birds including Nightjar, Crossbill,
Dartford Warbler, Hobby and Redstart.

Upton Park Country Park   195   1½ m NW of Poole centre
Signed entrance and car-park just south of A35 1m NW of its
junction with A350 at SY993933. Then paths south to marshes,
mudflats and hide.
Passage and winter waders and wildfowl.

**Parkstone Bay & Poole Boating Lake   195   ½ m-1m E of
Poole centre**
Car-park ¾m SE of Poole centre on the west side of Parkstone Bay
at SZ021904. Then footpath north to Boating Lake and around the
bay.
Passage and winter waders, wildfowl and gulls; winter Avocet.

Sandbanks & Whitley Bay   195   3m SE of Poole
Car-parks by B3369 along the spit at Poole Head, SZ050885 and a
further ½m SW at Sandbanks, SZ044875. Both have Poole Bay to
the south and Whitley Bay to the north.
Passage and winter waders and wildfowl; winter seaduck, divers
and grebes; passage and summer terns; winter Avocet.

Brownsea Island   195   2m S of Poole
Access permitted 1st April – 30th Sept.
Boats from Poole Quay ½m S of Poole centre, SZ012904, and from
Sandbanks at the SW end of B3369, SZ037872. Many tracks and
paths and hide.
Passage waders and wildfowl; summer and passage terns;
migrants; woodland birds including Nightjar and Golden Pheas-
ant; reedbed species.

Lytchett Bay   195   SY976924   2½m W of Poole
Passage and winter waders and wildfowl.

Holes Bay   195   SZ005917   1m NW of Poole centre
Passage and winter waders and wildfowl.

Upton Heath   195   SY985945   3m NW of Poole
Heathland birds including Nightjar and Dartford Warbler.

Canford Heath   195   SZ025955   3½m N of Poole
Heathland birds including Nightjar, Wood Lark and Dartford Warbler.

Branksome Chine   195   SZ068900   4m E of Poole
Migrants.

TIC	The Quay, Poole (0202 673322)
YH	As previous entry.
RF	Bakers Arms, Lytchett Minster
	Cock & Bottle, Morden
BB	Henbury Farm, nr Sturminster Marshall (0258 857306)
SC	Dairy Cottage, Trigon House, nr Wareham (09295 2097)
	(Quay Cottage, Brownsea Island) National Trust, Brownsea Island, Poole Harbour (0202 707744)

Stanpit Marsh   195   **1m SW of Christchurch**
Car-park by minor road ¼m S of B3059, 1m S of A35 at SZ173925. Then tracks and paths SW and W across the marshes and to the estuary.
Passage and winter waders and wildfowl.

Hengistbury Head   195   **1½m S of Christchurch**
Car-park at the end of minor road 1¼m E of B3059 on the south side of Christchurch Harbour at SZ163910. Then track west to the Head and north across Wick Hams.
Migrants; passage and winter waders, wildfowl and gulls; summer and passage terns; winter seaduck and divers; seawatching.

Little Haven   195   SZ183918   NE corner of Christchurch Harbour
Passage and winter waders.

St. Catherine's Hill   195   SZ145955   3m NW of Christchurch
Migrants; heathland birds including Dartford Warbler and Nightjar; summer warblers.

Sopley Common   195   SZ133977   5m NW of Christchurch
Woodland and heathland birds.

Avon Forest Park   195   SU127022   *3m N of Hurn*
Woodland and heathland birds.

TIC   Westover Road, Bournemouth (0202 291715)
YH   Cottesmore House, Cott Lane, Burley, Ringwood, Hants
      (04253 3233)
RF   Lamb Inn, Winkton, Sopley, nr Christchurch
      Saxon King, Southbourne (nr Hengistbury Head)

Holt Heath   **195**   **3m NE of Wimborne Minster**
Car-park by minor road 2m N of A31, 2½m SW of Three Legged
Cross at SU048036. Then many tracks and paths east.
Heathland birds including Dartford Warbler and Nightjar; wood-
land birds; winter raptors and Great Grey Shrike; migrants.

Holt Forest   **195**   **3m N of Wimborne Minster**
Park by minor road in Holt Wood 2m E of B3078 at SU034058. Then
track and path east through the woods. Also walkable from Holt
Heath.
Woodland birds including Redstart and Wood Warbler.

Boveridge Heath & Cranborne Common   **195**   **1–2m N of
Verwood**
Park by minor road near Stephen's Castle ½m N of B3081 at
SU090098. Then track NE through the woods and to the common.
Woodland and heathland birds including Dartford Warbler,
Nightjar and Crossbill.

Boys Wood   195   SU055095   *2m NW of Verwood*
Woodland birds.

Burwood   195   SU063142   *½m NE of Cranborne*
Woodland birds.

TIC   Avon Forest Park Centre, St. Leonards, Bournemouth
      (0425 478470)
YH   2 Crane Street, Cranborne, Wimborne (07254 285)
RF   Horton Inn, Horton, nr Verwood
      Drovers Inn, Gussage All Saints
BBE   Northill House, Horton, nr Wimborne (0258 840407)
SC   Chalbury Farm, Horton (0258 840246)

Duncliffe Wood   **183**   **2m W of Shaftesbury**
Park by minor road 1½m SW of B3091, 1½m S of A30 at ST834218.
Then track and footpath north to the woods and Duncliffe Hill.
Woodland birds and summer warblers.

Fontmell Down   183   3½m S of Shaftesbury
Park near the church in Compton Abbas just E of A350 at
ST871184. Then track and path SE up the hill.
Woodland, scrub and downland species; summer warblers;
Nightingale.

River Stour   183   4m W of Shaftesbury
Park in Stour Provost just west of B3092 at ST793216. Then paths
west, south and north beside the river.
River birds.

TIC	8 Bell Street, Shaftesbury (0747 53514)
YH	As previous entry.
RF	Blackmore Vale, Marnhull
RFBBE	Stapleton Arms, Buckhorn Weston, nr Gillingham (0963 70396)
	Crown, Marnhull, nr Sturminster Newton (0258 820224)
	The Ship, West Stour, nr Shaftesbury (0747 85640)
BBE	Sunridge Hotel, Bleke Street, Shaftesbury (0747 3130)
BBSC	Yew House, Marnhull (0258 820412)

Garston Woods   184   1½m N of Sixpenny Handley
Park by minor road 1½m N of B3081 at SU004194. Then signed
paths through the woods.
Woodland birds including Nightingale.

Pentridge   184   2½m E of Sixpenny Handley
Park near the church in Pentridge Village 1m E of A354 at
SU034177. Then tracks and path east, north and south to Pentridge
Hill, Blackbush and Bottlebush Downs and Martin Down.
Downland and scrub birds including Quail and Nightingale;
raptors including Hobby and harriers; Stone Curlew; migrants.

Martin Down   184   3½m NE of Sixpenny Handley
Car-park by A354, ½m NE of Woodygates, 2½m N of its junction
with B3081 at SU036200. Then tracks and paths SE to Blagdon Hill.
Summer warblers; scrub and downland birds including Nightingale, Quail, Hobby, possible Stone Curlew.

> *Shire Rock*   183   *ST972187*   *2m NW of Sixpenny Handley*
> *Woodland birds.*

TIC	As previous entry.
YH	As previous entry.
RF	Crown, Alvediston
	Horseshoe, Ebbesbourne Wake
	Star, Sixpenny Handley
BBE	The Barleycorn House, Deanland, Sixpenny Handley (0725 52583)
SC	(The Coach House, Church Street, Cranborne) The Old Vicarage, Cranborne (07254 253)

Durham, Cleveland & Tyne & Wear

Tynemouth & Priors Park　　88　　**7m NE of Newcastle centre**
Car-parks near the north pier east of A193 e.g. NZ375692 and
NZ372696. Then coast paths north or south.
Seawatching; migrants; winter seaduck, divers and northern
gulls.

Wallsend Swallow Pond　　88　　**4m W of Tynemouth**
Park by minor road ¾m SE of A191 on NW side of Wallsend at
NZ302693. Then footpaths across reserve and around pond.
Winter wildfowl; passage waders; summer warblers.

> ***Marden Park***　*88*　*NZ355714*　*2½m NW of Tynemouth*
> *Migrants.*

> ***Big Waters***　*88*　*NZ226735*　*5m N of Newcastle centre*
> *Wildfowl; summer warblers; passage waders; migrants.*

> ***St. Mary's Island***　*88*　*NZ352754*　*3m N of Whitley Bay*
> *Migrants; passage aind winter waders; seawatching.*

> ***Whitley Bay Cemetery***　*88*　*NZ346746*　*2m N of Whitley
> Bay centre*
> *Migrants.*

> ***Brier Dene***　*88*　*NZ349739*　*1m S of St. Mary's Island*
> *Migrants.*

> ***Gosforth Lake & Wood***　*88*　*NZ255703*　*4m N of New-
> castle centre*
> *Passage waders; wildfowl; woodland birds.*

TIC	Park Road, Whitley Bay, Tyne & Wear (091 252 4494)
YH	107 Jesmond Road, Newcastle-upon-Tyne (091 281 2570)
RF	Waterford Arms, Seaton Sluice (Northumberland)
BBE	Bay Hotel, Front Street, Cullercoats, Whitley Bay (091 252 3150)

Shibdon Pond   88   Blaydon, 4m SW of Newcastle centre
Park at swimming baths by B6317 ½m NW of its junction with A694 at NZ192627. Then footpath and marked trail around the pond.
Summer warblers; winter wildfowl; Water Rail; migrants.

Thornley Wood & Derwent Walk Country Park   88
1½m-2½m S of Blaydon
Car-park by minor road ¼m E of A694 at NZ182611. Then footpaths north and south. Also at Thornley Woodlands Centre by A694 ½m S of Winlaton Mill at NZ178604.
Woodland birds.

Throckley Pond & Tyne Riverside Country Park   88   4m
NW of Blaydon
Park near SW corner of Throckley ¾m S of B6528 at NZ152662. Then footpaths south, east and west.
Summer warblers and woodland birds including Redstart; winter wildfowl.

Ryton Willows   88   4m NW of Blaydon (S side of river)
Park by minor road on north side of Ryton, ½m N of A695 at NZ153647. Then footpaths north and east and nature trail.
Summer warblers; woodland birds; winter wildfowl; passage waders; migrants.

Pont Burn   88   4m NE of Consett
Park by B6310 ½m E of junction with A694 at NZ144562. Then track and footpaths south through the woods and by the river.
River and woodland birds including Redstart, Hawfinch and Wood Warbler.

> *Washingwell Wood   88   NZ219599   3m SE of Blaydon*
> *Woodland birds including Hawfinch and Crossbill.*

> *Chopwell Wood   88   NZ137585   5m NE of Consett*
> *Woodland birds including Long-eared Owl, Crossbill and Hawfinch.*

TIC	Central Library, Prince Consort Road, Gateshead, Tyne & Wear (091 477 3478)
YH	As previous entry.
RF	Black Bull, Blaydon
	Black Horse, Barlow, nr Blaydon
	Oak Tree Inn, Tantobie, nr Stanley

BBE   Chopwell Wood House, Chopwell Woods, Rowlands
Gill (0207 542765)
Oak Tree Cottage, Tantobie, nr Stanley (0207 235445)

Hamsterley Forest   92   10m W of Bishop Auckland
Car-park at end of minor road 4m W of Hamsterley at NZ067300.
Then many paths and tracks to the south and west.
Woodland and river birds including Redstart, Pied Flycatcher,
Wood Warbler and Dipper.

Whitton-le-Wear   92   3m W of Bishop Auckland
Car-park by minor road between Whitton-le-Wear and High
Grange at NZ160315. Then nature trail and hides.
Winter wildfowl; passage waders; woodland birds; summer
warblers; migrants.

**Bowlees Visitor Centre & Upper Teesdale   92   4m NW of
Middleton-in-Teesdale**
Car-park at centre ¼m N of B6277 at NY907283. Then trail up valley.
Also park 3m N of Newbiggin along minor road at Swinhope
Head, NZ898333, then walk east or west.
River, woodland and upland birds including Golden Plover, Dun-
lin, Merlin, Red and Black Grouse.

Burnhope Reservoir   92   10m W of Stanhope
View from minor road along dam at reservoir's eastern end,
NY847388.
Winter wildfowl.

Lune Moor   92   5m SW of Middleton-in-Teesdale
Park by B6276 near Hargill Bridge, NY885216, and take track and
footpath north up brook and to Hagworm Hill and Howden Moss.
Upland birds.

> *Stanhope & Muggleswick Commons   87   NY977447*
> *8m SW of Consett*
> *Upland birds.*
>
> *Derwent Reservoir   (see Northumberland)*
>
> *Selset & Grassholme Reservoirs   92   NY925215   3m SW*
> *of Middleton-in-Teesdale*
> *Winter wildfowl; gull roost.*
>
> *Langdon Common   92   NY850330   10m NW of*
> *Middleton-in-Teesdale*
> *Upland birds including Black Grouse.*
>
> *Cronkley Pasture   92   NY860293   ½m SW of Forest-in-*
> *Teesdale*
> *River birds; waders.*

Baldersdale Reservoirs 92 NY940185 7m NW of Barnard Castle
Winter wildfowl; gull roost.

McNeil Ponds 92 NZ132324 1m NW of Whitton-le-Wear
Passage and winter wildfowl.

TIC	43 Galgate, Barnard Castle, Durham (0833 690909)
YH	Langdon Beck, Forest-in-Teesdale, Barnard Castle (0833 22228)
	Low House, Edmundbyers, Consett, Durham (0207 55651)
RF	Three Tuns, Eggleston
	Victoria, Witton-le-Wear
RFBBE	High Force Hotel, nr Newbiggin, Barnard Castle (0833 22222/22264)
	Langdon Beck Hotel, Forest-in-Teesdale, nr Barnard Castle (0833 22267)
	Moorcock Inn, Eggleston (0833 50395)
BBE	Grove House, Redford, Hamsterley Forest, nr Bishop Auckland (038 888 203)
SC	Raby Estates Office, Middleton-in-Teesdale, nr Barnard Castle (0833 40209)
	Teesdale Hotel, Middleton-in-Teesdale, nr Barnard Castle (0833 40264)
	Eggleston Estate, Eggleston Hall, nr Barnard Castle (0833 50378)
	Klein Cottage, Romaldkirk, nr Barnard Castle (0833 50794)

Deepdale Wood & Beck 92 1–4m W of Barnard Castle
Park by B6277 ¼m north of its junction with A67 at NZ044166. Then footpaths west.
Woodland and river birds including Redstart and Dipper.

River Greta Valley 92 3m SE of Barnard Castle
Park by minor road just west of A66 at Greta Bridge, NZ085133. Then footpath west along river and through woods.
Woodland and river birds.

The Stang 92 5m SW of Barnard Castle
Car-parks by minor road through the forest 4m S of A66 at NZ024083. Then many tracks through woods.
Woodland birds including Black Grouse, Goshawk and Crossbill.

TIC	As previous entry.
YH	Blackton, Baldersdale, Barnard Castle, Durham (0833 50629)
RF	Morrilt Arms Hotel, Greta Bridge
RFBBE	Old Well Inn, 21 The Bank, Barnard Castle (0833 690130)

BBE West Roods Farm, Boldron, nr Barnard Castle (0833 690116)

SC The Rigg, Arkengarthdale, by Richmond, Yorks (0748 84272)

South Gare & Bran Sands 93 3m NW of Coatham from Tod Point Rd

Park near the end of the private road, which skirts the steelworks to the north, near the lifeboat station at NZ556274.

Migrants; seawatching; passage and winter waders; winter seaduck and divers.

Coatham Marsh & Locke Park 93 ½m SW of Coatham

Car-park off Tod Point minor road ½m W of Coatham at NZ586249. Then tracks to hides and east to Locke Park.

Passage and winter waders and wildfowl; passage terns; passerine migrants.

Scaling Dam Reservoir (part N. Yorks) 94 4m SE of Loftus

View from A171 and hide along northern side of reservoir at NZ744127. Also car-park at easternmost end.

Winter wildfowl and raptors; passage waders; winter gull roost.

> *Saltburn Hazel Grove* 94 NZ655216 NW *edge of Saltburn-by-the-Sea*
> *Migrants.*

> *Lockwood Beck Reservoir* 94 NZ670137 4m SE of *Guisborough*
> *Winter wildfowl and gulls.*

> *Guisborough Woods* 94 NZ620145 1m S of *Guisborough*
> *Woodland birds.*

> *Longnewton Reservoirs* 93 NZ364168 5m E of *Darlington*
> *Winter wildfowl.*

> *Kilton Beck* 94 NZ705180 1½m SW of Loftus
> *Woodland and river birds.*

TIC Regent Cinema Building, Newcomen Terrace, Redcar, Cleveland (0642 471921)
51 Corporation Road, Middlesborough (0642 243425)

YH Riftswood Hall, Victoria Road, Saltburn-by-the-Sea, Cleveland (0287 24389)

RF Victoria, Saltburn
Jolly Sailor, Moorsholm, nr Loftus
Ship, Saltburn
Lobster, Coatham Road, Redcar

BBE   Waterside House, 35 Newcomen Terrace, Redcar (0642 481062)
Zetland Hotel, 9 High Street, Marske (0642 483973)
Old Mill. Dalehouse, Staithes, nr Saltburn (0947 840683)
SC   4 Church Street, Marske, nr Redcar (0277 652778)

Hartlepool Headland   93   extreme eastern point of Hartlepool
Park as near the lighthouse as possible, NZ533338.
Migrants; seawatching; winter seaduck and divers.

> *Hartlepool Docks & Fish Quay*   93   *SW of Headland*
> *Winter seaduck, divers and northern gulls.*

North Gare, Seaton Carew & Greatham Creek   93   4m S of Hartlepool
Park at end of minor road 1m E of A178 at NZ535283. Then footpaths north towards Seaton Carew, east to the breakwater and south to Seaton Snook and Greatham Creek.
Migrants; seawatching; passage and winter waders; winter seaduck, divers, Snow Bunting and northern gulls.

Cowpen Marsh & Seal Sands   93   3m NE of Billingham
Car-park by A178 just south of the bridge over Greatham Creek at NZ507252, and tracks west and east to the hides.
Passage and winter waders and wildfowl.

Dorman's Pool & Reclamation Pond   93   4m E of Billingham
Park along minor road ½m E of A178, 1m N of its junction with A1046, at NZ516226. Then footpath north between the ponds.
Passage and winter waders and wildfowl.

> *Saltholme Pools*   93   *NZ506230   3m E of Billingham*
> *Passage waders and wildfowl.*

> *Charlton's Pond*   93   *NZ467233   ½m SE of Billingham station*
> *Winter wildfowl; passage waders and terns.*

> *Long Drag Pools*   93   *NZ515244   1m SE of Cowpen Marsh*
> *Passage and winter waders and wildfowl.*

TIC   Civic Centre, Victoria Road, Hartlepool, Cleveland (0429 266522)
Theatre Yard, off High Street, Stockton-on-Tees, Cleveland (0642 615080)
YH   As previous entry.

R   New Inn, Hartlepool Headland
RF   Billingham Arms Hotel, Billingham
    Stoney Oak, Billingham
BBE Staincliffe Hotel, The Cliff, Seaton Carew (0429 264301)

Castle Eden Dene 93 3m SW of Peterlee
Car-park and visitor centre ½m N of A181, immediately west of
A19, at NZ409387. Then footpaths east through woods and by the
burn.
Woodland birds and summer warblers including Wood Warbler
and Redstart.

Hurworth Burn Reservoir 93 6m W of Hartlepool
Park by minor road 3m E of Trimdon at NZ406334 and then tracks
north which cross the reservoir on the west and east sides.
Passage waders; passage and winter wildfowl.

   Crimdon Park & Beck *93 NZ483372 4m NW of*
   Hartlepool
   Migrants; seawatching; passage Little Gull and waders.

   Crookfoot Reservoir *93 NZ432314 2½m SE of*
   Hurworth Burn Reservoir
   Passage waders; winter wildfowl.

   Croxdale Wood & Marsh *93 NZ276387 4m NE of*
   Spennymoor
   Woodland birds; wildfowl and waders.

   Dene Mouth *88 NZ457407 1½m E of Peterlee*
   Gulls.

TIC As previous entry.
    20 The Upper Chare, Peterlee, Durham (091 586 4450)
YH Durham 6th Form Centre, The Sands, Providence Row,
    Durham City
RF Oaklands, Oakerside Park, Castle Eden

**Washington Waterfowl Park & Barmston Ponds 88 4m W
of Sunderland centre**
Car-park and visitor centre off minor road ½m S of A1231, 1½m W
of its junction with A19, at NZ330565. Then trails and hides.
Passage waders and terns; winter wildfowl; reedbed species.

   The James Steel Park *88 NZ320545 1m NW of*
   Penshaw
   Woodland birds.

Joe's Pond 88 NZ328486 1½m SW of Houghton-le-Spring
Summer warblers; winter wildfowl.

Ryhope 88 NZ416519 2m N of Seaham
Migrants.

Seaham Hall 88 NZ425505 1m NW of Seaham
Migrants.

Dawdon Blast Beach 88 NZ437475 1m S of Seaham
Migrants; summer warblers.

Chourdon Point 88 NZ443465 1½m SE of Seaham
Migrants; seawatching.

Hawthorn Dene & Quarry 88 NZ435463 2½m S of Seaham
Woodland birds and migrants.

TIC Crowtree Leisure Centre, Crowtree Road, Sunderland (091 565 0960)
YH As previous entry.
R Seaton Lane Inn, Seaton, nr Seaham
BBE Harbour View Hotel, North Terrace, Seaham (091 581 4386)

Marsden Cliffs & Quarry 88 **2m N of Whitburn**
Park by A183 at the southern edge of Marsden Bay, NZ406645. Then coastal path along cliffs and west of the main road to the quarry.
Summer seabird colonies; seawatching; migrants.

Whitburn Coastal Park 88 **½m E of Whitburn**
Continue coast path south from Lizard Point (when rifle range is not in use!) to Whitburn Bird Observatory and on to Souter Point, NZ416627.
Seawatching; migrants.

South Shields & The Leas 88 **E side of Town**
Car-parks between A183 and the shore e.g. near Trow Point 1m SE of South Pier at NZ382667. Then coast path south and north.
Winter seaduck, gulls, Lapland and Snow Bunting; passage waders; seawatching; migrants.

Whitburn Cemetery 88 NZ407622 centre of Whitburn
Migrants.

Whitburn Hall Churchyard   *88*   *NZ405617*   *S end of Whitburn*
Migrants.

Seaburn Cemetery   *88*   *NZ399604*   *1m SW of Whitburn*
Migrants.

TIC   Museum and Art Gallery, Ocean Road, South Shields (091 454 6612)
YH   107 Jesmond Road, Newcastle-upon-Tyne (091 281 2570)
RF   Mardsen Rattler, South Foreshore, South Shields
BB   Pier Guest House, 73 Ocean Road, South Shields (091 454 0013)

Essex

Stour Wood & Copperas Bay   169   4m W of Harwich
Park by B1352 2m W of Ramsey at TM189309. Then footpaths
through the woods and over the railway line to the shore and hide.
Woodland birds; summer warblers; Nightingale; passage and
winter waders and wildfowl.

Oakley Marshes   169   3m SW of Harwich
Park by B1414 ½m S of Little Oakley at TM215284 and take track and
footpath south to the shore and then east.
Waders and wildfowl.

Walton-on-the Naze   169   1–2m N of the town
Car-park above the cliffs at the north end of town at TM264235.
Then coast path north and northwest to Stone Point.
Passage and winter waders; winter wildfowl, Snow Bunting and
Twite; migrants.

TIC   Parkeston Quay, Harwich (0255 506139)
YHBBE East Bay House, 18 East Bay, Colchester (0206 867982)
RF   Swan, Beaumont, nr Thorpe-le-Stoken
             Swan, Stones Green, nr Thorpe-le-Stoken
             Lamb and Hoggit, Bradfield, nr Mistley
BBSC   Dimbols Farm, Wrabness, nr Harwich (0255 880328)
BBE   New Farm House, Spinnellis Lane, Wix, nr Harwich
             (0255 870365)

Colne Point   168 or 169   5m W of Clacton-on-Sea
Car-park at Lee-over-Sands, 2½m SW of St. Osyth, at TM107125.
Then footpaths east and west.
Migrants; passage and winter waders and wildfowl; winter Snow
Bunting.

St. Osyth Creek   168 or 169   2m N of Colne Point
Park by minor road ½m W of St. Osyth at TM115154 and take
footpath west along the south side of the creek.
Passage and winter waders and wildfowl.

TIC	23 Pier Avenue, Clacton-on-Sea (0255 423400)
YH	As previous entry.
RF	White Hart, St. Osyth
BBE	Chudleigh Hotel, Agate Road, Clacton (0255 425407)
	Chelsea House Christian Hotel, Marine Parade West, Clacton (0255 424018)

Abberton Reservoir   168   4m S of Colchester centre
Park by B1026 1m S of Layer de la Haye at TL963186 and take track east to the hide (20p). Also view from B1026 1m further south and from minor road 1m to the west which also crosses the reservoir at TL950166.
Autumn and winter wildfowl; passage waders, terns and raptors; breeding Cormorant and Common Tern; passerine migrants.

Fingringhoe Wick   168   4m SE of Colchester
Signed car-park and visitor centre at end of minor road 3m E of Abberton, ¾m E of South Green, at TM042195. Then trails to many hides.
Summer warblers; woodland birds including many Nightingale; winter wildfowl; passage and winter waders.

Old Hall Marshes   168   8m S of Colchester
Car-park near Old Hall Farm, 1½m N of Tollesbury 1m E of Bowrchiers Hall, at TL959123. Then footpaths east around the shore and north to Salcott Channel, or south towards Tollesbury.
Winter wildfowl, seaduck, divers and grebes, Short-eared Owl and Hen Harrier; passage waders; reedbed species including Bearded Tit; migrants.

Tollesbury Wick Marshes   168   9m S of Colchester
Park at east end of minor road 1m E of Tollesbury at TL967106 and take footpath north or south around the shore.
Birds as at Old Hall Marshes.

> *Cudmore Grove Country Park (Mersea Island)   168*
> *TM066144   7m SE of Colchester*
> *Winter wildfowl; passage and winter waders; migrants.*

> *Strood Channel & Ray Island   168   TM015150   3m S of Abberton*
> *Wildfowl and waders.*

TIC	1 Queen Street, Colchester (0206 46379)
YH	As previous entry.
RF	Rose, Peldon
	Anchor, Rowhedge
	Walnut Tree, Rowhedge
	Sun, Salcott-cum-Virley
	Queen's Head, Tolleshunt d'Arcy

BB	The Maltings, Mersea Island, Abberton (0206 35780)
BBE	Fosters, The Street, Salcott, nr Maldon (0621 860217)
	Bromans Farm, East Mersea, Mersea Island (0206 383235)
SC	Mistletoe Cottage, Great Wigborough (0206 35282)

Bradwell & Dengie Marshes   168   9m E of Maldon
Bradwell Bird Observatory, G Smith, 48 The Meads, Ingatestone
tel: 0277 354034
Park at the northernmost end of B1021 at Bradwell Waterside,
TL995078 and take coast path north or south. Also for Bradwell
Bird Observatory take minor road east from Bradwell for 2½m to its
end at TM032082. Then footpaths north or south.
Migrants; passage and winter waders and wildfowl; winter Twite,
Snow Bunting, Short-eared Owl and Hen Harrier.

> **Mundon Creek**   168   TL895025   4m SE of Maldon
> Passage and winter waders and wildfowl.

> **Ramsey Marsh**   168   TL940055   6m E of Maldon
> Wildfowl and waders.

TIC	The Maritime Centre, The Hythe, Maldon (0621 856503)
YH	As previous entry.
H/B	Bradwell Bird Observatory; see above.
RF	Cap and Feathers, Tillingham
	Green Man, Bradwell
	Kings Head, Bradwell

Two Tree Island   178   3m W of Southend centre
Car-park on the island, SE of Leigh-on-Sea railway station, at
TQ825854. Then footpaths and hide.
Passage and winter waders and wildfowl; migrants.

Hadleigh Country Park   178   5m W of Southend
Entrance and car-park by B1014 ½m SW of its junction with A13 at
TQ795868. Then footpaths through woods to shoreline of
Hadleigh Marsh.
Woodland birds; waders and wildfowl.

Wat Tyler Country Park   178   1½m S of Basildon
Car-park and visitor centre down minor road 1m S of A13, ¾m S of
Pitsea railway station, at TQ738866. Then trails.
Woodland and reedbed species; waders and wildfowl; migrants.

> **Belfairs Great Wood**   178   TQ820877   ½m N of Hadleigh
> Woodland birds.

> **Hockley Woods**   178   TQ830915   1m S of Hockley
> Woodland birds.

Langdon Hills Country Park   178   TQ680864   *3m NW of Corringham*
Woodland birds.

TIC	Civic Centre, Victoria Avenue, Southend-on-Sea (0702 355122)
YH	Wellington Hall, High Beach, Loughton (081 508 5161)
RF	Crooked Billet, Leigh-on-Sea
	Parsons Bar, North Shoebury
	Anchor, Great Wakering
BB	Mayflower Hotel, Royal Terrace, Southend (0702 340489)
SC	Lorkins Farm, Orsett, nr Tilbury (0375 891349)

Hanningfield Reservoir   **167**   **6m NE of Billericay**
View from minor road along dam at north end ½m S of West Hanningfield, TQ735995. Also 1½m NW of Brock Hill along the southern side at TQ723972.
Winter wildfowl; passage waders and terns.

Danbury Country Park   **167**   **1m SW of Danbury centre**
Car-park by minor road ½m S of A414, 2m E of A12, at TQ770047.
Then many footpaths.
Woodland birds.

Danbury Common   **167**   **1½m S of Danbury**
Car-parks by minor road 1m S of A414, 1m N of Bicknacre, at TQ784040. Then footpaths and nature trail north.
Summer warblers; woodland birds; Nightingale.

Blakes Wood & Lingwood Common   167   TQ775065   *1m NW of Danbury centre*
Woodland birds; Nightingale.

Woodham Walter Common   167   TQ790065   *1m SE of Little Baddow*
Woodland birds including Hawfinch and Redstart.

Norsey Wood   167   TQ685955   *1m NE of Billericay*
Woodland birds.

Marsh Farm Country Park   167   TQ814961   *1m S of Woodham Ferrers*
Passage and winter waders; wildfowl; winter Hen Harrier and Short-eared Owl.

TIC	As previous entry.
YH	As previous entry.
	Corner House, Netteswell Cross, Harlow (0279 21702)
RF	Hoop, Stock
	Bell, Woodham Ferrers
	Hurdlemakers Arms, Woodham Mortimer

BB   Eibiswald, 85 Mill Road, Stock, nr Billericay (0277 840631)
Chestnuts, Chestnut Walk, Little Baddow, nr Chelmsford (024 541 3905)

Epping Forest   167 or 177   8m S of Harlow
Conservation Centre, High Beach, Loughton tel: 071 508 7714
Car-park and conservation centre ½m W of A104 near High Beach at TQ412984. Then many footpaths. Also car-park and many paths through good woodland from Queen Elizabeth Hunting Lodge by A1069, ½m W of its junction with A104 at TQ404952.
Summer warblers; woodland birds including Hawfinch.

Weald Country Park   167 or 177   2m W of Brentwood
Car-parks in South Weald e.g. TQ574940, then footpaths north, or 1m north of village at park centre TQ570950.
Woodland birds; wildfowl.

Belhus Woods Country Park   177   3m S of Upminster
Car-park by minor road 1½m N of Aveley at TQ565825. Then footpaths east through woods to the lakes.
Woodland birds; summer warblers; reedbed species; wildfowl.

> ***Thorndon Country Park***   *177*   *TQ610915*   *2m S of Brentwood*
> *Woodland birds.*
>
> ***Parndon Wood***   *167*   *TL445070*   *3m N of Epping*
> *Woodland birds including Hawfinch.*

TIC   County Hall, Market Road, Chelmsford (0245 283400/283339)
YH   As previous entry.
RF   Green Man, Toot Hill, nr Chipping Ongar
       Tower Arms, South Weald, nr Brentwood
       Volunteer, Epping Forest
       Forest Gate, Epping Forest
BB   Half Way House Farm, Weald Road, South Weald, nr Brentwood (027721 0034)
       Newhouse Farm, Mutton Row, Stanford Rivers, nr Chipping Ongar (027736 2132)
BBE   Bonny Downs Farm, Doesgate Lane, Bulphan, nr Upminster (0268 42129)
       Bumbles, Moreton Road, Chipping Ongar (0277 362695)

Chalkney Wood & Colne Valley   168   4m SE of Halstead
Park by minor road 1m SE of Earls Colne at TL868283. Then footpaths south through wood and north to River Colne and pits.
Woodland birds; summer warblers; Nightingale; wildfowl; passage waders and terns.

TIC	1 Queen Street, Colchester (0206 712233)
YH	As previous entry.
RF	Dolphin, Stisted, nr Braintree
	Five Bells, Colne Engaine, nr Earls Colne
	Drum, Earls Colne
	Castle, Earls Colne
BB	Old House, Aldham, nr Colchester (0206 240456)
BBE	Elm House, 14 Upper Holt Street, Earls Colne (07875 2197)

Hatfield Forest Country Park   167   3m E of Bishops Stortford
Entrance and car-park from minor road 1m S of A120 at TL546199.
Then many paths and nature trail.
Woodland birds including Nightingale and Hawfinch; wildfowl.

> ***Garnetts Wood***   *167*   *TL635184*   *3m S of Great Dunmow*
> *Woodland birds including Nightingale.*

TIC	Council Offices, 2 The Causeway, Bishops Stortford (0279 655261)
YH	As previous entry.
RF	Dukes Head, Hatfield Broad Oak
	Ash, Burton End, nr Stansted
BB	Yarrow, 27 Station Road, Felsted, nr Great Dunmow (0371 820878)

Gloucestershire

Beachley Point   162   **2m S of Sedbury**
Park at the end of B4228 south from Sedbury at ST553908, then track under the Severn Bridge to pine trees and the point.
Migrants; seawatching.

Guscar Rocks   162   **4m SW of Lydney**
Park at the end of lane ¾m SE of A48 from Brookend at ST601991. Then cross the railway line to the shore and take the coast path NE toward Aylburton Warth or SE to overlook the rocks.
Winter wildfowl; passage and winter waders; migrants.

Bigsweir Wood & Lower River Wye   162   **6m W of Lydney**
Park by the A468 on the east side of Bigsweir Bridge, 1½m NW of St. Briavels at SO539051 and take track or path south between the river and woods.
Woodland and river birds including Pied Flycatcher and Kingfisher.

> *Sedbury Park*   162   *ST563943*   *1m NE of Sedbury*
> *Migrants.*

> *Pillhouse Rocks*   162   *ST569954*   *2m NE of Sedbury*
> *Winter wildfowl and waders.*

TIC	Market Place, Coleford (0594 36307)
YH	The Castle, St. Briavels, Lydney (0594 530272)
RF	Blacksmiths Arms, Alvington, nr Lydney
	Rising Sun, Woolaston Common, nr Lydney
RFBBE	George, St. Briavels, Lydney (0594 530228)
	Travellers Rest, Stowe Green, nr Coleford (0594 530424)
BB	Sylvia Farm, Brockweir, nr Chepstow (02918 514)
SC	Cinderhill Cottage, St. Briavels, nr Lydney (0594 530393)

Cannop Valley   162   3m NE of Coleford
Car-parks by B4234 south of its junction with A4136 e.g. at
SO614144 and SO609106.
Woodland birds including Pied Flycatcher, Redstart, Wood
Warbler and Hawfinch.

Nagshead   162   4m NW of Lydney
Signed RSPB car-park ½m N along track from B4431 immediately
west of Parkend village at SO607085 then waymarked trails.
Woodland birds including Pied Flycatcher, Redstart, Wood
Warbler, Nightjar, Firecrest and Hawfinch.

Speech House, Crabtree Hill & Woorgreens Marsh   162
2m SW of Cinderford
Car-park by B4226 1m NE of its junction with B4234 at SO623124
then paths and tracks NE to the marsh and Crabtree Hill or south
toward Saintlow Inclosure.
Woodland birds including Redstart, Pied Flycatcher; wildfowl;
passage waders.

> ***Symonds Yat***   *162   SO564160   2m N of Berry Hill*
> *Woodland birds; Peregrine.*

> ***Highbury Wood***   *162   SO539087   2½m SW of Coleford*
> *Woodland birds.*

> ***Walmore Common***   *162   SO740150   5m E of Cinderford*
> *Winter wildfowl.*

> ***Lord's Wood & River Wye (Herefordshire)***   *162*
> *SO547156   ½m   S of Great Doward*
> *Woodland and river birds.*

TIC	As previous entry.
	Cinderford Library, Belle Vue Road, Cinderford (0594 23184)
YH	Welsh Bicknor Rectory, Welsh Bicknor, Ross-on-Wye, Hereford (0594 60300)
RF	Red Hart, Awre, nr Blakeney
	Woodman, Parkend
BBE	Lower Viney Farm Guesthouse, Viney Hill, nr Blakeney (0594 510218)
	Brook House Restaurant, Bridge Street, Blakeney (0594 517101)
SC	(The Bungalow, Starve Beech, Drybrook) Old Kilns, Howle Hill, Ross-on-Wye (0989 62051)
	Purton Manor Cottage, Lydney (0594 842892)

Hasfield Ham   162   2m NE of Hartpury
View from minor road between Ashleworth and Hasfield especially from roadside hides at SO827265, ¼ m S of Colways Farm. Also
from Ashleworth Quay, SO818251, take path beside River Severn
to the NE, or from Haw Bridge on B4213 at SO844278 take the path
south along the west bank of the river.
Winter and passage wildfowl.

Coombe Hill Canal   162   4m SW of Tewkesbury
Park down lane just west of A38 opposite the junction with A4019
at Coombe Hill, SO888271, and take track and path westward
beside the disused canal.
Winter wildfowl; summer warblers.

Highnam Woods   162   3½ m W of Gloucester centre
Park by the church in Bulley, 1m N of A40 at SO763197, and take
track then footpaths east through the woods.
Woodland birds including Pied Flycatcher and Nightingale;
summer warblers.

> **May Hill & Newent Woods**   *162   SO696214   3½m SW of
> Newent*
> *Woodland birds; summer warblers; migrants.*

> **Castle Hill Wood**   *162   SO714208   3½m S of Newent*
> *Woodland birds.*

> **Walham Pits**   *162   SO822200   1m NW of Gloucester
> centre*
> *Summer warblers; passage wildfowl and waders.*

> **Sandhurst Pits**   *162   SO816234   3m N of Gloucester
> centre*
> *Summer warblers; wildfowl and passage waders.*

TIC   The Library, High Street, Newent (0531 822145)
            St. Michael's Tower, The Cross, Gloucester (0452
            421188/504273)
YH   As previous entry.
            Rock House, Cleeve Hill, Cheltenham (024267 2065)
RF   Canning Arms, Hartpury, nr Gloucester
            Farmers Arms, Apperley, nr Tewkesbury
            Yew Tree, Newent Woods, nr Newent
BB   Wood Cottage, Kitesnest Lane, Churcham, nr Gloucester
            (045 279 457)
BBE   Tyms Holm Guest House, Upper Apperley, nr Tewkes-
            bury (045 278 386)
SC   Home Farm, Two Mile Lane, Highnam, nr Gloucester
            (0452 26549)

Slimbridge   162   4m NW of Dursley
Entrance and car-park at SO723047 1m NW of Slimbridge village, at end of minor road 2m NW of A38.
Winter wildfowl; passage waders and terns; winter raptors.

Frampton Pools   162   6m N of Dursley
Park at the end of Frampton village green, ½m SW of B4071 down a 'no through road', at SO746076. Then track SE to the south pool and the marked paths to the northern pool.
Wildfowl; woodland birds including Nightingale; summer warblers; passage terns.

> ***Arlingham*** *162   SO706099   1m S of Arlingham village*
> *Winter wildfowl; passage waders.*

TIC	Subscription Rooms, Stroud (0453 76568)
YH	Shepherd's Patch, Slimbridge (0453 890275)
RF	George, Cambridge, nr Dursley
	Old Forge, Whitminster, nr Stonehouse
BB	Moorend Farm, Slimbridge (0453 890771)
BBE	Horseshoe View, Overton Lane, Arlingham (0452 740293)
SC	Lord's Rake, Moorend Lane, Slimbridge (0453 890322)

Minchinhampton Common   162   2½m S of Stroud
Park by minor road between Amberley and Minchinhampton, 1m E of A46 at SO855013, then many paths north or south.
Downland species; summer warblers; migrants.

Redborough Common   162   1m S of Stroud
Park by minor road ¼m N of Bagpath, 1m E of A46 at SO852036 and paths west.
Birds as Minchinhampton.

Stanley & Coaley Woods   162   3m NE of Dursley
Car-park by B4066 2m N of Uley at SO794014. Then paths NE through Stanley Wood and S across the minor road to Coaley Wood.
Woodland birds and summer warblers.

Silk Wood   162   3½m SW of Tetbury
Car-park and visitor centre ½m W of A433 from Westonbirt at ST848897 then tracks SW through the wood.
Woodland birds and summer warblers.

TIC	As previous entry.
YH	As previous entry.
RF	Ram, Woodcester, nr Stroud
	Black Horse, Amberley, nr Nailsworth
	Old Lodge, Minchinhampton Common
RFBBE	Amberley Arms, Amberley, nr Nailsworth

BBE   Apple Orchard House, Orchard Close, Springhill, nr
          Nailsworth (0453 832503)
          Burleigh Cottage, Burleigh, nr Stroud (0453 884703)
          Barley Hill, Watledge, Nailsworth (0453 832619)
SC   Ruscombe Farm, Ruscombe, nr Stroud (0453 64780)
          (Field House, Minchinhampton) Landmark Trust,
          Shottesbrooke, Maidenhead, Berks (0628 825925)

**Robins Wood Hill Country Park   162   2m S of Gloucester
centre**
Signed car-park and visitor centre ¼m E of the junction of A38 and
A4173 at SO838158. Then paths south up the hill.
Woodland birds; summer warblers; migrants.

**Cotswold Beechwoods & Cooper's Hill   163   2m S of
Brockworth**
Car-park by A46 2m SW of Brockworth at SO885138, then paths
NE to Cooper's Hill and Brockworth Wood and SE to Buckholt
Wood. Also from minor road 1m E of A46 at High Brotheridge,
SO896137, and paths north or south.
Woodland birds including Redstart, Wood Warbler and Haw-
finch; summer warblers; migrants.

> *Witcombe Reservoirs   163   SO905150   1m SE of
> Brockworth*
> *Winter wildfowl.*

> *Crickley Hill Country Park & The Scrubs   163
> SO928163   2m E of Brockworth*
> *Woodland birds; summer warblers; migrants.*

TIC   St. Michael's Tower, The Cross, Gloucester (0452
          421188/504273)
YH   As previous entry.
RF   Golden Heart, Brimpsfield, nr Brockworth
          Royal William, Cranham, nr Brockworth
BB   Gilberts, Brookthorpe, nr Gloucester
          Hill Farm, Upton St. Leonards, nr Gloucester (0452
          614081)

**Dowdeswell Reservoir & Lineover Wood   163   3m SE of
Cheltenham centre**
Park near the W end of the reservoir beside the A40 at SO987196
and take the Cotswold Way south to the wood and view the reser-
voir from the roadside.
Winter wildfowl; woodland birds and summer warblers.

Bourton Gravel Pits   163   1m SE of Bourton-on-the-Water
Park by minor road 1½m SE of A429, 1m W of Little Rissington at
SP180197. Then path north between the pits and track south to the
southern pit and River Windrush.
Winter wildfowl and river birds.

> *Pittville Lakes   163   SO950235   1m N of Cheltenham
> centre*
> *Winter wildfowl.*

> *Chedworth Woods   163   SP051133   8m SE of
> Cheltenham*
> *Woodland birds.*

> *Guiting Wood   163   SP066265   3m SE of Winchcombe*
> *Woodland birds.*

TIC	77 Promenade, Cheltenham (0242 522878)
YH	Rock House, Cleeve Hill, Cheltenham (0242 672065)
RF	Plough, Cold Aston, nr Bourton
	Royal Oak, Andoversford, nr Cheltenham
	Mill Inn, Withington, nr Cheltenham
BBE	Andoversford Nurseries, Upper Hannington, Andoversford (0242 820270)
	The Guest House, Guiting Power, nr Cheltenham (04515 470)
SC	(Kellam Cottage, Lower Slaughter) Old Manor Cottage, Upper Slaughter, nr Stow-on-the-Wold (0451 20927)

Oakley Wood   163   3–4m NW of Cirencester
Park by minor road 2m SW of A417, 1½m SW of Daglingworth at
SO970044, and tracks north or south.
Woodland birds including Nightingale; summer warblers.

> *Miserden Park   163   SO946090   7m NW of Cirencester*
> *Woodland birds.*

> *Frampton Common & River Frome   163   SO930030
> 2m E of Chalford*
> *Woodland and river birds.*

TIC	Corn Hall, Market Place, Cirencester (0594 23184)
YH	Duntisbourne Abbots, Cirencester (028 582 682)
RF	Bell, Sapperton, nr Cirencester
	Daneway, Sapperton, nr Cirencester
	Carpenters Arms, Miserden
BB	The Sleight, Coates, nr Cirencester (0285 770654)

Cotswold Water Park   163   4m S of Cirencester
Many pits viewable from minor roads and waymarked paths
between Somerford Keynes and the A419. Signed information
centre ¼m SW of A419 at SU073971 has full details of access.
Winter wildfowl and grebes; passage and winter waders; passage
and summer terns; Hobby, Nightingale, Little Ringed Plover.

Whelford Pools   163   2m SE of Fairford
Car-park ½m N of Whelford village, 1m S of A417 at SU174994,
then adjacent hides and paths to other pits west of the road, and
lane east for 1m to the eastern pits.
Winter wildfowl; passage waders and terns; summer warblers.

> *Edward Richardson Reserve   163   SP216007   1m N of
> Lechlade*
> *Wildfowl and summer warblers.*

TIC	As previous entry.
YH	As previous entry.
	Littleholme, Upper Inglesham, Highworth, Swindon, Wilts (0367 52546)
RF	Wild Duck, Ewen, nr Cirencester
	Masons Arms, Meysey Hampton, nr Fairford
	Greyhound, Siddington, nr Cirencester
BB	Moor Farm, Fairford (0285 712763)
BBE	Old Manor Farm, Ashton Keynes, nr Cricklade, Wilts (0285 861770)
	Upper Chelworth Farm, nr Cricklade (0793 750440)
	Little Court, Latton, nr Cricklade (0793 750788)
SC	(28 Beverstone Road, South Cerney) 201 Alexander Drive, Cirencester (0285 68056)

Greater London

Ruislip Common & Mad Bess Wood 176 TQ080895 1½ m NW of Ruislip
Woodland birds.

Park Wood 176 TQ095890 1m N of Ruislip
Woodland birds including Hawfinch and Wood Warbler.

Bayhurst Wood Country Park 176 TQ068890 2m NW of Ruislip
Woodland birds including Hawfinch.

Bentley Priory 176 TQ155930 1m NW of Stanmore
Woodland birds; summer warblers; migrants.

Old Park Wood 176 TQ045915 1m NW of Harefield
Woodland birds.

Brent Reservoir 176 TQ218877 between Neasden & West Hendon
Passage and winter wildfowl; summer warblers.

Darlands Lake 176 TQ243934 1m S of Totteridge
Wildfowl and woodland birds.

Hampstead Heath 176 TQ263867 1m N of Hampstead centre
Woodland birds; migrants.

Hanwell Springs 176 TQ148808 ½ m NW of Hanwell station
Woodland birds; wildfowl.

Walthamstow Reservoirs 177 TQ355895 between Walthamstow & Tottenham
Winter wildfowl and gulls. Permit from Thames Water (Central Division), New River Head, Rosebury House, London EC1 4TP tel: 071 837 3300.

Middlesex Filter Beds   177   TQ360867   1m SE of Upper Clapton
Migrants; Little Ringed Plover.

Walthamstow Marsh   177   TQ350877   ½ m N of Upper Clapton
Marsh and reedbed species.

William Girling & King George V Reservoirs   177   TQ370953 between Chingford & Enfield
Winter wildfowl and gulls. (Permit as for Walthamstow Reservoirs.)

Beckenham Place Park   177   TQ384705   1m NE of Beckenham centre
Woodland birds and summer warblers.

Petts Wood   177   TQ450690   1m S of Chislehurst
Woodland birds and summer warblers.

Ruxley Gravel Pits   177   TQ475700   2m E of Chislehurst
Passage and winter wildfowl.

Scadbury Park   177   TQ460705   1½ m NE of Chislehurst
Woodland birds and summer warblers.

Selsdon Wood   177   TQ365615   ¾ m SE of Selsdon
Woodland birds and summer warblers.

Addington Hills   177   TQ354644   2m SE of Croydon centre
Woodland birds; migrants.

Sydenham Hill Wood   177 or 176   TQ346726   ½ m NW of Upper Sydenham
Woodland birds; summer warblers; migrants.

Beddington Sewage Works   176   TQ295664   ¾ m E of Hackbridge
Passage waders; migrants.

Barn Elms Reservoirs & Park   176   TQ230770   E side of Barnes
Winter wildfowl, grebes and gulls; migrants.

Lonsdale Road Reservoir   176   TQ218775   W side of Barnes
Winter wildfowl.

Richmond Park   176   TQ200730   1–3m SE of Richmond
Wildfowl and woodland birds.

Wimbledon Common   176   TQ225720   1½ m NW of Wimbledon centre
Wildfowl; woodland birds and summer warblers.

Ham Lands   176   TQ169732   ½ m W of Petersham
Woodland birds; wildfowl; summer warblers; migrants.

TIC	Central Library, 14 High Street, Uxbridge, Middlesex (0895 50706)
YH	4 Wellgarth Road, Hampstead, NW11 7HR (081 458 9054)
RF	Six Bells, Ruislip
	Orange Tree, Totteridge Village
	Spaniards Inn, Hampstead
	Chequers, Tottenham
	College Arms, Walthamstow
	Bell, Rainham
	Bulls Head, Chislehurst
	Joiners Arms, Croydon
	Woodhouse, Sydenham Hill
	Bulls Head, Barnes

Hampshire & the Isle of Wight

Fritham Plain & Amberwood Inclosure   195   4m NW of Minstead
Car-parks at end of minor road at Fritham, SU230142. Then tracks and paths west and southwest.
Birds of prey; woodland birds including Redstart and Hawfinch.

Deadman Hill   184   4m NE of Fordingbridge
Car-parks by B3078 NE of Fordingbridge e.g. 1½m W of its junction with B3080 at SU206166 and open access to the north, down Millersford Bottom and to the south , down Blackgutter Bottom.
Dartford Warbler, Hobby and Nightjar; winter Great Grey Shrike, Hen Harrier and Merlin.

Hampton Ridge & Ogdens Purlieu   195   2–3m SE of Fordingbridge
Car-park by Latchmore Brook 1m W of Hungerford, 2m E of A338 at SU182125. Then open access NE to Hampton Ridge and SE to Hasley Inclosure & Ogdens Purlieu.
Dartford Warbler, Hobby and Woodlark; winter raptors and Great Grey Shrike.

Blashford & Mockbeggar Lakes   195   1–2m N of Ringwood
View from minor roads E of A338 from Blashford and Ibsley and from paths between and around the pits e.g. SU157078. Also fields between Ibsley and Harbridge W of A338 at SU147097 for winter Bewick's Swan (up to 300).
Passage waders and terns; passage and winter wildfowl; summer warblers.

Bolderwood Ornamental Drive   195   SU255066   3½m SW of Minstead
Woodland birds including Crossbill, Hawfinch, Redstart and Firecrest.

> **Withybed Bottom**   195   SU255105   1½m W of Minstead
> *Heathland and woodland birds.*

> **Acres Down & Highland Water Inclosure**   195
> SU267096   1½m SW of Minstead
> *Raptors and woodland birds.*

TIC	New Forest Museum & Visitor Centre, Lyndhurst (042128 2269)
YH	Cottesmore House, Cott Lane, Burley, Ringwood (04253 3233)
R	Royal Oak, Fritham, nr Lyndhurst
RF	Alice Lisle, Rockford, nr Blashford
RFSC	High Corner Inn, Linwood, nr Ringwood (0425 473973)
BB	Cottage Crest, Castle Hill, Woodgreen, nr Fordingbridge (0725 22009)
	Eyeworth Lodge, Fritham (0703 812256)
BBE	Landfall, Minstead Post Office, nr Lyndhurst (0703 813134)
BBSC	Acres Down Farm, Minstead (0703 813693)

Bishop's Dyke, Matley & Denny   196   2–4m SE of Lyndhurst

Car-park near Beaulieu Road railway station by B3056 3m SE of Lyndhurst at SU346064. Then tracks around the bog to the south and through Denny Woods and northwest across Matley Heath. Woodland and heathland birds including Hobby, Dartford Warbler, Crossbill and Hawfinch; winter Hen Harrier and Great Grey Shrike; summer raptors.

Calshot Marsh   196   2½m E of Blackfield

Car-park by the front ½m NE of Calshot from the end of B3053 at SU486016. Then path NW beside the marshes.
Passage and winter waders and wildfowl; winter gulls; migrants; seawatching.

Lepe Country PArk   196   2m S of Blackfield

Car-park by minor road near Stone Point at SZ456986. Then coast path west to the mouth of the Beaulieu River and east to Stansore Point.
Passage and winter waders and wildfowl; migrants; seawatching.

> **Beaulieu Heath**   196   SZ354994   3m SW of Beaulieu
> *Heathland birds.*

> **Sowley Pond**   196   SZ375965   4m E of Lymington
> *Passage and winter wildfowl.*

> **Ashlett Creek**   196   SU466034   1½m NE of Blackfield
> *Passage and winter waders.*

Eling Marsh   *196*   *SU368125*   *SE of Totton*
Passage and winter waders.

Lower Test Marshes   *196*   *SU366150*   *1m NE of Totton*
Reedbed species; passage terns and waders; migrants.

TIC	As previous entry.
YH	As previous entry.
RF	Jolly Sailor, Ashlett Creek, nr Fawley
BB	Bridge House, Ipers Bridge, Holbury, nr Beaulieu (0703 894302)
BBE	Dale Farm Guest House, Manor Road, Applemore, nr Dibden (0703 849632)
SC	Stationmasters House, Beaulieu Road Station, nr Beaulieu (042129 2984)
	New Farm Cottage, South Gorley, nr Fordingbridge (0425 52499)

Pennington Marshes & The Salterns   196   1–2m S of Lymington

Park near the end of minor road 1½m S of A337 at SZ318927. Then paths NE to The Salterns and Oxey Marsh and track south across Pennington Marshes to the sea wall and the coast path.
Passage and winter waders and wildfowl; summer terns; seawatching.

Keyhaven Marshes & Hurst Beach   196   2½m SW of Lymington

Car-park in Keyhaven 1m E of B3058 2m SE of Everton at SZ306915. Then coastal path NE around Keyhaven Marshes and SW to Hurst Beach. Or park ½m SW of the village at SZ300908 and take footbridge west to Hurst Beach.
Passage and winter waders and wildfowl; passage and summer terns; migrants; winter seaduck and divers; seawatching.

TIC	*St. Thomas Street Car-park, Lymington, Hants (0590 672422)
YH	As previous entry.
RF	Kings Head, Lymington
	Chequers, Pennington
	Gun, Keyhaven
SC	(Old Coastguard Cottages, Keyhaven) 19 Harpenden Road, St. Albans, Herts (0727 37473)

Farley Mount Country Park   185   4–5m W of Winchester

Car-parks by minor road 2–3m NW of A3090 e.g. SU407294. Then tracks and paths west to Parnholt Wood and east to West Wood, Crab Wood and Pitt Down.
Woodland and downland birds including Nightingale, Nightjar, Quail, Hobby and Buzzard.

Timsbury Gravel Pits   185   SU348242   2m N of Romsey
Passage and winter wildfowl.

Ampfield Wood   185   SU395240   3–4m NE of Romsey
Woodland birds including Nightingale, Nightjar, Woodcock
and Turtle Dove.

Squabb Wood   185   SU336220   2m NW of Romsey
Woodland birds including Hawfinch; summer warblers.

Marsh Court   185   SU354334   1½m S of Stockbridge
Passage and winter wildfowl; reedbed species.

Humbers Wood   185   SU360290   1½m S of Kings
Somborne
Woodland birds including Hawfinch and Nightingale.

Broughton Down   185 & 184   SU290330   1½m W of
Broughton
Woodland and downland birds; summer warblers.

TIC	Guildhall, The Broadway, Winchester (0962 840500/67871)
YH	The City Mill, 1 Water Lane, Winchester (0962 53723)
RF	John o'Gaunt, Horsebridge, nr Stockbridge
	Bear and Ragged Staff, Timsbury
	Mottisfont Post Office, Mottisfont, nr Romsey
BBE	Carberry Guest House, Salisbury Hill, Stockbridge (0264 810771)
	Kings Head Hotel, Hursley, nr Winchester (0962 75208)
SC	Dairy Cottage, Farley Farm, Braishfield, nr Romsey (0794 68265)
	The Parcel Office, Horsebridge Station, Kings Somborne, nr Stockbridge (0794 388071)

Harewood Forest   185   2–3m SE & E of Andover
Footpaths through the woods north and south from minor road
1m SE of B3400 at SU405450. Also south of A303 from SU404441.
Woodland birds including Nightingale, Wood Warbler and
Hawfinch.

Danebury Hill & Down   185   5½m SW of Andover
Car-park by minor road 2m SE of A343 at SU333377. Then tracks
and path west and southwest.
Winter Golden Plover; summer Quail and Stone Curlew; woodland and downland birds.

TIC	Town Mill Car-park, Bridge Street, Andover (0264 24320)
YH	Red Lion Lane, Overton, Basingstoke (0256 770516)

RF	Peat Spade, Longstock
	Hut, Leckford
	Crook & Shears, Upper Clatford, nr Andover
BBE	Turnpike Cottage, Salisbury Road, Middle Wallop (0264 781341)

Cheesefoot Head & Longwood Warren 185 3½m SE of Winchester

Car-park by A272 1¼m SE of its junction with A31 at SU529278. Then tracks south, southwest and north.
Downland birds including Quail and Stone Curlew; winter raptors and large finch flocks; migrants.

> ### Old Arlesford Pond & Watercress Beds 185 SU595333
> ¾m NE of New Arlesford
> Wildfowl; reedbed species including Cetti's Warbler; Winter Water Pipit.
>
> ### Avington Lake 185 SU527323 4m W of New Arlesford
> Passage and winter wildfowl.
>
> ### Twyford Down 185 SU485273 1½m S of Winchester
> Downland and scrub species; migrants.

TIC	The Guildhall, Broadway, Winchester (0962 840500/67871)
YH	The City Mill, 1 Water Lane, Winchester (0962 53723)
R	Flower Pots, Cheriton
RF	Bush, Ovington
BBE	Dellbrook, Hubert Road, St. Cross, Winchester (0962 65093)

Titchfield Haven 196 3m SW of Fareham

Car-park at the front 1m NW of Hill Head, 2½m S of A27, at SU531024. Public footpath up the NW side of the reserve and permits to enter the reserve from warden on site.
Reedbed species including Cetti's Warbler and Bearded Tit; passage waders, terns and gulls; seawatching; winter divers and grebes; migrants.

River Hamble & Hook Park 196 S & W of Warsash

Car-park by the estuary 2½m SW of A27 at SU489062. Then coast path north and south.
Passage and winter waders and wildfowl; reedbed species; passage and summer terns and gulls; migrants.

West Walk 196 2m NE of Wickham

Car-park by minor road 1m N of B2177 (formerly A333) at SU596124. Then footpaths north through the woods.
Woodland birds and summer warblers including Nightjar, Nightingale, Wood Warbler and Hawfinch.

Gilkicker Point 196   SZ606975 1½m S of Gosport centre
Migrants; seawatching.

TIC   Ferneham Hall, Osborn Road, Fareham (0329 221342)
YH   Wymering Manor, Cosham, Portsmouth (0705 375661)
RF   Osborne View, Hill Head
          Roebuck, Wickham

Farlington Marshes   196   3½m NE of Portsmouth centre
Car-park along track eastward from the south side of the
roundabout at the junction of A2030 and A27 at SU678044. Then
path and track around the marshes.
Passage and winter waders and wildfowl; reedbed species including Bearded Tit; migrants.

Langstone Harbour   197   1½m S of Havant centre
Car-park overlooking the harbour ¾m S of Brockhampton, ½m
SW of Langstone at SU708050. Then coast path around sewage
works or east to Langstone Bridge and mill.
Passage and winter waders and wildfowl; winter grebes.

Stoke Shore & Hayling Island   197   2½m S of Havant
Park by A3023 in Stoke at SU717029 and take coast path north or
south.
Birds as Langstone Harbour.

Sinah Common   197 & 196   SW tip of Hayling Island
Car-park at the point, SZ689999, then coast path south and east.
Migrants; passage and winter waders and wildfowl; winter
seaduck, divers and grebes; gulls.

Southsea Common & Castle   196   SZ640985   *S point of
Portsmouth
Migrants; seawatching.*

Fort Cumberland   196   SZ685995   *2½m E of Portsmouth
centre
Gulls; winter grebes and divers.*

Great Salterns Lake   196   SU675017   *2m NE of
Portsmouth centre
Passage and winter gulls, wildfowl and waders; migrants.*

Black & Eastoke Points   197   SZ750990   *SE end of
Hayling Island
Passage and winter waders and wildfowl; gulls; seawatching;
migrants.*

Langstone Mill   197   SU719049   *½m SE of Langstone
Passage and winter waders and wildfowl.*

TIC   1 Park Road South, Havant (0705 480024)
        *Seafront, Beachlands, Hayling Island (0705 467111)
YH   As previous entry.
RF   Royal Oak, Langstone
        Maypole, Hayling Island
BBE   Cockle Warren Cottage Hotel, 36 Seafront, Hayling Island (0705 464961)

Old Winchester Hill   **185**   **2m S of West Meon**
Car-park by minor road 2m SE of A32 from Warnford at SU648208. Migrants; woodland birds; summer warblers; downland birds.

Queen Elizabeth Country Park   **197**   **3½m SW of Petersfield**
Signed car-park and information centre on the east side of A3 at SU717186. Then many tracks eastward and west under the main road to Butser Hill where there are additional car-parks.
Woodland birds including Golden Pheasant and Hawfinch; summer warblers; downland birds.

TIC   County Library, 27 The Square, Petersfield (0730 68829)
YH   As previous entry.
RF   George, East Meon
BB   Brocklands Farm, West Meon, nr Petersfield (073086 228)
        Dunvegan Cottage, Frogmore Lane, East Meon (073087 213)

Fleet Pond   **186**   **N end of Fleet**
Park in Fleet Railway Station car-park, just SE of junction of B3013 and B3014, at SU816553. Also park at the end of residential roads along the SW side.
Passage and winter wildfowl; reedbed species; passage terns; woodland birds.

Yateley Common Country Park   **186**   **1m SE of Yateley**
Car-parks by minor road 1m N of A30 at SU823597 and on N side of A30 1–2m east of its junction with B3013. Then tracks east or north across the heath and through woodland.
Woodland and heathland birds including Nightjar, Nightingale, Redstart, Dartford Warbler and Hobby.

Alice Holt Forest   **186**   **4m SW of Farnham**
Car-parks off A325 3–5m S of its junction with A31 e.g. by minor road ¼m E at SU809415. Then many paths and forest walks through he woods.
Woodland birds and summer warblers including Nightingale, Hawfinch, Crossbill, Firecrest and Wood Warbler.

Eversley Gravel Pits   *186*   *SU806620*   *1½m NW of Yateley*
Wildfowl; Little Ringed Plover.

Wellington Country Park   *186*   *SU725627*   *4½m NW of Hartley Wintney*
Winter wildfowl; woodland birds.

Tundry Pond   *186*   *SU775525*   *3m S of Hartley Wintney*
Passage and winter wildfowl.

Chawton Park Wood   *186*   *SU673362*   *3m SW of Alton*
Woodland birds.

Selborne Common   *186*   *SU735333*   *4m SE of Alton*
Woodland birds including Nightingale and Wood Warbler.

TIC	Ghurka Square, Fleet Road, Fleet (0252 811151)
YH	Devil's Punch Bowl, nr Hindhead (042873 4285)
RF	Chequers, Well, nr Farnham
	Crown and Cushion, Minley Manor, nr Fleet
RFBBE	White Hart Inn, Holybourne, nr Alton (0420 87654)

ISLE OF WIGHT
Ferries: Lymington – Yarmouth Tel: 0590 71311
Portsmouth – Ryde/Fishbourne Tel: 0705 812011

Tennyson Down & Freshwater Marsh   **196**   **1–3m SW of Freshwater**
Car-park by Freshwater Bay by A3055 at SZ346858. Then paths east across the scrub covered down and along cliff tops, and north across the marsh.
Migrants; summer seabirds; reedbed species; summer warblers; Nightingale.

The Needles & Headon Warren   **196**   **3m SW of Freshwater**
Car-park above Alum Bay at west end of B3322 at SZ308854. Then paths north across Headon Warren and SW to the Coastguard lookout overlooking The Needles.
Migrants; summer seabirds; seawatching.

Yar Estuary & Fort Victoria Country Park   **196**   **W & S of Yarmouth**
Car-park in Yarmouth on east side of estuary just south of A3054 at SZ354895. Then path south beside River Yar or west toward Sconce Point and the country park.
Passage and winter waders; migrants; seawatching.

Newtown River & Marshes   **196**   **4–5m E of Yarmouth**
Car-park at western end of Newtown on east side of estuary, 1½m N of A3054 at SZ420907. Then path north around the nature reserve and to the hide. For the western side the Hamstead Trail runs north from A3054 ¾m W of Shalfleet.
Passage and winter waders and wildfowl.

Brighstone Forest   196   1½m N of Brighstone
Car-park by minor road 1½m N of B3399 from Brighstone at
SZ420845. Then paths and nature trail east to Brighstone and
Rowborough Downs and west across Westover Down.
Woodland and downland birds including Nightjar, Nightingale
and Turtle Dove.

TIC	*The Quay, Yarmouth, Isle of Wight (0983 760015)
YH	Hurst Mill, Totland Bay, Isle of Wight (0983 752165)
RF	Red Lion, Freshwater
	New Inn, Shalfleet, nr Newtown
BBE	The Nodes Country Hotel, Alum Bay Old Road, Totland Bay (0983 752859)
	Westgrange Country Hotel, Alum Bay Old Road, Totland Bay (0983 752227)
SC	National Trust, 35a St. James Street, Newport, Isle of Wight (0983 526445)

St. Catherine's Point   196   S tip of Island
Car-park 1m W of A3055 from Niton at SZ494758. Then path SW
through wood and scrub. Coast path and lighthouse at end of track
1m SW of Niton.
Migrants; seawatching.

**Luccombe Chine & Dunnose Landslip   196   2m S of
Shanklin**
Park in Luccombe village, ¾m SE of A3055 at SZ584800. Then
coastal path south.
Migrants.

**Bembridge Harbour & Ponds   196   between St. Helens &
Bembridge**
Car-park by B3395 at west end of harbour at SZ632885 and take
track east to the ponds. Also car-park ¾m NE of St. Helens on the
Duver at SZ637893 and paths south and west to view harbour and
north pond.
Passage and winter waders and wildfowl; reedbed species.

Culver Down & Whitecliff Bay   196   2m SW of Bembridge
Car-park at the end of minor road 1½m SE of B3395 at SZ636855.
Then coastal path north around Whitecliff Bay.
Migrants; winter seaduck and divers.

> ***Brading Marsh*** *196   SZ615870   ½m E of Brading*
> *Reedbed species; wildfowl and waders.*

> ***Wootton Creek*** *196   SZ555933   2½m W of Ryde*
> *Passage and winter waders, wildfowl and gulls; winter divers
> and grebes.*

Medina Estuary *196   SZ507918   ½m-2½m N of Newport*
Passage and winter waders, wildfowl and gulls.

TIC	67 High Street, Shanklin (0983 862942)
	The Esplanade, Sandown (0983 403886)
YH	Whitwell, Ventor (0983 730473)
	The Firs, Fitzroy Street, Sandown (0983 402651)
RF	Buddle, Niton
	Crab & Lobster, Bembridge
	Fishbourne, Wootton Bridge
	Wight Mouse Inn, Chale, nr Ventnor
BB	Briddlesford Lodge Farm, Wootton Bridge (0983 882239)
BBE	Clarendon Hotel, Chale, nr Ventnor (0983 730431)
	Pine Ridge Country House, Undercliff Drive, Niton (0983 730802)
	Springvale, St. Catherine's Road, Niton Undercliff (0983 730388)
	Ashlake Farmhouse, Wootton Creek (0983 882124)
SC	Lisle Combe Cottage, St. Lawrence, nr Ventnor (0983 852582)
	Harbour Farm Cottage, Embankment Road, Bembridge (0983 874080)

Hereford & Worcester

Clifford   148   3½m NE of Hay-on-Wye
Park at the end of minor road 1½m E of Clifford, 1½m E of B4350 at SO267463, then paths north or east beside the River Wye.
River birds; woodland birds; winter wildfowl; passage waders.

Olchon Valley   161   5–8m SE of Hay-on-Wye
Park by minor roads 2–4m NW of Longtown e.g. in car-parks at SO297299 and SO287330. Then paths to hills, woods and the Olchon Brook.
Woodland and upland species including Red Grouse, Peregrine, Ring Ousel, Redstart, Pied Flycatcher and Dipper.

Timberline Wood   161 or 149   2½m SE of Peterchurch
Park by minor road 1m S of B4352, 1½m SW of Madley, ½m S of Shenmore at SO395377. Then track and path SW to the wood.
Woodland birds including Pied Flycatcher, Redstart and Wood Warbler.

> *Mousecastle Wood   148   SO246426   1m E of Hay-on-Wye*
> *Woodland birds and summer warblers.*

> *Bradnor Hill   148   SO285585   1½m NW of Kington*
> *Hill birds; migrants.*

> *Hergest Ridge   148   SO255565   2½m W of Kington*
> *Hill birds; migrants.*

TIC   *The Car-park, Hay-on-Wye, Powys (0497 820144)
Town Hall Annexe, St. Owen Street, Hereford (0432 268430)
YH   World's End Lodge, Staunton-on-Wye (09817 308)

RF	Castlefield, Clifford
	Pandy, Dorstone
	Talbot Hotel, Kington
	Swan, Kington
RFBBE	Old Black Lion, Hay-on-Wye (0497 820841)
	Royal Oak, Hardwicke, nr Hay-on-Wye (04973 248)
BBE	The Gables, Michaelchurch Escley, nr Hay (098 123 287)
	Little Green, Newton, nr Vowchurch (098 123 205)
SC	Wye View, Wyeside, Clifford, nr Hay (04973 306)

Fishpool Valley & Bircher Common   148 or 149   7½ m SW of Ludlow

Car-park ½ m NW of B4362 from Cock Gate 2½ m NE of Mortimer's Cross at SO456661. Then paths and nature trails north and west through the woods and up the valley to Bircher and Leinthall Commons.

Woodland birds and summer warblers; raptors.

Mary Knoll   148 or 138   2½ m SW of Ludlow

Signed car-park by minor road, 2½ m W of B4361 from just south of the River Teme, at SO475732. Then many tracks and paths east down into the valley.

Woodland birds including Redstart, Wood Warbler, Woodcock, Goshawk; summer warblers.

Barnett Wood   148   1m W of Wigmore

Park by minor road 1m W of A4110 from Wigmore at the bottom of the hill at SO402691. Then track and paths south.

Woodland birds including Pied Flycatcher, Redstart and Wood Warbler.

TIC	Castle Street, Ludlow, Shrops (0584 875053)
YH	Ludford Lodge, Ludford, Ludlow, Shrops (0584 2472)
RF	Crown Inn, Aymestery
	Blue Boar, Ludlow
	Olde Oake, Wigmore
BBE	Brook Cottage, Lingen, nr Wigmore (0544 267990)
	Queens House, Wigmore (056 886 451)
SC	(Lynsdale, Lingen) School House, Lingen (0544 267735)

Queenswood Country Park & Dinmore Hill   149   4½ m S of Leominster

Car-park and visitor centre by A49 1¼ m S of its junction with A417 at SO506515. Then paths SW to the Country Park and Burghope Wood and E of the main road up Dinmore Hill.

Woodland birds and summer warblers including Redstart, Wood Warbler and Pied Flycatcher.

Bodenham Pits   149   5m S of Leominster
View from minor road 1½m W of A417, ½m W of Bodenham
village at SO520515.
Wildfowl; passage terns and waders; migrants; woodland birds.

>*Wellington Wood   149   SO484496   6m S of Leominster*
>*Woodland birds.*

>*Marston Stannett Woods   149   SO574555   5m SE of*
>*Leominster*
>*Woodland birds.*

TIC   6 School Lane, Leominster (0568 6460)
YH   World's End Lodge, Staunton-on-Wye (09817 308)
RF   Englands Gate, Bodenham
          Lamb, Stoke Prior, nr Leominster
BBE   Stretfordbury, nr Leominster (056 882 239)
          Great House Farm, Stoke Prior, nr Leominster (056 882
          663)
          Maund Court, Bodenham (056 884 282)
SC   (The Hollies, Ivington) Little Dilwyn, nr Leominster (056
          888 279)
          Vauld House Farm, Marden, nr Hereford (056 884 347)

Haugh & Sharpnage Woods   149   5m SE of Hereford
Car-park by minor road 1½m E of B4224 from Mordiford at
SO593366, then many paths north and south.
Woodland birds and summer warblers including Crossbill, Turtle
Dove and occasional Nightingale.

Capler Wood & River Wye   149   1½m SE of Fownhope
Park by minor road 1¼m S of B4224 from Fownhope at SO588327.
Then track and path south between the wood and the river, west
along the river bank, and north up Capler Hill.
Woodland and river birds including Kingfisher, Redstart, Wood
Warbler and Pied Flycatcher.

Queens Wood   149 & 162   5m NE of Ross-on-Wye
Car-park by minor road 2m SW of B4215 from Dymock, 1m S of
Kempley at SO677285. Then tracks and paths south.
Woodland birds and summer warblers.

>*Fishpool Hill   149   SO605343   1½m E of Fownhope*
>*Woodland birds and summer warblers.*

>*Westhide Wood   149   SO587434   5m NE of Hereford*
>*Woodland birds.*

>*Fiddler's Green & West Wood   149   SO575357   1m NW*
>*of Fownhope*
>*Woodland birds and summer warblers.*

Lugg Meadows   149   SO545405   2m E of Hereford centre Winter waders and gulls.

TIC	Town Hall Annexe, St. Owen Street, Hereford (0432 268430)
YH	Hatherley, 18 Peachfield Road, Malvern Wells, Worcs (0684 569131)
R	Forge & Ferry, Fownhope
RF	Green Man, Fownhope
	Moon Inn, Mordiford
	Royal Oak, Much Marcle, nr Ledbury
BBE	Orchard, Mordiford, nr Hereford (0432 73253)
	Bowens Country House, Fownhope (0432 77430)
	Wilton Oaks, Tarrington, nr Hereford (0432 79212)
SC	Hope Springs Farm, Mordiford (0432 73294)
	Overdine Farm, Fownhope (0432 77358)

Malvern Hills   150   2–7m S of Great Malvern
Many car-parks and paths e.g. by B4232 1m S of Upper Colwall at SO766421; at Wynds Point on A449 ¾m W of its junction with A4104 at SO762404; and by A438 at Hollybush 1½m NW of its junction with B4208 at SO759369.
Woodland birds; summer warblers; migrants.

Ravenshill Wood   150   5m E of Bromyard
Car-park by minor road 1½m S of A44 from Knightwick, 1m NW of Alfrick at SO740538, then paths west.
Woodland birds and summer warblers.

Old Storridge Common & Leigh Brook   150   SO745514 1m S of Alfrick Woodland and river birds including Redstart, Dipper and Kingfisher.

Old Hills   150   SO826487   4m SW of Worcester centre Woodland birds and summer warblers; migrants.

TIC	Winter Gardens Complex, Grange Road, Great Malvern (0684 892289)
YH	As previous entry.
RF	Chase Inn, Colwall, nr Great Malvern
	Railway, Malvern Wells
RFBBE	Talbot Hotel, Knightwick, nr Bromyard (0886 21235)
BBE	Cowleigh Park Farm, Malvern (06845 66750)
	Leigh Court, Leigh, nr Malvern (0886 32275)
	The Barrow, Suckley, nr Malvern (08864 208)
	Chirkenhill Farm, Leigh Sinton, Malvern (0886 32205)
SC	Acton Mill Farm, Suckley, nr Malvern (08864 227)

Bredon Hill   150   4m S of Pershore
Park in Ashton-under-Hill 1m W of A435, midway between Tewkesbury and Evesham at SO995384 and take the Wychaven Way and other paths NW up onto the hill.
Woodland and downland birds; migrants.

Tiddesley Wood   150   1m SW of Pershore
Park 1m SW of Pershore by the A4104, 1m SW of its junction with A44, near the church at SO937453. Then track west to the woods.
Woodland birds and summer warblers including Nightingale.

Eckington Bridge & River Avon   150   3m SW of Pershore
Park near Eckington Bridge at SO922423 and take path west beside the river on the south bank.
River birds.

TIC	19 High Street, Pershore (0386 554262)
YH	As previous entry.
RF	Defford Arms, Defford, nr Pershore
	Star, Aston-under-Hill
	Anchor, Eckington
BB	Lampitt House, Lampitt Lane, Bredon's Norton (0684 72295)
	Ashwoods, Harpley Road, Defford (0386 750870)
BBE	Home Farm, Bredon's Norton, nr Eckington (0684 72322)
SC	The Manor House, Manor Road, Eckington (0386 750997)

Upton Warren   150   4m NE of Droitwich
Car-parks by A38 east of Upton Warren village; along a track at the north end of the lake at SO937676; and at the sailing club by the south lake. Then paths to hides.
Passage and winter wildfowl; passage waders and terns; migrants.

Trench Wood   150   3–4m SE of Droitwich
Park in Sale Green 3m S of B4090, 1½m NE of Crowle at SO931580, then path NW to the wood and Dunhampstead.
Woodland birds and summer warblers including Nightingale.

Feckenham Moor   150   7m E of Droitwich
Park in Feckenham by B4090 at SP011612 and take track south to the hide.
Passage and winter wildfowl; passage waders; summer warblers.

> ***Pipers Hill***   *150   SO958650   4m NE of Droitwich*
> *Woodland birds and summer warblers.*

> ***Goosehill Wood***   *150   SO935607   3m SE of Droitwich*
> *Woodland birds; Nightingale.*

Grafton Wood 150 SO973558 7m SE of Droitwich
Woodland birds; Nightingale.

Nunnery Wood 150 SO875545 1½m E of Worcester centre
Woodland birds and summer warblers including Nightingale.

TIC Heritage Centre, St. Richard's House, Victoria Road, Droitwich (0905 774312)

YH Hemmingford House, Alveston, Stratford-on-Avon, Warks (0789 297093)

RF Firs, Dunhampstead, Sale Green, nr Droitwich
Rose and Crown, Feckenham
Bowling Green, Stoke Works, nr Upton Warren

BB Little Lodge, Broughton Green, Hanbury, nr Droitwich (052 784 305)

BBE Valley Farm, Hanbury Road, Hanbury, nr Droitwich (052 784 678)
Phepson Farm, Himbleton, nr Droitwich (090 569 205)

Shrawley Wood & River Severn 138 or 150 3m NW of Ombersley
Park in Frog Pool by B4196 2m NW of its junction with A4133 at SO800657, then track east to the woods and river.
Woodland birds; summer warblers; river birds including Kingfisher.

Holt & Grimley Pits 138 or 150 1.5–2m SW of Ombersley
View Holt Pits from lane to Holt ¼m E of A443, 1m SE of Holt Heath, at SO827623. For Grimley Pits, about 1m S, park by the church in Grimley ½m E of A443 at SO836607 and take path west.
Winter wildfowl; passage waders.

Hartlebury Common 138 1m E of Stourport-on-Severn
Car-park by B4193 ½m E of its junction with A4025 at SO825715, then many paths south.
Heathland birds and summer warblers.

Wilden Pool & Marshes 138 SO823730 1m NE of Stourport-on-Severn
Winter wildfowl; passage waders; summer warblers; migrants.

Abberley Hill 138 SO760670 4m SW of Stourport-on-Severn
Woodland birds and summer warblers.

Monk Wood 138 or 150 SO804610 3m SW of Ombersley
Woodland birds.

> *Great Pool* 150 *SO880635 W side of Droitwich*
> *Passage and winter wildfowl.*

TIC	Load Street, Bewdley (0299 404740)
YH	Malthouse Farm, Wheathill, Bridgnorth, Shrops (074 633 236)
RF	Plough Inn, Shenstone, nr Kidderminster
RFBBE	Crown & Sandys Arms, Ombersley (0905 620252)
	Admiral Rodney Inn, Berrow Green, Martley, nr Worcester (0886 21375)
BBE	Church Farm, Suffolks Lane, Abberley (0299 896316)

Wyre Forest 138 4m W of Kidderminster
Car-park and visitor centre by A456 2m W of Bewdley at SO752740, then nature trails and many paths and tracks northwards. For the northern half of the forest (Shropshire) car-parks by B4194 2–3m NW of Bewdley.
Woodland birds including Pied Flycatcher, Redstart, Hawfinch and Goshawk.

Devil's Spittleful 138 1½m SW of Kidderminster centre
Car-park at end of minor road ¼m W of B4549, which joins A456 and A45, at SO815752. Then paths westward.
Heathland and woodland birds.

Kingsford Country Park & Kinver Edge 138 3½m N of Kidderminster
Car-park by minor road 1m S of A458, 1½m SW of Kinver toward Kingsford, at SO824822. Then many paths through the woods east of the road.
Woodland and heathland birds.

> *Wassell Wood* 138 *SO795775 2m NW of Kidderminster centre*
> *Woodland birds.*

> *Hurcott Pool* 139 *SO852778 1½m NE of Kidderminster centre*
> *Passage and winter wildfowl.*

> *Eymore Wood* 138 *SO780796 4m NW of Kidderminster centre*
> *Woodland birds.*

TIC	*Severn Valley Railway, Comberton Hill, Kidderminster (0562 829400)
	Travellers Joy, The Old House, 47 High Street, Kinver, West Midlands (0384 872940)
YH	As previous entry.

RF	Brook, Callow Hill, nr Bewdley
	Hop Pole, nr Callow Hill
	Lock, Wolverley, nr Kidderminster
BB	Bullockhurst Farm, Rock, nr Bewdley (0299 22305)
BBE	Tanglewood, Button Oak, nr Bewdley (0299 401280)
SC	Dowles House, Dowles, nr Bewdley (0299 403137)

Clent Hills Country Park   139   2m E of West Hagley
Walton Hill car-park and visitor centre by minor road 1½m W of
B4551 from Romsley, 1m NE of Clent at SO943803. Then paths
south.
Woodland and downland birds; migrants.

Uffmoor Wood   139   3m NE of West Hagley
Park by minor road (Uffmoor Lane) ¾m S of A456, ¾m N of Clent
Hills visitor centre, at SO947812 and paths east.
Woodland birds and summer warblers.

Chaddesley Woods   139   3½m NW of Bromsgrove
Park by minor road 1m N of A448, ½m N of Woodcote Green at
SO914736, then paths and tracks SW.
Woodland birds.

Pepper Wood   139   1½m NW of Catshill
Park down lane at the N end of Fairfield, off B4091 at SO941750.
Then tracks and paths through the woods.
Woodland birds and summer warblers.

Lickey Hills Country Park   139   2m NE of Catshill
Car-park and visitor centre by B4096, ¼m W of its junction with
B4120 at SO996758, then paths through the woods south or north.
Woodland birds and summer warblers including Wood Warbler
and Redstart.

Bittell Reservoirs   139   1–2m N of Alvechurch
View lower reservoir from B4120 or minor road running north
from ½m NE of Barnt Green e.g.SP016744. Also park here and
take track north beside the upper reservoir.
Wildfowl; winter gull roost; passage waders and terns.

Arrow Valley Lake   150   1¼m E of Redditch centre
Car-park by B4497 ¼m S of its junction with A4023 at SP066676.
Then paths around the lake and north up the valley.
Wildfowl; woodland birds and summer warblers.

Waseley Hills Country Park   *139   SO972783   2½m N of*
Catshill
Woodland and downland birds.

Ipsley Alders   150   SP077676   2½m E of Redditch centre
Marshland and woodland birds.

TIC	47–49 Worcester Road, Bromsgrove (0527 31809)
YH	Hemingford House, Alveston, Stratford-on-Avon, Warks (0789 297093)
RF	Manchester Inn, Romsley
	Coach and Horses, Weatheroak Hill, nr Alvechurch
	Gate, Bournheath, nr Bromsgrove
	Swan, Chaddesley Corbett, nr Bromsgrove
BB	St. Elizabeth's Cottage, Woodman Lane, Clent, nr Hagley (0562 883883)
BBE	Hill Farm, Rocky Lane, Bourneheath, nr Bromsgrove (0527 72403)
SC	3 Twatling Road, Barnt Green, nr Alvechurch (021 455 1697)

Hertfordshire

West Hyde Pits   176   2m S of Rickmansworth
Park in West Hyde just east of A412 at TQ034911 and take path east between the pits. Also from ¼m S at TQ036904 another track bisects two pits to the east.
Passage and winter wildfowl; passage terns.

Stockers Lake   176   SE side of Rickmansworth
Park down minor road ½m SE of A412 at TQ044931 and path NE between the lake and Grand Union Canal.
Winter wildfowl and gulls; summer warblers and woodland birds.

Whippendell & Harrocks Woods   176 or 166   2½m NE of Rickmansworth
Car-park by minor road ¾m SE of Chandler's Cross at TQ073977, then many paths through Whippendell Woods to the east and north and Harrocks Wood a few hundred yards to the northwest.
Woodland birds including Hawfinch; summer warblers.

Maple Lodge   176   TQ036926   1m SW of Rickmansworth
Wildfowl; woodland birds and summer warblers.

Oxhey Woods   176   TQ106924   between Northwood & South Oxhey
Woodland birds.

Tolpits Gravel Pits   176 or 166   TQ097942   3m E of Rickmansworth
Winter wildfowl.

Cassiobury Park   176   TQ090974   1m W of Watford centre
Summer warblers; marshland birds; woodland birds.

TIC   46 High Street, Rickmansworth (0923 776611)
YH   Welders Lane, Jordans, Beaconsfield, Bucks (02407 3135)
RF   Clarendon Arms, Chandlers Cross, nr Watford
Plough, Harefield

BB   30 Hazelwood Road, Croxley Green, Rickmansworth
           (0923 33751/226666)

**Aldenham & Hillfield Park Reservoirs   176 or 166   2m SW
of Borehamwood**
For Hillfield Park, park by minor road ¼m N of A41 along the west
bank at TQ154960 then footpath around the reservoir. Aldenham
Country Park is about 1m to the SE, viewable from A411 which
runs by the south side of the reservoir at TQ170953.
Winter wildfowl; passage terns and waders.

Broad Colney Lakes   166   3m SE of St. Albans centre
Car-park by B5378 ½m N of its junction with B556 at TL176033.
Then paths east.
Winter wildfowl.

Bricket Wood Common   166   1m S of Bricket Wood
Park by minor 'no through road' south of the village on the east
side of the railway line e.g. at TL133006 and take tracks and paths
westward.
Woodland birds and summer warblers.

TIC   Town Hall, Market Place, St. Albans (0727 64511)
YH   Fairshot Court, Woodcock Hill, Sandridge, St. Albans
            (0727 51854)
RF   Three Horseshoes, Letchmore Heath, nr Radlett
            Crooked Billett, Colney Heath, nr St. Albans

Sherrardspark Wood   166   1½m S of Welwyn
Park by B197 1m N of its junction with B195, just east of the A1 at
TL225141. Then paths east through the woods.
Woodland birds.

Lemsford Springs   166   2m N of Hatfield centre
Park just west of junction 5 of A1 by the roundabout at TL224124.
Then paths west and south beside the old cress beds and to the
hide.
Water birds.

> ***Stanborough Reed Marsh*** *166   TL231105   1m N of*
> *Hatfield centre*
> *Reedbed species.*

> ***Brocket Hall Weir***   *166   TL215125   2m SE of*
> *Wheathampstead*
> *River and woodland birds.*

TIC	Campus West, The Campus, Welwyn & Hatfield (0707 332880)
YH	As previous entry.
RF	Brocket Arms, Ayot St. Lawrence, nr Welwyn
	Wicked Lady, Nomansland Common, nr Wheathampstead
	Crooked Chimney, Lemsford

Great Wood Country Park   166   **3m NE of Potters Bar**
Car-park just north of B157 1m W of Cuffley at TL282040, then many paths.
Woodland birds including Nightingale, Redstart and Wood Warbler.

Wormley Wood   166   **2–3m NE of Cuffley**
Car-park by minor road 2m west of A10, 1¼m S of Brickendon, at TL327065 and paths south.
Woodland birds and summer warblers including Nightjar and Grasshopper Warbler.

Cheshunt Pits   166   **1½m N of Waltham Abbey**
Car-park ¼m W of B194 1¼m N of its junction with A121 at TL376027 and paths west between the pits.
Winter wildfowl; summer warblers; passage waders; migrants.

> *Thunderfield Grove*   166   *TL337053   2½m NE of Cuffley*
> *Woodland birds and summer warblers.*

TIC	The Castle, Hertford (0992 584322)
YH	As previous entry.
RF	Coach and Horses, Newgate Street, nr Cuffley
	Woodman, Wormley, West End, nr Cheshunt

Hoddesdonpark Wood   166   **1½m W of Hoddesdon centre**
Park by minor road ½m W of A10 near the northwest corner of the wood at TL348088, then paths east and south.
Woodland birds and summer warblers including Hawfinch.

Spitalbrook Pits   166   **½m SE of Hoddesdon centre**
Park by minor road ½m E of A1170 just E of River Lee at TL385082, then track and path westward.
Winter wildfowl; passage terns and gulls.

Rye House Marsh   166   **1m NE of Hoddesdon centre**
Car-park just north of minor road ¼m NE of Rye House railway station, 1m SW of B181, at TL387100, then paths to hides.
Wildfowl; passage waders; reedbed species; summer warblers; migrants.

Great Amwell Pits   166   2½m N of Hoddesdon centre
Park by B181 at St. Margarets railway station, ½m W of Stanstead
Abbots at TL382118. Take towpath north beside the navigation
canal and pits from just east of the station.
Passage and winter wildfowl; passage waders and terns.

> ***Balls Wood*** *166   TL345105   2m NW of Hoddesdon centre*
> *Woodland birds and summer warblers.*

TIC   As previous entry.
YH   Corner House, Netteswell Cross, Harlow, Essex (0279
            21702)
RF   Galley Hall, Hailey, nr Hoddesdon
            Townshend Arms, Hertford Heath
BB   Marshall's Farm, Woodside, Thornwood, nr Epping
            (0378 74344)

Sawbridgeworth Marsh   167   ¾m NE of Sawbridgeworth
Park by minor road 1½m SW of A1060 from Little Hallingbury,
½m N of Sawbridgeworth railway station at TL494157, and path
west.
Marshland birds and summer warblers.

> ***Patmore Heath*** *167   TL446257   4m NW of Bishop's*
> *Stortford*
> *Woodland birds and summer warblers.*

TIC   Council Offices, 2 The Causeway, Bishop's Stortford
            (0279 655261)
YH   As previous entry.
RF   Nags Head, Little Hadham, nr Bishop's Stortford
            Hoops Inn, Perry Green, nr Sawbridgeworth
BB   Greys Farm, Ongar Road, Margaret Roding, nr Great
            Dunmow, Essex (024 531 509)
BBE   5 Willow Place, Hastingwood, nr Harlow (0279 28138)

Tring Reservoirs   165   1½m N of Tring
Car-parks by B489 1.5–2½m NE of A41, by north end of Wilstone
Reservoir at SP904135 and a further 1m NE by the top end of
Startops Reservoir at SP919141. Then paths around the waters and
to the hides.
Wildfowl; passage waders and terns; summer warblers; migrants.

Aldbury & Berkhamstead Commons   165   3–4m E of Tring
Car-park and information centre ½m W of B4506 at SP970131, then
many paths north and south. For Berkhamstead Common park by
B4506 further south, 2m S of Ringsall, e.g. SP977116, and paths
and tracks eastward.
Woodland birds and summer warblers including Redstart and
Wood Warbler.

TIC	The Library, Vernon Place, Dunstable, Beds (0582 471012)
YH	The Old Brewery House, Ivinghoe, Leighton Buzzard, Beds (0296 668251)
RF	Valiant Trooper, Aldbury, nr Tring
	Kings Arms, Tring
	White Lion, Startops End, nr Tring Reservoirs
	Angler's Retreat, Startops End, nr Tring Reservoirs
RFBBE	Chandos Arms, Main Street, Weston Turville (0296 613532)
BB	The Haven, 7 Lower Icknield Way, Aston Clinton, nr Tring (0296 630751)
BBE	Baywood Guest House, 98 Weston Road, Aston Clinton (0296 630612)

Oughtonhead Common   166   2m W of Hitchin centre
Park by minor road to Pirton 0.3m NW of B655 at TL158297 and take track and paths NE to the common.
Marshland birds and summer warblers; woodland birds.

> *Purwell Ninesprings   166   TL206293   1m SE of Hitchin railway station*
> *Woodland birds and summer warblers.*

TIC	Hitchin Library, Paynes Park, Hitchin (0462 434738)
YH	As previous entry.
RF	Cat and Fiddle, Pirton, nr Hitchin
	Green Man, Great Offley, nr Hitchin
	Old George, Ickleford, nr Hitchin
	Cricketers, Ickleford, nr Hitchin
BB	Beechlea, Kings Walden Road, Great Offley, nr Hitchin (046 276 703)
BBE	Pond Farm, High Street, Pulloxhill, nr Ampthill (0525 712316)

Therfield Heath   154   1m W of Royston
Park by minor road to Therfield ¼m SE of the roundabout on A505, at west end of Royston by-pass, at TL336403 and tracks east. Or by the north side of the heath ¾m W of A10, 1m E of A505, at TL348606 and paths south.
Downland and woodland birds; summer warblers.

TIC	Central Library, Southgate, Stevenage (0438 369441)
YH	1 Myddylton Place, Saffron Walden, Essex (0799 23117)
RF	Rose and Crown, Ashwell
	Cabinet, Reed, nr Royston
BBE	The Grange, Old North Road, Kneesworth, nr Royston (0763 48674)

Kent

Dungeness   189   2–4m SE of Lydd
RSPB Car-park and information centre signposted south from minor road 1½m SE of Lydd at TR063196, then paths to hides overlooking the pits. Other pits viewable from road east to Dungeness. For Dungeness Bird Observatory recording area park opposite the lighthouse, ¼m W of Britannia pub , at TR089169. Then many paths inland and to the hide on seaward side of the power station. Coast road north of Dungeness for Lydd Pits (TR078215) and Greatstone and Lydd Sands.
Migrants including many rarities; seawatching; winter seaduck, grebes and divers; passage waders and wildfowl; passage terns; summer Mediterranean Gull and Roseate Tern.

Walland Marsh   189   4m NW of Lydd
Park by the pub beside A259 1½m SW of Brookland at TQ978244, then path and track to the south.
Winter wildfowl; marsh and reedbed species; winter Hen Harrier.

Hamstreet Woods   189   TQ005338   5½m S of Ashford
Woodland birds; Hawfinch, Nightingale and Redstart.

TIC	*Light Railway Car-park, 2 Littlestone Road, New Romney (0679 64044)
	48 Cinque Ports Street, Rye, East Sussex (0797 222293)
YH	Guestling Hall, Rye Road, Guestling, Hastings, East Sussex (0424 812373)
R	Red Lion, Snargate
RF	Woolpack Inn, Brookland
	Plough, New Romney
	Smuggler's Inn, Dungeness
RFBBE	Star, St. Mary-in-the-Marsh, nr New Romney
BB	133 Coast Drive, Lydd-on-Sea (0679 21219)
BBE	Blue Dolphins Hotel, Dymchurch Road, New Romney (0679 63224)
	Rose and Crown, Swamp Road, Old Romney (0679 62270)

SC Dungeness Bird Observatory, Romney Marsh (0679 21309)
    Greatstone Cottages, 135 Coast Drive, Lydd-on-Sea (0679 20258)

Hemsted Forest 188 4½ m NE of Hawkhurst
Car-park by minor road 1½m N of B2086 from Benenden at TQ812344 then tracks north.
Woodland birds.

Bedgebury Forest 188 3m NW of Hawkhurst
Car-park by B2079 1¼ m N of its junction with A21 at TQ715338 and paths and tracks eastwards.
Woodland birds including Hawfinch and Crossbill.

Bewl Water 188 2m W of Bedgebury
See *Sussex*.

TIC *Vestry Hall, Stone Street, Cranbrook (0580 712538)
YH As previous entry.
RF King William IV, Benenden, nr Hawkhurst
    Oak and Ivy, Hawkhurst
BB Ockley Farm, Heartenoak Road, Hawkhurst (0580 52290)
BBESC Conghurst Farm, Conghurst Lane, Hawkhurst (0580 753331)

Bough Beech Reservoir 188 5m SW of Sevenoaks
Park and view from minor road at N end of the reservoir, 1¾m N of B2027 at TQ496492.
Winter wildfowl; autumn waders; passerine migrants; large winter gull roost.

Sevenoaks Wildfowl Reserve 188 N side of Sevenoaks
Open Wednesdays and weekends only.
Car-park and visitor centre signposted from A25, ½m E of its junction with A224, at TQ519568.
Winter wildfowl; passage waders; summer terns and Little Ringed Plover; woodland birds.

Lullingstone Park 188 6m N of Sevenoaks
Car-park by minor road 1m W of A225, 1½m N of Shoreham, at TQ516636 then paths north.
Woodland and parkland birds.

    Knole Park 188 TQ536546 1m SE of Sevenoaks centre
    Woodland birds including Hawfinch and Redstart.

    Toys Hill 188 TQ470515 4m SW of Sevenoaks
    Woodland birds.

TIC Buckhurst Lane, Sevenoaks (0732 450305)

YH	Crockham Hill House, Crockham Hill, Edenbridge (0732 866322)
	Cleves, Pilgrim's Way, Kemsing, Sevenoaks (0732 61341)
RF	Wheatsheaf, Bough Beech
	Cock, Ide Hill, nr Sevenoaks
	Dukes Head, Dunton Green, nr Sevenoaks
	Royal Oak, Shoreham, nr Otford
BB	Pond Cottage, Eggpie Lane, Weald, nr Sevenoaks (0732 463773)
SC	Whitepost Farmhouse, Chiddingstone Causeway, nr Penhurst (0892 870629)

Cliffe Pits   178   4m W of High Halstow
Park beside tracks west of Cliffe village e.g. TQ730768 and take tracks and paths around the ponds to the west and southwest.
Winter wildfowl, divers and grebes; passage and winter waders including Avocet; summer Garganey.

Halstow & St. Mary's Marshes   178   2m N of High Halstow
Park at Swigshole, at end of lane, 1½m N of A228, 1½m N of High Halstow at TQ788776. Then tracks north and east across the marshes to the coast path.
Winter waders and wildfowl; summer Garganey; marshland species.

Northward Hill   178   1m N of High Halstow
Park at the north end of the housing estate north of High Halstow centre at TQ784760 and follow RSPB signs and path to the reserve.
Woodland species including Nightjar, Hawfinch, Long-eared Owl; largest Heronry in Britain.

Allhallows   178   4m NE of High Halstow
Park at the sea front 1m N of Allhallows at TQ840786 then follow tracks east along the sea wall and across the marshes to Yantlett Creek and Stoke Lagoon.
Winter waders, raptors, Twite and Snow Bunting; passage waders and passerines; seawatching.

TIC	10 Parrock Street, Gravesend (0474 337600)
YH	As previous entry.
RF	Tudor Rose, Upnor, nr Rochester
BB	Haydown, Great Buckland, nr Cobham (0474 814329)
BBE	64 Main Road, Hoo, nr Rochester (0634 250570)

Burham Marsh & Pits   188   5m NW of Maidstone
Park by the church at Burham Court, 1m W of Burham, at TQ716619 and take track and path west. Also just west of New Hythe railway station 1¼m E of A228 at TQ708599 and track north around the pits.
Winter wildfowl; passage waders and terns; Bearded Tit, Cetti's Warbler and other reedbed species.

Trosley Country Park & Whitehorse Wood   188   3–4m W of Snodland
Signed car-park and visitor centre just E of A227, 2m N of its junction with M20, at TQ633612 then paths eastward.
Woodland birds including Hawfinch; summer warblers.

Mereworth & Hurst Woods   188   5–6m NE of Tonbridge
Park by minor road 2m N of A26 from Hadlow at S end of the woods, TQ629533, and take the Wealdway and other tracks north. Woodland birds including Hawfinch and Hobby; summer warblers.

> *Mote Park*   188   TQ775554   *1m SE of Maidstone centre*
> *Woodland birds; wildfowl.*

> *Holly Hill*   188   TQ670630   *2m NW of Snodland*
> *Woodland birds and summer warblers.*

> *Ryarsh Wood*   188   TQ655605   *1m N of Addington*
> *Woodland birds.*

TIC   The Gatehouse, Old Palace Gardens, Mill Street, Maidstone (0622 673581)
YH   As previous entry.
RF   Duke of Wellington, Ryarsh, nr Snodland
    Toastmasters, Burham
    Golden Eagle, Burham
BBE   Court Lodge Farm, The Street, Teston, nr Maidstone (0622 812570)
    Bydews Place, Farleigh Hill, nr Maidstone (0622 58860)

Chetney Marshes   178   4m N of Sittingbourne
Park just off A249 on the west side of Kingferry Bridge at TQ913693 and take the Saxon Shore Way NW beside the river and then west across the marshes to Funton Creek. Also view from minor road 1–2m NE of Lower Halstow.
Summer marshland species; passage and winter waders; wildfowl; winter raptors and Short-eared Owl.

Ham Green   178   2½m N of Newington
Park in Ham Green by minor road 1m N of Upchurch at TQ847688 and take track east to shore and path along the sea wall.
Winter wildfowl, divers and seaduck; passage and winter waders.

Eastcourt Meadows Country Park   178   4m NW of Newington
Signed car-park just N of B2004, ¼m NW of Lower Twydall on the N edge of Gillingham, at TQ807684. Then track north and The Saxon Shore Way west or east.
Winter wildfowl, waders and gulls; migrants.

TIC   Bridge Road Car-park, Sheerness (0795 665324)
YH   54 New Dover Road, Canterbury (0227 462911)

| RF | Plough and Harrow, Borden, nr Sittingbourne |
| BB | Woodlands, Pinks Corner, Groovehurst Road, Iwade, nr Sittingbourne (0795 73621) |

Elmley & Spitend Marshes   178   3–4m NE of Sittingbourne

Signed car-park south from A249 1m NE of Kingsferry Bridge, then 2m down track to Kings Hill Farm at TQ938680. Then tracks west or east toward Spitend Marshes.

Winter wildfowl; passage and winter waders; migrants.

Harty Marshes, Swale NNR & Shell Ness   178   E end of Isle of Sheppey

Car-park at the Ferry Inn at the end of minor road 3m S of B2231 at TR016660. Then track and paths NE across the marshes and along the seawall to Shell Ness.

Winter wildfowl and raptors; passage and winter waders; passerine migrants; seawatching; breeding birds include Garganey and Avocet.

TIC	As previous entry.
YH	As previous entry.
RF	Bell, Minster, nr Sheerness
BB	Innesmount, First Avenue, Eastchurch, Isle of Sheppey (0795 88419)
BBE	Isle of Sheppey Hotel, Halfway, Minster, Sheerness (0795 665950)

Murston Pits   178   2m NE of Sittingbourne

Park at the end of minor road 1¾m N of A2 from Bapchild, ½m W of Tonge Corner at TQ931654, then track SW or NE to the shore and around the pits.

Winter wildfowl and grebes; passage and winter waders; summer Garganey and terns; reedbed species; migrants.

Oare Marshes   178   2m N of Faversham

Park at the end of minor road 1m N of Oare at TR012641 then track north to the coast path.

Winter wildfowl; passage and winter waders; winter raptors, Short-eared Owl, Twite and occasional Snow Bunting.

Cleve & Nagden Marshes & The Swale   178 & 179   2–3m NE of Faversham

Park beside minor road at the sea front 2½m N of A299, 2m N of Graveney at TR062647 and take the Saxon Shore Way westwards.

Winter wildfowl, waders, raptors, buntings and Twite; migrants.

TIC	Fleur de Lis Heritage Centre, 13 Preston Street, Faversham (0795 534542)
YH	As previous entry.
RF	Shipwrights Arms, Oare
	Ship, Conyer, nr Faversham

BB   Forge Cottage, Lynsted, nr Sittingbourne (0795 521273)
            Moat House, Uplees, nr Oare (0795 536746)

Stodmarsh   179   6m NE of Canterbury
Car-park up lane ¼m N of Stodmarsh village, 2m N of A257 from
Littlebourne, at TR222609. Then paths around the reserve and NE
up to Grove Ferry bridge.
Wildfowl; passage waders, terns, passerines and raptors;
breeding Savi's and Cetti's Warbler, Bearded Tit; reedbed species.

Westbere Lakes & Marshes   179   1½m W of Stodmarsh
Park by the railway crossing on the S edge of Westbere village, ½m
S of A28 at TR196610. Then footpath across the railway line to the
lakes, reedbeds and River Stour.
Species similar to Stodmarsh.

Church Wood   179   2–4m NW of Canterbury centre
RSPB car-park ¼m along track NW of Rough Common, ½m W of
A290 at TR124594. Then track and paths west through the woods.
Woodland birds include Nightingale, Redstart and Hawfinch;
summer warblers.

Thornden & West Blean Woods   179   4m N of Canterbury
Car-park by minor road 1½m N of Tyler Hill at TR136628 then
signed paths. Also park by minor road ½m NE at TR144633 and
take track NE; or park 1m N of Calcott on A291 at TR174642 and
take track and paths westward.
Woodland birds including Redstart, Wood Warbler and Hawfinch; summer warblers.

Reculver   179   3m E of Herne Bay
Car-park near the front 2m NE of A299 at TR225693 then coast path
east or west.
Winter wildfowl; passage and winter waders; winter raptors,
buntings and Twite; migrants.

> ***East Blean Wood***   *179   TR190644   2½m S of Herne Bay*
> *Woodland birds.*
>
> ***Court Wood***   *179   TR075570   4m W of Canterbury*
> *Woodland birds.*

TIC   34 St. Margaret's Street, Canterbury (0227 766567/455567)
YH   As previous entry.
RF   Grove Ferry, Upstreet
            Fordwich Arms, Fordwich, nr Canterbury
            Gate Inn, Boyden Gate, nr Chislet
BB   Streete Farm House, Court Road, St. Nicholas-at-Wade,
            nr Birchington (0843 47245)
BBE   Crockshard Farmhouse, Wingham, nr Canterbury (0227
            720464)

SC Wingham Well Farm, Wingham, nr Canterbury (0227 720253)

Wye & Crundale Downs   189   2m SE of Wye
Car-park 2m along minor road from Wye to Hastingleigh at TR088454, then paths west and north.
Woodland species; summer warblers; Nightingale, Hobby.

Denge Wood   189   4½m NE of Wye
Park by minor road at Garlinge Green, 1¼m NW of Petham, 2m NW of B2068 at TR113526 and take lane SW and paths through woods.
Woodland birds including Nightingale and Hawfinch; summer warblers.

Hothfield Common   189   3m NW of Ashford centre
Car-park by A20 ½m SE of Tutt Hill at TR973458 then paths across the heath and through woods.
Woodland and heathland birds; summer warblers.

> *Kings Wood   189   TR025500   3m NW of Wye*
> *Woodland birds.*

> *Eastwell Park   189   TR010474   2½m W of Wye*
> *Woodland birds and wildfowl.*

TIC Lower High Street, Ashford (0233 37311 ext. 316)
YH As previous entry.
RF Tickled Trout, Wye
        Swan, Little Chart, nr Ashford
RFBBE Flying Horse, Boughton Aluph, nr Wye
        Kings Head, Church Street, Wye (0233 812418)
BBE The Old Rectory, Pluckley Road, Little Chart, nr Ashford (0233 713005)
SC Spring Grove Farm, Wye (0233 812425)

South Foreland   179   3m NE of Dover
Park in St. Margaret's near the shore at TR368445. Then take coast path south toward the windmill and lighthouse and areas of scrub and trees.
Migrants; frequent rarities.

Copt Point & The Warren   179   1m NE of Folkestone
Park by minor road 1m E of the town centre near the Point at TR240364 and walk east to the shore and sewage outfall and then north to The Warren.
Gulls, especially winter Mediterranean Gull; seawatching; migrants.

> *Dover Harbour   179   TR324405   ½m SE of town centre*
> *Winter gulls; seaduck.*

TIC	Townwall Street, Dover (0304 205108)
	Harbour Street, Folkestone (0303 58594)
YH	Charlton House, 306 London Road, Dover (0304 201314)
RF	Granville, St. Margaret's Bay, nr Dover
	Valiant Sailor, Chapel Le Ferne, nr Folkestone
BB	Hoptons Manor, Alkham Valley Road, South Alkham, nr Dover (0303 892481)
BBE	Crete Down, Crete Road West, Folkestone (0303 892392)
SC	Beachborough Park, Newington, nr Folkestone (0303 75432)

Sandwich Bay, Worth Marshes & Shell Ness   179   2m E of Sandwich

Park by the Bird Observatory 1½m along minor road E of Sandwich at TR355575. Footpaths lead SE across Worth Marshes and NE around the golf courses and along the shore to Shell Ness.

Migrants; frequent rarities; winter wildfowl, raptors and buntings; passage and winter waders; seawatching.

Pegwell Bay   179   3m SW of Ramsgate

Car-park and picnic site by A256 ¾m N of its junction with B2048 at TR342633 then paths north and south.

Passage and winter waders; passerine migrants.

TIC	Town Hall, High Street, Deal (0304 369576)
	*St. Peter's Church, Market Street, Sandwich (0304 613565)
YH	As previous entries (Dover and Canterbury).
RF	Crispin, Sandwich
	Market Inn, Sandwich
	St. Crispin, Worth
	Blue Pigeons, Worth
	Sportsman Inn, Pegwell Bay
RFBBE	Fleur de Lis Hotel, Sandwich (0304 611131)
SC	Sandwich Bay Bird Observatory, Guilford Road, Sandwich Bay, nr Sandwich (0304 617341)
	Ridgeway Farm, Woodnesborough Road, Sandwich (0304 612121)

Foreness Point   179   2½m E of Margate centre

Car-park by B2051 just west of a sharp dog-leg bend at TR380713. Then track NE to the Point and coast path further east to White Ness and North Foreland.

Migrants; seawatching; gulls at sewage outfalls.

TIC	Marine Terrace, Margate (0843 220241)
YH	54 New Dover Road, Canterbury (0227 462911)
R	Spread Eagle, Margate
BBE	Marylands Hotel, Marine Drive, Kingsgate, nr Broadstairs (0843 61259)
	Clintons, 9 Dalby Square, Cliftonville (0843 290598)

Lancashire

Martin Mere (Wildfowl Trust)   108   **4m NE of Ormskirk**
Car-park, visitor centre and entrance by minor road 2m NW of A59
from Burscough Bridge at SD428144. Then marked tracks to many
hides.
Wildfowl collection; winter wildfowl; passage and winter raptors,
waders and gulls; passage terns; summer Black-tailed Godwit and
Little Ringed Plover.

Mere Sands Wood   108   **5½m NE of Ormskirk**
Car-park and visitor centre just south off B5246, 1m NW of
Rufford, at SJ448158. Then tracks, nature trail and hide.
Wildfowl and woodland birds; passage waders; summer Little
Ringed Plover, Ruddy Duck and Turtle Dove.

> *Mere Brow Leisure Lakes* 108 *SJ410177 6m N of
> Ormskirk*
> *Winter wildfowl; passage waders and terns.*

TIC   112 Lord Street, Southport, Merseyside (0704
33133/500175)
RF   Legh Arms, Mere Brow
RFBBE Martin Inn, Martin Lane, nr Burscough
BB   Sandy Brook Farm, Scarisbrick, nr Southport (0704
880337)

Lever Park & Rivington Reservoir & Moor   109   **1–2m N of
Horwich**
Car-park and information centre by minor road on east side of
reservoir 1½m N of Horwich at SD628138. Then tracks by reser-
voir, through woodland and up onto moor. Also view reservoir
from roads by southern end and north around Anglezarke.
Woodland birds; winter wildfowl; moorland birds including Red
Grouse.

Jumbles Country Park & Reservoir   109   **3m N of Bolton**
Car-park and visitor centre at south end of reservoir ¼m W of A676
at SD737139. Then track north beside reservoir.
Woodland birds and winter wildfowl.

Wayoh Reservoir   109   5m N of Bolton
View from minor road crossing the reservoir 1m NW of
Edgeworth, SD732174, and from footpaths along the east and west
shores.
Winter wildfowl; passage waders; woodland birds; summer
warblers.

**Roddlesworth & Sunnyhurst Woods & Reservoir   103   2m
SW of Darwen**
Car-park by minor road 1m S of Tuckholes at SD665214. Then
footpaths west and northeast.
Winter wildfowl; woodland birds including Redstart and Wood
Warbler.

> *Belmont Reservoir   109   SD670170   5m NW of Bolton*
> *Winter wildfowl.*

TIC   Town Hall, Bolton (0204 36433)
YH   Mankinholes, Todmorden (0706 812340)
RF   Toby, Edgeworth
RFBBE   Black Dog Inn, Belmont (020 481 218)
            Strawberry Duck, Entwhistle

Hesketh Out Marsh & Bank   102   7m SW of Preston
Park at the end of minor road 1m N of Hesketh Bank, 3½m N of
A59 at SD438252. Then tracks east to River Asland and north to the
marsh embankment.
Winter wildfowl; passage and winter waders.

Hutton & Longton Marshes   102   6m SW of Preston
Park at end of minor road 1½m W of Longton, 2m N of A59, at
SD457254. Then footpaths and Ribble Way north.
Waders and wildfowl.

> *Cuerden Valley Country Park   102   SD568233   4m SE of*
> *Preston*
> *Woodland birds.*

> *Tun Brook Valley   102   SD591325   3m NE of Preston*
> *centre*
> *Woodland birds.*

TIC   The Guildhall, Lancaster Road, Preston (0772 53731)
R   Dolphin, Marsh Lane, Longton
RF   Anchor, Hutton
BBE   Garden Hotel, 19 Lathom Road, Southport (0704 30244)

Freckleton Flash   102   7m W of Preston
Park at east end of Freckleton, ¼m S of A584, at SD437290. Then
footpath and seawall south beside creek and flash.
Passage and winter waders and wildfowl.

Warton Bank & Aerodrome   102   7m SE of Blackpool
Park at end of minor road 1m S of Warton, 1m S of A584, at
SD403274. Then footpaths southeast and west.
Waders; winter wildfowl and raptors.

Fairhaven Lake & Squires Gate   102   3–5m S of Blackpool
Park and view from coast roads and car-parks between Lytham St.
Anne's and Blackpool e.g. near Fairhaven Lake at SD334275, St.
Anne's just north of the pier at SD317287 or Squires Gate at
SD305316.
Passage and winter waders; winter seaduck and divers;
seawatching.

Marton Mere   102   2m SE of Blackpool centre
Park ½m down track east of A587, 1m N of its junction with A583,
at SD336354. Then path east to the mere.
Passage waders; summer warblers; winter wildfowl; migrants.

> *Blackpool Airport* 102 *SD320310 between Lytham St.
> Anne's & Blackpool.*
> *Passage and winter waders, Short-eared Owl and raptors.*

TIC   The Square, Lytham St. Anne's (0253 725610)
RF   Ship, Freckleton
            Birley Arms, Warton
BBE   Ashfield Guest House, Lea Road, Lea, nr Preston (0772
            720201)

Rossall Point   102   W side of Fleetwood
Park by minor road along north coast, SD324482. Then track north
and promenade west by the golf course and to the point.
Seawatching; passage and winter waders; winter seaduck, divers,
Twite and Snow Bunting; migrants.

Stanah   102   1m NE of Thornton
Car-park by estuary shore 1m NE of B5412 at SD356433. Then coast
paths north and south.
Passage and winter waders, wildfowl and gulls.

> *Cleveleys* 102 *SD312435 3m S of Fleetwood*
> *Passage and winter waders, seaduck and divers.*

TIC   1 Clifton Street, Blackpool (0253 21623/25212)
RF   Mount Hotel, Fleetwood
            North Euston, Fleetwood

Stalmine Marshes   102   2m S of Knott End
Park at end of minor road 2m W of Stalmine at SD353454. Then
track and footpath north.
Passage and winter waders and wildfowl.

Pilling & Cockerham Marshes   102   4–6m NE of Knott End
Car-park at Lane Ends, just north of A588, 1m N of Stake Pool, at
SD415495. Then coast path east and west along the sea wall.
Passage and winter waders and wildfowl; winter raptors and
Twite.

Cockersand Point   102   5m SW of Lancaster
Park at end of minor road 2m W of B5272, 2m W of Upper
Thurnham, at SD432544. Then coastal path south to the point.
Seawatching; passage and winter waders; winter seaduck and
divers; passage terns; migrants.

Fishnet Point & Glasson Dock   102   3m SW of Lancaster
Park at end of B5290, 1m W of A588, at SD446562. Then short walk
NW to Fishnet Point.
Passage and winter waders and gulls; migrants.

TIC	7 Dalton Square, Lancaster (0524 32878)
YH	King's House, Slaidburn, Clitheroe (02006 656)
RF	Saracens Head, Preesall, nr Knott End
	Golden Ball, Pilling
	Caribou, Glasson Dock
	Shard Bridge Inn, Shard Lane, Hambleton
BB	White Lodge farm, Sower Carr Lane, Hambleton, nr Poulton (0253 700342)

Hollins Lane & Scorton Gravel Pits   102   6m S of Lancaster
Car-park by minor road just W of M6, 1½m N of Scorton, at
SD506505. Then footpaths north and south beside River Wyre and
pits. Also from minor road 1½m NE, SD519509, and take footpaths
northwest to the other pits.
Wildfowl; passage waders and terns; summer warblers.

Bleasdale Moors & Hareden Fell   102   9m SE of Lancaster
Park in Bleasdale, 3m NW of Chipping, 3m E of M6, at SD574456.
Then track and footpath north up onto the moors.
Moorland birds including Red Grouse, Golden Plover and Ring
Ousel.

Brock Valley   102   4m W of Chipping, 2½m W of M6
Car-park by bridge over River Brock, 1m W of Beacon Fell Country
Park at SD548431. Then footpaths north and south beside the river
and through woods.
Woodland and river birds including Pied Flycatcher, Redstart and
Dipper.

Stocks Reservoir & Gisburn Forest   103   8m N of Clitheroe
Park by northern shore of reservoir e.g. SD736563 and track and
footpath NE through the woods.
Winter wildfowl; woodland birds including Crossbill.

Grizedale 102 SD520483 3m NE of Garstang
Woodland and river birds.

Abbeystead Reservoir 102 SD560540 6m SE of
Lancaster
Wildfowl; woodland birds.

Beacon Fell Country Park 102 SD567428 5m SE of
Garstang
Woodland birds.

TIC	As previous entry.
	*The Community Centre Car-park, High Street, Garstang (09952 4430)
	M6 (Northbound), Bay Horse, Forton (0524 792181)
YH	As previous entry.
R	Fleece, Dolphinholme, nr Galgate
RF	Dog & Partridge, Hesketh Lane, nr Chipping
	Sun Inn, Chipping
	Bay Horse, Bay Horse Lane, nr Scorton
	New Holly, Forton, nr Scorton
	Inn at Whitewell, Whitewell, nr Clitheroe
RFBBE	Parker's Arms, Newton, nr Clitheroe (02006 236)
	Hark to Bounty Inn, Slaidburn, nr Clitheroe (02006 246)
BBE	Hough Clough Farmhouse, Chipping (09956 272)
	Gold Hill Country House, Woodhouse Lane, Slaidburn (02006 202)
	Old Mill House, Waggon Road, Lower Dolphinholme, nr Lancaster (0524 791855)
SC	(Dunsop Bridge Cottage) Northern Estates Manager, N.W. Water, Pennine House, Preston (0772 22200 ext 42355)
	Horns Farm, Church Street, Slaidburn (02006 288)

Clowbridge Reservoir   103   **3m SW of Burnley**
View from A682 by western shore, SD824283. Also track across the
northeastern corner.
Winter wildfowl.

Wycoller Country Park   103   **3m E of Colne**
Car-park by minor road at Wycoller, 2m NE of Trawden,
SD938394. Then footpath and nature trail.
Woodland, moorland and river birds.

Foulridge Reservoir   103   **1m N of Colne**
View from A56, ½m S of Foulridge, SD891415. Also from minor
road along the western side.
Winter wildfowl; passage waders and terns.

Whitemoor reservoir 103 SD877433 2m N of Colne
Winter wildfowl.

Upper Coldwell Reservoir   103   SD903363   *2m SE of Nelson*
Winter wildfowl; passage waders.

Pendle Hill   103   SD805415   *3m E of Clitheroe*
Moorland birds; migrants including spring Dotterel.

TIC   20a Scotland Road, Nelson (0282 692890)
          Burnley Mechanics, Manchester Road, Burnley (0282 30055)
YH   Glen Cottage, Birch Hall Lane, Earby, Colne (0282 842349)
          Longlands Hall, Longlands Drive, Lee Lane, Haworth, Keighley, W Yorks (0535 42234)
          Mankinholes, Todmorden (0706 812340)
RF   Kettledrum, Mereclough, nr Burnley
          Cross Gaits Inn, Blacko, nr Colne
RFBBE   Moorcock, Blacko, nr Colne (0282 64186)
BBE   Will o'th Moor Farm, Trawden, nr Colne (0282 864955)
          Higher Wanless Farm, Red Lane, Colne (0282 865301)

Sunderland Point & Middleton Marsh   102   **3m SE of Heysham**
Park at end of minor road by sea front, 1½m SW of Middleton, at SD414573. Then track and path SE beside the marsh and to the point.
Passage and winter waders; passage terns; migrants.

Heaton Marshes   97   **2m SW of Lancaster centre**
View from minor road on west side of River Lune ½m-1m N of Heaton e.g. SD448616. Or on the eastern bank park at end of minor road, 1m W of A588 1m W of Aldcliffe, SD460600, and footpath NW along the dyke.
Waders and wildfowl.

Heysham Harbour & Power Station   *97 & 102*
SD597397   S end of Heysham
Seawatching; passage terns; gulls; winter seaduck and divers; migrants.

TIC   Marine Road Central, Morecombe (0524 414110)
YH   Oakfield Lodge, Redhills Road, Arnside, Carnforth (0524 761781)
RF   Golden Ball, Heaton

Hest Bank   97   **3m NE of Morecambe**
Park by A5105 on west side of Hest Bank, SD467665. Then over railway by the level crossing and take track and footpath north.
Winter waders, wildfowl and raptors.

Carnforth Marsh   97   1½m NW of Carnforth
Park at end of minor road 1½m SW of Warton just over the railway line at SD487714. Then track by River Keer and around the marsh. Passage and winter waders and wildfowl.

Allen Pools & Heald Brow   97   3m NW of Carnforth
Car-park just west of railway line at Crag Foot SD475737. Then path south to hides on the sea wall and footpath west to the woods.
Passage and winter wildfowl and waders; woodland birds including Hawfinch; migrants.

Leighton Moss   97   4m NW of Carnforth
Car-park and visitor centre by minor road, 1½m E of Silverdale, ¼m E of railway line at SD478751. Then tracks to hides. Also public footpath across the reserve ¼m further along the road NE.
Bittern; Bearded Tit; summer warblers and Marsh Harrier; summer and winter wildfowl; passage waders and terns; migrants.

Morecambe Front   97   SD435646   N end of Morecambe
Passage and winter waders; winter seaduck, divers and grebes; seawatching.

Warton Lake   97   SD513725   2m NE of Carnforth
Winter wildfowl.

Warton Crag   97   SD494725   1½m N of Carnforth
Woodland birds; summer warblers; migrants.

Gait Barrows   97   SD476770   2m NE of Silverdale
Woodland birds; wildfowl.

Arnside Park & Blackstone Point (Cumbria)
B   97   SD436770   2m NW of Silverdale
Woodland birds; winter wildfowl and waders; migrants.

Jenny Browns Point & Jack Scout   97   SD460734   1½m
S of Silverdale
Passage and winter waders and wildfowl; migrants.

Hyning Scout Wood   97   SD502735   1m N of Wharton
Woodland birds and summer warblers.

TIC   As previous entry.
YH   As previous entry.
RF   Blue Anchor, Bolton-le-Sands
          New Inn, Yealand Conyers, nr Carnforth

RFBBE Wheatsheaf, Beetham, nr Milnthorpe (04482 2123)
BB Cotestones Farm, Sand Lane, Warton, nr Carnforth (0524 732418)
Brocco Bank, Beetham (05395 63834)
SC Brackenthwaite Farm, Yealand Redmayne, nr Carnforth (04482 3276)

Leicestershire

Eye Brook Reservoir   141   4m NW of Corby
Park by minor road over bridge at the very northernmost end, ½m SE of B664 at SP844971. Also view from road along NE and west shores.
Passage waders and terns; winter wildfowl and gull roost.

Rutland Water   141   1–4m E of Oakham
1. View from A6003 ½m N of Manton, 3m SE of Oakham at SK877053, especially for waders.
2. Park at southern shore 1½m NE of Manton at SK894055, then tracks west to hides and east.
3. Car-park by shore at Edith Weston, SK928057, especially for gull roost.
4. Car-parks ½m S of A606 along the north shore at SK924082, and SK909087 at Barnsdale.
5. Car-park and tracks to many hides at Egleton on the west shore at SK877073.
Winter wildfowl and grebes; passage and winter waders; passage terns; summer warblers, Oystercatcher, Little Ringed Plover, Common Tern and Hobby; reedbed species; woodland birds; passerine migrants; winter Long-eared Owl and Short-eared Owl.

Wardley Wood   141   1½m W of Uppingham
Park by minor road 1m N of B664 at SP834992, then footpath over bridge over Eye Brook and through the wood.
Woodland birds.

> *Owston Woods   141   SK790065   4m SW of Oakham*
> *Woodland birds.*

> *Launde Big Wood   141   SK785037   6m SW of Oakham*
> *Woodland birds.*

> *Saddington Reservoir   141   SP664913   5m NW of Market Harborough*
> *Winter wildfowl; passage waders.*

TIC	Civic Centre, George Street, Corby (0536 402551)
	Pen Lloyd Library, Adam & Eve Street, Market Harborough (0858 62649)
YH	Copt Oak, Markfield, Leicester (0530 242661)
	Capstone, 16 High Street, Thurlby, Bourne, Lincs (0778 425588)
RF	Noel Arms, Whitwell, nr Oakham
	Finches Arms, Upper Hambleton, nr Oakham
	Coach and Horses, Kibworth Beauchamp, nr Leicester
	White Horse, Empingham
RFSC	Kings Arms, Wing, nr Uppingham (057 285 315)
BBESC	Old Rectory, Belton-in-Rutland, nr Uppington (057 286 279)

Swithland Reservoir   129   3m SE of Loughborough
View from minor road at north end, 1m west of Rothley Plain to Quorndon road, at SK557148. Or from minor road at south end 1m east of Swithland at SK563133.
Winter wildfowl and gull roost; passage waders and terns; woodland birds.

Swithland Wood   129   4m S of Loughborough
Car-parks at south end by B5330 1½m NW of Cropston at SK537117 and at north end 1m W of Swithland at SK537129, then footpaths though the woods.
Woodland birds including Redstart, Wood Warbler and Hawfinch.

Cropston Reservoir   129   5m NW of Leicester
View from B5330 ½m west of Cropston at SK550112. Also car-park and footpath down the western shore and along the east side from end of track ¼m SW of B5328/B5330 junction, SK549107.
Winter wildfowl and gulls; passage waders and terns.

Bradgale Park Country Park   129   6m NW of Leicester
Car-park by minor road 1½m N of Newton Linford at SK524116 then tracks and path to the east.
Woodland and heathland birds.

Wanlip Country Park & Gravel Pits   129 & 140   4m N of Leicester centre
Park in Wanlip, SK602106, ½m S of B673. Then footpath SE beside and over the River Soar, along the Grand Union Canal and between the pits.
Passage and winter wildfowl; passage waders and terns; migrants.

Thornton Reservoir   140   8m NW of Leicester centre
View from minor road along the south side, ½m SE of Thornton village at SK474074.
Winter wildfowl; passage terns and gulls.

Blackbrook Reservoir   129   SK458175   5m W of
Loughborough
Winter wildfowl; passage waders and terns; summer warblers.

Groby Pool   140   SK522083   6m NW of Leicester centre
Winter wildfowl.

Beacon Hill Country Park   129   SK513147   3m SW of
Loughborough
Woodland birds.

TIC   2–6 St. Martin's Walk, Leicester (0533 511300)
John Storer House, Wards End, Loughborough (0509 230131)
YH   Copt Oak, Markfield, Leicester (0530 242661)
RF   Griffin, Swithland
Bradgale Arms, Cropston
BB   Leys Guest House, 67 Leicester Road, Anstey (0533 365929)

Kirby Bellars Gravel Pits   **129**   **3m W of Melton Mowbray**
Park at end of road ½m N of A607 at north end of Kirby Bellars, SK717183. Then footpath NW between the pits and by the River Wreake. Also view from minor road ¾m SE of Asfordby at SK710185.
Wildfowl; passage waders and terns.

Old Dalby Wood   129   SK680227   5m NW of Melton
Mowbray
Woodland birds.

Burrough Hill Country Park   129   SK766115   5m S of
Melton Mowbray
Woodland birds.

Ashby Woods   129   SK716136   4m SW of Melton
Mowbray
Woodland birds.

TIC   Melton Carnegie Museum, Thorpe End, Melton Mowbray (0664 69946)
YH   As previous entry.
RF   Crown, Old Dalby
Bell Inn, Frisby-on-the-Wreake, nr Asfordby
Stag and Hounds, Burrough-on-the-Hill
BB   Home Farm, Old Dalby (0664 822 622)
BBE   Manor House Farm, Saxelbye, nr Melton Mowbray (0664 812 269)
SC   White House Farm, Gaddesby Lane, Rearsby (066 474 225)

Stathern Woods   129   9m N of Melton Mowbray
Park by minor road ¾m E of Stathern village at SK783307, then footpaths north through the woods.
Woodland birds.

> ***Knipton Reservoir*** *130   SK315305   8m NE of Melton Mowbray*
> *Winter wildfowl.*

TIC	As previous entry.
YH	As previous entry.
	Capstone, 16 High Street, Thurlby, Bourne, Lincs (0778 425588)
RFBBE	Red House Inn, Knipton
SC	New Farm Cottage, Waltham Lane, Harby, nr Melton Mowbray (0949 60640)

Lincolnshire & South Humberside

Holbeach & Fosdyke Wash   131   6m NE of Holbeach
Car-park at end of minor road 1½m N of Holbeach St. Matthew,
4½m N of B1359 at TF408337. Then coast path east or north and
west to Fosdyke Wash and the mouth of the River Welland.
Passage and winter waders and wildfowl; winter Twite and Snow
Bunting.

Moulton Marsh   131   5½m NW of Holbeach
Park in Fosdyke Bridge by A17 at TF318324 and take path beside
the River Welland to the northeast along either bank. Also view
from minor road ¼m to the southeast.
Winter waders and wildfowl at high tide.

**Nene Mouth & Lutton Marsh   131   3–4m N of Sutton
Bridge**
View from minor road N from Sutton Bridge on the west side of the
River Nene. Also park near Guys Head, TF491257, and take coast
path north.
Passage and winter waders and wildfowl.

TIC	Ayscoughfee Hall, Churchgate, Spalding, Lincs (0775 725468)
YH	Thoresby College, College Lane, King's Lynn, Norfolk (0553 772461)
	Capstone, 16 High Street, Thurlby, Bourne, Lincs (0778 425588)
RF	Chequers, Gedney Dyke
	Old Black Lion, Gedney
BBE	Guy Wells Farm, Whaplode, nr Spalding, Lincs (0406 22239)

Frampton Marsh & The Scalp   131   5m SE of Boston
Park by minor road south of the River Witham Estuary, 3m W of
A16 from Kirton at TF354396. Then tracks and path east to the
point of The Scalp and southwest to Frampton and Kirton
Marshes.
Passage and winter wildfowl and waders; winter Twite; summer
terns; seawatching.

Boston Point   131   3–5m SE of Boston
Car-park at end of minor road on the north side of the river 2½m
SE of Fishtoft at TF380393. Then coast path east to the point and
west to the mouth of Hobhole Drain.
Passage and winter waders and wildfowl; migrants; winter Twite;
seawatching.

> *Freiston Low   131   TF400415   3m E of Fishtoft*
> *Passage and winter waders and wildfowl.*

TIC	The Pearoom Craft Centre, Station Yard, Heckington, nr Sleaford, Lincs (0529 60088)
YH	As previous entry.
RF	Moores Arms, Church End, Frampton Castle, Freiston
BBE	Mill House, Main Road, Stickney, nr Boston (0205 480298)

Baston Pits & Fen   130   3m N of Market Deeping
Park and view from minor road 2m E of Baston from A15 at
TF137146.
Summer warblers and wildfowl; winter wildfowl; passage terns.

Callan's Lane Wood   130   5m NW of Bourne
Car-park by minor road 2m W of A15, 1m W of Kirkby Underwood
at TF061271. Then track south through woods.
Woodland birds; summer warblers.

> *Bourne Wood   130   TF076204   1½m W of Bourne*
> *Woodland birds including Nightingale and Lesser-spotted*
> *Woodpecker.*

> *Langtoft Pits   130   TF114115   1½m NW of Market*
> *Deeping*
> *Passage and winter wildfowl; passage terns.*

> *Deeping St. James   130   TF183087   1½m SE of Deeping*
> *St. James*
> *Winter wildfowl.*

Morkery Wood   *130*   *SK955193*   *2m W of Castle Bytham*
Woodland birds and summer warblers.

TIC	The Museum, Broad Street, Stamford, Lincs (0780 55611)
YH	Capstone, 16 High Street, Thurlby, Bourne (0778 425588)
RF	Spinning Wheel, Baston, nr Market Deeping
RFBBE	Wishing Well, Dyke, nr Bourne (0778 422970)

Burton Gravel Pits   **121**   **2½m NW of Lincoln centre**
Park by minor road 1½m W of Burton, ¾m E of A57 at SK945740 and view from tracks and bridleway to the north around pits and woodland.
Wildfowl; woodland birds; summer warblers; passage terns.

Whisby Nature Park   **121**   **4m SW of Lincoln centre**
Signed car-park 1m N off A46 ½m N of Thorpe-on-the-Hill at SK912662, then track and paths north. Also from A46 ½m N of its junction with A1431 at SK918664.
Wildfowl; passage terns and waders; woodland birds including Nightingale; migrants; winter gull roost.

Hartsholme Country Park & Swanholme Lakes   *121*
SK943690   *2½m SW of Lincoln centre*
Woodland birds; summer warblers; wildfowl.

Potterhanworth Woods   *121*   *TF074670*   *1½m NE of*
Potterhanworth
Woodland birds.

Bardney Sugar Factory   *121*   *TF113683*   *1m SW of*
Bardney
Passage waders and wildfowl.

TIC	21 Cornhill, Lincoln (0522 512971)
YH	77 South Park, Lincoln (0522 22076)
RF	Chequers, Potterhanworth
BBE	The Village Farm, Sturton-by-Stow, nr Saxilby (0427 788309)
SC	Pantiles Cottage, The Old Hall, Potterhanworth, Lincoln (0522 791338)

Snipe Dales   **122**   **4m E of Horncastle**
Park just north of B1159 (formerly A1115) at Winceby, TF320683.
Then signed tracks north and east across the reserve.
Woodland birds; summer warblers including many Grasshopper Warblers.

Fulsby Wood   122   TF255620   *5m S of Horncastle*
Woodland birds.

Tattershall Pits   122   TF205570   *1m SW of Tattershall*
Wildfowl.

Kirkby Pits   122   TF236610   *2½m NE of Tattershall*
Passage and winter wildfowl; passage terns and gulls.

TIC	Money's Yard, Carre Street, Sleaford (0529 414294)
YH	Woody's Top, Ruckland, nr Louth, Lincs (0205 68651)
RF	Royal Oak, Mareham-le-Fen, nr Horncastle
	Leagate Inn, Coningsby, nr Tattershall
	Red Lion, Raithby
RFBBE	Crossed Keys, Salmonby, nr Horncastle
BB	Nags Head Cottage, Sotby, nr Horncastle (050 784 756)
BBE	The Penny Farthing Inn, Timberland, nr Metheringham (05267 359)

Gibraltar Point   122   3m S of Skegness
Large car-park and visitor centre at end of minor road south of
Skegness at TF556582. Then many tracks across the reserve and to
the hides.
Migrants; passage and winter waders and wildfowl; passage and
summer terns; winter Twite, Snow Bunting, Hen Harrier and
Short-eared Owl.

Chapel St. Leonards Pits   122   1–2m N of Chapel St. Leonards
View from minor road north of Chapel St. Leonards at TF558739
and ½m further north at TF555747.
Passage and winter wildfowl.

Anderby Creek   122   2½m N of Chapel St. Leonards
Car-park near the seafront 2½m E of A52 at TF553762, then paths
north or south.
Migrants.

Huttoft Bank   122   TF546776   *1m N of Anderby Creek*
Seawatching; migrants.

Well Vale   122   TF436735   *2m SW of Alford*
Woodland birds; summer warblers.

TIC	*Embassy Centre, Grand Parade, Skegness (0754 4821)
	*Dunes Entertainment Centre, Central Promenade, Mablethorpe (0507 472496)
YH	As previous entry.
R	Ship, Chapel St. Leonards

RFBBE The Vine, Vine Road, Skegness (0754 3018)
BBESC Gibraltar Point Bird Observatory, Skegness (0754 2677)

Saltfleetby & Theddlethorpe   113   3–6m NW of Mablethorpe
Park by A1031 at Salfleet Haven, TF456935, then track and coast path south. Also other car-parks further south, east of A1031 at TF467917 and TF477902.
Migrants; passage and winter waders; marshland birds.

Donna Nook & North Somercotes   113   N & E of North Somercotes
Car-park at Stonebridge at end of minor road 2½m N of A1031 from North Somercotes at TF423997. Then coast path NW to Somercotes Haven and Grainthorpe Haven and Marsh. Also coastal car-parks at south end of the reserve, 1–2m SE of North Somercotes, e.g. at TF444957.
Migrants; passage and winter waders and wildfowl; summer warblers and terns; winter Snow and Lapland Bunting, Twite, raptors and Short-eared Owl.

Covenham Reservoir   113   5m W of North Somercotes
Park by minor road along the north side 2m SW of A1031 at TF340963. Then perimeter path and hide.
Winter wildfowl and grebes; passage waders and terns; winter gull roost.

Tetney Haven & Northcoates Point   113   6m SE of Grimsby centre
Park at Tetney Lock 2m E of A1031 from Tetney at TA345025. Then track and path east, north and south of canal. Also car-park 2½m NE of A1031 at Horse Shoe Point, TA382017 and coast path north beside a disused airfield and south beside Grainthorpe Marsh.
Passage and winter waders and wildfowl; summer terns; migrants.

> *Legsby Wood & Linwood Warren* 112 *TF128875* *2m SE of Market Rasen*
> *Woodland birds including Nightjar and Long-eared Owl.*

> *Chapel Hill* 113 *TF130895* *1½m NE of Market Rasen*
> *Woodland birds.*

> *Bradley Wood* 113 *TA245058* *3m SW of Grimsby centre*
> *Woodland birds.*

> *Grimsby Docks* 113 *TA285110* *N extremity of Grimsby*
> *Winter seaduck and gulls; passage and winter waders.*

TIC	43 Alexandra Road, Cleethorpes, Humberside (0472 200220)
	Central Library, Town Hall Square, Grimsby (0472 240410)
YH	As previous entry.
RF	Greyhound, Marshchapel, nr Tetney
BB	The Grange, Grange Lane, Covenham, nr Louth (0507 86678)
BBE	Abbey Farm, North Ormsby, nr Louth (0472 840272)

North Killingholme Haven & Pits & Burkinshaw's Covert
113   3–4m NW of Immingham

View the Covert from minor road 1½m NW of A160 at TA164185. Continue north to the Haven and Pits at end of road at TA165200. Migrants; summer warblers; passage waders.

Barton Pits & Far Ings   112   1m N of Barton-upon-Humber

Car-park and information centre just east of A15 at the southern end of the Humber Bridge, TA026233. Then marked paths east or west to Far Ings and hides.

Passage and winter wildfowl and waders; reedbed species including Bearded Tit; migrants.

> ***Goxhill Haven***   *113*   *TA123255*   *2½m NE of Goxhill*
> *Passage and winter waders; migrants.*

> ***New Holland Pits***   *113*   *TA080243*   *3½m NE of Barton-upon-Humber*
> *Passage and winter waders and wildfowl.*

> ***Elsham Hall Country Park***   *112*   *TA027120*   *6m S of Barton-upon-Humber*
> *Woodland birds.*

TIC	Central Library, Town Hall Square, Grimsby (0472 240410)
	North Bank Viewing Area, Ferriby Road, Humber Bridge (0482 640852)
YH	As previous entry.
RF	Brocklesby Ox, Ulceby, nr Immingham
	Fox Inn, Ulceby, nr Immingham
BBE	Willow Tree Lodge, Pasture Road North, Barton-upon-Humber (0652 34416)

Winteringham Ings   112   4m W of Barton-upon-Humber

Park just south of A1077 1m W of South Ferriby on the west side of the drain at SE974208, then path west around the south side of the Ings.

Passage waders, terns and wildfowl.

Whitton   112   2½ m NW of Winteringham
Park by the church in Whitton at SE903245, then track SW and E.
Passage and winter waders; migrants.

Scotton Common   112   6m SW of Scunthorpe
Park by minor road 3m SW of Scotter (on A159) at SE840001. Then
tracks east through the woods.
Woodland birds including Nightjar and Long-eared Owl.

**Blacktoft Sands   112   9m NW of Scunthorpe (W of River
Trent)**
Car-park and information centre 1m E of Ousefleet at SE843232.
Then marked tracks to the hides.
Passage and winter waders and wildfowl; reedbed species in-
cluding Bearded Tit and Marsh Harrier.

Alkborough Cliff   112   SE878217   ¼m SW of Alkborough
Migrants.

Burton Wood   112   SE867165   1m SW of Burton upon
Stather
Woodland birds.

Broughton West Wood   112   SE954094   1m NW of
Broughton
Woodland birds.

Messingham Pits   112   SE914043   1m E of Messingham
Passage and winter wildfowl.

Winteringham Haven   112   SE935228   ¾m N of Winter-
ingham
Passage and winter waders.

TIC   Scunthorpe Library, Carlton Street, Scunthorpe, Humberside (0724 860161)
YH   As previous entry.
77 South Park, Lincoln (0522 22076)
RF   Dolphin, Althorpe, nr Scunthorpe
BBE   Olivers, Church Street, Scawby, nr Scunthorpe (0652
650446)

Norfolk

Welney Wildfowl Refuge   143   **6m SW of Downham Market**
Car-park, entrance, information centre, shop and hides by minor road 1½m NE of A1101 at TL546944.
Winter wildfowl and raptors; summer and passage waders.

TIC	District Library, Ely Place, Wisbech, Cambs (0945 583263)
YH	Ely 6th Form Centre, St. Audreys, Downham Road, Ely (0353 667423)
RF	Three Tuns, Welney
BBE	Greybridge House, Nordelph, nr Downham Market (03668 263)

Weeting Heath   143   **2m NW of Brandon**
Park by minor road between Weeting and Hockwold-cum-Wilton at TL763881. Permit from warden and views of heath from hides.
Heathland birds especially Stone Curlew.

Breckland Forest Walks   144   **1½m SE of Mundford**
Car-park by A134 SE of Mundford at TL814917. Then many tracks east and west through the woods.
Woodland and heathland birds.

Blackrabbit Warren & Madhouse Plantation   144   **3–5m S of Watton**
Park at Galley Hill 1¼m N of A1075 from Wretham at TL924927 and take the Peddars Way northward.
Woodland and heathland birds.

> ***East Wretham Heath***   *144*   *TL911880*   *4m NE of Thetford*
> *Woodland and heathland birds; wildfowl and passage waders.*

> ***Mickle Hill***   *144*   *TL876890*   *4m N of Thetford*
> *Woodland and heathland birds.*

Thompson Common   144   *TL935960   3½m SE of Witton*
Woodland birds and summer warblers.

Hockham Belt   144   *TL894855   3m NE of Thetford centre*
Woodland birds.

Snetterton Pits   144   *TL993916   3½m SW of*
Attleborough
Wildfowl; passage waders and terns.

TIC	White Hart Street, Thetford (0842 752599)
YH	Heath House, off Warren Close, Bury Road, Brandon, Suffolk (0842 812075)
RF	Old Railway Tavern, Eccles Road, nr East Harling
	Crown, Mundford
BBE	Church Cottage, Breckles, nr Attleborough (095 382 286)
	Thatched House, Pockthorpe Corner, Thompson, nr Attleborough (095 383 577)
	The Old Rectory, Weeting (0842 810265)
	Lynford Hall Forest Motel, Lynford, nr Thetford (0842 878351)
SC	Deacons Cottages, South Street, Hockwold, nr Thetford (0842 828023)
	Merton Estate Office, Merton, nr Walton (0953 883370)
	Fir Cottage, 26 St. Leonards Street, Mundford (0842 878389)

Breydon Water   134   **½m-3m W of Great Yarmouth centre**
Park at Great Yarmouth railway station, TG518082, or in the Asda Superstore car-park nearby.Then take footpath north along the shore to the hides. Also park near the church at Burgh Castle at TG476049 and take shore path north.
Passage and winter waders and wildfowl; winter Lapland and Snow Bunting and Twite; winter gulls.

Fritton Lake Country Park   134   **2m SW of Belton**
Car-park by A143 just east of Fritton at TG473004 then marked trails.
Woodland birds and wildfowl.

Strumpshaw Fen   134   **2m SE of Brundall**
Car-park by minor road beside the railway line 1½m SW of Strumpshaw village at TG343066. Then track east over railway line and paths around the reserve and to the hides.
Summer warblers including Cetti's warbler; Marsh Harrier and Bearded Tit; reedbed species.

Buckenham Marshes   134   *TG354045   4m SE of Brundall*
Winter Bean Geese.

Surlingham Marsh 134 TG305067 *5m E of Norwich centre*
Summer warblers including Cetti's; Bearded Tit; passage waders; wildfowl.

Rockland Broad 134 TG330050 *6m SE of Norwich centre*
Birds as Surlingham.

Great Yarmouth Cemetery 134 TG526083 *½m N of town centre*
Migrants.

TIC Town Hall, Hall Quay, Great Yarmouth (0493 846345)
The Guildhall, Gaol Hill, Norwich (0603 666071/761082)
YH 2 Sandown Road, Great Yarmouth (0493 843991)
112 Turner Road, Norwich (0603 627647)
RF Cock Tavern, Cantley, nr Reedham
Ferry Inn, Reedham
Albert Tavern, Southgates Road, Great Yarmouth
Bell, nr Fritton
New Inn, Rockland St.Mary
BB Pine Trees, Holly Lane, Blofield, nr Norwich (0603 713778)
Willow Cottage, Station Road, Reedham (0493 701388)
Rolling Acre, Wood's End, Bramerton, nr Norwich (05088 529)
BBE Old Hall Farm, South Walsham (060549 271)
SC (Reedham cottages) English Country Cottages, Claypit Lane, Fakenham (0328 51155)
(Upton cottage) Country Holidays, Spring Mill, Earby, Colne, Lancs (0282 445566)

Hickling Broad 134 **2½m NW of Martham**
Park by the church at Potter Heigham ¾m NE of A149 at TG419199. Then track north and footpath east and west along the south side of the broad. Also permits for reserve on north side, off Stubb Road, at TG427223.
Summer warblers usually including Savi's; Bearded Tit; woodland birds; passage waders.

Horsey Mere & Brayden Marshes 134 **3m N of Martham**
Car-park by B1159 ½m S of Horsey at TG456224. Then footpath along north shore of the mere and by the east side of the marsh. Birds as Hickling Broad plus winter wildfowl.

Winterton Dunes & Holmes 134 **N of Winterton**
Car-park at Winterton beach ½m E of B1159 at TG497196. Then footpath north on the inner side of the dunes.
Migrants; winter seaduck.

Waxham Marram Hills   134   4m NE of Stalham
Park by Waxham church just east of B1159 at TG442264. Then track east and path north and south on inner side of the dunes. Migrants.

Bacton Wood & Witton Heath   133   TG318313   2m E of North Walsham
Woodland and heathland birds.

Honing Common   133   TG337272   3m NW of Stalham
Summer warblers; woodland birds.

How Hill   134   TG373192   1½m NW of Ludham
Reedbed species; woodland birds; summer warblers; marshland birds.

TIC   As previous entry.
         *Station Road, Hoveton (0603 782281)
YH   As previous entry.
RF   Nelson Head, Horsey
         Sutton Staithe, Sutton
RFBBE Fishermans Return, Winterton (049 376 305)
BB   Street Farm, Horsey (0493 393212)
BBE   Magnolia Guest House, The Street, Catfield, nr Stalham (0692 80525)
SC   Crown House, Ludham (069 262 255)
         Min-y-don, St. Helen's Road, Walcott (0692 650798)
         (Marlow Cottage, Sea Palling) Norfolk Country Cousins, Point House, Ridlington, North Walsham (0692 650286)

Blickling Estate   133   2m NW of Aylsham
Park just off B1354 in Blickling at TG176286 and take tracks north or NW across the park.
Woodland birds including Wood Warbler and Hawfinch; wildfowl.

Lenwade Water   133   3m S of Reepham
Park and view from minor road just north of A1067 at TG105184. Summer warblers and wildfowl.

Sparham Pools   133   4m SW of Reepham
Park by minor road ½m NE of Lyng at TG074180 and take footpath east on the north side of the lake.
Summer warblers; woodland birds; wildfowl.

TIC   The Guildhall, Gaol Hill, Norwich (0603 666071/761082)
         *Red Lion House, 37 Market Place, Fakenham (0378 51981)

YH	1 Crerner's Drift, Sheringham (0263 823215)
	112 Turner Road, Norwich (0603 627647)
RF	Buckinghamshire Arms, Blickling, nr Aylsham
	Fox and Hounds, Lyng, nr Lenwade
	Mermaid, Elsing
BBSC	Rookery Farm, Church Street, Reepham (0603 871847)
BBE	Grey Gables Country House, Norwich Road, Cawston,
	nr Aylsham (0603 871259)
	Gillo's Guest House, Church Farm, Elsing (036 283 8236)
SC	Old Rectory Cottage, Salle Place, Salle, nr Reepham (0603
	870638)

Cley   133   7m W of Sheringham
Car-park and information centre (for permits) by A149 ½m east of
Cley village at TG054442. Then tracks to hides and around the
marshes. Also car-park at end of minor road north of Cley on the
west side of the marshes at TG048453.
Summer and passage waders and wildfowl; Bearded Tit, Avocet
and Bittern; many rarities.

Salthouse Heath   133   2½m N of Holt
Park by minor roads south of Salthouse e.g. NG072424 then many
tracks.
Summer Nightjar amd Nightingale; winter raptors; common
heathland birds.

Holt Lowes   133   1m SE of Holt
Park by minor road ¼m SE of A148, on the east side of Holt, at
NG086384. Then track south and footpath through woodland.
Woodland birds.

Salthouse Marshes & Kelling Quag   133   N of Salthouse
Car-park at end of beach road north of A149 ½m E of Salthouse at
NG083444. Then tracks west and east.
Passage waders; wildfowl; migrants; winter Shore Lark.

**Beacon Hill & The Roman Camp   133   2m SE of
Sheringham**
Car-park by minor road 1m south of West Runton at NG185414.
Then many paths east and west through the woods.
Woodland birds including Wood Warbler and Redstart; migrants.

Weybourne – Sheringham coast   133
Car-park at end of minor road north of Weybourne at NG111437.
Then coastal path east towards Sheringham.
Migrants; gulls and terns.

Walsey Hills & Snipes Marsh   133   NG063440   *1m W of Salthouse*
Migrants.

Kelling Heath   133   NG100418   *1½m SW of Weybourne*
Heathland birds.

Muckleburgh Hill   133   NG102432   *1m W of Weybourne*
Summer warblers; Nightingale; migrants.

The Hangs/Kelling Triangle   133   NG089410   *1½m N of Holt*
Woodland birds including Wood Warbler and Lesser Spotted Woodpecker.

Pretty Corner   133   NG155414   *1½m S of Sheringham*
Woodland birds.

West Runton   133   TG184432   *1½m E of Sheringham*
Migrants.

TIC	*Station Approach, Sheringham (0263 824329)
YH	1 Cremer's Drift, Sheringham (0263 823215)
RF	Bell, Wiveton, nr Cley
	Red Lion, Upper Sheringham
	George and Dragon Hotel, Cley
	Feathers, Holt
BBE	Flintstones, Wiveton (0263 740337)
BBESC	The Mill, Cley-next-the-Sea (0263 740209)
SC	(Cley cottages) The Berristead, Wilburton, Ely, Cambs (0353 740770)
	(Cley cottage) 47 Lyndale Avenue, London NW2 (081 431 2942)
	(Weybourne bungalow) 17 Ash Grove, Dunstable, Beds (0582 609827)
	(Cley cottages) Mill House, Little Braxted, Witham, Essex (0376 513008)
	(Hilltop House & Bean Cottage, Cley) English Country Cottages, Claypit Lane, Fakenham (0328 51155)

Blakeney Point   133   **3m NW of Blakeney**
Car-park at end of minor road 1m N of Cley at NG048453. Then long walk east to the point.
Large colonies of terns; migrants.

Blakeney Marshes   133   **1m NE of Blakeney**
Park by minor road ½m N of A149 on the north side of Blakeney village at NG029443. Then footpaths north around the marshes.
Passage and winter waders; migrants.

Morston Creek & Marshes   133   2m W of Blakeney
Park ¼m north of Morston at TG006443. Then Peddars Way
eastwards on south side of the creek towards Blakeney.
Passage waders; wildfowl; migrants.

Stiffkey & Warham Marshes   132   N & NW of Stiffkey
Car-park at end of minor road ½m N of A149, ½m W of Stiffkey, at
TF965439. Then Peddars Way east, or west beside the marshes and
to Warham pines.
Migrants; passage and winter waders and wildfowl.

Holkham Meals   132   2m NW of Wells
Car-park at end of minor road 1½m N of Wells at TF915455, then
tracks westwards. Also car-park at TF891447, 1½m W of Wells,
½m N of Holkham village.
Migrants including many rarities; winter geese; woodland birds.

> **Holkham Park**   132   TF893437   2m W of Wells
> Woodland birds including Hawfinch.

> **Wells Harbour**   132   TF923437   ½m NE of Wells
> Passage and winter waders and wildfowl.

TIC   *Staith Street, Wells-next-the-Sea (0328 710885)
YH   As previous entry.
           15 Avenue Road, Hunstanton (04853 2061)
RF   Kings Arms, Blakeney
           Crown Hotel, Wells
RFBBE Victoria Hotel, Holkham (0328 710469)
BB   Greengates, Stiffkey Road, Wells (0328 711040)
BBE   The Cobblers, Standard Road, Wells (0328 710155)
           Bramble Lodge, Morston Road, Blakeney (0263 740191)
           Ilex House, Bases Lane, Wells (0328 710556)
           Mill House Guest House, Northfield Lane, Wells (0328
           710739)
SC   (Blakeney cottage) 100 Patching Hall Lane, Chelmsford,
           Essex (0245 355210)
           The Lodge, Back Lane, Blakeney (0263 740477)
           52 High Street, Wells (0328 710337)
           (Blakeney house & cottage) 31 Bracondale, Norwich (0603
           624827)
           Armingland, Church Street, Stiffkey (032 875 581)

Titchwell   132   5m E of Hunstanton
Signed car-park just off A149 ½m west of the centre of Titchwell
village at TF750436. Then track north to hides and shoreline.
Summer Marsh Harrier, Bittern, Bearded Tit and usually Spoonbill; summer warblers; passage waders and terns; winter seaduck,
divers and grebes.

Holme 132 3m NE of Hunstanton
Car-park at end of minor road 1m N of A149 at TF697438. Then
Norfolk Coast Path east and west. Also track east for 1½m to
reserve car-park, hides etc.
Migrants; passage waders; winter Snow Bunting, seaduck, divers,
grebes and gulls; seawatching.

Thornham 132 4m E of Hunstanton
Park by minor road ½m N of A149, from west end of Thornham
village, at TF727438. Then footpath north and northwest.
Migrants; passage and winter waders; wildfowl; winter raptors
and Snow Bunting.

> *Norton Marshes* 132 *TF830445 2m N of Burnham
> Market*
> *Winter Lapland Bunting, Short-eared Owl and raptors.*

> *Barrow Common* 132 *TF790430 1½m SE of Brancaster*
> *Heathland birds; summer warblers; woodland birds.*

> *Brancaster Bay & Marshes* 132 *TF772453 1m N of
> Brancaster*
> *Migrants; passage waders; winter Snow Bunting, Lapland
> Bunting and Shore Lark; winter seaduck, divers and grebes.*

TIC	The Green, Hunstanton (04853 2610)
YH	As previous entry.
RF	Three Horseshoes, Titchwell
	Manor Hotel, Titchwell
	Lifeboat Inn, Thornham
RFSC	Jolly Sailors, Brancaster Staithe (0485 210314)
BBE	Briarfields, Main Street, Titchwell (0485 210742)
BBESC	St. Mary's House, Brancaster (0485 210774)
SC	Bay Tree Cottage, Thornham, nr Hunstanton (0485 26204)
	(The Saltings, Holme) English Country Cottages, Claypit Lane, Fakenham (0328 51155)

**Snettisham Coastal Park 132 2½m W of Snettisham
village**
Car-park at the end of the minor road west of Snettisham at
TF647335. Then tracks south by the gravel pits and to the hides,
and north toward Heacham.
Winter and passage waders and wildfowl; migrants; winter Snow
Bunting and Twite.

Roydon Common   132   4m NE of Kings Lynn
Park by track just south of minor road 2m west of Roydon at
TF680228 on the west side of the common.
Summer warblers, Nightjar and Nightingale; winter Hen Harrier
roost and occasional Great Grey Shrike.

Sandringham Country Park   132   7m NE of Kings Lynn
Car-park ¼m W of B1440, 1½m SE of Dersingham at TF689288.
Also 1m NE of A149 at TF683274. Then trails through woodland
and heathland.
Woodland and heathland birds including Redstart, Wood
Warbler, Crossbill and Nightjar.

Heacham   132   1m W of Heacham
Car-park at end of minor road west of Heacham at TF663368. Then
coastal path north and south.
Winter wildfowl, seaduck and gulls; passage waders; migrants.

> ***Ling Common*** *132   TF654237   3m NE of Kings Lynn*
> *Heathland and woodland birds.*

> ***Walton Common*** *132   TF737165   6m NW of Swaffham*
> *Summer warblers; woodland birds.*

> ***Admiralty Point*** *131   TF582247   5m NW of Kings Lynn*
> *Passage and winter waders and wildfowl.*

> ***Hunstanton Cliffs*** *132   TF675419   N side of Hunstanton*
> *Winter seaduck; seawatching.*

> ***Ringstead Downs*** *132   TF695402   1½m SE of*
> *Hunstanton*
> *Migrants; woodland birds.*

> ***Ken Hill Wood*** *132   TF675344   1m W of Snettisham*
> *Woodland birds.*

> ***Tottenhill Gravel Pits*** *132   TF635177   5m S of Kings*
> *Lynn*
> *Winter wildfowl.*

TIC The Old Gaol House, Saturday Market Place, Kings Lynn
(0553 763044)
YH As previous entry.
Thoresby College, College Lane, Kings Lynn (0553
772461)
H/B Courtyard Farm Bunkhouse, Ringstead (048525 369)

RF   Rose and Crown, Snettisham
Gin Trap Inn, Ringstead
King William IV, Sedgeford, nr Heacham
Three Horseshoes, Roydon
Red Cat Hotel, North Wootton, nr Kings Lynn

BBE   Shelbrooke Hotel, Cliff Terrace, Hunstanton (04853 2289)
St. Anne's Guest House, Neville Road, Heacham (0485 70021)
Snettisham Mill House, Station Road, Snettisham (0485 542180)

SC   Manor Farm, Heacham (0485 70567)
23 The Green, Hunstanton (0485 32448)

Northamptonshire

Salcey Forest   152   6m SE of Northampton
Car-park 1½m NE of Hartwell, ½m east of M1, at SP794517, then many paths through the forest.
Woodlandbirds including Nightingale, Woodcock and Grass-hopper Warbler.

Earls Barton Gravel Pits   152   6m E of Northampton
Park by minor road 2m S of Earls Barton 100yds south of the bridge over the River Nene, SP859619. Then footpath along the river and between the pits to the east.
Wildfowl; passage waders; summer warblers.

> *Clifford Hill Gravel Pits   152   SP800605   3m E of North-ampton centre*
> *Winter wildfowl; passage waders and terns.*

> *Billing Gravel Pits   152   SP830616   4½m E of North-ampton centre*
> *Winter wildfowl; passage waders; summer warblers.*

TIC	21 St. Giles Street, Northampton (0604 22677)
YH	Manor Farm, Vicarage Road, Bradwell, Milton Keynes (0908 310944)
RF	White Hart, Hackleton
	Old Cherry Tree, Great Houghton
BB	Quinton Green Farm, Quinton, nr Wootton (0604 862484)

Pitsford Reservoir   141 & 152   5m N of Northampton
Park and view from causeway which crosses the reservoir, 2½m east of the A508, at SP783703. Permits for north section and hides from the visitor centre in Holcot, east of the causeway at SP791698 or from warden, 84 Norton Road, Kingsthorpe.
Passage waders and terns; wildfowl; summer warblers and wood-land birds; passage migrants; winter gulls.

Ravensthorpe Reservoir   141   8m NW of Northampton
View from the causeway which crosses the reservoir at SP675711,
¾m NE of Ravensthorpe village. Also permit from Holcot, see
above.
Passage waders; winter wildfowl; summer warblers; woodland
birds.

Sulby & Welford Reservoirs   140 & 141   8m NE of Rugby
Park by minor road ¼m east of A50, just north of Welford, at
SP647808. Then footpath NE beside and between the reservoirs.
Wildfowl; summer warblers; woodland birds.

> *Stanford Reservoir   140   SP605805   5m NE of Rugby*
> *Wildfowl; passage waders and terns; summer warblers.*

> *Hollowell Reservoir   141   SP686730   10m NW of*
> *Northampton*
> *Winter wildfowl; passage waders and terns.*

> *Naseby Reservoir   141   SP670775   10m E of Rugby*
> *Wildfowl; woodland birds; passage waders and terns.*

TIC	As previous entry.
YH	Church Green, Badby, Daventry (0327 703883)
RF	Red Lion, Thornby
	Red Lion, East Haddon
	George, Brixworth
	Shoulder of Mutton, Welford
BBE	Wold Farm, Old, nr Pitsford (0604 781258)
	Woolleys Farm, Welford Road, Naseby (085 881 310)
SC	Estate Office, Althorp, nr Northampton (0604 42578)

**Daventry Reservoir & Country Park   152   1m N of
Daventry centre**
Car-parks by B4036 Daventry to Welton road e.g. SP576634, then
footpaths and nature trail.
Passage waders and terns; winter wildfowl.

Boddington Reservoir   151   8m SW of Daventry
View from minor road between Upper Boddington and Byfield,
SP496534. Also from track and footpath along east side to the dam
at the south end.
Wildfowl; passage waders and terns.

Badby Wood   152   3m S of Daventry
Park in Badby village just east of A361 at SP560587, then several
footpaths south to the wood and Badby Down.
Woodland birds including regular Redstart.

Drayton Reservoir *152 SP567647 2m N of Daventry*
Winter wildfowl.

Everdon Stubbs *152 SP605565 4m SE of Daventry*
Woodland birds.

High Wood *152 SP590547 5m SE of Daventry*
Woodland, scrub and meadow birds.

TIC Moot Hall, Market Square, Daventry (0327 300277)
YH As previous entry.
RF Old Plough, Braunston
Old Coach House, Ashby St. Ledgers
Carpenters Arms, Lower Boddington
Maltster's Arms, Badby
BBE Drayton Lodge, Daventry (0327 702449/76365)

St. James' Lake 152 ½m SW of Brackley centre
Park between the lakes by minor road to Hinton-in-the-Hedges
¼m west of A43 at SP582366.
Winter wildfowl; passage waders and terns; summer warblers.

Bucknell Wood 152 1½m NW of Silverstone
Car-park beside minor road to Abthorpe NW of Silverstone at
SP658448. Then many tracks through the woods.
Woodland birds including Lesser Spotted Woodpecker, and
occasional Wood Warbler, Redstart and Hobby.

Pentimore Woods 152 2m SW of Silverstone
Park by minor road 1½m S of A43 at SP668411, then tracks west
through the woods.
Woodland birds including Tree Pipit, occasional Nightjar and Firecrest.

Newbottle Spinney *151 SP516365 4m SE of Banbury*
Woodland birds.

TIC Banbury Museum, 8 Horsefair, Oxon (0295 259855)
YH As previous entry.
RF Bartholomew Arms, Blakesley
Bell, Brackley
Red Lion, Brackley
BBESC Walltree House Farm, Steane, nr Brackley (0295 811235)
SC Gingerbread Cottage, 16 Little London, Silverstone (0604
712059)

Thrapston Gravel Pits   141   6m E of Kettering
Park along minor road ¼m N of A604 ¼m W of its junction with A605 north at SP996788. Then footpaths west and north around the pits and by the River Nene.
Winter wildfowl and grebes; summer warblers, Common Tern and Little Ringed Plover; passage waders; migrants.

Barnwell Country Park   141   ½m S of Oundle
Car-park just west of the minor road south from Oundle centre to Barnwell at TL036874. Then many paths to gravel pits, river, meadows, reedbed and scrub.
Winter wildfowl; passage terns; summer warblers.

Ditchford Gravel Pits   153   1m W of Higham Ferrers
Park at end of minor road, ¾m west of A6 from Higham Ferrers centre, at SP953687. Then tracks west over the bridge over A45 and around the pits.
Wildfowl; passage waders and terns; winter gulls; passerine migrants.

Souther Wood   141   6m NE of Kettering
Park in Sudborough village just off the A6116 3m NW of Thrapston, SP973823. Take track to the NE on the other side of the major road through the woods.
Woodland birds including Nightingale.

> *Ringstead Gravel Pit   141   SP974750   3m SW of Thrapston*
> *Wildfowl; passage waders.*

> *Irchester Country Park   152   SP915660   1m NW of Irchester*
> *Woodland birds.*

> *Ashton Woods   142   TL090875   3½m SE of Oundle*
> *Woodland birds.*

TIC   Market Place, Oundle, Peterborough (0832 274333)
YH   As previous entry.
RF   Old Friar, Twywell
Vane Arms, Sudborough
Montagu Arms, Barnwell, nr Oundle
Bell, Little Addington, nr Irthlingborough
BBE   Dairy Farm, Cranford St. Andrew, nr Kettering (053 678 273)
Pear Tree Farm, Aldwincle, nr Thrapston (08015 614)

Geddington Chase   141   4m NE of Kettering
Park in Geddington village just east of A43 at SP898836 and take
bridleway and tracks north through the woods.
Woodland birds.

Brampton & Stoke Woods   141   2m N of Desborough
Park by minor road joining A6 and B669 at SP798849 and take
footpath north along the west side of the wood.
Woodland birds.

> *Wicksteed Park   141   SP880770   1½m SE of Kettering
> centre*
> *Wildfowl and woodland birds.*

> *Thorpe Malsor Reservoir   141   SP825794   3m W of
> Kettering*
> *Winter wildfowl.*

> *Cransley Reservoir   141   SP830782   3m W of Kettering*
> *Winter wildfowl.*

TIC   The Coach House, Sheep Street, Kettering (0536 410266)
YH   As previous entry.
RF   Overstone Arms, Pytchley
          Red Lion Hotel, Rothwell
          Fox, Wilbarston, nr Corby
BB   Grange Farm, Brampton Ash, nr Desborough (085 885
          215)

Northumberland

Seaton Sluice & Burn   88   **4m S of Blyth**
Park at the Kings Arms at the north end of Seaton Sluice,
NZ337767. Then footpath over bridge north to the old coastguard
lookout. Also footpath south immediately on the left by A193
north over the burn, NZ335767, beside the burn and through
woods to Holywell Dene.
Seawatching; passage waders; passerine migrants.

Holywell Pond & Dene   88   **2m SW of Seaton Sluice**
Park ¼ m NE of A192 at Holywell estate, NZ320746. Then footpath
north to pond and east to Holywell Dene.
Passage waders; winter wildfowl; passerine migrants.

Plessey Woods Country Park   88   **5m W of Blyth**
Car-park by A1068 1m N of its junction with A192 at NZ240800.
Then marked paths and nature trails south.
Woodland and river birds including Redstart and Dipper.

> ***Shankhouse Pool*** *88* *NZ276788* *3m SW of Blyth*
> *Passage waders.*

> ***Prestwick Carr*** *88* *NZ192737* *2m NE of Ponteland*
> *Summer warblers; waders.*

> ***Blyth Estuary*** *81* *NZ285824* *E of A189 over River Blyth*
> *Passage and winter waders.*

> ***Blyth Cemetery*** *88* *NZ319792* *2m S of Blyth centre*
> *Passerine migrants.*

TIC   Park Road, Whitley Bay (091 252 4494)
YH   107 Jesmond Road, Newcastle-upon-Tyne (091 281 2570)
RF   Waterford Arms, Seaton Sluice
            Ridley Arms, Stannington
            Kings Arms, Seaton Sluice

BBE	Bay Hotel, Front Street, Cullercoats, nr Whitley Bay (091 252 3150)
SC	Hiddlestone Cottage, Smallburn, nr Ponteland (0661 22861)

Derwent Reservoir & Pow Hill Country Park   87   5m W of Consett

Car-parks are by the dam at the eastern end just north of B6278 at Derwent Bridge, NZ033514; by minor road along the northwest shore e.g. at Millshield NZ014533; and on the south side by B6306 at Pow Hill, NZ010516.
Winter wildfowl and gull roost; passage waders; woodland birds.

Whittle Dene Reservoirs   87   4m NW of Prudhoe

View from B6318 and B6309 around their junction at NZ065683, 1m W of Harlow Hill.
Passage waders; winter wildfowl.

> ***Slaley Forest***   *87   NY980545   2m NW of Derwent Reservoir*
> *Woodland birds including Crossbill and Goshawk.*

> ***Coalgate Burn***   *87   NZ054486   4m SW of Consett*
> *Woodland and river birds including Pied Flycatcher, Redstart and Dipper.*

TIC	The Manor Office, Hallgate, Hexham (0434 605225)
	*Vicar's Pele, Market Place, Corbridge (0434 632815)
YH	Low House, Edmundbyers, Consett, Co. Durham (0207 55651)
	Acomb, Hexham (0434 602864)
RF	Manor House, Carterway Heads, nr Consett
	Highlander, Ovington, nr Prudhoe
	Bridge End Inn, Ovingham, nr Prudhoe
BBE	Rye Hill Farm, Slaley, nr Hexham (0434 73259)
	Morningside, Riding Mill, nr Hexham (043482 350)
SC	Lawn House, Slaley (043473 388)
	Stable Cottage, Newbiggin House, Blanchland, nr Consett (043475 210)

River Allen Valley   87 or 86   10m W of Hexham

Car-park by minor road ½m S of A69, over River Tyne and under railway line, at NY797642. Then footpaths south through woods and by river. Also footpaths east from minor road 1½m south at NY788624.
Woodland and river birds.

Grindon Lough   87 or 86   3m NW of Haydon Bridge
View from minor road, 2m N of A69, 1½m W of Grindon Hill, at NY806675.
Winter wildfowl.

> ***Nilston Rigg*** *87 or 86   NY826610   2½m SW of Haydon Bridge*
> *Winter wildfowl.*

> ***Irthing Gorge*** *86   NY636678   1m N of Gilsland*
> *River and woodland birds.*

TIC	*Military Road, Bardon Mill, Once Brewed (0434 344396)
	The Manor Office, Hallgate, Hexham (0434 605225)
YH	Acomb, Hexham (0434 602864)
	Military Road, Bardon Mill, Once Brewed (04984 360)
RF	Miners Arms, Acomb, nr Hexham
	Carts Bog Inn, Langley, nr Haydon Bridge
BB	Greenwood House, Whittis Road, Haydon Bridge (043484 220)
BBE	Anchor Hotel, John Martin Street, Haydon Bridge (043484 227)
SC	Birkshaw Farmhouse, Bardon Mill, nr Haydon Bridge (04984 394)
	Ashcroft Cottage, Bardon Mill (04984 409)
	Pagecroft Cottage, Haydon Bridge (043484 461/200)

Colt Crag Reservoir   87   10m N of Hexham
View from A68 by west shore at NY925781 and from track along the southern shore eastwards from A68 ½m south. Also from minor road across eastern end of reservoir 1m N of Little Swinburn.
Passage and winter wildfowl; passage waders; woodland birds.

Sweethope Loughs   80   3m NE of Colt Crag Reservoir
View from minor road along the north shore 2m E of A68 at NY935825 and take footpath through woods around the south side.
Winter wildfowl.

> ***Bavington Carr*** *87   NY992777   4m E of Colt Crag Reservoir*
> *Summer warblers and woodland birds.*

> ***Hallington Reservoirs*** *87   NY975771   2½m SE of Colt Crag Reservoir*
> *Winter wildfowl; passage waders.*

TIC	As previous entry.
	*Main Street, Bellingham (0434 220616)

YH	Woodburn Road, Bellingham, Hexham (0660 20313)
RF	Cheviot, Bellingham
BBE	The Old Vicarage, Kirkwhelpington (0830 40319)
	Warksburn House, Wark, nr Hexham (043472 389)
SC	Errington House, Errington, nr Hexham (043472 389)
	Little Walwick, Humshaugh, nr Hexham (043481 247)

Harbottle Crags   80   10m W of Rothbury
Car-park by minor road along the upper Coquet Valley, ¼m NW of Harbottle, NT927047. Then footpath SW up on to Harbottle Hills and Lough.
Upland birds including Red and Black Grouse, Merlin and Ring Ousel; winter wildfowl.

Holystone Burn & The Oaks   81 & 80   2½m S of Harbottle
Car-park ½m west of Holystone, 1m S of Sharperton, at NT952026. Then tracks and footpaths west through forestry and by the burn to The Oaks.
Woodland and river birds including Pied Flycatcher, Redstart and Dipper.

Catcleugh Reservoir   80   13m SE of Jedburgh
View from A68 along north side, NT740035.
Winter wildfowl; Goshawk.

Bakethin Reservoir   80   NW end of Kielder Water
Car-park at SE end ¼m N of Minor road, 2m S from Kielder, NY644912. Also view from minor road along W shore.
Winter wildfowl; woodland birds.

TIC	Tower Knowe, Kielder Water (0434 240398)
YH	7 Otterburn Green, Byrness (0830 20222)
RF	Cross Keys, Thropton, nr Rothbury
	Salmon, Holystone, nr Harbottle
RFBBE	Redesdale Arms, Rochester (0830 20668)
SC	Alwinton Farm, Harbottle (0669 50231)
	Low Alwinton, Harbottle (0669 50224)
	Charity Hall Cottage, Sharperton, nr Harbottle (0669 30208)

Simonside Hills   81   2½m SW of Rothbury
Car-park by minor road 2m NW of B6342 at NZ036997. Then tracks southwest up onto the hills.
Woodland and moorland birds; migrants.

Rothley Lake   81   4½m NW of Hartburn
Park by minor road ¼m N of B6342, ¼m W of Rothley crossroads, at NZ039900. Then paths through woods beside the lake.
Wildfowl; woodland birds.

Harwood Forest   81   8m SW of Rothbury
Park by minor road 1m W of B6342, 3m W of Rothley, at NZ003897.
Then tracks and footpaths north through forest to Redpath and
Fallowlees.
Woodland birds including Crossbill, Goshawk and Black Grouse.

Bolam Lake Country Park   81   3m S of Hartburn
Car-park and visitor centre 3m N of A696 from Belsay at NZ084821.
Then track through woods and around lake.
Wildfowl; woodland birds including Nuthatch.

Hartburn Lake   81   1½ m W of Hartburn
View from B6343 near the western end at NZ066866.
Winter wildfowl.

> *Rayburn Lake   81   NZ110927   5m N of Hartburn*
> *Passage waders; winter wildfowl.*

> *Fontburn Reservoir   81   NZ045935   5m NW of Hartburn*
> *Winter wildfowl.*

> *Cragside   81   NZ075023   1m E of Rothbury*
> *Woodland birds; wildfowl.*

> *Wallington Hall Woods   81   NZ025843   4m SW of
> Hartburn*
> *Woodland birds including Hawfinch.*

TIC   *National Park Information Centre, Church Street, Roth-
bury (0669 20887)
The Shambles, Alnwick (0665 510665)
YH   As previous entry.
RF   Queens Head, Rothbury
BBE   Whitton Farmhouse Hotel, Whitton, nr Rothbury (0669
20811)
Orchard Guest House, High Street, Rothbury (0669
20684)
SC   The Pele Tower, Whitton (0669 20410)
Whitton Grange, Rothbury (0669 20929)

Cresswell Pond   81   5m N of Newbiggin-by-Sea
Car-park and visitor centre at Blakemoor Farm ¾m N of Cresswell
at NZ284941. Also view from minor road along east side and footpath west and south opposite car-park at NZ284946.
Passage waders and terns; winter wildfowl; migrants.

Druridge Pools & Bay   81   3m N of Cresswell
Car-park by minor road at Druridge, NZ277961. Then track north
to pond.
Wildfowl; waders; migrants; winter seaduck and divers.

Newbiggin Point & Dunes   81   NE of Newbiggin centre
Park as near to the point as possible, NZ316882. Then footpath to
Newbiggin Point and north to Beacon Point and the dunes.
Seawatching; migrants; winter seaduck and divers.

> *Wansbeck Estuary   81   NZ304856   2m S of Newbiggin*
> *Passage and winter waders, wildfowl and gulls.*

> *Wansbeck Riverside Park   81   NZ258864   3m SW of*
> *Newbiggin*
> *Woodland birds; waders.*

> *Coney Garth Pond   81   NZ244873   1½m E of Pegswood*
> *Passage waders; winter wildfowl.*

> *Queen Elizabeth II Country Park   81   NZ285890   2m*
> *NW of Newbiggin*
> *Winter wildfowl.*

> *Warkworth Lane Pond   81   NZ275929   1m NW of*
> *Ellington*
> *Migrants; passage waders.*

TIC   The Chantry, Bridge Street, Morpeth (0670 510348)
       *Council Sub Offices, Amble (0665 712313)
YH   Rock Hall, Rock, Alnwick (066579 281)
RF   Forge, Ulgham, nr Ashington
RFBBE Old Ship Hotel, Front Street, Newbiggin

Hadstone Lake   81   3m S of Amble-by-the-Sea
Park by minor road which runs along the sea front 1m E of Hadston
at NU274000.
Passage waders; winter wildfowl; seaduck; migrants.

Low Hauxley   81   2m SE of Amble
Park by minor road just E of High Hauxley, NU280029, and take
track south to lake, hides and dunes.
Migrants; summer and passage terns; passage waders; winter
wildfowl and gulls.

Warkworth Harbour   81   ½m NW of Amble
Car-park just east of A1068 with views across the harbour on NW
side of Amble at NU263047. Also view from the main road along-
side the estuary SE of Warkworth. On the north side park at end
of minor road immediately east of the main road, north of River
Coquet at NU254063. Then coastal path south.
Passage and winter waders and wildfowl; winter seaduck, divers
Snow Bunting and Twite; migrants.

Coquet Island   81   1½m E of Amble
Boat trips around the island in spring and summer by Gordon
Easton tel: 0665 710384/712460.
Breeding terns including Roseate Tern, Puffins and Eider.

Alnmouth   81   4m SE of Alnwick
On the north side a footpath runs south beside the estuary
immediately east over the river. Also from car-park ¼m E of the
end of B1338, at NU252107, a footpath south crosses the golfcourse
and goes to the shore. Also car-park on the south side ½m E of
A1068 at NU246095, then footpaths north and south.
Passage and winter waders and wildfowl; winter seaduck, divers
and grebes; migrants.

> *Birling Carrs   81   NU254077   2½m S of Alnmouth*
> *Seawatching.*

> *Chevington Burn & Pond   81   NZ273983   4½m S of*
> *Amble*
> *Passage waders; migrants.*

TIC	As previous entry.
YH	As previous entry.
RF	Sun, Warkworth, nr Amble
BB	North Cottage, Birling, nr Amble (0665 711263)
BBE	Granary Hotel, Links Road, Amble (0665 710872)
	Westlea Guest House, 29 Riverside Road, Alnmouth (0665 830730)
	Bilton Barns, Alnmouth (0665 830427)
SC	20 South Avenue, Amble (0665 710303/710441)
	Green Batt Cottage, The Pinfold, Alnwick (0665 602429)
	Marine House Cottage, 1 Marine Road, Alnmouth (0665 830349)

Boulmer to Howick Haven   81   2m E of Longhoughton
Car-park at end of minor road 1½m NE of B1339 from Longhoughton at NU263156. Then coastal path north to Howick Haven
and south to Boulmer.
Migrants; passage waders; winter seaduck and divers;
seawatching.

**Arnold Reserve, Craster & Cullernose Point   81   S of
Craster**
Car-park on west side of village at NU256197. Then footpaths
south to woodland and scrub and along the cliffs to Cullernose
Point.
Migrants; summer seabirds.

TIC	*Car Park, Seafield Road, Seahouses (0665 720884)
	The Shambles, Alnwick (0665 510665)
YH	As previous entry.
RF	Jolly Fishermen, Craster
BBE	Cottage Inn, Dunston Village, Craster (066576 658)
SC	Farm Cottage, Red Steads, Howick, Alnwick (0665 77259)
	Proctors Stead, Craster, Alnwick (066576 613)

Castle Point   75   2m SE of Embleton

Park at end of minor road 1m E of B1339 at NU245224. Then coastal path east to the point.

Seawatching; summer seabird colonies; migrants; winter seaduck and divers.

Low Newton Pool & Newton Point   75   1½m NE of Embleton

Car-park on the north side of Low Newton 1½m E of B1339 at NU239247. Then walk south through the village and along footpath to reserve and hides, and NE along the shore to Newton Point.

Passage waders; winter wildfowl; migrants.

Beadnell Bay & Snook Point   75   2m S of Beadnell

Car-park by Newton Links House ¾m N of High Newton at NU235260. Then footpath north or south.

Passage and winter waders and gulls; winter seaduck and divers; passage and summer terns.

Seahouses & Annstead Burn   75   0–1m SE of Seahouses

Park near Seahouses Harbour, NU220322, and take coast path southeast to the Snook and Annstead Burn mouth.

Migrants; seawatching; passage waders; winter northern gulls.

Farne Islands   75   4m N of Seahouses

Information Centre: 16 Main Street, Seahouses Tel: 0665 720424

Daily boat trips from Seahouses harbour (Apr – end Sept).

Summer seabird colonies: 14 species including 20,000 pairs of Puffin, 14,000 pairs of Guillemot, 7,500 pairs of terns including 20 Roseate Tern and a Lesser Crested Tern in recent years, 1,500 pairs of Eider and 1,300 pairs of Shag.

> *Little Rock*   75   NU237286   *1m SE of Beadnell*
> *Migrants; seawatching.*

> *Monk's House Pool*   75   NU204336   *2m NW of Seahouses*
> *Passage waders.*

Scrog Hill & Castle Point 75 NU253215 *2m SE of Embleton*
Migrants; winter seaduck and divers.

TIC	As previous entry.
YH	30 Cheviot Street, Wooler (0668 81365)
RF	The Ship, Low Newton
RFBBE	Olde Ship Hotel, Seahouses (0665 720200)
BBSC	Newton Hall, Newton-by-the-Sea (0665 76239)
BBE	Beadnell Towers Hotel, Beadnell (0665 721211)
	St. Aidans Hotel, Seahouses (0665 720211)
SC	Keyholes, Newton-by-the-Sea, Alnwick (066576 221)
	31 St. Aidans, Seahouses (0661 843166)
	(Coastguard Cottage, Low Newton) National Trust, 18–20 Glendale Road, Wooler (0668 81611)

Bamburgh Castle & Harkess (Stag) Rocks   75   0.5–1m E & N of Bamburgh
Car-park by B1340 ¼m E of Bamburgh centre, NU183349. Then footpaths to the Castle Woods, south to the Dunes and north to Harkess Rocks.
Migrants; summer terns and auks; winter seaduck and divers.

Budle Point & Bay   75   2m NW of Bamburgh
Park in Budle by B1342, NU156351, and take footpath NE to Heather Cottages and Budle Point for views of the bay.
Passage and winter waders and wildfowl; summer terns; migrants.

Ross Links & Point   75   4m NW of Bamburgh
Park in Ross 2½m NE of A1 at NU134371. Then footpath east to the dunes and shore and north to the point.
Winter seaduck and divers; passage waders; summer terns; winter Snow Bunting and Twite.

Holy Island   75   7m NW of Bamburgh
Restricted tidal crossing.
Migrants – whole island. Passage and winter waders and wildfowl – The Lough and Sands. Winter seaduck, divers and gulls – The Harbour. Seawatching – Emmanuel Head.

Beal Point & South Low   75   1m NE of Beal
From minor road crossing to Holy Island at western end, NU080427, take coast path north.
Passage and winter waders and wildfowl.

Warren Burn 75 NU147337 *½m S of Warren Mill*
Migrants.

TIC   Belford Craft Gallery, 2/3 Market Place, Belford (06683 888)
YH   As previous entry.
RF   Victoria Hotel, Bamburgh
RFBBE   Lindisfarne Hotel, Holy Island (0289 89273)
            Crown & Anchor, Holy Island (0289 89215)
BB   Farne House, Holy Island (0289 89247)
            Manor House, Fenwick (0289 81381)
BBESC   Greenhill Farm, Bamburgh (06684 265)
SC   Cuddies Cottage, Fiddlers Green, Holy Island (0661 852345)
            White House, Fenkle Street, Holy Island (0289 306136)
            The Cottage, Radcliffe House, Bamburgh (043471 2073)
            Old School House, Church Street, Bamburgh (091 413 2135)
            Old Coach House, Radcliffe Road, Bamburgh (091 268 0869)

Berwick Harbour   75   mouth of the Tweed, S side
Car-park at Sandstell Point, NU006521, overlooks the harbour.
Winter seaduck, divers and northern gulls; passage and winter wildfowl.

Berwick Pier – Highfields   75   mouth of the Tweed, N side & northwards.
Car-park ½m E of Berwick centre near the coastguard station, NU006528. Then walk to end of pier southeast and north along coast path to golf course and Needles Eye.
Passage waders; winter seaduck, divers and gulls; migrants.

Cocklawburn Dunes   75   4m SE of Berwick
Park at end of minor road 1½m SE of Scremerston, east of A1 at NU032482. Then track and paths south to pool and dunes.
Passage and winter waders; migrants.

TIC   Castlegate Car Park, Berwick-upon-Tweed (0289 330733)
YH   As previous entry.
            Kirk Yetholm, Kelso, Roxburghshire (057382 631)
RF   Meadow House, Berwick
BB   The Steading, Low Cocklaw, nr Berwick (0289 86214)
BBE   The Old Vicarage, 24 Church Road, Tweedmouth, Berwick (0289 306909)
SC   Red House, Borwell Farm, Scremerston, nr Berwick (0289 308289)

College Valley & The North Cheviots　　74　　7m SW of Wooler

Park in Hethpool, 2m S of Westnewton, off B6351, at NT895285. Then track south by the burn and east toward Harelaw Cairn. River, woodland and upland birds including Dipper, Pied Flycatcher, Redstart, Ring Ousel, Dunlin, Golden Plover and Merlin.

Linhope & Comb Fell　　80 & 81　　10m S of Wooler

Park in Linhope at end of minor road 7m W of A697 at NT964163. Then paths west and north to the high hills. Upland birds.

TIC	*Bus Station Car Park, High Street, Wooler (0668 81602)
YH	30 Cheviot Street, Wooler (0668 81365)
RFBBE	Ryecroft Hotel, Wooler (0668 81459/81233)
BB	Earle Hill Head Farm, nr Wooler (0668 81243)
SC	Rose Cottage, High Humbleton, nr Wooler (0372 64284)
	Bewick Folly, Old Bewick, nr Wooler (06687 244)
	Kimmerston Farm, Wooler (06686 283)

Nottinghamshire

Attenborough Gravel Pits   **129**   **5m SW of Nottingham centre**
Car-park ¼m SE of Attenborough railway station, ¾m SE of A6005 down Attenborough Lane, at SK522343. Then paths around pits and to the hides.
Wildfowl; passage waders and terns; summer warblers and Common Tern; reedbed species.

Martin's Pond   **129**   **3m W of Nottingham centre**
Park along Russel Avenue, ¼m N of A609 on north side of Wollaton, at SK530403. Then footpath west to pond.
Summer warblers; wildfowl; passage waders.

> *Wollaton Park*   *129*   *SK528387*   *3m SW of Nottingham centre*
> *Wildfowl; woodland birds.*

TIC	14/16 Wheeler Gate, Nottingham (0602 470661)
	County Hall, Loughborough Road, West Bridgford, Nottingham (0602 823558)
YH	Shining Cliff, c/o 24 Bank View Road, Nether Heage (077385 3068)
RF	Boat and Horses, Attenborough, nr Beeston
BBE	Manor Hotel, Nottingham Road, Toton, Beeston (0602 733487)

Bestwood Country Park   **129**   **2½m SE of Hucknall**
Entrance ¾m W of A60 1½m N of B6004 at SK570463. Then many marked trails north through the woods.
Woodland birds and summer warblers.

Moorgreen Reservoir   **129**   **2m NE of Eastwood**
View from dam on B600, 1m NW of Moorgreen at SK482486, and take track along east side of reservoir through the woods.
Winter wildfowl; summer warblers; woodland bids; passage terns and gulls.

Brinsley Pits 129 & 120 SK448500 1½m NW of Brinsley
Winter wildfowl; passage waders and terns.

Oldmoor Wood 129 SK497418 4m NW of Nottingham centre
Woodland birds.

Sellers Wood 129 SK523454 2½m SW of Hucknall
Woodland birds; summer warblers.

TIC   As previous entry.
YH   As previous entry.
RF   Durham Ox, Brinsley, nr Eastwood
BB   Sun Inn Hotel, Market Place, Eastwood (0773 712940)
SC   Top House Farm, Mansfield Road, Arnold (0602 268330)

Radcliffe Gravel Pits **129** **1m NW of Radcliffe-on-Trent**
Park in Stoke Bardolph, 1½m S of A612 at SK647420. Then footpath south beside River Trent and around the pits.
Winter wildfowl; passage waders and terns.

Gunthorpe Pits **129** **3m NE of Radcliffe-on-Trent**
Park in Gunthorpe by A6097, 2m S of Lowdham at SK680437.
Then track and footpath west by River Trent and around the pits.
Or park in Bulcote ¼m S of A612 at SK658446 and tracks SE.
Wildfowl; summer warblers; passage terns and waders.

Hoveringham Pits **129** **5m NE of Radcliffe**
Park by minor road ½m SE of Hoveringham at SK704464. Then footpath NE beside the river and the pits.
Wildfowl; grebes; passage waders, terns and gulls; summer warblers.

Colwick Country Park 129 SK607395 2m W of Radcliffe
Winter wildfowl and gulls.

Holme Pierrepoint Country Park 129 SK610388 ½m S of Colwick Country Park
Winter wildfowl; passage terns and gulls.

TIC   As previous entry.
YH   As previous entry.
RF   Marquis of Granby, Hoveringham
        Black Horse, Caythorpe, nr Gunthorpe

BBE Springfield Hotel, Old Epperstone Road, Lowdham, nr Nottingham (0602 663387)

SC Eastwood Farm, Hagg Lane, Epperstone, nr Nottingham (0602 663018)
Criftin Farm, Epperstone, nr Nottingham (0602 652039)

Nomanshill Wood   120   2m NW of Ravenshead
Car-park by minor road ¼m N of B6020 at SK541558. Then track and footpaths north.
Woodland birds.

Blidworth Lodge   120   2m SE of Ravenshead
Car-park by minor road on west side of woods just north of the lodge at SK584534. Then take tracks east.
Woodland birds.

> *Oxton Bogs   120   SK615515   4m SE of Ravenshead*
> *Summer warblers; woodland birds.*

> *Rainworth Lake   120   SK585583   ½m SW of Rainworth*
> *Wildfowl; woodland birds.*

TIC Sherwood Forest Visitor Centre, Edwinstowe, nr Mansfield (0623 824490)

YH Shining Cliff, c/o 24 Bank View Road, Nether Heage (077385 3068)

RF Bird in Hand, Blidworth
Fox and Hounds, Lower Blidworth

BBE Willow Tree Guest House, 3 Mansfield Road, Papplewick, Hucknall (0602 632642)
18 Lea Road, Ravenshead (0623 793253)

SC Orchard Cottage, 53 Main Street, Papplewick (0636 813089)

Besthorpe & Girton Pits   121   8m N of Newark-on-Trent
Park in Besthorpe just W of A1133, 2m N of Collingham at SK825647 or in Girton ½m W of A1133 at SK820666. Then tracks and footpaths north and west from both sites around the pits.
Winter wildfowl; passage waders, terns and gulls; summer warblers; migrants.

Cottam   121   6m S of Gainsborough
Park in Cottam 4m N of A57 on the western side of the River Trent at SK819798. Then track SE between reservoirs and by the river and pits to the south.
Winter wildfowl; passage waders, terns and gulls.

Littleborough   121   2m N of Cottam
Park at east end of minor road in Littleborough, SK825825. Then tracks N and S beside the river and by the pits and Out Ings. Winter wildfowl; passage waders and terns; migrants.

Robin Hood Way & Southwell Trail   120   2m NW of Southwell
Car-park by minor road, 1m S of A617 from Kirklington, at SK676566. Then footpath along the disused railway west or east. Woodland birds and summer warblers.

> *Dunham Pits   121   SK817737   5m SW of Saxilby*
> *Winter wildfowl; passage waders.*

> *Winthorpe Lake   121   SK804577   2½m N of Newark centre*
> *Winter wildfowl; passage waders.*

> *South Muskham   121   SK790565   2m N of Newark centre*
> *Winter wildfowl.*

TIC	The Ossington, Beast Market Hill, Castlegate, Newark (0636 78962)
YH	77 South Park, Lincoln (0522 22076)
RF	Butchers Arms, Laneham, nr Cottam
	Muskham Ferry, North Muskham, nr Newark
	Wagon and Horses, Halam, nr Southwell
BBE	The Old Vicarage, Langford, nr Newark (0636 705031)
	Upton Fields House, Upton Fields, nr Southwell (0636 812303)
	Crown Cottage, High Street, East Markham, nr Retford (0777 870870)
	Hall House Farm, Church Lane, South Scarle, nr Newark (0636 892514)
	Old Vicarage, South Scarle (0636 892409)
SC	Averham Park Farm, Averham, nr Newark (0623 863676)

Lound Pits   120   4m N of East Retford
Park in Lound 3m E of A638 at SK693860. Then track (Chain Bridge Lane) east beside the pits. Winter wildfowl; passage waders and terns; migrants.

Sutton Pits   120   2½m NW of East Retford
Park by minor road ½m NE of Sutton village, 2m NE of A638 at SK685849. Then track south between the pits and to the River Idle. Wildfowl; passage waders and terns; summer warblers; migrants.

Torworth (Daneshill) Pits   120   5m NW of East Retford
Park by minor road ¾m E of Torworth (on A638) at SK666866. Then tracks north and south.

Summer warblers and Little Ringed Plover; woodland birds; winter wildfowl; passage waders and terns.

>*Treswell Wood*   120   *SK758797   4m E of East Retford*
>*Woodland birds; summer warblers.*

>*Eaton & Gamston Woods*   120   *SK726773   3m SE of East Retford*
>*Woodland birds and summer warblers.*

TIC	Amcott House Annexe, 40 Grove Street, Retford (0777 860780)
YH	77 South Park, Lincoln (0522 22076)
RF	Boat, Hayton
	Angel, Blyth
BB	Church Farm, Clarborough, nr Retford (0777 702768)
	White Horse Restaurant, Barnby Moor, Retford (0777 705986)
BBE	Priory Farm Guest House, Blyth (0909 76768)

Clumber Park   120   4m SE of Worksop
Car-park and information centre on northern side of Clumber Lake 2m E of B6005 (B6034 on O S Map 120) at SK624744. Then various described walks through the park and beside the lake.
Wildfowl; woodland birds including Redstart and Hawfinch.

Sherwood Forest Country Park & Budby South Forest   120 1–2m N of Edwinstowe
Car-parks by B6034 ¼m and ½m N of A6075 from Edwinstowe, e.g. SK627676. Then footpaths and tracks NW through the woods.
Woodland birds including Hawfinch, Redstart and raptors.

>*Rufford Country Park*   120   *SK646656   2m S of New Ollerton*
>*Wildfowl and woodland birds.*

>*Kirton Wood*   120   *SK708685   3m NE of New Ollerton*
>*Woodland birds and summer warblers.*

>*Manor Hills Wood*   120   *SK595757   2m S of Worksop*
>*Woodland birds.*

>*Great Lake*   120   *SK592723   4m S of Worksop*
>*Wildfowl.*

>*Thoresby Lake*   120   *SK630705   3m N of Edwinstowe*
>*Wildfowl.*

Langold Country Park   120   SK580863   1m SW of
Langold
Wildfowl and woodland birds.

Wellow Park   120   SK685675   2m E of New Ollerton
Woodland birds and summer warblers.

TIC	As previous entry.
	Sherwood Heath, Ollerton Roundabout, Ollerton (0623 824545)
YH	77 South Park, Lincoln (0522 22076)
	40 Bank Road, Matlock, Derbyshire (0629 582983)
RF	Harrow, Boughton
	Jug and Glass, Nether Langwith, nr Warsop
BB	Norton Grange Farm, Norton Cuckney, nr Mansfield (0623 842666)
	Old Orchard Cottage, Holbeck, nr Worksop (0909 720659)
BBE	3 Mill Lane, Edwinstowe (0623 823405)
BBSC	Blue Barn Farm, Nether Langwith, nr Mansfield (0623 742248)

Oxfordshire

Crays Pond & Common Woods   175   1m SE of Woodcote
Park by the minor road ½m NW of B4526 at SU651805 then tracks
east or west.
Woodland birds and summer warblers including Hawfinch,
Nightingale and Redstart.

North Grove   175   1m N of Woodcote
Park by A4074, 0.3m NW of its junction with B471 at SU638831,
then path NE through the wood.
Woodland birds.

>*New Copse* 175 *SU690808 1m W of Sonning Common*
>Woodland birds.

>*Sonning Eye* 175 *SU747763 1m NW of Sonning*
>Passage and winter wildfowl.

TIC	9 St. Martin's Street, Wallingford (0491 35351)
YH	Hill House, Reading Road, Streatley, Reading, Berks (0491 872278)
RF	Crooked Billet, Stoke Row, nr Sonning Common
BB	Tudor House, Farm Lane, Maidenditch, nr Pangbourne (0734 744482)
BBE	Shepherds, Shepherds Green, Rotherfield Greys, nr Henley (0491 7413)
SC	Estate Office, Mapledurham, nr Reading (0734 723350/723277)

Warburg   175   4m NW of Henley-on-Thames
Car-park and information centre at end of minor road 2m N of
A423 from Bix at SU721878, then many paths and nature trail.
Woodland birds including Golden and Lady Amherst's Phea-
sants; summer warblers.

Queen & Greenfield Woods   175   2½ m SE of Watlington
Park at Christmas Common, SU715933, and take the Oxfordshire
Way SE through Queen Wood and then the track SW through
Greenfield.
Woodland birds and summer warblers.

Aston Rowant   165   2m W of Stokenchurch
Car-park at the end of minor road 1m SW of A40 at SU732966, or in
a layby beside the A40 itself at SU743974.
Woodland birds and summer warblers including Hawfinch, Wood
Warbler and Nightingale; migrants.

> *Chinnor Hill   165   SP766002   1m SE of Chinnor*
> *Woodland birds and summer warblers; migrants.*

> *Watlington Hill   175   SU705935   1½m SE of Watlington*
> *Woodland birds; migrants.*

> *Blackmoor Woods   175   SU725935   1m E of Christmas*
> *Common*
> *Woodland birds and summer warblers.*

TIC	As previous entry.
YH	As previous entry.
RF	Bull and Butcher, Turville, nr Marlow
	Crown, Pishill, nr Henley
	Fox and Hounds, Christmas Common, nr Watlington
	Fox, Bix, nr Henley
BBE	Lower Farm, Berrick Salome (0865 891073)
	Beacon Cottage Country Guest House, Aston Hill, Aston Rowant, nr Chinnor (0844 51219)
SC	Myrtle Cottage, Manor Farm, Berrick Salome, nr Benson (0865 891208)

Lowbury Hill & Unhill Wood   174   5m SE of Didcot
Park by A417 3m SE of Blewbury at Kingstanding Hill, SU574838,
and take track along The Fair Mile ridge SW toward Lowbury Hill
or south across the valley to Unhill Wood and Moulsford Downs.
Downland and woodland birds including Quail; summer
warblers; migrants.

Little Wittenham   174 or 164   3½ m NE of Didcot
Car-park 1¼ m NW of A4130 from Brightwell-cum-Sotwell, ¾m S
of Little Wittenham at SU567924. Then many paths north through
the woods and down to the River Thames.
Woodland birds; summer warblers; river birds and winter
wildfowl.

Dorchester Pits   164   4½m NE of Didcot
View from A423 ¾m SE of Berinsfield at SU576953 and from minor road along the north shore. For pits to the SW use the car-park ¼m SE of A415 at SU571955 then footpaths around them.
Passage and winter wildfowl; passage waders and terns.

TIC   As previous entry.
YH   As previous entry.
RF   Red Lion, Brightwell, nr Wallingford
        Perch and Pike, South Stoke, nr Goring
BBE   Hacca's Cottage, Fieldside, East Hagbourne, nr Didcot (0235 814324)

Yew Down   174   2½m SE of Wantage
Park by B4494 at SU418842 and take the Ridgeway east.
Downland birds; migrants.

Whitehorse Hill   174   6m W of Wantage
Car-parks ½m S of B4507, 1m S of Woolstone, at SU296864. Then take the Ridgeway either east or west, or a track south toward Woolstone Down.
Downland birds and migrants.

TIC   *The Pump House, 5 Market Place, Faringdon (0367 22191)
YH   The Court Hill Ridgeway Centre, Court Hill, Wantage (02357 60253)
RF   White Horse, Woolstone
BBE   The Craven, Fernham Road, Uffington, nr Wantage (036782 449)

Badbury Hill & Eaton Wood   163   2m W of Faringdon
Car-park by B4019 near the top of the hill at SU262946. Then paths north through the woods and across the valley to Eaton Wood and Badbury Forest.
Woodland birds.

TIC   As previous entry.
YH   Littleholme, Upper Inglesham, Highworth, Swindon, Wilts (0367 52546)
RF   Plough, Coxwell
RFBBE   Apple Tree Inn, Buscot, nr Faringdon (0367 52592)
BB   Manor Farm, Kelmscott, nr Faringdon (0367 52620)
SC   (Lock Cottage, Buscot, nr Faringdon) National Trust, Coleshill Estate Office, nr Swindon (0793 762209)

Farmoor Reservoir   164   4m W of Oxford
Large car-park by B4017 at the east side of the reservoir, ½m S of
Farmoor Village at SP452063. Then track all around.
Winter wildfowl, grebes, divers and large gull roost; passage
waders and terns.

Stanton Harcourt Gravel Pits   164   7m W of Oxford
View from B4449 (formerly unclassified) 1m W of Staunton
Harcourt at SP403056 (the Old Vicarage Pit) and from tracks and
paths south of the road ¾m further west at SP390056.
Wildfowl; grebes; winter gull roost; passage waders and terns;
Little Ringed Plover; summer warblers.

> *Port Meadow   164   SP490086   1–2m NW of Oxford
> centre*
> *Winter wildfowl and gulls.*

> *Appleton Lower Common   164   SP425010   1m SW of
> Appleton*
> *Woodland and river birds.*

TIC	St. Aldates, Oxford (0865 726871)
YH	Jack Straw's Lane, Oxford (0865 62997)
RF	Mason Arms, South Leigh, nr Witney
	Harcourt Arms, Stanton Harcourt
	Dun Cow, Northmoor
BBE	Staddle Stones, Linch Hill, Stanton Harcourt (0865 882256)
	The Old Rectory, Church End, Standlake, nr Witney (086 731 559)
SC	Willowdene, 11 Back Lane, Ducklington, nr Witney (0993 2897)

Blenheim Park   164   4m NW of Kidlington
Park near the tourist information centre in Woodstock at SP446167
and cross the A34 to the east entrance and the grounds by Queen-
Pool (small admission charge). Then many paths around the lakes
and through the woodland.
Wildfowl and woodland birds including Hawfinch and Gadwall.

> *Wychwood Forest   164   SP323166   2–3m SW of
> Charlbury*
> *Woodland birds.*

TIC	*Hensington Road, Woodstock (0993 811038)
YH	The Laurels, The Slade, Charlbury (0608 810202)
RF	Kings Head, Woodstock
	Bell, Long Hanborough, nr Woodstock

BBE North Leigh Guest House, 28 Common Road, North Leigh, nr Witney (0993 881622)
   Woodman Inn, New Yatt Road, North Leigh (0993 881790)

SC (Wylcott Cottage, North Leigh) Holywell Cottage, New Yatt, nr Witney (099386 614)

Shotover Country Park & Horspath Common 164 3m E of Oxford centre

Car-park at the end of minor road 1m E of B4495 from New Headington or, approaching from the east, 2m W of Wheatley at SP566002. Then many paths and tracks.
Woodland birds and summer warblers; migrants.

Otmoor 164 4–5m E of Kidlington

Rifle range; access only when the red flags are not flying.
Park in Oddington, 2m E of B4027 from Islip, at SP553148. Take track east to the centre of the moor and then either north or south.
Woodland and heathland birds; summer and winter waders; winter wildfowl; summer warblers; Nightingale.

> ***Whitecross Green Wood*** *164* *SP604148* *7m E of Kidlington*
> *Woodland birds.*

TIC St. Aldates, Oxford (0865 726871)
YH Jack Straw's Lane, Oxford (0865 62997)
RF Plough, Noke, nr Kidlington
   Star, Stanton-St. John, nr Oxford
   Red Lion, Islip, nr Kidlington
BBE Manor Farm, Forest Hill, nr Oxford (08677 2434)
   Mead Close, Forest Hill, nr Oxford (08677 2248)

Grimsbury Reservoir 151 1½ m N of Banbury centre

Park ¼m E of A423, ½m W of A361, at SP458418 then path north around the reservoir.
Winter wildfowl and gulls; passage waders and terns.

Banbury Sewage Works 151 1m SE of Banbury centre

Park near the tourist information centre ¼m S of A422, from just east of the railway bridge, at SP464403. Then track southeast.
Passage and winter wildfowl and waders.

TIC Banbury Museum, 8 Horsefair, Banbury (0295 259855)
YH Church Green, Badby, Daventry, Northants (0327 703883)
RF Plough, Bodicote
   Moon and Sixpence, Hanwell

BB   Mill Barn, Lower Tadmarton, nr Banbury (029 578 349)
            The Old Manor, Cropredy, nr Banbury (029 575 235)
BBE   Mill House, North Newington, nr Banbury (029 573 212)
SC   (Millstone Cottages) Rye Hill Farm, Sibford Gower, nr
            Banbury (029 578 371)

Shropshire

Sowdley Wood   137   1–2m E of Clun
Park in Woodside ¾m SE of A488 from Clun at SO312802, then tracks east through woods.
Woodland birds including Pied Flycatcher, Redstart, Crossbill and Turtle Dove.

Colstey Woods & Sunnyhill   137   2m N of Clun
Car-parks at W side by A488 2m N of Clun at SO304842 and tracks east; or on E side of the woods 1¾m N of Clunton at SO334839 and paths westward.
Woodland birds and summer warblers including Pied Flycatcher, Redstart, Wood Warbler and Goshawk.

TIC	The Old School, Knighton, Powys (0547 528753)
YH	The Mill, Clun, Craven Arms (05884 582)
RF	Sun, Clun
BBE	New House Farm, Clun (0588 638314)
	Clun Forest Walks, 28/29 Clunton, nr Clun (05887 652)
	Woodside Farmhouse, Clun (05884 695)
SC	Upper House, Clunbury (05887 203)

Long Mynd   137   2m W of Church Stretton
Car-parks by minor roads west of Church Stretton from B4370 at the head of Carding Mill Valley at SO441948 and on the road to Ratlinghope 2m W of Church Stretton at SO421954 then many paths.
Woodland, river and upland birds including Red Grouse, Ring Ousel and Dipper; migrants including spring Dotterel.

Stiperstones   137   6m NW of Church Stretton
Car-park by minor road 3m E of A488, 2m E of Ratlinghope at SO370977, then paths and tracks north.
Upland birds.

Earls Hill   126   1m SE of Pontesbury
Park just south of Pontesford by A488 at SJ409063 and take lane
south for ¼m, then waymarked paths through woods and up the
hill.
Woodland birds and summer warblers including Pied Flycatcher,
Redstart, Wood Warbler and Raven.

TIC	*Church Street, Church Stretton (0694 723133)
	Castle Street, Ludlow (0584 875053)
YH	Bridges, Ratlinghope, Shrewsbury (058 861 656)
RF	Stiperstones Inn, Stiperstones
	Green Dragon, Little Stretton
RFBBE	Crown Inn, Wentnor, nr Church Stretton (058 861 613)
BB	Woolstaston House, Woolstaston, Church Stretton (06945 381)
BBE	Tankerville Lodge, Stiperstones (0743 791401)
SC	Bowdlers House, Woolstaston (06945 425)
	Keepers Cottage, Batchcott Hall, Church Stretton (06945 234)

Wenlock Edge   137   4m NE of Craven Arms
Car-park by minor road 2½m N of B4368 (from ½m W of its junc-
tion with B4365) at SO479876. Then paths NE or SW through the
woods.
Woodland birds and summer warblers including Pied Flycatcher,
Redstart and Wood Warbler; migrants.

Brown Clee Hill   138   2m S of Ditton Priors
Car-park by minor road 1m W of B4364 from Cleobury North at
SO607873 then tracks SW through woods and up onto the hill.
Woodland and upland birds including Wood Warbler, Goshawk,
Crossbill, Pied Flycatcher, Raven and Red Grouse.

**Hope Bowdler & Helmeth Hills   137 or 138   1–2m E of
Church Stretton**
Park by B4371 ¾m E of its junction with A49 at SO468933. Then
take track NE and paths off to Helmeth woods and Hope Bowdler
Hills to the east.
Woodland and hill birds; migrants.

> *Whitcliffe Common*   137 or 138   SO506742   ½m SW of
> Ludlow centre
> *Woodland and river birds; summer warblers; Hawfinch.*

> *Titterstone Clee*   137 or 138   SO594776   5m NE of
> Ludlow
> *Hill birds; migrants; Raven.*

Catherton Common 138 *SO625780* *2m E of Titterstone Clee*
Heathland birds.

Nortoncamp Wood 137 *SO445820* *1m SE of Craven Arms*
Woodland birds and summer warblers including Pied Fly-catcher, Redstart and Wood Warbler.

TIC	As previous entry.
YH	John Cadbury Memorial Hostel, Easthope, Much Wenlock (06943 363)
	Malthouse Farm, Wheathill, Bridgnorth (074 633 236)
RF	Swan, Aston Munslow, nr Diddlebury
	Kremlin, Clee Hill, nr Ludlow
	Crown, Munslow
BB	Hope Bowdler Hall, Hope Bowdler, Church Streton (0694 722041)
BBE	Gilberries Cottage, Wall-under-Heywood, Church Stretton (06943 400)
	Glebe Holme, Munslow (058 476 218)
	Heathwood House, Heath Farm, Tenbury Road, Clee Hill (0584 891021)
	Charlcotte Farm, Cleobury North (074 663 238)
BBESC	Strefford Hall, Strefford, nr Craven Arms (0588 672383)
SC	Cleeton Cottages, Old Hall Farm, Wall-under-Heywood (06943 253)
	Tana Leas Farm, Clee St. Margaret, Craven Arms (058 475 272)

Chelmarsh Reservoir **138** **3½m S of Bridgnorth**
Car-park at end of lane ½m N of Hampton, 1m E of B4555, at SO739876 then paths around the reservoir.
Winter wildfowl, grebes and gull roost; passage waders and terns; summer warblers.

Chorley Wood 138 *SO705840* *2m W of Woodhill*
Woodland birds including Redstart and Wood Warbler.

Borle Brook 138 *SO735824* *1m S of Woodhill*
Woodland and river birds including Dipper and Kingfisher.

TIC	The Library, Listley Street, Bridgnorth (0746 763358)
YH	As previous entry.
R	Halfway House, Eardington, nr Bridgnorth
RF	Fox and Hounds, Stottesdon, nr Chorley
RFBBE	Bull's Head Inn, Chelmarsh (0746 861469)
BB	Old Forge House, Hampton Lodge, nr Bridgnorth (0746 780338)
SC	Eudon Burnell Cottages, nr Bridgnorth (074 635 235)

Benthall Edge Wood   127   3½m NE of Much Wenlock
Car-park by the Ironbridge on the south side of the river ¾m N of
B4375 at SJ673033 then path west by the river and woods.
River and woodland birds including Redstart and Pied Flycatcher;
summer warblers.

**Easthope Wood & Blakeway Copse   138   1–5m SW of Much
Wenlock**
Car-parks by B4371 e.g. 1m SW of Much Wenlock at SO612997 or
3½m SW at SO574967, ½m SW of Presthope, then paths through
woods.
Woodland birds and summer warblers; migrants.

The Wrekin & Ercall   127   5m N of Much Wenlock
Park by minor road 1m S from junction 7 of M54, 1½m N of Little
Wenlock, at SJ637094. Then take tracks south to the Wrekin and
north to Lawrences Hill and The Ercall.
Woodland birds and summer warblers; wildfowl.

> ***Bannister's Copse***   127   *SJ615030   2m N of Much*
> *Wenlock*
> *Woodland and river birds.*

> ***Stirchley Grange***   127   *SJ698078   1m N of Stirchley*
> *Wildfowl and woodland birds.*

> ***Limekiln Wood***   127   *SJ654094   1½m N of Little Wenlock*
> *Woodland birds.*

TIC	*The Guildhall, Barrow Street, Much Wenlock (0952 727679)
YH	Colbrookdale Institute, Paradise, Colbrookdale, Telford (095245 3281)
RF	Wenlock Edge Inn, nr Easthope
	Longville Arms, Longville-in-the-Dale, nr Easthope
	George and Dragon, Much Wenlock
	Huntsman, Little Wenlock
	Bird in Hand, Ironbridge
BB	Mill Farm, Hughley, nr Much Wenlock (074 636 645)
BBE	Bridge House, Buildwas, nr Telford (095245 2105)
SC	The Grange, Much Wenlock (0952 727152)

Uffington Woods   126   3m NE of Shrewsbury centre
Park at the N end of Uffington ½m SE of B5062 at SJ529141 and
take path east through the woods.
Woodland birds.

Monkmoor & Shrewsbury Sewage Works   126   2m NE of Shrewsbury centre
Park at end of track 1m E of A49 at SJ526136, then path north or south beside the River Severn's west bank.
Winter wildfowl; river birds; migrants.

> *Bomere Pool & Wood   126   SJ500082   3m S of Shrewsbury centre*
> *Wildfowl; woodland birds and summer warblers.*

TIC   The Square, Shrewsbury, (0743 50761/50762)
YH   The Woodlands, Abbey Foregate, Shrewsbury (0743 60179)
RF   Corbet Arms, Upton Magna, nr Uffington
          Compasses, Bayston Hill, nr Shrewsbury
BB   Haughmond Farm, nr Shrewsbury (074 377 244)

Grinshill Hill   126   ¾m SE of Clive
Car-park at end of lane ½m S of minor road from Clive to Preston Brockhurst (on A49) at SJ524238, then paths through woods up the hill.
Woodland birds including Redstart and Pied Flycatcher.

> *Marton Pools   126   SJ446233   1½m NE of Baschurch*
> *Wildfowl; passage waders.*

> *Nesscliffe Hill   126   SJ385195   3m SW of Baschurch*
> *Woodland birds and summer warblers.*

> *Merrington Green Nature Trail   126   SJ465209   2½m SE of Baschurch*
> *Woodland birds and summer warblers.*

TIC   As previous entry.
YH   As previous entry.
RF   Red Lion, Myddle, nr Baschurch
          Bridgewater Arms, Harmer Hill
BBE   Vales Cottages, Valeswood, Nesscliffe (074 381 467)
          Fitz Manor Farm, Bomere Heath, Shrewsbury (0743 850295)
          Village Farm, Stanton (0939 250391)
SC   Booley Home Farm, Stanton, Shrewsbury (093 924 206)
          Prescott Lodge, Baschurch (0939 260495)
          Chapel Bungalow, Grinshill (093 928 214)

Llynclys Common & Llanmynech Hill   **126**   **1–2m SW of Llynclys**
Park just south of A495 1m W of its junction with A483 at SJ269239. Then take path up through the woods and south toward Llanmynech Hill.
Woodland birds and summer warblers including Pied Flycatcher, Raven and Redstart.

Melverley Green & Crewgreen   **126**   **4m SE of Four Crosses**
View flooded meadows from minor roads ¼m-1m N of B4393 from Crewgreen e.g. SJ334160.
Winter wildfowl.

> *Craig Sychtyn*   *126*   *SJ234255*   *3m NE of Llynclys*
> *Woodland birds and summer warblers.*

TIC	Mile End Services, Oswestry (0691 662488/657876)
YH	As previous entry.
RF	Bradford Arms, Llanmynech
	Cross Guns, Pant, nr Llynclys
RFBBE	Lion Hotel, Llanmynech (0691 830234)
BBE	April Spring Cottage, Nantmawr, nr Oswestry (0691 818802)
SC	Lloran Isaf, Llansilin, nr Oswestry (0691 70253)

The Mere, Ellesmere   **126**   **½m E of Ellesmere**
Car-park by A528 SE of Ellesmere beside SW side of the lake at SJ405347, then tracks around the perimeter.
Winter wildfowl and gull roost; passage terns; woodland birds.

Colemere Country Park   **126**   **2½m SE of Ellesmere**
Car-park at south end of the mere 1m NE of A528 just north of Colemere village at SJ436329, then path around the perimeter.
Winter wildfowl and gull roost; passage waders and terns; woodland birds and summer warblers.

Wood Lane Pit   **126**   **½m W of Colemere**
View from minor road west of Colemere village at SJ426328.
Passage waders; winter gulls.

Hanmer Mere (Clwyd)   **126**   **4m NE of Ellesmere**
View from minor road at north end, ¼m E of A539, 2m E of Penley, at SJ453396. Then take path south along the east side.
Passage and winter wildfowl; winter gull roost; Ruddy Duck, Great Crested Grebe.

Brown Moss   **126**   **2m SE of Whitchurch**
Car-parks by minor road beside east side of the lake ¾m E of A41, ½m W of Ash Magna e.g. at SJ564393.
Wildfowl; woodland birds and summer warblers.

Baggy Moor   **126**   **4–6m S of Ellesmere**
View from minor roads and lanes along the east side or park in
Bagley Marsh at SJ398277 and take track and path west across the
moor and over River Perry towards Haughton.
Wildfowl, waders, river and meadow birds; migrants.

> *White Mere*   *126*   *SJ414330*   *1m W of Colemere*
> *Winter wildfowl.*

> *Newton Mere*   *126*   *SJ425343*   *1m SW of Welshampton*
> *Winter wildfowl.*

> *Blake Mere*   *126*   *SJ415340*   *1m SE of Ellesmere*
> *Winter wildfowl and woodland birds.*

> *Whixall & Fenn's Mosses*   *126*   *SJ490360*   *5m SW of*
> *Whitchurch*
> *Heathland birds including Nightjar.*

TIC   Civic Centre, High Street, Whitchurch (0948 4577)
YH   Tyndwr Hall, Tyndwr Road, Llangollen, Clwyd (0978
          860330)
RFBBE Hanmer Arms, Hanmer, Clwyd
BBE   Frankton Manor, Welsh Frankton, nr Ellesmere (0691
          712454)
          Buck Farm, Hanmer, Clwyd (094 874 339)
SC   Keepers Cottage, Soulton Hall, Wem, nr Shrewsbury
          (0939 32786)

Somerset & Avon

Porlock Marsh & Bay   181   1m NW of Porlock
Car-park at the end of B3225, 2m NW of Porlock at SS865479, then coast path E between marsh and shore.
Passage and winter waders and wildfowl; migrants.

Horner Water   181   2m SE of Porlock
Car-park by minor road ¾m S of A39, ½m S of West Luccombe at SS898456, then path and track south through the woods and along the west bank of the river.
River and woodland birds including Dipper, Redstart and Pied Flycatcher.

Dunkery Hill   181   3m S of Porlock
Park by minor road at the top of the hill 2m S of Luccombe, 2m NW of B3224 at SS904420, then track west to Dunkery Beacon and beyond.
Moorland birds; winter raptors; migrants.

Dunster Beach   181   2½m SE of Minehead
Car-park at the seafront 1m E of A39, ½m E of Marsh Street at ST005446, then track and path NW towards the golf course and Warren Point.
Passage and winter waders and wildfowl; migrants.

> *Croydon Hill   181   SS975405   4m S of Minehead*
> *Woodland birds including Nightjar.*

> *River Barle Valley   181   SS860325   3½m S of Exford*
> *Woodland birds including Redstart and Pied Flycatcher; river birds including Dipper; summer warblers.*

TIC   The Market House, The Parade, Minehead (0643 702624)
YH   Alcombe Combe, Minehead (0643 2595)
   Exe Head, Exford, Minehead (0643 83288)

RFBBE	Ship Inn, Porlock (0643 862507)
	Dunkery, Wootton Courtenay, nr Minehead
BBE	The Lorna Doone Hotel, High Street, Porlock (0643 862404)
	Cloutsham Farm, Porlock (0643 862839)
	Fern Cottage, Allerford, nr Porlock (0643 862215)
SC	Burrow Farm, Wootton Courtenay, nr Minehead (0643 84361)
	Pack Horse, Allerford (0643 862475)

Wimbleball Lake & Hartford Bottom   181   10m S of Minehead
Car-park by B3190 1½m W of Upton at SS969286, then track down the hill to the reservoir and the wooded valley to the west. Other car-parks to view the reservoir are along the west side 1m SE of Brompton Regis at SS966307 and at the N end between the causeways at SS974318.
Passage and winter wildfowl; woodland and river birds including Redstart, Pied Flycatcher and Dipper.

Clatworthy Reservoir   181   4m E of Wimbleball Lake
Car-park by minor road along the east side ½m W of Clatworthy at ST044308, then path/track SW or NE around the reservoir.
Passage and winter wildfowl; woodland birds and summer warblers; migrants.

TIC	As previous entry.
YH	As previous entry.
RFBBE	Ralegh's Cross, Brendon Hills, nr Elworthy (0984 40343)
RF	Lowtrow Cross, Upton
BBE	Dassels Guest House, Dassels, nr Dulverton (03984 203)
	Springfield Farm, Dulverton (0398 23722)
SC	South Greenslade Farm, Brompton Regis, nr Dulverton (03987 207)
	Brook Cottage, Tolland, nr Taunton (09847 268)

Hodder's Combe   181   0–2m SW of Holford
Park on the west side of Holford, ¼m W of A39 at ST155411 and take track SW beside the river and through the woods up towards Thorncombe Hill.
River and woodland birds including Dipper, Redstart, Pied Flycatcher.

Staple Plantation & Beacon Hill   181   3m SE of Watchet
Car-park ¾m SE of A39 from West Quantoxhead at ST117410 then tracks east and south.
Woodland and hill birds including Nightjar and Whinchat.

Great Wood & Bagborough Hill   181   3m SW of Nether Stowey
Car-park near Triscombe Stone on SW edge of the plantation, at the end of minor road at ST164360, then track along the ridge to the south and around the southern edge of the woods.
Woodland and hill birds including Nightjar; migrants.

Lilstock Bay   181   3½m N of Nether Stowey
Car-park by the bay at the end of minor road 2m N of A39, 1m N of Kilton at ST173454, and coast path east or west.
Passage and winter waders and wildfowl.

> *Hawkridge Reservoir   182   ST205360   3m SE of Nether Stowey*
> *Passage and winter wildfowl.*

TIC   As previous entry.
YH   Sevenacres, Holford, Bridgwater (0278 74 224)
          Denzel House, Crowcombe, nr Taunton (09847 249)
RF   Hood Arms, Kilve, nr Watchet
          Plough, Holford
          Cottage Inn, Nether Stowey
BBE   Quantock House, Holford (0278 74439)
          Higher House, West Bagborough, nr Taunton (0823 432996)

Durleigh Reservoir   182   2m W of Bridgwater centre
Car-park at E end of reservoir by the dam, 1m S of A39 at ST275363. Also view from minor road along south side and from the hide at the SW corner.
Passage and winter wildfowl; passage waders.

Steart   182   6m N of Bridgwater
Car-park at Steart by minor road, 4m N of A39 from Cannington at ST275460, then track NE to Steart Point and the hides and SW to River Parrett. Also car-park 1m SW of Steart by Wall Common and coast path westward.
Passage and winter waders and wildfowl; winter raptors; migrants; seawatching.

> *Huntworth Pits   182   ST316350   1½m SE of Bridgwater centre*
> *Winter wildfowl; reedbed species including Cetti's Warbler.*

> *Chilton Trinity Pits   182   ST297395   1½m N of Bridgwater centre.*
> *Birds as Huntworth.*

TIC	*Town Hall, High Street, Bridgwater (0278 427652)
	Berrow Road, Burnham-on-Sea (0278 787852)
YH	As previous entry.
RFBB	Malt Shovel, Bradley Green, Cannington, nr Bridgwater (0278 653432)
BB	Heathfield Lodge, 2 Bridgwater Road, North Petherton, nr Bridgwater (0278 662232)
BBE	Swang Farm, Cannington (0278 378)
SC	Cox's Farm, Steart Bay, nr Bridgwater (0278 652322)

Langford Heathfield   181 or 193   3m NW of Wellington
Park by minor road along east side of the heath ½m W of Langford
Budville e.g. ST104234, then moorland paths westward.
Woodland birds and summer warblers; Nightingale.

Otterhead Lakes   193   7m S of Taunton
Park by minor road ½m W of B3170, just SE of Otterford church at
ST225142, then nature trail south.
Wildfowl; woodland birds and summer warblers.

> ***Wellington Hill***   *193 or 181   ST137175   2m S of*
> *Wellington*
> *Woodland birds; summer warblers.*

> ***Priors Park Wood***   *193   ST227164   5½m S of Taunton*
> *Woodland birds.*

> ***Staple & Curland Commons***   *193   ST272157   6½m SE of*
> *Taunton*
> *Woodland birds; summer warblers.*

TIC	The Library, Corporation Street, Taunton (0823 274785)
	*The Museum, 28 Fore Street, Wellington (0823 664747)
YH	As previous entry.
RF	Queens Arms, Pitminster, nr Taunton
	Half Moon, Stoke St. Mary
	Lamb and Flag, Blagdon Hill, nr Taunton
RFBBE	Winchester Arms, Trull, nr Taunton (0823 284723)
BBE	Hangeridge Farm, Wrangway, nr Wellington (0823 662339)
	Higher Dipford Farm, Trull (0823 275770/283497)
	Old Manor Farmhouse, Norton Fitzwarren, nr Taunton (0823 289801)

West Sedgemoor & Swell Wood   193   8m E of Taunton
Car-park by A378 ¾m NE of Fivehead at ST362239, then track to
hide and nature trail and path along southern edge of the moor.
Passage and winter wildfowl; summer waders including Black-
tailed Godwit. Woodland birds including Nightingale.

Aller Wood   182   7m SE of Bridgwater
Park down lane off minor road 1m W of High Ham, ¾m NE of
A372 at ST411312 and take track SW through the woods over-
looking the moors below.
Woodland birds and summer warblers; Nightingale.

> *Hurcot Hill*   *182*   *ST505305*   *2m NE of Somerton*
> *Woodland birds.*

TIC   The Library, Corporation Street, Taunton (0823 274785)
YH   As previous entry.
RF   Rising Sun, North Curry
        George Inn, Middlezoy, nr Bridgwater
BB   Hillards, High Street, Curry Rivel, nr Langport (0458
        251737)
BBE   The Jay's Nest, Stoke St. Gregory, nr Taunton (0823
        490250)
SC   Dykes Farm, Slough Lane, Stoke St. Gregory (0823
        490349)

Sutton Bingham Reservoir   194   3m S of Yeovil
View from minor road along west side of the reservoir 1½–2½m
SW of A37, e.g. from the causeway at the NW corner (ST546114).
Passage and winter wildfowl; passage waders, terns and gulls.

TIC   Petter's House, Petter's Way, Yeovil (0935 71279)
YH   The Chalet, Ivythorn Hill, Street, Somerset (0458 42961)
RF   Mandeville Arms, Hardington Mandeville, nr Yeovil
BBE   Halstock Mill, Halstock, nr Yeovil (093589 278)
        Barrows Country House, Weston Street, East Chinnock,
        Yeovil (093586 2390)
SC   Trill House, Thornford, nr Sherborne (0803 22747)

Westhay Moor   182   5m NW of Glastonbury
Park by minor road which runs along the southern edge of the
moor east of B3151, from 1m N of Westhay e.g. ST448433, and take
tracks north across the moor.
Passage and winter wildfowl; passage, winter and summer
waders.

Tealham & Tadham Moors   182   6–8m NW of Glastonbury
View from minor road crossing the moors NW of B3151 from 1½m
NE of Westhay e.g. ST405453. Also from track along the north side
of Norht Drain and minor roads south of Heath House and
Westham.
Passage and winter wildfowl; passage, winter and summer
waders.

Shapwick Heath   **182**   **5m W of Glastonbury**
View from minor road between Westhay and Shapwick, south of the South Drain and from tracks running east and west e.g. ST422406.
Marsh and woodland birds; summer warblers; Nightingale and Nightjar.

> *Ebbor Gorge*   *182*   *ST525485*   *2m NW of Wells*
> *Woodland birds and summer warblers.*

TIC	Town Hall, Market Place, Wells (0749 72552)
	*1 Marchant's Buildings, Northload Street, Glastonbury (0458 32954)
YH	As previous entry.
RF	Olde Burtle, Eddington
	Bird in Hand, Westhay
BB	Dove Cottage, Henton, nr Wells (0749 74604)
BBE	Yew Tree Country House, Sand, nr Wedmore (0934 712520)
	Ashcombe Farm, Steanbow, nr Glastonbury (074989 734)

Chew Valley Lake   **182 or 172**   **8m S of Bristol centre**
View from Herriott's Bridge where the A368 crosses the southernmost part of the lake at ST572583. Also track to the shore and hide, ½m NE of Herriott's Bridge at Sutton Wick (ST575593), or track N along SW shore to hides from ¼m SW of Herriott's Bridge or E from B3114 at ST554588. Two bays viewable from B3114 1–2m S of Chew Stoke and viewpoints from minor road E of Chew Stoke along the northern side of the lake.
Wildfowl; passage waders and terns; gulls; reedbed species including Bearded Tit; migrants.

Blagdon Lake   **182 or 172**   **1m N of Blagdon**
Viewable from minor road along the west side ½m N of A368 e.g. ST505596. Also track and hides along the southern side.
Wildfowl; gulls; passage waders and terns.

Cheddar Reservoir   **182**   **1m W of Cheddar**
Park by minor road off the Axbridge by-pass (A371) at the N end of the reservoir at ST438544, then track south and path around the perimeter. Access also from the Cheddar end ¼m W of A371 at ST448535.
Passage and winter wildfowl; passage terns and waders.

> *Mendip Forest*   *182*   *ST487547*   *2m NE of Cheddar*
> *Woodland birds; summer warblers; migrants.*

> *Brockley Combe Wood*   *182 or 172*   *ST483664*   *2m S of Backwell*
> *Woodland birds and summer warblers.*

Barrow Gurney Reservoirs 182 or 172 ST540677 4m SW of Bristol
Passage and winter wildfowl; passage terns and gulls.

TIC	*The Gorge, Cheddar, Somerset (0934 744071)
TIC	Town Hall, Market Place, Wells (0749 72552)
YH	Hillfield, Cheddar, Somerset (0934 742494)
RF	The Blue Bowl, West Harptree
BB	Aldwick Court Farm, Wrington, nr Bristol (0934 862305)
	The Farm, West Harptree
SC	Gournay Court, West Harptree (0761 221323)

Brean Down & Axe Estuary   182   2m SW of Weston-super-Mare
Car-park at end of minor road beside the shore, 2m N of Brean at ST296585, then paths west up onto the down and track east to the estuary mouth.
Migrants; passage and winter waders; seawatching.

Berrow Marsh & Manor   182   6m S of Weston-super-Mare
Park by B3140 in Berrow, 1½m N of Burnham-on-Sea at ST299515, then path west across the golf course to the marsh and shore. Also path west from Berrow church ¾m N at ST295524.
Passage waders; reedbed species; winter raptors; migrants.

Sand Point   182   3m N of Weston-super-Mare
Car-park at N end of minor road beside Sand Bay at ST331660 then paths west.
Migrants; seawatching; passage and winter waders.

River Brue Estuary 182 ST303475 1½m S of Burnham-on-Sea
Passage and winter waders and wildfowl; winter raptors.

Worlbury Hill 182 ST320626 1m N of Weston-super-Mare
Woodland birds; migrants.

TIC	Beach Lawns, Weston-super-Mare, Avon (0934 626838)
YH	As previous entry.
RF	Nut Tree, Worle, nr Weston-super-Mare
	Crossways, West Huntspill, nr Burnham-on-Sea
	Red Cow, Brent Knoll, nr Burnham-on-Sea
BBE	Purn House Farm, Bleadon, nr Weston-super-Mare (0934 812324)
	Kara Guest House, Hewish, nr Weston-super-Mare (0934 834442)

Steep Holm   182   6m W of Weston-super-Mare
Owned by the Kenneth Allsop Memorial Trust, Knock-na-Cre,
Milbourne Port, Sherborne, Dorset. Members may stay on the
island. Day trips on Saturdays April-October from Knightstone
Pier, Weston-super-Mare, at the N end of Weston Bay (ST313618)
10am-5pm.
Migrants; summer seabirds.

TIC   As previous entry.

**Severn Beach & New Passage   172   4–5m NE of
Avonmouth**
Park in Severn Beach by the railway station ¾m N of A403 at
ST539847, then coast path south or north. Also at the W end of
B4064 at New Passage, 1m NW of A403 at ST544864 and coast path
south along the sea wall.
Passage and winter waders and wildfowl; passage terns;
migrants.

Shepperdine   162   4m NW of Thornbury
Car-park at the Windbound Inn at the end of minor road ¾m NW
of Shepperdine at ST614961. Then coast path north and south.
Passage and winter waders and wildfowl.

**Littleton Warth & Brickpits   172 or 162   3½m W of
Thornbury**
Park at the end of minor road 1m NW of Littleton-on-Severn at
ST588910 and coast path north or south.
Reedbed species; migrants; passage and winter waders and
wildfowl.

> ***Wickwar Woods*** *172* *ST740873* *4m NE of Yate*
> *Woodland birds.*

TIC   14 Narrow Quay, Bristol, Avon (0272 260767)
YH   Hayman House, 64 Prince Street, Bristol (0272 337464)
           Mounton Road, Chepstow, Gwent (0291 622685)
RF   Boars Head, Aust
           Windbound Inn, Shepperdine
           Anchor, Oldbury-on-Severn
BBE   Green Farm Guest House, Falfield, nr Thornbury (0454
           260319)

Staffordshire

Kinver Edge   138   ½m-1m SW of Kinver
Park by minor road SW of Kinver e.g. SO835836 then many paths.
(Also see Hereford & Worcester: Kingsford Country Park & Kinver
Edge.)
Woodland birds including Redstart.

Highgate Common Country Park   138   4m N of Kinver
Car-parks by minor road 2½m N of A458, 1½m E of Bobbington
e.g. at SO837896, then many paths.
Woodland and heathland birds; summer warblers.

Enville Woods   138   *SO836864   2m N of Kinver*
Woodland birds including Crossbill.

Himley Wood   139   *SO870914   1m S of Wombourne*
Woodland birds.

Whittington Sewage Works   139   *SO872839   2m E of
Kinver*
Passage waders.

TIC	Travellers Joy, The Old House, 47 High Street, Kinver, West Midlands (0384 872940)
YH	Malthouse Farm, Wheathill, Bridgnorth, Shrops (074 633 236)
RF	Fox, Stourton, nr Kinver
	Whittington, Kinver
	Green Man, Swindon, nr Wombourne
BBE	Low Farm, Alveley, Arley, nr Kidderminster (02997 206)
	Tanglewood, Buttonoak, nr Bewdley (0299 401280)

Belvide Reservoir   127   4½m SW of Penkridge
Track runs along the west side from ½m W of Shutt Green at
SJ864096 north to the A5. For permit holders; car-park just west of
Shutt Green, 1¼m NW of Brewood, at SJ868098 and path along
the south side to the hides. Permits available from WMBC, Miss M.
Surman, 6 Lloyd Square, Niall Close, Edgbaston, Birmingham B15
3LX.
Wildfowl; winter gull roost; passage waders and terns; summer
warblers.

> *Gailey Reservoirs   127   SJ935105   2½m S of Penkridge*
> *Passage and winter wildfowl.*

> *Leecroft Rubbish Tip   127   SJ994098   1m E of Cannock*
> *centre*
> *Winter gulls.*

TIC   Prince of Wales Centre, Church Street, Cannock (0543
466453)
YH   Coalbrookdale Institute, Paradise, Coalbrookdale,
Telford, Shrops (0952 453281)
RF   Fox, Marston, nr Wheaton Aston
Admiral Rodney, Brewood
BBE   Moors Farm, Chillington Lane, Codshall, nr Wol-
verhampton (09074 2330)
Bargate House, Brewood (0902 850280)

Blithfield Reservoir   128   4m N of Rugeley
The B5013 crosses the reservoir at SK057238. Annual permits to
walk the shoreline and use the hides (8 at the last count!) from
WMBC (see Belvide Reservoir for address).
Winter wildfowl and gull roost; passage waders and terns;
migrants.

Cannock Chase   127 & 128   2–5m W of Rugeley
Many car-parks by minor roads north and east of Cannock
between A34 and A460 e.g. 1m SE of Brocton at SJ980184 and ½m
further south, then many paths east. Also 2m S of A460, 2m N of
Burntwood on the south side of Beaudesert Old Park, at SK045126
and paths north.
Woodland birds including Redstart, Pied Flycatcher, Crossbill and
Long-eared Owl; Nightjar; winter Great Grey Shrike and Hen
Harrier; migrants.

Branston Pits   128   3m SW of Burton upon Trent
Park just west of A38 at Branston, SK218214, and take the towpath
south beside the canal and pits.
Winter wildfowl; passage waders and terns.

Elford Pits   128   *SK180096*   *4m E of Lichfield*
Winter wildfowl; passage waders.

TIC	As previous entry. Town Hall, King Edward Place, Burton upon Trent (0283 45454)
YH	As previous entry. Copt Oak, Markfield, Leicester (0530 242661)
RF	Horseshoe Inn, Tatenhill, nr Branston, Burton upon Trent Chetwyn Arms, Brocton, nr Stafford
RFBBE	Crown, Abbots Bromley (0283 840227)
BBE	Marsh Farm, Abbots Bromley (0283 840323) Lower Newlands Farm, Newlands Lane, Blithbury, nr Rugeley (0283 840370)
SC	Priory Farm, Blithbury, nr Rugeley (088 922 269)

Copmere   **127**   **2m W of Eccleshall**
Park by minor road ½m SW of B5026, ¼m NE of Copmere End at SJ806295, then path around the east and north sides.
Winter wildfowl; woodland birds and summer warblers including Redstart and Wood Warbler; reedbed species.

Burnt Wood   **127**   **4m E of Market Drayton**
Park just south of B5026 ½m SE of its junction with A53 at SJ744354, then tracks south and west.
Woodland birds.

Loynton Moss   **127**   **4m SW of Eccleshall**
Park by minor road ¼m N of A519, 1½m SW of Woodseaves, at SJ781244. Then take track east toward the Shropshire Union Canal.
Woodland birds; summer warblers; reedbed species.

Tillington Marshes   **127**   **1m NW of Stafford centre**
Park by A5013 ¼m SE of junction 14 of M6 at SJ908249 and take track south between the pools and the River Sow to the hides.
Wildfowl; passage and winter waders; reedbed species; migrants.

Bishops Wood   127   *SJ744310*   *5m SE of Market Drayton*
Woodland birds.

Aqualate Mere   127   *SJ778205*   *2m NE of Newport*
Wildfowl; woodland birds; summer warblers.

TIC	The Ancient High House, Greengate Street, Stafford (0785 40204) Motorway Services M6, Keele

YH	The Woodlands, Abbey Foregate, Shrewsbury, Shrops (0743 60179)
RF	Junction, Norbury, nr Eccleshall
	Peel Arms, Ashley, nr Market Drayton
BBE	Glenwood, Croxton, nr Eccleshall (063 082 238)
	Kings Arms Hotel, Stafford Street, Eccleshall (0785 850294)
	Oulton House Farm, Norbury, nr Stafford (078 574 264)

Coombes Valley   119   3m SE of Leek
Car-park by minor road 1m SW of A523, 1m S of Bradnop at SK009535, then marked paths south.
Woodland and river birds including Redstart, Pied Flycatcher and Dipper.

Hawksmoor Wood   119   2m E of Cheadle
Park by B5417 1m SW of Oakamoor at SK039443 and track east or west.
Woodland birds including Pied Flycatcher and Redstart.

Manifold & Hamps Valleys   119   7m NW of Ashbourne
Car-park by minor road 1m E of Grindon, 1m SW of Wetton at SK099543, then track north or south.
Woodland and river birds including Redstart, Pied Flycatcher, Dipper and Common Sandpiper.

Dovedale   119   4–6m NW of Ashbourne
Car-park by minor road 1¼m W of A515 just west of Mildale, ¾m SE of Alstonefield at SK136547. Then take path south beside the river.
Woodland and river birds.

> *Froghall Woods   119   SK025484   1m S of Ipstones*
> *Woodland birds.*
>
> *Dimmingsdale   119   SK055430   1m NW of Alton*
> *Woodland birds.*
>
> *Ramshorn Common   119   SK075455   2m N of Alton*
> *Woodland birds.*
>
> *Castern Wood   119   SK115536   1½m SW of Alstonefield*
> *Woodland and river birds.*

TIC	Market Place, Leek (0538 381000)
	13 The Market Place, Ashbourne, Derbyshire (0335 43666)
YH	Ilam Hall, Ashbourne, Derbyshire (0335 29212)

RF	Red Lion, Ipstones, nr Froghall
	Jervis Arms, Onecote, nr Leek
	Olde Royal Oak, Wetton
	Izaak Walton, Ilam, nr Ashbourne
RFBBE	Greyhound Inn, Warslow, nr Leek (029 884 249)
BBE	Pethill Bank, Bottomhouse, Onecote, nr Leek (05388 555/277)
	Hillcrest House, Thorpe, nr Ashbourne (033 529 436)
	Blore Hall, Blore, nr Ashbourne (033 529 525)
BBSC	Old Furnace Farm, Greendale, Oakmoor, nr Cheadle (0538 702442)
SC	Summerhill Farm, Grindon, nr Leek (05388 264)
	Moorside Farm, Onecote (05388 567)

Trentham Park   127   4m S of Newcastle-under-Lyme
Car-park just west of A34 by SW edge of Trentham, near the junction of A34 and A5035 at SJ868407, then many paths.
Winter wildfowl; summer warblers; woodland birds including Redstart.

Hanchurch Woods   127 & 118   2m SW of Trentham
Car-park just south of minor road 2m NW of A51 from Stableford at SJ840397, then tracks north and south.
Woodland birds.

Park Hall Country Park   127   1½m NE of Longton
Car-park and visitor centre ¼m N of B5040, ½m W of A520 at SJ930448, then many paths.
Woodland and heathland birds including Whinchat and Stonechat.

> *Downs Bank   127   SJ902366   1½m N of Stone*
> *Woodland, river and heathland birds.*

> *Hem Heath Wood   118   SJ886410   1m E of Trentham*
> *Woodland birds including Wood Warbler and Redstart.*

TIC	Area Reference Library, Ironmarket, Newcastle-under-Lyme (0782 711964)
YH	Little Ranger, Oakamoor, Stoke-on-Trent (0538 702304)
RF	Mainwaring Arms, Whitmore
	Hunter, Saverley Green, nr Fulford
BBE	Home Farm Hotel, Swynnerton, nr Stone (078 135 241)
	The Hayes, Hayes Bank, Stone (0785 814589)

Westport Lake Park   118   2½m S of Kidsgrove
Car-park just west of A527 ½m NE of its junction with A500, 1m S of Tunstall, at SJ857501, then many paths.
Winter wildfowl and gull roost; passage waders and terns.

Greenway Bank Country Park   118   3½ m E of Kidsgrove
Car-park ¾m E of A527 from Brindley Ford, 1½m NW of Brown Edge at SJ890551, then many paths around the reservoir and through the woods.
Winter wildfowl; woodland and river birds including Dipper and Redstart.

> *Roepark   118   SJ856583   2½m NE of Kidsgrove*
> *Woodland birds.*

TIC   Town Hall, High Street, Congleton (0260 271095)
YH   Old School, Meerbrook, Leek (053 834 244)
BBE   Peacock Hay Farm, Talke, nr Kidsgrove (0782 773511)

Rudyard Reservoir & River Churnet   118   3m NW of Leek
Car-park at the south end of the reservoir ¼m N of B5331 1m W of A523 at SJ951583 and take the Staffordshire Moorlands Walks either north through the woods and beside the reservoir, or south down the River Churnet valley to Longsdon. Also car-park at the N end of the reservoir ¼m S of A523 from Ryecroft Gate at SJ938611.
Winter wildfowl; woodland birds and summer warblers including Redstart and Wood Warbler; river birds including Dipper and Kingfisher; passage waders.

Tittesworth Reservoir   118   2m N of Leek
Car-park at north end 1m NW of A53 ¼m SE of Meerbrook at SJ994604, or view from the causeway across the reservoir.
Winter wildfowl; passage waders.

The Roaches   119   3m NE of Leek
Car-park 1m Nw of A53 from upper Hulme at SK004622, then tracks north or south to the wooded cliffs and Hen Cloud.
Woodland and upland birds including Red Grouse, Twite, Redstart and Ring Ousel.

Back Forest & Black Brook   118 & 119   5m N of Leek
Park at Roach End 3m W of A53, 2½m N of Meerbrook at SJ996645, and paths north to wooded valley and NW along the ridge.
Woodland, river and upland birds including Black and Red Grouse, Twite, Ring Ousel, Redstart, Golden Plover and Dipper.

> *Stanley Pool   118   SJ935516   4½m SW of Leek*
> *Winter wildfowl.*

> *Deep Hayes Country Park   118   SJ960533   2½m SW of Leek*
> *Winter wildfowl and woodland birds.*

Longsdon Mill Pond *118 SJ953557 2m W of Leek*
Winter wildfowl and passage waders.

Swallow Moss *119 SK070603 1¾m NW of Warslow*
Moorland birds including Twite.

TIC	Market Place, Leek (0538 381000)
YH	As previous entry.
RF	Crown, Rushton Spencer, nr Leek
	Travellers Rest, Flash, nr Buxton
RFBBE	New Inn, Flash (0298 2941)
BBE	Fairboroughs Farm, Rudyard (02606 341)
	Bank End Farm, Longsdon, nr Leek (0538 383638)
SC	(New Lodge Cottage, Quarnford) Anchor Inn, Bolsover, Chesterfield (0246 823651)
	(Jasmine Cottage, Rudyard) Cullentra, Sutherland Road, Longsdon, Leek (0538 385030)

Suffolk

West Stowe Country Park & Gravel Pits   144 or 155   5m NW of Bury St. Edmunds
Car-park by minor road 1m E of A1101 at TL804713. Then paths south and west beside river and pits.
Woodland birds; wildfowl; passage waders and terns; summer Little Ringed Plover.

Cavenham Heath   155   8m NW of Bury St. Edmunds
Car-park 1m SW of A1101 by Icklingham to Tuddenham road at TL757727. Then marked trails.
Woodland and heathland birds including Nightjar and Whinchat.

Lakenheath Warren   143   2½ m SE of Lakenheath
Car-parks by A1065 on east side of Lakenheath Air Base e.g. TL756878, and tracks eastward.
Woodland and heathland birds including Nightjar.

> ***Botany Bay & Shepherds Fen***   *143   TL678854   2½m NW of Lakenheath*
> *Woodland birds; summer warblers.*

TIC	Athenaeum, Angel Hill, Bury St. Edmunds (0284 764667/757082)
	White Hart Street, Thetford, Norfolk (0842 752599)
YH	Heath House, off Warren Close, Bury Road, Brandon (0842 812075)
RF	Red Lion, Icklingham, nr Mildenhall
	Plough, Icklingham, nr Mildenhall
	Half Moon, Lakenheath
	Bull, Barton Mills, nr Mildenhall
BB	Eastleigh, West Stow, nr Bury St. Edmunds (0284 84264)
	30/31 Livermere Road, Timworth, nr Bury St. Edmunds (0284 848856)
BBE	The Olde Poste House, Culford, nr Bury St. Edmunds (0284 84310)
	North Stow Farm, Kings Forest, nr Bury St. Edmunds (0842 890356)

Wangford Warren   144   2½m S of Brandon
Car-park by B1106 at Mayday Farm, TL795835. Then track SW.
Woodland and heathland birds including Woodlark, Crossbill,
Nightjar, Goshawk and winter Great Grey Shrike.

Santon Downham   144   2–3m NE of Brandon
Several car-parks between A134 and B1107 e.g. between the Little
Ouse River and the railway line, ¾m SE of Santon Downham vil-
lage at TL827873; and SW of the village toward Brandon e.g.
TL808871. Then many tracks.
Woodland and heathland birds including Golden Pheasant,
Nightjar and Woodlark; river birds.

> *Brandon Country Park   144   TL788855   1m S of Brandon*
> *Woodland birds.*

> *Thetford Warren (Norfolk)   144   TL844840   2m NW of*
> *Thetford centre*
> *Woodland and heathland birds.*

TIC	As previous entry.
YH	As previous entry.
RF	Great Eastern, Brandon
	Duke of Wellington, Brandon
RFBBE	Dog & Partridge, East Wretham (095 382 245)
BBE	The Old Rectory, Weeting, nr Brandon (0842 810265)
	Cedar Lodge, West Tofts, nr Thetford (0842 878281)
BBSC	Brandon Lodge, 78 High Street, Brandon (0842 811236)
SC	(Brandon cottage) 28 Mustow Street, Bury St. Edmunds (0284 763053)
	Rymer Cottage, Rymer Farm, Barnham, nr Thetford (0842 890233)

Redgrave & Lopham Fens   144   5m W of Diss
Car-park at end of minor road 1½m SE of South Lopham at
TM046797. Then paths south.
Summer warblers; Nightingale; Bearded Tit; reedbed species;
woodland birds.

Knettishall Heath Country Park   144   6m SE of Thetford
Car-park by minor road 1½m W of Knettishall at TL956806. Then
many paths.
Woodland, heathland and river birds including Nightjar and
Hawfinch.

TIC	White Hart Street, Thetford, Norfolk (0842 752599)
YH	Heath House, off Warren Close, Bury Road, Brandon (0842 812075)

RF	White Elephant, Stuston, nr Diss
	Six Bells, Bardwell, nr Ixworth
BBE	Ingleneuk Guest House, Hopton Road, Garboldisham, nr Diss (095 381 541)
	Maltings Farm, Blo Norton Road, South Lopham (037 988 201)
SC	Driftway Cottage, Driftway, Badwell Ash, nr Bury St. Edmunds (03598 308)

Lowestoft Ness, Denes & Harbour   134   NE side of town

Car-park ¼m E of B1385, ¾m N of its junction with A12 at TM552954. Then walk south along the Denes and to the Ness and Harbour.

Migrants; gulls; winter waders; seawatching; summer Kittiwakes and Black Redstart.

Kessingland Denes   156   1–2m S of Kessingland

Car-park at the easternmost end of B1437 at TM536857. Then path south across the dunes to the gravel pits.

Migrants; winter Snow Bunting; passage waders; wildfowl.

Covehithe, Benacre Broad, Easton Wood & Broad   156   2½m-4½m S of Kessingland

Park at end of minor road ½m E of Covehithe, 2½m E of Wrentham at TM529819. Then coast path north to Benacre Broad and south along the cliffs to the other sites.

Migrants; passage waders; winter seaduck and divers, Snow and Lapland Bunting; summer ducks.

TIC	The Esplanade, Lowestoft (0502 565989/514274)
	*The Quay, Fen Lane, Beccles (0502 713196)
YH	2 Sandown Road, Great Yarmouth, Norfolk (0493 843991)
RF	Jolly Sailors, Pakefield, nr Lowestoft
	Crown, Southwold
BB	The Old Rectory, 157 Church Road, Kessingland (0502 740020)
BBE	Henstead Hall Country Hotel, Henstead, nr Kessingland (0502 740345)
	Quay House, Quay Lane, Reydon, nr Southwold (0502 722702)
SC	Sotterly Estate, Lower Green Farm, Sotterly, nr Beccles (0502 79850)

Blythburgh   156   4m W of Southwold

Park and view from A1095 ¼m N of Blythburgh village at TM453757. Also footpath around the south shore to hide and wood.

Passage and winter waders; migrants.

Walberswick & Westwood Marshes   156   1–2m W of Walberswick

Park by minor road SW of Walberswick at TM482743 and take paths north or south. Also excellent view of the marshes from the road 1½m further on at TM466737.

Marsh Harrier, Bearded Tit, Bittern, Nightingale; summer warblers including Savi's Warbler; passage waders; winter raptors and owls.

Corporation – Dingle Marshes   156   ½m-3m S of Walberswick

Park at the easternmost end of Walberswick nearest the beach and take the coastal path south beside the marshes, gravel pits and Dingle Hills.

Migrants; wildfowl; passage waders; Marsh Harrier, Bearded Tit; other reedbed species.

Dunwich & Westleton Heaths   156   1–2m E of Westleton

Park by minor road running east of Westleton e.g. at TM455695 and take path north. Also at TM449689 and footpath east. For Dunwich Heath car-park at end of road 2m S of Dunwich at TM476676 and footpaths north and west.

Heathland and woodland birds including Nightjar, Redstart and Nightingale.

Minsmere   156   3m SE of Westleton, 4m NE of Leiston

Follow signs to the reserve car-park from Eastbridge turning east off minor road between Eastbridge and Westleton. Car-park and reception centre at TM474682. Then trails to several hides. Also walk south down coast from Dunwich Heath car-park (see above) to public hide between the shore and the scrapes.

Summer terns, Avocet, Redstart, Nightingale, Nightjar, Cetti's Warbler, other warblers; Marsh Harrier, Bittern, Bearded Tit; heathland and woodland birds; passage waders and terns; migrants; wildfowl.

TIC	*Waveney Local Office, Town Hall, Southwold (0502 722366)
YH	Heath Walk, Blaxhall, Woodbridge (0728 88206)
RF	White Hart, Blythburgh
	Crown, Westleton
	Eel's Foot, Eastbridge
	Bell Hotel, Walberswick
RFBBE	Ship, Dunwich (072 873 219)
BB	Barn Cottage, Mill Street, Westleton (072 873 437)
	Dickon, Main Street, Walberswick (0502 724046)
BBE	Green Farm, Cookley, nr Halesworth (098 685 209)
BBESC	Priory Farm, Darsham (072 877 459)

SC (Westleton cottage) Bagwell House, Odiham, Hants
(Old School Cottage, Chediston) 5 Hawkrodge, Shoe-
buryness (0702 584514)
The Old School, Dunwich (072 873 570)
(Dunwich bungalow) 2 Camps Hall Cottages, Castle
Camps, Cambridgeshire (079 984 643)

North Warren & Thorpeness Meare   156   3m SE of Leiston
Car-park ¼m E of B1122 at North Warren, 2m N of Aldeburgh,
TM455587. Then tracks and footpaths N and NE across the reserve
and to the Meare.
Summer warblers; woodland and heathland birds; wildfowl; passage waders and terns; migrants; seawatching from Thorpe Ness
point itself.

**Aldeburgh Marshes & Alde Estuary   156   1m SW of
Aldeburgh**
Park at south end of Aldeburgh near where the road ends at
TM464560. Then footpath east and south by the River Alde and
around the southern edge of the marsh. Also at Snape Maltings,
TM392574 and footpath along the south shore of the estuary.
Waders and wildfowl; migrants; winter seaduck.

Orford & Havergate Island   169   10m E of Woodbridge
Car-park at Orford Quay, at S end of B1084, TM426497. Then
coastal path south around Chantry Point and Marshes. Seasonal
boat trips to Havergate Island from Orford Quay.
Summer terns; Avocets; passage and winter waders; winter
wildfowl.

TIC   *The Cinema, High Street, Aldeburgh (0728 453637)
Sea Front, Felixstowe (0394 276770)
YH   As previous entry.
RF   Mill Inn, Aldeburgh
Golden Key, Snape
Jolly Sailor, Orford
RFBBE Kings Head, Orford (0394 450271)
BBE   Wateringfield, Golf Lane, Aldeburgh (072 845 3104)
The Forge, Church Road, Blaxhall (072 888 346)
Gemini Cottage, 7 Long Row, Snape Road, Sudbourne
(0394 450207)
SC   The House in the Clouds, The Uplands, Thorpeness (081
252 0743/072 885 3787)
Quayview, Quay Street, Orford (0394 450229)
Barn Hall, Thorpeness (072 885 3105)
Old Brewery Cottage, Quay Street, Orford (0394 450275)

Sutton Common & Rendlesham Forest   169   3–5m SE of Woodbridge

Car-park by B1083 2m SE of its junction with A1152 at TM307476 and at TM335472 by minor road 3m SE of B1083. Then tracks north across the common and through the woods.

Heathland and woodland birds including Nightjar, Crossbill and occasional Goshawk; summer warblers.

Oxley Marshes   169   7m SE of Woodbridge

Park by minor road 1m E of Hollestay at TM368438. Then footpaths east and south by river and to the pits.

Passage waders; winter widlfowl and seaduck; summer terns.

Ramsholt & Shottisham Creek & Stonner Point   169   5m SE of Woodbridge

Park at Ramsholt Quay 2½m west of Alderton at TM307414 and take footpath north by the River Deben.

Passage and winter waders and wildfowl; summer warblers; migrants.

TIC	As previous entry.
YH	As previous entry.
RF	Ramsholt Arms, Ramsholt
	Plough, Sutton
	Fox, Hollesley
BB	Priory Cottage, Butley Low Corner, Butley, nr Woodbridge (0394 450382)
	Church Farm, School Lane, Hollesley, nr Woodbridge (0394 411792)
BBE	The Old House, Eyke, nr Woodbridge (0394 460213)

Felixstowe Ferry   169   2½m NE of Felixstowe centre

Park near end of the minor road northeast from Felixstowe at TM328377 and take footpaths north or south.

Passage and winter waders; winter wildfowl, seaduck and divers; seawatching; migrants.

Landguard Point   169   2½m SW of Felixstowe centre

Car-park near the beach at end of minor road (Manor Terrace) ½m S off A154 at TM290326. Then track south along the shore to the point.

Migrants; passage waders; winter seaduck; seawatching.

Waldringfield & Kirton Creek   169   3–5m S of Woodbridge

Park at the easternmost end of Waldringfield at TM286446. Then coastal path north, or south to Kirton Creek.

Passage and winter waders and wildfowl.

> **Martlesham Creek** 169 TM265473 1m S of Woodbridge
> Waders and wildfowl.

> **Brookhill Wood** 169 TM218440 4m E of Ipswich centre
> Woodland birds.

> **Thorpe Common & Trimley Marshes** 169 TM255375
> 3m NW of Felixstowe
> Waders; wildfowl; migrants.

TIC	As previous entry.
YH	As previous entry.
RF	Ferry Boat, Felixstowe Ferry
	Black Tiles, Martlesham
	Hand in Hand, Trimley St. Martin, nr Felixstowe
BBE	The White House, Bucklesham, nr Ipswich (047 388 325)
	Redhouse, Bridge Road, Levington, nr Ipswich (047 388 670)
BBESC	Orwell Meadows, Priory Lane, Nacton, Ipswich (0473 726666)

Alton Water 169 5m SW of Ipswich centre

View from minor road ¼m N of Tattingstone where it crosses the reservoir at TM136375. Also view from ½m south of the village. At the southern end there is a car-park, 1m N of B1080 between Sutton and Holbrook, at TM164357.
Winter wildfowl; passage waders and terns.

Pin Mill & Hall Point 169 6m SE of Ipswich

Park at the end of minor road ½m N of B1456 and Chelmondiston at TM206379. Then footpaths east through woods and north to Woolverstone Park and Hall Point.
Waders; winter widlfowl; woodland birds.

> **Shotley Marshes** 169 TM247351 3m SE of
> Chelmondiston
> Passage and winter waders and wildfowl.

> **Holbrook Bay** 169 TM174347 6m S of Ipswich
> Passage and winter waders; winter wildfowl.

TIC	Town Hall, Princes Street, Ipswich (0473 258070)
YH	East Bay House, 18 East Bay, Colchester, Essex (0206 867982)
RF	Butt & Oyster, Pin Mill
	Boot, Freston
	Queens Head, Erwarton
	Compasses, Holbrook

BBE   Mill House, Holbrook (0473 328249)
Old Rectory, Harkstead (0473 34586)
Grange, Chelmondiston (0473 84238)
SC   Mill Malthouse, The Mill, Holbrook (0473 327127)

Wolves Wood   155   2m NE of Hadleigh
Car-park by A1071, 2½m E of its junction with A1141, at TM054436. Then footpaths.
Summer warblers; woodland birds; Nightingale.

Felshamhall Wood   155   6m SE of Bury St. Edmunds
Park by minor road 3m E of A134, 1m W of Gedding, at TL935581 and path south and west through the woods.
Birds as at Wolves Wood.

*Groton Wood   155   TM977430   3m W of Hadleigh
Woodland birds.*

TIC   Toppesfield Hall, Hadleigh (0473 822922)
YH   Monks Croft, Bury Road, Alpheton, Sudbury (0284 828297)
RF   Crown, Buxhall
Kings Head, Bildeston, nr Chelsworth
RFBBE Peacock, Chelsworth (0449 740758)
Bell, Kersey, nr Hadleigh (0473 823229)
BBE   Mount Pleasant Farm, Offton, nr Ipswich (047 333 8896)
Red House Farm, Kersey, nr Ipswich (0787 210245)
SC   Bridge House, Kersey, nr Hadleigh (0473 823770)

Surrey

Frensham Common & Ponds   186   3m S of Farnham
Car-parks by the Little Pond ¾m E of A287 at SU857417 and at the
north end of Great Pond just W of A287, ¾m S of Frensham at
SU847406. Also many tracks across the common in between.
Passage and winter wildfowl; passage terns and waders; reedbed
species; winter gull roost; woodlark.

Thursley Commons   186   4m SW of Godalming
Car-park by minor road 1½m S of B3001 from Elstead at SU900417,
then paths and tracks east and south.
Woodland and heathland birds including Dartford Warbler,
Hobby, Nightingale, Woodlark, Nightjar, Redstart and winter
Great Grey Shrike.

> *Puttenham Ponds   186   SU912457   4m E of Farnham*
> *Passage and winter wildfowl; woodland birds and summer*
> *warblers.*

> *Hankley Common   186   SU885415   4½m SE of Farnham*
> *Heathland and woodland birds including Nightjar and Hobby.*

> *Devil's Punch Bowl & Beacon Hill   186   SU895360*
> *2–3m N of Haslemere.*
> *Woodland and Heathland birds including Hobby, Crossbill and*
> *Firecrest.*

> *Witley Common   186   SU930405   3m SW of Godalming*
> *Woodland birds; summer warblers.*

TIC	Locality Office, South Street, Farnham (0483 861111)
YH	Devil's Punch Bowl, 1m N of Hindhead (042873 4285)
RF	Barley Mow, Tilford, nr Farnham
	Three Horseshoes, Thursley
BB	Sycamore, Sands Road, The Sands, Farnham (02518 2117)
SC	Mrs Ransom, Bowlhead Green Farm Cottage, Bowlhead Green, nr Hindhead

Sidney Wood   186   6m SE of Godalming
Car-park by minor road 1¼m W of A281 from Alfold Crossways at
TQ026351, then tracks and path south through the wood.
Woodland birds and summer warblers including Nightingale and
Redstart.

Winkworth Arboretum   186   2m SE of Godalming
Car-park by B2130 2m SE of A3100 at SU990412, then track east.
Also car-park on eastern side ½m S of Thorncombe Street.
Woodland birds; summer warblers; wildfowl.

> *Hydon Heath   186   SU978400   2½m S of Godalming*
> *Woodland birds; summer warblers.*

> *Hambledon Hurst   186   SU965374   4m S of Godalming*
> *Woodland birds.*

> *Hascombe Hill   186   TQ005390   4m SE of Godalming*
> *Woodland birds; summer warblers.*

TIC   Guildford House Gallery, 155 High Street, Guildford
         (0483 444007)
YH   As previous entry.
         Radnor Lane, Holmbury St. Mary, Dorking (0306 730777)
RF   White Horse, Hascombe, nr Godalming
         Sun, Dunsfield, nr Cranleigh

Frimley Gravel Pits   186   between Frimley & Farnborough
Car-park at Farnborough North railway station, ½m E of A325 at
SU877566, then track east between the pits.
Wildfowl; summer warblers and Little Ringed Plover; passage
terns and waders; reedbed species.

Pirbright Common   186   2m SW of Pirbright
Park by minor road between A321 and A324, 1¼m SW of B3012 at
SU912550, then tracks and paths east and south *if the red flags are
not flying*. (This is a military training area.)
Heathland and woodland birds including Dartford Warbler,
Redstart, Nightjar, Hobby; winter raptors and Great Grey Shrike
occasionally.

Send Gravel Pits   186   3m SE of Woking centre
Park and view from minor roads between A247 and B367, 1½m N
of A3, e.g. TQ040564. Also marked paths around the pits.
Passage and winter wildfowl; passage terns and waders; summer
Little Ringed Plover.

Bagshot Heath & Olddean Common 186 *SU887628*
2m W of Bagshot.
Heathland and woodland birds including Woodlark, Hobby,
Crossbill and Redstart.

TIC The Library, Pinehurst, Farnborough, Hants (0252 513838)
YH Polesdon Lacey, Dorking (0372 52528)
RF New Inn, Send, nr Woking
Saddler's Arms, Sendmarsh, nr Woking
White Hart, Pirbright

Staines Reservoir 176 **1m N of Staines**
Park by A3044 (Staines Moor Road) 1m N of its junction with A30 at TQ046730, then track east between the reservoirs.
Passage and winter wildfowl and grebes; passage waders, terns and passerines.

Queen Mary Reservoir 176 **2m SE of Staines**
Entrance at NE corner of the reservoir by the A308 at Littleton Common, TQ080704 (the junction of Staines Road West and Ashford Road). Permit from Thames Water (Central Division), New River Head, Rosebury Avenue, London EC1 4TP. Tel: 071 837 3300.
Passage and winter wildfowl; winter gull roost.

Island Barn Reservoir & Field Common Gravel Pits 176
2m N of Esher
Park at the end of minor road 2m N of A317, about ½m E of Queen Elizabeth II Reservoir, at TQ130668. Then paths north and south to gravel pits and east to Island Barn Reservoir.
Passage and winter wildfowl; migrants.

Shepperton Gravel Pits 176 **3m E of Staines**
Park just S of B376 (Laleham Road) at Shepperton Green, TQ068678, then path south between the pits.
Passage and winter wildfowl; migrants.

Walton Reservoirs 176 *TQ120685* *2m NE of Walton-on-Thames*
Passage and winter wildfowl. (Permit as for Queen Mary Reservoir.)

Virginia Water & Valley Gardens 176 *SU975690* *4m SW of Staines.*
Wildfowl and woodland birds.

Chobham Common 176 *SU965655* *2m N of Chobham*
Woodland and heathland birds; migrants.

TIC	Town Hall, New Zealand Avenue, Walton-on-Thames (0328 710885)
YH	Edgeworth House, Mill Lane, Windsor, Berks (0753 861710)
RF	Three Horseshoes, Laleham, nr Chertsey Swan, Staines
BB	37 Gloucester Drive, Wraysbury (0784 64858)

Great Bookham Common   187   3m W of Leatherhead
Park at Bookham railway station, 1½m N of A246 at TQ127556, then paths and tracks north over the footbridge through the woods. Or park by minor road at the west end of the common, 1¼m S of A245 from Stoke D'Abernon, at TQ134570 and paths east.
Woodland birds and summer warblers.

Ashtead Common   187   2m N of Leatherhead
Car-park by B280 1½m W of Epsom at TQ183611, then tracks and paths south toward Ashtead.
Woodland birds and summer warblers include Hawfinch and Redstart.

> ***Ockham Common***   *187   TQ080585   2m SE of Byfleet*
> *Woodland birds and summer warblers.*

> ***Engham Ponds***   *187   TQ116553   1½m NW of Great Bookham*
> *Wildfowl; summer warblers.*

> ***Horton Country Park***   *187   TQ190630   2m NW of Epsom*
> *Woodland birds; summer warblers; winter wildfowl.*

TIC	As previous entry.
YH	Polesdon Lacey, Dorking (0372 52528)
RF	King William IV, Mickleham, nr Leatherhead Plough, Effingham
BBE	Apple Tree Cottage, 3 Oakshade Road, Oxshott (037284 2087)

Ranmore Common   187   2–3m W of Dorking
Car-parks by minor road 2–3m W of A24 at TQ142504 and TQ126503 then paths north.
Woodland birds and summer warblers including Redstart and Wood Warbler.

Effingham Forest & Hackhurst Downs   187   5m W of Dorking
Car-park by minor road 1½m SW of A246, 2½m S of East Horsley at TQ092510 then tracks south. Also tracks north from Abinger Hammer on A25 at TQ093476.

Woodland birds and summer warblers including Nightingale, Redstart, Wood Warbler, Hobby and Nightjar.

Pewley Down & The Chantries   186   1–2m SE of Guildford
Car-park down minor road ½m E of A281 at TQ004484 then North Downs Way eastward.
Woodland birds and summer warblers including Nightingale.

TIC   Guildford House Gallery, 155 High Street, Guildford
             (0483 444007)
YH   As previous entry.
RF   Black Horse, Gomshall

Box Hill Country Park   187   1m NE of Dorking
Car-parks by minor road 1½m W of Box Hill, 1m E of A24, at TQ180513 then many paths.
Woodland birds and summer warblers.

Headley Heath   187   3m SE of Leatherhead
Car-parks by B2033 ½m and 1m NW of its junction with B2032, S of Headley at TQ205539 and TQ206533. Then take paths west.
Woodland and heathland birds including Nightjar; summer warblers.

TIC   As previous entry.
YH   As previous entry.
RF   Royal Oak, Brockham, nr Dorking

Holmwood Common   187   2–3m S of Dorking
Car-park by minor road 1m E of A24 from South Holmwood at TQ184454, then paths NW through the woods.
Woodland birds and summer warblers.

Leith Hill & Wotton Common   187   4½m SW of Dorking
Car-park by minor road 1½m N of B2126, 2½m NW of A29, at TQ131434. Then tracks east and north.
Woodland birds including Redstart, Wood Warbler and Hobby.

Hurt Wood & Holmbury Hill   187   3½m NE of Cranleigh
Car-parks by minor road 1½m SE or SW of Peaslake at TQ098433 and TQ080428 and take tracks east.
Woodland birds and summer warblers including Redstart and Nightjar.

Glovers Wood   187   1m W of Charlwood
Park at the end of minor road on the west side of Charlwood at TQ235411 then path west through the woods.
Woodland birds and summer warblers.

Winterfold Heath & Woods 187 TQ058428 2.5–3m N *of Cranleigh.*
Woodland birds and summer warblers including Nightjar and Crossbill.

Abinger Common 187 TQ115455 4m SW of Dorking
Woodland birds.

Hammonds Copse 187 TQ213445 3m NW of *Charlwood*
Woodland birds.

Reffolds Copse 187 TQ193435 1m N of Newdigate
Woodland birds.

TIC	As previous entry.
YH	Radnor Lane, Holmbury St. Mary, Dorking (0306 730777)
RF	Plough, Coldharbour, nr Sutton
	Abinger Hotel, Abinger Common
	Surrey Oaks, Newdigate
BB	Bulmer Farm, Holmbury St. Mary (0306 730210)
BBE	Crossways Farm, Raikes Lane, Abinger Hammer, nr Dorking (0306 730173)
SC	Westland Farm, Ockley Road, Ewhurst, nr Cranleigh (0483 277270)

Nutfield Marsh Gravel Pits 187 1½m NE of Red Hill
Car-park at the east end of Mercers Lake by minor road ½m SE of South Merstham, 1½m NW of A25, at TQ300518. Then paths north and south around the pits.
Passage and winter wildfowl; passage and winter waders and terns; summer warblers and Little Ringed Plover.

Godstone Reservoirs 187 ½m W of Godstone
Park by A25 just west of the junction with the B2236, at TQ349516, then track north between the lakes.
Passage and winter wildfowl; Little Ringed Plover; summer warblers.

Hedgecourt Lake 187 TQ355404 3m NW of East *Grinstead*
Wildfowl; woodland birds and summer warblers.

TIC	Katharine Street, Croydon (081 760 5630)
YH	Crockham Hill Rise, Crockham Hill, Edenbridge, Kent (0732 866322)
RF	Dog & Duck, Outwood, nr Smallfield
	Whyte Harte, Bletchingley
BBE	Oaklands, Felcourt, nr Lingfield (0342 834705)

Sussex

Thorney Island   197   6m SW of Chichester
Park by the church at the end of minor road at West Thorney 2m S
of the A27, SU769024, then coast path north or south.
Passage and winter waders and wildfowl; gulls; summer terns;
migrants.

**East Head and Chichester Harbour   197   6½m NW of
Selsey Bill**
Car-park by the sea front ¾m SW of West Wittering at SZ772978,
then coast path NW.
Passage and winter waders and wildfowl; winter grebes, seaducks
and divers; summer and passage terns; gulls.

West Itchenor   197   2m NE of West Wittering
Park by the front at West Itchenor 1½m N of the B2179 at
SU799015, then coast path west or east.
Birds as Thorney Island.

Selsey Bill   197   7m S of Chichester
Car-park at the end of minor road ½m W of the B2145 at SZ844930,
then walk south to the Bill and east to the east side, or northwest
along the coast. Also car-park by the east side 1m NE of the Bill at
SZ866934 and coast path N or S.
Migrants; seawatching; winter divers, grebes and seaducks.

Pagham Harbour   197   6m S of Chichester
Car-park and information centre at Sidlesham Ferry by the B2145
1½m S of Sidlesham at SZ856964, then paths around the harbour
and to the hides. Also car-park at the end of minor road in Church
Norton at the S end of the harbour at SZ873956, then paths NW
and S to the spit and the Severals. Also on the N side of the
harbour, S of Pagham itself, at SZ884966 and coast path N.
Passage and winter waders and wildfowl; winter raptors, Twite
and Short-eared Owl; migrants; winter seaducks, divers and
grebes.

Chichester Gravel Pits   197   1m E and SE of Chichester centre
Park by minor road ½m S of the A27 from Westhampnett at SU884056, then path west between the gravel pits. Other pits viewable from the B2145 north of North Mundham e.g. just south of the A27 at SU868036 and the path SE.
Passage waders; wildfowl; gull roost; passage and summer terns; migrants.

Kingley Vale   197   5m NW of Chichester
Car-park 1m N of East Ashling (on B2178) at SU825088, then track and nature trail north across Stoke Down.
Woodland, downland and scrub species and summer warblers including Nightingale; Golden Pheasant, Hawfinch; migrants.

TIC	St. Peter's Market, West Street, Chichester (0243 775888)
	Belmont Street, Bognor Regis (0243 823140)
YH	Warningcamp, Arundel (0903 882204)
RF	Crab and Lobster, Sidlesham
	Old House at Home, Chidham, nr Southbourne
	Crown and Anchor, Dell Quay, Chichester
BB	Lark Rise, Shipton Green, Itchenor, nr Chichester (0243 512390)
SC	Hunston Mill, Selsey Road, Chichester (0243 783375)

Arundel Wildfowl & Wetland Trust Reserve   197   1m N of Arundel
Car-park and visitor centre at TQ024084 by minor road 1½m N of A27 (from the east end of the by-pass), then tracks to the hides.
Reedbed species; passage waders; passage and winter wildfowl.

Burton Mill Pond   197   2½m S of Petworth
Car-park and information centre by minor road at the N end of the lake 1m SE of A285 at TQ979181.
Wildfowl, reedbed species and woodland birds.

> **Waltham Brooks**   *197   TQ026162   6m N of Arundel*
> *Passage and winter wildfowl; passage waders.*

> **Northpark Wood**   *197   TQ054155   2m S of Pulborough*
> *Woodland birds.*

> **Littlehampton Golf Course**   *197   TQ020014   ½m SW of Littlehampton centre*
> *Migrants.*

TIC	61 High Street, Arundel (0903 882268/882419)
YH	As previous entry.

RF   The Swan, Fittleworth, nr Pulborough
           The George and Dragon, Houghton, nr Arundel
BB   Marsh Acres, South Lane, Houghton (0798 831854)
           Portreeves Acre, The Causeway, Arundel (0903 883277)
           New House Farm, Broadford Bridge Road, West Chil-
           tington, nr Pulborough (07983 2215)

The Mens   197   3½m NE of Petworth
Park by minor road ¼m SE of A272 at TQ026235, then path north
through the woods.
Woodland birds.

Petworth Park   197   0–2m NW of Petworth
Car-park by A283 1½m NW of Petworth at SU966238, then paths
east.
Woodland birds including Hawfinch.

Ebernoe Common   197   4m N of Petworth
Car-park in Ebernoe by church at SU976278, 1½m NE of A283,
then paths south.
Woodland birds including Nightingale and Hawfinch.

Black Down   186 & 197   2m SE of Haslemere
Car-park by minor road 1½m SE of B2131 at SU923306, then tracks
and paths south.
Woodland birds; summer warblers; Nightingale.

Lavington Common   197   3m SW of Petworth
Park by minor road 1½m W of A285, 2m NE of Graffham, at
SU946187, then paths and tracks north and south.
Heathland and woodland birds including Nightjar and Dartford
Warbler.

Iping Common   197   2½m W of Midhurst
Car-park ¼m S of A272, ½m W of Stedham at SU854220 and tracks
west and east.
Heathland and woodland birds including Nightjar.

>   *Ambersham Common   197   SU914195   2m SE of
>   Midhurst*
>   *Heathland and woodland birds.*
>
>   *Graffham Down   197   SU923165   4m SE of Midhurst*
>   *Woodland birds and summer warblers.*
>
>   *Lickfold Mill Pond   197   SU938258   3½m NW of
>   Petworth*
>   *Wildfowl.*

TIC	As previous entry.
YH	As previous entry.
	Devil's Punch Bowl, 1m N of Hindhead. (0428 734285)
RF	Horseguards, Tillington, nr Petworth
	Halway Bridge, Lodsworth, nr Midhurst
	Lickfold Inn, Lickfold, nr Midhurst
BB	Mill Farm, Trotton, nr Midhurst (0730 813080)

Cissbury Ring & Lychpole Hill 198 3–4m N of Worthing

Car-park by minor road, 1¼m E of A24, 1m E of Findon at TQ137086, then tracks south to Mount Carvey and SE below Lychpole Hill Woods.

Woodland birds; summer warblers; downland birds; migrants.

Adur Estuary & Shoreham Beach 198 by Shoreham-by-Sea

Car-parks are on the west side of the bridge by A259 at TQ211050, then path north beside the estuary; at the harbour mouth, 1½m E of A259 at TQ233045; and by Widewater just S of A259 at TQ206044 (½m SW of the bridge).

Passage and winter waders and wildfowl; winter grebes, divers and seaduck; seawatching.

TIC	Town Hall, Chapel Road, Worthing (0903 210022)
YH	Tottington Barn, Truleigh Hill, Shoreham-by-Sea (0903 813419)
RF	Village House Hotel, Findon, nr Worthing
	Red Lion, Shoreham-by-Sea
RFBB	Castle Hotel, The Street, Bramber (0903 812102/815993)
BBE	Nash Hotel, Horsham Road, Steyning (0903 814988)

Seaford Bay & Tide Mills 198 between Seaford & Newhaven

Park at the NW end of Seaford front, ½m S of A259 at TV467997 and take the path heading NW.

Winter seaduck and divers; passage waders and terns; migrants.

Cuckmere Haven 199 2m E of Seaford

Car-park by A259 at Exceat, 2½m W of East Dean at TV518994, then tracks and path S either side of the river. Also park at South Hill Farm, 1m S of A259 at TV504981 and tracks west and east.

Passage waders; migrants; winter wildfowl and seaduck; seawatching.

Lullington Heath 199 2m NW of East Dean

Car-park just off minor road at the S end of Jevington, 2m N of A259 at TQ563013, then tracks SW toward Friston Forest or NW to the heath.

Heathland and scrub species; summer warblers, Nightingale, Dartford Warbler; migrants; raptors.

Arlington Reservoir   199   4m SW of Hailsham
Car-park by B2108 (formerly a minor road) 1½m N of A27, ½m N of Berwick Railway Station at TQ527074, then track around the reservoir.
Passage waders and terns; passage and winter wildfowl and gulls.

Beachy Head   199   3m SW of Eastbourne
Many parking areas by the minor road between Birling Gap, 1½m S of East Dean (on A259) and the B2103. e.g. at Belle Tout, TV562958 and paths east or west; by Beachy Head Hotel, TV590957, then paths east to Whitbread Hollow and SW towards the lighthouse.
Migrants; seawatching.

> *Lewes Levels* 198   TQ415075   *1–2m S of Lewes*
> *Winter wildfowl; summer and passage waders.*

> *Langney Point*   199   TQ644010   *2m NE of Eastbourne*
> *Seawatching; winter seaduck; passage waders and terns.*

> *Manxey Level*   199   TQ650070   *1½m N of Pevensey*
> *Winter waders and wildfowl.*

> *Horse Eye Level*   199   TQ630087   *2m E of Hailsham*
> *Winter waders and wildfowl.*

> *Combe Hill*   199   TQ575023   *3m NE of East Dean*
> *Woodland and scrub species; summer warblers.*

TIC	3 Cornfield Road, Eastbourne (0323 411400/27432)
	Station Approach, Seaford (0323 897426)
YH	Bank Cottages, Telscombe, Lewes (0273 37077)
	Frog Firle, Alfriston, Polegate (0323 870423)
	East Dean Road, Eastbourne (0323 21081)
RF	Market Cross Inn, Alfriston, nr Seaford
	Plough and Harrow, Litlington, nr Seaford
	Golden Galleon, Exceat Bridge, nr Seaford
SC	Gilbert Estate, Birling Manor, East Dean, nr Eastbourne (0323 422217)
	(Alfriston Cottage, Seaford) Seaford Cottage, Alfriston Road, High and Over, Seaford (0323 890049)
	(Crangon & Danny Cottages, Birling Gap & Alfriston) National Trust, Scotney Castle, Lamberhurst, nr Tunbridge Wells (0892 890651)
BB	Pleasant Rise Farm, Alfriston (0323 870545)
BBE	Birling Gap Hotel, East Dean, nr Eastbourne (03215 3163/3197)
RFBBE	Alfriston Wingrove Inn, Alfriston (0323 870276)

Ashdown Forest   187 & 188   4–6m SE of East Grinstead
Car-parks by minor roads 1½m E of Wych Cross (the junction of
A275 and A22) at TQ443326 (there is a visitor centre here) and
1–1½m NE of Nutley (3m SE of Wych Cross) at TQ455288. Then
use the many paths north and south.
Woodland and heathland birds including Hawfinch, Nightjar and
Crossbill; summer warblers; migrants.

Weirwood Reservoir   187   2m S of East Grinstead
Car-park by minor road overlooking the reservoir near the western
end, 2m S of B2110 at TQ384342 and path along the north shore.
Passage waders; passage and winter wildfowl; summer warblers;
woodland birds.

Ardingly Reservoir   187   3m N of Haywards Heath
View from minor road 1m W of Ardingly (on B2028) where it
crosses the reservoir at TQ333298 and paths along the shore from
either end of the causeway.
Wildfowl; woodland birds; passage terns and gulls.

> ***Chaily Common*** *198   TQ386217   4m SE of Haywards
> Heath centre*
> *Heathland and woodland birds*

> ***Ditchling Common Country Park*** *198   TQ336184   1m
> E of Burgess Hill*
> *Heathland and woodland birds.*

> ***Wapsbourne Woods*** *198   TQ395237   4m E of Haywards
> Heath*
> *Woodland birds.*

> ***Hedgecourt Lake (Surrey)*** *187   TQ355404   3m NW of
> East Grinstead*
> *Wildfowl; reedbed species; summer warblers and woodland
> birds.*

TIC   Horsham Museum, The Causeway, Horsham (0403
         211661)
         Monson House, Monson Way, Tunbridge Wells, Kent
         (0892 515675)
YH   Blackboys, Uckfield (082582 607)
RF   The Cat, West Hoathly, nr East Grinstead
         White Hart, Selsfield Common, nr East Grinstead
BBE   Acorn Lodge, Turner's Hill Road, East Grinstead (0342
         23207)
SC   Coppers, 20 Luxford Road, Lindfield, Haywards Heath
         (04447 3284)

Bewl Water   188   7m SE of Tunbridge Wells
Car-parks at the visitor centre, 1m SW of A21 at the north end of
the reservoir, at TQ676387, then path around the reservoir, and
1½m N of B2099, on the southern side near Chessons Farm, at
TQ673320, then path to hide overlooking the reserve. Also a minor
road crosses the extreme eastern end 1m S of A21 at TQ700320.
Passage waders, terns and gulls; passage and winter wildfowl;
summer warblers; woodland birds; migrants.

TIC	As previous entry.
YH	As previous entry.
RF	Brown Trout, Lamberhurst
	Elephant's Head, Hook Green, nr Lamberhurst
BB	Cock Farm, Stonegate, nr Wadhurst (0580 200305)
BBE	Furnace Farm, Furnace Lane, Lamberhurst (0892 890788)
SC	Birch Cottage, five Ashes, Mayfield, nr Crowborough (082 585 265)

Fore Wood   199   4m NW of Hastings centre
Park near the church in Crowhurst 2m S of A2100 at TQ756125,
then marked trails west to the woods.
Woodland birds and summer warblers including Hawfinch.

**Fairlight Country Park & Covehurst Bay   199   3m NE of
Hastings centre**
Car-park ¼m S of minor road at W end of Fairlight, 2m E of A259 at
TQ860116, then tracks and paths south, east and west through
woods and scrub overlooking the bay.
Migrants; woodland birds; summer warblers; winter seaduck and
divers.

Pett Pools and Shore   189   2m S of Winchelsea
View from the minor road between the pools and the sea, 1½m SW
of Winchelsea Beach at TQ903145.
Passage and winter waders and wildfowl; winter seaduck and
divers.

Rye Harbour   189   2m SE of Rye
Car-park at end of minor road at Rye Harbour, 2m SE of A259 at
TQ940190, then tracks and path S and SW to the hides.
Passage and winter wildfowl and waders; summer and passage
terns; reedbed species; migrants; seawatching; winter Snow and
Lapland Buntings and Twite.

> *Powdermill Reservoir*   199   TQ797195   *6m N of
> Hastings*
> *Woodland birds; wildfowl.*
>
> *Guestling Wood*   199   TQ863145   *4m NE of Hastings*
> *Woodland birds.*

TIC	48 Cinque Ports Street, Rye (0797 222293)
	4 Robertson Terrace, Hastings (0424 718888)
YH	Guestling Hall, Rye Road, Guestling, Hastings (0424 812373)
RF	Two Sawyers, Pett, nr Hastings
	Queen's Head, Icklesham, nr Winchelsea
	Queen's Head, Rye
	William the Conqueror, Rye Harbour
BB	Strand House, Winchelsea (0797 226276)
	The Old Vicarage, Rye Harbour (0797 222088)
	Cliff Farm, Iden Lock, nr Rye (0797 8331)
SC	(Coastguard Cottage, Rye Harbour) Mill House, Peasmarsh, nr Rye (0797 21340)

Warwickshire & West Midlands

Bartley Reservoir   139   3m SE of Halesowen
View from minor roads around the reservoir, ¾m NE of Frankley,
e.g. from Scotland Lane along the west bank at SO999807.
Winter wildfowl and gull roost.

Edgbaston Reservoir   139   2m W of Birmingham centre
Car-park by east shore ½m W of Ladywood, ½m N of Hagley Road
(A456) at SP045866, then paths around reservoir.
Winter wildfowl and gull roost.

Saltwells Wood   139   3m NW of Halesowen
Park by minor road ½m E of A4036, from roundabout ¼m N of its
junction with A4100, at SO935867. Then paths through woods to
the north.
Woodland birds and summer warblers including Wood Warbler.

> ***Pensnett Pools*** 139 *SO915885* *2m SW of Dudley*
> *Winter wildfowl.*

> ***Sheepwash Park*** 139 *SO973916* *2m NE of Dudley*
> *Wildfowl; winter gull roost; migrants.*

TIC 39 Churchill Precinct, Dudley, W Midlands (0384 50333)
YH Cambrian Halls, Brindley Drive, off Cambridge Street,
Birmingham (0527 70712)
RF Fox and Grapes, Pensnett
Wharf, Old Hill, Cradley Heath
Wall Heath Inn, Wall Heath, nr Kingswinford
RFBBE Saltwells Inn, Saltwells, Brierley Hill (0384 69224)

Sandwell Valley Country Park   139   1½m E of West Bromwich
Car-park ¾m down Forge Lane /Park Lane south of A4041, 1¼m NE of junction 1 of M5, at SP027922. RSPB reserve car-park and visitor centre ½m NE, ¼m S of B4167 at SP036931.
Passage and winter wildfowl; passage waders and terns; woodland birds; migrants.

Chasewater   139   2m NW of Brownhills
Car-park at south end of reservoir ½m N of A5, from ¼m E of its junction with A452, at SK036072. Then paths around the shore.
Winter wildfowl and gull roost; passage waders and terns.

Sutton Park   139   1½m W of Sutton Coldfield
Park just off A452 at Banners Gate, 1m SE of its junction with A4041 at SP090955, then paths east. Also from 1m east of here at SP107952 and from B4151 at north end.
Woodland birds; summer warblers; wildfowl; migrants.

TIC   As previous entry.
YH   As previous entry.
R   George and Dragon, Clayhanger, nr Brownhills
RF   Wheel Inn, Brownhills
RFBBE Plough and Harrow, Pinfold Hill, Shenstone, nr Lichfield (0543 480377/480826)

Kingsbury Water Park   139   5m S of Tamworth
Car-parks from minor road joining A4091 and A4097; one just E of the canal at Broomey Croft, SP202969; and another ½m N of Bodymoor Heath ¼m E of M42 at SP210964. Then many paths north and south around the lakes.
Winter wildfowl and gull roost; summer warblers, Little Ringed Plover and Common Tern; passage terns.

Lea Marston Pits   139   1½m S of Kingsbury
View from minor road ¼m SE of A4097 from Marston at SP213943.
Passage and winter wildfowl; passage waders.

Alvecote Pools   140   3m E of Tamworth
Car-park 1¼m N of B5000 ½m SE of Alvecote at SK250044, then path north from the road and over the railway line. Also view from minor road on north side ½m S of Shuttington.
Passage and winter wildfowl; summer warblers; passage waders and terns.

> *Dosthill Gravel Pits   139   SP205987   3½m S of Tamworth*
> *Passage and winter wildfowl; passage terns and waders.*

TIC	Marmian House, Lichfield Street, Staffs (0827 311222)
YH	As previous entry.
	Copt Oak, Markfield, Leicester (0530 242661)
R	Bird in Hand, Austrey, nr Polesworth
RF	Royal Oak, Kingsbury
	Green Man, Middleton, nr Tamworth
BBE	Monwode Lea Farm, Over Whitacre, nr Coleshill (0675 81232)

Bentley & Monks Park Woods   140   2m SW of Atherstone
Park by B4116 at Bentley, ¼m SW of Bentley Common, at SP283957 and take track SE. Or park at east end of this track ½m NE of Birchley Heath at SP293950 and walk NW and view from minor road to the NE.
Woodland birds.

Hartshill Hayes Country Park   140   2m S of Atherstone
Car-park by minor road ¾m NW of Hartshill, ¾m N of B4114 at SP316944, then paths through the woods.
Woodland birds; summer warblers.

Seeswood Pool   140   2½m SW of Nuneaton centre
View from B4102 ¼m SW of its junction with B4112 at SP329905.
Passage and winter wildfowl; passage waders and terns.

> *Bedworth Sloughs   140   SP350872   ¾m W of Bedworth centre*
> *Passage and winter wildfowl; passage waders; migrants especially autumn Swallow roost.*

TIC	Nuneaton Library, Church Street, Nuneaton, Warks (0203 384027)
YH	As previous entry.
RF	Rose Inn, Baxterley, nr Atherstone

Coombe Country Park & New Close Wood   140   4m E of Coventry centre
Signed car-park N of A427 2m west of Brinklow at SP404797, then many paths around the lake and through the wood. Track south of the main road, opposite the entrance, leads to New Close Wood.
Wildfowl and woodland birds.

Wappenbury Wood   140   6m SE of Coventry centre
Park ½m W of B4453, 1½m W of A423 from Princethorpe, at SP382709. Then take track and path north through the woods.
Woodland birds including Nightingale.

Draycote Water Country Park   151 & 140   4m SW of Rugby
Car-park just W of A426 1½m SW of M45 and Dunchurch at
SP466692. To drive around the perimeter get permit from the garage in Kites Hardwick (½m S of entrance on A426).
Winter wildfowl, sawbills, divers, huge gull roost; passage waders, terns and passerines.

Crackley Woods   140   1¼m N of Kenilworth centre
Park by minor road ¾m N of A429, ½m NW of Crackley, at
SP287737, then path east through woods.
Woodland birds and summer warblers.

> *Brandon Marsh   140   SP388754   4m SE of Coventry
> centre*
> *Wildfowl; summer warblers; migrants.*

> *Stoke Floods   140   SP374790   2½m E of Coventry centre*
> *Wildfowl and reedbed species; summer warblers.*

> *Piles Coppice   140   SP385770   3½m SE of Coventry
> centre*
> *Woodland birds and summer warblers.*

TIC   Central Library, Coventry, W Midlands (0203 82311/2)
YH   Church Green, Badby, Daventry, Northants (0327
703883)
RF   Raven, Brinklow, nr Coventry
Malt Shovel, Bubbenhall, nr Kenilworth
RFBBE   Dun Cow Hotel, Dunchurch, nr Rugby
Golden Lion Inn, Easenhall, nr Rugby (0788 832265)
BBE   Marton Fields Farm, Marton, nr Rugby (0926 632410)
BBESC   Snowford Hall Farm, Hunningham, nr Leamington (0926
632297)

Earlswood Lake & Clowes Wood   139   4m W of Dorridge
Car-park by B4102 1¼m N of its junction with B4101 by east side of
the lake at SP116738. Also from minor road ¼m NE of The Lakes
railway station at Terry's Green, SP112738 and take path around
western half of the lake and through Clowes Wood.
Wildfowl; passage terns; woodland birds and summer warblers
including Wood Warbler.

> *Windmill Naps   139   SP093725   5m SW of Dorridge*
> *Woodland birds.*

TIC   Civic Square, Alcester Street, Redditch, Worcs (0527
60806)
YH   Cambrian Halls, Brindley Drive, off Cambridge Street,
Birmingham (0527 70712)

RF	Bulls Head, Earlswood
BBE	Norton House, 230 Norton Lane, Earlswood (05646 2348)

Newbold Comyn Country Park   151   1m E of Leamington Spa centre
Signed car-park just N of A425, 1¼m W of Radford Semele, at SP330655, then many paths and nature trail.
Woodland and river birds.

Ufton Fields   151   2½m W of Southam
Park by minor road ½m S of A425 from Ufton at SP378615, then path north.
Winter wildfowl; summer warblers.

Bishop's Bowl   151   3m SW of Southam
Park just W of B4451 ½m S of its junction with B4452, 1m N of Bishop's Itchington, at SP390590. Then nature trail around the lakes and through the woods.
Wildfowl; summer warblers.

> *Chesterton Fish Ponds   151   SP360580   4½m SW of Southam*
> *Wildfowl.*

TIC	Royal Pump Room, The Parade, Leamington Spa, Warwickshire (0926 311470)
YH	Church Green, Badby, Daventry, Northants (0327 703883)
RF	White Hart, Ufton, nr Southam
	Harvester, Long Itchington, nr Southam
	Shakespeare, Harbury, nr Southam
	Two Boats, Long Itchington
RFBBE	Old New Inn, Farm Street, Harbury (0926 613027)
BBE	Hill Farm, Lewis Road, Radford Semele, nr Leamington Spa (0926 337571)
BBESC	Sharmer Farm, Fosse Way, Radford Semele (0926 612448)
SC	Holt Farm, Southam (092 681 2225)

Edge Hill Woods   151   3½m SW of Fenny Compton
Park in Edge Hill 1m N of A422, ½m W of Ratley, at SP375475, then paths into woods to the west and tracks north and south.
Woodland birds; migrants.

Wormleighton Reservoir   151   2m E of Fenny Compton
Park by minor road ½m N of Claydon, 1½m E of A423, at SP461513, then path west beside Oxford Canal to the reservoir (¾m).
Passage waders and wildfowl.

Burton Dassett Country Park   *151*   *SP395520*   *1½m W of Fenny Compton*
Downland and scrub species.

TIC	The Green, Cropredy, Oxon (0295 758203)
YH	As previous entry.
RF	Castle, Edge Hill
	George and Dragon, Fenny Compton
BBE	Nolands Farm, Oxhill, nr Pillerton Priors (0926 640309)
	Crandon House, Avon Dassett, nr Banbury (029 577 652)
	Willowbrook House, Lighthorne Road, Kineton (0926 640475)

Whichford Wood   **151**   **1¼ m NE of Long Compton**
Park by minor road 1m SW of Whichford, 1m NE of A34 from Long Compton, at SP296343, then track and paths south.
Woodland birds and summer warblers.

TIC	Talbot Court, Stow-on-the-Wold, Gloucs (0451 31082)
YH	Stow-on-the-Wold, Cheltenham, Gloucs (0451 30497)
RF	Gate, Upper Brailles, nr Shipston-on-Stour
BBE	Archways, Crockwell Street, Long Compton (060 884 358)

Wiltshire

Shear Water & Aucombe Down   183   2½ m SW of
Warminster
Car-park by the lake, 1m W of A350 fron Crockerton, at ST855420,
then track around the north side of the Water and west through the
woods.
Woodland birds including Crossbill; winter wildfowl.

Brimsdown Hill   183   **5m SW of Warminster**
Park by minor road 3m W of Longbridge Deveril, 1m SE of Horn-
ingsham at ST826404, then track south to the hill top and ridge to
SW.
Woodland, scrub and downland birds; summer warblers;
migrants.

Clanger & Picket Woods   183   ST875545   2m N of Westbury
Woodland birds and summer warblers including Nightingale.

> *Westbury Pits*   *183*   *ST864519*   *1m NW of Westbury*
> *centre*
> *Passage and winter wildfowl.*

TIC   The Central Car-park, Three Horseshoes Mall, War-
minster (0985 218548)
*The Library Car-park, Edward Street, Westbury (0373
827158)
YH   Bathwick Hill, Bath, Avon (0225 65674)
RF   Bath Arms, Horningsham, nr Warminster
Dove, Corton, nr Warminster
Cross Keys, Corsley, nr Warminster
BB   Welam House, Bratton Road, West Ashton, nr Trow-
bridge (0225 755908)
BBESC Spinney Farmhouse, Chapmanslade, nr Westbury (0373
88412)

Somerford Common & Ravensroost Wood   173   4m NW of Wootton Bassett
Park by minor road 2¼m W of B4696, 4m W of Purton at SU022876, then track north through the wood and south ¼m to Somerford Common.
Woodland birds and summer warblers including Redstart and Nightingale.

Coate Water   173   2m SE of Swindon centre
Car-park at the north end near the dam, ¼m S off A4259 at SU176826, then path around the lake to the hides.
Passage waders and terns; passage and winter wildfowl; summer warblers.

> ***Braydon Pond*** *173   ST998883   5½m NW of Wootton Bassett*
> *Winter wildfowl.*

> ***Lydiard Park*** *173   SU103845   2½m NE of Wootton Bassett*
> *Woodland birds.*

TIC   32 The Arcade, Brunel Centre, Swindon (0793 530328)
YH   Littleholm, Upper Inglesham, Highworth, Swindon (0367 52546)
RF   Three Crowns, Brinkworth, nr Wootton Bassett
BB   Bullocks Horn Farm, Charlton, nr Malmesbury (0666 7458)
     Little Cotmarsh Farm, Broad Town, Wootton Bassett (0793 731322)
     Parsonage, Chiseldon, nr Swindon (0793 740204)
BBE   Dolls Guest House, The Street, Latton, nr Cricklade (0793 750384)

Marlborough Downs   173   5m NW of Marlborough
Park by minor road at Hackpen Hill, 1½m SE of A4361 at SU129746, and take the Ridgeway N towards Barbury Hill or S to Fyfield Down.
Downland birds including Stone Curlew, Quail and Hobby; winter raptors; migrants; winter Golden Plover and possible Great Grey Shrike.

West Woods   173   3m SW of Marlborough
Park down lane ¼m SE of Lockeridge (1m S of A4) at SU153673, then tracks and paths south through the woods.
Woodland birds and summer warblers including Redstart.

Pewsey Downs & Wansdyke   173   6m SW of Marlborough
Park by minor road 1¼m NE of Alton Barnes at SU116637 then tracks east or west along Wansdyke to Horton Down.
Downland birds including Stone Curlew and Quail; migrants; winter raptors.

TIC	*St. Peter's Church, High Street, Marlborough (0672 53989)
	*The Great Barn, Avebury (06723 425)
YH	Bathwick Hill, Bath (0225 65674)
RF	Who'd a Thought It, Lockeridge, nr Marlborough
	Up the Garden Path, Manton, nr Marlborough
BBE	Bayardo Farm, Clatford Bottom, nr Marlborough (0672 55225)
	Windmill House, Winterbourne Monkton, nr Marlborough (06723 446)

Savernake Forest   173 & 174   0.5–4m SE of Marlborough
Posterne Hill car-park is just north of A346, 1m SE of the centre of Marlborough, at SU197678, then many tracks and marked trails to the SE.
Woodland birds including Wood Warbler, Redstart, Turtle Dove, Nightjar and Nightingale.

Chilton Foliat & Littlecote   174   2m NW of Hungerford
Park by the church in Chilton Foliat by the B4192, ¼m W of its junction with the B4001 at SU317705, then path south across the river, west along minor road and track through Littlecote Park and meadows by the River Kennet. Also view the lake from the B4192 just east of the village.
River and water meadow species; summer warblers, winter wildfowl.

> *Ramsbury Manor Lake   174   SU263711   1m SW of Ramsbury*
> *Winter wildfowl; river birds.*

> *Bedwyn Common   174   SU257656   5m SE of Marlborough*
> *Woodland birds; summer warblers.*

> *Wilton Water   174   SU264620   2m SW of Great Bedwyn*
> *Wildfowl.*

> *Wilton & Bedwyn Brails   174   SU275625   &   284625*
> *1½m S of Great Bedwyn*
> *Woodland birds.*

TIC	As previous entry.
YH	Court Hill Ridgeway Centre, Court Hill, Wantage, Oxon (02357 60253)
RF	Harrow, Little Bedwyn Cross Keys, Great Bedwyn Bell, Ramsbury
BBE	The Old Vicarage, Burbage, nr Marlborough (0672 810495)

Salisbury Plain   184   10–15m NW of Salisbury
View from A360 between Tilshead and West Lavington and from track NE from Gore Cross (SU008510). Also from minor road SW of Tilshead to Chitterne. *When artillery ranges are not in use and the red flags are not flying* the minor road/track E of Tilsbury to the Bustard Hotel (SU092462) and the track north from West Down (SU054476) to Market Lavington (SU024535) may be explored.
Summer downland birds include Quail, Stone Curlew and Hobby; scrub species including Whinchat; winter raptors.

Steeple Langford Gravel Pits   184   5m NW of Wilton
Car-park by minor road ¼m S of A36 from Steeple Langford, just south of the river at SU036370 and view from the footpath 200yds north on the east of the road.
Passage and winter wildfowl.

Fonthill Lake   184   10m W of Wilton
Park by minor road 1m S of B3089 from Fonthill Bishop at ST934317, view from here and path south beside the lake. Also from the bridge just south of Fonthill Bishop at ST934326.
Passage and winter wildfowl.

> ***Compton Down***   *184   SU034277   4½m SW of Wilton*
> *Downland birds; migrants; Hobby.*

> ***Langdean Bottom***   *184   ST935364   2½m N of Fonthill Bishop*
> *Woodland birds.*

> ***Grovely Woods***   *184   SU066336   2½m NW of Wilton*
> *Woodland birds.*

> ***Porton Down***   *184   SU215356   5m SE of Amesbury*
> *Downland birds and scrub species.*

TIC	Redworth House, Flower Lane, Amesbury (0980 623255) Fish Row, Salisbury (0722 334956)
YH	Milford Hill House, Milford Hill, Salisbury (0722 27572)

RF   Royal Oak, Great Wishford, nr Wilton
          Kings Arms, Fonthill Bishop
          Beckford Arms, Fonthill Bishop
BBE   Rollestone Manor, Shrewton, nr Larkhill (0980 620216)
          Stoke Farm, Broadchalke, nr Salisbury (0722 780209)
          Porton Hotel, Porton, nr Salisbury (0980 610203)
BBESC Scotland Lodge, Winterborne Stoke (0980 620493)

Britford Water Meadows   184   2m SE of Salisbury centre
Park in Britford, ½m E of A338 at SU161280, then tracks east to the River Avon across the meadows.
Winter wildfowl; river birds.

Pepperbox & Dean Hills   184   5½m SE of Salisbury
Car-park by A36 1¼m NW of its junction with A27 at SU212248, then track and path NE along the ridge past Pepperbox and on towards Dean Hill (SU250260).
Downland and woodland birds; migrants.

> ***Whiteparish Common***   *184   SU255224   1m SE of Whiteparish*
> *Woodland birds and summer warblers.*

> ***Langley Wood***   *184   SU225205   1½m E of Redlynch*
> *Woodland birds.*

> ***Blackmoor Copse***   *184   SU235294   5½m E of Salisbury*
> *Woodland birds.*

TIC   Fish Row, Salisbury (0722 334956)
YH   As previous entry.
RF   Radnor Arms, Nunton, nr Salisbury
          Appletree Inn, Morgans Vale, Redlynch
BBE   St. Marie's Grange, Alderbury, nr Salisbury (0722 710351)

Yorkshire & North Humberside

Spurn Head   113   8m SE of Withernsea
Toll ½m S of Kilnsea. Car-park at the Information Centre/Observatory, TA419150, and near the lighthouses at the southern end, TA405114.
Migrants; seawatching; many rarities.

Kilnsea – Easington   113   7m SE of Withernsea
Park in Kilnsea, TA416158, and explore the triangle of land to the SW and the coast north to Beacon Lane Pool and Easington.
Migrants; passage waders; passage and winter wildfowl.

Skeffling   113   2m SW of Easington
Park at end of minor road south of Skeffling at TA370184 and take coast path east or west.
Passage and winter waders and wildfowl.

TIC	75–76 Carr Lane, Hull, Humberside (0482 223559)
YH	The Friary, Friars Lane, Beverley, N. Humberside (0482 881751)
RF	Plough Inn, Hollym
	Crown and Anchor, Kilnsea
SC	Spurn Bird Observatory, Kilnsea, via Patrington, Hull

Cherry Cob & Stone Creek   113   5m SW of Patrington
Park at end of minor road 4m S of Keyingham at Stone Creek, TA234189. Then coast path NW to Cherry Cob and Foulholme.
Passage and winter wildfowl and waders.

Paull and Hedon Haven 107   2m SW of Hedon
Park near the lighthouse at the front, TA166263, and take the coast path south to the mouth of Thorngumbold Drain , or north beside Hedon Haven Estuary.
Passage and winter wildfowl, waders and gulls.

Hull Docks & Holderness Drain   107   TA137286   3m E
of Hull centre
Passage waders; winter northern gulls.

Kelsey Pits   107   TA238265   1m NW of Keyingham
Passage and winter wildfowl.

TIC	As previous entry.
YH	As previous entry.
R	Crown Inn, Paull
RF	Shakespeare Inn, Hedon
	White Horse, Ottringham

Hornsea Mere   107   **1m SW of Hornsea**
Signed car-park at Kirkholme Point at east end of the mere, ¼m
west of B1242 at TA198474, and footpath along the south side from
minor road ½m SW of B1242.
Passage waders and terns; winter wildfowl; Bittern, Bearded Tit,
other reedbed species; migrants.

Tophill Low Reservoirs   107   **5m NE of Beverley**
Park at end of minor road 3m east of A164 at Wilfholme Landing,
TA062472 and take the bridleway or footpath north between the
Beverley and Barmston Drain and the reservoirs.
Passage and winter wildfowl; passage waders; migrants; summer
warblers.

Hornsea Beach   107   TA212474   1m E of B1242
Winter seaduck; seawatching.

Burshill   107   TA096480   1½m W of Brandesburton
Passage and winter wildfowl.

Grimston   107   TA285354   3m SE of Aldbrough
Migrants.

TIC	*Floral Hall, Esplanade, Hornsea, Humberside (0964 532919)
YH	As previous entry.
RFBBE	George & Dragon, Aldbrough (0964 527230)

Brough Creek & Welton Ings   106   **between Brough &
North Ferriby**
Park on the south side of Brough, 1½m SW of A63, ¼m S of the
railway line at SE936284. Take the coastal footpath SE beside the
estuary toward Welton Ings.
Passage and winter waders and wildfowl.

Faxfleet Ness & Weighton Lock   106   3½m SE of Gilberdyke
Park in Faxfleet, 3m S of B1230 at SE864243. Take track or coast path NE to the mouth of the Market Weighton Canal or SW to Faxfleet Ness.
Passage and winter waders and wildfowl; reedbed species; migrants.

Saltmarshe Delph   106   4½m SW of Gilberdyke
View from minor road along the south side 1½m NW of Saltmarshe at SE775247, or from hide on the north bank.
Summer warblers; reedbed species; winter wildfowl.

> ***North Cliffe Wood***   *106   SE864370   3m SW of Market Weighton*
> *Woodland birds.*

> ***Broomfleet Ponds***   *106   SE866280   1m NW of Broomfleet*
> *Summer warblers; reedbed species; passage and winter wildfowl.*

> ***Humber Bridge Country Park***   *106   TA020255   2m E of North Ferriby*
> *Summer warblers; migrants; passage and winter waders.*

TIC   North Bank Viewing Area, Ferriby Road, Humber Bridge (0482 640852)
YH   As previous entry.
R   Buccaneer, Brough
RF   Black Horse, Ellerker
BBESC   Rudstone Walk Farmhouse, South Cave, nr Brough (0430 422230)

Skipwith Common   106 or 105   4½m NE of Selby
Park in Skipwith 1½m N of A163 at SE665385 and take track and footpath south to the common.
Heathland and woodland birds including Nightjar and Long-eared Owl.

Allerthorpe Common   106   3m SW of Pocklington
Car-park by minor road 1m SW of A1079 at SE755481. Then many tracks and paths through the woods.
Woodland birds.

Pocklington Canal   106   4m SW of Pocklington
Park in Melbourne 1½m E of B1228 at SE747443 and take track N and towpath east or west beside the canal.
Winter wildfowl and passage waders; summer warblers.

Seavy Carr   106 SE758448 3½m SW of Pocklington
Passage waders; summer warblers.

Wheldrake Ings   106 SE700440 1½m SE of Wheldrake
Passage and winter wildfowl; passage waders.

Derwent Bridge   106 SE707364 ½m W of Bubwith
Winter wildfowl; passage waders.

Hagg Wood   106 SE685525 2½m SW of Stamford Bridge
Woodland birds.

TIC	Park Street, Selby, N Yorks (0757 703263)
YH	Peter Rowntree Memorial Hostel, Haverford, Waterend, Clifton, York (0904 653147)
RF	St. Vincent Arms, Sutton-upon-Derwent
BB	Grange Farm, Sutton-upon-Derwent (0904 85265)
BBE	Derwent Lodge, Low Catton, nr York (0759 71468)
SC	The Coach House, Storwood Manor, Storwood, nr York (0759 318518)

Fairburn Ings   105   **2m NE of Castleford centre**
Park in Fairburn ¼m SW of A1 at SE471277 and take path south to hides. Also view from minor road west of Fairburn beside the north shore, and, further west, from footpath SW of Newton Farm, SE445278.
Passage waders, terns and wildfowl; winter wildfowl and gull roost; summer warblers.

Bishop Wood   105   **4m W of Selby**
Park by minor road 1m SE of B1222 e.g. SE555334. Then many tracks and nature trails north or south.
Woodland birds and summer warblers.

Ledston Park   105 SE445310 3m N of Castleford
Woodland birds.

Pontefract Park   105 SE446224 2m SE of Castleford centre
Passage waders; migrants.

Swillington Ings   104 SE390280 3m NW of Castleford centre
Passage waders and terns; passage and winter wildfowl.

TIC	As previous entry.
YH	As previous entry.

RF   The Chequers, Claypit Lane, Ledsham, nr Castleford
BBE   The Cocked Hat Hotel, London Road, South Milford, nr
          Selby (0757 683945)
          Mill Farm, Gorse Lane, South Milford (0977 682979)

Thorpe Marsh   **111**   **4m N of Doncaster**
Park by minor road 1½m SW of Barnby Dun, 3m NE of A19 at
SE594087. Then tracks north over bridge.
Summer warblers and waders; passage and winter wildfowl.

Potteric Carr   **111**   **1½m SE of Doncaster centre**
Car-park at end of track 1m SW of A638 on SW edge of Bessacarr at
SE598010. Then path west and south. Also car-park on the west
side off A6182 at SE590014.
Passage and winter wildfowl; summer warblers; reedbed species;
passage waders and terns.

Sprotborough Flash   **111**   **2½m SW of Doncaster**
Park at south side of Sprotborough 1m N of A630, on the north side
of bridge over the River Don at SE537015. Then path SW between
the river and the lake, or track on the north side.
Passage and winter wildfowl; summer warblers; woodland birds;
reedbed species; Kingfisher.

Denaby Ings   **111**   **4m SW of Doncaster**
Car-park by minor road 1m NE of A6023, 1½m NE of Mexborough
at SE498008. Then track to the hide.
Passage waders and terns; winter widlfowl; summer warblers and
Little Ringed Plover; reedbed species.

> ***Thorne Waste & Goole Moors***   *112*   *SE730160*   *4m S of
> Goole*
> *Woodland birds including Nightjar, Redstart and Nightingale;
> spring Dotterel; winter raptors including Hen Harrier roost.*

> ***Sandall Beat Wood***   *111*   *SE613040*   *2½m NE of
> Doncaster centre*
> *Woodland birds and summer warblers; Nightingale.*

TIC   Central Library, Doncaster, S Yorks (0302 734309)
YH   Langsett: c/o 7 New Bailey, Crane Moor, Sheffield (0742
        884541)
RF   Cadeby Inn, Cadeby, nr Conisburgh

Thrybergh Reservoir   **111**   **3m NE of Rotherham centre**
Signed car-park and visitor centre from A630 about 1m NE of
Thrybergh at SE474963.
Passage and winter wildfowl; winter gull roost.

Rother Valley Country Park   111   6½m SE of Sheffield centre
Signed car-parks from B6058 and A618 to the north of Killamarsh. Also paths west from minor road ½m W of A618 at SE460830, 1m W of Wales and M1.
Passage and winter wildfowl; passage terns and waders; winter gull roost.

> ***Ulley Reservoir   111   SE455876   6½m E of Sheffield centre***
> *Passage and winter wildfowl and gulls.*

TIC   Central Library, Walker Place, Rotherham, S Yorks (0709 823611)
YH   As previous entry.
RF   Ship Inn, Kilnhurst, nr Swinton
          Royal Oak, Ulley

Wintersett Reservoirs   111 or 110   5½m NE of Barnsley centre
Car-park 1m NW of Ryhill, 1½m NW of B6428, between the reservoirs at SE375154. Also view from minor road across the eastern arm.
Passage and winter wildfowl; passage terns and waders; winter gulls.

Newmillerdam Country Park   111 or 110   5½m N of Barnsley centre
Car-park by A61 at SE332157, then many tracks and paths around the lakes and through the woods.
Woodland birds; summer warblers; winter wildfowl.

Carlton Marsh   111 or 110   3m NE of Barnsley centre
Car-park by minor road 1½m E of B6132 from Carlton at SE378104, then paths south.
Summer warblers; passage and winter wildfowl.

Worsborough Mill Country Park   111 or 110   2m S of Barnsley centre
Signed car-park west from A61 2½m N of junction 36 of M1 at SE352033. Also track across southern end of the reservoir to the hide from A61 at SE347031.
Passage waders; woodland birds; passage and winter wildfowl; Kingfisher; reedbed species.

Bretton Country Park   110   5½m NW of Barnsley centre
Car-park by A637 ½m N of junction 38 of M1 at SE295125. Then trails around the lakes and through the woods.
Passage and winter wildfowl; passage terns; woodland birds; summer warblers.

Stony Cliffe Wood   *110*   *SE272155*   *2m SW of Hornbury*
Woodland birds.

Wombwell Wood   *111 or 110*   *SE375027*   *3m SE of*
Barnsley centre
Woodland birds.

Broomhill Flush   *111*   *SE415030*   *1m E of Wombwell*
Passage waders and wildfowl; summer warblers.

Howell Wood   *111*   *SE435095*   *5½m NE of Barnsley*
centre
Woodland birds.

TIC   56 Eldon Street, Barnsley, S Yorks (0226 206757)
YH   As previous entry.
RF   Kings Arms, Heath, Warmfield, nr Wakefield

Langsett & Midhope Reservoirs   110   3m NW of Stocksbridge
View from minor road off A616 south from Langsett at SE213005.
Winter wildfowl and gull roost; passage waders; woodland birds.

Midhope Moors & Margery Hill   110   4m W of Stocksbridge
From western end of track on the south side of Langsett reservoir
at SK203998, take track SW up onto the moors and Mickleton Edge
south toward Margery Hill.
Upland birds including Red Grouse, Golden Plover, Merlin, Hen
Harrier, Ring Ousel, Peregrine and Short-eared Owl.

Ingbirchworth Reservoir   110   2½m NW of Penistone
View from minor road along the southern side ¾m west of
Ingbirchworth on A629. Or from car-park on the north side at
SE215064.
Passage waders and terns; winter wildfowl.

Winscar Reservoir   *110*   *SE150025*   *5m W of Penistone*
Passage and winter wildfowl.

Ewden Beck   *110*   *SK243968*   *2m SW of Stocksbridge*
Woodland and river birds including Redstart and Dipper.

TIC   49–51 Huddersfield Road, Holmfirth, W Yorks (0484
687603)
YH   As previous entry.
RF   Cubley Hall, Mortimer Road, nr Penistone
BBSC   Weaver's Cottages, 3–5 Tenter Hill, Thurlstone, nr Penistone (0226 763350)

Eccup Reservoir   104   5m N of Leeds centre
Car-park ½m W of A61, 1½m N of its junction with A6120, at
SE308416. Then track and path around the reservoir.
Passage and winter wildfowl; large winter gull roost including
regular northern species; passage terns; woodland birds.

Fewston & Swinsty Reservoirs   104   4½m N of Otley
Car-park between the reservoirs 1½m W of B6451, 1m S of A59, at
SE187537. Then track around Swinsty Reservoir. Also view from
causeway om minor road on the eastern side of Swinsty at
SE198536.
Passage and winter wildfowl; woodland birds.

> *Thruscross Reservoir   104   SE155575   2m NW of*
> *Blubberhouses*
> *Passage and winter wildfowl.*

> *Lindley Wood Reservoir   104   SE215495   2m NE of*
> *Otley*
> *Woodland birds and winter wildfowl.*

TIC Council Offices, 8 Boroughgate, Otley, W Yorks (0943
   465151)
YH The Old Rectory, Linton-in-Craven, Skipton, N Yorks
   (0756 752400)
RF Queens Head, Kettlesing, nr Harrogate
   Stone House, Thruscross, nr Blubberhouses
BB Old Hall Farm, Clifton, nr Otley (0943 463972)

Bolton Park Woods   104   6m NW of Ilkley
Car-park ¼m E of B6160, 1½m N of A59, 1m N of Bolton Abbey at
SE077553. Then nature trail north through woods and beside River
Wharfe.
Woodland and river birds including Pied Flycatcher, Redstart,
Dipper, Kingfisher and Common Sandpiper.

Grass & Bastow Woods   98   1½m NW of Grassington
Footpath east up through the woods from minor road 2m NW of
Grassington (on B6265) at SD982656.
Woodland birds and summer warblers.

> *Hebden Moor   98   SE045660   3m NE of Grassington*
> *Upland birds including Golden Plover, Red Grouse and Ring*
> *Ousel.*

TIC 8 Victoria Square, Skipton, N Yorks (0756 792809)
   *Grassington National Park Centre, Hebden Road, N
   Yorks (0756 752748)
YH As previous entry.

RF	Craven Arms, Appletreewick, nr Skipton
BBE	Haughside, Appletreewick (0756 72225)
SC	Highcroft, Burnsall, nr Skipton (0756 72668)
	Estate Office, Bolton Abbey, nr Skipton (0756 71227)

Malham Tarn & Moss   98   4m NE of Settle
Car-park by minor road N of Malham, ¼m W of the tarn at
SD883673. Then track east and footpaths and nature trail to Tarn
Moss, around the tarn and through the woods.
Summer warblers and woodland birds; passage and winter wild-
fowl; Red Grouse; winter Twite and large gull roost.

**Clapham Lake & Ingleborough Common   98   3m SE – 2m E
of Ingleton**
Park in Clapham ¼m E of A65 at SD746693. Then track north
beside the lake, Clapham Beck and woods and up to Ingleborough.
Passage and winter wildfowl; woodland and river birds including
Dipper and Redstart; Upland birds including Twite, Red Grouse,
Ring Ousel, Golden Plover and Dunlin.

> *Semer Water   98   SD920870   2m SW of Bainbridge*
> *Passage and winter wildfowl.*

> *Fountains Fell   98   SD870710   3m NW of Malham Tarn*
> *Upland birds including Golden Plover and Dunlin.*

TIC	Town Hall, Cheapside, Settle, N Yorks (07292 5192)
	Pen-y-Ghent Cafe, Horton-in-Ribblesdale, N Yorks (07296 333)
YH	John Dower Memorial Hostel, Skipton, N Yorks (07293 321)
	Taitlands, Stainforth, Settle, N Yorks (07292 3577)
RF	Rose & Crown, Bainbridge
RFBBE	Game Cock, Anstwick, nr Settle (04685 226)
	Queen Victoria, Kirkby Malham
	Buck Inn, Malham (07293 316)
BBE	Park Bottom Country Guest House, Litton (075 677 235)
	The Mains, Woodlands, Giggleswick (07292 2576)
SC	Scalegill, Kirkby Malham (07293 293)

Leighton & Roundhill Reservoirs   99   4m SW of Masham
View from minor road around the west side 4m SW of A6108 e.g. at
SE155786.
Passage and winter wildfowl.

Gouthwaite Reservoir   99   2–4m NW of Pateley Bridge
View from minor road along the west shore 2–4m NW of B6265 e.g.
at SE123705.
Passage and winter wildfowl; passage waders and terns; winter
gull roost.

Studley Park   99   2m SW of Ripon
Entrance and car-park off B6265 2m SW of Ripon centre at
SE278704. Then many paths.
Woodland and river birds including Hawfinch, Pied Flycatcher,
Redstart, Dipper and Kingfisher.

> *Birk Gill & Witton Moor*   99   SE130824   6m W of
> *Masham*
> *River, woodland and upland birds.*

> *Thornton Reservoir*   99   SE180880   4m SE of Leyburn
> *Passage and winter wildfowl.*

> *Mile House Gravel Pits*   99   SE216821   1m N of Masham
> *Passage and winter wildfowl.*

TIC	*Southlands Car-park, off High Street, Pateley Bridge, N Yorks (0423 711147)
	*Minster Road, Ripon, N Yorks (0765 4625)
YH	Lilac Cattage, Ellingstring, nr Masham, Ripon, N Yorks (0677 60216)
RF	Yorke Arms, Ramsgill, nr Pateley Bridge
BBE	Pasture House, Healey, nr Masham (0765 89149)
	Haregill Lodge, Ellingstring (0677 60272)
	Longside House, Ramsgill (0423 75207)
SC	(Fountains Abbey & Studley Royal cottages, nr Ripon) National Trust, 27 Tadcaster Road, Dringhouses, York (0904 702021)

Whitestone Cliff & Gormire Lake   100   5m E of Thirsk
Car-park by A170 at the top on the east side of Sutton Bank, 2½m E
of Sutton-under-Whitestonecliffe at SE516830. Then Cleveland
Way north along the top of Whitestone Cliff to South Woods, and
path down to Gormire Lake below.
Woodland birds and summer warblers including Redstart and
Wood Warbler; winter wildfowl.

Roulston Scar   100   2½m SE of Sutton-under-Whitestonecliffe
Car-park by minor road at the top of the hill 1½m N of Kilburn at
SE516812. Then track, footpaths and nature trail west and north.
Woodland birds.

Castle Howard Lake   100   5m W of Norton
Park in Coneysthorpe 2½m S of B1257 at SE714714. Then track and
path south beside the lake and around the woods.
Passage and winter wildfowl; summer warblers and woodland
birds.

Ashberry Wood & River Rye   100   SE573850   2½m NW
of Helmsley
Woodland and river birds including Redstart, Wood Warbler
and Kingfisher.

Hovingham High Wood   100   SE646747   2m SW of
Hovingham
Woodland birds.

TIC	*14 Kirkgate, Thirsk, N Yorks (0845 22755)
	*Sutton Bank Visitor Centre, Sutton Bank, Thirsk, N Yorks (0845 597426)
YH	Carlton Lane, Helmsley, N Yorks (0439 70433)
RF	Forrester's Arms, Kilburn
RFBB	Worsley Arms, Hovingham
BBE	High House Farm, Sutton Bank, Cold Kirby (0845 597557)
SC	(School House, Sutton-under-Whitestonecliffe) Thornborough House Farm, South Kilvington, Thirsk (0845 22103)

Levisham Moor & Beck   100   **6m NE of Pickering**
Park by A169 near High Horcum and take paths south or west from
hairpin bend at bottom of the hill (SE850941), down Levisham
Beck and up onto the moor.
Woodland, river and moorland birds including Dipper, Redstart,
Golden Plover and Red Grouse.

Dalby Forest & Bridestones   101   **4½m NE of Thornton Dale**
Car-park by minor road at Adderstone Rigg, 2½m E of A169, 4m N
of A170 at SE883905. Then many tracks south through the forest
and northwest to Bridestones and Grime Moor.
Woodland, river and moorland birds including Nightjar, Crossbill
and Red Grouse.

Thornton Dale & Dalby Beck   100   **3m NE of Thornton Dale**
Car-park in Low Dalby on the east side of the river at SE856874.
Then track south through the woods and beside the river.
River and woodland birds including Dipper and Crossbill.

TIC	*Eastgate Car-park, Pickering, N Yorks (0751 73791)
	St. Nicholas Cliff, Scarborough, N Yorks (0723 373333)
YH	The Old School, Lockton, Pickering, N Yorks (0751 60376)
RF	Moor Cock, Langdale End (closed on Sunday)
RFBBE	New Inn, Cropton, nr Pickering (07515 330)
	Horseshoe, Levisham (0751 60240)
BB	Vivers Mill, Pickering (0751 73640)

BBESC Easthill Guest House, Thornton Dale, nr Pickering (0751 72722)

SC (Keldy Castle, Forest Cabins, nr Cropton) Forest Holidays, Forestry Commission, 231 Corstophine Road, Edinburgh (031 334 2576)

Flamborough Head   101   4m NE of Bridlington

Car-parks near the head itself at east end of B1259, TA250707; at South Landing, ½m S of Flamborough village, TA230695; Danes Dyke, 1m SW of Flamborough at TA215695; and at NE end of B1255, 1½m NE of Flamborough at TA239719. Coast path around the peninsula especially from South Landing eastwards.

Migrants; seawatching; seabird colonies; winter divers, seaduck and grebes; summer warblers and woodland birds.

Bempton Cliffs   101   4m N of Bridlington

Car-park at end of minor road 1½m N of Bempton (on B1229) at TA197740. Then coastal path east or west.

Summer seabird colonies including 700 pairs of Gannet; winter seaduck, divers and grebes; migrants.

Barmston Lagoons & Fraisthorpe Sands   107 & 101   4–5m S of Bridlington

Car-park at end of minor road ½m E of Barmston, 1m E of A165 at TA172594. Then coast path south to the mouth of Barmston Main Drain and north to the lagoons and sands.

Passage waders; migrants; winter Lapland and Snow Bunting, divers and seaduck.

> ### Bridlington Harbour   101   TA185665   SE side of Bridlington
> *Winter gulls, seaduck and divers.*

TIC 25 Prince Street, Bridlington, Humberside (0262 673474)

YH The Whitehouse, Burniston Road, Scarborough (0723 361176)

RF Seabirds, Flamborough
Viking Inn, nr Flamborough

RFBBE Royal Dog & Duck, Flamborough

BBE Aaheather Cottage, 12 Chapel Street, Flamborough (0262 851036)

SC Grange Farm cottages, Marton, nr Bridlington (0262 674522)

Broxa Forest & River Derwent   101   7m NW of
Scarborough
Car-park by minor road 3½m NW of Scalby, 2½m W of Cloughton
at SE966945. Then track through the forest to the west and path
down to the River Derwent.
Woodland and river birds including Nightjar, Turtle Dove, Dipper
and Kingfisher.

Forge Valley & Scarwell Wood   101   3½m SW of
Scarborough
Car-park by minor road 2m N of West Ayton (on A170) at
SE984875. Then paths south and NE beside the river and through
the woods.
Woodland birds, summer warblers and river birds including Dipper and Hawfinch.

Filey Brigg & Country Park   101   1m N of Filey
Signed car-park at end of minor road N of Filey at TA121818. Then
path along the coast east to Filey Brigg.
Migrants; seawatching; winter seaduck and divers.

Cornelian Bay & Woods   101   2½m SE of Scarborough
Park at end of track ½m E of A165 at TA057862. Then footpath
south between the bay and wooded cliff.
Migrants; summer warblers; passage and winter waders; winter
seaduck and divers.

Scarborough Castle & Harbour & Scalby Ness   101   NE
side of town
Park near the castle at the extreme NE corner of town at TA053887.
The harbour is on the south side of wooded area around the castle.
Also coastal road around North Bay to Scalby Ness.
Migrants; winter northern gulls; seawatching; winter seaduck and
divers; passage and winter waders.

> **Filey Dams**   101   TA107808   ½m W of Filey centre
> *Migrants; passage waders.*

> **Wykeham Forest**   101   SE943888   6m W of Scarborough
> *Woodland birds including Turtle Dove and Nightjar.*

> **Scarborough Mere & Olivers Monument**   101   TA035860
> *1m S of Scarborough centre*
> *Passage and winter wildfowl; migrants.*

TIC   St. Nicholas Cliff, Scarborough, N Yorks (0723 373333)
YH   The White House, Burniston Road, Scarborough (0723
361176)
RF   The Bull, Gristhorpe, nr Filey

BBE The Grainary, Keasbeck Hill Farm, Harwood Dale, nr
Scarborough (0723 870026)
Cober Hill, Newlands Road, Cloughton, nr Scarborough
(0723 870310)
SC Gowland Farm, Gowland Lane, Cloughton (0723 870924)

Hayburn Wyke & Beast Cliff 101 **5½ m N of Scarborough**
Park by minor road 1½m E of A171, ½m E of Crowdon at
TA004977. Then track and path south to the Wyke and then north
along the coast path (Cleveland Way) to the wooded Beast Cliff.
Migrants; woodland birds including Redstart and Pied Flycatcher.

Boggle Hole & Robin Hood's Bay 94 **5½ m SE of Whitby**
Car-park at end of minor road 2½m NE of A171 above the Bay at
SE954039. Then Cleveland Way north or south.
Migrants; winter seaduck and divers.

> *Falling Foss* 94 *SE890035* *5m S of Whitby*
> *Woodland and river birds including Pied Flycatcher, Kingfisher
> and Dipper.*

> *Ravenscar & Old Peak* 94 *SE980020* *7½m SE of
> Whitby*
> *Migrants; seawatching; winter seaduck.*

> *Hawkser Bottoms* 94 *SE941083* *3m SE of Whitby*
> *Migrants.*

TIC New Quay Road, Whitby, N Yorks (0947 602674)
YH Bogle Hole, Mill Beck, Flying Thorpe, Whitby (0947
880352)
RSC The Laurel, Robin Hood's Bay
RF Dolphin, King Street, Robin Hood's Bay
The Bryherstones, Cloughton Newlands
BBE Crag Hill, Ravenhall Road, Ravenscar (0723 870925)
SC (Chapel Cottage, Peakside, Ravenscar) National Trust, 27
Tadcaster Road, Dringhouses, York (0904 702021)
Fern House, Swan Farm, High Hawsker, nr Whitby (0947
880682)

Runswick Bay & Kettleness 94 **6m NW of Whitby**
Car-park at N end of the bay 1m E of A174 at NZ807162. Then coast
path south beside the woods and shore round to Kettle Ness.
Migrants; seawatching; winter seaduck; passage and winter
waders.

Sandsend   94   3m NW of Whitby
Car-parks by A174 along the sea-front e.g. at NZ872121. Then
tracks and paths up wooded valleys and north to Deepgrove
Wyke.
Migrants; woodland birds; passage and winter waders and
seaduck.

> *Whitby Harbour   94   NZ900110   centre of Whitby*
> *Winter gulls.*
>
> *Scaling Reservoir   (see Cleveland)*
>
> *Lealholm Moor   94   NZ745105   9m W of Whitby*
> *Moorland birds including Red Grouse, Golden Plover and*
> *Dunlin.*

TIC   As previous entry.
YH   East Cliff, Whitby, N Yorks (0947 602878)
RF   Beehive, Newholm, nr Whitby
            Royal, Runswick
RFBBE   Horse Shoe, Egton Bridge, nr Whitby (0947 85245)
BBE   Ugthorpe Lodge Hotel, Ugthorpe, nr Whitby (0947
            840331)
            Ellerby Hotel, Ellerby, Saltburn-by-sea (0947 840342)

Spaunton Moor   94 or 100   4½m N of Kirkbymoorside
Park by minor road on top of the moor at SE717938. Then path
southwest or east.
Moorland birds including Red Grouse, Merlin, Golden Plover and
Dunlin.

Beck Hole   94   1½m NW of Goathland
Park by bridge over Eller Beck at NZ823023. Then footpath along
the northern river bank and through woods.
Woodland and river birds.

> *Danby High Moor   94   NZ690014   4½m S of Danby*
> *Moorland birds.*
>
> *Grosmont   94   NZ826056   6m SW of Whitby*
> *Woodland and river birds including Dipper and Kingfisher.*
>
> *Northdale Rigg   94 or 100   SE736970   1½m NE of*
> *Rosedale Abbey*
> *Moorland birds including Merlin, Golden Plover and Ring*
> *Ousel.*
>
> *Rudland Rigg   100   SE650955   6m NW of Kirkbymoorside*
> *Moorland birds including Merlin and Hen Harrier.*

TIC	*Ryedale Folk Museum, Hutton-le-Hole, N Yorks (07515 367)
YH	Westerdale Hall, Westerdale, Whitby, N Yorks (0287 60469)
	Wheeldale Lodge, Goathland, Whitby (0947 86350)
RF	Anglers Rest, Glaisdale
	White Horse, Rosedale Abbey
	Blacksmith's Arms, Lastingham
RFBBE	Lion, Blakey Ridge, nr Kirkymoorside (07515 320)
BB	House Farm, Farndale (0751 33207)
BBE	Whitfield House Hotel, Darnholm, Goathland, nr Whitby (0947 86215)
SC	Beckside Cottage, Glaisdale, nr Whitby (0947 87365)

Borders

Craik Forest   79   10m SW of Hawick
Car-park at Craik just north of minor road 5½m SW of B711 at
NT348080, then many tracks and forest trails.
Woodland and moorland birds including crossbills, Goshawk,
Black Grouse and Short-eared Owl.

Alemoor Loch   79   7m W of Hawick
View from B711 2–3m W of Roberton from the bridge at NT396148
and ½m further west by the north shore at the western end of the
loch.
Wildfowl; passsage waders.

**St. Mary's Loch & Loch of the Lowes   73 & 79   15m SW of
Selkirk**
Car-park between the two lochs beside the A708 at NT237205. Also
parking places along the western shores.
Summer and winter wildfowl; hillside birds.

Whitlaw Wood   79   NT500133   *1m S of Hawick centre*
Woodland and river birds.

TIC	*Common Haugh Car-park, Hawick (0450 72547)
YH	Snoot, Roberton, Hawick (0450 88224)
RFBBE	Tibbie Shiels Inn, St. Mary's Loch (0750 42231)
	Gordon Arms, Mountbenger, nr Selkirk (0750 82222/82232)
	Tushielaw Inn, Ettrick Valley, by Selkirk (0750 62205)
BBE	West Buccleuch Hotel, Ettrick Valley, by Selkirk (0750 62230)
	Fir Cottage Guest House, Ettrick Bridge, by Selkirk (0750 52236)
SC	Hyndhope Hill Cottage, Ettrick Bridge, by Selkirk (0750 52213)

Elibank Forest   73   4m E of Innerleithen
Car-park by minor road on south side of River Tweed at NT395367,
then many tracks through the woods and onto the surrounding
hills.
Woodland and hill birds including Goshawk and Black Grouse.

Lindean Reservoir   73   2m E of Selkirk
Car-park by minor road to Lindean Moor, 1m N of A699 at
NT506293, then path around the reservoir to the hide.
Summer and winter wildfowl and grebes; summer warblers.

> *Plora Wood*   73   NT344366   *1m E of Innerleithen*
> *Woodland birds.*

> *St. Ronans*   73   NT326375   *½m W of Innerleithen*
> *Woodland birds.*

> *Gunknowe Park*   73   NT522374   *2m NW of Melrose*
> *Winter wildfowl; summer warblers and woodland birds.*

TIC	*Halliwell's House, Selkirk (0750 20054)
	*Bank Street, Galashiels (0896 55551)
YH	Priorwood, Melrose (0896 822521)
	Old Broadmeadows, Yarrowford, Selkirk (0750 76262)
RF	Queens Head, Selkirk
	Burts Hotel, Melrose
RFBBE	Traquair Arms Hotel, Innerleithen (0896 830229)
BBE	13 High Cottages, Walkerburn, nr Innerleithen (0896 87252)
	Clovenfords Hotel, Clovenfords, nr Galashiels (0896 85203)
SC	Holiday Cottages Ltd, Lilliesleaf, Melrose (08357 481/485)

Yetholm Loch   74   6m SE of Kelso
Park at end of track ¼m S of B6352, 1m W of Town Yetholm, by the
north end of the loch at NT805284.
Wildfowl; marshland birds.

Hoselaw Loch & Din Moss   74   5m SE of Kelso
View from minor road 1½m-2m NE of B6352 e.g. at NT805318.
Winter wildfowl; passage waders; woodland and marsh birds.

The Hirsel   74   1m NW of Coldstream
Car-park and visitor centre 1m N of A698 from just west of
Coldstream at NT828402. Then many paths through the woods
around the lake and to the hide.
Passage and winter wildfowl; woodland birds including Pied
Flycatcher and Hawfinch; river birds including Dipper and Com-
mon Sandpiper.

River Teviot   *74*   *NT675255*   *2m SW of Kelso*
River birds; winter wildfowl.

Bermersyde Moss   *74*   *NT616340*   *7m W of Kelso*
Wildfowl; summer warblers and marshland birds.

TIC	*Turret House, Kelso (0573 23464)
	*Henderson Park, Coldstream, Berwickshire (0890 2607)
YH	Kirk Yetholm, Kelso (057 382 631)
RF	Newcastle Arms Hotel, Coldstream
RFBBE	Plough Hotel, Yetholm
	Border Hotel, Kirk Yetholm (057 382 237)
BBE	Collingwood Arms Hotel, Cornhill-on-Tweed, nr Coldstream (0890 2424/2556)
BBESC	Lochside, Yetholm, nr Kelso (057 382 349)
SC	Birgham Haugh, nr Coldstream (0890 83223)
	Karingal, Lochton, Birgham, Coldstream (0890 83205)

Duns Castle Country Park   **74 or 67**   **1–2m NW of Duns**
Car-park ½m SW of B6365 at NT778554, then many trails through woodland and by Hen Poo.
Woodland birds and summer warblers including Wood Warbler and Pied Flycatcher.

Watch Water Reservoir   **74 or 67**   **2m SW of Longformacus**
Park and view from minor road beside east shore at NT664565.
Winter wildfowl.

Moneynut Water   **67**   **NW of Abbey St. Bathans**
Park by minor road running NW up the valley beside the river, 3m N of B6355, e.g. NT736634.
River birds including Dipper and Kingfisher; woodland birds including Pied Flycatcher and Redstart.

Hule Moss & Greenlaw Moor   *74*   *NT715490*   *2m N of Greenlaw*
Winter wildfowl and passage waders.

TIC	As previous entry.
YH	Abbey St. Bathans, Duns (03614 217)
RFBBE	Waterloo Arms Hotel, Chirnside, nr Duns (0890 81520)
	Cross Keys Hotel, Greenlaw (03616 247)
SC	Shannobank, Abbey St. Bathans (03614 242)
	Horseupcleugh, Longformacus, nr Duns (03617 225)

St. Abbs Head & Mire Loch   67   4m NW of Eyemouth

Car-park near the end of minor road 1½m N of B6438 to St. Abbs at NT913693 just before the lighthouse; or at junction with B6438 and walk. Footpath to lighthouse and around Mire Loch.

Summer seabirds; seawatching; migrants including frequent rarities.

Coldingham Bay & Buskin Burn   67   2m S of St. Abbs Head

Park along minor road 1m E of Coldingham village e.g. NT915663 and walk across the valley southeast toward Yellow Craig on the coast.

Passerine migrants; seabirds; winter seaduck and divers.

> *Eyemouth Bay*   67   NT945645   *N side of town*
> *Passage and winter gulls and seaduck.*

> *Burnmouth & Breeches Rock*   67   NT957611   *2m SE of Eyemouth*
> *Migrants; summer seabird colonies.*

TIC	*Auld Kirk, Eyemouth, Berwickshire (08907 50678)
	Castlegate Car-park, Berwick-on-Tweed, Northumberland (0289 330733)
YH	The Mount, Coldingham, Eyemouth (08907 71298)
RF	Craw Inn, Auchencrow, nr Eyemouth
BB	Ebba Strand, St. Abbs (08907 71329)
BBE	St. Abbs Haven Hotel, Coldingham Bay (08907 71491)
	Shieling Hotel, Coldingham Bay (08907 71216)
	Stoneshiel Hall, Reston, nr Eyemouth (08907 61267)
	Northfield House, St. Abbs (08907 71556)
SC	Lumsdaine Farm, nr Coldingham (08907 71218/71584)
	West Loch House, nr Coldingham (08907 71270)

Dumfries & Galloway

Castle Loch   78   4m W of Lockerbie
Car-park by A709 1m SE of Lochmaben at NY089819 overlooks the loch.
Winter wildfowl; summer Great Crested Grebe and warblers.

Hightae Mill Loch   78   ½m S of Castle Loch
Car-park by B7020 1½m S of Lochmaben at NY086802, then foot-paths.
Wildfowl; woodland birds; summer warblers; migrants.

> *Kirk Loch   78   NY080825   W side of Lochmaben*
> *Wildfowl.*

> *Mill Loch   78   NY078833   N side of Lochmaben*
> *Wildfowl; migrants.*

TIC   Whitesands, Dumfries (0387 53862)
YH   Lotus Lodge, Wanlockhead, Biggar, Lanarkshire (0659 74252)
H/B   The Walk Inn Bunkhouse, Wanlockhead (0659 74360)
BBE   Balcastle Hotel, Lochmaben (0387 810239)
           Royal Four Towns Hotel, Hightae, nr Lockerbie (038781 0402)
SC   (Lochmaben cottage) 60 Nunholm Road, Dumfries (0387 69167)

Caerlaverock (Wildfowl Trust)   84 & 85   8m SE of Dumfries
Open mid Sept – end April, £2 entry to observation towers and hides.
Signed car-park east to Eastpark, NY053657, from B725 1½m S of Bankend.
Winter wildfowl including 12,000 Barnacle Geese; passage waders.

Caerlaverock (NCC)   84   next to above site
Car-parks by B725 3m S of Bankend at NY018653, then open
access. Also park at Hollands Farm 1¼m E of B725 at NY043658.
Winter wildfowl, waders and raptors.

**Kirkconnel Merse & Nith Estuary   84   4–6m SE of
Dumfries**
View from B725 between Kelton and Glencaple e.g. NX995688.
Winter wildfowl; passage and winter waders.

TIC	Whitesands, Dumfries (0387 53862)
YH	Kendoon, Dalry, nr Glenhoul, by Castle Douglas
RF	Nith Hotel, Glencaple
	Swan Hotel, Kingholm Quay, nr Dumfries
BBE	Kirkland House Hotel, Ruthwell, nr Clarencefield (038787 284)
	Hurkledale Farm, Cummertrees, nr Annan (04617 228)
SC	Conheath, Glencaple (038777 205)

Carse Bay & Sands   84   10m S of Dumfries
Park at seafront of Carsethorn 1m E of A710 at NX992599.
Winter wildfowl and seaduck; passage and winter waders.

Southerness Point   84   13m S of Dumfries
Park at the end of minor road 2½m S off A710 at NX977543.
Winter wildfowl, seaduck and divers; passage and winter waders;
seawatching.

Dalbeattie Forest   84   1–3m SE of Dalbeattie
Park up track just north of Barnbarroch (on A710) at NX843566.
Then many paths through the forest to the north.
Woodland birds.

> *Lot's Wife & Mersehead Sands*   84   NX910558   *7m SE
> of Dalbeattie*
> *Winter wildfowl; passage and winter waders; passerine
> migrants.*

> *Kipford*   84   NX836554   *5m S of Dalbeattie*
> *Waders and wildfowl.*

> *Castlehill Point & Rough Island*   84   NX854524   *2m S
> of Kipford*
> *Winter waders, wildfowl and seaduck; summer terns.*

> *Drummains Reedbed*   84   NX984609   *1m NW of
> Carsethorn*
> *Reedbed species; winter waders and wildfowl.*

TIC	As previous entry.
	*Town Hall, Dalbeattie (0556 610177)
YH	As previous entry.
RF	Pheasant, Dalbeattie
RFBBE	Criffel Inn, New Abbey (038 785 244)
BBE	Millbrae Guest House, Rockcliffe, nr Dalbeattie (055 663217)
	Cavens House, Kirkbean, nr Dumfries (038 788 234)
SC	(Southerness cottage) Wendy Cottage, Auchenlarie, nr Gatehouse of Fleet (055 724 261)
	(Port Donnel Cottage, Rockcliffe) National Trust for Scotland, 5 Charlotte Square, Edinburgh (031 226 5922)
	Ingleston Farm, nr New Abbey (038 785 204)

Balcary Bay & Point   84   2m SE of Auchencairn
View from minor road SE of A711 from Auchencairn, also park at
end (NX822495) overlooking the bay and walk to the point.
Passage and winter waders and wildfowl; summer seabirds.

Manxman's Lake & Milton Sands   83 or 84   1–3m S of Kirkcudbright
View from A711 south of Kirkcudbright and from minor road
south beside the estuary south of Mutehill e.g. NX686486 and
NX678468.
Passage and winter waders and wildfowl.

River Dee Estuary   83 or 84   2m SW of Kirkcudbright
View from B727 ½m-2m SW of its junction with A755 and from
car-park overlooking Goat Well Bay at NX657487.
Passage and winter waders and wildfowl.

TIC	*Harbour Square, Kirkcudbright (0557 30494)
YH	As previous entry.
RF	Balcary Bay Hotel, Auchencairn
	Selkirk Arms Hotel, Auchencairn
BBE	Solwayside Guest House, Auchencairn (055 664 280)
	Marks Farm, nr Kirkcudbright (0557 30854)
SC	Auchenshore, Auchencairn (055 664 244)
	Hall of Auchencairn, Auchencairn (055 664 281)

Loch Ken   84   4m NW of Castle Douglas
View from minor road along the west shore, e.g. NX718665,
leaving B795 north at Glenlochar.
Wildfowl including winter geese and swans; passage waders.

Kenmure Holms & Woods   77   1m S of New Galloway
Car-park on west side of A762 at NX633767. Then footpaths west
into woodlands and view the marshes east from the road.
Woodland birds including Pied Flycatcher and Wood Warbler;
wildfowl and waders; summer warblers.

Threave Wildfowl Refuge   84   2m SW of Castle Douglas
Open Nov – March only.
Car-park ¼m up lane north of A75 at Kelton Mains Farm,
NX746616. Then tracks to visitor centre, the hides and the river.
Winter wildfowl; river birds; migrants.

> *Carlingwark Loch   84   NX763615   S side of Castle
> Douglas*
> *Wildfowl.*

> *Bennan Forest   77 or 84   NX654720   4m S of New
> Galloway*
> *Woodland birds including Crossbill and Nightjar.*

TIC   *Markethill, Castle Douglas (0556 2611)
YH   As previous entry.
RFBBE   Kings Arms Hotel, Castle Douglas (0556 2097)
BBE   Garry House, Mossdale, nr New Galloway (06445 253)
             Ken Bridge Hotel, New Galloway (06442 211)
SC   Troquhain, Balmaclellan, nr New Galloway (06442 212)
             (Millbank & Kelton Mill cottages, Threave) National Trust
             for Scotland, 5 Charlotte Square, Edinburgh (031 226
             5922)

Carstramon Wood   83   3m N of Gatehouse of Fleet
Park by minor road ½m E of B796 on the east side of the Water of
Fleet e.g. NX590600, then many paths.
Woodland birds including Pied Flycatcher, Redstart and Wood
Warbler.

Fleet Forest   83   1m S of Gatehouse of Fleet
Car-park by B727 at NX606562, ½m E of its junction with B786 in
Gatehouse. Then many forest tracks to the south.
Woodland birds including Crossbill.

Fleet Bay   83   3m SW of Gatehouse of Fleet
Car-park at end of minor road at Sandgreen, NX577521, 2m SE of
A75 on the east side of the estuary. Then coastal paths.
Winter wildfowl; passage and winter waders and gulls.

Cree Estuary East   83   N & S of Creetown
View from A75 0–2m north and south of Creetown e.g. ½m S at
NX473576.
Winter wildfowl and waders.

Stronard Forest 83 NX452645 2½m SE of Newton Stewart
Woodland and river birds.

TIC	*Car Park, Gatehouse of Fleet (05574 212)
	*Dashwood Square, Newton Stewart (0671 2431)
YH	Minnigaff, Newton Stewart (0671 2211)
RF	Murray Arms Hotel, Gatehouse of Fleet
BBE	Hill of Burns Country House, Creetown (067 182 487)
	The Boathouse, Creetown (067 182 335)
	The Bobbin Guest House, Gatehouse of Fleet (05574 229)
SC	Rusko, Gatehouse of Fleet (05574 215)

Wood of Cree   77   4m NW of Newton Stewart
Park by minor road which runs parallel to A714 on the east side of River Cree at NX382708. Then footpath through the woods.
Woodland, moorland and river birds including Pied Flycatcher, Redstart and Dipper.

Glentrool   77   9m N of Newton Stewart
Car-park at the eastern end of Loch Trool at NX415804. Then footpaths and trails through the lakeside woods and up onto the hill tops to the northeast.
Woodland and upland birds including Pied Flycatcher, Redstart, Golden Eagle, Peregrine, Black Grouse, Short-eared Owl and Hen Harrier.

Cairnsmore of Fleet 77 NX510660 5m E of Newton Stewart
Upland birds including Golden Eagle, Golden Plover and Peregrine.

Murrays Monument 77 NX490721 5m NE of Newton Stewart
Woodland birds including Golden & Lady Amherst's Pheasants, Crossbill and Goshawk.

TIC	As previous entry.
YH	As previous entry.
RFBBE	Creebridge House Hotel, Newton Stewart (0671 2121)
BBE	Auchenleck Farm, Minnigaff, Newton Stewart (0671 2035)
	House o'Hill Hotel, Bargrennan, nr Newton Stewart (067184 243)
	Crown Hotel, Newton Stewart (0671 2727)
SC	Borgan, Bargrennan (0671 84247)
	Skaith Farm, nr Newton Stewart (0671 2774)

Cree Estuary West   83   **6m SE of Newton Stewart**
View from minor road running N from Wigtown on the western
side of the estuary, e.g. NX444578. Also car-park by River
Bladnoch ½m SE of Wigtown centre at NX439547.
Waders; wildfowl; winter raptors.

Garlieston Bay   83   **6m SE of Wigtown**
Park at the front in Garlieston ¼m E of B7004 at NX477464. Then
track and paths north around the bay.
Waders; winter seaduck; passerine migrants.

> **Burrow Head**   83   *NX450342*   *13m S of Wigtown*
> *Seawatching; migrants.*

TIC	As previous entry.
YH	As previous entry.
RFBBE	The Steampacket Hotel, Isle of Whithorn (09885 334)
	Harbour Inn, Garlieston (09886 685)
SC	Stannock Farm, Isle of Whithorn (09885 266)

Loch Ryan   82   **N of Stranraer**
View from A77 along the east and south shores, especially from
Cairnryan, NX062686.
Winter grebes, divers, seaduck and other wildfowl; passage and
winter waders.

Torrs Warren & Luce Sands   82   **3m SW of Glenluce**
Access down a track through forest east of A715, ¼m S of its junc-
tion with A748, at NX144564.
Waders; wildfowl; woodland birds; passerine migrants.

> **The Wig**   82   *NX040680*   *4m N of Stranraer*
> *Winter wildfowl, waders and Twite; migrants.*

> **West Freugh Airfield**   82   *NX110545*   *5m SE of Stranraer*
> *Winter wildfowl and raptors including Hen Harrier roost.*

> **Black Loch & White Loch**   82   *NX110610*   *3m E of*
> *Stranraer*
> *Wildfowl.*

> **Loch Magillie & Soulseat Loch**   82   *NX100590*   *3m SE*
> *of Stranraer*
> *Wildfowl.*

TIC	*Port Rodie Car-park, Stranraer (0776 2595)
YH	As previous entry.
RFBBE	George Hotel, Stranraer (0775 2487/2488)
	Arkhouse Inn, Stranraer (0776 3161)

BBE	Low Balyett Farm, nr Stranraer (0776 3395)
	Bucks Head Hotel, Stranraer (0776 2064)
SC	Grusey House, Sandhead, Stranraer (0776 83309)
	Meikle Mark Farm, nr Stranraer (0776 2366)

Mull of Galloway   82   3m S of Drummore
Park at end of minor road just before the lighthouse at NX157304.
Seawatching; cliff seabird colonies; migrants.

Drummore Harbour & Bay & Cailiness Point   82
NX138368   Drummore
Winter gulls and seaduck; passage waders.

Grennan Plantation   82   NX127397   2m N of Drummore
Woodland birds; migrants.

TIC	*Port Rodie Car-park, Stranraer (0776 2595)
YH	Minnigaff, Newton Stewart (0671 2211)
RF	Queens Hotel, Drummore
RFBBE	Ship Inn, Drummore (077 684 383/296)
SC	Killaser, Ardwell, by Stranraer (077 686 294)

Portpatrick Harbour   82   7m SW of Stranraer
Park at the harbour front, the extreme western end of A77, at
NW999541.
Winter gulls; breeding Black Guillemot.

Black Head   82   2½m NW of Portpatrick
Car-park 1½m along minor road west of A764, ¼m before the light-
house at NW983567.
Seawatching; breeding seabirds; winter seaduck and divers.

Corsewall Point   82   10m NW of Stranraer
Park by the lighthouse, NW982727, at the end of minor road which
runs NW from where A718 becomes B738.
Seawatching; migrants.

TIC	As previous entry.
YH	As previous entry.
RFBBE	Crown, Portpatrick (077 681 261)
BBE	Downshire Arms Hotel, Portpatrick (077 681 300)
	Carlton Guest House, Portpatrick (077 681 253)
SC	North Park, Kirkcolm, nr Stranraer (0776 853666)
	Glaick, Leswalt, by Stranraer (077 687 286)

Fife

Inverkeithing Bay   65   SE of Inverkeithing
View from West Ness ¾m E of B981 at the SE corner of the Inner Bay at NT136820, and coast path south toward North Queensferry. Winter wildfowl, seaduck, grebes and divers; passage and winter waders; passage and summer terns.

Lochore Meadows Country Park   58   1m NE of Kelty
See Tayside.

Culross   65   NS975856   *3m SE of Kincardine*
Passage and winter waders.

Torry Bay   65   NT020860   *2m E of Culross*
Passage and winter waders and wildfowl.

Dalgety Bay & Braefoot Point   65 or 66   NT176833
2½m E of Inverkeithing
Passage and winter waders; winter seaduck and divers; migrants; summer terns.

TIC	Forth Road Bridge, by North Queensferry, Fife (0383 417759)
	4 Kirk Gate, Burntisland (0592 872667)
	*Glen Bridge Car-park, Chalmers Street, Dunfermline (0383 720999)
YH	Glendevon, Dollar, Clakmannanshire (025 981 206)
	Back Wynd, Falkland (0337 57710)
RF	Hawes Inn, Queensferry
	Ship Inn, Limekilns, nr Rosyth
	Old Inn, Carnock
	Aberdour Hotel. Aberdour, nr Dalgety Bay
	Pitfrane Arms, Crossford, nr Dunfermline
BBE	Seal Bay House, 42 The Wynd, Dalgety Bay (0383 822790)
	Woodhead Farm, Culross (0383 880270)

Largo Bay   59   0–4m E of Leven
View from car-parks on the north side of the mouth of the River Leven, on the east side of the town, at NO383005; 1m to the NE at NO390014; just south of the bridge on the south side of Lower Largo, halfway around the bay at NO416025; and from Ruddons Point on the east side at NO005454.
Passage and winter waders; winter seaduck, divers and grebes; passage and winter gulls.

Kilconquar Loch   59   1½m NW of Elie
View from B941 along the north side at NO485021.
Early autumn Little Gulls; summer and winter wildfowl.

Fife Ness & Crail Airfield   59   1–2m NE of Crail
Car-parks at the end of minor road by the golf course, ¼m before the lighthouse at NO630099, and ½m E of minor road northeast of Crail on the northern side of the disused airfield at NO630088. Then tracks to the coast and NE to Fife Ness. Also car-park ½m east of Kingsbarns, 2½m NW of the Ness at NO603124 and coastal path SE to Cambo and the golf course.
Migrants including frequent rarities; seawatching.

Isle of May   59   island 5m SE of Anstruther
Boats from Anstruther Harbour, NO568038. Tel:0333 310860. Also boats from Crail, tel:0333 50484.
Bird observatory, hostel-type accommodation for up to 6 people; open April-October. Contact Mrs. R. Cowper, 9 Oxgangs Road, Edinburgh, EH10 7BG Tel:031 445 2489.
Migrants including many rarities spring and autumn; summer seabird colonies; seawatching.

> ***Elie Ness*** *59   NT497995   ½m SE of Elie*
> *Migrants; seawatching.*

TIC	South Street, Leven (0333 29464)
	*Scottish Fisheries Museum, Anstruther (0333 310628)
	*Crail Museum & Heritage Centre, Marketgate, Crail (0333 50869)
YH	As previous entry.
R	Ship, Elie
RF	Dreel, Anstruther
RFBBE	Golf Hotel, Crail (0333 50206)
	Smugglers Inn, Anstruther (0333 310506)
BBE	The Elms Guest House, Elie (0333 330404)
	Balcomie Links Hotel, Crail (0333 50237)
SC	Isle of May Bird Observatory (see above)
	Elie Letting, The Park, Bank Street, Elie (0333 330219)

Cameron Reservoir   59   **4m SW of St. Andrews**
Car-park ½m W of A915 at the east end of the reservoir at
NO478114. Then track beside the north and west banks.
Wildfowl.

Eden Estuary & St. Andrews Bay   59   **2–3m NW of St.**
Andrews
Car-park near the end of minor road north of St. Andrews between
the shore and the golf course at NO498193. View from here and
from the north end of the peninsula at Out Head. Also view from
¼m N of A91 along the south side of the Estuary, 3m NW of St.
Andrews, at NO467192, and from the bridge at Guardbridge, a
further mile to the west, at NO454188.
Winter divers, grebes and seaduck; passsage and winter waders;
migrant pipits, wheatears and waders on the golf courses.

Morton Lochs   59   **1½m SE of Tayport**
Car-park and hides ¾m E of B945 at NO465264.
Summer warblers; passage waders; winter wildfowl.

Tentsmuir Point & Tayport   59   **7m N of St. Andrews**
Car-park in Tayport ¼m E of B945 at NO463280, then track east
around the bay to the Point. Also car-park by the shore 3m NE of
Leuchars at NO499243 and coast path north to Tentsmuir Point.
Passage and winter waders and seaduck; summer and passage
terns; winter Snow Bunting.

> *Greenside Scalp*   59   *NO427288*   *2m W of Tayport*
> *Passage and winter waders.*

TIC	South Street, St. Andrews (0334 72021)
YH	As previous entry.
RF	Ma Bells, St. Andrews
	Taybridge Halt, Wormit, nr Newport-on-Tay
BBE	Pinewoods Hotel, St. Michaels, nr Leuchars (033 483 8262)
	Milton Farm, Leuchars (033 483 281)
SC	Estate Office, Craigie Farm, Leuchars (033 483 218)
	(Dairsie cottage) 7 Randolph Crescent, Edinburgh (031 225 2709)
	(Hill of Tarvit, Cupar) National Trust for Scotland, 5 Charlotte Square, Edinburgh (031 226 5922)

Balmerino   59   **4m SW of Newport-on-Tay**
View from minor road beside the estuary 2½m N of A914 at
NO358253.
Passage and winter waders, wildfowl, seaduck and divers.

Lindores Loch   59   2½ m SE of Newburgh
View from B937 ½m-1m SE of its junction with A913 e.g.
NO270164.
Wildfowl.

Newburgh   58   NW side of the town
Park just north of A913 at west end of the town at NO231185 and
view from coast path to the west.
Passage and winter waders and wildfowl.

TIC   As previous entry.
YH   As previous entry.
BBE   Homehill, Grange of Lindores, nr Newburgh (0337
           40742)

Grampian

Glen Tanar   44   3m SW of Aboyne
Park at the visitor centre (open Apr–Sept) at end of minor road 2m
SW of B976 at NO475957. Then tracks through the forest to the
south and southwest.
Scottish Crossbill, Capercaillie, Black Grouse, Golden Eagle,
Goshawk and Merlin.

**Kinord & Davan Lochs & Muir of Dinnet NNR   37   5m NE
of Ballater**
Car-park by A97 1½m N of its junction with A93 at NO430997.
Then marked paths to woods, lochs and moorland. Or view Loch
Davan at its north end from A97.
Winter wildfowl; woodland, moorland and marshland birds;
migrants.

Glen Muick & Lochnagar   44   6m SW of Ballater
Car-park and visitor centre at end of minor road, which runs the
length of Glen Muick SW from B976, at NO309853. Then tracks
west up onto Lochnagar and north along the west side of the River
Muick.
Woodland and upland birds including Ptarmigan, Dotterel, Snow
Bunting, Golden Eagle, Black Grouse and Goshawk.

Glen Quoich & Beinn a Bhuird   43   *NO085930*   4m NW
of Braemar
River, Woodland and upland birds.

Morrone Birkwood   43   *NO130900*   1½m SW of Braemar
Woodland birds.

TIC	*Balnellan Road, Braemar (03397 41600)
	*Station Square, Ballater (03397 55306)
	*Ballater Road Car-park, Aboyne (03398 86060)
YH	Deebank Road, Ballater (0338 55227)

H/B	Braemar Outdoor Centre, 15 Mar Road, Braemar (03397 41242)
	Jenny's Bothy, Delachuper, Corgarff, nr Strathdon (09756 51446)
	Glen Avon Hotel Bunkroom, The Square, Tomintoul, nr Braemar (08074 218)
RF	Fife Arms, Braemar
RFBBE	Boat Inn, Charlestown Road, Aboyne (03398 86137)
BBE	Moorfield House Hotel, Chapel Brae, Braemar (03397 41244)
	Arbor Lodge, Aboyne (03398 86101)
	Profeits Hotel, Dinnet (03398 85229)
SC	Birchwood, Chapel Brae, Braemar (03383 681)
	Estate Office, Dinnet (033985 341/342)
	Oldyleiper, Birse, Aboyne (0339 2232)

Mouth of River Don   38   2m N of Aberdeen centre
Car-park at end of minor road ¼ m E of A92 on the north side of the river at NJ952095. Then take path east.
Passage waders; winter northern gulls, seaduck and divers.

Blackdog Rock   38   6m N of Aberdeen
Park at end of track east off A92 at NJ965141. Then walk north and south along the shore.
Winter divers and seaduck including regular King Eider.

Girdleness   38   1½ m E of Aberdeen centre
Car-parks along minor road east of A956, on the south side of the mouth of the River Dee, at NJ965056.
Seawatching; winter northern gulls; migrants.

> *Balmedie   38   NJ977177   7m N of Aberdeen*
> *Winter waders and Snow Bunting; summer terns.*

> *Loch of Skene   38   NJ785075   9m W of Aberdeen*
> *Winter wildfowl.*

> *Crathes   38   NO730970   3m E of Banchory*
> *Woodland birds.*

> *Drum   38   NJ790010   3m W of Peterculter*
> *Woodland birds.*

> *Bennachie Forest   38   NJ680210   5m W of Inverurie*
> *Woodland and moorland birds.*

> *Fowlsheugh   45   NO880790   4m S of Stonehaven*
> *Large summer seabird colonies.*

TIC	St. Nicholas House, Broad Street, Aberdeen (0224 632727)
YH	The King George VI Memorial Hostel, 8 Queens Road, Aberdeen (0224 646988)
RF	Heugh Hotel, Westfield Road, Stonehaven Boars Head, Kinmuck, nr Inverurie Thainstone House Hotel, Inverurie Grants Arms, Monymusk, nr Inverurie
BB	Bellfield Farm, Kingswells, nr Aberdeen (0224 740239)
BBE	Blackdog Heights, Bridge of Don (0224 704287) Millcroft Guest House, Old Rayne, nr Inverurie (04645 210) Park Hill Lodge Hotel, Kemnay, nr Inverurie (0467 42789)
SC	Millbank Cottage, Sauchen, by Inverurie (03303 379) Woodlands Cottage, Woodlands of Durris, nr Banchory (03308 625) (Kennels Cottage, Drum Castle) National Trust for Scotland, 5 Charlotte Square, Edinburgh (031 226 5922)

Sands of Forvie   38   12m N of Aberdeen
Car-park at Forvie Centre by B9003, 1m E of A975 at NK034289.
Then tracks along the shore to Rockend.
Summer terns and Eider; winter seaduck, divers and Snow Bunting; passage waders.

Ythan Estuary   38   immediately W of Sands of Forvie
Car-park ¼m E of Newburgh at NK003246 and track east to the shore. Also car-park on eastern side of the bridge over River Ythan, by A975 at NK004270. Then track south by the estuary. Also parking by A975 1m north along the eastern bank at NK006283 and track north to the hide.
Winter wildfowl; passage and winter waders; migrants.

Bullers of Buchan & Long Haven Cliffs   30   4m S of Peterhead
Car-park along track ½m S of A952 at NK116393. Then paths along the cliffs north and south.
Large summer seabird colonies.

> *Meikle Loch   30   NK030310   4m SW of Cruden Bay*
> *Wildfowl; passage waders and terns.*

> *Cotehill Loch   38   NK026293   N end of Sands of Forvie*
> *Wildfowl; passage waders and terns.*

> *Cruden Bay Woods   30   NK094365   E side of Cruden Bay village*
> *Migrants.*

Peterhead Bay   30   NK130455   *SE side of Peterhead*
Winter northern gulls, seaduck and divers.

Ugie Estuary   30   NK121474   *N side of Peterhead*
Passage waders.

TIC	As previous entry.
	*Market Street Car-park, Ellon (0358 20730)
	*54 Broad Street, Peterhead (0779 71904)
YH	As previous entry.
RF	Udny Arms Hotel, Newburgh
RFBBE	New Inn, Market Street, Ellon (0358 20425)
BBE	Kilmarnock Arms Hotel, Cruden Bay (0779 812213)
SC	Hayhillock, Ellon (0358 20318)
	North Aldie Farm, Cruden Bay (0779 84256)

Loch of Strathbeg & Rattray Head   30   between Fraserburgh & Peterhead
Signed car-park 1m N of A952 from Crimond at NK056581, then tracks to hides.
Part of the Loch viewable from minor road, by the southern end, 2m E of A952 at NK088578, which continues east to Rattray Head.
Passage and winter wildfowl; summer warblers; winter seaduck and divers offshore, Snow Bunting; seawatching; migrants.

Fraserburgh Harbour & Kinnaird Head   30   NJ999674
Winter northern gulls, divers and seaduck; seawatching.

St. Fergus Lagoon   30   NK106534   *3m S of Rattray Head*
Passage waders.

Scotstown & Kirkton Head   30   NK117510   *3m N of Peterhead*
Migrants; winter seaduck and divers; passage waders; seawatching.

TIC	As previous entry.
	*Saltoun Square, Fraserburgh (0346 28315)
YH	As previous entry.
BBE	Strathlea, Crimond, nr Fraserburgh (0346 32379)
SC	Kirktown, Tyne, nr Fraserburgh (03464 231)

Banff Bay   29   between Banff & Macduff
View from roads around the bay e.g. at Meavie Point at the NW corner, NJ690647, by the mouth of River Deveron at NJ694640, and from Macduff Harbour at NJ703646.
Winter seaduck, divers and northern gulls.

Troup Head   29   2m NE of Gardenstown
Car-park ½m N of B9031 at NJ836660. Then path northeast to Lions
Head and then coast path north to Downie Bay and the point.
Summer seabirds; migrants; seawatching.

> *Gardenstown Harbour & Gamrie Bay*   29   *NJ799650*
> *6m E of Macduff*
> *Winter seaduck and divers.*

TIC	*Collie Lodge, Banff (02612 2419)
YH	1 Old Edinburgh Road, Inverness (0463 231771)
RF	The Highland Haven, Shore Street, Macduff
RFBBE	Pennan Inn, Pennan, nr Gardenstown (03466 201)
BBE	Knowes Hotel, Market Street, Macduff (0261 32229)
BBESC	Carmelite House Hotel, Low Street, Banff (02612 2152)
SC	(Pennan cottage) Upper Crichie, Stuartfield (0771 24206/24369)
	(Gardenstown cottages) Country Holidays, Spring Mill, Earby, Colne, Lancs (0282 445566)
	Montcoffer Farm, Banff (02612 2597)

Spey Bay   28   4m W of Buckie
Car-parks at north end of B9104, on the eastern side of the mouth
of the River Spey at NJ348656, and by B9013 3m N of its junction
with A96 at NJ255670. Also tracks NE to Boar's Head Rock at
NJ290677.
Passage waders; passage and winter seaduck including regular
Surf Scoter and King Eider.

Lossiemouth   28   SE end of Lossiemouth
Car-park ½m SE of A941 on SW side of the estuary at NJ238702.
Passage and winter waders; winter seaduck and northern gulls.

> *Buckie Harbour*   28   *NJ430660   NE end of Buckie*
> *Winter northern gulls and seaduck.*

TIC	As previous entry.
YH	As previous entry.
RF	Gordon Arms Hotel, Fochabers
RFBBE	Grant Arms Hotel, Fochabers (0343 820202)
BBE	Spey Bay Hotel, Spey Bay (0343 820424)
SC	Maryhill Farm, Buckie (0542 31284/31646)

Culbin Forest, The Bar & Dunes   27   3m NW of Forres
Car-park at Cloddymoss off minor road 2m N of Brodie Castle at
NH982599. Then tracks through the forest to the Bar and Dunes.
Also car-park at Kingsteps (Highland), 1m NE of Nairn at
NH901573 and tracks NE.
Crested Tit, Capercaillie, Long-eared Owl, Scottish Crossbill,
terns and waders; wildfowl and seaduck.

Findhorn Bay   27   2m N of Forres
View from minor road and tracks along the southern side e.g. from
NJ036616, or along the eastern side from B9011 2m NW of Kinloss.
Passage and winter waders and wildfowl; summer terns and
Osprey.

Burghead Harbour & Bay   27 & 28   W of Burghead
Park and view from the pier at NW end of Burghead, NJ108691,
and from Findhorn at the western end, NJ043648.
Winter seaduck, divers and grebes.

Darnaway Forest & Findhorn Gorge   27   NH996514
5m SW of Forres
Woodland and river birds.

TIC	*Falconer Museum, Tolbooth Street, Forres (0309 72938)
	17 High Street, Elgin (0343 542666/543388)
YH	1 Old Edinburgh Road, Inverness (0463 231771)
RFBBE	Crown & Anchor, Findhorn (0309 30252)
BBE	Culbin Sands Hotel, Findhorn (0309 30252)
SC	Braemar, Rafford, Forres (0309 73676)
	(Findhorn cottage) Balmalcolm, Kinrossie, Perth (08215 233)
	Snab of Moy, Dyke, Forres (03094 280)
	(Brodie Castle, Forres) National Trust for Scotland, 5 Charlotte Square, Edinburgh (031 226 5922)

Highland

Ariundle Woods   40   2m NE of Strontian
Car-park at end of track 1½m NE of A861 from Strontian at
NM830635, then many paths.
Woodland and river birds including Redstart, Wood Warbler and
Dipper.

Kentra Moss & Bay   40   2m NW of Acharacle
View from B8044 1–2½m NW of Acharacle e.g. NM660690, and at
the end of the road at NM634701.
Waders and wildfowl.

> *Glenmore Bay   47   NM590620   2m NW of Glenborrodale*
> *Passage waders; winter wildfowl; woodland birds.*

> *Strontian   40   NM814615   ¼m S of Strontian bridge*
> *Passage waders.*

> *Sallachan Point   40   NM990615   2m SW of Corran*
> *Passage waders and wildfowl.*

> *Loch nan Gabhar   40   NM968632   3m W of Corran*
> *Summer wildfowl; woodland birds.*

TIC	Cameron Square, Fort William (0397 3781)
	*Ballachulish, Argyll (08552 296)
YH	Glencoe, Argyll (08552 219)
	Glen Nevis, Fort William (0397 2336)
BBE	Ardshealach, Acharacle, Ardnamurchan, Argyll (096 785 301)
	Strontian Hotel, Strontian (0967 2029)
	Ardgour Hotel, Ardgour, Corran, Fort William (08555 225)
SC	(Acharacle cottage) Durn, Isla Road, Perth (0738 21121)

Rhum   39   10m W of Mallaig
Passenger ferry from Mallaig (OS Map 40, NM675970) on Mon,
Wed, Fri & Sat. Caledonian MacBrayne tel: 0687 2233.
Permission needed to stay on the island overnight from: NCC
warden, The White House, Kinloch, Rhum tel: 0687 2026.
Full board accommodation available at Kinloch Castle.
Summer seabirds including large Manx Shearwater colony;
Red-throated Diver, Peregrine, Golden Eagle, White-tailed Eagle,
Merlin; woodland birds.

> *Canna*   4m NW of Rhum (boat from Mallaig or Rhum)
> *Seabirds; Corncrake; migrants.*

> *Eigg*   4m SE of Rhum (boat from Mallaig or Rhum; also
> *Glennig (summer only))*
> *Summer seabirds and Red-throated Diver; Corncrake.*

TIC	Mallaig, Invernesshire (0687 2170)
YH	Garramore, Morar, Mallaig (06875 268)
BBE	Kinloch Castle, Rhum (see above)
	Laig Farm Guest House, Eigg (0687 82437)
SC	(Tighard, Canna) National Trust for Scotland, 5 Charlotte Square, Edinburgh (031 226 5922 or 0687 2466)

Isle of Skye   32 & 33
Frequent ferries from Kyle of Lochalsh (OS Map 33, NG761272).

Cuillin Hills   NG440230   Isle of Skye
Ptarmigan, Golden Eagle, Greenshank.

Loch Sligachan   NG500310   Isle of Skye
Golden Eagle, Black-throated Diver; waders.

Kilmuir   NG380705   Isle of Skye
Corncrake; migrants.

Dunvegan Harbour   NG250480   Isle of Skye
Winter northern gulls; waders.

TIC	Meall House, Portree, Isle of Skye (0478 2137)
	*Broadford, Isle of Skye (04712 361)
YH	Uig, Skye (047 042 211)
	Glenbrittle, Skye (047 842 278)
	Creachan Cottage, Raasay (off Skye) (047 862 240)
	Broadford, Skye (04712 442)
	Kyleakin, Skye (0599 4585)
	Ardvasar, Sleat, Skye (04714 260)

H/B	Sligachan Hotel Bunkhouse (047 862 2137)
	Uiginish Lodge, Dunvegan, Skye (047 022 445)
	Raasay House, Isle of Raasay (047 882 266)
RFBBE	Old Inn, Carbost (047 842 205)
	Ardvasar Hotel, Ardvasar (04114 223)
	Sligachan Hotel, Sligachan (047 852 303)
	Hotel Eilean Iarmain, Isle of Ornsay (04713 332)
BBE	Duntulm Castle Hotel, Duntulm (047 052 213)
SC	Bidwell, Point of Sleat, Ardvasar (04714 242/217)
	Skye Leisure, Sligachan (047 852 303)
	Macleod Estate Office, Dunvegan Castle (047 022 206)
	2 Sartle, Staffin (047 062 202)

Glen Affric   25 & 26   4–10m SW of Cannich
Several car-parks by minor road SW of A831 from Cannich e.g. at NH283282 and at NH200234. Then tracks north and south and beside the river.
River, woodland and upland birds including Golden Eagle, Ptarmigan, divers, Goshawk, Capercaillie and Black Grouse.

> ***Balmacaan Woods***   *26*   *NH501290*   *1m SW of Drumnadrochit*
> *Woodland birds.*

> ***Urquhart Bay Wood***   *26*   *NH520296*   *1m E of Drumnadrochit*
> *Woodland birds; summer warblers.*

TIC	23 Church Street, Inverness (0463 234353)
	*Car-park, Fort Augustus (0320 6367)
YH	Allt Beithe, Glen Affric, Cannich, Beauly, Inverness-shire
	Cannich, Beauly (04565 244)
	Glenmoriston, Inverness (0320 51274)
RFBBE	Lewiston Arms, Lewiston, Drumnadrochit (04562 225)
BBE	Chisholm Stone House, Struy, by Beauly, Inverness-shire (046 376 222)
	Cnoc Hotel, Struy (046 376 264)
	Glen Affric Hotel, Cannich (04565 214)

Kintail Forest   33   2m NE of Shiell Bridge
Car-park and visitor centre at Morvich, 1¼m NE of A87 at NG961211, then track SE beside River Croe.
Upland and river birds including Golden Eagle, Ptarmigan and Red-breasted Merganser.

Kintail Country Park & Inverinate Forest   33   4–6m NE of Shiell Bridge
Car-park 1½m up track on N side of Strath Croe, 2m NE of A87 at NG976222, then tracks north.
River, woodland and upland birds including Dipper, Golden Eagle, Ptarmigan and Black-throated Diver.

> *Shiell Bridge & Loch Duich* 33 *NG930195 ½m-4m NW of Shiell Bridge*
> *Passage and winter waders and wildfowl; winter divers and seaduck.*

TIC	*Shiell Bridge, Ross & Cromarty (0599 81264)
YH	Glenshiel, Kyle, Ross & Cromarty (0599 81243)
RFBBE	Plockton Hotel, Plockton, nr Buirinish (059 984 250)
BB	Camuslongart Guest House, Ardelve (059 985 357)
BBE	Ratagan House Hotel, Ratagan, Glenshiel, Ross-shire (059 981 272)
	Loch Duich Hotel, Ardelve, Dornie, nr Kyle of Lochalsh (059 985 357)
SC	(Balmacara Cottages) National Trust for Scotland, 5 Charlotte Square, Edinburgh (031 226 5922)
	(Inverinate cottage) 55 Warrington Road, Harrow, Middx (081 427 3872)
	(Inverinate) Little Dalcross, Croy, Inverness (06678 224)

Loch Ruthven   26   9m NE of Foyers
Car-park 1m W of B851 from East Croachy at the east end of the loch, NH637281, then path to the hide.
Summer Slavonian Grebe and Red-throated Diver; woodland birds; Black Grouse.

Farigaig Forest   26   2m NE of Foyers
Car-park by B852 along the east side of Loch Ness at NH522237, then trails through the woods and by the river.
River and woodland birds.

TIC	As previous entry.
YH	1 Old Edinburgh Road, Inverness (0463 231771)
BBE	Aberarder House, Strathnairn, Inverness-shire (08083 383)
	Foyers Hotel, Foyers (04563 216)
SC	Abersky, Torness, Dores, Inverness-shire (046 375 252)
	Gorthleck Mains, Gorthleck, Inverness-shire (04563 282)
	Ruthven Holiday Homes, Aberarder by Dores, Inverness-shire (08083 283)

Abernethy Forest   36   6m SW of Grantown-on-Spey
Park by minor road 1½m south of Nethy Bridge at NH996187 and explore the Caledonian forest to the east.
Capercaillie, Scottish Crossbill, Crested Tit and Osprey.

Loch Garten   36   2m E of Boat of Garten
Car-park at NH978184 1½m along minor road SE of B970, then tracks and hide.
Osprey, Crested Tit, Capercaillie, Black Grouse and Scottish Crossbill.

Glenmore Forest & Pass of Ryvoan   36   5–7m W of Aviemore
Car-park by minor road at eastern end of Loch Morlich, 4m E of B970 from Coylumbridge at NH977097, then track east up the valley.
Woodland and upland birds including Golden Eagle, Capercaillie, Black Grouse, Crested Tit, Scottish Crossbill and Redstart.

Loch Insh & Insh Marshes   35   5m NE of Kingussie
View from minor road ½m south of Kincraig at NH837046. Or car-park 1½m SE of Kingussie at NH775998, then tracks to hides overlooking the marshes and scrapes.
Summer Goldeneye and other ducks; summer warblers; passage waders and wildfowl; winter swans and geese.

Carn Ban Mor   35 & 36   8m SE of Kingussie
Park by minor road 4m S of Feshiebridge just before the road ends at Achlean, NN852977. Then track east up on to Carn Ban Mor and plateau to the south and east.
Ptarmigan, Dotterel, Golden Eagle, possible Snow Bunting, Lapland Bunting and Snowy Owl.

> ***Findhorn Valley*** *35   NH737197   10m NW of Aviemore*
> *Golden Eagle; river birds.*

> ***Craigellachie*** *36   NH888126   just west of Aviemore*
> *Woodland birds; Peregrine.*

> ***Inverdruie Fish Farm*** *36   NH897117   ½m SE of Aviemore*
> *Summer Osprey.*

> ***Whitewell*** *36   NH915087   3m SE of Aviemore*
> *Black Grouse, Scottish Crossbill; woodland birds.*

> ***Woods of Glentromie*** *35   NN779969   3m SE of Kingussie*
> *Woodland and river birds.*

TIC	Grampian Road, Aviemore (0479 810363)
	54 High Street, Grantown-on-Spey (0479 2773)
YH	Aviemore, Inverness-shire (0479 810345)
	Glen More, Loch Morlich, Aviemore (0479 86238)
	Viewmount, Kingussie (05402 506)
H/B	Glenfeshie Hostel, Balachcroick House, Glenfeshie, Kincraig (05404 323)
RF	Tomatin Inn, Tomatin, nr Findhorn Bridge
	Creel Bar, High Street, Kingussie
	Tyree, Grantown-on-Spey
BBE	Brieriach, Kincraig (05404 369)
	March House Guest House, Kincraig (05404 388)
	Dochlaggie Farm, Boat of Garten (0479 83242)
	Ossian Hotel, Kincraig (05404 242)
SC	(Feshie Bridge bungalow) Torwood, Moss-side Road, Nairn (0667 54974)
	Dell of Abernethy, Nethy Bridge, Inverness-shire (0479 82643)
	Tigh Beag, Nethy Bridge (0479 82293)
	Birchfield, Nethy Bridge (0479 82613)

Beauly Firth   26   2–6m W of Inverness
View from South Kessock pier at east end of the firth, 1m E of the south side of Kessock Bridge, at NH655473. Also from Clachnaharry pier a further ¾m W at NH644467, and Longman Point by the south end of Kessock Bridge at NH666470. For the north side of the firth, car-park in North Kessock at NH654479, just south of A9. Also view from minor road west along shoreline to A832 west of Milton; e.g. Corgrain Point, NH596486.
Passage and winter wildfowl and waders.

Udale Bay & Newhall Point & Burn   21   5m W of Cromarty
Car-park by the south end of the bay by B9163 at NH711651 and view from minor road along west shore and from Newhall Point, NH709671.
Waders and wildfowl; woodland birds; migrants.

Sutors of Cromarty   21   1m E of Cromarty
Car-park at end of minor road east from A832 in Cromarty at NH807671, then tracks west and south.
Migrants; seawatching.

>
> ***Munlochy Bay***   26   *NH656536   4m N of Inverness*
> *Passage and winter waders and wildfowl.*
>
> ***Gallowhill Wood***   26   *NH600495   4m W of North Kessock*
> *Woodland birds.*

TIC	23 Church Street, Inverness (0463 234353)
	North Kessock, by Inverness (0463 73505)
YH	1 Old Edinburgh Road, Inverness (0463 231771)
RFBBE	Royal Hotel, Fortrose (0381 20236)
	North Kessock Hotel, North Kessock
	Ord Arms Hotel, Muir of Ord (0463 870286)
BBE	Royal Hotel, Cromarty (03817 217)
	Marine Hotel, Rosemarkie, Fortrose (0381 20253)
SC	(Avoch Cottage, nr Fortrose) Springfield, Culbokie, Ross-shire (034 987 603)
	Reelig Estate, Reelig Glen, Kirkhill, Inverness (0463 83208)
	Cullicudden Farm, Culbokie, by Dingwall (034 987 609)

Nigg Bay   21   3–5m NE of Invergordon
View from B9175 along the east shore 3–4m S of A9 e.g. NH795710, and from B817 along the west side e.g. by Balintraid Pier, 1m SW of Barbaraville at NH741711.
Passage and winter waders and wildfowl.

Loch Eye   21   3½m SE of Tain
View from minor road along west shore 1–2m NE of B9165 from Just west of Fearn railway station e.g. NH827806.
Passage and winter wildfowl.

Tarbat Ness   21   3m NE of Portmahomack
Car-park at end of minor road NE from Portmahomack at NH945874, then coast paths north and south and to small plantations.
Migrants; seawatching.

Inver Bay   21   5m E of Tain
View from shore at Inver 2m W of B9165, 3m SW of Portmahomack at NH862828.
Passage and winter waders and wildfowl.

Tain Bay   21   ½m N of Tain
Car-park just north of the railway line on the north side of Tain, ¼m N of B9174 at NH781827. Then path southeast.
Passage and winter waders and wildfowl.

Cambuscurrie Bay   21   4m NW of Tain
View from Ferry Point 1¼m NW of A9 at NH733858.
Passage and winter waders and wildfowl.

> ***Alness Point***   21   NH658680   *1m S of Alness*
> *Passage and winter waders and wildfowl.*

> ***Alness Bay***   21   NH635670   *2m SW of Alness*
> *Passage and winter waders and wildfowl.*

Ben Wyvis   20   NH460680   8m NW of Dingwall
Upland birds including Ptarmigan, Golden Eagle and Dotterel.

Balintore Airfield   21   NH840760   6m SE of Tain
Passage waders, pipits etc.

Rockfield Cliff   21   NH927835   1m SE of Portmahomack
Summer seabirds.

Morrich More   21   NH820845   3m NE of Tain
Summer and passage waders and terns; passsage and winter wildfowl.

TIC	*Bonar Bridge, Sutherland (08632 333)
	*The Square, Strathpeffer, Ross & Cromarty (0997 21415)
	The Square, Dornoch, Sutherland (0862 810400)
YH	Strathpeffer, Ross & Cromarty (0997 21532)
RFBBE	Morven House Hotel, Alness (0349 882323)
BBE	Tigh Gorm, Main Street, Portmahomack, Ross-shire (086 287 606)
	Balblair House, Edderton, nr Tain (086 282 272)
	The Sycamores, Balintore, nr Tain (086 283 2322)
SC	Old House of Ardross, Alness, Ross-shire (0349 882906)

Dornoch Point & Firth   21   **1m S of Dornoch**
Car-park ½m E of Dornoch centre by the shore at NH807895, then tracks and coast path south to the dunes and Dornoch Point. Winter seaduck, divers and waders; migrants; winter Snow Bunting.

Loch Fleet   21   **4m N of Dornoch**
Car-park at west end by A9 at NH776984, or by minor road along the south shore at Skelbo, NH795953 and walk east to Coul dunes and the loch mouth. Also from minor road south of Golspie to Littleferry, NH806956.
Winter seaduck including regular Surf Scoter and King Eider, divers and grebes; passage and winter waders; migrants; winter Snow Bunting; woodland birds including Scottish Crossbill.

Newton Point   21   NH711877   5m W of Dornoch
Passage and winter waders and wildfowl.

Meikle Ferry   21   NH729870   4m SW of Dornoch
Passage and winter waders and wildfowl.

Spinningdale   21   NH670892   8m W of Dornoch
Woodland birds including Wood Warbler, Redstart and Pied Flycatcher.

Kyle of Sutherland 21 NH603929 1¼m NW of Bonar Bridge
Woodland and river birds; passage and winter wildfowl and waders.

Ardgay 21 NH601904 1m SW of Bonar Bridge
Passage and winter wildfowl and waders.

TIC	As previous entry.
YH	Carbisdale Castle, Culrain, Ardgay, Sutherland (054 982 232)
BBE	Kyle house, Dornoch Road, Bonar Bridge, Sutherland (08632 360)
	Bridge Hotel. Bonar Bridge (08632 685)
	Evelix Farm Guest House, Evelix, nr Dornoch (0862 810271)
	Trevose Guest House, Cathedral Square, Dornoch (0862 810269)
SC	Skibo Castle Estate, Clashmore, nr Dornoch (086288 236)
	Embo House, nr Dornoch (0862 810260)
	Cambusavie Farmhouse, Dornoch (04083 3184)

Beinn Eighe   19 & 25   west of Kinlochewe
Car-park at visitor centre 1m NE of Kinlochewe by A832 at NH020630, then tracks and trails westwards. Also car-park 2m further NW at NH001650 and trails south. *Access restricted 1st Sept–21st Nov.*
Upland birds including Ptarmigan, Merlin, Golden Eagle; woodland birds including Redwing; summer divers and waders.

Upper Loch Torridon   24 & 25   west of Torridon
Car-park and visitor centre by A896 ½m SE of Torridon at east end of the loch, NG905557. Also car-parks along north shore 2m NW of Torridon at NG869576 and track north, and by A896 along the south side.
Waders, woodland birds, winter wildfowl; raptors; upland birds including Ptarmigan, Golden Eagle and divers.

Gruinard Bay 19 NG960930 10m NE of Poolewe
Winter seaduck and divers.

Rubha Mor 19 NG865960 10m N of Poolewe
Summer waders and divers.

Redpoint 19 NG725687 7m SW of Gairloch
Seawatching; migrants.

Rassal Ashwood 24 NG844433 4m NW of Lochcarron
Woodland birds.

> **Strathcarron Marshes**   25   NG930420   *1m SW of Strath-carron*
> *Wildfowl and waders.*

TIC	Achtercairn, Gairloch, Ross & Cromarty (0445 2130)
	*Main Street, Lochcarron, Ross & Cromarty (05202 241)
YH	Torridon, Achnasheen, Ross & Cromarty (044 587 284)
	Dinbaig, Achnasheen
	Carn Dearg, Gairloch (0445 2219)
H/B	Glen Cottage, Torridon (044 587 268)
	Kinlochewe Bunkhouse, Kinlochewe Hotel, Kinlochewe (044 584 253)
RF	Ledgowan Lodge Hotel, Ledgowan, Achnasheen
RFBBE	Old Inn, Gairloch (0445 2006)
BBE	Churchfield, Kinlochewe (044 584 250)
	Upper Dinbaig, nr Torridon (044 581 227)
	The Croft, Aultbea, Ross-shire (044 582 352)
	Harbour View, Badachro, Ross-shire (044 583 316)
	Badachro Inn, Badachro, (044 583 255)
	Ocean View Hotel, Laide, nr Aultbea, (044 582 385)
SC	17 Port Henderson, nr Gairloch (044 583 278)
	5 Obinan, Laide, nr Aultbea (044 582 307)
	(Kinlochewe bungalow) 1 Thorntrees Ave, Lea, Preston, Lancs (0772 727157)

Inverpolly & Coigach   15   8–12m N of Ullapool
Car-park and visitor centre by A835 2m SW of Elphin at NC187093 and trails west. Also minor road west from Drumrunie 2½m further south. Also car-park at NC108095 on north side of Loch Lurgainn.
Upland and woodland birds including Ptarmigan, Golden Eagle, Redwing, Greenshank and divers.

> **Point of Stoer**   15   NC022355   *9m NW of Lochinver*
> *Seawatching; seabird colonies.*

> **Eddrachillis Bay**   15   NC120330   *7m N of Lochinver*
> *Divers and seaduck.*

> **Raffin**   15   NC004328   *8m NW of Lochinver*
> *Seawatching; seabird colonies; moorland birds including Great Skua.*

> **Reiff & Rubha Mor**   15   NB966145   *5m NW of Achiltibuie*
> *Divers, summer waders; winter seaduck.*

> **Achnahaird Bay**   15   NC016140   *3m N of Achiltibuie*
> *Passage waders and seaduck.*

> **Badentarbat Bay**   15   NC010090   W of Achiltibuie
> Winter seaduck and divers; summer seabirds.

> **Ullapool & Loch Broom**   19 & 20   NH128938
> Winter (& sometimes summer) northern gulls; divers.

> **Achadhantuir Woods**   15   NC085250   2m NW of
> Lochinver
> Woodland birds including Pied Flycatcher, Redstart and
> Redwing.

TIC	*West Shore Street, Ullapool (0854 2135)
	*Main Street, Lochinver (05714 330)
YH	Shore Street, Ullapool (0854 2254)
	Achininver, Achiltibuie, Ullapool
	Achmelvich, Recharn, Lairg, Sutherland (05714 480)
RFBBE	Drumbeg Hotel, Drumbeg (05713 236)
	Kylesku Hotel, Kylesku, Sutherland (0971 2231)
BBE	Cruachan Guest House, Stoer, Sutherland (05715 303)
	Ferry Boat Inn, Shore Street, Ullapool
BBESC	Birchbank, Knockan, nr Elphin, Sutherland (085486 203/215)
SC	Dornie House, Achiltibuie, by Ullapool (085482 271)
	Tighnuilt, Inverkirkaig, nr Lochinver (05714 233)

Kyle of Durness   9   **2m SW of Durness**
View from A838 along the eastern shore e.g. NC382646 and
NC366620. Also from ferry pier ½m NW of A838 at NC377662.
Passage and winter waders, seaduck and divers.

Faraid Head & Balnakeil Bay   9   **1–2m NW of Durness**
Car-park in Balnakeil 1m NW of Durness at NC392687 and walk
north to the point and cliffs on the east side.
Summer seabirds; passage and winter waders, seaduck and
divers; migrants; seawatching; Corncrake.

Loch Hope & Ben Hope   9   **8m SW of Tongue**
Park by minor road along east side of the loch e.g. at the south end
at NC459506 and 2m north at NC468542. Then tracks east.
Summer divers and Greenshank; Golden Eagle and other upland
birds; woodland birds.

Handa Island   9   **3m NW of Scourie**
Boat Mon-Sat from Tarbet (NC164489) 15th Apr–10th Sept, tel:
0971 2156 for details. Overnight stay only by arrangement with the
RSPB Highland Office, tel: 046 381496.
Summer seabirds including Arctic & Great Skua, Red-throated
Diver and Eider; migrants; Rock Dove.

Loch Eriboll　9　NC400550　*9m W of Tongue*
Divers and seaduck; raptors.

Strath Beag　9　NC390514–540　*0–2m S of Loch Eriboll*
Waders, river and woodland birds.

Clo Mor　9　NC305733　*3m E of Cape Wrath*
Summer seabirds (highest cliffs in Britain); Rock Dove; Greenshank.

Cape Wrath　9　NC260748　*10m NW of Durness*
Summer seabirds and seawatching.

TIC	*Sango, Durness, Sutherland (097 181 259)
YH	Smoo, Durness, Lairg, Sutherland (097 181 244)
RF	Oasis, Durness
	Sango Sands, Durness
BBE	Cape Wrath Hotel, Durness, (097 181 274)
	Far North Hotel, Durness, (097 181 221)
	Minch View, Scouriemore, Scourie, Sutherland (0971 2110)
SC	(Kinlochbervie & Scourie) Estate Office, Achfary, Sutherland (097 184 221)

Kyle of Tongue　10　**1½m NW of Tongue**
Park and view from minor road on east side of the causeway, ½m NE of A838 at NC592588, and from car-parks on the causeway itself.
Passage and winter waders and wildfowl.

Skelpick　10　**8m SE of Tongue**
Park at Skelpick at the end of minor road 4m S of A836 from Invernaver, on the east side of River Naver, at NC726553. Then take track to the southeast and along Skelpick Burn towards Loch Mor area.
Summer divers and waders; woodland and river birds; Hen Harrier.

Invernaver & Torrisdale Bay　10　**1m S of Bettyhill**
Park in Invernaver just north of A836 at NC707599 and walk along coast north and then inland.
Summer divers, Greenshank and Short-eared Owl; passage waders; migrants.

Strathy Point　10　**8m NE of Bettyhill**
Car-park at end of minor road 2½m N of A836 from Strathy at NC828696.
Seawatching; migrants; winter seaduck and divers; Corncrake.

> **Borgie Forest**   10   NC663577   3½m SW of Bettyhill
> Woodland birds.

> **Naver Forest**   10   NC689419   13m S of Bettyhill
> Woodland birds.

> **Loch Naver**   16   NC620370   17m S of Bettyhill
> Woodland, upland and moorland birds; divers.

TIC   *Bettyhill, Sutherland (06412 342)
YH   Tongue, Lairg, Sutherland (084 755 301)
RFBBE Melvich Hotel, Melvich (06413 206)
BBE   Tongue Hotel, Tongue, (084 755 206/207)
           Dunveaden House, Bettyhill, (06412 273)
           Bettyhill Hotel, Bettyhill, (06412 352)
SC   (Bettyhill house) Hoy Farm, Halkirk, Caithness (084 783 544)
           Glaickbea, Skerray, nr Tongue, Sotherland (06412 432)

Dunnet Head   12   **8m NE of Thurso**
Car-park at northernmost end of B855 near the lighthouse at ND203766, then paths southwest and southeast.
Seabird colonies including Great Skua; Rock Dove; seawatching; migrants.

Dunnet Bay & Woods   12   **0–2m NE of Castletown**
Car-park by A836 at NE corner of the bay at ND219706, or at the south end at Castletown itself, ND198685. Views of the bay and nearby woodland at both sites.
Winter divers, seaduck and other wildfowl; passage waders; migrants.

Duncansby Head   12   **2m E of John o'Groats**
Car-park at east end of minor road east of A9 from John o'Groats at ND403734.
Seawatching; migrants.

Noss Head   12   **3m NE of Wick**
Car-park by minor road 2m NE of Wick airport ½m before the lighthouse at ND384546. Then paths along the coast and inland.
Summer seabird colonies; seawatching; migrants; winter seaduck.

> **Holborn Head**   12   ND108716   2m NW of Thurso
> Seawatching; winter divers and seaduck; migrants.

> **Thurso Harbour & Bay**   12   ND119687   N side of Thurso
> Winter northern gulls, divers and seaduck; passage waders.

Green Folds   *12*   *ND210495*   *10m W of Wick*
Summer waders and divers.

Brough Head   *12*   *ND371631*   *6m S of John o'Groats*
Summer seabird colonies.

Ackergill Links   *12*   *ND342567*   *4m NW of Wick*
Passage waders; migrant pipits etc.

Wick Bay   *12*   *ND370505*   *½m E of Wick*
Winter northern gulls, divers and seaduck.

TIC	Whitechapel Road, off High Street, Wick, Caithness (0955 2596)
	*Riverside, Thurso (0847 62371)
	*Country Road, John o'Groats (095 581 373)
YH	Canisbay, John o'Groats, Wick, Caithness (095 581 424)
RF	Upper Deck, Scrabster, nr Thurso
RFBBE	Rosebank Hotel, Thurso Street, Wick (0955 3244)
BBE	Northern Sands Hotel, Dunnet (084 784 270)
	Berriedale Arms Hotel, Mey, nr Thurso (084 785 244)
SC	Pentland View, Scarfskerry, Caithness (084 785 357)

Lothian

Tyninghame & John Muir Country Park   67   1–3m W of Dunbar
Car-park ½m N of West Barns, off A1087, by Belhaven Bay at NT652787. Then take coastal paths east across the river to Belhaven and Long Craigs and west around the south side of the Tyne estuary. Also car-park on the north side of the estuary at the end of Limetree Walk at NT626809 and paths east and south along the shoreline.
Winter seaduck and divers; passage and winter waders; winter Snow Bunting and Shore Lark; woodland birds and passerine migrants.

Seacliff   67   6m NW of Dunbar
Car-park ½m E of A198 from Auldhams, 2m N of Whitekirk, at NT603846 and coast path west.
Migrants; winter seaduck and divers.

Barns Ness   67   3m SE of Dunbar
Car-park near the end of minor road ½m N of East Barns, 1½m NE of A1 at NT718772 and tracks west around the bay and east to the lighthouse.
Migrants; seawatching.

> **Bass Rock**   67   NT603873   *island 3m NE of North Berwick*
> *Large seabird colonies especially Gannet. Spring and summer boat trips from North Berwick Harbour. Tel: 0620 2838 (24 Victoria Road, North Berwick)*

TIC	Town House, High Street, Dunbar (0386 63353)
	Quality Street, North Berwick (0620 2197)
YH	Abbey St. Bathans, Duns, Berwickshire (03614 217)
	The Mount, Coldingham, Eyemouth, Berwickshire (08907 71298)
RF	Battleblent Hotel, West Barns
BB	Kiloran House, East Linton, nr Dunbar (0620 860410)

BBE St. Beys Guest House, Bayswell Road, Dunbar (0368 63571)

SC Whitekirk Mains, Whitekirk, nr North Berwick (0620 87245)

Stonelaws Farm, East Linton (0620 87207)

Whiteadder Reservoir 67 9m SE of Gifford
Car-park near the eastern end of the reservoir by B6355, 1½m NW of Cranshaws at NT666634. Then many paths.
Wildfowl, woodland and moorland birds including Redstart and Black Grouse.

Humbie Glen 66 5m SW of Gifford
Park by Humbie church ½m N of Humbie and the junction of A6137 and B6371 at NT461637 and take many paths north through the woods and beside the river.
Woodland and river birds including Wood Warbler, Redstart and Dipper.

Crichton Glen 66 2m E of Gorebridge
Park by Crichton church ½m SW of the village on the B6367 at NT381616 and take path south.
Woodland and river birds; summer warblers.

Fala Moor 66 NT425585 5m SE of Gorebridge
Moorland birds; winter wildfowl.

TIC As previous entry.
Granada Service Area, A1, nr Old Craighall (031 653 6172)
YH As previous entry.
RF Tweeddale Arms Hotel, Gifford
BBE Goblin Ha' Hotel, Gifford (0620 81244)
Long Newton Farm, Gifford (0620 81210)
SC Under Bolton, nr Haddington (0620 81318)

Aberlady Bay 66 2m SW of Gullane
Car-park by A198 ¾m E of Aberlady at NT473806. Then take bridge over the estuary and path north along the east shore toward Gullane Point. Also path north from A198 at Aberlady along the western shore to Aberlady Point and Graigelaw Point.
Winter divers, grebes, seaduck and geese; passage and winter waders; passage migrants and frequent rarities; winter Snow and Lapland Buntings, Short-eared and Long-eared Owls.

Gullane Bay & Point 66 1m NW of Gullane
Car-park by shore ½m N of A198 from Gullane at NT476832. Then coast path west to the point and NE to Black Rocks Wood.
Seawatching; winter divers and seaduck; passerine migrants.

Gosford Bay & Ferny Ness   66   1–2m SW of Aberlady
View from car-park by A198 at the south end of the Bay near the Ness at NT442776.
Passage and winter grebes, seaduck and gulls; seawatching; migrants.

> *Drem & Fenton Barns*   66   *NT515805   3m E of Aberlady
> Winter wildfowl.*

TIC   Quality Street, North Berwick (0620 2197)
YH   7 Bruntsfield Crescent, Edinburgh (031 447 2994)
RF   Waggon, Aberlady
        Open Arms, Dirleton, nr Gullane
BBE   Golf Hotel, Aberlady (08757 682)
        Cedar Grove House, Dirleton (0620 85227)

Mouth of River Esk   66   N side of Musselburgh
Park at the end of minor road running north along the east bank of the river from A199, at NT346736 and footpath north around the seawall to lagoons and scrape.
Passage and winter waders; seaduck; winter divers and gulls.

Duddingston Loch   66   2m SE of Edinburgh centre
Car-park by minor road by the north side of the loch, ¾m SW of A1 down Duddingston Road, at NT283726. Then path SW to overlook the water.
Winter wildfowl and Water Rail; reedbed species; migrants; summer warblers.

Leith Docks & Portobello   66   2–3m N & NE of Edinburgh centre
Park ¼m east of A199 3m E of Edinburgh centre at NT303745, then coast path north toward lagoons and sewage outlet or south toward Joppa. Also just north of A901 at Newhaven, by the docks at NT257772.
Winter divers, grebes, seaduck and gulls; passage and winter waders.

> *Hermitage of Braid   66   NT255705   2m S of Edinburgh centre
> Woodland birds.*

> *Colinton Dell   66   NT215695   4m SW of Edinburgh centre
> Woodland and river birds.*

TIC   Waverley Market, Princes Street, Edinburgh (031 557 1700)
        Scottish Travel Centre, 14 South St. Andrew Street, Edinburgh (031 557 5522)

YH   As previous entry.
18 Eglington Crescent, Edinburgh (031 337 1120)

Gladhouse Reservoir & Moorfoot Valley   66   6m SE of Penicuik

View from minor road at the north end, 1½m SE of B6372, at NT302545. Also from car-parks at the SW corner (NT293527) and NE corner at NT308543. Moorfoot Valley path from the SW corner, NT293527.

Passage and winter wildfowl; passage waders; migrants.

Roslin Glen   66   3m NE of Penicuik

Park by B7006 by the SE side of Roslin at NT274632 then path east and north beside the River Esk. Or park just west of B7003 ½m to the southwest at NT266627.

Woodland and river birds.

> *Rosebery Reservoir   66   NT310567   5½m SE of Penicuik*
> *Passage and winter wildfowl; woodland and river birds.*

> *Edgelaw Reservoir   66   NT300582   5m SE of Penicuik*
> *Passage and winter wildfowl; woodland birds.*

> *Portmore Loch (Borders)   66   NT260505   7m S of Penicuik*
> *Winter wildfowl and gull roost.*

TIC   The Library, White Hart Street, Dalkeith (031 663 2083)
YH   As previous entry.
RF   Old Howgate Inn, Howgate, nr Penicuik
RFBBE   Old Original Inn, Roslin (031 440 2384)
BBE   Royal Hotel, Roslin (031 440 2029)
SC   Halton Knowe Farm, Eddleston, nr Peebles (07213 282)

Drum Sands & River Almond   66 or 65   4m E of Queensferry

Car-park on east side of the mouth of the River Almond at the north end of Cramond, NT190770. Then coast path east, track out to Cramond Island at low tide and path south beside the river.

Passage and winter waders; river birds.

Dalmeny Shore Walk & Hound Point   65   1–4m E of Queensferry

Either coast path NW over the footbridge from the above site or park at Hawes Inn car-park, by B924 just west of the Forth Bridge, at NT138784 and coast path east to Hound Point for the best seawatching.

Passage and winter waders, wildfowl and seaduck; woodland birds; migrants; summer and passage terns; seawatching.

TIC   Forth Road Bridge, by North Queensferry, Fife (0383 417759)
YH   As previous entry.
RF   Cramond Inn, Cramond
          Hawes Inn, Queensferry
          Moorings, Queensferry

Blackness   65   4m NE of Linlithgow
Park near the end of B903 at Blackness, NT053800, then track out to the castle and coast paths east or west.
Passage and winter waders and wildfowl; winter seaduck and divers; summer and passage terns.

Linlithgow Loch   65   N side of Linlithgow
Car-park just north of A803 by the south shore of the loch at NT001772, then path all around.
Great Crested Grebe; wildfowl; reedbed species; summer warblers; woodland birds; migrants.

Beecraigs Country Park   65   2m S of Linlithgow
Car-parks by minor roads south of Linlithgow e.g. just south of the visitor centre at NT007743. Then paths around the loch and through the wood.
Woodland birds including Long-eared Owl and Crossbill; winter wildfowl.

Muiravonside Country Park (Central)   65   3m SW of Linlithgow
Car-park ½m S of B825 at NS964755, then tracks east through the woods and beside the River Avon.
Woodland and river birds; summer warblers.

> *Lochcote Reservoir   65   NS975736   2½m SW of Linlithgow*
> *Passage and winter wildfowl.*

TIC   Burgh Halls, The Cross, Linlithgow (0506 844600)
YH   As previous entry.
RF   Four Marys, High Street, Linlithgow
BBE   Belsyde Farm, Lanark Road, Linlithgow (0506 842098)
         William Craigs, nr Linlithgow (0506 834888)

Threipmuir Reservoir & Pentland Hills   65   2–4m S of Balerno
Car-park by minor road just north of where it crosses the reservoir
at NT164637. Then paths along the north shore to the east and
south over the bridge and up onto the Pentland Hills.
Passage and winter wildfowl; marshland birds; summer warblers;
passage waders, gulls and terns; winter Hen Harrier and Short-
eared Owl; upland birds including Red Grouse and Ring Ousel.

Harperrig Reservoir   65   5m SE of West Calder
Car-park ¼m S of A70 at the west end of the reservoir, NT88606,
then path all around the shore.
Passage and winter wildfowl; passage waders.

West Water Reservoir (Borders)   65   2m W of West Linton
Park by minor road ½m NW of A702 from West Linton centre at
NT142522. Then track west for 1½m to the reservoir.
Passage and winter wildfowl; summer and passage waders.

*Almondell & Calder Wood Country Park   65   NT090690
6m NE of West Calder
Woodland and river birds.*

*Tailend Moss   65   NT003676   3½m N of West Calder
Marshland birds; winter wildfowl.*

*Cobbinshaw Reservoir   65   NT015575   3m S of West
Calder
Winter wildfowl.*

TIC	Horsemarket, Ladyacre Road, Lanark (0555 61661)
YH	As previous entry.
R	Grey Horse Inn, Balerno
RF	Linton, West Linton
BB	Whitecroft Farm, East Calder (0506 881810)
BBE	Westlands, West Linton (0968 60873)
	Ratho Park Hotel, Kirknewton, nr East Calder (031 333 1242)
SC	Slipperfield House, West Linton (0968 60401)
	(Dunsyre Cottages) Lee & Carnwath Estates, Estate Office, Carnwath (0555 840273)

Orkney

to Orkney:
by air: British Airways tel: 0856 2233
        Loganair   tel: 0856 3457
by boat: P & O Scottish Ferries   tel: 0856 850655
        Thomas & Bews   tel: 0955 81353

TIC   Broad Street, Kirkwall (0856 2856)
          Ferry Terminal Building, Pierhead, Stromness (0856 850716)

MAINLAND   OS Map 6

Loch of Graemeshall   7m SE of Kirkwall
View from B9052 1½m E of St. Mary's at HY490018.
Summer wildfowl and waders; reedbed species; migrants.

Deerness   easternmost peninsula of Mainland
Whole peninsula (which is almost an island) excellent for migrants. e.g. Mull Head area HY590090, Mirkady HY540070, Point of Ayre HY590040 and any areas of cover.

Copinsay   island 3m SE of Deerness
Day-trips from Skaill at east end of B9050, HY588065.   tel:085 674 252
Summer seabird colonies; Rock Dove; Twite; migrants.

St. Peter's Pool & Bay of Suckquoy   6m SE of Kirkwall
View from A960 at HY516046 and HY543037.
Passage waders, ducks, gulls and terns.

Berstane Wood   1m SE of Kirkwall centre
View from minor road at HY468103.
Migrants; winter Long-eared Owl roost.

Scapa Flow   6m S of Kirkwall
View from Churchill Barriers joining Mainland to Burray e.g.
ND480997.
Passage and winter waders; winter Great Northern Diver and
seaduck.

> *Kirkwall Harbour   HY445110*
> *Winter northern gulls.*

YH   Old Scapa Road, Kirkwall (0856 2243)
BBE   Heathfield Farmhouse, St. Ola (0856 2378)
      Karona, St. Mary's, Holm (0856 78346)
SC   Schoolhouse, Deerness (0856 74268)

Bay of Firth   4m NW of Kirkwall
View from A965 e.g. at HY396124 or HY376129.
Winter seaduck; passage and winter waders.

Hobbister & Waukmill Bay   5m SW of Kirkwall
Park down minor road ½m S of A964 at HY384065 or at HY396070
on the main road. Best area south of A964 and NE of Loch of
Kirbister.
Summer raptors and moorland species; passage and winter
waders; winter divers and seaduck.

Loch of Stenness & Loch of Harray   4m W of Finstown
Car-park by B9055 running between the two lochs at HY296134.
Wildfowl.

> *Stromness Harbour   HY256093*
> *Winter northern gulls.*

> *Binscarth Wood   HY350141   ½m W of Finstown*
> *Migrants; winter Long-eared Owls.*

YH   As previous entry.
        Hellihole Road, Stromness (0856 850589)
RFBBE   Ferry Inn, Stromness (0856 850280)
BBE   Ardeonaig, Houton, Orphir (0856 81356)
        Braes Hotel, Stromness (0856 850495)
        Ramsquoy, Stenness (0856 850316)
SC   Swanbister Cottage, Orphir (0856 81 212/261)
        Roadside Cottage, Orphir

Burgar Hill & Lowries Water   8m N of Finstown
Park at end of track on the top of Burgar Hill, 1m SW of A966, at
HY343260. Hide overlooks Lowries Water.
Wildfowl and moorland waders; Red-throated Diver.

Lower Cottascarth   4m N of Finstown
Park along track north of Settiscarth, 1m W of A966, at HY369194, then path to hide.
Summer moorland birds including Short-eared Owl, Hen Harrier, Merlin and skuas.

Birsay Moors   7m NW of Finstown
View from B9057 between Dounby and Stenso (A986 to A966) e.g. HY343243.
Moorland birds.

> **Eynhallow Sound**   *HY386268   1½m NE of Evie*
> *Winter seaduck and divers.*

YH	As previous entry.
BBE	Riff, Rendall (0856 76541)
BBESC	Woodwick House, Evie (0856 75330)
SC	Midhouse, Evie (0856 75210)
	Quayfree, Rendall
	Midland, Rendall (0856 75 259/281)

The Loons   10m N of Stromness
Park by minor road ¼m E of B9056 from Marwick, at HY246242, then path to hide.
Summer ducks, waders, Arctic Tern and Corncrake; winter wildfowl.

Brough Head   NW extremity of Mainland
Car-park at end of minor road ½m N of western end of A966 at HY244284.
Seawatching; migrants.

Marwick Head   3m S of Brough Head
Car-parks along minor roads 1m W of B9056 at HY233252 and HY230242. Then coastal paths.
Summer seabird colonies including Rock Dove.

> **Loch of Banks**   *HY275233   2m NW of Dounby*
> *Waders and wildfowl; winter Hen Harrier roost.*

YH	As previous entry.
BBE	Links House, Birsay (0856 72221)
BBESC	Quoylonga, Marwick, Birsay (0856 72225)
SC	(Birsay cottage) Orkney Self-catering, Finstown (0856 76397)
	Newan, Birsay (0856 72251)

HOY   7   SW of Mainland
by boat: Passenger and car ferry from Houton (HY318040) on Mainland to Lyness on Hoy.   tel: 085 681 397
Passenger ferry from Stromness.
Skuas, Red-throated Diver, Ring Ousel, Peregrine; migrants; moorland birds; Merlin, Hen Harrier and Short-eared Owl.

Rackwick   ND200990
Summer offshore Manx Shearwater and Storm Petrel gatherings.

Rora Head   ND174993
Seawatching.

Sneuk Head   ND210953
Manx Shearwaters.

Heldale Water   ND265924
Skuas.

South Walls   ND330900
Winter Barnacle Geese; migrants.

Hurliness   ND290893
Passage waders.

YH	Rackwick Outdoor Centre, Hoy
	Hoy Outdoor Centre, Hoy
BBE	Stoneyquoy, Lyness, Hoy (0856 79234)
	Old Custom House, Longhope, Hoy (0856 70442)
	Burnmouth Guest House, Hoy (0856 79297)

BURRAY & SOUTH RONALDSAY   7   SE of Mainland
Access: via Burray and Churchill Barriers road from Mainland.

Churchill Barriers   causeways joining Mainland & Burray, Burray & S Ronaldsay.
Winter seaduck; summer skuas and terns.

Echna Loch & Bay   ND474967
Passage and winter wildfowl.

Liddel   ND460836
Migrants.

Widewall Bay   ND425920
Winter seaduck and divers; passage waders.

Aikers   ND454913
Wildfowl and waders.

YH   Old Scapa Road, Kirkwall (0856 2243)
BBE   Rufford, Burray (0856 73329)
            Bellevue House, St. Margaret's Hope, South Ronaldsay
            (0856 83294)
BBESC   South Cara, South Ronaldsay (0856 83275)
SC   Briarlea, Burray (0856 73 225/253)

ROUSAY   6   2m N of Mainland
Ferry: Car and passenger ferry from Tingwall (Mainland),
      HY404229, to Brinian (Rousay).   tel:085 675 360
Summer Red-throated Diver; moorland birds including skuas,
Hen Harrier, Merlin, Short-eared Owl and Golden Plover.

Brings   HY385343
Arctic and Great Skuas, Arctic Terns.

Moss of Catagreem   HY410310
Moorland birds.

Faraclett Head   HY448338
Migrants.

Scabra Head   HY364313
Summer seabirds.

Trumland   HY427276
Moorland birds including Merlin, Hen Harrier, Short-eared Owl
and skuas.

BBE   Old Manse, Sourin, Rousay (0856 82375)

STRONSAY   5   NE of Mainland
by air: Loganair from Kirkwall.   tel: 0856 2494
by sea: Passenger ferries from Kirkwall, Eday and Sanday.   tel:
      0856 2044

Rothiesholm Peninsula   HY620220
Summer skuas, waders and wildfowl.

Lea Shun   HY660213
Waders and wildfowl.

Mill Bay   HY670270
Winter seaduck and divers; passage and winter waders.

Meikle Water   HY665245
Wildfowl and waders.

Oyce of Huip   HY640300
Passage waders and wildfowl.

Burgh Head   HY698230
Migrants; seawatching.

Bay of Holland   HY630240
Waders; winter seaduck and divers.

BBE   Clifton House, Stronsay (08576 378)

WESTRAY   5   **N of Mainland**
by air: Loganair from Kirkwall.   tel: 0856 2494
by sea: Passenger and car (lift-on) ferry from Kirkwall.   tel: 0856
    2044

Noup Head   HY392500
Huge summer seabird colonies; seawatching.

Stanger Head   HY510428
Seabird colonies; migrants.

Loch of Burness   HY430480
Waders and wildfowl.

Bay of Tuquoy   HY454448
Waders; winter seaduck and divers.

Bay of Pierowall   HY445486
Winter northern gulls, seaduck and divers.

The Ouse and Bay of Skaill   HY456512
Waders.

BBE   Pierowall Hotel, Westray (08577 472/208)
BBESC   Sand o'Gill, Westray (08577 374)

PAPA WESTRAY   5   **NE of Westray**
by air: Loganair from Kirkwall.   tel: 0856 2494
by sea: Passenger and car (lift-on) ferry from Kirkwall and neigh-
    bouring islands.   tel: 0856 2044
Summer Corncrake, seabirds; migrants; Twite.

North Hill   HY500550
Summer Arctic Skuas and terns, waders and gulls.

Mull Head   HY500558
Seawatching; migrants.

Loch of St. Tredwell   **HY495505**
Passage and summer waders and wildfowl.

YHBBE Beltane House, Papa Westray (08574 267/238)

SANDAY   5   NE of Mainland, N of Stronsay
by air: Loganair from Kirkwall.   tel: 0856 2494
by sea: Passenger and car (lift-on) ferry from Kirkwall and neigh-
          bouring islands.   tel: 0856 2044

North Loch   **HY755460**
Winter wildfowl.

Northwall   **HY750445**
Summer wildfowl, terns and waders; migrants.

Lamaness Firth   **HY685426**
Passage and winter waders.

Whitemill   **HY690462**
Summer waders and Short-eared Owl.

Plain of Fidge Golf Course   **HY710410**
Migrants.

Gump of Spurness   **HY604355**
Moorland birds including Arctic Skua and Short-eared Owl.

BBE   Kettletoft Hotel, Sanday (08575 217)

EDAY   5   NW of Stronsay
by air: Loganair from Kirkwall.   tel: 0856 2494
by sea: Passenger and car (lift-on) ferry from Kirkwall and neigh-
          bouring islands.   tel: 0856 2044

Mill Loch   **HY565367**
Summer Red-throated Diver.

Fers Ness   **HY530345**
Winter seaduck and divers.

Vinquoy Hill Plantation   **HY564384**
Migrants.

Red Head   **HY570407**
Summer seabirds.

YH   London Bay, Eday (08572 283)
BBE   Merry Dancers Inn, Eday (08572 221)

North Ronaldsay   5   most NE of the Orkneys
by air: 'Loganair from Kirkwall. tel: 0856 2494
by sea: 'Passenger and car (lift-on) ferry from Kirkwall and neighbouring islands. tel: 0856 2044
Migrants and many rarities; seawatching; summer waders, wildfowl and seabirds.

BBE   North Ronaldsay Bird Observatory, N Ronaldsay (08573 267)
SC   Quoybanks, N Ronaldsay (08573 260)

Shetland

to Shetland:
by air: British Airways   tel: 0595 3162
              Loganair   tel: 0595 84246
by boat: P & O Ferries   tel: 0224 572615

TIC   The Market Cross, Lerwick (0595 3434)
YH   Islesburgh House, Lerwick (0595 2144)

Fair Isle   4   between mainland Shetland & Orkney
The premier birdwatching island in western Europe.
Summer seabirds; migrants including many rarities.

by air: 'Loganair from Kirkwall (Orkney), or Tingwall (Lerwick).
'Eight seater also available for charter from Tingwall to Fair Isle
and other islands, also to the Scottish mainland, Orkney, the
Faroes and Norway. Loganair Ltd, Tingwall Airport, Gott, Shetland tel: 0595 84246

by sea: Mr. J. W. Stout, Skerryholm, Fair Isle tel: 03512 222
From Grutness Pier, Sumburgh, once or twice weekly; and from
Lerwick Harbour fortnightly May – Sept (MV Good Shepherd IV)

BBE   Utra, Fair Isle (03512 209)
              full board at Fair Isle Bird Observatory Lodge (03512 258)

Sumburgh Head   4   southernmost point of mainland
Park at end of minor road near lighthouse, HU408081, or the
Sumburgh Hotel area just south of A970, HU400097.
Summer seabirds; seawatching; migrants.

Pool of Virkie   4   immediately N of Sumburgh airport
View from minor road skirting the northern shore, ½m E of A970,
e.g. HU398115.

Loch of Hillwell   4   ¼ m E of Hillwell
Park by minor road between Ringasta and Hillwell, HU376143, and walk south around the loch and down the burn.
Wildfowl; waders; migrants.

Loch of Spiggie   4   2m W of Boddam
View from minor road at north end ¾m W of B9122 at HU373176.
Winter wildfowl; passage waders; summer terns and skuas and Red-necked Phalarope.

Boddam Voe   4   ¾m SE of Boddam
View from minor road along the north shore, HU400155, ½m SE of A970.
Winter seaduck, divers and gulls.

> *Scatness   4   HU387095   1m SW of Sumburgh airport*
> *Wildfowl; waders; migrants.*

> *Burn of Sevdale   4   HU390214   1m E of Bigton*
> *Migrants.*

> *Bay of Quendale   4   HU367127   ½m S of Quendale*
> *Gulls; seaduck; divers; passage waders.*

> *The Nev, Fitful Head   4   HU343147   2m NW of Quendale*
> *Seawatching.*

H/B   Northlynn, Toab, Virkie (0950 60498)
BBE   Meadowvale Hotel, Virkie (0950 60240)
       Mainland Guest Hosue, Dunrossness (0950 60517)
       Lunnabister, Dunrossness (0950 60480)
       Jorvik, Bigton (05902 295)
SC   (Scatness cottage) 3 Ferry View, Ulsta, Yell (095 782 285)
       The Knowe, Toab, Virkie
       (Quendale cottage) 57 King Harald Street, Lerwick (0595 2170)

Mousa   4   uninhabited island off E coast of mainland Shetland HU460240
Access by boat from Sand Lodge, Sandwick. Mr. Tom Jamieson, Leebitton, Sandwick tel: 09505 367
Seabird colonies including skuas and storm petrels; passage waders and migrants.

Scalloway Harbour   4   4m W of Lerwick
View from minor road south of A970 near the castle, HU404393.
Winter northern gulls; migrants.

Gremista Copse   4   1½m N of Lerwick
By the North Burn of Gremista, ¼m N of A970 along minor road, HU464433.
Migrants.

Lochs of Tingwall & Asta   4   3m W of Lerwick
View from B9074 1½m & 2½m south of Veensgarth e.g. HU416434.

> *Lerwick Sewage Outfall & Loch of Clickimin   4*
> *HU467408   SW edge of Lerwick*
> *Winter northern gulls and wildfowl.*

> *Strand Plantation   4   HU433460   1¼m N of Veensgarth*
> *Migrants.*

BB	Seafield House, Sound, Lerwick (0595 2054)
BBE	Brylyn Guest House, Port Arthur, Scalloway (059 588 407)
	Carriden, Shurton Brae, Gulberwick (0595 4768)
SC	Leagarth, East Voe, Scalloway (059 588 376)
	Burland, Trondra, Scalloway (059 588 430)

Bressay   4   island 1m E of Lerwick
Car ferry from Lerwick harbour. Shetland Islands Council, Lerwick (0595 2024)
Migrants especially around habitation; seawatching from Bard Head and Loder Head.

Noss   4   (mid May–end Aug only) island E of Bressay
Short ferry (inflatable) from Bressay across Noss Sound operated by Nature Conservancy Council tel: 0595 3345
Huge seabird colonies including 7,000 pairs of Gannet, Great and Arctic Skuas.

BBE	Maryfield House, Bressay (059582 207)
SC	(Bressay cottage) Vaarie, Voe (08068 360)

Papa Stour   3   island off west mainland coast
by sea: 'Passenger ferry (MV Koada) from West Burrafirth (HU255568) Mon, Wed, Fri & Sat. Shetland Islands Council, Lerwick tel: 0595 2024/86335
by air: 'Loganair, Tingwall tel: 0595 84246
Summer seabirds; seawatching; pasage waders, wildfowl and passerines.

BBE	Longhouse, Papa Stour (059573 238)
	Hurdiback, Papa Stour (059573 227)

Tresta & Tresta Voe   3   10m NW of Lerwick
Park by A971 at HU364381, search trees around the chapel, view
the Voe from minor road south.
Migrants; winter seaduck and divers.

Sandness   3   mainland side of Sound of Papa
Park near the Pier at HU187579. Seawatch across the sound, walk
south and east to the lochs for migrants.

Weisdale   3   between A970 and A971
Park along B9075 1–2m N of A971 from the head of Weisdale Voe,
e.g. HU396545 and search the plantations and cover north and
south in the valley.
Migrants.

BBE   Bixter House, Bixter (059581 200)
        Old Manse, Sand, Bixter (059586 271)

Lunna Ness   3   NE corner of Mainland
Take minor road on north from end of B9071 for 2–3m, search
roadside trees and West Lunna Voe, HU483694.
Migrants.

Garths Voe   3   E end of Sullom Voe
View from B9076 at Laxobigging, HU408736.
Winter seaduck, divers and northern gulls.

Houb of Scatsa   3   1m SW of Garths Voe
View from road at HU396727.
Passage waders.

Esha Ness   3   NW corner of Mainland
Park at end of minor road ½m NW of B9078 at HU210785 and walk
north and south.
Summer seabirds, waders and skuas; seawatching; migrants.

Ronas Hill   3   6m NE of Esha Ness
Park by A970 at North Collafirth, HU353837, and walk westwards.
Migrants; occasional Snowy Owl.

> ***Voxter Plantation & Voe*** *3   HU367702   1½m NE of*
> *Brae*
> *Migrants; winter seaduck and divers.*

> ***Gaza Strip*** *3   HU350727   ½m SW of Sullom*
> *Migrants.*

H/B   Voxter Centre, 4 Havragord, Brae (080622 417)
RFBBE   The Booth, Hillswick (080623 348)
BBE   Braewick Cottage, Eshaness (080623 385)
            Mossbank House, Mossbank (0806 242 596)

SC   (Nibon cottage) Inches, Bells Road, Lerwick (0595 5413)
(Nibon cottage) Buster, Brae (080622 230)
Houster, Loch End, North Roe (08063 231)
(Graven, Sullom Voe) Bank House, Gairloch, Ross-shire
(0445 2305)
Easthouse, Grobsness, Voe (08068 339)

WHALSAY   2   island off NE Mainland coast
by air: Flights from Lerwick by Loganair   tel: 0595 842246 advance
      bookings   tel: 08065 253
by sea: Car ferry from Vidlin, nr north end of B9071 at HU480655.
      tel: 08066 259
Summer divers and skuas. Migrants.

Skaw   HU590664
Migrants.

Symbister Harbour   HU537624
Winter northern gulls.

BBE   Lingaveg Guest House, Marrister, Symbister (08066 489)
       Hillhead, Skaw (08066 288)
SC   West Green, Symbister (08066 284)

Out Skerries   2   islands 5m NE of Whalsay
by sea: Passenger and vehicle ferry from Lerwick Tues & Fri, and
from Vidlin Sat & Sun. tel: 08065 226
by air: Loganair flights Mon, Wed & Thurs April–Oct, from
Tingwall, Lerwick. tel: 0595 84246
Migrants; summer seabirds.

BBESC Rocklea, East Isle (08065 228)

Foula   4   island 15m W of Mainland
by sea: Passenger ferry from West Burrafirth, Mainland
(HU255568) on Tues & Thurs. tel: 0595 86 335
by air: Flights April–Oct from Tingwall, Lerwick. tel: 059584 246
Summer seabirds including many Great Skuas, Storm and Leachs
Petrels and Manx Shearwater; migrants.

H/B   Freyers (03933 3233)
BBE   Broadfoot (03933 3239)
BBESC Freyers (03933 3233)
SC   The Haa (03933 3232)
       Leraback (03933 3226)

YELL 1 & 2 across Yell Sound NE of Mainland
Car ferry from Boath of Toft at north end of A968 (HU437763). tel:
095 782 259/268

Burravoe HU520799 SE corner of island
Park and search any cover in the area.
Migrants.

Hamnavoe HU486807 2m W of Burravoe
Passage waders; winter seaduck and divers.

Lumbister HU490950 E of Whale Firth
Park by A968 at HU509974 and walk westwards and south.
Summer divers, waders and skuas.

BBE   Pinewood Guest House, Upper Toft, Aywick (0957 2077)
       Manse, West Sandwick (095786 211)
       Manse, Ravensgeo (0957 2288)
SC   Isleview, Basta, Mid-Yell (0957 2216)
       North Haa, West Sandwick (095786 262)
       2 Greenbank Road, Cullivoe (095784 268)

FETLAR 2 island E of Yell
Ferry from Unst and North Yell. tel: 095782 259/268
Snowy Owl; View from end of minor road in centre of island ¼m SE
of Skutes Water, HU626916.
Red-necked Phalarope; On Loch of Funzie by B9088, HU655901.

Lamb Hoga SW peninsula of island
Summer seabirds e.g. HU623875.

Tresta Beach between Lamb of Hoga and Tresta
View from track between Papil Water and the sea, HU606905.
Passage waders and seabirds, especially evening shearwaters in
summer.

Funzie E end of island
Migrants.

Grunnigeo ½m W of Papil Water, HU593903
Summer seabirds especially Storm Petrel at night.

BBE   St. Rogvalds Guest House (095783 240)
BBESC Leagarth (095783 226)

UNST   1   northernmost island
by air: Flights Mon–Fri from Tingwall, Lerwick.   tel: 059584 246
by sea: Car ferry from Yell (Gutcher, HU549993).   tel: 095782
    259/268
Snowy Owl; occasional on Gallow Hill in SW corner of the island.

Baltasound   HP623088   on A968
Migrants.

Hermaness   HP605184   NW extremity
Seabirds including Gannet and Skuas, also a summer Black-
browed Albatross in recent years.

Loch of Cliff   HP600120
Winter seabirds and northern gulls.

Valla Field   HP585070
Skuas and Merlin.

H/B   Cloudin Hostel, Uyeasound (095785 237)
BBE   Clingera Guest House, Baltasound (095781 579)
    Baltasound Hotel (095781 334)
SC   (Unst cottages) The Old Rectory, Hasfield, Gloucs
    (045278 713)
    Kelda, Baltasound (095781 643)

Strathclyde & Central

Ailsa Craig   76   island 10m W of Girvan
Boat trips from Girvan Harbour (NX183982) and from Brodick, Isle of Arran (NS023359).
Summer seabirds including 25,000 pairs of Gannets.

Ballantrae Shingle Beach & Stinchar Estuary   76   10m SW of Girvan
Car-park by the sea front at Ballantrae ¼m W of A77 at NW082825. Then coast path south along the spit.
Passage waders; summer terns; seaduck; winter divers.

Culzean Country Park   76 & 70   8m N of Girvan
Car-park at visitor centre (open April–Oct) at NS235104, signposted off A719 2m NE of Maidens at NS244098. Then woodland and coast trails.
Seaduck; passage waders; woodland birds.

>*Girvan Harbour*   76   NX183982   *¼m W of A77 in Girvan*
>*Passage waders; winter gulls.*

>*Turnberry Point*   76   NS196073   *5½m N of Girvan*
>*Seawatching; migrants; winter divers.*

TIC	*Bridge Street, Girvan, Ayrshire (0465 4950) *Culzean Castle & Country Park, Culzean, Strathclyde (06556 293) 39 Sandgate, Ayr (0292 810363)
YH	Craigwell Road, Ayr (0292 262322) Minnigaff, Newton Stewart, Wigtownshire (0671 2211)
RF	Kings Arms, Girvan Kirkmichael Arms, Kirkmichael, nr Maybole

BBE   Hotel Westcliffe, Girvan (0465 2128)
            Thistleneuk Guest House, 19 Louisa Drive, Girvan (0465 2137)
            (Segganwell Cottages, Culzean) National Trust for Scotland, 5 Charlotte Square, Edinburgh (031 226 5922)
            (Lendalfoot cottage) 50 Dalrymple Street, Girvan (0465 4421/2378)

Bogton Loch & Dalmellington Moss   70   1m W of Dalmellington
View from B741 ¾m W of A713 at NS461060 and track down west side of the loch.
Marshland birds; summer warblers; winter and passage wildfowl; winter Hen Harrier roost.

New Cumnock Lochs & Marsh   71   3–5m SE of Cumnock
View from A76 1–2m NW of New Cumnock (e.g. NS594163) and tracks south from it. Also minor roads and tracks 0–1m north of Connel Park.
Wildfowl; summer warblers; passage waders.

Ayr Gorge   70   2½m SW of Mauchline
Park by B743 on the west side of Failford at NS456261 and track south beside river and woods.
Woodland and river birds.

TIC   Glasnock Street, Cumnock, Ayrshire (0290 23058)
            The Burns Memorial Tower, Kilmarnock Road, Mauchline, Ayrshire (0290 51016)
YH   As previous entry.
            Kendoon, Dalry, Castle Douglas
BBE   The Mill, Dalmellington (0292 550357)
            Lochside House Hotel, New Cumnock (0290 38629)
            Duncraig House, 44 Barskimning Road, Mauchline (0290 50096)

Doonfoot Bay   70   2m S of Ayr
Car-park at Greenan by minor road ½m N of A719, on the north side of Doonfoot at NS315194 and coast path east or west.
Winter wildfowl and gulls; passage and winter waders.

Troon   70   5m S of Irvine
Park near the western end of B749 to Troon lighthouse at NS306314 and overlook the north and south bays.
Winter seaduck and gull roost.

Garnock Estuary   70   **1m W of Irvine**
Car-park 1½m W of A737 on the south side of the estuary at
NS305381 and view from shore to the east.
Passage and winter waders; winter seaduck and wildfowl.

Shewalton Pits   70   **2m S of Irvine**
Park by minor road south of the River Irvine, just east of A737 ½m
NW of its junction with A78 at NS326370. The reserve is to the east
and also pit on west side of A737.
Passage waders; passage and winter wildfowl; summer warblers.

> *Eglington Country Park* 70 NS320420 *2m N of Irvine
> centre*
> *Woodland and river birds.*

TIC   39 Sandgate, Ayr (0292 284196)
            *Municipal Buildings, South Beach, Troon, Ayrshire
            (0292 317696)
YH   Craigwell Road, Ayr (0292 262322)
RF   Anchorage Hotel, Troon
            Wheatsheaf Inn, Symington, nr Troon
RFBBE   Finlayson Arms Hotel, Coylton, nr Ayr (0292 570298)
BBE   Damar, Broomlands Drive, Irvine (0294 78075/71017)

Falls of Clyde   71 or 72   **1m S of Lanark**
Park near visitor centre at south end of New Lanark, ½m S of A73
on east side of the River Clyde at NS883427. Then trails south
beside the river and through the woods. Also woodland and
nature trail on west side of the river at NS879415.
Woodland and river birds including Dipper and Kingfisher.

Cleghorn Glen   72   **1½m NE of Lanark**
Park by A706 near the bridge over Mouse Water at NS905453 and
path NW beside the river and through the woods.
Woodland and river birds.

> *Crossford Glen* 72 NS820467 *4m NW of Lanark*
> *Woodland and river birds.*

> *Medwin Water* 64 NS980440 *1½m S of Carnwarth*
> *Passage waders; winter wildfowl.*

> *South Medwin* 64 NT052467 *5m E of Carnwarth*
> *Winter wildfowl.*

> *Douglas Estate* 72 NS845317 *8m SW of Lanark*
> *Woodland birds; winter wildfowl; waders.*

TIC	Horsemarket, Ladyacre Raod, Lanark (0555 61661)
YH	Lotus Lodge, Wanlockhead, Biggar, Lanarkshire (0659 74252)
BBE	Kirkfield House, Kirkfieldbank, nr Lanark (0555 65273)
SC	Carmichael Estate Office, West Mains, Carmichael, nr Biggar (08993 336)

Lochwinnoch   63   10m E of Largs

Nature centre car-park ½m SE of Lochwinnoch village by A760, ½m W of its junction with A737 at NS359581. Then trail to three hides.

Wildfowl; passage waders; summer warblers and woodland birds.

Farland Head & Ardneil Bay   63   7m S of Largs

Park at west end of B7048 2m W of West Kilbride at NS176488, then coast path north or south.

Winter seaduck; passage waders; seawatching; migrants.

Great Cumbrae   63   island 1–4m SW of Largs

Frequent ferry from Largs Pier, NS201595. Then A860 around island.

Seabirds; summer terns; passage waders and wildfowl; migrants.

> ***Largs Bay***   *63*   *NS200600*   *NW side of Largs*
> *Passage waders; winter seaduck, gulls and divers.*

> ***Muirshiel Country Park***   *63*   *NS313632*   *3½m NW of Lochwinnoch*
> *Woodland, river and hill birds including Dipper, Red Grouse and Hen Harrier.*

> ***Munnoch Reservoir***   *63*   *NS250477*   *3m E of West Kilbride*
> *Passage and winter wildfowl.*

TIC	Promenade, Largs, Ayrshire (0475 673765)
YH	Craigwell Road, Ayr (0292 262322)
	11 Woodlands Terrace, Glasgow (041 332 3004)
RF	Glenboyd Hotel, Seamill
	Eglington Arms, Beith
BB	High Beltrees, Lochwinnoch (0505 842376)
BBE	The College, Millport, Great Cumbrae Island (0475 530353)

Lunderston Bays & Inverkip   63   6m SW of Greenock

Car-park by A770 at north end of the bay 1¼m NW of its junction with A78 at NS204746. Then coast path south to Ardgowan Point and Inverkip.

Passage and winter waders, wildfowl and gulls.

West Ferry   64   5m E of Port Glasgow
Park off north side of roundabout at junction 31 of M8 overlooking
the estuary at NS402731.
Passage and winter waders and wildfowl.

Old Kilpatrick   64   1m N of Bishopton
Park at end of lane ½m N of B815, 1m N of A8, at NS435727.
Passage and winter waders and wildfowl.

Gourock Bay   63   NS245775   2m NW of Greenock centre
Passage and winter waders.

Parklea   63   NS350741   2m E of Port Glasgow
Passage and winter waders and wildfowl.

Loch Tom   63   NS260720   3m SW of Greenock
Wildfowl and woodland birds.

TIC   Municipal Buildings, Clyde Square, Greenock, Ren-
frewshire (0475 24400)
YH   As previous entry.
RF   Spinnaker Hotel, Gourock
BB   The Forresters, Station Road, Inverkip (0475 521433)
East Morningside, Langbank (0475 54219)

Baron's Haugh   64   1½m S of Motherwell centre
Entrance ½m S of Motherwell Civic Centre at south end of
Knoweton, NS755552, or from railway bridge ¼m W of Knoweton
at NS748558.
Wildfowl; summer warblers; passage waders.

Possil Loch   64   2m N of Glasgow centre
Park just west of A879 2½m S of its junction with A807 at NS584695
and enter reserve on east side of the main road.
Wildfowl and passage waders; summer warblers.

**Strathclyde Country Park   64   between Motherwell &
Hamilton**
Several car-parks beside the loch on the east side and at the
southern end e.g. east of junction 6 of M74 at NS731566 and paths-
around. Also the section east of the motorway viewable from
Hamilton services 1m N of junction 6.
Passage and winter wildfowl; passage waders; summer warblers;
winter gull roost.

Mugdock Wood   64   NS545765   1½m N of Milngavie
Woodland birds.

Hogganfield Loch   64   NS643674   *3m E of Glasgow centre*
Winter wildfowl and gull roost.

Bishops Loch   64   NS687670   *3m NW of Coatbridge*
Reedbed species; wildfowl.

Drumpelier Country Park   64   NS705665   *2m NW of*
Coatbridge
Winter wildfowl.

Hillend Reservoir   65   NS836670   *5m E of Airdrie*
Passage waders, terns and wildfowl.

TIC	35 St. Vincent Place, Glasgow (041 204 4400)
	Roadchef Services, M74 northbound, nr Hamilton (0698 285590)
YH	As previous entry.
R	Camphill Vaults, Bothwell, nr Stonefield
	Quarry Inn, Twecher, nr Kirkintilloch
BBE	Oriel Villa, 77 Fallside Road, Bothwell (0698 812465)

Cardross Bay   **63**   **S side of Cardross**
Park by Cardross railway station ¼m S of A814 at NS345774 and
view from the shore over the bridge.
Passage and winter waders and wildfowl.

Ardmore Point   **63**   **2m NW of Cardross**
Car-park at end of minor road ½m SW of A814 at NS325786, then
path around the peninsula.
Passage and winter wildfowl and waders; migrants.

Rhu   **56**   **1½m NW of Helensburgh**
Park and view from car-park just west of A814 at Rhu Marina,
NS272835.
Passage and winter waders and gulls.

Balmaha & Inchcailloch   **56**   **8m N of Dumbarton**
Car-park in Balmaha near SE corner of Loch Lomond by B837 at
NS421901. Then shore path north and frequent boat trips over to
Inchcailloch.
Winter wildfowl; woodland birds including Wood Warbler and
Redstart.

Ben Lomond   **56**   **9m NW of Balmaha**
Car-park by minor road ¼m N of the Rowardennan Hotel at
NS361986. Then steep track NE for 4m up to Ben Lomond.
Upland and woodland birds including Ptarmigan, Ring Ousel,
Crossbill and Peregrine.

TIC	Tourist Information Desk, Glasgow Airport, Inchinnan Road, Paisley (041 848 4440)
	*The Clock Tower, Helensburgh, Dunbartonshire (0436 72642)
	*Balloch Road, Balloch, Dunbartonshire (0389 53533)
YH	Arden, Alexandria, Dunbartonshire (0389 85226)
	Luss, Alexandria (0436 86635)
RF	Salmon Leap Inn, Drymen, nr Balmaha
	Ardencaple Hotel, Rhu, nr Balmaha
BB	Lomond Bank, Balmaha (036087 213)
BBE	Kirkton House, Darleith Raod, Cardross (0389 841951)
	Croftburn, Croftamie, Drymen (0360 60796)
	Rowardennan Hotel, Loch Lomond, by Drymen (036087 273)

ARRAN   69   island 10m W of Ardrossan
Car ferry from Ardrossan (OS Map 70, NS224423) to Brodick on Arran (NS023360) and, in summer only, from Claonaig on the Kintyre Peninsula (NR875560) to Lochranza at the north of the island (NR926510).

Brodick Country Park, Merkland Wood & Goatfell
Car-park signposted off A841 2m north of Brodick, then woodland trails and track up onto Goatfell.
Woodland birds including Nightjar; summer warblers; upland birds including Golden Eagle.

Lochranza
Park by minor road off A841 near northern point of the island e.g. NR934510 which overlooks the bay.
Winter seaduck and divers; passage waders.

Sliddery Water
Take minor road north up the glen from A841 in the SW corner of the island e.g. NR953260.
Woodland and river birds.

>   *Glen Lorsa & Loch Tanna*   NR930390–440
>   *Upland birds including divers.*

>   *Cock of Arran Woods*   NR965515
>   *Woodland birds; migrants.*

TIC	The Pier, Brodick, Isle of Arran (0770 2140)
	*Lochranza, Isle of Arran (0770 83320)
YH	Lochranza, Isle of Arran (0770 83631)
	Whiting Bay, Brodick, Isle of Arran (0770 7339)

RFBBE   Lochranza Hotel, Lochranza (0770 83223)
               Hotel Ormidale, Brodick (0770 2293)
               Catacol Bay Hotel, Catacol (0770 83231)
               Cameronia Hotel, Whiting Bay (0770 7254)
BBE   Benvaren, Lochranza (0770 83647)
               Glencloy Farmhouse, nr Brodick (0770 2351)
               The Lagg Hotel, Kilmory (0770 87255)
               Torlin Villa, Kilmory (0770 87240)
SC   Bellevue Farm, Sliddery (0770 87238)
               Largiemeanoch, Whiting Bay (0770 7563)
               Cir Mhor, Sannox (0770 81248/81661)
               (Brodick Castle) National Trust for Scotland, 5 Charlotte
               Square, Edinburgh (031 226 5922)

KINTYRE PENINSULA   **62 & 68**   **west of Arran**

West Loch Tarbert   **62**   **5m SW of Tarbert**
View from B8024 along the northern shore 2–5m SW of Tarbert e.g.
NR843677 near Dubhchladach, and at NR803627 3m further
southwest.
Winter seaduck, divers and grebes; woodland birds.

Loch Caolisport   **62**   **8m NW of Tarbert**
View from B8024 along southern shore e.g. at NR726706 and
NR756753, and from minor road along the north shore at
NR763774.
Winter seaduck, divers and grebes; woodland birds.

Campbeltown Loch   **68**   **1–2m E of Campbeltown**
Park by minor road along south side of the bay at NR745195.
Winter seaduck, divers and northern gulls; passage and winter
waders.

Machrihanish   **68**   **5m W of Campbeltown**
Park in the village by B843, NR636207 and walk west to the point or
north along the shore to the river mouth.
Autumn seawatching; winter seaduck and divers; passage
waders.

> ***Carradale Point & Bay***   *68*   *NR815370*   *12m N of*
> *Campbeltown*
> *Winter seaduck; seawatching.*

> ***Keil Point & Glen Breackerie***   *68*   *8m SW of Campbeltown*
> *Migrants; river and woodland birds; winter seaduck and divers.*

TIC   Campbeltown, Argyllshire (0856 52056)
RF   Kilberry Inn, Kilberry, nr Tarbert
RFBBE Tarbert Hotel, Tarbert (08802 264/847)

BBE   Osmary Farm, Southend, nr Campbeltown (058683 665)
Ardell House, Machrihanish (058681 235)
Ashbank Hotel, Carradlae (05833 650)
SC   Creggan, Skipness, nr Tarbert (08806 225)
Carskiey Estate, Southend (058683 241/672)
(Machrihanish bungalow) Hamster Cottages, Whitehill,
Biggar, Lannark (08993 775)
(Kilberry cottages) Ardlarach, Ardfern, by Lochgilphead
(08525 284)

ISLAY   60   island west of Kintyre Peninsula
Ferries daily from Kennacraig on the Kintyre Peninsula by West
Loch Tarbert (OS Map 62, NR818626) run by Caledonian Mac-
Brayne, tel: 0475 33755. Also flights by Loganair twice weekly from
Glasgow, tel: 041 889 3181.

Loch Gruinart   NW corner of Islay
View from B8017 or minor roads running north along the east
shore e.g. NR283669, NR294690 and NR278682. Also car-park by
Aoradh Farm, NR275673.
Winter wildfowl and raptors; passage and winter waders.

Bridgend & Bowmore Harbour   4m SE of Loch Gruinart
View from A847 which runs around the bay e.g. NR322627 on the
north side, or NR334613 along the south. Also from the pier at
Bowmore, NR310600.
Passage and winter waders; winter wildfowl, seaduck, divers,
grebes and gulls.

Mull of Oa   SW tip of the island
Car-park at end of minor road 4m SW of Port Ellen at NR280423.
Then track SW to the Mull and surrounding cliffs.
Summer seabird colonies; Golden Eagle, Peregrine, Chough;
seawatching; migrants.

> *Loch Gorm   NR230660   3m SW of Loch Gruinart*
> *Winter wildfowl; summer terns.*

> *Machir Bay   NR206634   2m SW of Loch Gorm*
> *Passage waders; winter seaduck and divers; Chough.*

> *Claddach & Portnahaven   NR165525   13m SW of Loch
> Gruinart*
> *Seawatching; migrants.*

TIC   Bowmore, Isle of Islay (049 681 254)
RF   Port Charlotte Hotel, Port Charlotte
RFBBE Harbour Inn, Bowmore (049 681 330)

BBE   Loch Gruinart Guest House, Gruinart (049 685 212)
           Islay Hotel, Port Ellen (0496 2260)
SC   Islay Field Centre, Port Charlotte (049 685 288/218)
           Lorgba House, Port Charlotte (049 685 208)
           58 Port Wemyss, Portnahaven (049 686 282)

COLONSAY   **61**   **island 6m N of Islay**
Ferry three days a week from Oban (OS Map 49, NM856298) run by Caledonian MacBrayne tel: 0475 33755.

The Strand   **NR365900**   **3m SW of Scalasaig**
Passage and winter waders.

Kiloran Bay   **NR400980**   **2½m N of Scalasaig**
Winter wildfowl; passage waders; Chough.

Loch Fada   **NR388957**   **1m NW of Scalasaig**
Wildfowl.

Oronsay   **NR355885**   **S of The Strand**
Summer raptors and waders; migrants.

TIC   As previous entry.
RFBBE Isle of Colonsay Hotel (09512 316)
BBE   Baleromindobh Farm (09512 305)
SC   Machrins Farm (09512 312)
           Isle of Colonsay Hotel (09512 316)

Taynish   **55**   **6–8m SW of Crinan**
Park at south end of Tayvallich by B8025 at NR739868, then track south through the woods and beside the shoreline.
Woodland birds and passage waders.

Loch Gilp   **55**   **0–2m S of Lochgilphead**
View from A83 which runs around the shoreline e.g. NR864876 on the east side, and from Ardrishaig on the west side, NR855854.
Passage and winter waders and wildfowl; passage terns; winter seaduck and gulls.

Loch Crinan & Knapdale Forest   **55**   **6m NW of Lochgilphead**
Car-park at the westernmost end of Crinan Canal at NE corner of Crinan at NR788944 for views of the loch and paths through the woods. Also view from Islandadd Bridge 1½m SE of the village and forest walks from B8025 1½m SW of Bellanoch, NR784906.
Passage and winter wildfowl and waders; woodland birds; winter gulls.

Loch Craignish   55   5m N of Crinan
View from B8002 along the north shore ½m-3m SW of A816, NE
and SW of Ardferne.g. NM809046 and NM780018.
Passage and winter divers and wildfowl; passage waders.

Inverliever Forest & Loch Awe   55   12m SE of Oban
Many parking places along minor roads beside the north
shoreline of Loch Awe and Loch Avich e.g. NM942154, NN008193,
NM915138. Then tracks through the forest and up onto the sur-
rounding hills.
Woodland birds including Pied Flycatcher, Black Grouse and
Goshawk; divers, Golden Eagle, Peregrine, Hen Harrier; summer
waders.

> **Ulva Lagoons & Loch na Cille**   *55   NR713820, 697805*
> *4–5m SW of Tayvallich*
> *Passage waders and winter wildfowl.*

> **Loch Sween**   *55   NR735818   4m SW of Kilmichael*
> *Winter wildfowl.*

TIC	*Lochnell Street, Lochgilphead, Argyllshire (0546 2344)
	Argyll Square, Oban (0631 63122)
YH	Inveray, Argyllshire (0499 2454)
RF	Crinan Hotel, Crinan
RFBBE	Kilmartin Hotel, Kilmartin (05465 244)
	Galley of Lorne Inn, Ardfern (08525 284)
	Kilmory Rest, Kilmory, nr Lochgilphead
BBE	Dunchragaig, Kilmartin, nr Lochgilphead (054 684 209)
	Tayvallich Inn, Tayvallich (05467 282)
BBESC	Lunga, Ardfern (08525 237)
SC	Duntrune Castle, Kilmartin (05465 283)

Loch Feochan   49   4m S of Oban
View from A816 1–4m SW of Kilmore e.g. at eastern end,
NM873242 and near junction with B844 at NM835226.
Passage waders; winter wildfowl; passage and summer terns.

Oban Harbour & Bay   49   W side of Oban
Park near the railway station by A816 overlooking the harbour at
NM858299.
Winter (and sometimes summer) northern gulls; seaduck and
divers.

Loch Etive   49 & 50   0–7m E of Connel
View from A85 along the south shore east of Connel e.g.
NM937347 and minor road along the north side. Also from the
jetty 1m N of Taynuilt, NN011325 (OS Map 50).
Winter wildfowl; seaduck and divers.

Dunstaffnage Bay   49   *NM883343*   *3m NE of Oban*
Passage waders; seaduck; winter divers and gulls.

Ledaig Point & Ardmucknish Bay   49   *NM895353*
1–3m NW of Connel
Passage waders; passage and summer terns; seaduck and divers.

Glen Nant   50   *NN020273*   *1–2m SE of Taynuilt*
Woodland birds including Wood Warbler and Redstart.

TIC   as previous entry.
YH   Esplanade, Oban (0631 62025)
H/B   Jeremy Inglis Hostel, 21 Airds Crescent, Oban (0631 65065/63064)
RF   Oban Inn, Stafford Street, Oban
RFBBE   Falls of Lora Hotel, Connel (063 171 483)
BBE   Ichrachan House, Taynuilt (08662 641)
             Foxholes Hotel, Cologin, Lerags, nr Oban (0631 64982)
SC   Kilbride Farm, Lerags (0631 62878)
             Airds Bay House, Taynuilt (08662 232)

Loch Crenan   49   2–4m NE of Benderloch
View from jetty at west end of the loch 1½m N of A828 at NM909423 and from A828 along the south shore e.g. NM946414. Seaduck and divers; passage waders; passage and summer terns.

Glen Crenan   50   *NN035488*   *0–5m NE of Loch Crenan*
Woodland, river and upland birds.

Loch Laich   49   *NM923465*   *1½m NE of Port Appin*
Passage waders and wildfowl; passage and summer terns.

TIC   As previous entry.
YH   As previous entry.
RF   Airds Inn, Port Appin
BBE   Bracken, Tralee Bay, Benderloch, nr Oban (063172 467)
             Linnhe House, Port Appin (063173 245)
SC   Mrs Campbell, Achnacree Bay, North Connel, nr Oban (063171 288)
             Kinlochlaich House, Appin (063173 342)

MULL   47,48 & 49   island west of Oban
Ferries from Oban or Lochaline (OS Map 49, NM674443) run by Caledonian MacBrayne tel: 0475 34531. Also flights by Loganair from Glasgow.

Summer seabirds & White-tailed Eagle
Iona & Sound of Iona   48   NM290230
Calliach Point   47   NM348544
Quinish Point   47   NM410570
Calgary Bay   47   NM360510

Passage and winter waders
Loch Don   49   NM735330
Mouth of River Ba   47   NM535410
Calgary Bay   47   NM360510
An Leth-onn   48   NM535285
An Caolas   48   NM305205
Loch na Lathaich   48   NM370230

Upland birds
Glen More & Ben More   48   NM530330

Seawatching
Sound of Iona   48   NM299234
Rubha nan Cearc   48   NM315258
Treshnish Point   48   NM335485

Winter northern gulls
Tobermory Harbour   47   NM505552

Seaduck & divers
Sound of Mull   47 & 49   NM670430
Loch na Keal   47 or 48   NM500380
Loch Scridain   48   NM460260
Sound of Iona   48   NM299234
Loch Tuath   48 or 47   NM400440

Summer breeding birds, migrants and woodland birds
Ross of Mull   48   NM400200

TIC   *Main Street, Tobermory, Isle of Mull (0688 2182)
     Argyll Square, Oban (0631 63122)
YH   Tobermory, Isle of Mull (0688 2481)
BBE   Dungrianach, Fionnphort (06817 417)
     Argyll Hotel, Iona (06817 334)
     Druimard Country House, Dervaig, nr Tobermory (06884 345/291)
     Pennygale Lodge, Craignure (06802 333)
     Argyll Arms Hotel, Bunessan (06817 505)
SC   (Bunessan cottage) Welwyn, Firbank Terr, Cambus-barron, Stirling (0786 72900)
     (Calgary cottage) 136a Abbots Road, Abbots Langley, Herts (09277 63924)
     Mrs Scott, Glenaros, nr Salen (06803 337/340)

TIREE   46   island 25m W of Mull
Ferries from Oban, Lochaline and Tobermory (Mull) run by Caledonian MacBrayne. Flights by Loganair from Glasgow Mon–Sat.

Summer seabirds
Ceann a'Mhara (SW extremity)   NL933405

Summer duck, Red-throated Divers and waders
Most Lochs.

Wildfowl, seaduck and divers
Lochs; especially Loch a'Phuill   NL955420
Balephuil Bay   NL950400
Gott Bay   NM055405
Hynish Bay   NM010430

Passage and winter waders
Balephetrish Bay   NM005475
Aerodrome & The Reef   NM005455
Salum & Vaul Bays   NM055490
Traigh Mhor   NM050472
the western beaches   e.g. NL935450

Migrants
especially Hynish (NL980380) to Balemartine (NL985415) in the SW.

COLL   46   island NE of Tiree
Ferries as for Tiree. Flights by Loganair.
Winter wildfowl; summer waders and seabirds; passage and winter waders; migrants; summer divers and wildfowl.

TIC   As previous entry.
BBE   Scarinish Hotel, Scarinish, Tiree (08792 308)
    Isle of Coll Hotel, Coll (08793 334)
BBESC   Tiree Lodge Hotel, Scarinish (08792 353/368)
SC   The Cottage, Balinoe, Tiree (08792 371)
    Estate Office, Coll (08793 339)

Inversnaid   56   12m NW of Aberfoyle
Car-park at end of minor road by Loch Lomond 4m W of the northern end of B829 from Stronachlachar at NN337088. Then take West Highland Way north through the woods and beside the loch. Woodland and river birds including Pied Flycatcher, Redstart, Wood Warbler and Dipper.

Achray Forest   57   1–3m N of Aberfoyle
Guide maps etc. from David Marshall Lodge ½m N of Aberfoyle at
NN520015. Then several car-parks by A821 to the north and tracks
east or west.
Woodland and upland birds including Black Grouse, Hen Harrier
and Long-eared Owl.

Loch Achray & The Trossachs   57   4m N of Aberfoyle
Car-parks at the west end of the loch by A821 e.g. at NN505068 and
1m west at the end of A821 at NN495072. Then many paths
through the woods and beside the lochs.
Wildfowl and woodland birds including Pied Flycatcher, Redstart
and Wood Warbler.

> *Lake of Menteith   57   NN584009   3m E of Aberfoyle*
> *Winter wildfowl.*

> *Loch Ard   57   NN470015   3m W of Aberfoyle*
> *Wildfowl.*

> *Pass of Leny   57   NN595090   2½m NW of Callander*
> *Woodland and river birds.*

TIC   *Main Street, Aberfoyle, Perthshire (08772 352)
YH   Kinlochard, Stirling (08777 256)
      Rowardennan, by Drymen, Glasgow (036 087 259)
RF   Myrtle, Callander
      Altskeith Hotel, Kinlochard, nr Aberfoyle
BBE   Inverard Hotel, Loch Ard Road, Aberfoyle (08772 229)
      The Inn, Strathyre, nr Callander (08774 224)
      Creagan House, Strathyre (08774 638)
SC   Creag Darach, Milton of Aberfoyle, Perthshire (08772
      476)
      Strathyre cabins, Forestry District Office, Aberfoyle
      (08772 383 or 087730 323)
      Leny House, Leny Estate, Callander (0877 31078)

Cambus Pool   58   2½m W of Alloa centre
Park on the west side of River Devon just west of Cambus, ¼m SW
of A907 at NS853940. Then path south beside the river to the pool
and River Forth.
Passage waders; winter wildfowl and gulls; migrants.

Longcarse & Tullibody Inches   58   1½m SW of Alloa
Park 1m W of Alloa centre ¼m S of A907 at NS870933 and take
tracks south to the River Forth and the islands.
Passage and winter waders and wildfowl.

Gartmorn Dam Country Park   58   2m NE of Alloa
Car-park and visitor centre at end of minor road 1m E of A908 ½m
E of New Sauchie at NS910940. Then paths around the reservoir
and to the hide.
Winter wildfowl.

**Wood Hill Wood, The Roundal & Ben Buck   58   3–5m N of
Alloa**
Car-park ½m N of A91 between Alva and Tillicoultry at NS898975.
Then tracks through the woodland and up onto the high ground to
the north via Mill Glen.
Woodland and upland birds including Pied Flycatcher, Wood
Warbler, Ring Ousel, Golden Plover and Merlin.

> ***Dollar Glen***   *58   NS964994   1m N of Dollar*
> *Woodland and river birds including Pied Flycatcher, Wood*
> *Warbler, Dipper and Ring Ousel.*

TIC	*Clock Mill, Upper Mill Street, Tillicoultry (0259 52176)
YH	Argyll Lodging, Castle Wynd, Stirling (0786 73442)
	Glendevon, Dollar, Clackmannanshire (025 981 206)
RF	Kings Seat, Dollar
	Strathallan Hotel, Dollar
	Mansfield Arms, Sauchie, nr Alloa
BBE	Strathallan Hotel, Chapel Place, Dollar (02594 2205)
	Soroba House Hotel, Main Street, Blairingone, Dollar (02594 2785)

Skinflats   65   1m NW of Grangemouth
Park by minor road 1m E of A905, 1m NE of Skinflats village, at
NS921840. Then tracks south to lakes and foreshore.
Passage and winter waders; winter wildfowl; passage terns;
migrants.

Kinneil Sewage Works   65   2m W of Bo'ness
Park near the end of minor road by sewage works ¾m N of A904
and E side of the mouth of River Avon at NS962812. Then track NE
overlooking the settling lagoons.
Passage and winter waders and wildfowl.

TIC	The Steeple, High Street, Falkirk (0324 20244)
	Burgh Halls, The Cross, Linlithgow, West Lothian (0506 844600)
YH	As previous entry.
	18 Eglington Crescent, Edinburgh (031 337 1120)
RF	Whyteside House Hotel, Polmont, nr Bo'ness
BBE	Hollywood House, 25 Grahamsdyke Road, Bo'ness (0506 823260)
	Kinglass Farm, Bo'ness (0506 822861)

Tayside

Loch Leven   58   1m SE of Kinross
Car-parks by B9097 along the southern shore at NT171993 and at
the Vane Farm Nature Centre NT160991, both about 2m E of junction 5 of M90. Also on the north side car-parks ½m E of Kinross at
the end of minor road at NO127017 and along minor road joining
B996 and A91 at NO134042.
Exceptional site for summer and winter wildfowl; passage waders;
summer and passage terns.

Lochore Meadows Country Park (Fife)   58   1m NE of Kelty
Car-park just east of B996 ¼m N of its junction with A909 at
NT153949, then track to hide.
Wildfowl and wetland birds.

> *Moncreiffe Hill Wood   58   NO130200   2½m SE of Perth
> centre*
> *Woodland birds.*

TIC	45 High Street, Perth (0738 38353)
	*Kinross Service Area, M90, nr Kinross (0577 63680)
YH	107 Glasgow Road, Perth (0738 23658)
RF	Nivingston House, Cleish, nr Kinross
	Bein Inn, Glenfarg, nr Kinross
BBE	The Grange, Scotlandwell, nr Kinross (059 284 220)
	Lomond Country Inn, Main Street, Kinnesswood, nr Kinross (059 284 253/317)
SC	Colliston, Glenfarg (05773 434)
	(St. Andrews House, Falkland) National Trust for Scotland, 5 Charlotte Square, Edinburgh (031 226 5922)

Pond of Drummond   58   2m S of Crieff
View from A822 by the east side of the lake 1m N of Muthill at
NN863186.
Winter wildfowl; woodland birds.

Gorthy Wood   58   6m NE of Crieff
Park by minor road ¾m N of A85, 2m W of Keillour Castle at
NN954249, then tracks north through the forest.
Capercaillie, Black Grouse, Crossbills.

> **Dupplin Loch & Cairnie Wood**   58   NO030200   5m SW
> of Perth
> Winter wildfowl; woodland birds.

> **Kinkell Bridge**   58   NN933166   5m SE of Crieff
> Winter geese.

> **Carsebreck & Rhynd Lochs**   58   NN865095   7m S of
> Crieff
> Winter wildfowl.

> **Muckle Burn**   57   NN807076   4m NE of Dunblane
> Black Grouse; river birds.

TIC	90 High Street, Auchterarder, Perthshire (0764 63450)
	*High Street, Crieff, Perthshire (0764 2578)
YH	As previous entry.
	Glendevon, Dollar, Clackmannanshire (025 981 206)
RF	Oakbank Inn, Turret Bridge, Crieff
	Royal Hotel, Comrie
BBE	Clathybeg, Findo Gask, nr Crieff (073 873 213)
	Nether Coul, Auchterarder (0764 63119)

Kingoodie   53   4½m W of Dundee centre
View from minor road along the shore 1m S of A85 1½m SW of
Invergowrie e.g. NO333294.
Passage and winter waders and wildfowl.

> **Port Allen**   53   NO251212   1¼m S of Errol
> Passage and winter waders; migrants.

> **Seaside**   53   NO282244   2m NE of Errol
> Passage and winter waders; migrants.

> **Invergowrie Bay**   54   NO349299   S side of Invergowrie
> Passage and winter waders and wildfowl.

TIC	4 City Square, Dundee (0382 27723)
YH	107 Glasgow Road, Perth (0738 23658)

Broughty Ferry   54   5m E of Dundee
Park near Broughty Castle ¼m S of A930 at NO465304 or by coastal road to the east toward Barnhill.
Spring Little Gull; winter northern gulls; winter seaduck and divers; passage waders.

Carnoustie   54   south side of Carnoustie
Car-park ¼m S of the railway line at the end of track at NO562340. Passage waders and terns; winter seaduck and divers; migrants; Little Gull.

Monikie Reservoirs   54   4m NW of Carnoustie
Car-park on west side of the reservoirs ½m N of B961 at NO503384. Winter wildfowl.

Crombie Country Park   54   5m NW of Carnoustie
Car-park ¼m N of B961, ¼m W of its junction with B9128 at NO527403. Then take paths to hides, around the reservoir and through the woods.
Winter wildfowl; woodland birds.

Arbroath Harbour, Whiting Ness & Seaton Cliffs   54   0–1m E of Arbroath
Park near the harbour, NO644406, and by the coast road 1m east, at NO657413. Also walk the coast path and nature trail to the NE.
Winter gulls, waders, seaduck and divers; summer seabirds; migrants.

> ***Dighty Water***   *54   NO486317   between Broughty Ferry & Monifrieth*
> *Passage and winter waders and gulls; passage terns.*

> ***Buddon Burn***   *54   NO516322   1m E of Monifrieth*
> *Passage and winter waders; passage and summer terns.*

TIC   Market Place, Arbroath (0241 72690/76680)
          *The Library, High Street, Carnoustie (0241 52258)
YH   As previous entry.
RF   Fisherman's Tavern, Fort Street, Broughty Ferry
          Glencoe Hotel, Links Parade, Carnoustie
BBE   Brax Hotel, Links Parade, Carnoustie (0241 53032)
SC   15 Long Row, Westhaven, Carnoustie (0241 52428)

Lunan Bay   54   4m S of Montrose
Car-park overlooking the bay ¼m E of minor road near the Lunan Bay Hotel at NO691516, and paths south to the mouth of Lunan Water.
Seaduck, divers and grebes; passage and summer terns; migrants.

Montrose Basin   54   0–2m W of Montrose
View from A935 along the north side, or from minor road north of
A934 along the western side between Maryton and Barnhead. Also
park at Old Montrose, NO675572, and take path north by the shore
around the Lurgies to Bridge of Don. (Keys for the hide are £5 for
life, tel: 0674 76335).
Passage and winter waders and wildfowl.

Mouth of River Esk   45   3m N of Montrose
Park by the south side of the river ½m NE of A92 at NO729622 and
walk east beside the estuary.
Passage and winter waders; seaduck and divers; migrants.

St. Cyrus (Grampian)   45   4m N of Montrose
Car-park 1½m NE of A92 near Kirkside at NO742634 then tracks to
the north.
Passage and winter waders; summer warblers and terns;
migrants; autumn and winter seaduck and divers.

> *Usan   54   NO726546   2m SE of Montrose*
> *Migrants; seawatching.*

TIC   *The Library, High Street, Montrose (0674 72000)
YH   Clova, Kirriemuir, Angus (05755 236)
BB   Lunan Lodge, Lunan (02413 267)
BBE   Balmoral Hotel, Friockheim, nr Arbroath (02412 224)
SC   (House of Dun, nr Montrose) National Trust for Scotland,
5 Charlotte Square, Edinburgh (031 226 5922)

Balgavies Loch   54   4½m E of Forfar
Car-park by A932 overlooking the loch at NO534507, 1m W of
Milldens.
Winter wildfowl; summer warblers.

Loch of Kinnordy   54   1½m W of Kirriemuir
Car-park by B951 along the south side of the reserve at NO361539,
then path to hides. Or view from the road itself.
Wildfowl including Ruddy Duck; summer warblers; passage
waders; wetland birds.

Loch of Lintrathen   53   6m W of Kirriemuir
View from B951 by the north end at NO282557. Also from minor
roads which encircle the loch.
Winter wildfowl; woodland birds; passage and summer grebes
and Osprey.

> *Forfar Loch   54   NO440505   1m W of Forfar*
> *Winter wildfowl; passage waders.*

Montreathmont Forest 54 NO570550 *7m NE of Forfar*
Woodland birds including Long-eared Owl and Capercaillie.

TIC	*Bank Street, Kirriemuir, Angus (0575 74097)
	*The Library, West High Street, Forfar (0307 67876)
YH	As previous entry.
H/B	Round House, Knockshannoch Lodge, Glenisla, Alyth (057 582 238)
RF	Commercial Inn, Letham, nr Forfar
BBE	Inshewan House, Inshewan, nr Forafar (030 786 328)
	Thrums Hotel, Bank Street, Kirriemuir (0575 72758)
SC	Castle Cottage, Balgavies, nr Forfar (030 781 535)

Glas Maol & Caenlochan Forest   43   9m S of Braemar
Car-park by A93 near the Ski Rescue Post 5m N of Spittal of
Glenshee at NO139780. Then take tracks SE up onto the high
ground.
Upland birds including Golden Eagle, Ptarmigan, Dotterel,
Golden Plover, Snow Bunting.

Glen Doll   44   3½m-6m NW of Clova
Car-park at the head of Glen Clova, 3½m NW of Clova from B955,
at NO284762. Then take tracks west, Jocks Road, and southwest,
Kilbo Path.
Upland, river and woodland birds including Golden Eagle,
Dotterel, Golden Plover, Twite, Capercaillie and Black Grouse.

Loch & Glen Lee   44   3–6m W of Tarfside
Car-park at the head of Glen Esk ar Auchronie, NO447805. Then
take road and track west beside the river and the northern side of
the loch and beyond up the glen.
Wildfowl, wetland, river and upland birds including Ring Ousel,
Golden Eagle, Peregrine, summer waders.

Glen Isla 43 NO190680 *5m E of Spittal of Glenshee*
Upland and river birds including Golden Eagle.

TIC	*Balnellan Road, Braemar, Aberdeenshire (03397 41600)
	22 Atholl Road, Pitlochry, Perthshire (0796 2215/2751)
YH	As previous entry.
H/B	As previous entry.
	Milton of Clova Bunkhouse, Ogilvy Arms Hotel, Milton of Clova (05755 222)
RFBBE	Clova Hotel, Glen Clova (05755 222)
BBE	Purgavie Hotel, Glenisla (05756 213)
	Dalmunzie House Hotel, Spittal of Glenshee (025 085 224)
	Blackwater Inn, Blackwater, nr Glenshee (025 082 234)

SC   Dalhousie Estates Office, Brechin (03562 4566)
          Middlehill Farm, Glen Clova, nr Kirriemuir (05754 262)
          Finegand, Glenshee (025 085 234)
          Dalnaglar Castle, Glenshee (025 082 232)

Loch of Lowes   53   1½m NE of Dunkeld
Car-park, visitor centre and hide ¼m E of A923 by the southwest corner of the loch at NO041436.
Summer Osprey; summer and winter wildfowl and grebes; woodland birds.

The Hermitage   53   1m SW of Dunkeld
Car-park just south of A9 1m W of its junction with A822 at NO013422, then forest walks from here.
Woodland and river birds.

> ***Stormont Loch***   *53*   *NO193423*   *2m S of Rattray*
> *Passage and winter wildfowl.*

> ***Loch of Clunie***   *53*   *NO115443*   *4m W of Rattray*
> *Passage and winter wildfowl.*

TIC   *The Cross, Dunkeld, Perthshire (03502 688)
          *Wellmeadow, Blairgowrie, Perthshire (0250 2960)
YH   107 Glasgow Road, Perth (0738 23658)
RFBBE Bridge of Cally Hotel, nr Rattray (025 086 231)
BBE   Ninewells Farm, Snaigow, nr Dunkeld (073 871 272)
          Atholl Arms Hotel, Dunkeld (03502 219)
SC   Riemore Lodge, Butterstone, nr Dunkeld (03504 234/205)
          Delvine Gardens, Spittalfield, nr Rattray (073 871 259)

Birks of Aberfeldy   52   ½m SW of Aberfeldy
Car-park just south of A826 ¼m S of its junction with A827 at NN855485. Then take marked trails south.
Woodland and river birds including Redstart, Wood Warbler and Dipper.

Loch Faskally   52   0–1½m NW of Pitlochry
Car-parks by the dam just south of Pitlochry railway station, ¼m S of A924, at NN936578; and 1m NW by the B8019 at NN922591 and many paths.
Passage and winter wildfowl; woodland birds.

Tummel Forest & Loch   52 & 43   5m NW of Pitlochry
Car-park and visitor centre (April–Sept) by B8019 along the northern shore of the loch at NN864597. Then take tracks north through the forest.
Woodland birds including Black Grouse, Capercaillie, crossbills, Redstart and Wood Warbler; wildfowl.

Killiecrankie   43   4m NW of Pitlochry
Car-park, visitor centre and trails by A9 just before Killiecrankie
village at NN917626. Also car-park and marked trails at Balrobbie
Farm ½m W of the village at NN907627.
Woodland and river birds including Pied Flycatcher, Black Grouse
and Dipper.

Atholl   43 & 42   7–15m NW of Pitlochry
From Old Blair, 1½m N of A9 at NN867666, tracks lead north up
Glen Tilt and northwest up to Glen Bruar and onto the high
ground.
Woodland, river and upland birds including Golden Eage, Ptar-
migan, Dotterel and Black Grouse.

> *Ben Vrackie   43   NN950633   3m N of Pitlochry*
> *Hill and upland birds.*

TIC	*8 Dunkeld Street, Aberfeldy, Perthshire (0887 20276)
	22 Atholl Street, Pitlochry (0796 2215/2751)
YH	Golden Jubilee Hostel, Braeknowe, Knockard Road, Pit-lochry (0796 2308)
RF	Killiecrankie Hotel, Killiecrankie
	Aileen Chraggan, Weem, nr Aberfeldy
RFBBE	Crown Hotel, Aberfeldy (0887 20448)
	Ballinluig Inn, Ballinluig, nr Pitlochry (079 682 242)
	Bruar Falls Hotel, Calvine, nr Pitlochry (079 683 243)
	Struan Inn, Calvine, nr Pitlochry (079 683 208)
BBE	Tigh-na-Caorann, Crieff Road, Aberfeldy (0887 20993)
SC	Vale of Atholl County Cottages, Bridge of Tilt, Blair Atholl (079 681 467)
	Auchanross, Strathtay, nr Pitlochry (08874 374)
	Castle Menzies Home Farm, Aberfeldy (0887 20260)
	(Kennels Cottage, nr Killiecrankie) Forestry Commission, 231 Corstorphine Road, Edinburgh (031 334 0303)

Drummond Hill Forest   51   ¼m-2m NW of Kenmore
Car-parks ¼m N of A827, ½m N of Kenmore at NN771461, then
tracks west; and by the loch just south of A827 at NN762453 and
tracks north.
Capercaillie, Pied Flycatcher and Crossbill.

Dunalastair Water   51   2m E of Kinloch Rannoch
View from B846 along the north side or minor road beside the
marshland to the south.
Summer and winter wildfowl; summer and passage waders.

Rannoch Forest & Carn Gorm   51   3–5m SW of Kinloch Rannoch
Car-parks along minor road by the south shore of Loch Rannoch
e.g. at NN616569. Then tracks south through the forest and up
onto Carn Gorm and Carn Mairg.
Woodland and upland birds including Capercaillie, Ptarmigan,
Black Grouse and Short-eared Owl.

> *Rannoch Moor 51 & 41 NN410550 0–5m SW of Rannoch Station*
> *Moorland birds including Red-throated Diver, Merlin, Green-shank and other waders.*

TIC	As previous entry.
YH	As previous entry.
	Loch Ossian, Corrour by Fort William, Invernesshire
H/B	Balgies Bunkhouse, Bridge of Balgie, Glen Lyon, Aberfeldy (08876 221)
RF	Kenmore Hotel, Kenmore
RFBBE	Fortingall Hotel, Fortingall, nr Aberfledy (08873 367)
	Bunrannoch Hotel, Kinloch Rannoch (08822 367)
BBE	Ben Lawers Hotel, Lawers, nr Aberfeldy (05672 436)
	Glen Rannoch House, Kinloch Rannoch (08822 307)
	Cuilmore Cottage, Kinloch Rannoch (08822 218)
	Moor of Rannoch Hotel, Rannoch Station (08823 238)
SC	Springbank, Fearnan, nr Aberfeldy (08873 340)
	Duneaves Farm, Fortingall, nr Aberfeldy (08873 337)
	Carie, Rannoch Station (08822 341)
	(Tigh-na-Coille Cottage, by Loch Rannoch) Forestry Commission, 231 Corstorphine Road, Edinburgh (031 334 0303)

Western Isles

Sea ferries: Caledonian MacBrayne, The Ferry Terminal, Gourock
PA19 1QP.   Tel: 0475 33755

Butt of Lewis   8   N extremity of Lewis
Park near the lighthouse at NB520664.
Seawatching; migrants; summer seabirds.

Loch Stiapavat   8   2m SE of Butt of Lewis
View from B8014 ½m N of A857, NB535644, or from footpath
across the northern end joining B8014 and B8013, NB526644.
Wildfowl especially in winter; migrants.

TIC   4 South Beach Street, Stornoway, Isle of Lewis (0851
        3088)
YH   Garenin, Carloway, Isle of Lewis
RFBBE Cross Inn, Cross, Ness (085 181 378)
        Harbour View Tearoom, Port of Ness (085 181 735)
BBE   Eisdean, Fivepenny Ness (085 181 240)
SC   5a Adabrook, Port of Ness (085 181 616)
        (Habost bungalow) 42 Moray Park Avenue, Culloden,
        Inverness (0463 792276)

Stornoway Harbour   8   0–2m S of Stornoway
Park near Ferry harbour at NB422327 and walk the shoreline road
south. Also view from minor road southwest of Sandwick e.g.
NB441316.
Winter gulls including Glaucous and Iceland, waders and
seaduck.

Stornoway Woods   8   ½m W of Stornoway
Park at the gardens on the west side of the estuary at NB419333 and
follow paths through woods to the north and south.
Woodland birds and migrants.

Melbost Sands & Loch Branahuie   8   3m E of Stornoway
Park by A866 at NB478323 and walk west to view the loch and
further to Melbost Point.
Passage waders; winter seaduck especially Long-tailed Duck;
summer terns.

> *Eye Peninsula   8   4–8m E of Stornoway*
> *Seawatching; winter seaduck and divers; migrants.*

> *Broad Bay & Traigh Chuil   8   NB462384   4m NE of*
> *Stornoway*
> *Passage and winter waders; winter seaduck.*

> *Gob Steinish   8   NB447341   1½m NE of Stornoway*
> *Passage and winter waders and wildfowl.*

> *Upper Laxdale   8   NB360380   4–6m NW of Stornoway*
> *Upland birds.*

> *Blar nam Faoileag   8   NB410440   5–6m N of Stornoway*
> *Upland birds.*

TIC	As previous entry.
YH	As previous entry.
H/B	Bayble Bunkhouse, Burncrook, Upper Bayble, Point, (Eye Peninsula) (0851 870 863)
	Cromore Centre, Cromore (0851 88 383)
RF	Coffee Pot, Stornoway
BBE	The Old Manse, Knock, Point (0851 870 281)
	3 Aignish, Point (0851 870 900)
	Hebridean Guest House, Bayhead, Stornoway (0851 2268)
	Tower Guest House, 32 James Street, Stornoway (0851 3150)
SC	5a Knock, Point (0851 870 537)
	(Seisiader cottage, Point) 6 Braeside Park, Ballock, Invernesshire (0463 792075)
	132 Newmarket, Laxdale, nr Stornoway (0851 2015)
	1 Lower Sandwick, Stornoway (0851 4282)

Loch Eilaster area   13   3m S of Carloway
Park by A858 2m N of Breasclete by Loch na Muilne, NB206378,
and take track east.
Summer waders; birds of prey.

Uig Sands   13   1–2m W of Timsgarry
Park and view from minor road ¼m N of Crowlista at NB043344, or
½m S of Carnish at NB035315, or ½m N of Ardroil at NB049329.
Passage and winter waders.

Gallan Head 13 NB054394 *3m N of Timsgarry*
Seawatching; migrants.

Glen Valtos 13 NB075345 *2m E of Timsgarry*
Migrants.

TIC	As previous entry.
YH	As previous entry.
H/B	Garenin Hostel, Garenin, Carloway
RF	Callanish Tearoom, Callanish
BBE	Baile-na-Cille Guest House, Timsgarry (085 175 242)
	Scaliscro Lodge, Uig (085 175 325)
	Garymilis, Kirkibost, Bernera (0851 74341)
SC	(Callanish house) Riverdale, Breasclete, Isle of Lewis (085 172 218)
	28a Callanish, Lewis (085 172 271)
	5 Hacklete, Great Bernera, Lewis (0851 74269)
	(Reef cottage, Uig) Wester Craigie Dhu, Cardney, Dunkeld, Perthshire
	(Uig House) 6 Westfield Terrace, Aberdeen (0224 641614)

Sound of Harris   18   between Harris & North Uist
View from minor road south of Leverburgh e.g. NG025846, or from Leverburgh Pier, NG012864. Also ferries from Leverburgh to islands in the sound.
Winter divers, seaduck and wildfowl.

Luskentyre   14   5m SW of Tarbert
View from minor road to Luskentyre along the northern shoreline e.g. NG074987 and NG082980. Also park just west of Luskentyre and walk west across the dunes to overlook the Sound of Taransay.
Passage and winter waders, gulls and wildfowl; winter seaduck including regular Surf Scoter.

Northton   18   3m NW of Leverburgh
Park at end of minor road just NW of Northton at NF987904 and walk track northwards.
Wildfowl; waders; migrants; winter seaduck and divers; seawatching.

West Loch Tarbert 14 NB130015 *NW of Tarbert*
Winter seaduck, divers and gulls.

Morsgail Forest 14 NB120180 *12m NW of Tarbert*
Upland birds; summer waders and loch species.

Clisham 14 NB155073 *4m N of Tarbert*
Upland birds including Golden Eagle.

TIC	As previous entry.
	*Tarbert, Isle of Harris (0859 2011)
YH	Kyles, Stockinish, Harris
	Rhenigidale, North Harris
H/B	Cromore Centre, Cromore (0851 88 383)
RF	Rosevilla Tearoom, Tarbert
BBE	Ardvourlie Castle Guest House, Ardvourlie (0859 2307)
	Minch View House, Tarbert (0859 2140)
	Old Post Office House, Northton (085982 206)
	Suil na Mara, Isle of Scalpay (085 984 278)
	1 Quidinish, Flodabay (085 983 311)
BBESC	Eilean Glas Lighthouse, Isle of Scalpay, Harris (0859 84345)
SC	Tigh na Seallach, Bowglass, Harris (0859 2411)
	(Cliasmol bungalow) 3 Amhuinnsuidhe, Amhuinn-suidhe, Harris (085 986 230)
	Bayview, 1 Drinnishader, Harris (085 981 213)
	3 Scadabay, Scadabay (085 981 206)
	8 Grosebay, Harris (085 983 251)
	(Borve bungalow) School Side, Leverburgh, Harris (085 982 265)

St. Kilda   18   40m W of the main islands
To stay on the island contact National Trust for Scotland, 5 Charlotte Square, Edinburgh Tel: 031 226 5922 who organise the cruises and holidays.
The seabird island with huge colonies of most species including 60,000 pairs of Gannet. Also very good but underwatched for migrants and vagrants.

SOUTH UIST & BENBECULA   22
Loch Druidibeg
View from B890 which runs along the northern shore between its junction with A865 and Lochskipport e.g. NF795385.
Wildfowl, divers, waders, Corncrake, Twite and raptors; migrants; woodland birds along the road.

Loch Bee
View from A865 where it crosses the loch, NF782427.
Wildfowl.

Ardivachar Point & North Bay
Park at the west end of minor road which runs west of A865 north of Loch Bee, at NF741458. Then take paths north.
Seawatching.

Rubha Ardvule
Park at end of minor road 2m W of A865 at NF717298.
Seawatching; migrants; winter seaduck.

Loch Boisdale Harbour   NF794184   *S end of island*
Winter gulls including Iceland and Glaucous, seaduck and divers.

Howmore   NF753364   *3m SW of Loch Druidibeg*
Waders; Corncrake.

Loch Hallan   NF740220   *1m NW of Daliburgh*
Wetland birds; wildfowl.

Loch a Mhoil & Bun na Feathlach   NF740355   *4m SW of Loch Druidibeg*
Passage and winter wildfowl and waders.

Benbecula Aerodrome
View from B892 between its junction with A865 and Balivanich e.g. NF792557.
Passage waders and pipits.

Balivanich   NF770555
Migrants; gulls.

Oitir Mhor   NF830569   *4m NE of Balivanich*
Passage and winter waders.

Cuinabunag   NF765527   *1½m S of Balivanich*
Summer waders; marshland birds.

Loch Fada   NF773521   *2m S of Balivanich*
Wildfowl; summer waders.

TIC	*Lochboisdale, South Uist (08784 286)
YH	Howmore, South Uist
RFBBE	Orasay Inn, Lochcarnan, nr Ardivachar (08704 298)
	Polochar Inn, Pollachar, South Uist (08784 215)
BBE	Grianaig Guest House, Garrypallie, nr Lochboisdale (08784 406)
	Inchyra Guest House, 27 Liniclate, Benbecula (0870 2176)
	20 Balivanich, Benbecula (0870 2129)
	Borrodale Hotel, Daliburgh, South Uist (08784 444)
	Lochboisdale Hotel, Lochboisdale, S Uist (08784 332)
SC	4 Milton, South Uist (08785 320)
	(South Lochboisdale house) East Farmhouse, Wylye, Warminster, Wilts (09856 219)

NORTH UIST   18 & 22
Balranald & Loch Paible
Park down track ¼m S of Hougharry, 1m W of A865 at NF706707.
Then follow waymarked paths to the south.
Summer wildfowl, waders including Red-necked Phalarope,
divers and Corncrake; passage waders; winter wildfowl and
raptors.

Vallay Strand
View from A865 along the southern shore 1–2m W of Malaclete
e.g. at NF772738 and NF789730.
Passage waders.

Griminish Point
2m N of A865 at NF724766.
Seawatching.

Guala na h-Imrich Plantation
½m E of the minor road north from Ardheisker to Malaclete, at
NF797703.
Migrants.

Aird an Runair
Parking as for Balranald. Then track west to the point, NF687705.
Seawatching especially in May for Long-tailed Skua.

Loch Scadavay & Skealtar
View from A867 1–3m W of Lochmaddy e.g. NF870672 or
NF900683.
Summer divers, waders, Arctic Skua.

Ben Langass Plantation
½m S of A867 2m SW of Loch Scadavay at NF845655.
Migrants.

Newton
1–2m S of Newtonferry by B893 e.g. NF884764.
Summer waders and Corncrake; migrants.

Vallaquie Strand
View from B893 3m S of Newtonferry at NF873747.
Waders and wildfowl.

Loch Maddy
View from pier at easternmost end of the loch at NF920680.
Winter seaduck and gulls including Iceland and Glaucous.

Loch Aulasary
View from minor road 4m NE of Lochmaddy e.g. NF953744.
Winter wildfowl and seaduck.

TIC	*Lochmaddy, North Uist (08763 321)
YH	Claddach Baleshare Hostel, Claddach Baleshare
	Ostram House, Lochmaddy (08763 368)
	Bernaray Hostel, Isle of Bernaray
RFBBE	Westford Inn, Claddach Kirkibost (08764 653)
BBE	Langass Lodge Hotel, Locheport (08764 285)
	Sealladh Traigh, Claddach Kirkibost (08764 248)
	The Old Courthouse, Lochmaddy (08763 358)
SC	Balard, Malaglate, Sollas (08766 242)
	16 Knockintorran, Bayhead (08765 353)
	Lag Gorm, 5a Machair Illeray (08764 278)

Anglesey

all Anglesey   **OS Map 114**

TIC   Marine Square, Salt Island Approach, Holyhead (0407 2622)
Station Site, Llanfair P.G. (0248 713177)
YH   Tan-y-Bryn, Bangor, Gwynedd (0248 353516)

South Stack   2m W of Holyhead
Car-parks near end of minor road at extreme NW corner of Holy Island, SH206823. Then tracks to cliffs, heathland and Elin's Tower lookout (April–Sept).
Summer seabird colonies; seawatching; migrants; heathland birds; Chough and Peregrine.

Holyhead Mountain & North Stack   1½m W of Holyhead
Park by minor road ½m W of Llaingoch at SH232827. Then path NW, on the eastern side of the mountain, beside quarries and to North Stack.
Birds as South Stack.

Penrhos Nature Reserve   2m SE of Holyhead
Signed car-park overlooking Beddmanarch Bay off A5 on the western side of Stanley Embankment at SH275805. Then tracks through woods and to the ponds.
Migrants; passage and winter waders and wildfowl; terns and gulls.

Inland Sea   3m SE of Holyhead
Park on the east side of Four Mile Bridge on B4545, 1m W of Valley, at SH282785. Then path north by the shore.
Passage and winter waders and wildfowl; terns.

> **Penrhosfeilw Common**   *SH215800   2½m SW of Holyhead*
> *Heathland birds; migrants; Chough.*

Soldiers Point   SH236836   *1m NW of Holyhead Harbour*
Seawatching; winter seabirds; migrants.

Holyhead Harbour   SH250831   *N end of A5*
Winter divers, grebes, Black Guillemot, gulls.

Rhoscolyn Head   SH257755   *S end of Holy Island*
Migrants; Chough; seabirds.

Gromlech   SH264772   *1m NW of Rhoscolyn*
Reedbed species; migrants.

BBE   The Old School, Rhoscolyn (0407 741593)
             Highground Hotel, Trearddur Bay (0407 860078)
BBESC The Old Rectory, Rhoscolyn (0407 860214)
             Tan y Cytiau Country House, South Stack Road, nr
             Holyhead (0407 762763)
SC   Celyn, Holyhead Mountain (0407 3761/4034)

Llyn Llywenan   5m E of Holyhead, 2m E of A5025
View from minor road at northern end of the lake, 1½m N of
B5109, at SH347823.
Wildfowl; summer warblers; reedbed species.

Llyn Alaw   4m SW of Amlwch
Car-park at end of minor road 2m NW of Llanerchymedd,
SH405866. Then signed track north to the hide. Also car-park and
visitor centre at southern end, SH374856.
Wildfowl; passage waders and terns; winter raptors; summer
warblers; migrants.

Cemlyn Bay   6m W of Amlwch
Car-parks at E and W ends of the lagoon, 1½m W of Tregele on
A5025, SH328935 or SH336932.
Summer terns; wildfowl; waders.

Cemaes Bay & Wylfa Head   4½m W of Amlwch
Car-park at end of minor road 1m N of Tregele at SH356938. Then
paths north and east.
Passage waders; winter seaduck and divers; summer terns;
migrants; seawatching.

Point Lynas   2½m E of Amlwch
Park by lane up to the lighthouse at SH479931 and walk north to
the point.
Migrants; summer seabirds; seawatching.

Traeth Dulas   4m SE of Amlwch
Park by the estuary at end of minor road, 1m E of Llaneuddog on A5025, at SH476882. Then take coastal path north and south. Passage and winter waders and wildfowl.

> **Llyn Llygerian**   SH346900   1½m SW of Llanfechell
> Wildfowl; summer warblers.

> **Carmel Head**   SH297930   NW corner of main island
> Seawatching; summer seabirds; Chough; migrants.

> **Dinas Gynfor**   SH388953   3½m NW of Amlwch
> Seawatching.

> **Alaw Estuary**   SH306820   3m E of Holyhead
> Passage and winter waders and wildfowl.

> **Moelfre**   SH517867   1½m NE of Llanallgo
> Seabirds; seawatching; migrants.

> **Mynydd Bodafon**   SH470850   5m SE of Amlwch
> Woodland and heathland birds.

RF   Crown Hotel, Bodedern
          Parciau Arms, Marian-glas, nr Benllech
          Pilot Boat, Dulas
BBE   Llwydiarth Fawr, Llanerchymedd (0248 470321)
          Tre'r Ddôl Farm, Llanerchymedd (0248 470278)
BBESC Hafod Country House, Cemaes Bay (0407 710500)
SC   (Clegir Mawr) National Trust, North Wales Holiday cottages, Station Road, Deganwy, Conwy (0492 82492)

Valley Lakes (Dinam, Penrhyn & Traffwll)   2m SE of Valley
Car-park by minor road near SE corner of Llyn Penrhyn at SH315766 and paths westward between the lakes.
Wildfowl; reedbed species; summer warblers.

Valley Airfield   2½m SE of Valley
View from car-park by minor road 2m SW of A5, just over the railway line at SH309764.
Passage and winter waders and raptors; migrants.

Llyn Maelog   4m SE of Valley
Park by south shore beside A4080 ½m SE of Rhosneigr at SH324726 and paths beside the east and west shores.
Wildfowl and grebes; passage terns; reedbed species; migrants.

Llyn Coron   1½m NE of Aberffraw
Car-parks by A4080 at SH375693. Then footpaths north beside the west and east shores.
Wildfowl; reedbed species; passage and winter wildfowl and raptors.

Cefni Reservoir   2m NW of Llangefni
Car-park at northern end of reservoir by B5111 at SH452783. Then track to the hide.
Wildfowl; passage waders; woodland birds; summer warblers.

> *Rhosneigr SH316728 4m SE of Valley*
> *Summer terns including Roseate Tern.*
>
> *Tywyn Aberffraw SH355685 ½m SE of Aberffraw*
> *Waders; wildfowl; heathland birds; migrants.*
>
> *Llyn Padrig SH364727 3m N of Aberffraw*
> *Wildfowl and waders.*
>
> *Llyn Hendref SH397765 4m W of Llangefni*
> *Wildfowl and waders.*
>
> *Afon Cefni Dingle SH455762 ½m NW of Llangefni*
> *Woodland birds.*

RF	Crown Hotel, Bodedern
BBE	Sealands Hotel, Rhosneigr (0407 810834)
	Bull Hotel, Valley (0407 740351)
SC	Bodwina Farm, Gwalchmai (0407 720233)

Cob Pool   3m E of Aberffraw
View from car-park by A4080 ¼m SE of the bridge over River Cefni at SH410685.
Passage and winter waders and wildfowl.

Llyn Rhos Ddu   4½m SE of Aberffraw
Car-park and hide ¼m down track SW of A4080 from Pen-lôn at SH427647.
Wildfowl.

Llanddwyn Island, Newborough Forest & Warren   5m SE of Aberffraw
Car-park at end of minor road 2m SW of Newborough at the southern end of the forest at SH405635. Then footpaths west to Llanddwyn Island and southeast to Newborough Warren and Abermenai Point.
Woodland birds; migrants; winter seaduck, divers and raptors; Black Guillemot; summer terns; passage and winter waders and wildfowl.

Malltraeth Marsh   SH452717   2½m S of Llangefni
Waders and wildfowl.

Malltraeth Sands   SH405665   1½m NW of Newborough
Passage and winter waders and wildfowl.

Traeth Gwyllt   SH478648   3½m E of Newborough
Passage and winter waders, wildfowl and gulls.

Moel-y-don   SH518678   2½m SW of Llanfair P.G.
Birds as Traeth Gwyllt.

Llyn Parc Mawr   SH415670   1m NW of Newborough
Wildfowl; passage waders; woodland birds.

RF	White Lion, Newborough
	Mermaid, Brynsiencyn
BBE	Swn-y-Mor, Malltraeth (0407 840676)
	Plas Trefarthen, Brynsiencyn (0248 73379)
SC	(Llangaffo cottage) 34 Cae Cnyciog, Llanfair P.G. (0248 714824)
	Feisdon Bach, Malltraeth (061 980 3253)

Afon Cadnant Estuary   **1m NE of Menai Bridge**
Park by A545 at SH560727 and view estuary from the eastern side of the road.
Passage and winter waders and wildfowl.

Fryars Road   **1m N of Beaumaris**
View from car-park by B5109 at SH612776 and coastal path north.
Passage and winter waders, wildfowl and gulls.

Black Point, Penmon   **2m NE of Llangoed**
Car-park near lighthouse at end of minor road ¾m NW of Penmon at SH640813.
Migrants; winter seaduck and divers; summer seabirds; Black Guillemot.

Red Wharf Bay   **1½m SE of Benllech, 5m NW of Menai Bridge**
Park at the end of minor road overlooking the bay 1½m NE of Pentraeth (on A5025) at SH534798. Also car-park on the western side of the bay ¾m NE of A5025 at SH529812.
Passage and winter waders and wildfowl; winter seaduck and divers.

Church Island   SH552717   W side of Menai Bridge
Passage and winter waders and wildfowl; woodland birds.

Gallows Point   *SH598752*   *½m SW of Beaumaris*
Passage and winter waders and wildfowl.

Lleiniog   *SH621792*   *2m NE of Beaumaris*
Passage waders and terns; winter wildfowl and seabirds.

Llyn Bodgylched   *SH585770*   *1½m NW of Beaumaris*
Wildfowl.

Fedw Fawr   *SH606819*   *1½m N of Llangoed*
Seabirds including Black Guillemot.

Mynydd Llwydiarth   *SH544789*   *3m SE of Benllech*
Woodland birds.

Cors Goch   *SH495814*   *1½m SW of Benllech*
Marsh and heathland birds including Nightjar.

RF   Ship, Red Wharf Bay
Olde Bulls Head, Beaumaris
Gazelle, Menai Bridge
Owain Glendwr, Llanddona
Liverpool Arms, Menai Bridge
BBE   Bryn Tirion Hotel, Red Wharf Bay (0248 852366)
Plas Cichle Farm, nr Beaumaris (0248 810488)
SC   Glendale, Llangoed, nr Beaumaris (0248 78294)

————————————————————————

Clwyd

Rhos-on-Sea & Colwyn Bay   116   **4m NE of Conwy**
Park and view from sea front in Rhos e.g. at SH843813 1m N of
A546.
Winter seaduck and divers; passage and winter waders; passage
terns; gulls; seawatching.

Llandulas & Abergele Roads   116   **2½m NW of Abergele**
View from car-park on seafront just north of the railway line ¼m N
of A55 from Llandulas at SH906786. Also walk east along the shore
and car-parks by the shore at Pensarn 2m E e.g. at SH949788.
Winter seaduck and divers; passage and winter waders; migrants;
winter gulls.

> *Clwyd Estuary & Marine Lake*   116   *SJ003800   1½m
> SW of Rhyl centre*
> *Passage and winter waders and wildfowl.*

> *Coed Bryndansi*   116   *SH854740   3m S of Colwyn Bay*
> *Woodland birds.*

> *Gopa Wood*   116   *SH935770   1m SW of Abergele*
> *Woodland birds.*

TIC	Station Road, Colwyn Bay (0492 530478)
	Central Promenade, Rhyl (0745 355068)
YH	Foxhill, Nant-y-Glyn, Colwyn Bay (0492 530627)
RF	White Lion, Llanelian-yn-Rhos, nr Old Colwyn
	Plough, Old Colwyn
	Mountain View, Mochdre, nr Colwyn Bay
BBE	Cabin Hill Hotel, College Avenue, Rhos-on-Sea (0492 44568)
SC	The Granary, Betws-yn-Rhos, Abergele (0492 60259)

Point of Ayr   116   4m NE of Prestatyn
Park at end of minor road at Talacre, 1½m NE of A548 at SJ125850.
Then paths south along the sea wall to hide and west toward The
Warren.
Passage and winter waders; winter seaduck, divers,raptors, Twite
and Snow Bunting; seawatching; migrants.

> *Llyn Helyg   117   SJ115774   5m SE of Prestatyn*
> *Winter wildfowl and woodland birds.*

> *Mostyn Bank   117   SJ143820   5m E of Prestatyn*
> *Passage and winter waders and wildfowl.*

> *Graig Fawr   116   SJ060804   2m SW of Prestatyn*
> *Woodland and heathland birds; summer warblers; migrants.*

> *Nant Felinblwm   116   SJ137810   S of Pen-y-ffordd*
> *River and woodland birds including Pied Flycatcher and
> Dipper.*

> *Gronant Warren   116   SJ088842   2m NE of Prestatyn*
> *Winter seaduck; summer terns; reedbed species.*

TIC   *Scala Cinema, Prestatyn (07456 4365)
           Central Promenade, Rhyl (0745 355068)
YH   As previous entry.
RF   Bells of St. Marys, Gronant, nr Prestatyn
           Rock Inn, Lloc
           Smugglers Inn, Point of Ayr

Bagillt & Flint Marsh   117   ½m-1½m NW of Flint
Park just off A548 toward the northern end of Bagillt at SJ223754
and take path across the marsh to the northeast and along dyke
southeast to Flint Marsh.
Waders; wildfowl; migrants; winter raptors.

Nant-y-Flint   117   2m SW of Flint
Park by minor road ¾m NE of A55 from Pentre Halkyn, at
SJ216725 and take track south beside river and through the wood.
Woodland and river birds including Hawfinch and Dipper.

**Shotton Steelworks Pools   117   ½m-1½m NE of Connah's
Quay**
Three year permit, map and access details from Public Relations,
BSC, Shotton Steelworks, Deeside, Clwyd, CH5 2NH.
Also public footpath from Hawarden Bridge railway station,
SJ312695, ruńs NW beside River Dee and a few pits.
Passage waders; winter wildfowl; summer Common Tern and
warblers; migrants.

Connah's Quay   117   NW side of Connah's Quay
Entry by permit only from Deeside Naturalists Soc, 38 Kelsterton Road, Connah's Quay, CH5 4BJ. Entrance via the Electricity Generation Station gates by A548 opposite Kelsterton College at SJ284705. Then tracks to visitor centre and hides and further NW to Oakenholt Marsh.
Passage and winter waders and wildfowl; passage terns and gulls; migrants.

> *Whelston Marsh   117   SJ214764   1½m NW of Bagillt*
> *Passage and winter waders and wildfowl.*

> *Shotwick Lakes & Range Pools   117   SJ310722   2m N of Shotton*
> *Passage and winter wildfowl; passage waders; passage and summer terns; migrants.*

> *Bryn Celyn   116   SJ191768   1m S of Greenfield*
> *Wildfowl; woodland birds.*

TIC	*Town Hall, Earl Street, Mold (0352 59331)
	Craft Centre, Ruthin (08242 3992)
YH	Hough Green House, 40 Hough Green, Chester (0244 680056)
	Holt Hostel, Maeshafn, Mold (035 285 320)
RF	Sir Gawain & the Green Knight, Connah's Quay
	Old Quay House, Connah's Quay
	Britannia Inn, Halkyn
	Royal Oak, Holywell
BB	The Hall, Lygan-y-Wern, Pentre, Halkyn (0352 780215)
BBE	Greenhill Farm, Bryn Celyn, Holywell (0352 713270)
	Groes Farm, Middle Hill, Northop (0352 86322)
	Oakenholt Farm, Chester Road, Flint (03526 3264)

Moel Fammau Country Park & Clwyd Forest   116   5m SW of Mold
Car-park by minor road , 1½m SW of A494 from Tafarn-y-Gelyn, at SJ172612. Then tracks north through woods and onto moorland. Woodland and moorland birds including Red and Black Grouse, Merlin and Goshawk.

Loggerheads Country Park   116   3m SW of Mold
Car-park by A494 at SJ198626, then trails north beside Afon Alun. Woodland and river birds including Dipper, Pied Flycatcher, Hawfinch and Crossbill.

> *Llyn Gweryd   116   SJ174550   4m SE of Ruthin*
> *Winter wildfowl; woodland and hillside birds.*

Ysceifiog Lake 116 SJ146716 1½m SE of Caerwys
Woodland birds; summer warblers; winter wildfowl.

Penycloddan Hill & Moel Arthur 116 SJ138668
1m NE of Llangwyfan
Woodland and hill birds.

Craig-adwy-wynt 116 SJ122544 2½m S of Ruthin
Woodland birds.

Rhewl 116 SJ105597 2m NW of Ruthin
Woodland and river birds.

TIC	As previous entry.
YH	As previous entry.
RF	White Horse, Cilcain, nr Mold
	Griffin, Llanbedr, nr Ruthin
BB	Argoed Guest House, Llanfwrog, nr Ruthin (08242 3407)
SC	Garden Cottage, Bathafarn Hall, Llanbedr, nr Ruthin (08242 2187)
	Tynywern Farm, Corwen Road, Ruthin (08242 2079)
	Bryn Nannerch, Nannerch, nr Mold (0352 741249)

Llyn Brenig 116 7m SW of Denbigh

Car-park at northern end 1m down track south of B4501 at SH984575. Then paths to view reservoir to the west, and east to moorland and plantation.
Winter wildfowl; Red and Black Grouse, Crossbill, Hen Harrier, Merlin and Short-eared Owl.

Llyn Aled 116 4m W of Llyn Brenig

Park by minor road along northern shore 1m NW of A543 at SH916578 and walk west, northwest or northeast.
Winter wildfowl; moorland birds including Golden Plover, Dunlin, Hen Harrier and Merlin.

Alwen Reservoir 116 SH950537 2m SW of Llyn Brenig
Winter wildfowl; woodland and moorland birds.

Clocaenog Forest 116 SJ005535 2m SE of Llyn Brenig
Woodland birds including Crossbill, Goshawk and Long-eared Owl.

Melin-y-Wig 116 SJ046494 5m SE of Llyn Brenig
Woodland and river birds including Pied Flycatcher, Wood Warbler and Dipper.

Llyn y Cwrt 116 SJ906513 3m NW of Cerrigydrudion
Passage and winter wildfowl; woodland birds.

TIC	as previous entry.
	Royal Oak Stables, Betws-y-coed (06902 426/665)
YH	The Old Mill, Cynwyd, Corwen (0490 2950)
RF	Sportsmans Arms, Bylchau
RFBBE	Red Lion, Cyffylliog, nr Ruthin (08246 664)
BBE	Growine Farm, Glasfryn, nr Cerrigydrudion (049 082 447)

North Berwyn & Ceiriog Valley   125   7m SW of Llangollen
Park in Pentre at end of minor road 2m NW of the end of B4500 at
SJ136347. Then track and path north or south along the Ceiriog
Valley, NE to Y Fawnen, and west toward Cadair Bronwen.
River, moorland and woodland birds including Red and Black
Grouse, Hen Harrier, Merlin, Short-eared Owl, Golden Plover,
Dunlin, Dipper, Kingfisher and Pied Flycatcher.

Ceiriog Forest & Moel Fferna   125   5m SW of Llangollen
Car-park by minor road 3m W of B4500 at SJ166384. Then tracks
and footpaths north. Also at end of minor road 1½m SW of A5
from Glyndyfrdwy, SJ134407.
Woodland, upland and river birds including Black Grouse, Merlin, Ring Ousel and Dipper.

Pistyll Rhaeadr   125   3½m NW of Llanrhaeadr
Car-park at end of minor road 3½m NW of the end of B4580 at
SJ074296. Then track and footpaths north up Nant y Llyn toward
Cadair Berwyn.
Upland birds including Peregrine, Ring Ousel, Golden Plover,
spring Dotterel, Hen Harrier and Merlin.

> *Penbwlch* 125 *SJ090365* *3½m SE of Cynwyd*
> *Upland birds including Red Grouse, Hen Harrier and Merlin.*

> *Hafod-y-calch* 125 *SJ060425* *1m N of Cynwyd*
> *River birds.*

TIC	Town Hall, Llangollen (0978 860828)
YH	Tyndwr Hall, Tyndwr Road, Llangollen (0978 860330)
RF	Green Inn, Llangedwyn
	Hand, Chirk
RFBBE	Britannia Inn, Horse Shoe Pass, Llangollen (0978 860144)
BBE	Abbey Grange Hotel, Llangollen (0978 860753)
	Ty'n Celyn, Tyndwr, Llangollen (0978 861117)
SC	(Home Farm Cottage, Chirk Castle) National Trust North Wales Holiday Cottages, Station Road, Deganwy, Conwy (0492 82492)
	(Rhewl cottage) 7 Thornhurst Avenue, Oswestry, Shrops (0691 655179)
	(Llangollen house) Penlan, Tregeiriog, Llangollen (069172 488)

Gresford Flash   117   2m N of Wrexham centre
View from minor road ½m N of A5156 1m SW of Gresford at
SJ346536.
Wildfowl; passage and winter gulls; summer warblers; migrants.

Eglwyseg   117   6m SW of Wrexham
Car-park at end of minor road, 3½m SW of B5426 from Minera, at
SJ234485. Then track and footpaths south along escarpment, SE to
Ruabon Mountain, and SW down Offas Dyke Path.
Upland, moorland and woodland birds including Red Grouse,
Hen Harrier, Peregrine, Golden Plover and Ring Ousel.

Erddig Park   117   1½m SW of Wrexham centre
Park at northern end of Park ½m SE of A483 at SJ329489. Then
track and footpaths south through park, beside river and woods.
Also entrance from minor road at the southern end ½m N of
Sontley at SJ334477.
Woodland and river birds.

> ***Nant-y-Ffrith Reservoir***   *117   SJ243530   6m NW of*
> *Wrexham*
> *Winter wildfowl.*

> ***Llyn Cyfynwy***   *117   SJ216546   8m NW of Wrexham*
> *Winter wildfowl; Red Grouse; Great Crested Grebe.*

> ***Moel-y-Faen Quarries***   *116   SJ186480   4m NW of Llan-*
> *gollen*
> *Chough, Peregrine, Ring Ousel.*

> ***Llantysilio Mountain***   *116   SJ147454   5m NW of Llan-*
> *gollen*
> *Upland birds including Merlin, Hen Harrier and Short-eared*
> *Owl.*

TIC   As previous entry.
       *Memorial Hall, Town Centre, Wrexham (0978 357845)
YH   As previous entry.
       Holt Hostel, Maeshafn, Mold (035285 320)
RF   City Arms, Minera
       Griffin, Gresford
       Kings Head, Bwlchgwyn
       Sun Inn, Rhewl, nr Llangollen
BBE   Grove Guest House, 36 Chester Road, Wrexham (0978
       354 288)
       Buck Farm, Hanmer (094 874 339)

Dyfed

Ynys-Hir   135   4½m SW of Machynlleth
Car-park and reception centre at end of track 1m N of A487 from
Furnace Bridge (just south of Eglwysfach), at SN682962. Then
nature trail, hides etc.
Woodland birds including Pied Flycatcher, Redstart and Wood
Warbler; passage and winter waders and wildfowl; winter raptors.

Ynyslas   135   3m N of Borth
Car-park on beach at end of minor road 1m N of B4353 at
SN610943. Then paths across dunes and along shore east and
west.
Passage and winter waders and wildfowl; winter seaduck; gulls;
migrants; seawatching.

Cwm Rheidol   135   6m E of Aberystwyth
Car-park and information centre by minor road on north side of
River Rheidol, 3m E of Capel Bangor at SN696796. Then nature
trail and footpaths beside river, around reservoir and through
woods on the south side over the bridge.
Woodland and river birds; passage and winter wildfowl.

> ***Aberystwyth Harbour***   *135   SN580807   ½m S of*
> *Aberystwyth centre*
> *Passage and winter gulls.*

> ***Upper Borth***   *135   SN604887   5m N of Aberystwyth*
> *Passage and winter gulls; winter divers and seaduck;*
> *seawatching.*

> ***Borth Bog (Cors Fochno)***   *135   SN630910   7m NE of*
> *Aberystwyth*
> *Marshland and heathland birds; winter raptors; Hen Harrier;*
> *Black Grouse.*

> ***Clarach Bay***   *135   SN586839   2m N of Aberystwyth*
> *Passage and winter gulls, seaduck and divers.*

Nant-y-moch Reservoir *135 SN740880 6m E of Talybont*
Passage and winter wildfowl.

Plynlimon *135 SN790870 8m E of Talybont*
Upland birds.

Llyn yr Oerfa *135 SN728798 2m SW of Ponterwyd*
Passage wildfowl.

Llyn Frongoch *135 SN722754 1½m SW of Devil's Bridge*
Passage and winter wildfowl.

Rheidol Gravel Pits *135 SN667786 1½m SE of Capel Bangor*
Passage and winter wildfowl; passage waders.

TIC	Terrace Road, Aberystwyth (0970 612125/611955)
	Canolfan Owain Glyndwr, Machynlleth (0654 2401/702401)
YH	Morlais, Borth (0970 871498)
	Glantuen, Ystumtuen, Aberystwyth (0970 85693)
RFBBE	Dyffrn Castell, nr Ponterwyd, Aberystwyth (0970 85237)
	White Lion & Black Lion, Talybont, Aberystwyth (0970 86245)
BBE	Erwbarfe Farmhouse, Devil's Bridge (097085 251)
	Neuadd Parc Farm, Caple Bangor, Aberystwyth (0970 84260)

Cors Caron (Tregaron Bog) 146 2m N of Tregaron

Park by B4343 at SN684614. Then path along the old railway line north leading to hide.
Winter wildfowl and raptors; Red Kite; summer warblers; marshland species.

Llyn Fanod *146 SN603644 5m NW of Tregaron*
Passage and winter wildfowl.

Llyn Eiddwen *135 SN606670 4m SE of Llanrhystud*
Passage and winter wildfowl.

Llyn Derigch *146 SN570500 2m NW of Lampeter*
Passage and winter wildfowl.

Pencarreg Lake *146 SN536456 3½m SW of Lampeter*
Passage and winter wildfowl.

Cwm Gwenffrwd *146 SN596598 5m W of Tregaron*
River and woodland birds.

TIC	Terrace Road, Aberystwyth (0970 612125/611955)
	*The Harbour, Aberaeron (0545 570602)
YH	Blaencaron, Tregaron (09744 441)
RF	Three Horseshoes, Llangeitho
	Cross Inn,Rhos-yr-Hafod
RFBBE	Talbot, Tregaron (09744 208)
BBE	Neuaddlas, Tregaron (09744 380/8905)
BBESC	Abermeurig Mansion Farm, Lampeter (0570 470216)

Afon Pysgotwr & Cefn Cnwcheithinog   146   8m N of Llandovery

Park by minor road 2½m N of Rhandirmwyn by bridge over River Twyi at SN773458. Then over bridge and track then footpath beside woodland and river, on north side of the river, up the Afon Doethie up onto the hill.

Woodland, river and upland birds including Pied Flycatcher, Dipper, Common Sandpiper, Goosander, Merlin, Peregrine and Red Kite.

> ***Llyn Brianne***   *146 & 147   SN795490   10m N of Llandovery*
> *Passage and winter wildfowl.*

> ***Mynydd Mallaen***   *146   SN735445   6m N of Llandovery*
> *Upland birds.*

> ***Afon Gwenlais to Rhyd Ddu***   *146   SN745414–SN713430   5m NW of Llandovery*
> *River and upland birds.*

TIC	*Broad Street, Llandovery (0550 20693)
YH	Hafody Pant, Cynghordy, Llandovery (05505 235)
	Tyncornel c/o S Wales Office, 1 Cathedral Road, Cardiff (0222 231370)
RF	Neuadd Fawr, Cilycwm
RFBBE	Royal Oak, Rhandirmwyn (05506 201)
BBE	Llwyncelyn Guest House, Llandovery (0550 20566)
SC	Ysgabor, Cwm Croiddur, Cilycwm, Llandovery (0550 20188)

Newquay   145   20m SW of Aberystwyth

Park in Newquay by the sea front at the north end of A486, SN389602, and take coastal path west from the north end of town. Summer seabird colonies; seawatching; heathland birds; migrants.

Lochtyn   145   4½m SW of Newquay
Park in Llangranog near juntion of B4321 and B4334 at SN316538.
Then coastal path north from the sea front.
Summer seabird colonies; seawatching; Chough.

> ***Traeth Penbryn***   145   *2½m NE of Aberporth*
> *Winter seaduck and divers.*

TIC   *Church Street, Newquay (0545 580865)
YH   The Glyn, Church Street, Newquay (0545 560337)
RF   Crown Inn, Llwyndafydd, nr Newquay
            Brynhoffnant Inn, Brynhoffnant
BBE   Llwynwermod Farm, Maenygroes, nr Newquay (0545
            560083)
BBESC   Tŷ Hen Farm, Llwyndafydd, nr Newquay (0545 560346)

Teifi Estuary   145   2m NW of Cardigan
View from B4548 2–2½m N of its junction with A487 at SN165485
and SN164495. Also from B4546 on the west side.
Passage and winter waders and wildfowl.

Cemaes Head   145   4m NW of Cardigan
Car-park at end of B4546 2m N of St. Dogmaels at SN153486. Then
Pembrokeshire Coast Path northwest to the point.
Seawatching; summer seabirds; winter seaduck and divers;
migrants; Chough and Peregrine.

> ***Pentŵd Marshes***   145   *SN186454   1m SE of Cardigan*
> *Marshland birds; passage waders; wildfowl; reedbed species.*

> ***Afon Cych***   145   *SN270376   3m SE of Abercych*
> *River and woodland birds.*

TIC   *Theatre Mwidan, Bath House Road, Cardigan (0239
            613230)
YH   Sea View, Poppit, Cardigan (0239 612936)
RF   Pendre Inn, Cilgerran
            Ferry Inn, St. Dogmaels
BBE   Ffynonwen County Guest House, Aberporth (0239
            810312)
SC   (Church Cottage, Llandygwydd) Landmark Trust,
            Shottesbrook, Maidenhead (0628 825925)

Strumble Head   157   4m NW of Fishguard
Park beside minor road just before end of minor road to lighthouse
at SM895413. Then coastal path east or west and seawatching
lookout below parking area.
Seawatching; migrants; Chough.

Dinas Island   157   4m NE of Fishguard
Car-park 1m N of A487 ½m NE of Bryn-henllan at SN014400. Then
circular coastal path around the headland.
Migrants; seawatching; summer warblers; Chough and Peregrine.

Cwm Gwaun   157   4m SE of Fishguard
Park in Pontfaen 1m N of B4314 at SN027341 and take footpaths
through woods on south side of river. Also car-parks on the south
side of Cilrhedyn Bridge, SN005347, and paths through woods
and by river on the north side. Also 2m further east at SN045349.
Woodland and river birds including Pied Flycatcher, Wood
Warbler, Redstart and Dipper.

Pengelli Forest   145   5m E of Newport
Park by minor road 1½m NE from A487, at SN123395, then
marked paths southeast through woods.
Woodland birds including Pied Flycatcher, Redstart and Wood
Warbler.

Nyfer Estuary & Newport Bay   145   ½m-1½m N of Newport
Car-park at end of minor road near The Bennet 1½m N of Newport
at SN055406. Then paths north and south. Also view estuary from
southern side e.g. SN050397, ½m north of A487.
Winter seaduck and divers; passage and winter waders.

> *Fishguard Harbour*   157   SM955385   1½m N of
> Fishguard centre
> *Winter seaduck, divers and gulls.*

> *Goodwick Moor*   157   SM945375   1m NW of Fishguard
> centre
> *Summer warblers; marsh and reedbed species.*

> *Coed Llwyngoras*   145   SN097390   3m E of Newport
> *Woodland and river birds.*

> *Llys-y-fran Reservoir*   157   SN035245   8m SE of Fish-
> guard
> *Passage and winter wildfowl; winter gull roost.*

> *Mynydd Preseli & Pantmaenog Forest*   145   SN075322
> 4–5m SE of Newport
> *Woodland and hill birds; migrants.*

TIC	*4 Hamilton Street, Fishguard (0348 873484)
YH	Castell Mawr, Tref Asser, Goodwick (03485 233)
RF	Freemasons Arms, Dinas
	Llys-y-fran Visitor centre, Llys-y-fran Reservoir

RFBBE Trewern Arms, Nevern (0239 820395)
Gelli Fawr, Pontfaen
Golden Lion, Newport
BBE Piccola Calabria, New Hill, Goodwick (0348 874101)
Cilwene Hill Farm, Dinas Cross, nr Newport (03486 239)
Penlan Oleu, Llanychaer, Fishguard (034882 314)
SC Gelli Fawr, Pontfaen

St. David's Head   157   2½m NW of St. Davids
Car-park at Whitesands Bay at end of B4583, 1½m NW of St.
Davids at SM734272. Then coastal path NW to cliffs and area of
willow and reeds.
Summer seabird colonies; seawatching; migrants; heathland
birds; passage waders.

Ramsey Island   157   3m W of St. David's
Boat trips daily (Easter–end Sept) from St. Justinian, 2m W of St.
David's at SM724252 tel: 0437 720438. Also accommodation avail-
able on the island tel: 0437 781234.
Summer seabird colonies and Short-eared Owl; migrants; Chough
and Peregrine.

Porthllisky & Merry Vale   157   1–2m SW of St. David's
Car-park by minor road 1m SW of St. David's at the end of Merry
Vale, SM740243. Then coastal paths south beside Porth Clais
around Porthllisky Bay and on to Pendal-aderyn, SM715234. Also
tracks up Merry Vale and car-park at St. Justinian and coast path
south.
Migrants; summer seabirds; heathland birds; Chough.

Dowrog & Tretio Commons   157   2–3m E of St. David's
Park and view from minor roads crossing the commons NW of
A487 e.g. at SM773274 and SM790283. Also take paths and tracks
across the commons and to ponds on Dowrog.
Summer warblers; winter raptors including Hen Harrier roost;
passage wildfowl and waders; migrants; Short-eared Owl.

> **Trefeiddan Common**   157   SM734250   1½m W of St.
> David's
> Passage and winter wildfowl and raptors; migrants; reedbed
> species.

> **Waun Vachelich & St. David's Airfield**   157   SM785262
> 2m E of St. David's
> Winter raptors including Hen Harrier; passage waders;
> migrants.

Treleddyd Common 157 SM755272 1½m N of St. David's
Winter raptors; heathland birds.

TIC *City Hall, St. David's (0437 720392)
YH Llaethdy, St. David's (0437 720345)
11 Ffordd-yr-Afon, Trevine, Haverfordwest (0348 831414)
RF Farmers Arms, Trevine, Haverfordwest
BBE Ramsey House, Lower Moor, nr St. David's (0437 720321)
BBESC Llanddinog Old Farmhouse, Solva (0348 831224)
Trevaccoon Farm, nr St. David's (0348 831438)
Ramsey Island, via St. Justinian, St. David's (0437 781234)

Skomer Island   157   island 10m W of Milford Haven
Boats daily from April to Sept from Martin's Haven 2½m W of Marloes at SM760090. Details from Dale Sailing Company, Dale Haverfordwest tel: 0646 636349, and from Dyfed Wildlife Trust, 7 Market Street, Haverfordwest, SA61 1NF tel: 0437 765462 who have some self-catering accommodation available on the island. Summer seabirds including 100,000 pairs of Manx Shearwater and 1,000 Storm Petrel; Short-eared Owl and Chough; migrants.

Skokholm   157   island 3m S of Skomer
Weekly boat from Martin's Haven by Dale Sailing Company. Weekly full board accommodation available late March – mid Sept, details from Dyfed Wildlife Trust (see above). Also some day trips during July and August.
Migrants; summer seabirds including 6,000 pairs of Storm Petrel.

Grassholm   157   island 7m W of Skomer
Weekly boat trips from Martin's Haven, every Monday (must be booked). Contact Dale Sailing Co. (see above). Landing from Mid June–Sept only.
Summer seabirds including 30,000 pairs of Gannet.

Pickleridge Pools & The Gaun   157   ½m N of Dale
Car-park by B4327 overlooking the bay at SM808066. Then path NE.
Passage and winter waders, wildfowl and divers; migrants.

Marloes Mere   157   1m W of Marloes
Car-park overlooking the Mere by minor road ½m W of Marloes Court at SM780083 and tracks and paths north and west.
Passage and winter wildfowl and waders; migrants.

Rickets Head 157 SM854188 5m NW of Haverfordwest
Winter seaduck and divers; passage and winter waders.

Borough Head & Goultrop Roads   *157   SM840126   6m SW of Haverfordwest*
Migrants; winter seaduck and divers; seawatching.

St. Brides Woods   *157   SM800105   1½m N of Marloes*
Migrants.

Wooltack Point   *157   SM754094   2½m W of Marloes*
Seawatching; summer seabirds; Chough.

Dale Point & Dale Roads   *157   SM816053   ½m SE of Dale*
Winter divers and seaduck; migrants.

St. Ann's Head   *157   SM805028   2m S of Dale*
Migrants; Chough.

Bicton Reservoirs   *157   SM844076   ½m E of St. Ishmaels*
Passage waders and wildfowl.

Monk Haven   *157   SM827064   ½m SW of St. Ishmaels*
Migrants.

Sandyhaven   *157   SM855075   1½m E of St. Ishmaels*
Passage and winter waders and wildfowl; migrants.

Dale Airfield   *157   SM794070   1m NW of Dale*
Passage waders; passerine migrants.

TIC	*Car-park, Broad Haven (0437 781412)
	*40 High Street, Haverfordwest (0437 766141)
YH	Runwayskin, Marloes, Haverfordwest (0646 636667/636662)
	Broad Haven, Haverfordwest (0437 781688)
RF	Lobster Pot, Marloes
RFBBE	The Druidstone, nr Broad Haven (0437 781221)
SC	The Druidstone, as above.

Western Cleddau   157 or 158   3m SE of Haverfordwest
Park in Little Milford 1m SE of Lower Freystrop at SM969116. Then path north and east beside the estuary.
Passage and winter waders and wildfowl.

Pill   *157 or 158   SM914056   E side of Milford Haven*
Passage and winter waders.

Hazelbeach   *157 or 158   SM957050   3m E of Milford Haven*
Passage and winter waders and gulls.

Burton Ferry   *157 or 158*   *SM978050*   *4½m E of Milford Haven*
Passage and winter waders, gulls and wildfowl.

Llangwm   *157 or 158*   *SM995093*   *4½m SE of Haverfordwest*
Passage and winter waders.

TIC	*40 High Street, Haverfordwest (0437 766141)
YH	Broad Haven, Haverfordwest (0437 781688)
RF	Jolly Sailor, Burton, nr Neyland
RFBBE	Denant Mill Inn, Dreenhill, nr H'west (0437 66569)
BBESC	Dreenhill Farm, Dale Road, Haverfordwest (0437 764494)

Landshipping Quay   **158**   **4m SE of Haverfordwest**
View from minor road ½m S of Landshipping at SN009107. Also road and path south beside the shore.
Passage and winter waders, wildfowl and gulls.

Lawrenny Quay   **158**   **3½m NE of Pembroke**
View from minor road south of Lawrenny e.g. SM016063.
Passage and winter waders, gulls and wildfowl; woodland birds; migrants.

Cosheston Point   **158**   **2m N of Pembroke**
Park in Cosheston, SN003036, ½m N of A477. Then track and footpath west to the point.
Passage and winter waders, gulls and wildfowl.

Pembroke River   *158*   *SM946027*   *1m SW of Pembroke Dock*
Passage and winter waders, wildfowl and gulls.

Pembroke Docks   *158*   *SM962038*   *2½m NW of Pembroke*
Winter gulls and divers.

Hakin Point   *158*   *SN033043*   *3m NE of Pembroke*
Passage and winter waders; woodland birds.

TIC	*Drill Hall, Pembroke (0646 682148)
YH	Manorbier, Tenby (0834 871803)
R	The Cresselly Arms, Cresswell Quay
RF	Cosheston Brewery, Cosheston, nr Pembroke
	Ferry Inn, Pembroke Ferry

Angle Bay   157   6m W of Pembroke
Park in Angle at end of B4320 at SM866028 and take the Pembrokeshire Coast Path east or north.
Passage and winter waders; winter wildfowl, divers and gulls.

Elegug Stacks   158   6m SW of Pembroke
Park at end of minor road 2m S of B4319 at SR926945 and take coast path east. *NB access only when red flag is not flying.*
Summer seabird colonies.

St. Govan's Head   158   5½m S of Pembroke
Car-park at end of minor road 2½m S of B4319 and 1½m S of Bosherston at SR967930. Then track east to the point.
Seawatching; migrants.

Bosherston Fish Ponds & Broad Haven   158   4½m S of Pembroke
Park by Bosherston church 1½m S of B4319 at SR966947 and take paths east around ponds and SE to Broad Haven. Also car-park at Broad Haven, SR977937.
Passage and winter wildfowl and waders; summer warblers; reedbed species; migrants.

Barafundle Bay & Stackpole Head   158   1½m E of Bosherston
Take coastal path east from Broad Haven or park in Stackpole Quay, ¾m SE of Stackpole at SR993957 and take the coastal path south.
Summer seabird colonies; seawatching; migrants; winter seaduck and divers.

TIC	As previous entry.
YH	As previous entry.
RF	The St. Govan's, Bosherston
BBE	Gupton Farm, Castlemartin, nr Pembroke (064681 268)
SC	(Stackpole Estate Cottages) National Trust, Kings Head, Bridge Street, Llandeilo (0558 823911)

Saundersfoot Bay & Monkstone Point   158   2–3m N of Tenby
Park ¼m E of B4316 just south of Saundersfoot Harbour at SS137044 and take coast path south to the point. Also view bay from Coppet Hall Point ¾m NE of Harbour, car-parking at SS139054.
Seaduck and winter divers; passage waders and gulls; migrants.

Pendine – Telpyn Point   158   3–5m NE of Saundersfoot
Park near the church by B4314 ¾m N of its junction with A4066 at the top of the hill at SN228087. Then track and path south down valley to Ragwen Point, then coast path west across Marros Sands to Telpyn Point.
Winter seaduck and divers; migrants; passage and winter waders.

East Marsh & Ginst Point   159   4½ m S of St. Clears
Park at end of minor road 1m S of A4066 at SN289079 and take track east beside the marsh and on to Ginst Point *if ammunition testing not in progress.*
Passage and winter waders; winter seaduck and divers; migrants.

Laugharne & Sir John's Hill   159   4m SE of St. Clears
Park in Laugharne, by A4066, at SN302107 and take track and path south beside the Taf Estuary and around the southern side of the hill.
Passage and winter waders; migrants.

TIC	*The Croft, Tenby (0834 2402)
	*The Harbour, Saundersfoot (0834 811411)
YH	The Old School, Pentlepoir, Saundersfoot (0834 812333)
R	New Three Mariners, Laugharne
RF	New Inn, Amroth, nr Saundersfoot
BBE	Brook House Farm, Pendine Road, Laugharne (099421 239)

Ferryside   159   3m NW of Kidwelly
Park near the railway station at SN366104 and view the Afon Twyi from west side of the railway line nearby, and from the minor road to the south.
Passage and winter waders; winter divers, grebes and seaduck.

Kidwelly Quay   159   1m SW of Kidwelly
Park and view from the end of minor road 1m SW of A484 from Kidwelly at SN397064. Also take path south.
Passage and winter waders and wildfowl.

Burry Port Power Station   159   ½ m S of Burry Port
Park at the sea front by the power station ½m S of B4311 at SN448002. View from here and walk east to the point.
Passage and winter waders; winter seaduck, divers and gulls.

Machynys & Penrhyn Gwyn   159   2m S of Llanelli centre
Park down track ½m SW of Morfa at SS509979 and walk SW to the point and along dyke beside the marsh to Tir Morfa and Morfa-Bacas (SS544978).
Passage and winter waders and wildfowl; migrants.

Pembrey Burrows   159   SS408995   1½m S of Pembrey
Passage and winter waders; winter seaduck, divers and raptors.

Pembrey Creek   159   SS437999   1m SE of Pembrey
Passage and winter waders.

Pwll   159   SN485006   2½m E of Burry Port
Passage and winter waders, wildfowl and gulls.

Salmon Point Scar   159   SN360075   3m W of Kidwelly
Passage and winter waders and wildfowl; winter seaduck and divers.

Lliedi Reservoirs   159   SN515043   3m N of Llanelli
Winter wildfowl.

Old Castle Pond   159   SN500004   1m W of Llanelli centre
Winter wildfowl.

Morfa-Bacas & Penclacwydd   159   SN535978   2m SE of Llanelli
Passage and winter waders and wildfowl; migrants.

TIC	*Lammas Street, Carmarthen (0267 231557)
	Pont Abraham Services, Junction 49 M4, nr Cross Hands (0792 883838)
YH	The Old School, Pentlepoir, Saundersfoot (0834 812333)
	The Old Lifeboat House, Port Eynon, Swansea (0792 390706)
RF	Farriers Arms, Cwmbach, nr Llanelli
BBE	Pen-y-bac Farm, Mynyddgarreg, Kidwelly (0554 891200)

Dryslwyn Water Meadows   159   **4m SW of Llandeilo**
Park by B4297, 1m N of its junction with B4300 at SN553204 and view the valley eastwards from the Old Castle hill. Also view meadows from B4300 to the SE e.g. from SN570196.
Winter wildfowl, especially White-fronted Geese, and Golden Plover.

Dynevor Castle Woods & Lakes   159   **1m SW of Llandeilo centre**
Car-park by A40 ¼m W of its junction with A483, by ambulance station at SN626226. Then follow marked footpath southwest through parkland and woods to the castle remains and lakes.
Woodland birds including Pied Flycatcher, Redstart, Wood Warbler and Lesser Spotted Woodpecker; winter wildfowl.

Carreg Cennen Woods   159   **3m SE of Llandeilo**
Car-park by minor road 3m E of A483, 1m E of Trapp at SN666194. Then footpaths south and east.
Woodland birds and summer warblers including Pied Flycatcher, Wood Warbler, Redstart.

Black Mountain   160   7m SE of Llandeilo
Car-park by A4069 3m N of Brynamman at SN734187 and walk line of hills east or west.
Hill and upland birds including Peregrine, Raven, Golden Plover and Merlin.

Talley Lakes   146   6m N of Llandeilo
View from minor road above western shore west off B4302 at Talley e.g. at SN627335. Open access around the southern lake. Winter wildfowl; summer warblers and woodland birds.

Brechfa Forest   146   7m NW of Llandeilo
Car-park by minor road, 1½m N of B4310 from Brechfa, at SN522323 and tracks through forest. Also other minor roads through forest to the east.
Woodland birds including Crossbill, Goshawk and Long-eared Owl.

TIC	As previous entry.
	*Broad Street, Llandovery (0550 20693)
YH	The Old Red Lion, Llandeu, Llangadog (05504 679/634)
RF	Cennen Arms, Trapp, nr Llandeilo
RFBBE	Forest Arms, Brechfa
	Red Lion, Llandybie, nr Ammanford (0269 851202)
BBE	Ty Isaf, Trapp, nr Llandeilo (0558 823099)

Glamorgan

Salthouse Point   159   4m SW of Gorseinon
Park and view from end of track, ½m W of B4295, ½m NW of
Crofty, at SS524957.
Passage and winter waders and wildfowl; gulls; winter seaduck
and divers.

**Whiteford Burrows & Berges Island   159   4m NW of
Llanrhidian**
Park in Cwm Ivy, ½m NW of Llanmadoc at SS438936, and take
track and marked paths north across the burrows to Whiteford
Point.
Passage and winter waders and wildfowl; winter seaduck, divers
and grebes, raptors and gull roost; passage terns; migrants.

Worms Head   159   SW corner of Gower Peninsula
Car-park in Rhossili at western end of B4247, 3m W of A4118, at
SS416879. Then coastal path to the point.
Migrants; winter seaduck and divers; summer seabirds;
seawatching.

Oxwich   159   3m S of Llanrhidian
Car-park and reserve information centre 1½m S of A4118 at the
southern end of the bay at SS503864. Then marked trails north
around the marsh and south to Oxwich Wood and Point.
Summer warblers including Reed and Cettis; Bearded Tit; other
reedbed species; passage and winter wildfowl; passage raptors,
waders and terns; woodland birds; migrants; seawatching.

Blackpill   159   3m SW of Swansea centre
Park and view from car-park by A4067 at the seaward end of the
Clyne Valley at SS619906.
Large winter gull roost including regular Ring-billed, Mediter-
ranean and northern gulls; passage and winter waders; passage
terns and gulls; winter seaduck and divers.

Burry Holms   *159*   *SS403926*   *2m NW of Llangennith*
Winter seaduck and divers; seawatching; passage waders;
migrants.

Mewslade Bay–Overton Cliff   *159*   *SS420870–460847*
3m S & SE of Llangennith
Summer seabirds; migrants.

Port-Eynon Point   *159*   *SS467845*   *¾m S of Port Eynon*
Seawatching; migrants.

Broad Pool   *159*   *SS510910*   *1m SE of Llanrhidian*
Passage waders and wildfowl; heathland birds.

Nicholaston Woods & Burrows   *159*   *SS515880*   *3m̃ SE*
of Llanrhidian
Woodland birds; passage and winter waders and gulls;
migrants.

Park Woods   *159*   *SS534903*   *2m NW of Southgate*
Woodland birds.

Ilston Cwm   *159*   *SS555896*   *1½m N of Southgate*
Woodland and river birds.

Penard Pill   *159*   *SS539880*   *1m W of Southgate*
Passage and winter waders, wildfowl and gulls.

Pwlldu Valley   *159*   *SS575873*   *1½m E of Southgate*
Woodland and river birds; migrants.

Bishop's Wood   *159*   *SS594880*   *2½m E of Southgate*
Migrants; woodland birds.

Gelli-hir Woods & Fairwood Common   *159*   *SS567924*
1½m S of Three Crosses
Woodland and heathland birds; passage and winter raptors.

Mumbles Head   *159*   *SS630874*   *4m SW of Swansea centre*
Seawatching; migrants; winter seaduck, divers and gulls.

Llanrhidian Common Wood   *159*   *SS508926*   *1m NE of*
Llanrhidian
Woodland birds; migrants.

TIC   Singleton Street, Swansea, West Glam (0792 468321)
*Oystermouth Square, Mumbles, Swansea (0792 361302)
YH   The Old Lifeboat House, Port Eynon, Swansea (0792
390706)

RF	Joiners Arms, Bishopston
	Greyhound, Oldwalls, nr Llanrhidian
BBE	Broad Park Guest House, Rhosili, Gower (0792 390515)
SC	(Burrows Cottage, Llanmadoc) National Trust, Kings Head, Bridge Street, Llandeilo, Dyfed (0558 823911)

Baglan Bay & Neath Estuary   170   3m SW of Neath
Park and view from track south off A483, 1½m SW of its junction with A48, at SS724929.
Passage and winter waders.

Cwm Clydach   159   3m N of Clydach
Car-park by minor road from Clydach to Ammanford at SN682053. Then marked trail and footpaths west and south through woods and beside River Clydach.
Woodland and river birds including Dipper, Pied Flycatcher, Redstart and Wood Warbler.

> *Lliw Reservoirs 159 SN655037 & SN663065 3–4m NW of Clydach*
> *Passage and winter wildfowl.*

> *Crymlyn Bog 170 SS700960 3m E of Neath*
> *Reedbed species; passage and winter wildfowl.*

> *Pant-y-Sais & Tennant Canal 170 SS713940 3m SW of Neath*
> *Summer warblers; reedbed species.*

> *Craig Gwladus 170 SS765994 2m N of Neath*
> *Woodland birds.*

TIC	*Aberdulais Basin, Aberdulais, nr Neath, W Glam (0639 633531)
	*Beefeater Restaurant, Sunnycroft road, Baglan, W Glam (0639 823049)
YH	Glyncornel, Llwynypia, M Glam (0443 430859)
RFBBE	Wernoleu Hotel, Pontamen Road, Ammanford (0269 2598)
BBE	Trehaven, Penlan Road, Rhyd-y-Fro, Pontardawe, Swansea (0792 830174)
	Bryn Haul Farm, Rhiwfawr, Swansea Valley (0639 830259)

Kenfig Pool & Sker Point   170   3m NW of Porthcawl
Car-park and reserve centre by minor road at Kenfig 2m W of
junction 37 of M4 at SS802812. Then tracks around the Pool and to
hides and across the dunes to Kenfig sands and Sker Point.
Passage and winter waders, wildfowl, grebes and divers; summer
warblers; reedbed species; passage terns and gulls; migrants;
seawatching.

> ### Eglwys Nunydd Reservoir   170   SS794857   2m N of
> Kenfig
> Winter wildfowl; passage terns and gulls.

> ### Margam Abbey & Craig Fawr   170   SS803865   3m N of
> Kenfig
> Woodland birds and summer warblers.

TIC   *The Old Police Station, John Street, Porthcawl, M Glam
        (065671 6639)
        Sarn Park Services, Junction 36 M4, nr Bridgend, M
        Glam (0656 654906)
YH   As previous entry.
RF   The Prince of Wales, Kenfig
BBE   Ty'n y Caeau, Margam Village, nr Port Talbot (0639
        883897)

Ogmore Estuary   170   4m SW of Bridgend
Car-parks ¼m W of B4524 by the sea front in Ogmore at SS863754
and by river 1m NE of Ogmore at SS874763.
Passage and winter waders; passage terns and gulls; winter
seaduck and divers.

Nash Point & Cwm Nash   170   4m W of Llantwit Major
Car-park at end of minor road 1m SW of Marcross at SS917683.
Then coastal path north to Cwm Nash and up the wooded valleys.
Migrants; passage waders; seawatching.

East Aberthaw   170   4m SE of Llantwit Major
Park in East Aberthaw ¾m S of B4265 at ST035666. Then track and
footpath west under the railway and south beside the pools.
Passage and winter waders; wildfowl and gulls.

Limpert Bay & Summerhouse Point   170   3m SE of
Llantwit Major
Park at the end of minor road 1m S of B4265 south of West
Aberthaw at ST019664. Then coastal path west to Summerhouse
Point and SE to Breaksea Point.
Passage waders, gulls and wildfowl; migrants.

Llantwit Major Beach *170   SS956675   1m SW of*
Llantwit Major
Passage and winter waders.

Porthkerry Country Park *170 & 171   ST090670   1m W*
of Barry
Woodland birds; migrants.

Little Island *171   ST111666   S side of Barry*
Passage and winter waders, gulls and wildfowl.

TIC	*The Promenade, Barry Island, S Glam (0446 747171)
	Sarn Park Services, Junction 36 M4, nr Bridgend, M Glam (0656 654906)
YH	As previous entry.
	1 Wedal Road, Roath Park, Cardiff (0222 462303)
RF	The Pelican, Ogmore
	Green Dragon, Llancadle, nr St. Athan
BBE	Downs Farmhouse, Wick Road, Llantwit Major (04465 4252)
	21 West Farm Road, Brigadon Hill, Ogmore by Sea (0656 880183)

Lavernock Point   171   2½m S of Penarth
Car-park at end of minor road ¾m SE of B4267 at ST186683. Then coastal paths north and southwest.
Migrants; seawatching.

Cosmeston Lakes   171   2m SW of Penarth centre
Car-park just off B4267, 1m NW of Lavernock Point, at ST179694. Then tracks and paths around the lakes and woods.
Winter wildfowl; summer warblers; woodland birds; migrants.

Flat Holm   171   island 4m SE of Penarth
Permits required for landing. Access details from Flat Holm Project Manager, Harbour Road, Barry, S Glam.
Migrants.

Coed-y-Bedw   171   2m N of Radyr
Park by minor road ½m NW of A470 and B4262 at ST116827. Then footpaths through the woods.
Woodland birds including Pied Flycatcher, Redstart and Wood Warbler.

Rumney Estuary   171   2m NE of Cardiff centre
View from minor road along the west and south side east of Pengam, ½m-1m SE of A4161 e.g. ST215775, ST220770. Also from sea wall along north shore and from Rumney Great Wharf, e.g. ST223777 and eastwards.
Passage and winter waders and wildfowl; winter seaduck; gulls.

Penarth Flats   171   ST185733   1m N of Penarth centre
Passage and winter waders and gulls.

Roath Park Lake   171   ST185795   2m N of Cardiff centre
Winter gulls and wildfowl.

Lisvan & Llanishen Reservoirs   171   ST186820   3½m N
of Cardiff centre
Winter wildfowl.

TIC	8–14 Bridge Stre, Cardiff, S Glam (0222 227281)
	*The Promenade, Barry Island, S Glam (0446 747171)
YH	1 Wedal Road, Roath Park, Cardiff (0222 462303)
RF	Captain's Wife, Swanbridge, Sully, nr Penarth

Llwyn-on Reservoir   160   4½m NW of Merthyr Tydfil
View from car-parks by A470 along the eastern shore e.g.
SO013117, or at the northern end 1m north.
Winter wildfowl.

Taf Fechan   160   2½m N of Merthyr centre
Park by minor road 1¼m NW of A465 on the northern side of the
river at SO044097. Then footpaths beside the river and through
woods.
Woodland and river birds including Pied Flycatcher, Wood
Warbler and Dipper.

Craig-y-Llyn   170   4m NW of Treherbert
Park by A4061 3½m N of Treherbert at SN923030 and take track
and footpaths westward.
Woodland and upland birds including Ring Ousel, Peregrine and
Raven.

Penmoelallt Forest   160   SO005100   3m NW of Merthyr
Tydfil
Woodland birds.

TIC	14a Glebeland Street, Merthyr Tydfil, M Glam (0685 79884)
YH	Tai'r Heol, Ystradfellte, Aberdare, M Glam (0639 720301)
	Llwyn-y-Celyn, Libanus, Brecon, Powys (0874 4261)
RF	Old White Horse, Pontneddfechan
SC	Granary Cottages, Ystraggynwyn, Torpantau, Merthyr Tydfil (0685 83358)

Gwent

Peterstone Wentlooge   171   **5m NE of Cardiff centre**
Park 1m NE of Peterstone Wentlooge by B4239 at ST273810. Then track south to the sea wall and coast path west toward Peterstone Great Wharf.
Passage and winter waders; winter seaduck and gulls; passage terns.

St. Bride's Wentlooge   171   **4½m SW of Newport centre**
Park at end of minor road ½m S of B439 at ST300816. Then coast path NE or SW.
Passage and winter waders and wildfowl; winter seaduck and gulls; passage terns; migrants.

> *Sluice Farm & Rumney Great Wharf*   171   *ST256790*
> *4m NE of Cardiff*
> *Birds as Peterstone Wentlooge.*

TIC   8–14 Bridge Street, Cardiff (0222 227281)
Newport Museum & Art Gallery, John Frost Square, Newport (0633 842962)
YH   1 Wedal Road, Roath Park, Cardiff (0222 462303)
RF   Church House Inn, St. Brides Wentlooge
BB   Chapel Guest House, Church Road, St. Brides Wentlooge (0633 681018)

Llandegfedd Reservoir   171   **2m E of Pontypool**
Car-park at southern end 1½m E of A4042 at ST328985. Also view from minor road along west side and at end of minor road 1½m S of A472 at the northern end, SO333006.
Winter wildfowl and gull roost; passage waders and terns.

> *Five Locks Canal*   171   *ST287968*   *N end of Cwmbran,*
> *¾m W of A4051*
> *River and woodland birds including Kingfisher.*

Sor Brook 171 ST332966 1½m S of Llandegfedd
Reservoir
River and woodland birds.

Priory Wood 161 SO354056 4m NE of Pontypool
Woodland birds including Pied Flycatcher, Redstart and
Hawfinch.

Llanvihangel Gobion 161 SO348089 6m NE of Pon-
typool
River birds; winter wildfowl; passage waders.

TIC Newport Museum & Art Gallery, John Frost Square, Newport (0633 842962)
YH Glyncornel, Llwynypia, Mid Glamorgan (0443 430859)
RF Beaufort Arms, Monkswood
BBESC Pentwyn Farm, Little Mill, nr Pontypool (049528 249)

Gold Cliff **171** **5m SE of Newport centre**
Park by minor road through Goldcliff at ST367831. Then footpath SW on the western side of the creek or SE to Gold Cliff point and coastal path eastward. Or park at Gold Cliff Point itself, at southern end of minor road by the sea wall at ST374822, and coastal path west.
Passage and winter waders; migrants; seawatching.

Porton Grounds **171** **2½m S of Magor**
Park at end of minor road ½m S of Redwick at ST416834. Then coastal path east or west.
Passage and winter waders and wildfowl.

Magor & Cold Harbour Pills **171** **2½m SE of Junction 23 of M4**
Park by Magor Pill Farm at ST433857, 1m S of B4245. Then track and footpaths south to the shore.
Passage and winter wildfowl, gulls and waders.

Magor Fen **171** **¼m S of Magor**
Park in Magor ¼m S of B4245 near the church at ST425868. Then footpath south across Whitewall Common to the reserve and hide. Also from minor road along the east side of the common at ST428866 and paths west.
Passage and winter wildfowl; summer warblers; reedbed species.

Wentwood Reservoir & Forest **171** **4m N of Magor**
Car-park at northern end of reservoir 2m N of A48 at ST428938. Then many tracks and marked trails through the woodland.
Passage and winter wildfowl; woodland birds including Redstart, Wood Warbler, Crossbill, Nightjar and Hawfinch.

Usk Valley Walk 171 ST390933 4½m NW of Magor
Woodland birds.

Nedern Brook 171 ST485895 1m NE of Caldicot
Winter wildfowl; migrants.

TIC As previous entry.
YH Mountain Road, Chepstow, Gwent (0291 622685)
RFBB Hanbury Arms, High Street, Uskside, Caerleon (0633 420340)

Sugar Loaf 161 3m NW of Abergavenny
Car-park by minor road 1m N of A40 at SO268166. Then paths east and north.
Woodland and hill birds including Pied Flycatcher and Raven; migrants.

Blorenge 161 3m SW of Abergavenny
Park by B4246 at Pen-ffordd-goch Pond 1½m N of Blaenavon and take footpath NE up onto the hill.
Passage wildfowl; moorland and hill birds including Red Grouse.

Ysgyryd Fawr 161 3m NE of Abergavenny
Car-park by B4521 1½m W of A65 at SO328164. Then footpaths north through woods and up onto hill.
Woodland, hill and scrub species including Stonechat, Whinchat and Redstart; summer warblers.

Vale of Ewyas 161 8m N of Abergavenny
Park in Llanthony, about halfway up the valley 6m NW of A465, at SO287276. Then footpaths west or east up onto moorland.
River, woodland and upland birds including Dipper, Red Grouse, Peregrine and Redstart.

Cwm Clydach 161 SO210124 2m E of Brynmawr
Woodland and river birds.

Strawberry Cottage Wood 161 SO315214 4m N of
Abergavenny
Woodland and river birds.

TIC *Swan Meadow, Cross Street, Abergavenny (0873 77588)
YH Capel-y-Ffin, Abergavenny (0873 890650)
RFBBE Rock & Fountain, Old Rock Road, Clydach
Old Pandy Inn, Pandy (0873 890208)
BBE The Wenallt, Gilwern (0873 830694)
Little Treadam, Llantilio Crossenny, Abergavenny (060085 326)
SC Troedrhiwmwn c/o Cwmbuchill, Llanthony, Abergavenny (0873 890619)

Wynd Cliff & Wye Valley Walk   162   2½ m N of Chepstow
Car-park by A466 ¾m NE of St. Arvans at ST526973. Then foot-path south through woods and beside River Wye and nature trail to Wynd Cliff.
Woodland and river birds including Pied Flycatcher, Redstart and Kingfisher.

> **Great Barnet's Wood**   162   ST513944   1½m NW of Chepstow centre
> Woodland birds.

> **Chepstow Park Wood**   162   ST502984   3m NW of Chepstow
> Woodland birds including Nightjar and Redstart.

> **Beacon Hill & Trelleck Common**   162   SO510053   7m N of Chepstow
> Woodland birds including Nightjar, Crossbill and Turtle Dove.

TIC	*The Gatehouse, High Street, Chepstow (02912 3772)
YH	Mounton Road, Chepstow (0291 622685)
RF	Carpenter's Arms, Shirenewton
BBE	Parva Farmhouse, Tintern, nr Chepstow (02918 411)
SC	Tor y Mynydd Farm, Devanden, nr Chepstow (0600 860417)

Gwynedd

Bardsey Island   **123**   **island 4m SW of Aberdaron**
Access by boat from Pwllheli or Porth Meudwy. Bookings for Sat–
Sat stay at the observatory or farmhouses. Details from Bardsey
Island Trust Secretary, 38 Walthew Avenue, Holyhead. tel: 0407
2633
Migrants; summer seabirds including Manx Shearwater.

Porth Meudwy & Pen-y-Cil   **123**   **1–2m SW of Aberdaron**
Park by minor road 1m SW of Aberdaron, near Cwrt, SH160262.
Then track south down the valley and along the coast to Pen-y-Cil.
Migrants; summer seabirds; Chough.

Aberdaron Bay   **123**   **W end of B4413**
Park in Aberdaron, SH173264, and take coastal paths southwest to
Porth Meudwy, SH164256, and small valley to the west.
Winter seaduck, divers and gulls; migrants.

Porth Dinllaen   **123**   **7m NW of Pwllheli**
Car-park ¼m N of B4417 on the western side of Morfa Nefyn at
SH282406. Then track and path NW by the golf course and to the
northern end of the promontory.
Seawatching; winter seaducks and divers; migrants; Chough;
passage and winter waders.

Morfa Gors, Abersoch   **123**   **½m S of Abersoch**
Car-park near the shore on south side of Abersoch, ½m S of town
centre at SH314276. Then take track south.
Migrants; passage waders; winter seaduck and divers.

> *Trwyn Cilan*   *123*   *SH295232*   *3m SW of Abersoch*
> *Migrants; summer seabirds; Chough; seawatching.*

> *Pwllheli Harbour*   *123*   *SH380345*   *SE side of Pwllheli*
> *Winter gulls; passage waders.*

Morfa Abersoch   123   SH415357   2m NE of Pwllheli
Passage waders; winter seaduck and raptors; migrants.

Braich y Pwll   123   SH136258   2m W of Aberdaron
Seawatching; summer seabirds; heathland birds; migrants.

Penrhyn Glas   123   SH336439   6m NW of Pwllheli
Summer seabirds; Chough; migrants.

Trefor Pier   123   SH376475   8m N of Pwllheli
Seawatching; winter seaduck.

Afon Hen   123 or 115   SH410484   2m NE of Trefor
Woodland birds including Pied Flycatcher and Redstart.

TIC   *Village Hall, Abersoch (075 881 2929)
*Y Maes, Pwllheli (075 861 3000)
High Street, Porthmadog (0766 512981)
YH   Snowdon Ranger, Ryhd Ddu, Caernarfon (028 685 391)
Pen-y-Garth, Harlech (0766 780285)
RF   Ty Coch, Porth Dinllaen
Bryncynan, Morfa Nefyn
St. Tudwal's Hotel, Abersoch
Glyn-y-Weddw Arms, Llanbedrog
Tu Hwnt I'r Afon, Rhydyclafdy, nr Pwllheli
BBE   Carreg Plas Guest House, Aberdaron (0758 86308)
Bronhuelog Hotel, Lon Garmon, Abersoch (0758 812177)
Old Rectory Hotel, Boduan, nr Nefyn (0758 720923/721363)
SC   Bay View, Aberdaron (0758 86214)
Ty'n Morfa Farm, Llanengen, nr Abersoch (0758 812240)
Tan-y-Ffordd, Mynytho, nr Pwllheli
(Bwthyn yr Ardd) National Trust, North Wales Holiday cottages, Station Road, Deganwy, Conwy (0492 82492)
Bardsey Bird Observatory (hostel & houses); see Bardsey Island.

Foryd Bay   115   **3m SW of Caernarfon**
View from minor road along the east side, 2m W of A487, e.g. SH454596 and SH454588. Also footpath along the west bank. Passage and winter waders and wildfowl.

Llyn Padarn Country Park   115   ¾m E of Llanberis
Car-park ½m E of A4086 at SH586602. Then tracks and paths north through the woods and south to the quarries.
Woodland birds including Pied Flycatcher and Redstart; Chough and Peregrine.

Nantgwynant   115   3m NE of Beddgelert
Car-park just north of Bethania and A498 at SH627507. Then tracks through the woods and beside the river.
Woodland and river birds.

Pass of Aberglaslyn   115   1½m S of Beddgelert
Car-park just east of the bridge by A4085 at SH595463. Then tracks north beside the river and over the hills.
River, woodland and moorland birds.

> *Llyn-y-gader & Beddgelert Forest   115   SH570520   2m NW of Beddgelert*
> *Woodland birds; winter wildfowl.*

TIC	Oriel Pendeitsh, Caernarfon (0286 672232)
YH	Llwyn Celyn, Llanberis, Caernarfon (0286 870280)
RF	Newborough Arms, Bontnewydd
	Bull Inn, Deiniolen, nr Bethesda
	Cwellyn Arms, Rhydd-Ddu, nr Beddgelert
RFBBE	Goat, Llanwnda (0286 830256)
BBE	Sygun Fawr Country House, Beddgelert (0766 86258)
	Pengwern Farm, Saron, Llanwnda, nr Caernarfon (0286 830717)
	Bryn Eisteddfod Hotel, Clynnog Fawr, nr Caernarfon (0286 86431)
SC	Fort Belan, Llanwnda (0473 348982)
	Old Bakery, Rhostryfan, nr Caernarfon (0286 830881)
	Bryn Beddau, Bontnewydd, nr Caernarfon (0286 830117)

Port Penrhyn & Bangor Flats   115   1m NE of Bangor centre
Car-park at south end of the harbour, ¼m E of A5 at Abercegin, SH593725. Then short walk north to view the flats.
Passage and winter waders, wildfowl and grebes; gulls; migrants.

Aberogwen   115   2m E of Bangor
Car-park by the shore at end of minor road 1m N of A55 at SH615724, and coast paths east and west.
Passage and winter waders and wildfowl; woodland birds; migrants.

Coedydd Aber & The Carneddau   115   2–4m S of Llanfair-fechan
Car-park by the bridge on minor road ¾m SE of Aber (on A55) at SH663720. Then tracks and paths south through the woods and up to Aber Falls and the high ground around Bera Bach, SH673677.
Woodland, river and upland birds including Ring Ousel, Merlin, Dipper and spring Dotterel.

Llanfairfechan   115   6m NE of Bangor
View from car-park by the front in the village, just north of the
railway line at SH678754, and coast path southwest.
Winter seaduck, divers and grebes including regular Surf Scoter;
passage and winter waders and raptors; winter Snow Bunting and
Twite; migrants.

> *Conwy Morfa   115   SH770790   1½m NW of Conwy*
> *Winter seaduck, waders, raptors and gulls.*

> *Caerhun Roman Fort   115   SH776704   4½m S of Conwy*
> *Woodland birds including Hawfinch.*

TIC   *Theatr Gwynedd, Deiniol Road, Bangor (0248 352786)
        *Conwy Castle Visitor Centre, Conwy (0492 592248)
        Chapel Street, Llandudno (0492 76413)
YH   Tan y Bryn, Bangor (0248 353516)
        Penmaenbach, Penmaenmawr (0492 623476)
        Rhiw Farm, Rowen, Conwy (0492 531406)
RF   George & Dragon, Conwy
        Union Hotel, Bangor
BBE   Rainbow Court, Pentir, nr Bangor (0248 353099)
BBESC The Towers, Promenade, Llanfairfechan (0248 680012)
SC   Capel Ogwen, Penrhyn Park, nr Bangor (0248
        351055/362254)
        Norbrit, Fernbrook Road, Penmaenmawr (0492 622248)

Great Orme   115   1m N of Llandudno
Several car-parks on the head e.g. at the northern end near the
lighthouse at SH754842, then many paths and tracks.
Migrants; summer seabirds; winter seaduck, divers, grebes and
Snow Bunting; passage and winter waders; seawatching.

Little Orme   116   2m E of Llandudno
Park by A546 at the eastern end of Llandudno Bay, SH807823.
Then footpaths north across the headland.
Migrants; summer seabird colonies; seawatching.

Conwy Estuary   116   1½m SE of Conwy
Park and view from A470 ½m-1m S of Llandudno Junction e.g.
SH804767 and SH801756.
Passage and winter waders and wildfowl.

> *Tal-y-cafn Bridge   115   SH786718   3½m S of Conwy*
> *Passage and winter waders and wildfowl.*

TIC   As previous entry.
YH   As previous entry.
        Foxhill, Nant-y-Glyn, Colwyn Bay (0492 530627)

RF   Queens Head, Glanwydden, nr Llandudno
          Farmer's Arms, Deganwy, nr Llandudno
BBE   Glenvine Guest Hosue, 45 Church walks, Llandudno
          (0492 75850)
          Bryn-y-Bia   Lodge,   Craigside,   Llandudno   (0492
          49644/40459)

Coed Hafod   116   1½m NE of Betws-y-coed
Park by A470 1½m N of its junction with A5, just north of Drapers Field Centre at SH805576. Then signed footpaths through the woods.
Woodland birds including Pied Flycatcher, Redstart and Wood Warbler.

Bryn-y-fawnog   115   2m NW of Betws-y-coed
Car-park by minor road 1½m N of A5 at SH778592. Then nature trail and tracks west through the forest.
Woodland birds including Crossbill and Goshawk.

Llyn-y-Parc Woods   115   1m N of Betws-y-coed
Car-park north of the bridge at junction of A5 and B5106 in Betws at SH791568. Then marked trails north through the forest to the lake or west by the river.
Woodland birds including Goshawk; river birds including Dipper and Grey Wagtail.

Llyn Elsi & Gwydyr Forest   115   1m SW of Betws-y-coed
Park just south off A55 ¾m W of Betws at SH781566 and take footpath and tracks south and west through the woods and to the lake, or to the moorland to the west.
Woodland birds including Black Grouse and crossbill; winter wildfowl.

Llyn Idwal & Devil's Kitchen   115   4½m SE of Bethesda
Car-park just off A5 at Pen-y-benglog, SH648604, then track south.
Upland birds including Ring Ousel, Raven and Peregrine.

TIC   *Royal Oak Stables, Betws-y-coed (06902 426/665)
YH   Plas Curig, Capel Curig, Betws-y-coed (06904 225)
          Lledr House, Pont-y-Pant, Dolwyddelan (06906 202)
RF   Pont-y-Pair Hotel, Betws-y-coed
          Waterloo Arms, Betws-y-coed
RFBBE Ty Gwyn, Betws-y-coed (06902 383)
          White Horse, Capel Garman
BBE   Church Hill Hotel, Vicarage Road, Betws-y-coed (06902
          447)
          Fairy Glen Hotel, Dolwyddelan Road, Betws-y-coed
          (06902 269)

SC Rhyd-y-Creua Farm, Betws-y-coed (06902 343)
   Dolwen, Glasgwm Road, Penmachno, nr Betws-y-coed
   (06903 417)
   (Betws-y-coed cottages) National Trust, North Wales
   Holiday Cottages, Station Road, Deganwy, Conwy (0492
   82492)

Bala Lake (Llyn Tegid) 125 SW of Bala
Car-parks at northern end between A494 and B4403 e.g. just off
A494 at SH924356 and at the southern end by B4403, 1½m NE of
Llanuwchllyn at SH893308.
Passage and winter wildfowl; winter gull roost.

Penllyn Forest 125 3m SE of Bala
Park by minor road 2½m SE of B4391, SH958324. Then tracks
beside the river and through the forest.
Woodland and river birds including Dipper, Crossbill, Goshawk
and Black Grouse.

Llyn Celyn 125 or 124 5m NW of Bala
Car-parks along the northern shore by A4212 and at the western
end at SH846404.
Passage and winter wildfowl.

TIC *High Street, Bala (0678 520367)
YH Plas Rhiwaedog, Rhos-y-Gwaliau, Bala (0678 520215)
RF White Lion Royal Hotel, Bala
   Olde Bulls Head, Bala
BBE Frondderw Hotel, Stryd-y-Fron, Bala (0678 520301)
   Bala Lake Hotel, Bala (0678 520344/520111)
SC Ceniarth, Llanuwchllyn, Bala (06784 686)
   Ty Capel, Llwyn Einion, Bala (0678 520572)

Llyn Trawsfynydd 124 4m S of Ffestiniog
Car-parks at southern end of the llyn by minor road 1m W of A470
at SH702348, and at the northern end ¼m W of A470 at SH695384
then nature trail westward.
Passage and winter gulls and wildfowl; passage waders; migrants.

Coed Llyn y Garnedd 124 4½m W of Ffestiniog
Car-park by A487 2m NW of Penrhyndeudraeth at SH635404.
Then path NE through the woods under the railway line and on to
Llyn Mair.
Woodland birds including Pied Flycatcher, Redstart and Wood
Warbler; winter wildfowl.

Afon-y-Glyn & Glastraeth   124   3m NE of Harlech
Park along track north of A496, ½m NW of Tygwyn station at
SH599358. Then track west along the shore and NE over bridge
and along the dyke by Glastraeth.
Passage and winter waders, wildfowl and raptors; migrants.

Shell Island & Morfa Dyffryn   124   3m SW of Harlech
Park at end of minor road 1m W of Llanbedr at SH568272. Then
tracks and paths southwest.
Passage and winter waders, wildfowl and raptors; migrants.

Porthmadog Cob   124   ½m SE of Porthmadog
Park and view from A487 by the tollgate at the eastern end of
causeway, SH585380.
Passage and winter waders and wildfowl.

Coed Cymerau   124   1½m NW of Ffestiniog
Car-park by A496 1½m N of junction with B4391 near Pengwern at
SH694434. Then footpaths north and south.
Woodland and river birds.

> ***Black Rock Sands***   *124   SH530372   2m SE of Criccieth*
> *Winter seaduck and divers.*

> ***Criccieth***   *124   SH512378   SE side of Criccieth*
> *Winter seaduck and divers.*

> ***Morfa Harlech***   *124   SH569316   1m W of Harlech*
> *Winter seaduck; migrants.*

> ***Coed Crafnant***   *124   SH617289   2½m SE of Harlech*
> *Woodland and river birds.*

> ***Cwm Bychan & Rhinog***   *124   SH645315 – SH657290*
> *4m E of Harlech*
> *Woodland and upland birds including Ring Ousel, Peregrine*
> *amd Red Grouse.*

> ***Portmeirion***   *124   SH586370   1½m SE of Porthmadog*
> *Woodland birds; migrants; passage and winter waders and*
> *wildfowl.*

TIC *High Street, Blaenau Ffestiniog (0766 830360)
High Street, Porthmadog (0766 512981)
YH Caerblaidd, Llan Ffestiniog, nr Blaenau Ffestiniog (0766
762765)
Pen-y-garth, Harlech (0766 780285)
RF Grapes, Maentwrog
Prince of Wales, Criccieth
White Lion, Trawsfynydd

RFBBE Victoria Inn, Llanbedr
BBE Pensarn Hall, Llanbedr (034123 236)
Gwrach Ynys House, Ynys, Talsarnau (0766 780742)
Henfaes Hotel, Porthmadog Road, Criccieth (0766 522396)
Old Mill Farmhouse, Fron Oleu Farm, Trawsfynydd (0766 87397)
SC Ger-yr-Allt, Llanystumdwy, Criccieth (0766 522132)
5 Bron-y-Graig, Harlech (0766 780614)
Y Fedw, Llanbedr (034123 408)

Coed y Brenin 124 **4m N of Dolgellau**
Car-park by A470 just north of the bridge over Afon Gamlan near Ganllwyd, SH727244. Then tracks east, west and beside the river. Woodland and river birds including Dipper, Pied Flycatcher, Crossbill, Goshawk and Black Grouse.

Cutiau Marsh 124 **2m NE of Barmouth**
Park and view from A496 by the mouth of Afon Dwynant at SH635173.
Passage and winter waders and wildfowl.

Mawddach Estuary 124 **4m W of Dolgellau**
Park by A493 at Penmaenpool, near the toll bridge at SH695185 and take 'Penmaenpool to Morfa Mawddach Walk' which runs along the shore southwestward.
Passage and winter waders; woodland birds.

Morfa Mawddach 124 **1m N of Fairbourne**
View from end of minor road north from Fairbourne, SH616148, and from footpath along the south side of the marsh.
Passage and winter waders and gulls; winter seaduck and divers; seawatching.

> ***Coed Garth Gell*** 124 *SH685200* *3½m NW of Dolgellau*
> *Woodland birds.*

> ***Torrent Walk*** 124 *SH755185* *2m E of Dolgellau*
> *Woodland and river birds.*

> ***Arthog Bog*** 124 *SH641148* *1m NE of Morfa Mawddach*
> *Wetland birds.*

TIC *The Old Library, Barmouth (0341 280787)
*The Bridge, Dolgellau (0341 422888)
YH Kings, Penmaenpool, Dolgellau (0341 422392)
RF George III, Penmaenpool
RFBBE Fairbourne Hotel, Fairbourne

BBE   Llwyndu Farmhouse, Llanaber, nr Barmouth (0341 280144)

SC   Rowen Farm, Talybont, nr Barmouth (03417 336) (Nantlas and Plas Cregennan Lodge) National Trust, North Wales Holiday Cottages, Station Road, Deganwy, Conwy (0492 82492)

Cadair Idris   124   **4m S of Dolgellau**
Park by B4405 ¼m SW of its junction with A487 at SH730114 and take path north through the woods and up Afon Cau to Llyn Cau. Woodland and upland birds including Ring Ousel and Peregrine.

Cwm Cadian   124   **2m S of Corris**
Car-park by A487 3½m N of Machynlleth at SH756055. Then many paths and tracks northwest.
Woodland birds including Pied Flycatcher, Crossbill and Goshawk.

Aber Dysynni & Broadwater   135   **2m NW of Tywyn**
Park at end of minor road 2m NW of Tywyn beside the railway line at SH567027. Then footpaths northwest to the point and SE along the southern side of Broadwater.
Passage and winter waders; winter seaduck, divers and gull roost; seawatching; migrants.

> ***Tal-y-Llyn***   *124*   *SH720100*   *5m S of Dolgellau*
> *Winter wildfowl.*

> ***Craig yr Aderyn***   *124*   *SH644066*   *5m NE of Tywyn*
> *Cormorant colony; Chough; Peregrine.*

> ***Aberdyfi***   *135*   *SN610957*   *3½m SE of Tywyn*
> *Passage and winter waders and wildfowl; seaduck and gulls.*

> ***Tarren Cwmffernol***   *135*   *SH655020*   *4m E of Tywyn*
> *Upland birds.*

TIC   *Craft Centre, Corris (065473 244)
        *High Street, Tywyn (0654 710070)
        *The Wharf, Aberdovey (0654 72321)

YH   Old School, Old Road, Corris, Machynlleth, Powys (065473 686)

RF   Slater's Arms, Corris
        Ty'n y Cornel, Tal-y-llyn

RFBBE   Braich Goch Hotel, Corris (065473 229)

BBE   Dulas Valley Hotel, Corris (065473 688)

SC   Llwyngwern Farm, nr Machynlleth (0654 2492)

Powys

Lake Vrynwy   125   9m SE of Bala
Many parking places by B4393 which runs around the lake e.g. at
southern end by the dam at SJ017192 for information centre and
nature trail, or by the northwest shore at SH965220 then tracks
through woods and up onto Bryn Mawr and Cefn Glas.
Woodland and upland birds including Crossbill, Firecrest,
Goshawk, Long-eared Owl, Short-eared Owl, Hen Harrier,
Redstart, Pied Flycatcher and Black Grouse; passage waders; river
birds.

> *Dyfnant Forest   125   SH994148   3m S of Lake Vrynwy*
> *Woodland birds including Crossbill, Goshawk and Black*
> *Grouse.*

> *Tanat Valley   125   SJ116245   4m NW of Llanfyllin*
> *River birds including Dipper and Kingfisher.*

> *Mynydd Waun Fawr   125   SJ015055   5m W of Llanfair*
> *Caereinon*
> *Upland birds.*

TIC	*High Street, Bala, Gwynedd (0678 520367)
YH	Plas Rhiwaedog, Rhos y Gwaliau, Bala (0678 520215)
RF	Cann Office Hotel, Llangadfan
RFBBE	Cain Valley Hotel, High Street, Llanfyllin (0691 84366)
	Lake Vrynwy Hotel, Llanwddyn (0691 73692)
BBE	Cyfie Farm, Llanfihangel-yng-Ngwynfa, Llanfyllin (0691 84451)
	Tynymaes Farm, Llanwddyn (0691 73216)
BBSC	Lluest Fach, Foel, Llangadfan (093888 351)
SC	Wales Cottage Holidays, The Bank, Newtown, Powys (0686 628200)

Vrynwy Confluence   126   8m NE of Welshpool
View from minor road from Crewgreen (on B4393) to Melverley or take footpath east or west on the southern side of the river from SJ329157, ¼m north of Crewgreen.
Winter wildfowl; passage waders; river birds.

> *Leighton Flats   126   SJ236065   1½m SE of Welshpool*
> *Winter wildfowl.*

> *Breidden Forest   126   SJ300140   6m NE of Welshpool*
> *Woodland birds.*

> *Tirymynach   126   SJ270128   4½m NE of Welshpool*
> *River birds; winter wildfowl.*

> *Gaer-fawr Hill   126   SJ224130   3m N of Welshpool*
> *Woodland birds; summer warblers.*

> *Llyn Du   125   SJ173128   5½m NW of Welshpool*
> *Passage waders and winter wildfowl.*

TIC   Vicarage Gardens Car-park, Welshpool (0938 552043)
YH   The Woodlands, Abbey Foregate, Shrewsbury (0743 60179)
            Bridges, Ratinghope, Shrewsbury (058 861 656)
RF   Horseshoe, Arddln
BBE   Tynllwyn Farm, Welshpool (0938 553175)
            Moat Farm, Welshpool (0938 553179)
            Royal Oak Hotel, The Cross, Welshpool (0938 552217)
BBESC   Gungrog House Farm, Rhallt, nr Welshpool (0938 553381)
SC   As previous entry.

Llyn Clywedog   136   4m NW of Llanidloes
View from B4518 along the eastern side e.g. SN922883, or from minor road on the western shore at SN887893. Also nature trail beside the lake and through woods from SN905874.
Passage and winter wildfowl.

Uwch-y-coed   136   9m NW of Llanidloes
Park along track which runs SW from minor road to Glaslyn west of B4518 at SN835950 and continue SW beside lakes and over moorlands and to crags to the west.
Upland birds including Red Grouse, Merlin, Peregrine, Ring Ousel, Golden Plover, Hen Harrier and Red Kite.

> *Hafren Forest   136   SN855855   6m W of Llanidloes*
> *Woodland and upland birds.*

Trannon & Brynamlwg 136 SN910960 5m SE of Llandbrynmair
Upland birds including Golden Plover, Dunlin, Short-eared Owl and Hen Harrier.

Llyn Ebyr 136 SN980880 3m NE of Llanidloes
Wildfowl and woodland birds.

Llyn Mawr 136 SO010970 7m NW of Newtown
Wildfowl and upland birds.

Marsh's Pool 136 SN927813 2½m SW of Llanidloes
Passage and winter wildfowl.

TIC	*Central Car-park, Newtown (0686 625580)
	*Longbridge Street, Llanidloes (05512 2605)
YH	Glantuen, Ystumtuen, Aberystwyth, Dyfed (097085 693)
RF	Red Lion, Trefeglwys
RFBBE	Star Inn, Dylife (06503 345)
BBE	Esgairmaen Farm, Fan, nr Llanidloes (05516 272)
SC	As previous entry.

Elan Estate 147 4m SW of Rhayader
Minor roads run beside the reservoirs and up the Elan and Claer-wen valleys. Many parking places, and open access, on foot, to over 70 square miles, e.g. SN905616 and track SW towards Drygarn Fawr, SN886688 and track west up onto moorland at Trumau and Pantllwyd.
Woodland and upland birds including Red Kite, Dunlin, Golden Plover, Merlin, Peregrine, Ring Ousel, Pied Flycatcher and Redstart; winter wildfowl.

Gilfach & Wyloer 147 or 136 SN960715 2½m N of Rhayader
River, woodland and upland birds.

Cefn Cennarth 147 SN965756 5m N of Rhayader
Woodland birds including Pied Flycatcher, Redstart and Wood Warbler.

Llandrindod Lake Woods 147 SO065605 1m SE of Llandrindod centre
Woodland birds; summer warblers.

Bailey Einon 147 SO085614 1½m E of Llandrindod Wells
Woodland and river birds.

TIC	Old Town Hall, Llandrindod Wells (0597 822600)
	*Elan Valley Visitor Centre, Rhayader (0597 810898)
YH	As previous entry.
	Dolgoch, Tregaron, Dyfed (09744 680)
	The School, Glascwm, Llandrindod Wells (0982 570367)
RF	Elan Valley Visitor Centre Cafe, Elan Village (Apr-Oct)
	Triangle Inn, Rhayader
	Llanerch, Llandrindod Wells
	Carole's Tea Room, Rhayader
BBE	Flickering Lamp, Elan Valley, nr Rhayader (0597 810827)
	Beili Neuadd Farm, Rhayader (0597 810211)
	Elan Hotel, Rhayader (0597 810373)
	Disserth Farm, Howey, nr Llandrindod Wells (0597 89277)
	Brynhir Farm, Chapel Road, Howey (0597 822425)
SC	Wales Cottage Holidays, The Bank, Newtown (0686 628200)

Llyn Heilyn & Gwaunceste Hill   148   5m SW of New Radnor
Park by A481 ¼m SW of its junction with A44 at SO166583. Then track SW above the road and to moorland.
Wildfowl; passage waders; migrants; moorland birds including Red Grouse, Merlin and Peregrine.

Radnor Forest   148   1–4m N of New Radnor
Park at top of hill 1m NW of New Radnor at SO205617. Then track north along the east side of the valley and up to Black Mixen and Shepherd's Well.
Woodland and upland birds including Crossbill, Goshawk, Ring Ousel, Merlin and Peregrine.

Burfa Camp   148   2½m SW of Presteigne
Park just north of B4362 2m NE of its junction with A44 at SO277609. Then track east around the hill.
Woodland birds and summer warblers.

Beacon & Pool Hills   148 or 136   7m NW of Knighton
Park by minor road 1½m N of B4356 on the west side of the hill at SO154766 and tracks east.
Upland and hill birds including Red Grouse and Ring Ousel.

> ***Maelinydd*** *148   SN130709   8m NE of Llandrindod Wells*
> *Moorland birds; passage waders.*

TIC	The Old School, Knighton (0547 528753)
	*The Old Market Hall, Presteigne (0544 260193)
YH	The School, Glascwm, nr Llandrindod Wells (0982 570367)
	Old Primary School, Knighton (0547 528807)

RFBBE	Eagle Hotel, New Radnor (054421 208)
	Severn Arms Hotel, Penybont, nr Llandrindod Wells (0597 87224/87334)
BBE	Milebrook House Hotel, Milebrook, nr Knighton (0547 528632)
SC	Kinverley, The Knapp, Walton, nr Presteigne (054421 229)
	Highbrook Farm, New Radnor (054421 670)
	Penwhimpen, Yardro, Walton (054421 240)

Llanbedr Hill   148   2½m NW of Painscastle
Park by minor road 2m N of B4594 at SO147484. Then tracks west across moorland.
Moorland birds including Red Grouse and winter Hen Harrier.

Pwll Patti   161   1m W of Glasbury
Park and view from B4350 1m W of A438 at SO166393.
Winter wildfowl including Bewicks and Whooper Swans.

River Wye   161   0–2m W of Glasbury
Park by B4350 ¼m W of its junction with A438 on the western side of Glasbury village at SO175393 and take marked path westwards beside the river to Glangwye.
Passage and winter wildfowl; passage waders; woodland and river birds including Goosander, Kingfisher and Common Sandpiper.

> *Glasbury Bridge   161   SO180393   E side of Glasbury*
> *Passage waders; migrants.*

> *Rhosgoch   148   SO195485   2m NE of Painscastle*
> *Woodland and marshland birds; summer warblers; winter wildfowl.*

> *Llan Bwch Llyn   148   SO120464   3m W of Painscastle*
> *Wildfowl; passage waders; woodland birds; summer warblers.*

> *Brechfa Pool   161   SO119376   3½m SW of Glasbury*
> *Winter wildfowl; passage waders.*

> *Dderw Pool   161   SO143376   2½m SW of Glasbury*
> *Passage waders and wildfowl.*

TIC	*The Car-park, Hay-on-Wye (0497 820144)
	Old Town Hall, Llandrindod Wells (0597 822600)
YH	The Old School, Glascwm, nr Llandrindod Wells (0982 570367)
RF	Maesllwch Arms, Glasbury
	Maesllwch Arms, Painscastle
	Harp, Glasbury

BB   Fforddfawr Farmhouse, Glasbury (04974 332)
Newhouse Farmhouse, Bryngwyn, nr Painscastle (04975 671)
BBE   The Forge, Glasbury, nr Hay-on-Wye (04974 237)
Goblaen House, Glasbury (04974 332)
SC   Welsh Holiday Cottages, The Bank, Newtown (0686 628200)
Cae Mawr Cottage, Clyro, nr Hay-on-Wye (0497 820730)

Llangorse Lake   161   5m SE of Brecon
Park and view from northern shore ¾m SW of Llangorse village (on B4560) at SO127272. Or from southern shore by the church at SO134263 and footpath west along the shore.
Winter wildfowl; passage waders, terns and gulls; reedbed species; migrants.

Talybont Reservoir   161   8m SE of Brecon
View from minor road along NW shore 3m SW of B4558 from Talybont e.g. at SO091178.
Winter wildfowl; passage waders; woodland birds.

Craig y Cilau & Mynydd Llangatwg   161   3m SW of Crickhowell
Park by minor road 2½m W of A4077 toward B4360 at SO186168. Then paths south by crags and woodland and up onto moorland. Upland and woodland birds including Ring Ousel, Raven, Peregrine, Redstart and Golden Plover.

> *Priory Grove   160   SO047293   ½m N of Brecon centre*
> *Woodland and river birds.*

> *Pwll-y-wrach   161   SO165326   1½m SE of Talgarth*
> *Woodland and river birds.*

> *Pentwyn & Ponsticill Reservoirs   160   SO055144*
> *4m N of Merthyr Tydfil*
> *Passage and winter wildfowl.*

> *Mynydd Llangynidr & Trevil Quarries (Gwent)   161*
> *SO120140   4m N of Tredegar*
> *Upland birds including Ring Ousel, Peregrine and Red Grouse.*

TIC   The Mountain Centre, Libanus, Brecon (0874 3366)
*Cattle Market Car-park, Brecon (0874 2485)
*Watton Mount, Brecon (0874 4437)
YH   Ty'n-y-caeu, Groesffordd, Brecon (0874 86270)
Llwyn-y-celyn, Libanus, Brecon (0874 4261)

RF	White Swan, Llanfrynach
	Star, Talybont
	Old Ford Inn, Llanhamlach
RFBBE	Red Lion Hotel, Llangorse (0874 84238)
	Bear Hotel, Crickhowell (0873 810408)
BBE	The Old Rectory Hotel, Llangattock, nr Crickhowell (0873 810373)
SC	Trefeinon Farm, Llangorse (0874 84607)
	Pregge Mill Cottage, Pregge Lane, Crickhowell (0873 811157)

Pont Melin-fach   160   8m NW of Aberdare
Car-park by minor road 2½m N of A465 and 3m W of A4059 at
SN907105. Then path south or north beside River Neath.
Woodland and river birds including Dipper, Pied Flycatcher and
Redstart.

Craig Cerrig Gleisiad   160   7m SW of Brecon
Park by A470 2m S of its junction with A4215 at SN972223. Then
tracks southwest up to moorland and crags.
Upland birds including Ring Ousel, Red Grouse and Peregrine.

Traeth Mawr   160   SN970253   5m SW of Brecon
Heathland and moorland birds.

Carreg Lwyd   160   SN860150   5m NE of Ystradgynlais
Upland birds including Ring Ousel, Merlin and Peregrine.

Beacons Reservoir   160   SN987185   8m NW of Merthyr Tydfil
Passage and winter wildfowl.

Cantref Reservoir   160   SN994160   6½m NW of Merthyr Tydfil
Passage and winter wildfowl.

Usk Reservoir   160   SN828286   6m W of Sennybridge
Passage and winter wildfowl; woodland birds.

Disgwylfa   160   SN820180   5m N of Ystradgynlais
Upland birds.

Craig-y-nos Country Park   160   SN844156   4m NE of Ystradgynlais
River and woodland birds including Pied Flycatcher and Dipper.

TIC	As previous entry.
	14a Glebeland Street, Merthyr Tydfil, Mid Glamorgan (0685 79884)

YH As previous entry.
Tai'r Heol, Ystradfellte, Aberdare, Mid Glam (0639 720301)

RF New Inn, Ystradfellte
Three Horseshoes, Brecon
Gremlin Hotel, Brecon
Six Bells, Brecon

BBE Pengelli Fach Farm, Ponsticill, Vaynor, nr Merthyr (0695 722169)

BBESC Brynfedwen Farm, Trallong Common, Sennybridge (0874 82505)

SC Wern y Marchog Farm, Cantref, nr Brecon (0874 86329)

THE KIT

Binoculars & Telescopes:-
You can spend from £50 to £500+ on a pair of binoculars so it's important that they are suitable for birdwatching and suited to you. Several establishments have a rural setting where you can try out a wide range of binoculars and telescopes on the surrounding countryside e.g. Focus Optics, Church Lane, Corley, Coventry (0676 40501/42476) and Focalpoint, 14 Cogshall Lane, Comberbach, Northwich, Cheshire (0606 891098). Some others have 'field weekends' at various nature reserves around the country e.g. In Focus, 204 High St, Barnet, Herts (081 449 1445). If you are unable to take advantage of these facilities try out some other birdwatchers optics (most are quite friendly if you smile!) and if they suit you go mail order. Most reputable companies will accept return within a couple of weeks if you're not happy. Many of the bigger firms also do secondhand equipment at about half or less of the 'new' prices. These are usually very good buys especially if you are buying £500 worth of binoculars or telescope for £200-£300 as the more expensive models *generally* do not wear out in a lifetime or two, if used properly.

Here is a selection of equipment in various price brackets with the generally available price as at Jan 1991:-

Binoculars:-

under £100:
   Carl Zeiss 8 × 30 Jenoptem (£50)
   Carl Zeiss 10 × 50 Jenoptem (£80)
   Carl Zeiss 8 × 30 Deltrintem (£60)

These are East German Zeiss models so with the new set up may not be so cheap in the future. (The West German equivalent of the 8 × 30's are over £400!) The 8 × 30's are small, light, of good quality and very good value. Many of the bigger birdwatchers have never used anything else. The 10 × 50's are also very good value but much bigger and heavier and really only easily used by an adult with big hands!

under £200:
   Mirador 8 × 42 (£110)
   Mirador 10 × 42 (£115)
   Nikon 8 × 30 CF (£199)
   Bausch & Lomb Custom 8 × 36 (£190)
   Bausch & Lomb 10 × 40 (£199)
   Optolyth Osiris 8 × 40 (£140)
   Optolyth Osiris 10 × 40 (£140)
All very good binoculars. The Bausch & Lomb models are half this price in the U.S. where they are made!

under £300:
   Optolyth Alpin 8 × 40 (£225)
   Optolyth Alpin 10 × 40 (£230)
Excellent optics, suitable for all sized hands, extremely light.

under £400:
  Swarovski Habicht SLC 8 × 30 (£325)
  Swarovski Habicht Diana 10 × 40 (£350)
The 8 × 30's are probably the best binoculars of this specification for birdwatching. The 10 × 40's have been largely unchanged for many years and are of a very high quality.

under £500:
  Optolyth 8 × 56 (£450)
  Optolyth 9 × 63 (£450)
  Carl Zeiss 10 × 40 (£490)
It cannot be long before Zeiss come up with a new roof prism 8 × 40 and/or 10 × 40 to take on Leica and Bausch & Lomb in the top price bracket. The Optolyth models are big and heavy but superb as regards light gathering.

under £600:
  Bausch & Lomb Elite 8 × 42 (£590)
  Bausch & Lomb Elite 10 × 40 (£590)
The best birdwatching binoculars available at present. They were £699 when first on the market in this country in 1989! In the U.S. and Canada they are available for about £350, so you could fly over and buy a pair and still save a few pounds on the U.K. price! Roll on the GATT talks getting around to us birdwatchers!

  Leica (Leitz) 8 × 42 (£560)
  Leica (Leitz) 10 × 42 (£560)
The new replacement for the old Trinovid 8 × 40 and 10 × 40. For the birdwatcher they are not as good as their predecessors but still excellent optically and totally waterproof and dustproof. If you can find a pair of the old style 8 × 40's secondhand for less than £300 buy them!

  Carl Zeiss 8 × 56 (£570)
Big and heavy but excellent light gathering.

Telescopes:-

under £150:
  Mirador Merlin 30 × 75 (£120)
Excellent value with an eyepiece assembly turning through 360 degrees so adaptable as 'offset' or 'straight through'.

under £200:
  Opticron Classic 30 × 75 (£160)
Another very good value telescope.

under £300:
  Kowa TS 601 & 602 with 25× eyepieces (c. £240)
The 601 is the offset eyepiece model, the 602 'straight through'. Both models have 60mm objective lenses. The modern versions of the first use-able telescopes for the birdwatcher which Kowa brought to our shores in the mid 1970's. Still excellent value.

under £450:
  Kowa TSN1 & TSN2 with 25× eyepiece (£350)
  Kowa TSN1 & TSN2 with 30× eyepiece (£400)
Both models have 77mm objective lenses. The TSN 1 is the offset model. The 30× wide angle eyepiece is well worth the money. Brilliant telescopes.

under £600:
  Nikon Fieldscope ED II 20-45 × 60 (£550)
The best birdwatching telescope available in our opinion. Although only a 60mm object lens light gathering is extraordinary. Very light, compact and worth every penny.

under £700:
  Kowa TSN3 & TSN4 with 25× eyepiece (£610)
  Kowa TSN3 & TSN4 with 30× eyepiece (£660)
With 77mm object lens as the TSN1 & 2 except that the 3 & 4 have fluorite lens elements. Expensive but excellent. Fluorite is a crystal with exceptional light transmission qualities formerly only found on those very expensive long camera lenses clustered behind the goal mouth! It's about time that it was used in binoculars although it seems that the next innovation is to be diamond coated lenses.

under £2,150:
  Questar 3.5″ and 30-50× lens (c. £2,149.99)
A superb piece of equipment but a bit on the expensive side! Doubled in price over the last ten years but so has everything I suppose! A mirror system 'telescope' quite unlike other models mentioned here. There are a few birdwatchers with them so have a look through one if you get the chance.

Tripods:-
  Manfrotto 144 with 200 head & quick release plate (c. £105)
This is an excellent tripod for the birdwatcher and one of the few suitable for taller people without crouching. It is usable with a straight-thru telescope by anyone from 2′2″ to 6′5″, or with an angled eyepiece, 6′8″ or more! If you buy one check that the nuts and bolts are secure. They can come off if loosened too much but fortunately are easily replaceable. Indeed there is little that can go wrong with it. Buy a black rather than silvery one – you don't want to flush everything within a quarter of a mile! As with all tripods keep the legs slippery with a finger-dab of cooking oil (virgin olive of course) or a drop of your mum's (or your own) sewing-machine oil if you want to show off! You won't be too popular with your life insurer if your tripod legs squeal on extending just when a crowd has gathered to see the last Eskimo Curlew which promptly flies off into the sunset never to be seen again!
  If you're not so tall and want something smaller, lighter and a bit cheaper, the *Velbon* D500, D600, D700 are all excellent at about £60-£80.

Notebook:-
  Survival Aids Waterproof Notebook (c. £3.00)
Useable in the rain. Pencil writing can be erased from the Polyart paper (64 sides). Refill pads available. Invaluable for taking field notes or sketches in poor conditions. from Survival Aids Ltd, Morland, Cumbria, or your local 'outdoor' shop.

Clothing:-
'Barbour' Durham jacket (with built-in hood).
'Barbour' lined leggings.
'Buffalo' Double P clothing.
Phoenix Gore-tex anoraks.
We've tried the above and they are all excellent. To be weatherproof for less than £100 is difficult. Beware of cheap immitations and wild claims – birdwatchers often find themselves in appallingly wet conditions and there are few short cuts to comfort. Ask your outdoor shop for expert advice if necessary as there are a large number of different makes on the market but few that will keep you dry and warm in a squall whilst buntin' huntin' in the Cairngorms!

Books:-
A selection of some of the better and more useful works:
Kingfisher Field Guide to the Birds of Britain & Europe £10.95
Mitchell Beazley Birdwatchers Pocket Guide £5.95
The Birds of Britain & Europe, by Heinzel, Fitter & Parslow (Collins) £7.95
The three best field guides although none are totally comprehensive and faultless. We're still waiting for that!

Bird groups & monographs:-
Seabirds; Shorebirds; Wildfowl; (Croom Helm) £19.95 to £22.95
Three works in an excellent series.
Collins Guide to Birds of Prey of Britain & Europe £14.95
The MacMillan Field Guide to Bird Identification £14.95
Deals with about 90 'problem' species. Very useful.

General:-
Biographies for Birdwatchers (Academic Press) £17.50
Birds of the Western Palearctic vols I-IV (OUP) £70 per vol.
The Illustrated Encyclopedia of Birds (Headline) £30
The Birds of Siberia – The Yenisei (Alan Sutton Ltd) (£2.95)
The Birds of Siberia – To the Petchora Valley (£2.95)
Population Trends in British Breeding Birds (BTO) £17

Children 6-10 yrs:-
Usborne First Nature 'Birds' £2.50
Amazing Birds (Dorling Kindersley) £3.99
'Ladybird' guides 99p
Seven guides on various groups of birds.

Magazines & Journals:-
'Birdwatching' monthly from newsagents. £1.60
Easily the best magazine for the birdwatcher in Britain with a lot of interest for birdwatchers of all levels.

'Birding World' monthly by subscription. £18 a year to Stonerunner, Coast Rd, Cley, Norfolk.
A relatively new journal and still developing and improving. Generally for the hardened birder with most of the content on rarities and identification problems. Often has excellent recent photographs of rare birds in both black & white and colour. Prides itself on being 'first with the news' but has slipped a week or so (at least!) over the last year or so.

'British Birds' monthly by subscription. £31.20 a year from Fountains, Park Lane, Blunham, Beds.
Has a varied content from breeding biology to identification and behaviour. Often has good colour photographs. A bit expensive.

'Birds' 3 issues a year (used to be 4) to members of the RSPB. £16 annually from The Lodge, Sandy, Beds.
Occasional interesting articles and good photographs but very poor compared with its equivalent from the Audobon Society in the USA. Tends to be packed with adverts and short on content. RSPB members deserve better.

'Bird Life' 6 issues a year to members of the junior branch of the RSPB, the Young Ornithologists Club. Membership £8.50
An excellent magazine also available to adult (over 18) 'supporters' and easily the best for the beginner birdwatcher and the under 12's.

'Bird Study' 3 issues a year. £9 to members of BTO (£32.50 to others!)
Has some papers of general interest to all birdwatchers but has developed a tendency in recent years to have too many papers from university departments trying to increase their output of published material to obtain more finance from a minimum of new research, and/or justify their existence. Only an extremely small percentage of BTO members can understand the statistics contained therein and the style of paper accepted should be geared to them, not to the ornithological academic. There are other journals for such material.

'BTO News' 6 issues a year to members of BTO. Membership £14 annually from BTO, Beech Grove, Tring, Herts.
An excellent publication of 20 pages per issue at present, packed with interest for all birdwatchers. Membership of the British Trust for Ornithology should be the first £14 every birdwatcher spends on bird conservation in Britain.

'Birder's World' 6 issues a year from newsagents. £1.95 each.
An American journal generally available for the last couple of years from U.K. newsagents. Superb colour photography puts our magazines in the shade. Also many interesting articles mostly in a 'chatty' U.S. style. Buy it for the photographs alone.

Sound Recordings:-

British Bird Vocabulary by Victor Lewis.
Six volumes of two cassettes covering song and calls of more than 120 species. Excellent quality and playing time per species.
Details from Victor Lewis, Rosehill, Lyonshall, Herefordshire, HR5 3HS.

British Wildlife Habitats by Richard Margoschis.
A series of 6 cassettes of which numbers 1,2,4 & 5 are of most interest to the birdwatcher. Excellent in every way.
£5.50 each from R. Margoschis, 80 Mancetter Rd, Atherstone, Warks CV9 1NH.

British Bird Songs & Calls & More British Bird Sounds compiled by Ron Kettle.

A double and a single cassette compilation. More than 160 species in all. £13.99 and £5.99 respectively.

A Sound Guide to Waders in Britain by John Burton et al.
A single cassette from Pinnacle at £4.50

Woodland and Garden Birds.
A double cassette compilation from Pinnacle at £9.50

All the Bird Songs of Europe by J.C. Roche.
Four compact discs covering nearly 400 species. £75. No announcement of species and accompanying booklet not very good, and even more of a nuisance when driving! Very high quality and reasonably comprehensive. Like field guides we still await some very obvious improvements. A collection of cassettes or CD's for British birds with good recording time for each species and English announcements surely is not too much to ask?

Bird information by telephone:-
Available in the U.S. for many years this is a comparitively recent phenomenon in Britain. The 0898 numbers cost 44p per minute peak rate and 33p per minute cheap rate at present (Jan 91). Unnecessarily expensive, but another British Telecom monopoly. Most of the organisers contribute some of their profits to conservation.

0898 884 503 BTO News Line – all profits go to the BTO.
0898 700 227 General bird news
0898 884 501 Nationwide rare bird news (news in: 0205 358 050)
0898 700 222 Nationwide rare bird news (news in: 0263 741 140)

local rare bird news:
0898 700 240 SE England (news in: 081 676 0209)
0898 700 245 E Anglia (news in: 0603 763388)
0898 700 246 NE England (news in: 0423 509113)
0898 700 247 Midlands (news in: 0905 754154)
0898 700 249 NW England (news in: 051 336 6188)
0898 700 234 Scotland (news in: 0292 611994)

COUNTY BIRD RECORDERS & THE B.T.O.'s REGIONAL REPRESENTATIVES

The County Bird Recorders and the Regional Representatives of the British Trust for Ornithology are the principal gatherers of bird information at the county or area level. They are all voluntary and unpaid and devote a huge amount of time to other birdwatchers and bird conservation. Make yourself useful and help, if you are able, with recording and surveying work in your area.

COUNTY BIRD RECORDERS
The County Recorders are usually attached to the county's birdwatching society who often have field meetings and other events well worth attending, especially to meet other birdwatchers. Submitting your bird records to the relevant County Recorder is an important part of the 'Good Birdwatchers Code of Conduct' (which you will have read in the intro!). Nothing was ever learnt without the gathering of information especially in science and nature conservation. Your recorder will tell you how, when and which records he or she wants. Or get hold of a recent copy of your county/regional bird report (usually present in the local reference library) and you will see the sort of records required. Also (very important!!) if you see an unusual or rare bird or you don't know what it is give him/her a ring. Quickly. Not in a fortnights time! County Recorders are a difficult species to replace and tend to suicide when told weeks after the event that 'I had this little bird with a blue tail and red bits in my garden for a whole week until the cat ate it. I've never seen one like it before – what was it?' Be kind to your Recorder and he or she will live for years – and probably look after you in return!

County Recorders – England:-

Avon: H.E. Rose, 12 Birbeck Rd, Bristol (0272 303298/681638)
Beds: P. Trodd, White Garth, West Parade, Dunstable (0582 609017)
Berks: P.E. Standley, 7 Llanvair Drive, South Ascot (0344 23502)
Bucks: A.V. Harding, 15 Jubilee Terrace, Stony Stratford (0908 565896)
Cambs: C.A.E. Kirtland, 22 Montgomery Rd, Cambridge (0223 63092)
   Hunts & P'borough: J.S. Clark, 7 Westbrook, Hilton, Cambs (0480 830472)
Cheshire: T. Broome, 9 Vicarage Lane, Poynton, Stockport
Cleveland: J.B. Dunnett, 43 Hemlington Rd, Stainton, Middlesborough (0642 595845)
Cornwall: S.M. Christophers, 5 Newquay Rd, St.Columb Major (0637 881279)
   Scilly: W.H. Wagstaff, 42 Sally Port, St.Mary's (0720 22212)
Cumbria: M.F. Carrier, 6 Brackenrigg, Armathwaite, Carlisle (06992 218)
Derbys: R.W. Key, 3 Farningham Close, Spondon, Derby (0332 678571)
Devon: P.W. Ellicott, Wyatts, Trusham, Newton Abbot (0626 852329)

Dorset: M. Cade, 12 Littlemoor Rd, Preston, Weymouth (0305 833166)
Durham: T. Armstrong, 39 Western Hill, Durham (091 386 1519)
Essex:
  J. Miller, 450a Baddow Rd, Great Baddow, Chelmsford (0245 73734).
  M. Dennis, 173 Collier Row Lane, Romford (0708 761865)
Gloucs: G.R. Avery, 12 Hemmingsdale Rd, Hempsted, Gloucester (0452 305002)
Gtr London: M.J. Earp, 63 Ivinghoe Rd, Bushey, Watford (081 950 5906)
Gtr Manchester: P. Hill, 10 Woodlands Ave, Rochdale (0706 48118)
Hampshire: E.J. Wiseman, Normandy Farm, Normandy Lane, Lymington (0590 675906)
  I.o.W: J. Stafford, Westering, Moor Lane, Brighstone (0983 740280)
Hereford: K.A. Mason, The Sett, Common Hill, Fownhope, Hereford (043 277 546)
Herts: P. Walton, Twin Oaks, Rabley Heath, Welwyn (0438 811760)
Kent: I.P. Hodgson, 73 Middle Deal Rd, Deal (0304 366203)
Lancs & M'side: M. Jones, 31 Laverton Rd, St.Annes-on-Sea (0253 721076)
Leics: R.E. Davis, 31 Tysoe Hill, Glenfield, Leicester (0533 873896)
Lincs & S. Humbs: G.P. Catley, 13 West Acridge, Barton-on-Humber (0652 34752)
Norfolk:
  P.R. Allard, 39 Mallard Way, Bardwell, Gt. Yarmouth (0493 657798)
  M.J. Seago, 33 Acacia Rd, Thorpe St.Andrew, Norwich (0603 34351)
Northants: R.W. Bullock, 25 Westcott Way, Favell Green, Northampton (0604 27262)
Northumbs: M.S. Hodgson, 31 Uplands, Monkseaton, Whitley Bay (091 252 0511)
Notts: J.A. Hopper, 4 Shipley Rise, Carlton, Nottingham (0602 874682)
Oxon: J.W. Brucker, 65 Yarnton Rd, Kidlington, Oxford (08675 2845)
Shrops: J. Sankey, 11 Mardol Terr., Smithfield Rd, Muck Wenlock (0952 727761)
Somerset: B. Rabbitts, Flat 3, 17 The Esplanade, Burnham-on-Sea (0278 789068)
Staffs: Mrs G. Jones, 4 The Poplars, Lichfield Rd, Abbots Bromley, Rugeley (0283 840555)
Suffolk: R.B. Warren, 37 Dellwood Ave, Felixstowe (0394 270180)
Surrey: J.J. Wheatley, 6 Boxgrove Ave, Guildford (0483 573152)
Sussex: P. James, 23 Islingword Place, Brighton (0273 673609)
Tyne & Wear: as Northumberland.
Warwickshire: S. Haynes, 4 Spinney Close, Arley, Coventry (0676 42066)
West Midlands: T. Hextell, 49 Cradley Croft, Handsworth, Birmingham (021 551 4984)
Wilts: R. Turner, 14 Ethendun, Bratton, Westbury (03808 30862)
Worcs: S.M. Whitehouse, 5 Stanway Close, Blackpole, Worcester (0905 54541)
Yorks & N. Humbs: G.R. Bennett, Kingsfield, Strawberry Gardens, Hornsea (0964 532251)

Scotland:-
Borders: R. Murray, 4 Bellfield Cres., Eddleston, Peebles (07213 677)
Central: C.J. Henty, Edgehill East, 7 Coneyhill Rd, Bridge of Allan (0786 832166)
Dumfries & Galloway:
  E.C. Fellowes, West Isle, Islesteps, Dumfries (0387 62094)
  A.D. Watson, 54 Main St, Dalry, Castle Douglas (06443 246)
Fife: D.E. Dickson, 45 Hawthorn Terr, Thornton, Fife (0592 774066)

Grampian: K. Shaw, 4 Headland Court, Newton Hill, Stonehaven (0569 30946)
Moray: J.H. Cook, Rowanbrae, Clochan, Buckie (05427 296)
Highland:
E.W.E. Maughan, Burnside, Harbour Rd, Reay, Thurso (084 781 315)
A.R. Mainwood, 13 Ben Bhraggie Drive, Golspie, Sutherland (04083 3247)
Lothian:
P.R. Gordon, 4 Craigelaw, Longniddry, East Lothian (08757 588)
C.C. McGuigan, 10 Blair St, Edinburgh (031 220 4778)
Orkney: C.J. Booth, 34 High St, Kirkwall (0856 2883)
Shetland: D. Suddaby, 92 Sandveien, Lerwick (0595 5643)
Strathclyde:
B. Zonfrillo, 28 Brodie Rd, Glasgow (041 557 0791).
I.P. Gibson, 2 Fulton Cres, Kilbarchan, Renfrew.
M. Madders, Smithy Cottage, Lochdon, Craignure, Mull.
R.H. Hogg, 11 Kirkmichael Rd, Crosshill, Maybole, Ayrshire (06554 317)

Wales:-

Clwyd: P. Rathbone, Wern, Llanarmon-yn-Ial (08243 676)
Dyfed:
Pembs: J.W. Donovan, 5 Dingle Lane, Crundale, H'fordwest (0437 762673)
Carms: D.H.V. Roberts, 6 Ger-y-coed, Pontyates, Llanelli (0269 860325)
Cards: P.E. Davis, Felindre, Aberarth, Aberaeron (0545 570870)
Glamorgan:
M: J.R. Smith, 15 Milton Drive, Bridgend
S: P. Bristow, 10 Lisvane St, Cathays, Cardiff (0222 227104)
W: H.E. Grenfell, 14 Brynn Terr, Mumbles, Swansea (0792 360487)
Gwent: B.J. Gregory, Monmouth School, Monmouth (0600 4953)
Gwynedd & Anglesey: T. Gravett, Tyddyn Llan, Eglwsbach, Colwyn Bay (0492 650774)
Merioneth R. Thorpe, Tan-y-Garth, Friog, Fairbourne (0341 250560)
Powys:
Rads; P.P. Jennings, Garnfawr, Hundred House, Llandrindod Wells (0982 570334)
Brec: M.F. Peers, Gorse Bank, Llangammarch Wells (05912 341)
Mont: B. Holt, Scops Cottage, Pentrebeirdd, Welshpool (093 884 266)

REGIONAL REPS

These are the British Trust for Ornithology's Regional Representatives. They organise the Trust's survey work etc and are their main contacts with the membership nationwide. First join the BTO and then contact your RR if you want to take part in the various species and habitat surveys, or any of the other BTO schemes.
BTO Membership: £14 a year includes 6 issues of BTO News. Details from Membership Unit, BTO, Beech Grove, Tring, Herts HP23 5NR. tel: 044 282 3461

Regional Reps – England:-

Avon: R.L. Bland, 11 Percival Rd, Bristol (0272 734828)
Beds: E. Newman, 15 Birchmead, Gamlingay, Sandy (0767 50964)

Berks: contact BTO.
Bucks: A.F. Brown, Ridersway, Poyle Lane, Burnham (0628 604769)
Cambs: R.G. Clarke, New Hythe House, Reach, Cambridge (0638 742447)
Cheshire:
  Mid: R.S. Leigh, 19 Queen St, Knutsford (0565 2417)
  N & E: C. Richards, 13 The Green, Handforth, Wilmslow (0625 524527)
  S: C. Lythgoe, 11 Waterloo Rd, Haslington, Crewe (0270 582642)
Cleveland: R. McAndrew, 5 Thornhill Gdns, Hartlepool (0429 277291)
Cornwall: S.F. Jackson, 2 Trelawney Cottages, Falmouth (0326 313533)
  Scilly: J.W. Hale, Langarth, St.Agnes (0720 22364)
Cumbria:
  N: J.C. Callion, The Cherries, Scawfield, High Harrington (0946 830651)
  S: R.I. Kinley, 16 Underley Hill, Kendal (0539 27133)
Derbys: G.P. Mawson, Moonpenny Farm, Farwater Lane, Dronfield, Sheffield (0246 415097)
Devon: H.P. Sitters, Whistley House, Axtown Lane, Yelverton (0822 854876)
Dorset: contact BTO.
Durham: D.L. Sowerbutts, 9 Prebends Field, Gilesgate Moor, Durham (091 386 7201)
Essex:
  NW: G.Smith, 48 The Meads, Ingatestone (0277 354034)
  NE: P. Dwyer, 48 Churchill Ave, Halstead (0787 476524)
  S: G.E. Edwards, 3 Dalmation Rd, Southend (0702 619233)
Gloucs: R.Purveur, 5 Northfield Sq, Gloucester (0452 502102)
Hants: G.C. Evans, Waverley, Station Rd, Chilbolton, Stockbridge (0264 74697)
  I.o.W: J. Stafford, Westering, Moor Lane, Brighstone (0983 740280)
Hereford: K.A. Mason, The Sett, Common Hill, Fownhope (043277 546)
Herts: C. Dee, 8 The Barons, Thorley Park, Bishops Stortford (0279 755637)
Kent: G.F.A. Munns, Spring Place, St.Aubyn's Close, Orpington (0689 35325)
Lancs:
  NW: D.J. Sharpe, 17 Greenwood Ave, Bolton-le-Sands (0524 822492)
  E: A.A. Cooper, 28 Peel Park Ave, Clitheroe (0200 24577)
  S: D. Jackson, 38 Broadwood Drive, Fulwood, Preston (0772 864214)
Leics: C. Measures, 28 Oakfield Ave, Birstall (0533 676476)
Lincs:
  W: Mrs A. Goodall, 22 Laburnum Drive, Cherry Willingham, Lincoln (0522 752188)
  S: R.& K. Heath, 56 Pennytoft Lane, Pinchbeck, Spalding (0775 67055)
  E: R.K. Watson, 8 High St, Skegness (0754 810645)
  N: I. Shepherd, 38 Lindsey Rd, Cleethorpes, S. Humbs (0472 697142)
London: K.F. Belton, 8 Dukes Close, Fully Hill, Farnham, Surrey (0252 724068)
Manchester: R.G. Williams, 2 Milwain Rd, Stretford (061 865 1401)
Merseyside: A.S. Duckels, 16 The Spinney, Freshfield, L'pool (07048 76676)
Norfolk:
  NE: contact BTO.
  NW: M. Barrett, Walnut Pastures, Hall Lane, Thornham (048526 484)
  SW: A.M. Waterman, East Anglian Field Study Centre, Stowbridge (0366 383949)
  SE: K. Johns, 9 Broom Ave, Thorpe St.Andrew, Norwich (0603 32355)
Northants: P.W. Richardson, 10 Bedford Cottages, Gt. Brington (0604 770632)

Northumbs: T. Cadwallender, 22 South View, Lesbury, Alnwick (043473 509)
Notts: Mrs.L. Milner, 6 Kirton Park, Kirton, Newark (0623 862025)
Oxon:
 S: Mrs.C. Ross, Duck End Cottage, Sutton, Stanton Harcourt (0865 881552)
 N: M.F. Oliver, 1 The Bakery, Northend, Leamington Spa (029 577 699)
Shrops: C.E. Wright, 6 St.Annes Rd, Collegefields, Shrewsbury (0743 50372)
Somerset: contact BTO.
Staffs:
 N: F.C. Gribble, 22 Rickerscote Ave, Stafford (0785 54166)
 S: P.K. Dedicoat, 2 The Elms Paddock, Pattingham, W'hampton (0902 700514)
Suffolk: M.T. Wright, 15 Avondale Rd, Ipswich (0473 710032)
Surrey: E.F.J. Garcia, 2 Busdens Close, Milford, Godalming (0483 425620)
Sussex: A.B. Watson, 83 Buckingham Rd, Shoreham (0273 452472)
Warks: J.A. Hardman, Red Hill House, Red Hill, Alcester (0789 763159)
West Mids: J.R. Winsper, 32 Links Rd, Hollywood, B'ham (021 430 8191)
Wilts:
 W: R. Turner, 14 Ethendun, Bratton, Westbury (0380 830862)
 E: S.B. Edwards, Hazeldene, Medbourne Lane, Liddington, Swindon (0793 790500)
Worcs: G.H. Green, Windy Ridge, Pershore Rd, Little Comberton, Pershore (038674 377)
Yorkshire:
 N: C.M. Hind, Valmont Ridge, The Green, Richmond (0748 3572)
 SE: K. Hayhow, 42 Middlefield Rd, Grange Estate, Rotherham (0709 370650)
 NE: S. Cochrane, 4 Pinewood Ave, Filey (0723 515480)
 SW: A.H.V. Smith, 16 Silverdale Close, Sheffield (0742 362953)
 N.Humbs: F. Moffatt, 102 Norwood, Beverley, Hull (0482 868718)

Scotland:-

Borders: R.J. Robertson, 99 Howden Rd, Jedburgh (0835 62719)
Central: M.E. Philips, Pitsulie Cottage, Shiresmill, Dumfermline (0383 880381)
Dumf & Galloway: R. Mearns, Connans Knowe, Kirkton, Dumfries (0387 710031)
 Kirk: G. Shaw, Kirriereoch, Bargrennan, Newton Stewart (0671 84288)
 Wig: G. Sheppard, The Roddens, Leswalt, Stranraer (077687 685)
Fife: N. Elkins, 18 Scotstarvit View, Cupar, Fife (0334 54348)
Grampian:
 A. Webb, 17 Rubislaw Terr, Aberdeen (035 887 307)
 R.M. Laing, 87 Johnston Gdns East, Peterculter, Aberdeen (0224 732642)
 M.J.H. Cook, Rowanbrae, Clochan, Buckie (05427 296)
Highland:
 E.W.E. Maughan, Burnside, Harbour Rd, Reay, Thurso (084 781 315)
 G. Bates, 105 Strathy Point, Strathy, Thurso (06414 234)
 D.S. Whitaker, Clunes, Achnacarry, Spean Bridge (0397 81722)
 R.L. Swann, 14 St.Vincent Rd, Tain (0862 4329)
 A.D.K. Ramsay, Tain Royal Academy, Scotsburn Rd, Tain (0862 2121)
 A. Currie, Glaiseilean, Harrapool, Broadford, Skye (04712 344)
Lothian: G.D. Smith, 16 Stewart Ave, Currie (031 449 5366)
Orkney: C.J. Corse, Garrisdale, Lynn Park, Kirkwall (0856 4484)

Shetland: J.D. Okill, Heilinabretta, Cauldhame, Trondra (0595 88450)
Strathclyde:
  M. Madders, Smithy Cottage, Lochdon, Craignure, Mull (06802 347)
  D. Evamy, The Anchorage, Tarbert, Argyll (08802 881)
  D.W. Warner, Castle Cottage, Brodick, Arran (0770 2462)
  B.D. Kerr, 95 Portland St, Troon (0292 316723)
  M. Ogilvie, Glencairn, Bruichladdich, Islay (049 685 218)
  J.J. Sweeney, 9 Townhead Terr, Paisley (041 848 7406)
Tayside:
  K. Slater, 71 Patrick Allen Fraser St, Arbroath (0241 78266)
  R.E. Youngman, Atholl Bank, East Moulin Rd, Pitlochry (0796 2753)
W Isles: P.R. Boyer, 10 Baile na Cille, Balivanich, Benbecula (0870 2686)

Wales:-

Anglesey: J. Clark, Glan Dwr, Llyn Traffwll, Holyhead (0407 741536)
Clwyd:
  E: J.C. Peters, Whitewell Farm, Penymynydd, Chester (0244 542887)
  W: R.D. Corran, Tir Eithin, Maes-y-Bryn, Berthengam, Holywell (0745
    560150)
Dyfed:
  Cards: R. Squires, Cae'r Berllan, Eglwysfach, Machynlleth (065 474 265)
  Carms: D.H.V. Roberts, 6 Ger-y-coed, Pontyates, Llanelli (0269 860325)
  Pembs: G.H. Rees, 22 Priory Ave, Haverfordwest (0437 762877)
Glamorgan:
  M & S: R. Poole, 45 Fairway, Bargoed (0443 833301)
  W: R.J. Howells, Ynys Enlli, 14 Dolgoy Close, West Cross, Swansea
Gwent: S.J. Tyler, Yew Tree Cottage, Lone Lane, Penallt (0686 24829)
Gwynedd:
  Caers: J. Barnes, Fach Goch, Waunfawr, Caernarfon (028685 362)
  Merioneth: Mrs.M.M. Cooper, Bryn Hyfryd, Llanfachreth, Dolgellau
    (0341 422937)
Powys:
  Rads: P.P. Jennings, Garnfawr, Hundred House, Llandrindod Wells
    (0982 570334)
  Brec: G.C. Cundale, Redwing, Cusop, Hay-on-Wye (0497 820396)
  Mont: K. Stott, Wilderley, Garth, Guilsfield, Welshpool (0938 2332)
Channel Isles: I.J. Buxton, Le Petit Huquet, La Rue du Huquet, Jersey
    (0534 55845)

THE BIRDS & THE WEATHER FOR 1990

This chapter gives you a brief summary of the weather, month by month, and a selection of the more unusual bird records, day by day, for 1990.

Some birds remaining from 1989:
Red-breasted Nuthatch Holkam to 6/5. **Dark-eyed Junco** Portland to 25/3; Church Crookham to 7/3. **Spotted Sandpiper** Cavendish Dock, Barrow to 1/5. **Terek Sandpiper** Blyth to 9/5. **Rose-coloured Starling** Portland to 4/3; Paynters Lane End, Cornwall to 31/3. **Green-winged Teal** Martin Mere to 25/2. **Ring-necked Duck** Timsbury, Hants to 4/3. **Night Heron** Roath Park, Cardiff to 16/2. **Black Duck** Lochwinnoch to 2/3. **Kentish Plover** Burnham-on-Sea to 17/3; Reeds Island, River Humber to 4/3. **Surf Scoter** 1-4 St. Andrews, Fife to 18/2. **King Eider** Ythan Estuary to 25/5. **Shorelark** 5-6 Salthouse to 5/5. **Great Grey Shrike** Thursley Common to 15/2; Blackgutter Bottom, New Forest to 20/2; Raunceby Warren to 31/3; Mayday Farm, Suffolk to 10/3.

JANUARY

The month was very mild for January with maximum daytime temperatures up 3°C on average, and a particularly mild spell mid-month. On average rainfall was 35% above normal with the extremes along the east coast of England where precipitation was less than usual and northwest Scotland where it was twice the norm. The south and west were cloudier than normal whilst the east was some 30% up on usual sunshine hours. After the first week, which was largely cold with night frosts and light winds, a succession of depressions crossed the Atlantic dominating the weather with almost continual westerly winds often reaching gale or storm force from mid-month onwards.

Violent storms, with hurricane force westerly winds in places, swept the country from 25th to 26th. There was snow in the north and very heavy rain in the west of Britain.

1st	**Richard's Pipit** Snettisham to 13/3. **American Wigeon** Tring Reservoir. **Dartford Warbler** East Tilbury, Essex. **Ring-necked Duck** Loch Insh to 4/2.
2nd	**Serin** Grove, Portland.
3rd	**Waxwing** 12, Stornoway.
4th	**Serin** Starcross, Devon to 13th. **Kumlien's Gull** Banff Harbour to 21/4.
5th	**Garganey** Wilstone Reservoir to 10/2.
6th	**Ring-billed Gull** Felixstowe; St. Mary's, Scillies.
7th	**Great Grey Shrike** Arnfield Reservoir.
9th	**Great Grey Shrike** Longside, Grampian.
10th	**White-tailed Eagle** Scolt Head to Hunstanton.
11th	**Bonaparte's Gull** Long Rock Pool, Marazion.

12th	**Red Kite** Overton, Hants to 26th. **White-tailed Eagle** Humber Estuary. **Oystercatcher** 32,000 Caerlaverock.
13th	**Ring-billed Gull** Ryde, Isle of Wight to 19/2. **Firecrest** 8, Dungeness. **Great Grey Shrike** Priory Country Park to 3/2. **Red Kite** Woodbridge, Suffolk.
14th	**Ring-necked Duck** Llanfanod, Dyfed.
15th	**Green-winged Teal** Daventry Reservoir. **Black Brant** Hamford Water, Essex. **Bewick's Swan** 5,984 Welney, Norfolk. **Whooper Swan** 686 Welney.
16th	**Ring-billed Gull** 4 Par Beach, Cornwall. **White-tailed Eagle** Rhos Point, Gwynedd.
17th	**Ring-billed Gull** Point of Ayr. **Waxwing** 32, Guisborough, Cleveland to 21st.
18th	**Surf Scoter** Barmston, Humberside.
19th	**Great Grey Shrike** Essex University to 4/2; Silkstone, Yorkshire. **Naumann's Thrush** Chingford, Gtr. London to 9/3.
20th	**Ring-billed Gull** Draycote Water.
21st	**Surf Scoter** Flamborough Head.
23rd	**Pomarine Skua** Irvine Harbour to 27th. **Ring-billed Gull** 2, Plym Estuary.
25th	**Great Skua** 10, Exemouth. **Little Gull** 100, Seaforth. **White-billed Diver** Wyre Sound, Orkney to 26th.
26th	**Green-winged Teal** Titchfield Haven. **Pomarine Skua** Northampton town centre. **Sabine's Gull** Selsey Bill. **Little Auk** 3, Corsewall Point.
27th	**Surf Scoter** 8, Eden Estuary. **Bonaparte's Gull** Dee Estuary. **Ring-billed Gull** Pennington Flash to 28th. **Great Shearwater** Dungeness. **Ring-necked Duck** Alresford Pond.
28th	**Rough-legged Buzzard** Massingham Heath, Norfolk to 26/3. **American/Pacific Golden Plover** nr Okehampton. **Mediterranean-Gull** 30, Copt Point, Kent. **Dartford Warbler** Bridgwater Nature Reserve. **Ring-necked Duck** Roadford Reservoir, Devon.
29th	**King Eider** Tayport, Tayside to 11/2. **Great Grey Shrike** Carlton Colville, Suffolk.
30th	**Green Heron** Starcross, Devon to 3/2.

FEBRUARY

Another very mild month with average maximum daytime temperatures 2.6°C above the norm. It was also a very wet month with twice the usual rainfall although sunshine hours were about average in most places. All that rain was brought by an almost continuous succession of deep depressions crossing the Atlantic with frequent gales from the westerly half. These were especially from the southwest hence the very mild temperatures generally. Temperatures reached 15°C in South Devon on the 5th and 18.5°C in London on the 23rd whilst winds gusted to between 95 and 100 mph in Devon on the 7th and in northern England on the 26th. The only colder spells were from 11th to 16th and between 26th and 28th when winds came down from the northwest accompanied by snow in Scotland and northeast England and wintry showers and some night frosts elsewhere.

2nd	**Green-winged Teal** Slimbridge. **Little Auk** Cley.
3rd	**Leach's Petrel** 3, Dungeness. **American Wigeon** Gladhouse Reservoir to 10th.

| 4th | **Green-winged Teal** Draycote Water. **White-tailed Eagle** Minsmere. **Pomarine Skua** Dungeness. **Waxwing** 15, Ashington, Northumberland. **Black Duck** Loch of Spiggie to 4/5. |

4th **Green-winged Teal** Draycote Water. **White-tailed Eagle** Minsmere. **Pomarine Skua** Dungeness. **Waxwing** 15, Ashington, Northumberland. **Black Duck** Loch of Spiggie to 4/5.
5th **Sabine's Gull** Budleigh Salterton.
6th **Green-winged Teal** Sevenoaks to 4/3. **Ring-billed Gull** Stromness Harbour to 2/3. **Sabine's Gull** Keyhaven, Hants.
7th **Swallow** St. Mary's, Scillies. **Red Kite** Flixborough, Lincs to 18th.
9th **Little Egret** 2, Hayling Island. **Black Brant** Loch Gruinart to 24/3. **Crane** Hengistbury Head.
10th **Ring-billed Gull** Porthellick, St. Mary's to 3/8. **Sabine's Gull** Portland. **Red-rumped Swallow** Saltfleetby.
11th **American Wigeon** Roseberry Reservoir to 22nd; 2, Martin Mere to 6/3. **Green-winged Teal** Blakeney Freshmarsh. **White-tailed Eagle** Blakeney. **Ring-billed Gull** Newton Point, Mid-Glamorgan.
12th **Leach's Petrel** 3, Dunster Beach. **Little Auk** Dunster Beach.
13th **White-tailed Eagle** Walberswick to 14th. **Ring-billed Gull** Radipole Lake to 15th. **Yellow-browed Warbler** St. Columb Major, Cornwall to 4/3.
14th **White-billed Diver** Whalsay. **Great Grey Shrike** Usk Reservoir.
15th **Waxwing** 14, Inverness.
16th **American Robin** Mount Joy, Cornwall. **Little Egret** Whitchurch, Hants to 2/3. **White-tailed Eagle** Cley. **Red-throated Diver** 112, Gibralter Point. **Barnacle Goose** 11,500 Caerlaverock. **Richardson's Canada Goose** Caerlaverock.
17th **Little Ringed Plover** 2, Lincoln. **Ring-billed Gull** Taff/Ely Estuary. **Pine Bunting** Bigwaters Nature Reserve to 16/3.
18th **American Wigeon** Ulverston, Cumbria to 25th. **Green-winged Teal** Cley to 22nd. **Serin** Portland.
19th **Waxwing** 7, Norwich.
20th **Mediterranean Gull** 30, Copt Point. **Shorelark** Cresswell Pond, Northumberland.
21st **Bonaparte's Gull** Plymouth. **Sandwich Tern** Dungeness.
22nd **White-fronted Goose** 1,000 Elmley.
23rd **Ring-billed Gull** 2, Blackpill to 24th; Lodmoor. **Great Spotted Cuckoo** Lundy.
24th **Bonaparte's Gull** River Erme to 1/3. **Sabine's Gull** Stranraer. **Night Heron** Avon Valley, Hants. **Sand Martin** Trent Valley, Staffs; Leighton Moss.
25th **White-fronted Goose** 3,200 Slimbridge. **Sardinian Warbler** Newquay, Cornwall. **Wheatear** Lakenheath.
26th **Little Auk** Bude Harbour. **Sand Martin** Billing Pits, Northants; Exeter. **Sabine's Gull** Rhymney Estuary.
27th **Waxwing** 28, Thornaby, Cleveland to 28th.
28th **Bonaparte's Gull** Herdhill Scar, Cumbria. **Wheatear** Elan Valley, Powys.

MARCH

A month dominated for the most part by a succession of depressions coming in from the west. Unlike February the depression centres were generally further north, crossing to the north of Scotland. With high pressure to the south and east for much of the time this resulted in generally dry and very mild conditions in the south and east of England but extremely wet weather in the Highlands and Western Scotland.

There were exceptions to this pattern. The first two days of the month had the winds in the north and northwest resulting in heavy falls of snow in Scotland and some moderate accumulations over eastern England for a time. The 24th and 25th were particularly chilly with strong winds from the northwest again bringing snow to Scotland from a depression centred just to the south of Iceland. Other than these brief periods southwest winds predominated over England and Wales and the month was mild, sunny and much drier than usual. Temperatures mid-month reached 22°C in Norfolk and 15-17°C widely from 16th to 19th.

High pressure built from the southwest from the 26th onwards and March ended warm and sunny with light winds from the southeast over most of Britain.

1st	**Waxwing** 28, Thornaby, Cleveland. **Sabine's Gull** Souter Pt., Co.Durham.
2nd	**Green-winged Teal** Titchfield Haven. **Bonaparte's Gull** Portland. **Ring-billed Gull** Eyebrook Res. to 7th.
3rd	**Green-winged Teal** Roadford Res. to 10th. **Grey Phalarope** Salthouse to 6th. **Red-throated Diver** 183 off Hornsea.
4th	**American Wigeon** 3, Martin Mere to 7th. **Green-winged Teal** Welney to 15th. **Little Auk** Llanfairfechan, Gwynedd.
5th	**Iceland Gull** 7, Fraserburgh.
6th	**Red Kite** Royston, Herts.
7th	**Iceland Gull** 16, Ullapool.
8th	**White-tailed Eagle** Berney Marshes, Suffolk. **Sardinian Warbler** Stratton, nr Bude to 22nd. **Cuckoo** Tibberton, Worcs.
9th	**Ring-billed Gull** 3, Blackpill to 12th.
10th	**Spoonbill** Minsmere. **Green-winged Teal** Arundle Wildfowl Trust to 24th.
11th	**Spoonbill** Titchwell. **American Wigeon** Greatham Creek, Cleveland to 16th. **Red Kite** Barton Mills, Suffolk. **White-tailed Eagle** Walberswick. **Bonaparte's Gull** Kenilworth and Draycote Water to 31st. **Ring-billed Gull** 2, St. Mary's to 31st. **Garganey** 7, Marazion. **Crane** Frampton, Lincs. **Turtle Dove** Blows Downs, Bedfordshire.
12th	**White-tailed Eagle** Minsmere to 13th. **Red Kite** Hardy's Monument, Dorset.
13th	**Red Kite** Norwood Country Park, London. **Ring-billed Gull** Aber, Gwynedd to 14th.
14th	**American Wigeon** Cley to 18th. **White-tailed Eagle** Berney Marshes and 15th. **Ring-billed Gull** Par Beach. **Serin** Portland to 16th.
15th	**Mediterranean Gull** 40, Copt Pt., Kent.
16th	**Red Kite** Middleton, Norfolk.
17th	**Night Heron** 5, Scillies; Skomer to 24th; Radford Park Lake, Devon to 24th; Frampton, Lincs to 31st. **Green-winged Teal** Berney Marshes to 24th. **Red Kite** Lancaster University. **Baillon's Crake** Keyhaven, Hants. **Dartford Warbler** Waxham, Norfolk. **Woodchat** Plymouth to 25th; Portland to 7/4. **Garganey** 7, Curry Moor, Somerset. **Black-browed Albatross** Hermaness to 7/4.
18th	**Night Heron** High Wycombe; Heysham Harbour and Moss to 1/4. **Black Brant** King George V Res. **American Wigeon** Musselburgh. **Black-winged Stilt** Tresco to 16/4. **Great Spotted Cuckoo** Woolston Eyes, Cheshire. **Serin** Pagham. **Ortolan** Hengistbury Head. **Laughing Gull** Ferrybridge, Weymouth. **Common Tern** 2, Pitsford Res. **Red-footed Falcon** Holyhead, Anglesey.

19th **Red Kite** Mayday Farm, Suffolk. **Alpine Swift** Scotney Court Gravel Pit, Kent/Sussex; New Milton, Hants; Bournemouth. **Woodchat** Thurlestone, Devon & 20th. **Ring-billed Gull** Chew Valley Lake.

20th **Squacco Heron** St. Mary's to 12/4. **Purple Heron** St. Mary's. **White-tailed Eagle** Massingham Heath, Norfolk. **Bonaparte's Gull** Swanpool, Cornwall. **Great Spotted Cuckoo** Dawlish Warren to 29th. **Scop's Owl** Portland. **Alpine Swift** Bromsgrove, Hants; Swanage.

21st **Green-winged Teal** Cley to 31st. **Crane** 3, over Manchester centre. **Bonaparte's Gull** St. Marys to 31st. **Alpine Swift** Lymington; Stamford, Lincs. **Woodchat** East Prawle & 22nd. **Red Kite** Staveley, Derbys & 22nd.

22nd **Purple Heron** Axmouth. **Alpine Swift** Shoebury Ness, Essex.

23rd **Black-winged Stilt** Penally, Dyfed to 27th. **Alpine Swift** Broadstairs.

24th **Night Heron** Dymchurch & 25th; Par Beach to 26th. **American Wigeon** Bavelaw, Lothian to 27th. **Alpine Swift** Sandwich Bay and Deal. **Waxwing** 20, Newcastle centre to 29th. **Ring-billed Gull** Lound, Lincs.

25th **Night Heron** Alresford Pond. **Black-winged Stilt** Haytor Bog to 2/4. **Great Spotted Cuckoo** Sandwich Bay. **Alpine Swift** Crumbles, Sussex; Dartford Marshes, London. **Woodchat** Hope's Nose, Torquay to 2/4. **Serin** Porthcurno. **Common Swift** Lymington. **Kildeer** Upper Teesdale.

26th **Night Heron** 2-4, Par Beach to 5/4; nr Swansea. **Surf Scoter** Burghead, Grampian. **Black Kite** Yetminster, Dorset. **Alpine Swift** Boscombe, Dorset; Fareham, Hants.

27th **Night Heron** Weymouth to 29th. **Black Wheatear** St. Marys.

28th **Surf Scoter** 3, Gosford Bay to 4/4. **Black Kite** Winfrith, Dorset. **Spotted Crake** St. Agnes, Scillies to 30th. **Ring-necked Duck** Bittell Res.

29th **Waxwing** 5, Norwich to 2/4. **Golden Oriole** Tresco. **Pied Flycatcher** Ryde, Isle of Wight.

30th **Green-winged Teal** Fairburn Ings to 1/4. **Ring-billed Gull** Flint, Clwyd to 2/4. **Richards Pipit** Portland & 31st. **Subalpine Warbler** Caertillion Cove, Cornwall to 21/4.

31st **Purple Heron** Bere Ferrers, Devon to 28/4. **Rough-legged Buzzard** Knock of Braemory, Grampian to 2/4. **Black-winged Stilt** Northam Burrows to 3/4; Cogden Beach, Dorset to 3/4. **Caspian Tern** Hastings pier. **Wryneck** St. Mary's. **Great Grey Shrike** Holkham; Stratford-on-Avon. **Shoveler** 1,000 Dungeness; 800, Seaford, Sussex.

APRIL

Another very dry month generally and above average sunshine. Some very cold nights early in the month. The first four days were cold with the wind in the north bringing wintry showers and widespread night frosts with temperatures down to −10°C in places. High pressure in mid-Atlantic and a low over the continent were the systems responsible. Although still cool the wind direction backed to the southwest on the 5th and the next day further around to the east or southeast with temperatures of 8-10°C by day and frosts at night in the north. The 7th to 9th were largely sunny with just a few showers in the east as a ridge of high pressure extended over the country towards Denmark. On the 10th a cold front pushed down from the northwest bringing milder air behind it, a lot of cloud and some showers.

With a low centred over Iceland and high pressure towards the Azores this generally westerly flow continued to the 18th with day temperatures of 10-13'C, a lot of sunshine and a little rain in places. A low centred over Britain on the 19th brought very variable winds and thundery showers to most areas. As it moved away eastward northeast winds set in for a couple of days bringing cold winds to the east and south. The period 22nd to 25th was one of warm, sunny weather with light winds and temperatures reaching 15-19°C by day in many areas. However, another cold front came down from the northwest over the following 48 hours with some rain behnid it, mainly in the west. The last few days of the month were dominated by an area of high pressure coming in from the Atlantic which brought almost unbroken sunshine to most parts and temperatures of more than 20°C to some regions.

1st	**Crane** Baggy Moor, Shrops to 3rd. **Great Snipe** Thurlby, Lincs. **Common Scoter** 7,250 Dungeness. **Black-eared Wheatear** Borrowdale, Cumbria. **Alpine Swift** Bude, Cornwall. **Spotted Crake** Filey; Pennington Flash to 17th.
2nd	**Waxwing** 11, Gateshead. **King Eider** 2, Don mouth, Aberdeen to 28th. **Little Gull** 220, Seaford, Essex.
3rd	**Rough-legged Buzzard** St. Clears, Dyfed. **Great Spotted Cuckoo** North Lancing, Sussex to 2/5. **Woodchat** St. Martins. **Franklin's Gull** Bere Ferrers, Devon. **Collared Pratincole** St. Agnes, Scillies & 4th. **Purple Heron** St. Marys to 5th.
4th	**Night Heron** 3, St. Marys; Portland. **Penduline Tit** Minsmere.
5th	**Red Kite** Preston. **Rough-legged Buzzard** Cley.
6th	**Red Kite** Rushden, Northants. **Bonaparte's Gull** 1-2, Seaforth to 30th.
7th	**Black Stork** Kingston Common, Hants to 8th. **Green-winged Teal** Hornsea Mere to 18th. **Surf Scoter** 4-6, Largo Bay to 30th. **Rustic Bunting** Portland. **Red Kite** Charminster, Dorset.
8th	**Spotted Crake** St. Marys. **Black Kite** Haldon Forest.
9th	**White-billed Diver** Whalsay. **Lesser Scaup** Lound Lagoons & Rother Valley to 23rd. **King Eider** Tresta Voe, Shetland. **Black Kite** nr Wareham. **Rough-legged Buzzard** Cley. **Purple Heron** Curbridge, Hants.
10th	**American Wigeon** Breydon Water.
11th	**Ring-necked Duck** 2, Holywell Pond; Benbecula. **American Golden Plover** Frampton-on-Severn to 20th. **American Wigeon** Elmley Marshes to 21st.
12th	**Red-footed Falcon** Pennington Flash. **Black Stork** nr Ringwood. **Cattle Egret** Calbourne Mill, Isle of Wight.
13th	**Red-rumped Swallow** Minsmere & Walberswick & 14th. **Richard's Pipit** Coatham Marsh.
14th	**Spotted Crake** Great Wakering, Essex. **Black Scoter** Dornoch, Highland & 15th. **Green-winged Teal** Wheldrake Ings to 16th.
15th	**Red-rumped Swallow** Westbere, Kent to 22nd. **Night Heron** Rosemarket, Dyfed. **Great Grey Shrike** Arnfield Res., Derbys to 21st. **Little Shearwater** Portland.
16th	**Gyr Falcon** Tingwall to 17th. **Purple Heron** Tresco. **Night Heron** Littlehampton; Dungeness; Hayhead Wood, W Midlands to 22nd.
17th	**Gyr Falcon** Islay. **Penduline Tit** St. Catherine's Pt.
18th	**American Wigeon** Gladhouse Res. **Red-footed Falcon** Rye Harbour.
19th	**Blue-winged Teal** Theale Gravel Pit.

20th **Great Skua** 10, Southwold. **Great Grey Shrike** Filey Brigg to 25th.

21st **King Eider** Ythan Estuary. **Green-winged Teal** Pingewood Gravel Pit, Berks. **Great Grey Shrike** Scaling Dam to 26th. **Ring Ousel** 17, Spurn.

22nd **Alpine Swift** Worth Matravers. **Rustic Bunting** South Gare. **Woodchat** Littlehampton Golf Course to 24th. **Red-rumped Swallow** 2, Dungeness. **Black Stork** Fritham, New Forest. **Night Heron** Oxwich Marsh.

23rd **Red-rumped Swallow** 2, Worthing. **Black-eared Wheatear** South Uist. **Arctic Redpoll** Fair Isle.

24th **Night Heron** nr Bournemouth & 25th. **Arctic Tern** 100, Farmoor Res. **Serin** 6, Portland. **Bonaparte's Gull** Grimsby Docks & 25th.

25th **Little Bunting** 2, Portland. **Bee-eater** Red Rocks. **Cattle Egret** Walpole St. Andrew, Norfolk. **Night Heron** St. Marys to 30th.

26th **Yellow-headed Blackbird** Fair Isle to 30th. **Ring-necked Duck** Clumber Park to 6/5. **Ring-billed Gull** Whisby Pits, Lincs to 29th. **Spotted Crake** Appleton Res.

27th **Gull-billed Tern** 2, Selsey Bill. **Black-winged Stilt** West Charlton Marsh, Devon. **Purple Heron** Dagenham Chase. **Night Heron** Rye Harbour to 30th.

28th **Ortolan** Portland. **Crane** Filey Brigg. **Great Grey Shrike** Seahouses to 29th. **Siberian Stonechat** Fair Isle. **Bluethroat** Farne Islands. **Tawny Pipit** Reculver. **Red-rumped Swallow** Broadstairs. **Sabine's Gull** Severn Beach. **King Eider** Aberdysynni, Gwynedd.

29th **Night Heron** 2, Dungeness. **Black Kite** Hunstanton; Benacre & Kessingland. **Long-tailed Skua** Hayling Island. **Red-rumped Swallow** Selsey Bill. **Richard's Pipit** Portland. **Tawny Pipit** St. Just Airfield; Horsey, Norfolk. **Little Bunting** Dungeness. **Pomarine Skua** 31, Dungeness. **Ortolan** Portland.

30th **Black-winged Stilt** Farlington Marshes to 2/5. **Alpine Swift** Hillfield Park Res., Herts. **Woodchat** Benacre. **Red-rumped Swallow** St. Marys. **Pomarine Skua** 36, Hurst, Hants.

MAY

The first six days were very warm with high pressure over the North Sea and the low countries. The light winds came from the east and southeast and temperatures were generally 20-25°C. On the 6th and 7th a cold front moved down from the nothwest across the whole country with a low pressure system forming in it's wake and introducing much cooler and fresher conditions with rain in Scotland particularly. With the slack area of low pressure over most of the country until the 13th winds were light and variable with a good deal of sunshine, a few scattered showers and maximum daytime temperatures around 15-17°C.

A more vigorous low moved up from the southwest during the 14th and 15th bringing southwesterly winds and some heavy rain to many western and northern areas including more than and inch in N Wales and Newcastle. From the 17th to 21st the weather was largely determined by an area of high pressure moving slowly southeast from Iceland into the North Sea and bringing largely northeasterly winds. Fronts crossed Scotland and down over England and Wales from 22nd to 24th, although pressure was generally high all around, and it was mainly sunny and warm with just a few showers in Scotland. Eventually the high pressure became firmly established until the 28th with light south or southeast winds, a lot of sunshine and temperatures around 15-20°C.

Low pressure moved in from the Atlantic on the 29th with a succession of fronts coming in from the west pushing the high away into the continent and introducing a west to southwest airflow by the month's end and some rain to Scotland, Wales and western England on the 29th and 30th. As for most of the spring little of the rain in May found it's way across to the southeast of England.

1st   **Purple Heron** over Wolverhampton; 2, Carn Naun Pt., Cornwall. **Red-rumped Swallow** Slough. **Savi's Warbler** Skomer. **Ortolan** Greatstone, Kent. **Little Bunting** Dungeness. **Wheatear** 300, Fair Isle. **Bee-eater** Portland. **Black Tern** 750, New Passage, Avon. **Kentish Plover** Earls Barton Pits.

2nd   **Black Stork** 2, over Maddingley; over Watford; Ibsley, New Forest. **White Stork** over Cotswold Water Park. **Short-toed Eagle** Brading, Isle of Wight & 7th. **Pomarine Skua** 29, Dungeness. **Shore Lark** Flambo' Head & 3rd. **Red-throated Pipit** Pegwell Bay; 2, St. Martins. **Woodchat** Wick, Christchurch. **Ortolan** St. Martins. **Arctic Tern** 80, Staines Res. **White-winged Black Tern** Highbridge, Somerset. **Blue-winged Teal** Theale Gravel Pit. **Black Tern** 1,000, Holkham; 220, Belvide Res.; 170, Draycote Water.

3rd   **American Wigeon** Kinniber, Tayside. **Bonaparte's Gull** Longtown, Cumbria; Dungeness; Plym Estuary to 9th. **Night Heron** 2, Rye Harbour; 1-2, St. Marys to 15/6. **Red-rumped Swallow** Dungeness; Sumburgh Head & 4th. **Collared Pratincole** Abbotsbury. **Ortolan** Minsmere. **Subalpine Warbler** Skomer. **Tawny Pipit** St. Agnes, Scillies; Staines Res. & 4th. **Roller** nr Biggleswade, Beds. **Purple Heron** Nuneaton & Alvecote Pools.

4th   **White-billed Diver** South Uist. **Black-eared Wheatear** Skomer. **Tawny Pipit** St. Martins. **Red-rumped Swallow** Dungeness; Cromer. **Red-footed Falcon** Farlington Marshes. **American Wigeon** Hirsel Lake, Borders to 6th. **Night Heron** Ouse Washes & 5th.

5th   **Red-footed Falcon** Barling, Essex; Wet Moor, Somerset. **Woodchat** Dungeness. **Lesser Grey Srike** Kirk Yetholme, Borders. **Melodious Warbler** Barn Elms Res. **Richard's Pipit** Lundy to 8th. **Red-rumped Swallow** Winterton; Spurn. **Marsh Sandpiper** River Avon, Devon. **White Stork** nr Bourne, Lincs.

6th   **Pectoral Sandpiper** Stocks Res., Lancs to 8th; 2, West Mainland, Orkney. **Spotted Crake** Skokholm. **Red-footed Falcon** Kislingbury Gravel Pit. **Purple Heron** nr Rye. **Great White Egret** R Avon, Dorset. **Subalpine Warbler** Lundy. **Great Reed Warbler** Kilnsea. **Red-rumped Swallow** Flambo' Head. **Black Kite** Tunstall, Suffolk.

7th   **Black-winged Stilt** Skokholm. **Woodchat** Foulness Island; Prawle Pt. **Serin** 3, Portland. **Laughing Gull** Polperro. **Tawny Pipit** Sandwich Bay; Walton-on-the-Naze. **Short-toed Lark** Portland; Blakeney Pt. to 10th. **Alpine Swift** Siddlesham Ferry. **Red-necked Phalarope** Lochwinnoch to 10th. **Marsh Sandpiper** Connah's Quay & 8th. **Black Kite** Odiham, Hants. **Squacco Heron** Elmley to 14th. **Night Heron** Coate Water.

8th   **Rough-legged Buzzard** St. Kilda. **Red-footed Falcon** East Stoke, Dorset. **Red-breasted Flyctcher** Hollingbury Camp, Sussex. **Yellow-browed Warbler** Skokholm. **Citrine Wagtail** Worth Marshes, Kent to 10th. **Tawny Pipit** Waxham & 9th. **Kumlien's Gull** South Walney. **Laughing Gull** Penzance Harbour to 14th. **Pectoral Sandpiper** Scatness. **American Golden Plover** Fetlar. **Crane** 1-4, Esha Ness, Shetland to 6/6. **Green-winged Teal** Holywell Pond to 13th. **Purple Heron** Westbere, Kent to 12th.

9th **Night Heron** Holland Haven. **Tawny Pipit** Portland. **Subalpine Warbler** Portland. **Rustic Bunting** Filey Dams & 10th. **Black-eared Wheatear** Church Norton. **Red-rumped Swallow** Southwold. **Short-toed Lark** Fair Isle. **Bee-eater** 2, Vidlin, Shetland to 18th. **Broad-billed Sandpiper** Inner Marsh Farm, Cheshire to 13th.

10th **Night Heron** Hull; Salthouse & Cley & 11th. **Long-tailed Skua** Durlston Head **Franklin's Gull** Loch of Hillwell. **Red-throated Pipit** Scaling Dam & 11th. **Red-footed Falcon** Lundy; Greenabella Marsh, Teeside to 21st. **Black-winged Stilt** Lisvane Res., S Glam.

11th **Red-rumped Swallow** Cley; Southend. **Ortolan** Lowestoft to 14th; Lundy. **Spotted Crake** Llyn Llywenan, Anglesey to 14th.

12th **Lesser Grey Shrike** Kirton Marsh, Lincs. **Little Egret** 4, Rye. **Tawny Pipit** Portland. **Ortolan** Butterwick Marsh, Lincs. **Red-throated Pipit** Burnham Norton, Norfolk. **Black-winged Stilt** Stanpit Marsh & 13th. **Red-footed Falcon** North Creake, Norfolk.

13th **Red-footed Falcon** Westhay Moor, Somerset to 16th; Witham Marsh, Lincs. **Golden Oriole** 3, St. Marys. **Red-throated Pipit** Blakeney Pt. **Tawny Pipit** Gibraltar Pt. & 14th; nr Llanwrst, Gwynedd. **Red-rumped Swallow** Cuckmere Valley. **Caspian Tern** Church Norton. **Terek Sandpiper** Farlington Marshes to 23rd. **Black Kite** nr Gillingham, Kent; Bryher & Tresco.

14th **Tawny Pipit** Durlston Country Park; Winterton & 15th. **Night Heron** Southwold to 20th. **Matsudaira's Storm Petrel** Ferrybridge, Weymouth & 15th.

15th **Marsh Warbler** Heysham & 16th. **Little Bunting** Fair Isle. **Marsh Sandpiper** Cotehill Loch & 16th. **Red-footed Falcon** Holme.

16th **Ring-necked Duck** Swillington Ings & 17th. **Squacco Heron** St. Martins to 1/6. **Red-throated Pipit** Cley. **Red-rumped Swallow** nr St. Albans to 19th. **Bonaparte's Gull** Penzance Harbour. **Greater Yellowlegs** Beacon Ponds, Humberside. **Marsh Sandpiper** Lakenheath Washes, Norfolk. **Wilson's Phalarope** Findhorn Bay. **Pectoral Sandpiper** Findhorn Bay to 20th. **Crane** 3, Holme. **White Stork** Derwent Valley, Tyne & Wear.

17th **Marsh Sandpiper** Pentney Gravel Pit, Norfolk. **Great Reed Warbler** Aberlady Bay. **Marsh Warbler** Bough Beech Res. **Black Kite** Two Tree Island, Essex.

18th **Rough-legged Buzzard** North Uist. **Savi's Warbler** Besthorpe Pits, Notts to 10/6. **Little Bittern** Hinton Parva, Dorset. **Red-necked Phalarope** Rutland Water. **Black-winged Stilt** Cliffe, Kent. **Ring-necked Duck** Fairburn Ings. **Night Heron** 2, St. Marys to 29th.

19th **Marsh Sandpiper** Llwynhendry WWT, Dyfed. **Pallas's Sandgrouse** Loch of Hillwell, Shetland to 4/6. **Red-throated Pipit** Kelling Quag. **Thrush Nightingale** Isle of May & 20th. **Short-toed Lark** Cheddar Reservoir. **Great Reed Warbler** North Thoresby, Lincs. **Bluethroat** 3, Hartlepool Headland.

20th **White-billed Diver** Balranald. **White-tailed Eagle** Thornton Dale, Yorks. **Serin** Arncliffe, Yorks to 31st. **Marsh Sandpiper** Pumphouse Marsh, Cheshire & 21st. **Pechora Pipit** Skomer. **Black Kite** Skokholm. **Ortolan** Fair Isle & 21st. **Subalpine Warbler** Blakeney Pt. **Tawny Pipit** Fair Isle to 26th. **Red-footed Falcon** Cley.

21st **Black Kite** St. Marys & St. Agnes to 4/6. **Alpine Swift** Durlston Country Park. **Short-toed Lark** Ness Point, Yorks. **Black-eared Wheatear** nr Brighstone, Isle of Wight. **Icterine Warbler** Flambo' Head to 23rd.

22nd **Red-footed Falcon** Dronfield, Derbys to 27th; Seaforth Nature Reserve. **White Stork** over High Holburn, central London. **Buff-**

breasted Sandpiper Severn Beach & 23rd. **Bee-eater** St. Marys. **Red-rumped Swallow** Littlehampton.

23rd **Ortolan** Fair Isle to 25th. **Red-footed Falcon** Salthouse Heath & 24th.

24th **Scarlet Rosefinch** Fair Isle. **Lesser Crested Tern** Farne Islands & Cleveland coast to 19/8. **Gyr Falcon** Hoy, Orkney to 7/6.

25th **Woodchat** Filey Brigg. **Red-footed Falcon** 2, Bishop's Dyke, New Forest.

26th **Subalpine Warbler** Skomer. **Black Stork** Bishop's Dyke. **Great White Egret** Rutland Water. **Black-browed Albatross** Hermaness.

27th **Ancient Murrelet** Lundy to 4/7. **Crane** 3, South Mills, Beds. **Alpine Swift** Ashington, Northumberland. **Alpine Accentor** Alum Bay, Isle of Wight to 6/6. **White-throated Robin** Skokholm to 30th. **Ortolan** Portland. **Bee-eater** St. Marys & St. Agnes. **Red-footed Falcon** Cotswold Water Park & 28th. **King Eider** Deer Sound, Orkney to 2/6. **Cory's Shearwater** 2, Portland Bill.

28th **Matsudaira's Storm Petrel** Ferrybridge, Weymouth to 30th. **Kentish Plover** Christchurch Harbour. **Bee-eater** Spurn. **Black Stork** nr Salisbury. **Ring-necked Duck** Westhay Moor. **Rustic Bunting** Sumburgh to 30th. **Scarlet Rosefinch** Fair Isle to 30th; North Ronaldsay; Prawle Pt. to 30th. **Subalpine Warbler** North Ronaldsay. **Bluethroat** 3, Fair Isle. **Short-toed Lark** Fair Isle & 29th.

29th **Spotted Sandpiper** Draycote Water. **Alpine Swift** Hemel Hempstead. **Red-throated Pipit** Fair Isle. **Icterine Warbler** Fair Isle; North Ronaldsay. **Woodchat** Kilnsea to 31st. **Black-headed Bunting** Marloes, Dyfed & 30th.

30th **Rustic Bunting** 2, Sumburgh. **Scarlet Rosefinch** nr Cramlington, Northumberland. **Red-breasted Flycatcher** Fair Isle. **Terek Sandpiper** Breydon Water & 31st. **Great White Egret** Loch Lochy, Highland to 1/6.

31st **Glossy Ibis** Roath Park, Cardiff. **Barred Warbler** Scalloway to 3/6. **Spotted Sandpiper** Elland Gravel Pit to 2/7. **Red-footed Falcon** Rainham Marshes to 17/6. **Purple Heron** Middleton Marshes, Suffolk.

JUNE

Generally June was cool with half the usual sunshine hours for that month. Although it was again largely a dry period in the southeast the north and west of Britain had well above average rainfall.

The first week saw a succession of depressions crossing the Atlantic from about Newfoundland to the north of Scotland. This brought showery and sometimes very wet conditions, a cool northwesterly airflow and temperatures typically only 12-15°C, although in east Norfolk on the 1st it reached 25°C. A ridge of high pressure to the west of Ireland parted two areas of low pressure on the 10th and this pulled down more cool air bringing north to northeasterly winds until the 13th. The high pressure gradually established itself over the southeast of England over the next few days bringing winds in from the southeast and raising temperatures a few degrees.

Low pressure dominated the rest of the month. A system to the west of Ireland from the 18th to 21st pushed a succession of fronts across the whole of Britain bringing considerable amounts of rain to the west and some showers to the east. Eventually this low forced itself across Scotland and into the North Sea by the 26th bringing cool west and northwest winds behind it. Somewhat warmer, showery weather came later in the month as a low formed off southern Ireland and winds went around to the south and southeast.

1st **Great White Egret** Bunarkaig, Highland. **Scarlet Rosefinch** North Ronaldsay; Holm, Orkney; 1-2, Lundy to 9th. **Marsh Warbler** Towcester. **Icterine Warbler** Souter Pt., Durham. **Collared Flycatcher** Loch Druidibeg.

2nd **Scarlet Rosefinch** Fetlar. **Black Stork** New Forest. **Black-headed Wagtail** St. Marys & 3rd. **Least Tern** Rye Harbour to 12/7. **Spoonbill** 3, Minsmere.

3rd **Scarlet Rosefinch** Sumburgh Hotel & 4th. **Pectoral Sandpiper** Loch of Strathbeg to 12th. **Surf Scoter** Murca, Grampian to 18th. **King Eider** 2, Ythan Estuary. **Great White Egret** Loch Drona, Highland.

4th **Alpine Swift** nr Garstang, Lancs. **Red-footed Falcon** Gibralter Pt. to 15th. **Great White Egret** Cromarty Firth. **Squacco Heron** Aveton Gifford, Devon to 6th. **Shore Lark** Skokholm.

5th **Golden Oriole** 3, Sandwich Bay. **Red-breasted Flycatcher** St. Kilda. **Scarlet Rosefinch** N Ronaldsay.

6th **Marsh Warbler** Dunnet Head. **Bee-eater** Hilbre Island. **Broad-billed Sandpiper** Cley. **Tree Swallow** St. Marys to 10th. **Red-footed Falcon** Theale Gravel Pits. **Surf Scoter** Bressay & 7th. **King eider** Murca, Grampian. **Black Stork** Flitcham, Norfolk. **Purple Heron** Minsmere.

7th **Wilson's Phalarope** Slimbridge to 10th. **Broad-billed Sandpiper** Titchwell. **Red-footed Falcon** Colne Pt.

8th **Woodchat** Flotta, Orkney & 9th. **Marsh Warbler** N Ronaldsay. **Swift** 10,000 Rutland Water.

9th **Pectoral Sandpiper** Hayle Estuary & 10th.

10th **Rustic Bunting** St. Kilda & 11th. **Great Reed Warbler** Chapel Rossan Bay, Dumfries & Galloway. **Scarlet Rosefinch** 2, Stronsay.

11th **Scarlet Rosefinch** Portland. **Crane** 2, Lakenheath. **Black Kite** Leiston, Suffolk.

12th **Crane** Hurstpierpoint, Sussex.

13th **Icterine Warbler** Skokholm. **Scarlet Rosefinch** 2, Iona.

14th **Great Reed Warbler** Iken Cliff, Suffolk. **Red-necked Phalarope** Elmley, Kent.

15th **Lesser Yellowlegs** Gibraltar Pt. to 17th. **Greenish Warbler** Portland & 16th. **Alpine Swift** Colliford Lake. **Night Heron** Denaby Ings to 28th.

16th **Terek Sandpiper** Breydon Water. **Kentish Plover** Dawlish Warren. **Black Kite** Easton Broad.

17th **Broad-billed Sandpiper** Kingston, Morayshire to 19th. **Red Kite** Grimspound, Dartmoor & 18th.

19th **Greenish Warbler** Skomer. **Kentish Plover** Cley to 21st.

20th **Richard's Pipit** North Duffield Carrs, Yorks to 26th. **Red-footed Falcon** Chelmer Valley, Essex to 10/7. **Marsh Sandpiper** Sidlesham Ferry to 9/7. **American Golden Plover** Sandwich Bay to 23rd. **Cory's Shearwater** Hope's Nose, Devon.

21st **Black Stork** Leighton Moss.

22nd **Blue-winged Teal** Cley to 12/7.

23rd **Lesser Grey Shrike** Salcott, Essex to 2/7. **Broad-billed Sandpiper** Greatham Creek. **Red-footed Falcon** Cley. **Black Stork** Sanday. **Night Heron** Rye Harbour. **White-billed Diver** Yell.

24th **Ring-billed Gull** Teesmouth Reclamation Pond to 30th. **Storm Petrel** 100, Hope's Nose, Devon.

26th	**Red-footed Falcon** 3, Bishop's Dyke, New Forest.
27th	**Caspian Tern** Rye Harbour.
28th	**Alpine Swift** Colliford Lake. **Red-footed Falcon** Sandwich Bay.
30th	**Black-eared Wheatear** Rossendale, Lancs. **Little Shearwater** Flambo' Head.

JULY

A month rather of two halves. The first somewhat changeable and the second generally settled and hot with no rain anywhere over most of Britain between the 17th and 26th. Many parts of southeast England had no rain to speak of all month.

The month began with a low centred over Scotland pulling cool and showery northwesterlies across most of Britain. Further fronts came in from the Atlantic between the 4th and 10th bringing rain or showers to most parts particularly on the 4th when almost everywhere had between 0.5" and 1" of rain. Winds were still from the west or northwest and temperatures generally 15-19°C. From the 10th a large area of high pressure slowly moved up from the southwest bringing hot and sunny weather to the south and southeast until the 15th when a weak cold front crossed all areas. This was only a temporary 'blip' however as immediately behind the front high pressure built over Britain with a return to temperatures in the range of 25-27°C in many places inland. The high pressure persisted until the 27th and temperatures reached 30-32°C in some places on the 20th.

From the 27th to 30th a series of cold fronts came in from the west bringing some much needed rain to most parts (other than SE England!). The 31st was dry and sunny as high pressure formed again over central England.

1st	**Swift** 10,000 Spurn. **Scarlet Rosefinch** Spurn & 2nd.
2nd	**Yellow-breasted Bunting** Lundy. **Green-winged Teal** Blacktoft to 7th. **Great White Egret** Welney.
3rd	**Surf Scoter** Murca, Grampian to 11/8. **American Golden Plover** Sidlesham Ferry. **Spotted Sandpiper** Farmoor Res. & 4th.
5th	**Night Heron** Denaby Ings to 18th.
6th	**Red-necked Phalarope** 1-2, Cley to 12th; N Ronaldsay.
7th	**Matsudaira's Storm Petrel** Tynemouth. **Night Heron** Cley. **Pied Wheatear** Newhaven, Sussex to 9th.
8th	**Pectoral Sandpiper** Cley to 1/8.
9th	**Franklin's Gull** Sutton Bingham Res. & 10th.
10th	**Red-necked Phalarope** Bowness, Cumbria.
12th	**Stilt Sandpiper** Cliffe Pools to 22nd. **Red-footed Falcon** Kelling Quagg. **Night Heron** Otley Gravel Pits. **Bee-eater** Loch of Strathbeg. **Rose-coloured Starling** Stronsay. **Marsh Warbler** Stronsay.
13th	**White-rumped Sandpiper** South Gare to 3/8. **Black Kite** St. Marys & 14th.
14th	**Richard's Pipit** Lundy to 21st. **Tawny Pipit** Cropston Res.; Poole Harbour. **Savi's Warbler** 3, Minsmere to 28th.
15th	**Bee-eater** Bempton. **White-winged Black Tern** Leighton Moss & Dockacres Pits. **Great White Egret** Hickling Broad. **Pacific Golden Plover** Ouse Washes & 16th. **Honey Buzzard** 4, Haldon Hill. **Caspian Tern** Dungeness.
16th	**Sabine's Gull** Dunbar Castle. **King Eider** Don Mouth. **Pectoral Sandpiper** Rockcliffe, Cumbria. **Caspian Tern** Sale Water Park. **Night Heron** nr Llandeilo, Dyfed. **Bee-eater** 2, BarnardsGreen, Worcs. **Red-footed Falcon** Langley Mill, Derbys/Notts & 17th.
17th	**Red Kite** Crookham, Hants. **Great Northern Diver** Rutland Water to 21st.

19th   **White-rumped Sandpiper** Blackmoorfoot Res. & 20th. **Great White egret** Scaling Dam. **Bee-eater** Great Wakering.
20th   **Bee-eater** Belstead, Suffolk.
21st   **Bonaparte's Gull** Millbrook Lake & 22nd.
22nd   **Caspian Tern** Cley. **Pacific Golden Plover** Pilling Marsh to 24/8. **Broad-billed Sandpiper** Hornsea Mere.
23rd   **Great White Egret** Welney & 24th. **Red Kite** Botley, nr Oxford. **White-rumped Sandpiper** Saltholme Pools & Greatham Creek to 1/8.
24th   **Tawny Pipit** Portland. **Black Stork** Bempton.
25th   **King Eider** Fair Isle to Oct. **Two-barred Crossbill** 2, Fair Isle to 7/8. **Spotted Crake** Belvide Reservoir. **Pacific Golden Plover** Stanpit Marsh to 27th.
26th   **Night Heron** Berwick. **Broad-billed Sandpiper** Gibraltar Pt. & 27th. **Pectoral Sandpiper** Kellet Pool, Lancs; 1-2, Fagbury Reserve, Suffolk to 9/8. **Red-necked Phalarope** Canvey Island. **Black Kite** Haldon Hill & 27th.
27th   **Cory's Shearwater** 51, Porthgwarra. **'yellow-legged'Herring Gull** 36, Dungeness. **Black Stork** Barnwell, Northants & 28th.
28th   **Cory's Shearwater** 1,000+ Porthgwarra. **Marsh Warbler** Landguard Pt. **Black Stork** Ellough Airfield, Suffolk & 29th. **Broad-billed Sandpiper** Cley to 31st. **Greenish Warbler** Fife Ness.
29th   **Black Stork** Kessingland & Hemley, Suffolk. **Red-footed Falcon** Sand, Shetland. **Ferruginous Duck** Fairburn Ings to 27/8. **Great Shearwater** 6, Porthgwarra. **Red-backed Shrike** 2, Pool of Virkie.
30th   **Great Shearwater** Prawle Point.
31st   **Two-barred Crossbill** Hoy, Orkney to 12/8. **Bonaparte's Gull** Gairloch, Ross. **Curlew Sandpiper** 129, Cliffe Pools, Kent.

AUGUST

Most of the month was hot and dry. Over Britain as a whole second only to August 1976 since records began.

High pressure with light south to southeast winds prevailed for the first three days. It was very hot in places with 36°C (97°F) at Barbourne (Worcs.) on the 2nd and a record breaking 37°C (99°F) at Cheltenham the next day, the highest temperature ever recorded in Britain. Many stations recorded 32°C or more although in Scotland it was only 20-25°C. Cold fronts pushed across the whole of Britain over the 4th and 5th bringing temperatures down to this level everywhere and some rain to Scotland on northwest winds.

This 'light'westerly weather kept conditions at a comfortable level until the 14th with a large high pressure system in mid-Atlantic and lows around Iceland. It was generally dry and sunny everywhere with just a few showers in Scotland. A depression moved south over Scotland on the 15th-18th bringing fresh to strong NW winds. The first rainfall of the month was recorded inmany areas and in some parts of the east and southeast of England it was the first appreciable precipitation for several months. More than 0.5″ fell in some places on the 19th and even more on the East Anglian coast the next day as the low moved away into the North Sea and further fronts crossed from the west. The Atlantic high extended a ridge behind these fronts bringing a return to warm and sunny weather over England and Wales from 22nd-24th with accompanying light SE or variable winds.

Fronts came in from the west on 25th bringing W or SW winds over England and Wales and easterlies to Scotland. There were thunderstorms in many central areas and it felt 'sticky'with temperatures around 25°C. It was generally dry over the 26th and 27th with an area of high pressure over Denmark and winds from the S or SE swinging around to the SW then W by the 29th. Rain came in to the west and southwest of the country and some showers to the east on the 30th and 31st with temperatures a pleasant 20°C.

1st   **Pectoral Sandpiper** N Ronaldsay; Cley to 3rd. **Melodious Warbler** Prawle Pt.; Worthing & 2nd. **Broad-billed Sandpiper** Cley.

2nd   **Pacific Golden Plover** Oakenholt Marsh to 4th. **Alpine Swift** Illogan, Cornwall. **King Eider** Greyhope Bay, Grampian to 11th.

3rd   **White-rumped Sandpiper** Cley to 14th.

4th   **Aquatic Warbler** 6-8, Church Cove, Gunwalloe to 8th. **Hoopoe** Durlston Country Park to 11th. **Caspian Tern** Doonfoot &Martnaham Lochs to 6th. **Red-necked Phalarope** Pitsford Res. **Buff-breasted Sandpiper** Whitburn to 8th. **Pectoral Sandpiper** Loch of Strathbeg. **Spotted Crake** Radipole to 11th. **King Eider** Ythan Estuary to 18th.

5th   **Melodious Warbler** St. Agnes; Portland & 6th. **Rose-coloured Starling** St. Agnes & 6th. **Red-necked Phalarope** Snettisham. **Marsh Sandpiper** Dungeness. **Broad-billed Sandpiper** Blakeney Harbour & 6th. **Great White Egret** Pagham Harbour.

6th   **Sardinian Warbler** Pett Level. **Red-footed Falcon** Cley. **Great White Egret** Newton Marsh, Isle of Wight.

7th   **Bee-eater** Hadstone Carr. **Stilt Sandpiper** Trimley Marshes to 18th. **Pectoral Sandpiper** Farlington Marshes to 14th. **Pacific Golden Plover** Cley & 8th.

8th   **Pectoral Sandpiper** Rudyard Res., Staffs. **Long-billed Dowitcher** Weaver Bend to 13th. **Great White Egret** Dungeness.

9th   **Spotted Crake** Tresco to 13th.

10th   **Aquatic Warbler** Penclacwydd, Dyfed. **Black Stork** Teme Valley, Powys to 5/9. **White Stork** Egham. **Pectoral Sandpiper** Kelling Quag & 11th.

11th   **Pectoral Sandpiper** Cley; Ringley Sewage Works, Gtr Manchester to 18th. **Purple Heron** 2, Burnham Norton. **Icterine Warbler** Lizard.

12th   **Aquatic Warbler** Kenfig. **Red-footed Falcon** Hadleigh Downs, Essex. **Icterine Warbler** Lundy to 16th. **Woodchat** St. Catherine's Pt., Isle of Wight. **Semi-palmated Sandpiper** Oldbury Power Station, Avon to 14th.

13th   **Little Egret** 5, Penclacwydd, Dyfed. **Pectoral Sandpiper** Old Hall Marshes. **Red-necked Grebe** 38, Gosford Bay.

14th   **Melodious Warbler** Portland. **Pectoral Sandpiper** Abberton Res. to 18th. **Purple Heron** Portland.

15th   **Terek Sandpiper** Cresswell Pond. **White-rumped Sandpiper** Whitburn to 29th.

16th   **Great Shearwater** 14, Pendeen; 15, St. Ives. **Pectoral Sandpiper** Cley; Salthouse; Pennington Flash. **Sabine's Gull** 2, St. Ives. **Barred Warbler** N Ronaldsay & 17th. **Greenish Warbler** Fair Isle. **Two-barred Crossbill** Fair Isle. **Red-necked Phalarope** Lacock Gravel Pit, Wilts.

17th   **Two-barred Crossbill** 3-4, Rendall, Orkney to 22nd. **Pectoral Sandpiper** Gib. Point; Aveton Gifford, Devon. **Long-tailed Skua** 6, over Wilstone Res., Tring. **Ferruginous Duck** Hanningfield Res. to 19th.

18th   **Wilson's Phalarope** Porthleven & Hayle Estuary to 28th. **Icterine**

Warbler South Walney. **Red-necked Phalarope** Church Wilne Res., Derbys to 22nd. **Golden Eagle** Mellor Moor, Derbys.

19th **Red-necked Phalarope** Abberton Res. to 24th. **Black Tern** 450, Dungeness. **Caspian Tern** Weirwood Res. **Great Shearwater** 9, Porthgwarra. **Black-browed Albatross** Skokholm.

20th **Aquatic Warber** 2, Kenfig. **Pectoral Sandpiper** nr Castleford to 6/9. **Long-tailed Skua** 4, Holmpton, Humberside. **Red-necked Phalarope** Snettisham. **White-rumped Sandpiper** Sidlesham Ferry to 27th. **Blue-winged Teal** Titchwell to 4/10.

21st **Woodchat** St. Martins to 7/9. **Lesser Yellowlegs** Staines Res. to 8/9.

22nd **Ortolan** Portland. **Icterine Warbler** Church Norton to 23rd. **Sabine's Gull** 2, Flambo' Head. **Red-necked Phalarope** Minsmere. **Little Egret** 11, Brands Bay, Poole Harbour.

23rd **Two-barred Crossbill** Fair Isle. **Woodchat** nr Marlborough, Wilts. **Bonaparte's Gull** Torpoint to 26th. **Long-billed Dowitcher** Draycote Water to 26th.

24th **Dartford Warbler** Barns Ness, Lothian. **Icterine Warbler** Blakeney. **Red-necked Phalarope** Cley to 29th. **White-rumped Sandpiper** Minsmere to 28th.

25th **Greenish Warbler** Blakeney Pt.; Wells Wood; Reculver; Filey Brigg to 28th. **Barred Warbler** N Ronaldsay. **Icterine Warbler** Holme Dunes; Portland to 28th. **Melodious Warbler** Church Norton. **Black Stork** over Kennington Oval.

26th **Icterine Warbler** Wells & 27th; Beachy Head. **Arctic Warbler** Fair Isle & 27th. **Bonelli's Warbler** Isle of Grain & 27th. **Melodious Warbler** St. Just, Cornwall. **Pectoral Sandpiper** 1-2, Drift Res. to 16/9. **Black-eared Wheatear** Bulverhythe, Sussex & 27th. **Ortolan** Sidlesham Ferry to 29th. **Black Stork** Old Hall Marshes & 27th. **Ferruginous Duck** Priory Water, Leics. **Cory's Shearwater** Newtonhill, Grampian.

27th **Marsh Warbler** Whitburn. **Red-necked Phalarope** N Killingholme. **Melodious Warbler** Hollingbury Camp, Sussex. **Yellow-breasted Bunting** Fair Isle & 28th. **Scarlet Rosefinch** Reculver. **Two-barred Crossbill** Yesnaby, Orkney. **Woodchat** Filey Brigg. **Greenish Warbler** Unst; Sizewell, Suffolk to 30th. **Barred Warbler** 3, Fair Isle & 28th; Holland Haven to 30th. **Citrine Wagtail** Fair Isle to 30th. **White-winged Black Tern** West Thurrock Power Station, Essex to 6/9. **Marsh Sandpiper** Eden Estuary. **Pectoral Sandpiper** Stanpit Marsh to 2/9.

28th **Tawny Pipit** Spurn/Kilnsea & 29th. **Barred Warbler** Stronsay. **Icterine Warbler** Dungeness; West High Down, Isle of Wight; St. Marys. **White-winged Black Tern** Oare Marshes, Kent. **Pectoral Sandpiper** Grafham Water to 30th. **Night Heron** Pitsford Res.

29th **Barred Warbler** 3, N Ronaldsay to 1/9. **Icterine Warbler** St. Martins; Alum Bay, Isle of Wight; Whitburn. **Tawny Pipit** Waxham. **Red-necked Phalarope** Rye Harbour to 2/9. **White-rumped Sandpiper** St. Marys.

30th **Spotted Crake** Penclacwydd, Dyfed to 2/9. **Great White Egret** Clyst Estuary, Devon. **Sabine's Gull** 2, Pendeen. **American Golden Plover** N Ronaldsay to 2/9.

31st **Aquatic Warbler** 2, Kenfig.

SEPTEMBER

September was sunnier than average over Britain but also slightly colder due to a few cold nights towards the month's end. It was yet another very dry month generally even though the 29th and 30th brought wet weather everywhere for a time. For example some parts had only 0.25" of rain all month until the last day produced 1" or more.

With a slack area of low pressure centred over the Irish Sea the 1st and 2nd had winds light and from the SW or W. Very warm weather was still widespread with temperatures up to 26°C. A deepening depression to the south of Iceland brought a more vigorous NW airstream the next two days with a large high in mid-Atlantic and the remnants of hurricane Gustav to the west of that. A warm front followed by a cold one crossed all parts on the 5th with southerly winds veering NW to W and strengthening to near gale force over some western areas. The high moved east across Britain on the 7th and dominated the weather until the 16th, bringing sunny weather and temperatures aroud 20°C for most of England and Wales but nearer to 15°C in Scotland. Showers had been quite widespread on the 6th and a few in the east and north on the 7th but otherwise the period was dry everywhere. This spell was broken by a low over Iceland pushing a cold front southeastwards across Britain. Again there was a large high in mid-Atlantic and a dying hurricane further west, this time Isidore. The cold front brought showers to the north and west and as the low deepened and moved east to the north of Scotland on the 19th it brought gale force winds from the NW to many places. These winds continued over the 20th to 23rd but as the depression slipped down towards Denmark they veered to the NE over Scotland on the 24th and over most of Britain the next day, with showers in many places and temperatures averaging 15°C.

An area of high pressure formed to the south of Iceland on the 25th and moved SE down over Britain during the next three days. This brought settled, sunny weather with winds between N and E veering to SW by the 27th as the high slipped away south into the continent. Fronts stretching the width of the Atlantic gradually pushed SE over the whole of Britain from the 28th to 30th bringing mild SW winds and rain to nearly all areas.

1st **Icterine Warbler** Wells Dell. **Pectoral Sandpiper** Stanpit Marsh & 2nd; St. Fergus Lagoon & 2nd; Eyebrook Res. **Black Stork** Benacre. **Great White Egret** Stour Valley, Kent to 17th. **Ring-necked Duck** Anglers Country Park, Yorks to 11th; Marden Quarry to 3rd. **King Eider** Fair Isle to Oct. **Spotted Crake** 1–2, St. Marys to 5th. **American Golden Plover** Foula & 2nd. **Temminck's Stint** Abberton Res to 18th.

2nd **Icterine Warbler** All Hallows, Kent; Lundy. **Black Tern** 120, Tilbury. **Cory's Shearwater** South Gare. **Black Kite** Letheringsett, Norfolk; Chippenham, Cambs. **Swallow** 17,000 Marton Mere.

3rd **Swallow** 7,000 Landguard Pt. **Serin** Dungeness. **Black Kite** N Wootton. **Temmincks Stint** Dosthill G Pit & 4th. **White-winged Black Tern** Skokholm. **Red-necked Phalarope** Rye Harbour & 4th. **Icterine Warbler** Soar, Devon.

4th **Icterine Warbler** Grutness; Durlston Country Park; Thorpeness, Suffolk. **Ortolan** Lundy. **Tawny Pipit** Littlehampton Golf Course. **Black Kite** Snailwell, Cambs. **Long-toed Stint** S Uist to 7th.

5th **Baikal Teal** Fort Henry Ponds, Leics to 14th.

6th **Sooty Shearwater** 63, St. Ives. **Wilson's Petrel** Strumble Head. **Great Shearwater** Strumble Head. **Lesser Yellowlegs** Powderham, Exe Estuary. **Baird's Sandpiper** St. Fergus Lagoon to 18th. **American Wigeon** Wath Ings. **Semi-palmated Sandpiper** Ogmore Estuary to 17th. **Scarlet Rosefinch** 2, N Ronaldsay.

7th **Great Shearwater** 2, Strumble Head. **Little Shearwater** Flambo' Head; Hartlepool Headland. **Arctic Skua** 117, Shell Ness, Kent.

Little Egret 7, Exe Estuary. **Melodious Warbler** Portland & 8th. **Aquatic Warbler** 1–2, Skomer to 9th. **Pectoral Sandpiper** Wheldrake Ings. **Barred Warbler** Fife Ness. **Rose-coloured Starling** St. Marys to 9th.

8th   **Sabine's Gull** 4, Flamborough Head. **Pectoral Sandpiper** Tophill Low Res; Aveton Gifford, Devon. **Ortolan** 1–2, Portland to 17th. **Tawny Pipit** Reculver. **Greenish Warbler** Holme.

9th   **Olivaceous Warbler** Hengistbury Head. **Icterine Warbler** Portland. **Melodious Warbler** Weirwood Res. **Greenish Warbler** Gib Point. **Black Kite** Reculver. **Red Kite** Rostherne Mere. **Curlew Sandpiper** 90, Ythan Estuary; 37, Rutland Water. **Scarlet Rosefinch** Cruden Bay to 17th. **Ortolan** Cruden Bay. **Cory's Shearwater** Flambo' Head. **Pectoral Sandpiper** Hornsea Mere to 17th. **Buff-breasted Sandpiper** Druridge Bay; St. Marys Airfield & Tresco to 23rd. **Wilson's Phalarope** Snettisham. **Hoopoe** Easington to 15th. **Yellow-breasted Bunting** Fair Isle to 14th.

10th   **Wilson's Phalarope** Holy Island. **Rose-coloured Starling** Thanet. **Ferruginous Duck** Cropston Res to 3/11. **Broad-billed Sandpiper** Hauxley. **Gyr Falcon** Harlech to 26th. **Sabine's Gull** Blithfield Res. **Spoonbill** Fleet, Dorset.

11th   **Ortolan** 3, Durlston Country Park. **Icterine Warbler** Church Norton & 12th. **Yellow-breasted Bunting** Gib Point. **Scarlet Rosefich** Tynemouth. **Citrine Wagtail** Fair Isle to 13th. **Woodchat** Fair Isle. **Marsh Sandpiper** Hodbarrow, Cumbria. **Cory's Shearwater** Anstruther, Fife; Seaton Sluice.

12th   **Barred Warbler** Lilstock, Somerset to 14th. **Red-breasted Flycatcher** Sandwich Bay. **Sabine's Gull** Hartlepool Bay. **Spotted Sandpiper** Mere Sands Wood, Lancs. **American Wigeon** Titchwell. **Surf Scoter** Lunan Bay. **Hoopoe** Holkham. **Icterine Warbler** St. Agnes to 14th.

13th   **Ring-billed Gull** Seaforth to 26th. **Pectoral Sandpiper** Chew Valley Lake to 17th. **Scarlet Rosefinch** Gibraltar Point. **Yellow-browed Warbler** Benacre.

14th   **Black Stork** Radipole & 15th. **American Wigeon** Messingham Pits. **Cory's Shearwater** Brough, Orkney. **White-rumped Sandpiper** N Ronaldsay. **Long-billed Dowitcher** Fair Isle & 15th. **Icterine Warbler** Holland Haven. **Spotted Crake** Wath Ings. **Hoopoe** Abberton Res. **Yellow-browed Warbler** Ladywell Park, London. **Serin** St. Aldhelm's Head. **Tawny Pipit** Portland.

15th   **Tawny Pipit** Blakeney Pt. **Barred Warbler** Bamburgh. **Yellow-browed Warbler** Southwold. **Rose-coloured Starling** Davidstow Airfield. **Spotted Crake** Dorking, Surrey. **Lazuli Bunting** nr Seaton, Cornwall to 26th. **Golden Eagle** Betws-y-coed to 18th. **Gull-billed Tern** 2, Athafield, Isle of Wight. **American Wigeon** Seaforth. **Marsh Sandpiper** Double Bay, Northumbs. **Baird's Sandpiper** 2, St. Fergus Lagoon to 18th. **Pectoral Sandpiper** Colliford Lake. **Long-billed Dowitcher** Slidderywater Foot, Arran to 17th. **Pied-billed Grebe** Ellesmere to Dec.

16th   **Black Stork** nr Penzance. **Baird's Sandpiper** Witham mouth, Lincs. **Emperor Goose** Stornoway to Dec. **Ring-necked Duck** Pitsford Res to 23rd. **Red Kite** Whiteadder Res to 23rd. **Scarlet Rosefinch** Pothgwarra. **Melodious Warbler** TrevoseHead. **Yellow-browed Warbler** St. Marys; North Cotes, Lincs; Cruden Bay. **Tawny Pipit** West High Down, Isle of Wight. **Barred Warbler** Walton-on-the-Naze; Kirkwall, Orkney. **Red-throated Pipit** Red Rocks to 18th. **Bluethroat** 3, Fair Isle. **Red-breasted Flycatcher** Blakeney Pt.

17th   **Citrine Wagtail** Portland. **Barred Warbler** Dungeness. **Yellow-browed Warbler** Pagham. **Little Bunting** Kilnsea. **Ring-billed Gull** Marlow, Bucks. **Night Heron** Ironbridge, Shrops to 29th. **Surf Scoter** Hartlepool Bay. **Black-browed Albatross** off Strumble Head. **Kentish Plover** Breydon Water.

18th   **Melodious Warbler** Portland to 24th. **Pectoral Sandpiper** Stithians Res; nr Stornoway. **Spotted Crake** Marsworth Res, Tring; Titchfield Haven.

19th   **Buff-breasted Sandpiper** Tresco & 20th. **Grey Phalarope** Alresford Pond; Cley. **Sabine's Gull** 10, St. Ives.

20th   **Yellow-throated Vireo** Kenidjack Valley to 27th. **Red-eyed Vireo** Cot Valley to 30th. **Grey Phalarope** 48, S Uist; Kidwelly Quay; Loch of Strathbeg to 24th. **Ring-billed Gull** Bideford to 24th; Aberdeen. **Spotted Crake** Tresco.

21st   **American Golden Plover** Scatness, Shetland. **Kentish Plover** Shell Ness, Kent to 26th. **Snow Goose** Meikle Loch to 23rd. **Greater Flamingo** Gibraltar Point. **Arctic Redpoll** St. Kilda.

22nd   **Little Egret** 8, Studland & 23rd. **Great Shearwater** Landguard Pt & Lowestoft; 2, Mull of Galloway. **Grey Phalarope** Blithfield Res to 24th. **Leach's Petrel** 550, New Brighton. **Wilson's Phalarope** Pennington Flash. **Sabine's Gull** Humphrey Head; 3, Seaforth; New Brighton; Filey Brigg. **American Golden Plover** St. Kilda to 24th. **Little Shearwater** Pendeen. **American Wigeon** Messingham Pits to 11/10. **Little Bunting** Fair Isle; Unst. **Two-barred Crossbill** Kergord, Shetland. **Red-breasted Flycatcher** Fair Isle. **White's Thrush** Sumburgh Farm, Shetland. **Yellow-browed Warbler** Stronsay; Holm, Orkney; St. Klda; 2, Cruden Bay.

23rd   **Hoopoe** Stronsay. **Ring-billed Gull** Whitby Marina. **Baird's Sandpiper** Benacre Broad. **King Eider** Loch Fleet. **Great Shearwater** Flambo' Head. **Sabine's Gull** 1-2, Lowestoft & 24th. **Wilson's Phalarope** Martin Mere & Burton Marsh to 5/10. **Buff-breasted Sandpiper** St. Marys to 25th. **Long-billed Dowitcher** Drift Res. **Parrot Crossbill** Fair Isle. **Booted Warbler** Kilnsea & 24th. **Lanceolated Warbler** Fair Isle. **Olive-backed Pipit** 1-3, Fair Isle to 2/10. **Richard's Pipit** 2, West Runton, Norfolk. **Yellow-browed Warbler** Evie, Orkney; Holy Island to 1/10; Tynemouth; Filey Brigg. **Pechora Pipit** St. Kilda. **Ortolan** 4, Landguard Pt.

24th   **Scarlet Rosefinch** 2, N Ronaldsay. **Richard's Pipit** 2, Fair Isle. **Yellow-browed Warbler** South Gare; N Ronaldsay; 2, Lucke Park, Cleveland. **Ring-necked Duck** Stithians Res to 1/10. **Pectoral Sandpiper** Blacktoft Sands. **Buff-breasted Sandpiper** Hauxley. **Long-tailed Skua** 10, Hound Pt, Lothian.

25th   **Hoopoe** West Runton & 26th. **Grey Phalarope** Cley. **Red-necked Phalarope** Cley. **Long-billed Dowitcher** Lynn Pt, Norfolk to 15/10. **Cory's Shearwater** Flambo' Head. **Sabine's Gull** Tynemouth. **Yellow-browed Warbler** St. David's Head; Filey. **Melodious Warbler** St. Marys & 26th. **Pechora Pipit** Scalloway. **Icterine Warbler** Kenfig. **Red-eyed Vireo** St. Marys & 26th.

26th   **Scarlet Rosefinch** 2, Fair Isle. **White's Thrush** Eyemouth, Borders. **Red-breasted Flycatcher** Portland. **Siberian Stonechat** Salthouse; Fair Isle to 30th. **Olive-backed Pipit** Sumburgh Hotel to 30th. **Black-throated Thrush** N Ronaldsay to 28th. **Yellow-browed Warbler** Scoughall, Lothian; Sandwich Bay; Potters Barn Park, Merseyside; nr Seaforth. **Arctic Warbler** St. Kilda. **Barred Warbler** St. Abbs Head to 2/10. **Spoonbill** 2, Lodmoor.

27th   **Lesser Yellowlegs** Kidwelly Marsh & Quay to 19/11. **Yellow-**

browed Warbler Dungeness. **Black Stork** Binstead, Isle of Wight.

28th **Melodious Warbler** Prawle Pt. **Icterine Warbler** Prawle Pt. to 30th. **Tawny Pipit** Skomer. **Rose-coloured Starling** Skomer. **Yellow-browed Warbler** Lowestoft.

29th **Lesser Grey Shrike** Whalsay to 14/10. **Citrine Wagtail** Quendale, Shetland & 30th. **Olive-backed Pipit** N Ronaldsay & 30th. **Icterine Warbler** N Uist to 9/10. **Aquatic Warbler** Etwall, Derbys to 2/10. **Sabine's Gull** Dungeness & 30th. **Grey Phalarope** Druridge Bay. **Green-winged Teal** Chew Valley Lake to Dec. **Long-tailed Skua** Hound Pt. **Curlew Sandpiper** 104, East Tilbury, Essex.

30th **Scarlet Rosefinch** 2, N Ronaldsay. **Two-barred Crossbill** 1-2, Sandringham to 22/10. **Red-eyed Vireo** Spurn to 1/10. **Woodchat** Prawle Point to 14/10. **Red-breasted Flycatcher** 2, Fair Isle; St. Marys; S Uist; Hengistbury Head; East Fleet, Dorset & 1/10. **Dusky Warbler** Fair Isle. **Melodious Warbler** 2, Portland; Loch Eynort to 2/10. **Aquatic Warbler** Titchfield Haven. **Lanceolated Warbler** Fair Isle. **Swainson's Thrush** FairIsle to 3/10. **Ring-necked Duck** Billing Gravel Pit. **Cory's Shearwater** Dunbar. **White-winged Black Tern** 2, Inverkeithing Harbour.

OCTOBER

Overall a mild and wet month with rainfall 1.5 to 2 times normal in many places from Sussex to Strathclyde. Average temperatures were 0.5 to 3.5°C above the usual for October in most areas of England and Wales whilst sunshine hours were near to normal.

A depression between Iceland and Greenland pushed a cold front across the whole of Britain as it moved eastwards over the first few days of the month. Winds were strong and from the SW at first veering W behind the front. There was a lot of rain in Scotland on the 2nd and then in England and Wales the following day. On the 5th and 6th another area of low pressure moved quickly eastwards across Scotland bringing more heavy rain to NW England and Scotland particularly with 1–2 inches recorded in some places. High pressure was to dominate the weather for a change over the 7th to 9th with an anticyclone to the SW of Iceland maintaining a generally westerly airflow over most of Britain. Winds were predominantly NW on the 7th although N to NE over S and SW England. However everywhere had SW winds on the 8th, light over the south of England but fresh to strong in northern parts. The wind continued to come largely from the SW until the 11th with fronts bringing rain to Scotland trying to move south over the rest of the British Isles. Their progress was hampered by warm air to the south which, as winds backed further to the south and even SE at times over the 12th to 15th, raised temperatures to near record levels for October reaching 22°C in many places. The inevitable low to the south of Iceland with its attendant troughs and fronts eventually began to have it's own way from 15th bringing a SW airflow and showers, many thundery. A spin-off from this was a depression forming in the western Channel on the 16th and as this moved slowly NE over the following two days it turned winds to the SE and E over all of Britain. This brought a lot of heavy rain to the eastern half and temperatures of 15–18°C in the south and 11–14°C in the north.

A low to the west of Ireland and a large high over Scandinavia from the 19th to 26th kept the SE run of winds over all of Britain. It was generally dry until the 24th when fronts moving in from the SW brought rain to much of England and Wales. The depression gradually pushed eastwards bringing further rain and introducing a westerly airflow from the 27th to the month's end. As this low had been gathering moisture for some time to the west of Ireland rain was torrential in most areas on the 28th with 1–2 inches widely and 0.5" at least almost everywhere. It was the wettest day in Britain for three years. The low eventually passed into the North Sea and winds went around to a strong northwesterly on the 31st bringing showers and cooler weather (11–13°C) generally.

1st Ortolan St. Marys. **Melodious Warbler** Portland; St. Marys to 3rd. **Barred Warbler** St. Abbs Head. **Little Bunting** Balivanich, W Isles. **Tawny Pipit** Portland. **Olive-backed Pipit** Stronsay; Fair Isle; N Ronaldsay to 5th. **Short-toed Lark** Whalsay. **Long-tailed Skua** 5, Hound Pt, Lothian. **Honey Buzzard** Hilbre Island.

2nd Ruppell's Warbler Whalsay to 18th. **Olive-backed Pipit** Whalsay to 4th; 2, Fair Isle. **Yellow-browed Warbler** 2, Durlston Country Park; 9 Scillies. **House Martin** 15,000 Dungeness. **Two-barred Crossbill** nr Clun, Shrops to 6/11. **Barred Warbler** Landguard Pt. **Melodious Warbler** East Soar, Devon; S Uist. **Icterine Warbler** Nanquidno. **Red-throated Pipit** Fair Isle. **Red-rumped Swallow** Hadleigh, Essex. **Buff-breasted Sandpiper** Snettisham to 4th. **Black Kite** nr Drift, Cornwall to 10/11.

3rd Sabine's Gull 2, Dungeness. **Whiskered Tern** Strumble Head. **Little Bunting** N Ronaldsay. **Rustic Bunting** Fair Isle; Tresco & 4th. **Honey Buzzard** Warwick. **Spotted Crake** St. Marys. **White's Thrush** Stronsay. **Olive-backed Pipit** Whalsay & 4th; 2, Kergord, Shetland to 6th. **Short-toed Lark** 1-2, N Ronaldsay to 12th. **Little Auk** 6, Whitburn.

4th Alpine Swift St. Margaret's Bay, Kent. **Arctic Redpoll** 3, Whalsay. **Barred Warbler** Stronsay. **Icterine Warbler** Prawle Pt to 7th. **Bluethroat** St. Marys to 14th. **American Wigeon** Messingham Pits.

5th Olive-backed Pipit 2, Whalsay to 8th; 2, Kergord, Shetland; 2, Vidlin, Shetland. **Yellow-browed Warbler** 3, Kergord; 7, St. Marys. **Arctic Redpoll** Kergord. **Buff-breasted Sandpiper** Chew Valley Lake. **Little Bunting** Stronsay. **Scarlet Rosefinch** 3, St. Marys. **Greenish Warbler** Whalsay to 7th. **Greater Flamingo** Breydon Water & 6th. **Great Shearwater** St. Marys.

6th Olive-backed Pipit 2, Kergord; Geosetter, Shetland. **Soft-plumaged Petrel** Strumble Head. **Little Gull** 60, Fife Ness. **Greater Flamingo** Gib Point & 7th. **Hoopoe** Staines Res. **Little Bunting** Benbecula. **Blackpoll Warbler** Sumburgh Head. **Arctic Redpoll** 3, Unst. **Arctic Warbler** Unst to 8th. **Icterine Warbler** N Uist. **Snowy Owl** Unst to 8th. **Cory's Shearwater** Filey Brigg.

7th Cory's Shearwater Spurn; Snettisham. **Great Shearwater** Snettisham; Flambo' Head. **Surf Scoter** St. Andrews Bay. **Red-throated Thrush** Easington, Humberside. **Sora Rail** Skomer. **Grey-cheeked Thrush** St. Agnes & 8th. **Barred Warbler** Keyhaven; St. Abbs Head. **Melodious Warbler** Portland to 16th; St. Marys to 14th. **Purple Heron** Stopton, Devon. **Red-breasted Flycatcher** Porthgwarra. **Ring-necked Duck** Hule Moss. **Ferruginous Duck** Druridge Bay; Eccles Tarn, Cumbria. **Rough-legged Buzzard** S Uist to 28th. **American Golden Plover** Troon. **Pectoral Sandpiper** Pitsford Res to 17th. **Siberian Stonechat** Whitburn & 8th; Wick Hams nr Christchurch. **Snowy Owl** Sumburgh. **Terek Sandpiper** Blyth Estuary to Dec. **Two-barred Crossbill** 1-2, Bedgebury Pinetum to 13/11.

8th Serin Heysham. **Melodious Warbler** Radipole Lake. **Scarlet Rosefinch** 2, Lundy to 17th. **Bonaparte's Gull** St. Marys. **Two-barred Crossbill** Haldon Forest & 9th. **Radde's Warbler** Tresco.

Greater Flamingo Landguard Pt; Minsmere. **Aquatic Warbler** St. Agnes to 17th. **Siberian Stonechat** South Stack,Anglesey. **Tawny Pipit** Burnham Norton. **Crane** 4, Landguard Pt. **Ring-necked Duck** Tresco to 17th. **American Wigeon** Vane Farm to 5/12. **Barred Warbler** Skokholm.

9th   **Wilson's Petrel** S Walney. **Forsters Tern** Par Beach. **Long-billed Dowitcher** Westwood Pool, nr Droitwich to 20th. **Ring-necked Duck** Bogton Loch, Strathclyde. **Tawny Pipit** Tresco. **Greenish Warbler** Tresco. **Rustic Bunting** Lundy. **Richard's Pipit** Lundy. **Melodious Warbler** St. Levan, Cornwall to 14th.

10th   **Melodious Warbler** Lundy to 20th. **Little Bunting** Lundy & 11th. **Little Egret** Chew to 24th. **Black-billed Cuckoo** St. Marys. **Swainson's Thrush** 1-2, St. Marys to 24th. **Scarlet Rosefinch** 3, Bryher.

11th   **Barred Warbler** St. Marys to 15th. **Red-necked Phalarope** Scarborough. **American Golden Plover** Bryher, St. Martins & Tresco to 17th. **Surf Scoter** St. Andrews. **American Wigeon** Pennington Flash & 12th.

12th   **Gull-billed Tern** Loch Ryan. **Gyr Falcon** Strumble Head. **Little Bunting** Lundy to 15th; St. Marys. **Red-breasted Flycatcher** 2, Porthgwarra. **Red-throated Pipit** nr Littlehampton. **Richard's Pipit** 3, St. Marys to 19th. **Short-toed Lark** Blakeney Point. **American Golden Plover** Rother Valley Country Park to 16th. **Ferruginous Duck** Hollowell Res. **Purple Heron** Slapton Ley.

13th   **Red-breasted Flycatcher** Girdleness; Stronsay. **Penduline Tit** 6, Ely, Cambs; Cley. **Tawny Pipit** Durlston. **Olive-backed Pipit** Tresco. **Red-throated Pipit** Plymouth & 14th. **Richard's Pipit** 3, Trevose Head, Cornwall. **Little Bunting** St. Marys to 17th. **Red-rumped Swallow** Trevail, Cornwall. **Scarlet Rosefinch** Cot Valley. **Long-billed Dowitcher** Camel Estuary. **Two-barred Crossbill** Stockhill, Somerset. **Radde's Warbler** Flambo' Head. **Yellow-browed Warbler** 5, Hartlepool Headland. **Barred Warbler** Toab, Shetland. **Honey Buzzard** Blakeney Pt. **Green-winged Teal** Martin Mere to Dec.

14th   **Parrot Crossbill** Whalsay. **Siberian Stonechat** N Ronaldsay; Stiffkey. **Ferruginous Duck** Penicuik; Brothers Water; Crumbles, Sussex. **Richard's Pipit** Gib Point; 3, Donna Nook. **Red-throated Pipit** Ladybrook Valley, nr Stockport. **Olive-backed Pipit** 2, Portland. **Great Grey Shrike** Frensham Common to Dec. **Isabelline Shrike** Donna Nook & 15th. **Lesser Yellowlegs** Nanjizal, Cornwall. **Little Bunting** N Ronaldsay. **Rustic Bunting** Lands End to 17th. **Golden Oriole** N Ronaldsay. **Short-toed Treecreeper** St. Margarets Bay, Kent to 21st. **Pallas's Warbler** Whalsay. **Barred Warbler** 3, N Ronaldsay. **Melodious Warbler** 2, St. Marys. **Marsh Warbler** Kergord, Shetland & 15th. **Grey-cheeked Thrush** Slimbridge. **Short-toed Lark** St. Agnes & 15th. **Spoonbill** 3, Arne. **Ring-necked Duck** Marden Park. **Surf Scoter** Marros, Dyfed & 15th. **Honey Buzzard** Thornbury, Avon. **Bonaparte's Gull** Newman's Flash, Cheshire.

15th   **Red-breasted Flycatcher** Rame Head to 20th; 3, Fair Isle; 2, St. Martins. **Richard's Pipit** Barns Ness. **Olive-backed Pipit** St. Marys. **Little Bunting** Tresco to 17th. **Radde's Warbler** Barns Ness. **Icterine Warbler** Happisburgh. **Long-billed Dowitcher** Caerlaverock to Dec. **Pectoral Sandpiper** Sennen, Cornwall; Crowan Res to 22nd. **Sociable Plover** Welney to 30th.

16th   **Pallas's Warbler** Eswick, Shetland. **Richard's Pipit** Cropston Res; Aberlady Bay. **Oive-backed Pipit** Fair Isle. **Red-throatedPipit** St. Marys to 21st. **Melodious Warbler** Portland. **Icterine Warbler**

Gt.Yarmouth Cemetery. **Sardinian Warbler** Cot Valley. **Red-eyed Vireo** Lundy to 18th. **Rustic Bunting** 1-2, Tresco to 22nd. **Spotted Crake** St. Marys; St. Agnes to 18th; Tresco to 19th.

17th **Great White Egret** Bardsey. **Hoopoe** Monmouth Golf Course to 21st. **Red-breasted Flycatcher** Durlston. **Yellow-breasted Bunting** Spurn. **Ortolan** St. Agnes; N Ronaldsay. **Siberian Stonechat** N Ronaldsay; Llanfairfechan & 18th. **Dusky Warbler** Salthouse. **Penduline Tit** 3, Tresco & 18th. **Rose-coloured Staring** nr Skelmersdale.

18th **Redwing** 26,000 Flambo' Head; 12,000 Donna Nook. **Goldcrest** 3,000 Donna Nook. **Pallas's Warbler** Marsden; Flambo' Head; Grimston, Humbs. **Radde's Warbler** Seaburn; Bardsey. **Dusky Warbler** St. Marys Island, Tyne & Wear; Inner Farne & 19th. **Lanceolated Warbler** Bardsey. **Barred Warbler** Stronsay. **Icterine Warbler** Ceibwr, Dyfed. **Olive-backed Pipit** 2, Fair Isle; Blakeney Pt; Donna Nook; Hauxley. **Rustic Bunting** Newbiggin to 21st. **Little Bunting** St. Marys to 20th; Fair Isle; Flambo' Head; Farne Islands to 25th. **Siberian Stonechat** St. Marys Island. **Parrot Crossbill** 5, Donna Nook. **Arctic Tern** 40, Draycote Water. **Arctic Redpoll** 1-2, Blakeney Pt to 21st. **Short-toed Treecreeper** Dungeness to Dec. **Isabelline Wheatear** St. Marys, Scilly to 2/11. **Waxwing** 40, Fair Isle. **Red-rumped Swallow** N Ronaldsay. **White-winged Black Tern** Draycote Water & 19th. **Long-billed Dowitcher** Durleigh Res to 23rd.

19th **Fieldfare** 9,500 Gib Point. **Dusky Warbler** Druridge Bay; North Cotes; Saltfleetby; Holkham & 20th; Fair Isle. **Radde's Warbler** Aldburgh, Humbs; Holkham. **Pallas's Warbler** 1-3, Filey to 23rd; Tynemouth. **Booted Warbler** Inner Farne. **Barred Warbler** Newbiggin & 20th. **Greenish Warbler** Cruden Bay. **Bonelli's Warbler** St. Agnes. **Parrot Crossbill** 3, Filey. **Marsh Warbler** Portland. **Little Bunting** 2, Fair Isle; South Gare. **Ring-necked Duck** 2, Looe Pool. **Siberian Stonechat** Hartlepool Headland; Kenidjack Valley. **Pied Wheatear** Holme, Norfolk to 21st. **Grey-cheeked Thrush** St. Marys to 25th. **Olive-backed Pipit** St. Agnes. **Red-breasted Flycatcher** Soar, Devon; nr Titchwell, Norfolk. **Richard's Pipit** Lundy.

20th **Fieldfare** 13,000 Stonecreek, Humbs. **Robin** 1,500 Spurn. **Solitary Sandpiper** Malaclete, N Uist. **Wilson's Phalarope** S Walney. **Olive-backed Pipit** nr Skegness; Boulby, Cleveland; Cruden Bay; 2, Druridge Bay. **Pechora Pipit** Lands End & 21st. **Red-throated Pipit** Flambo' Head. **Richard's Pipit** Penclacwydd, W Glam. **Siberian Stonechat** Scatness, Shetland & 21st; Flambo' Head; Cruden Bay. **Pallas's Warbler** Kilnsea; Priors Park, Hartlepool; Wells, Norfolk; Donna Nook; Muchalls, Grampian. **Dusky Warbler** Filey & 21st; Flambo' Head & 21st; Minnis Bay, Kent & 21st. **Parrot Crossbill** 3, Gib Point; 2, Donna Nook. **Little Bunting** Gib Point; Benbecula. **Red-rumped Swallow** Chew Lake. **Bee-eater** Holywell Bay, Cornwall. **Yellow-browed Warbler** 2, Cruden Bay. **Rough-legged Buzzard** Balranald to 24th.

21st **Fieldfare** 15,000 Ripon; 10,000 Fairburn Ings. **Eye-browed Thrush** Tresco. **Hermit Thrush** Trevose Head. **Isabelline Wheatear** Kilnsea to 23rd. **Siberian Stonechat** Cruden Bay; Bamburgh. **Night Heron** Dalston, Cumbria & 22nd. **Short-toed Lark** Treen, Cornwall to 30th; St. Marys. **Olive-backed Pipit** Woodhorn Cemetery, Northumbs to 23rd. **Barred Warbler** Filey; Bamburgh. **Pallas's Warbler** 2, Marsden Hall; Sumburgh Head to 23rd; Cruden Bay; Spurn; Whitburn Churchyard; Skate-raw, Lothian & 22nd. **Radde's Warbler** nr Donna Nook & 22nd. **Dusky Warbler** Kilnsea & 22nd. **Red-breasted**

Flycatcher 3, Gib Point. **Great Grey Shrike** 3 Spurn; Prawle Pt to 23rd; Skate-raw to 24th. **Serin** 2, Cot Valley to 24th. **Blyth's Pipit** Skewjack, Cornwall to 1/11. **Parrot Crossbill** 4, Holme; 2, Gib Point to 26th. **Pine Bunting** Bamburgh & 22nd. **Rustic Bunting** Flambo' Head.

22nd **Richard's Pipit** 2, Balmedie, Grampian. **Olive-backed Pipit** 2, Portland. **Blackpoll Warbler** St. Marys to 25th. **Surf Scoter** Telpyn Pt, Dyfed. **White-tailed Eagle** St. Margarets Bay, Kent. **Pallas's Warbler** nr Lizard to 24th; Denburn Wood, Fife to 26th. **Serin** 2, St. Agnes. **'humei' Yellow-browed Warbler** Cruden Bay. **Barred Warbler** Fife Ness & 23rd. **Bee-eater** Tresco & St. Agnes to 9/11. **Long-billed Dowitcher** Braunton, Devon.

23rd **Saker Falcon** Sheringham. **White-tailed Eagle** Spurn. **Rough-legged Buzzard** Walberswick. **Tawny Pipit** Hartlepool Headland. **Olive-backed Pipit** Fair Isle; 2, St. Marys & 24th. **Pallas's Warbler** Sumburgh Head; St. Marys. **Icterine Warbler** St. Agnes. **Melodious Warbler** Nanquidno. **Penduline Tit** 5, Titchfield Haven. **Arctic Redpoll** 2, Stronsay. **Little Bunting** Fair Isle. **White-billed Diver** Holme, Norfolk.

24th **Great Reed Warbler** Big Water NR. **Sardinian Warbler** nr Treen, Cornwall & 25th. **Barred Warbler** Waxham. **Pallas's Warbler** Stronsay. **Dusky Warbler** Stronsay; Cley to 27th; St. Marys. **Waxwing** 40, Lerwick. **Collared Flycatcher** Lundy. **Melodious Warbler** 2, Lundy. **Bluethroat** St. Marys. **Tawny Pipit** Portland to 30th. **Olive-backed Pipit** 2, Fair Isle; St. Agnes. **Ferruginous Duck** Swithland Res; New Swillington Ings, Yorks. **Black Brant** Swalecliffe, Kent to Dec. **Purple Heron** Reculver.

25th **Little Bunting** St. Marys. **Rustic Bunting** N Foreland, Kent & 26th. **Serin** 2, St. Marys. **Firecrest** 15, Dungeness. **Bonelli's Warbler** Porthgwarra to 28th. **Melodious Warbler** St. Marys to 28th. **Red-rumped Swallow** Overstrand, Norfolk. **Rough-legged Buzzard** Isle of Sheppey. **Surf Scoter** Burghhead, Grampian to 27th; Skokholm.

26th **Baird's Sandpiper** Hartland Pt to 30th. **Pallas's Warbler** Stromness. **Radde's Warbler** Tresco to 28th. **Siberian Stonechat** Flambo' Head. **Olive-backed Pipit** St. Marys. **Red-necked Phalarope** Gib Point. **Ring-necked Duck** Dockacres G Pits to end Dec.

27th **White-tailed Eagle** Wyberton, Lincs; Snettisham & Sandringham. **Swift** Breydon Water. **Parrot Crossbill** Sandwich Bay. **American Golden Plover** nr Lands End to end Dec. **Red-eyed Vireo** Seaburn, Tyne & Wear to 29th. **Rose-coloured Staring** Crail. Fife to 2/11. **Radde's Warbler** Flambo' Head; Craster. **Sardinian Warbler** Scarbo' Castle. **Siberian Stonechat** 1-2 Flambo' Head to 29th. **Olive-acked Pipit** N Ronaldsay. **Barred Warbler** Skokholm.

28th **Olive-backed Pipit** Whalsay. **Dusky Warbler** Frakkafield, Shetland to 1/11. **Red-rumped Swallow** 2, Tyninghame, Lothian. **Razorbill** 10,000 Strumble Head. **Richard's Pipit** Milton Keynes to 30th. **Red-throated Pipit** nr Treen. **Waxwing** 50-100 Inverness to Dec. **Little Bunting** Filey & 29th. **Grey Phalarope** Priory Water, Leics.

29th **Laughing Gull** Sunderland Docks. **Arctic Redpoll** Cley.

30th **Red Kite** Louth, Lincs. **Little Bunting** Fetlar. **Arctic Redpoll** 2, Unst.

31st **Grey Phalarope** Ellesmere to 8/11. **Rough-legged Buzzard** Spurn.

NOVEMBER

A tendency for winds to come from either the east or north for much of the month resulted in eastern England being wetter than usual and the west of Britain much drier. Overall rainfall was well below normal over the British Isles. Day time maximum temperatures were average for November but there were comparitively few cold nights.

With low pressure over Scandinavia and high pressure mid-Atlantic the first four days of the month saw cold, northerly winds over the whole of Britain with showers or longer periods of rain in most places and snow over the Scottish mountains. The high moved east to N Scotland over the 5th to 7th bringing lighter winds from the eastern half.

As fronts approached from the SW on the 8th winds freshened from the SE over the whole country. These fronts slowly pushed NE across Britain over the next four days bringing some showers, and winds eventually veering to the SW everywhere by the 13th. Fresh west to northwest winds then dominated until the 20th with a low by then positioned in the North Sea.

Winds were very light and variable or from the north by the 22nd, bringing the only widespread frosty night of the month, before freshening from the south or SE on the 23rd as a depression moved in from the Atlantic. This low positioned itself over southern England until the 26th bringing NE winds and some heavy rain to the SE. As the low moved NE towards the Baltic a high formed over Northern Ireland which kept mainly light winds from the N or NE until the end of the month, with just a few showers in the east and north of the British Isles.

1st	**Double-crested Cormorant** St. Mary's, Scillies to 4th. **Whiskered Tern** Ellesmere to 3rd. **Richard's Pipit** Snettisham to 5/12. **Pallas's Warbler** East Soar, Devon. **Olive-backed Pipit** St. Martin's Scillies & 2nd. **Shore Lark** Walton-on-the-Naze to 6th. **Pectoral Sandpiper** St. Mary's & 2nd.
2nd	**Desert Wheatear** Beeley Moor, Derbys. **Two-barred Crossbill** Rhinefield, New Forest to 16th. **Yellow-browed Warbler** Littlehampton Golf Course. **Olive-backed Pipit** St. Mary's to 5th. **Alpine Swift** nr Leyland, Lancs. **Green-winged Teal** Martin Mere to end Dec. **American Wigeon** Messingham. **Snow Goose** 4 Montrose Basin; Martin Mere to 4th. **Greater Flamingo** Elmley to Dec: Southwold.
3rd	**Grey Phalarope** Farlington Marshes; Seasalter, Kent; Shell Ness. **Rough-legged Buzzard** Spurn; Boyton, Suffolk to 20th. **Surf Scoter** Seaton Sluice & 4th. **Iceland Gull** Cley; Felixstowe to end Dec. **Little Auk** 2 Abberton Res. **Sardinian Warbler** Porthgwarra. **Yellow Warbler** Helendale, Lerwick & 4th. **Little Bunting** Keyhaven. **Alpine Accentor** Rough Tor, Cornwall. **Richard's Pipit** Parrett Estuary to 6th.
4th	**Cetti's Warbler** Marton Mere, Lancs. **Rough-legged Buzzard** Dunwich. **Desert Wheatear** Pagham. **Great Grey Shrike** Bishop's Dyke, New Forest to Dec. **Parrot Crossbill** 10-30 Kirkby Moor, Lincs to Dec. **Pallas's Warbler** Dunwich Monastery. **Shore Lark** Barmston. **Little Auk** 1,500 Flamborough Head. **Sabine's Gull** Waxham. **Long-tailed Skua** Hornsea. **American Wigeon** 1-2 Stenhouse Res. to Dec. **Snow Goose** Carnforth, Lancs to 24th.
5th	**Parrot Crossbill** 6 Holkham. **Dusky Warbler** Holme to 11th. **Little Auk** 670 Flambo' Head. **Black-winged Stilt** Titchwell. **White-tailed Eagle** Hickling area to 15/12. **Cory's Shearwater** Flambo' Head.
6th	**Parrot Crossbill** 5 Hamsterley Forest to Dec. **Hoopoe** Cromer to 8th.

Red Kite nr Boston. **Surf Scoter** Nairn to 9th. **King Eider** Don Mouth to end Dec. **Black Brant** Breydon Water to Dec.

7th **Dusky Warbler** 2 Holme. **Short-toed Treecreeper** Sandwich Bay. **Firecrest** 10 Dungeness.

9th **Iceland Gull** 3 Lerwick. **Ring-necked Duck** Poole Park Lake to Dec. **Spoonbill** Exe Estuary. **Great Grey Shrike** Wentwood Forest to Dec.

10th **'humei' Yellow-browed Warbler** Aldborough, Humbs to 14th. **Dusky Warbler** Blacktoft & 11th.

11th **Hoopoe** Rainham, Notts. **Waxwing** 300 Scarborough. **Parrot Crossbill** 44 Kirkby Moor, Lincs. **Two-barred Crossbill** Derwentdale, Yorks. **Pallas's Warbler** Gunners Park, Essex. **Tawny Pipit** Reculver. **Red-rumped Swallow** Swanage & 12th; Layer de la Haye Pits, Essex to 16th. **Shore Lark** Holkham Gap. **Surf Scoter** Filey Bay. **Green-winged Teal** Blithfield Res. to 27th.

12th **Green-winged Teal** 2 Martin Mere. **Shore Lark** Snettisham. **Parrot Crossbill** 5–9 Lockwood Beck Res. to Dec.

13th **Parrot Crossbill** 10–38 Chopwell Wood, Tyne & Wear to 23rd. **Little Egret** 12 Poole Hbr.

14th **Spoonbill** 3 Arne. **Cory's Shearwater** Sandwich Bay. **Richard's Pipit** Skomer to 25th.

15th **Shore Lark** 2 Thornham Pt.

16th **Bee-eater** Hope's Nose, Devon.

17th **Pallas's Warbler** Pagham. **Waxwing** 60 Lowestoft. **Ring-billed Gull** Ryde, Isle of Wight to Dec. **Grey Phalarope** Titchfield Haven.

18th **Waxwing** 110 Guisborough. **Crane** Wilstone Res. **Grey Phalarope** Cley; Abberton Res. **Ring-billed Gull** Chew to end Dec; Shoreham.

19th **Parrot Crossbill** 5–12 Mayday Farm to Dec.

20th **Rough-legged Buzzard** Massingham Heath to 28th. **Hoopoe** Maidenhead, Berks to 28th. **Black-bellied Dipper** Tinwell, Lincs to Dec.

21st **Hoopoe** Sutton-on-Trent to 25th. **Two-barred Crossbill** Wakering Great Wood; Northants to 28th.

22nd **Waxwing** 250 Aberdeen to Dec; 200 Edinburgh to Dec. **Parrot Crossbill** Wakering Great Wood to Dec.

23rd **Rough-legged Buzzard** Fritton Lake, Suffolk to Dec. **Iceland Gull** Flambo' Head.

24th **Parrot Crossbill** 6–10 Harwood Forest to Dec. **Ross's Gull** Barmston, Humbs. **American Wigeon** Vane Farm to end Dec. **Spoonbill** Withymoor Pool, Stourbridge.

25th **Spoonbill** Venus Pool, Shrewsbury to 29th. **Grey Phalarope** Abberton Res; Audenshaw Res & 26th. **Snowy Owl** Pool of Virkie. **Richard's Pipit** Spurn. **Two-barred Crossbill** Linford Arboretum, Norfolk to end Dec. **Water Pipit** 18 Chew. **Waxwing** 80 Newcastle.

26th **Grey Phalarope** Northam Burrows to 1/12.

27th **Yellow-browed Warbler** Marsh Mills, Plymouth to 9/12. **Arctic Redpoll** Holkham Pines. **American Wigeon** Exe Estuary.

28th **Penduline Tit** Radipole. **Pallas's Warbler** Filey & 29th. **Surf Scoter** Colwyn Bay to 30th. **Iceland Gull** Littlehampton.

29th **Desert Wheatear** Southwold to 5/12. **White-tailed Eagle** Highcliffe & Hengistbury Head. **Parrot Crossbill** Elan Valley & 30th.

30th **Glossy Ibis** Welches Dam, Ouse Washes to 4/12.

DECEMBER

Not only wetter and much windier in most places than the average December it was also the coldest since 1981 throughout the British Isles.

High pressure dominated the first week with light winds mainly from the west and north and some widespread fog in central areas. From 7th a cold front pushed down across the whole of Britain bringing snow and strong winds to most areas. The cold winds had veered to the NE by the 10th bringing more snow to southern areas. Daytime maxima rarely reached 5°C over much of Britain until the 20th when high pressure and winds from the east gave way to a depression over northern Scotland and its attendant westerlies. Low pressure centred around Iceland dictated the weather for the rest of the month bringing often strong winds from the westerly half. There was a lot of rain over England and Wales and blizzard conditions over Scotland for much of the last week.

1st	**Pallas's Warbler** Benacre Broad & 2nd. **Crane** 2 Dungeness. **Long-billed Dowitcher** Dungeness & Denge Marsh to 24th. **Rough-legged Buzzard** nr Orford to 31st. **Snow Goose** 1–2 Loch of Strathbeg to 31st.
2nd	**Surf Scoter** Llandulas to 19th. **Long-billed Dowitcher** Fremington Pill, Devon. **Parrot Crossbill** 14 nr Market Rasen. **Green-winged Teal** Llyn Traffwll, Anglesey to 6th. **Greater Flamingo** nr Walberswick to 5th.
5th	**Lesser White-fronted Goose** Slimbridge to 11th. **Night Heron** Brixham. **'humei' Yellow-browed Warbler** nr South Stack & 6th. **Yellow-browed Warbler** Cardiff. **Shore Lark** Snettisham.
6th	**Laughing Gull** Corby, Northants. **Yellow-billed Cuckoo** Sandy.
7th	**Franklin's Gull** Dawlish Warren. **Arctic Redpoll** 1–4 Holkham Pines & Wells Wood to 31st.
9th	**Two-barred Crossbill** Sandringham. **Little Auk** 2,300 Girdle Ness. **White-billed Diver** Whalsay to 31st. **Iceland Gull** 2 Ullapool. **Glaucous Gull** 2 Ullapool. **Waxwing** 270 Edinburgh. **Parrot Crossbill** 2 Wakerley Great Wood, Northants.
10th	**Little Auk** 670 Sheringham.
11th	**Great Northern Diver** Ringstead G Pits, Northants to 14th.
12th	**Sabine's Gull** Margate. **Little Auk** 3,800 Whitburn. **Iceland Gull** Radipole Lake.
13th	**Two-barred Crossbill** Mortimore Forest, Ludlow. **Little Auk** 1,850 Flambo' Head. **Grey Phalarope** South Gare. **Surf Scoter** Burgh Head, Grampian. **Greater Flamingo** Minsmere to 25th.
14th	**Surf Scoter** Culbin Bar. **Spoonbill** Taw Estuary to 31st.
15th	**Rough-legged Buzzard** Fingringhoe Wick to 31st. **Surf Scoter** 2–4 Musselburgh to 31st. **Smew** 15 Wraysbury. **Little Egret** West Wittering.
16th	**American Wigeon** Cotswold Water Park to 21st. **Parrot Crossbill** 7 Castle Eden Dene to 24th; 13 Lockwood Beck Res; 16 nr Market Rasen. **Ring-necked Duck** Little Sea, Studland.
17th	**Arctic Redpoll** Tollesbury Wick. **Great Northern Diver** Chasewater to 31st; Hanningfield Res. & 18th. **Ivory Gull** Lerwick to 21st.
19th	**Iceland Gull** Ullswater.
20th	**Snow Goose** 2 Penrith.
21st	**Ring-necked Duck** Clatworthy Res. **Great Shearwater** Flambo' Head. **Snowy Owl** nr Wainfleet, Lincs to 31st.
22nd	**Grey Phalarope** King George V Res. to 31st. **Ring-necked Duck** Timsbury G Pits to 31st. **Waxwing** 280 Rosyth. **Red Kite** Coate Water. **Little Auk** 1,700 Filey Brigg; 600 Flambo' Head.

23rd **Rough-legged Buzzard** 2 nr Orford. **King Eider** Ythan Estuary to 31st. **Red Kite** Wells. **Waxwing** 200 Blaydon, nr Newcastle.

24th **Shore Lark** Druridge Bay to 31st. **Iceland Gull** Foremark Res. to 31st. **American Wigeon** nr Lympstone, Devon to 31st.

25th **Grey Phalarope** South Gare.

26th **Shore Lark** 2 Shell Island, Gwynedd & 27th.

27th **Iceland Gull** 2 Taff Estuary.

28th **Glaucous Gull** 8 Unst. **Red Kite** Weybourne.

29th **Franklin's Gull** Brighton Marina. **Green-winged Teal** 2 nr Southport.

30th **Rough-legged Buzzard** Colne Marsh. **Grey Phalarope** Abberton Res. & 31st; Seaton Sluice. **Ring-billed Gull** Sinah G Pit, Hants; Radipole Lake. **Iceland Gull** 2 Newquay, Cornwall.

31st **Red Kite** Orford; Kings Lynn. **Waxwing** 380 Edinburgh. **Ring-billed Gull** 2 Radipole Lake.

SPECIES CHECKLISTS

The lists below include species recorded up to December 1990. The total for England is 550, Scotland 486 and Wales 408. Altogether, with the 8 species listed at the end only seen in Ireland, the Isle of Man and the Channel Islands, the total is 585 for the British Isles. Some of the more distinguishable or interesting subspecies which have occurred are also listed (but omitted from the totals above) and appear as their scientific names underneath the specific vernacular.

	E	S	W						
Red-throated Diver:	●	●	●						
Black-throated Diver:	●	●	●						
Great Northern Diver:	●	●	●						
White-billed Diver:	●	●							
Pied-billed Grebe:	●	●	●						
Little Grebe:	●	●	●						
Great Crested Grebe:	●	●	●						
Red-necked Grebe:	●	●	●						
P.g. holbollii:		●							
Slavonian Grebe:	●	●	●						
Black-necked Grebe:	●	●	●						
Black-browed Albatross:	●	●	●						
Fulmar:	●	●	●						
Soft-plumaged Petrel:	●		●						
Capped Petrel:	●								
Bulwer's Petrel:	●								
Cory's Shearwater:	●	●	●						
Great Shearwater:	●	●	●						
Sooty Shearwater:	●	●	●						
Manx Shearwater:	●	●	●						
P.p. mauretanicus:	●	●	●						

	E	S	W						
P.p. yelkouan:	●								
Little Shearwater:	●	●	●						
Wilson's Petrel:	●	●	●						
White-faced Petrel:	●	●							
Storm Petrel:	●	●	●						
Leach's Petrel:	●	●	●						
Madeiran Petrel:	●								
Matsudaira's Petrel:	●								
Gannet:	●	●	●						
Cape Gannet:		●							
Cormorant:	●	●	●						
Double-crested Cormorant:	●								
Shag:	●	●	●						
Dalmatian Pelican:	●								
White Pelican:	●	●							
Magnificent Frigatebird:		●							
Bittern:	●	●	●						
American Bittern:	●	●	●						
Little Bittern:	●	●	●						
Night Heron:	●	●	●						
Green Heron:	●	●							
Squacco Heron:	●	●	●						
Cattle Egret:	●		●						
Little Egret:	●	●	●						
Great White Egret:	●	●	●						
Grey Heron:	●	●	●						
Purple Heron:	●	●	●						
Black Stork:	●	●	●						
White Stork:	●	●	●						
Glossy Ibis:	●	●	●						
Spoonbill:	●	●	●						
Greater Flamingo:	●								
Mute Swan:	●	●	●						
Bewick's Swan:	●	●	●						

	E	S	W						
C.c. columbianus:	●								
Whooper Swan:	●	●	●						
Bean Goose:	●	●	●						
Pink-footed Goose:	●	●	●						
White-fronted Goose:	●	●	●						
Lesser White-fronted Goose:	●	●	●						
Greylag Goose:	●	●	●						
Snow Goose:	●	●	●						
Ross's Goose:	●	●							
Emperor Goose:	●	●							
Canada Goose:	●	●	●						
B.c. minima/hutchinsii:	●	●							
Barnacle Goose:	●	●	●						
Brent Goose:	●	●	●						
B.b. nigricans:	●								
Red-breasted Goose:	●	●	●						
Egyptian Goose:	●	●	●						
Ruddy Shelduck:	●	●							
Shelduck:	●	●	●						
Wood Duck:	●	●	●						
Mandarin:	●	●	●						
Wigeon:	●	●	●						
American Wigeon:	●	●	●						
Falcated Duck:	●								
Gadwall:	●	●	●						
Baikal Teal:	●	●							
Teal:	●	●	●						
A.c. carolinensis:	●	●	●						
Mallard:	●	●	●						
Black Duck:	●	●	●						
Pintail:	●	●	●						
Garganey:	●	●	●						
Blue-winged Teal:	●	●	●						
Shoveler:	●	●	●						

	E	S	W						
Marbled Duck:	●								
Red-crested Pochard:	●	●	●						
Pochard:	●	●	●						
Ring-necked Duck:	●	●	●						
Ferruginous Duck:	●	●	●						
Tufted Duck:	●	●	●						
Scaup:	●	●	●						
Lesser Scaup:	●								
Eider:	●	●	●						
S.m. borealis:		●							
King Eider:	●	●	●						
Steller's Eider:	●	●							
Harlequin:	●	●							
Long-tailed Duck:	●	●	●						
Common Scoter:	●	●	●						
M.n. americana:	●	●							
Surf Scoter:	●	●	●						
Velvet Scoter:	●	●	●						
Bufflehead:	●	●							
Barrow's Goldeneye:		●							
Goldeneye:	●	●	●						
Hooded Merganser:	●		●						
Smew:	●	●	●						
Red-breasted Merganser:	●	●	●						
Goosander:	●	●	●						
Ruddy Duck:	●	●	●						
White-headed Duck:	●								
Honey Buzzard:	●	●	●						
Black Kite:	●	●	●						
Red Kite:	●	●	●						
White-tailed Eagle:	●	●	●						
Bald Eagle:		●							
Egyptian Vulture:	●								
Griffon Vulture:	●								

	E	S	W							
Black Vulture:			●							
Short-toed Eagle:	●									
Marsh Harrier:	●	●	●							
Hen Harrier:	●	●	●							
Pallid Harrier:	●	●								
Montagu's Harrier:	●	●	●							
Goshawk:	●	●	●							
A.g. atricapillus:	●									
Sparrowhawk:	●	●	●							
Buzzard:	●	●	●							
B.b. vulpinus:	●									
Rough-legged Buzzard:	●	●	●							
Spotted Eagle:	●									
Golden Eagle:	●	●	●							
Osprey:	●	●	●							
Lesser Kestrel:	●	●	●							
Kestrel:	●	●	●							
American Kestrel:	●	●								
Red-footed Falcon:	●	●	●							
Merlin:	●	●	●							
F.c. coumbarius:		●								
Hobby:	●	●	●							
Eleonora's Falcon:	●	●								
Saker Falcon:	●	●								
Gyr Falcon:	●	●	●							
Peregrine:	●	●	●							
F.p. anatum/tundrius:	●									
Red Grouse:	●	●	●							
Ptarmigan:	●	●								
Black Grouse:	●	●	●							
Capercaillie:	●	●								
Red-legged Patridge:	●	●	●							
Grey Patridge:	●	●	●							
Quail:	●	●	●							

	E	S	W						
Pheasant:	●	●	●						
Golden Pheasant:	●	●							
Lady Amherst's Pheasant:	●	●	●						
Water Rail:	●	●	●						
Spotted Crake:	●	●	●						
Sora Rail:	●	●	●						
Little Crake:	●	●	●						
Baillon's Crake:	●	●	●						
Corncrake:	●	●	●						
Moorhen:	●	●	●						
Allen's Gallinule:	●								
American Purple Gallinule:	●								
Coot:	●	●	●						
Crane:	●	●	●						
Sandhill Crane:	●	●							
Little Bustard:	●	●							
Houbara:	●	●							
Great Bustard:	●	●	●						
Oystercatcher:	●	●	●						
Black-winged Stilt:	●	●	●						
Avocet:	●	●	●						
Stone Curlew:	●	●	●						
Cream-coloured Courser:	●	●	●						
Collared Pratincole:	●	●	●						
Oriental Pratincole:	●								
Black-winged Pratincole:	●	●	●						
Little Ringed Plover:	●	●	●						
Ringed Plover:	●	●	●						
Semipalmated Plover:	●								
Killdeer:	●	●	●						
Kentish Plover:	●	●	●						
Greater Sand Plover:	●	●	●						
Caspian Plover:	●	●							
Dotterel:	●	●	●						

	E	S	W						
American Golden Plover:	●	●	●						
Pacific Golden Pover:	●	●	●						
Golden Plover:	●	●	●						
Grey Plover:	●	●	●						
Sociable Plover:	●	●	●						
White-tailed Plover:	●								
Lapwing:	●	●	●						
Great Knot:		●							
Knot:	●	●	●						
Sanderling:	●	●	●						
Semipalmated Sandpiper:	●		●						
Western Sandpiper:	●	●							
Red-necked Stint:	●								
Little Stint:	●	●	●						
Temminck's Stint:	●	●	●						
Long-toed Stint:	●	●							
Least Sandpiper:	●	●	●						
White-rumped Sandpiper:	●	●	●						
Baird's Sandpiper:	●	●	●						
Pectoral Sandpiper:	●	●	●						
Sharp-tailed Sandpiper:	●	●	●						
Curlew Sandpiper:	●	●	●						
Purple Sandpiper:	●	●	●						
Dunlin:	●	●	●						
Broad-billed Sandpiper:	●	●	●						
Stilt Sandpiper:	●	●							
Buff-breasted Sandpiper:	●	●	●						
Ruff:	●	●	●						
Jack Snipe:	●	●	●						
Snipe:	●	●	●						
G.g. delicata:		●							
Great Snipe:	●	●							
Short-billed Dowitcher:	●								
Long-billed Dowitcher:	●	●	●						

	E	S	W						
Woodcock:	●	●	●						
Black-tailed Godwit:	●	●	●						
Hudsonian Godwit:	●	●							
Bar-tailed Godwit:	●	●	●						
Little Whimbrel:	●								
Eskimo Curlew:	●	●							
Whimbrel:	●	●	●						
N.p. hudsonicus:		●							
Curlew:	●	●	●						
Upland Sandpiper:	●	●	●						
Spotted Redshank:	●	●	●						
Redshank:	●	●	●						
Marsh Sandpiper:	●	●	●						
Greenshank:	●	●	●						
Greater Yellowlegs:	●	●	●						
Lesser Yellowlegs:	●	●	●						
Solitary Sandpiper:	●	●							
Green Sandpiper:	●	●	●						
Wood Sandpiper:	●	●	●						
Terek Sandpiper:	●	●							
Common Sandpiper:	●	●	●						
Spotted Sandpiper:	●	●	●						
Grey-tailed Tattler:			●						
Turnstone:	●	●	●						
Wilson's Phalarope:	●	●	●						
Red-necked Phalarope:	●	●	●						
Grey Phalarope:	●	●	●						
Pomarine Skua:	●	●	●						
Arctic Skua:	●	●	●						
Long-tailed Skua:	●	●	●						
Great Skua:	●	●	●						
South Polar Skua:	●								
Great Black-headed Gull:	●								
Mediterranean Gull:	●	●	●						

	E	S	W						
Laughing Gull:	●	●	●						
Franklin's Gull:	●	●							
Little Gull:	●	●	●						
Sabine's Gull:	●	●	●						
Bonaparte's Gull:	●	●	●						
Black-headed Gull:	●	●	●						
Slender-billed Gull:	●								
Ring-billed Gull:	●	●	●						
Common Gull:	●	●	●						
Lesser Black-backed Gull:	●	●	●						
Herring Gull:	●	●	●						
Thayer's Gull:	●								
Iceland Gull:	●	●	●						
L.g. kumlieni:	●	●							
Glaucous Gull:	●	●	●						
Great Black-backed Gull:	●	●	●						
Ross's Gull:	●	●	●						
Kittiwake:	●	●	●						
Ivory Gull:	●	●	●						
Gull-billed Tern:	●	●	●						
Caspian Tern:	●	●	●						
Royal Tern:	●		●						
Lesser Crested Tern:	●	●	●						
Sandwich Tern:	●	●	●						
Roseate Tern:	●	●	●						
Common Tern:	●	●	●						
Arctic Tern:	●	●	●						
Aleutian Tern:	●								
Forster's Tern:	●	●	●						
White-cheeked Tern:	●								
Bridled Tern:	●	●	●						
Sooty Tern:	●	●	●						
Little Tern:	●	●	●						
Least Tern:	●								

	E	S	W						
Whiskered Tern:	●	●	●						
Black Tern:	●	●	●						
White-winged Black Tern:	●	●	●						
Guillemot:	●	●	●						
Brünnich's Guillemot:	●	●							
Razorbill:	●	●	●						
Black Guillemot:	●	●	●						
Ancient Murrelet:	●								
Little Auk:	●	●	●						
Puffin:	●	●	●						
Pallas's Sandgrouse:	●	●	●						
Rock Dove:	●	●	●						
Stock Dove:	●	●	●						
Wood Pigeon:	●	●	●						
Collared Dove:	●	●	●						
Turtle Dove:	●	●	●						
Rufous Turtle Dove:	●								
Ring-necked Parakeet:	●	●	●						
Great Spotted Cuckoo:	●	●	●						
Cuckoo:	●	●	●						
Black-billed Cuckoo:	●	●							
Yellow-billed Cuckoo:	●	●	●						
Barn Owl:	●	●	●						
Scop's Owl:	●	●	●						
Eagle Owl:	●	●							
Snowy Owl:	●	●	●						
Hawk Owl:	●	●							
Little Owl:	●	●	●						
Tawny Owl:	●	●	●						
Long-eared Owl:	●	●	●						
Short-eared Owl:	●	●	●						
Tengmalm's Owl:	●	●							
Nightjar:	●	●	●						
Red-necked Nightjar:	●								

	E	S	W						
Egyptian Nightjar:	●								
Common Nighthawk:	●	●							
Chimney Swift:	●								
Needle-tailed Swift:	●	●							
Swift:	●	●	●						
Pallid Swift:	●		●						
Pacific Swift:	●								
Alpine Swift:	●	●	●						
Mottled Swift:	●								
Little Swift:	●	●	●						
Kingfisher:	●	●	●						
Belted Kingfisher:	●								
Blue-cheeked Bee-eater:	●								
Bee-eater:	●	●	●						
Roller:	●	●	●						
Hoopoe:	●	●	●						
Wryneck:	●	●	●						
Green Woodpecker:	●	●	●						
Yellow-bellied Sapsucker:	●								
Great Spotted Woodpecker:	●	●	●						
Lesser Spotted Woodpecker:	●	●	●						
Eastern Phoebe:	●								
Calandra Lark:	●	●							
Bimaculated Lark:	●	●							
White-winged Lark:	●								
Short-toed Lark:	●	●	●						
Crested Lark:	●	●	●						
Woodlark:	●	●	●						
Skylark:	●	●	●						
Shore Lark:	●	●	●						
E.a. alpestris:		●							
Sand Martin:	●	●	●						
Tree Swallow:	●								
Crag Martin:	●		●						

	E	S	W					
Swallow:	●	●	●					
Red-rumped Swallow:	●	●	●					
Cliff Swallow:	●							
House Martin:	●	●	●					
Richard's Pipit:	●	●	●					
Blyth's Pipit:	●	●						
Tawny Pipit:	●	●	●					
Olive-backed Pipit:	●	●	●					
Tree Pipit:	●	●	●					
Pechora Pipit:	●	●	●					
Meadow Pipit:	●	●	●					
Red-throated Pipit:	●	●	●					
Rock Pipit:	●	●	●					
Water Pipit:	●	●	●					
American Pipit:	●	●						
Yellow Wagtail:	●	●	●					
Citrine Wagtail:	●	●						
Grey Wagtail:	●	●	●					
Pied Wagtail:	●	●	●					
Cedar Waxwing:	●	●						
Waxwing:	●	●	●					
Dipper:	●	●	●					
C.c. cinclus:	●	●						
Wren:	●	●	●					
Northern Mockingbird:	●							
Brown Thrasher:	●							
Gray Catbird:	●							
Dunnock:	●	●	●					
Alpine Accentor:	●	●	●					
Rufous Bush Robin:	●							
Robin:	●	●	●					
Thrush Nightingale:	●	●	●					
Nightingale:	●	●	●					
L.m. africana:		●						

	E	S	W						
Siberian Rubythroat:		●							
Bluethroat:	●	●	●						
Red-flanked Bluetail:	●	●							
White-throated Robin:			●						
Black Redstart:	●	●	●						
P.o. ochruros/phoenicuroides:	●								
Redstart:	●	●	●						
P.p. samamisicus:	●	●							
Daurian Redstart:		●							
Moussier's Redstart:			●						
Whinchat:	●	●	●						
Stonechat:	●	●	●						
S.t. maura/stejnegeri:	●	●	●						
S.t. variegata:	●								
Isabelline Wheatear:	●	●							
Wheatear:	●	●	●						
Pied Wheatear:	●	●	●						
Black-eared Wheatear:	●	●	●						
Desert Wheatear:	●	●	●						
White-crowned Wheatear:	●								
Black Wheatear:	●	●							
Rock Thrush:	●	●	●						
Blue Rock Thrush:	●	●	●						
White's Thrush:	●	●							
Siberian Thrush:	●	●							
Varied Thrush:	●								
Wood Thrush:	●								
Hermit Thrush:	●	●							
Swainson's Thrush:	●	●	●						
Gray-cheeked Thrush:	●	●	●						
Veery:	●								
Ring Ousel:	●	●	●						
T.t. alpestris/amicorum:	●	●							
Blackbird:	●	●	●						

	E	S	W						
Eye-browed Thrush:	●	●							
Dusky Thrush:	●	●	●						
T.n. naumanni:	●								
Black-throated Thrush:	●	●							
T.r. ruficollis:	●								
Fieldfare:	●	●	●						
Song Thrush:	●	●	●						
Redwing:	●	●	●						
Mistle Thrush:	●	●	●						
American Robin:	●	●							
Cetti's Warbler:	●		●						
Fan-tailed Warbler:	●								
Pallas's Grasshopper Warbler:	●	●							
Lanceolated Warbler:	●	●	●						
Grasshopper Warbler:	●	●	●						
River Warbler:	●	●	●						
Savi's Warbler:	●	●	●						
Moustached Warbler:	●								
Aquatic Warbler:	●	●	●						
Sedge Warbler:	●	●	●						
Paddyfield Warbler:	●	●							
Blyth's Reed Warbler:	●	●							
Marsh Warbler:	●	●	●						
Reed Warbler:	●	●	●						
A.s. fuscus:	●								
Great Reed Warbler:	●	●	●						
Thick-billed Warbler:		●							
Olivaceous Warbler:	●	●	●						
Booted Warbler:	●	●							
Icterine Warbler:	●	●	●						
Melodious Warbler:	●	●	●						
Marmora's Warbler:	●								
Dartford Warbler:	●	●	●						
Spectacled Warbler:		●							

	E	S	W							
Subalpine Warbler:	●	●	●							
Sardinian Warbler:	●	●	●							
Rüppell's Warbler:	●	●								
Desert Warbler:	●									
Orphean Warbler:	●	●								
Barred Warbler:	●	●	●							
Lesser Whitethroat:	●	●	●							
S.c. blythi:	●	●	●							
Whitethroat:	●	●	●							
Garden Warbler:	●	●	●							
Blackcap:	●	●	●							
Green Warbler:	●									
Greenish Warbler:	●	●	●							
Two-barred Greenish Warbler:	●									
Arctic Warbler:	●	●	●							
Pallas's Warbler:	●	●	●							
Yellow-browed Warbler:	●	●	●							
P.i. humei:	●									
Radde's Warbler:	●	●	●							
Dusky Warbler:	●	●	●							
Bonelli's Warbler:	●	●	●							
Wood Warbler:	●	●	●							
Chiffchaff:	●	●	●							
Willow Warbler:	●	●	●							
Goldcrest:	●	●	●							
Firecrest:	●	●	●							
Spotted Flycatcher:	●	●	●							
Red-breasted Flycatcher:	●	●	●							
Collared Flycatcher:	●	●	●							
Pied Flycatcher:	●	●	●							
Bearded Tit:	●	●	●							
Long-tailed Tit:	●	●	●							
Marsh Tit:	●	●	●							
Willow Tit:	●	●	●							

	E	S	W						
P.m. borealis:	●								
Crested Tit:	●	●							
Coal Tit:	●	●	●						
Blue Tit:	●	●	●						
Great Tit:	●	●	●						
Red-breasted Nuthatch:	●								
Nuthatch:	●	●	●						
Wallcreeper:	●								
Treecreeper:	●	●	●						
Short-toed Treecreeper:	●								
Penduline Tit:	●		●						
Golden Oriole:	●	●	●						
Brown Shrike:		●							
Isabelline Shrike:	●	●	●						
Red-backed Shrike:	●	●	●						
Lesser Grey Shrike:	●	●	●						
Great Grey Shrike:	●	●	●						
L.e. pallidirostris:	●	●							
Woodchat Shrike:	●	●	●						
Jay:	●	●	●						
Magpie:	●	●	●						
Nutcracker:	●	●	●						
N.c. caryocatactes:	●								
Chough:	●	●	●						
Jackdaw:	●	●	●						
Rook:	●	●	●						
Carrion Crow:	●	●	●						
Raven:	●	●	●						
Daurian Starling:		●							
Starling:	●	●	●						
Rose-coloured Starling:	●	●	●						
House Sparrow:	●	●	●						
Spanish Sparrow:	●	●							
Tree Sparrow:	●	●	●						

	E	S	W						
Rock Sparrow:	●								
Snow Finch:	●								
Yellow-throated Vireo:	●								
Philadelphia Vireo:	●								
Red-eyed Vireo:	●	●	●						
Chaffinch:	●	●	●						
Brambling:	●	●	●						
Serin:	●	●	●						
Citril Finch:	●								
Greenfinch:	●	●	●						
Goldfinch:	●	●	●						
Siskin:	●	●	●						
Linnet:	●	●	●						
Twite:	●	●	●						
Redpoll:	●	●	●						
Arctic Redpoll:	●	●	●						
Two-barred Crossbill:	●	●	●						
Crossbill:	●	●	●						
Scottish Crossbill:		●							
Parrot Crossbill:	●	●	●						
Trumpeter Finch:	●	●							
Scarlet Rosefinch:	●	●	●						
Pallas's Rosefinch:		●							
Pine Grosbeak:	●	●							
Bullfinch:	●	●	●						
Hawfinch:	●	●	●						
Evening Grosbeak:		●							
Black-and-white Warbler:	●	●	●						
Golden-winged Warbler:	●								
Tennessee Warbler:		●							
Northern Parula:	●								
Yellow Warbler:		●	●						
Chestnut-sided Warbler:		●							
Blackburnian Warbler:		●	●						

	E	S	W						
Cape May Warbler:		●							
Magnolia Warbler:	●								
Yellow-rumped Warbler:	●	●							
Blackpoll Warbler:	●	●	●						
American Redstart:	●	●							
Ovenbird:	●	●							
Northern Waterthrush:	●								
Yellowthroat:	●	●							
Hooded Warbler:	●								
Wilson's Warbler:	●								
Summer Tanager:		●							
Scarlet Tanager:	●								
Rufous-sided Towhee:	●								
Lark Sparrow:	●								
Savannah Sparrow:	●	●							
Song Sparrow:	●	●	●						
White-crowned Sparrow:	●	●							
White-throated Sparrow:	●	●	●						
Dark-eyed Junco:	●	●	●						
Lapland Bunting:	●	●	●						
Snow Bunting:	●	●	●						
Pine Bunting:	●	●							
Yellowhammer:	●	●	●						
Cirl Bunting:	●	●	●						
Rock Bunting:	●		●						
Ortolan:	●	●	●						
Cretzschmar's Bunting:		●							
Yellow-browed Bunting:	●	●							
Rustic Bunting:	●	●	●						
Little Bunting:	●	●	●						
Chestnut Bunting:		●	●						
Yellow-breasted Bunting:	●	●	●						
Reed Bunting:	●	●	●						
Pallas's Reed Bunting:		●							

	E	S	W						
Red-headed Bunting:	●	●	●						
Black-headed Bunting:	●	●	●						
Corn Bunting:	●	●	●						
Rose-breasted Grosbeak:	●	●	●						
Blue Grosbeak:	●	●							
Indigo Bunting:	●	●							
Painted Bunting:	●	●							
Bobolink:	●	●							
Yellow-headed Blackbird:	●	●							
Northern Oriole:	●	●	●						

The following eight species have been recorded in the British Isles but not in England, Scotland or Wales:

Yellow-nosed Albatross:	off Malin Head, Co.Donegal, Eire 26/9/1963.
Brown Booby:	nr Castletown Bearhaven, Co.Cork, Eire 28/9/1990.
American Coot:	Ballycotton, Co.Cork, Eire 7/2–4/4/1981.
Elegant Tern:	Greencastle Point, Carlingford Lough, Co.Down, N Ireland 22/6–3/7/1982 and then at Ballymacoda, Co.Cork, Eire on 1/8/1982.
Mourning Dove:	Calf of Man, Isle of Man 31/10/89.
Lesser Short-toed Lark:	30, Derrymore Island, Tralee Bay, Co.Kerry, Eire 4/1/1956. 5, Great Saltee, Co.Wexford, Eire 30/3/1956. (4 still present on 31/3). 2, nr Belmullet, Co.Mayo, Eire 21/5/1956. 5, Great Saltee, Co.Wexford, Eire 22/3/1958. (1 seen 23/3, 2 on 24/4 and 4 on 25/3).
Siberian Blue Robin:	Banquette Valley, Sark, Channel Islands 27/10/1975.
Fox Sparrow:	Copeland Island, Co.Down, N Ireland 3 & 4/6/1961.

During the decade 1981–1990 50 species were added to the British Isles list:-

1981 American Coot. Ballycotton, Co. Cork 7/2–3/4
Rock Sparrow. Cley 14/6
Pacific Swift. North Sea oil rig, Beccles & Shadingfield 19/6
Oriental Pratincole. Dunwich, Suffolk 22/6–8/7
Lark Sparrow. Landguard Point 30/6–4/7
Hudsonian Godwit. Blacktoft 10/9–3/10
Magnolia Warbler. St.Agnes 27–28/9
Grey-tailed Tattler. Dyfi Estuary 13/10–17/11

1982 Savannah Sparrow. Portland 11–16/4
Marmora's Warbler. Midhope Moor, Yorks 15/5–24/7
White-crowned Black Wheatear. Kessingland, Suffolk 1–5/6
Elegant Tern. Greencastle, Co.Down 22/6–3/7
Lesser Crested Tern. Cymryan Bay, Anglesey 13/7
Long-toed Stint. Saltholme Pool, Cleveland 28/8–1/9
Northern Mockingbird. Saltash, Cornwall 29/8
Little Whimbrel. nr Sker Point, Mid Glamorgan 30/8–6/9
South Polar Skua. St.Ives 14/10
Chimney Swift. Porthgwarra 21–27/10, two 23–25/10
Varied Thrush. Nanquidno, Cornwall 9–25/11
1983 Least Tern, Rye Harbour 8/6
White-throated Robin. Calf of Man 22/6
Green Warbler. St.Mary's 26/9–4/10
Cliff Swallow. St.Mary's & St.Agnes 10–27/10
1984 none (everyone stayed indoors!)
1985 Daurian Starling. Fair Isle 7–28/5
Chestnut-sided Warbler. Fetlar 20/9
Brown Shrike. Sumburgh 30/9–2/10
Philadelphia Vireo. Galley Head, Eire 12–17/10
Wilson's Warbler. Rame Head 13/10
1986 Red-necked Stint. Blacktoft 22–29/7
1987 Lesser Scaup. Chasewater 8/3–25/4
Eastern Phoebe. Slapton 22/4
Wood Thrush. St.Agnes 7/10
Two-barred Greenish Warbler. Gugh, Scillies 21–27/10
1988 Moussier's Redstart. Dinas Head, Dyfed 24/4
Daurian Redstart. Isle of May 29–30/4
Pallas's Rosefinch. North Ronaldsay 2/6–14/7
Crag Martin. Stithians Reservoir 22/6
Double-crested Cormorant. Charlton's Pond, Cleveland 8/12–29/4/89
1989 Golden-winged Warbler. Larkfield, Kent 7/2–9/4
Thayer's Gull. Galway City 17–31/3
White-cheeked Tern. Dungeness 13/5
Matsudaira's Storm Petrel. Tynemouth 23/7
Great Knot. Scatness, Shetland 15/9
Red-breasted Nuthatch. Holkham Woods 13/10–6/5/90
Mourning Dove. Calf of Man 31/10
1990 Short-toed Eagle. Brading, Isle of Wight 2–7/5
Ancient Murrelet. Lundy 27/5–4/7
Tree Swallow. St.Mary's 6–10/6
Yellow-throated Vireo. Kenidjack Valley 20–27/9
Brown Booby. nr Castletown Bearhaven, Co. Cork 28/9

And here are 50 for the future:-

Wandering Albatross
Southern Giant Petrel
Cape Petrel
Grey Petrel
Audubon's Shearwater
White-tailed Tropicbird
Audouin's Gull
Antarctic Tern
Brown Noddy
Least Bittern
Yellow-crowned Night Heron
Yellow Rail
Whip-poor-will
Northern Flicker
Eastern Kingbird
Great Crested Flycatcher
Eastern Wood-Pewee
Acadian Flycatcher
Purple Martin
Ruby-crowned Kinglet
Solitary Vireo
Warbling Vireo
Black-winged Warbler
Black-throated Green Warbler
Prairie Warbler
Bay-breasted Warbler
Black-throated Blue Warbler
Palm Warbler
Mourning Warbler
Canada Warbler
Vesper Sparrow
Chipping Sparrow
Lincoln's Sparrow
White-rumped Swift
Mourning Wheatear
Masked Shrike
Siberian Accentor
Black-throated Accentor
Olive-tree Warbler
Brown Flycatcher
Mugimaki Flycatcher
Gray's Grasshopper Warbler
Black-faced Bunting
Oriental Greenfinch
Siberian Meadow Bunting
White-throated Rock Thrush
Willet
Asiatic Dowitcher
Pintail Snipe
Lesser Sand Plover

(That ought to guarantee Spoon-billed Sandpiper and Upcher's Warbler!)

INDEX